AMERICAN DIARIES
1902-1926

Theodore Dreiser

THEODORE DREISER

AMERICAN DIARIES 1902-1926

Edited by

THOMAS P. RIGGIO

Textual Editor

JAMES L. W. WEST III

General Editor

NEDA M. WESTLAKE

University of Pennsylvania Press
Philadelphia 1983

The preparation of this volume was made possible in part by grants from the American Council of Learned Societies, and from the Program for Editions of the National Endowment for the Humanities, an independent federal agency.

Designed by Adrianne Onderdonk Dudden

first printing 1982
second printing, with corrections, 1983

Library of Congress Cataloging in Publication Data

Dreiser, Theodore, 1871–1945.
  American diaries, 1902–1926.

  Includes bibliographical references and index.
  1. Dreiser, Theodore, 1871–1945—Diaries.
  2. Authors, American—20th century—Biography.
  I. Riggio, Thomas P.   II. West, James L. W.
  III. Westlake, Neda M.   IV. Title.
  PS3507.R55Z467 1981   818'.5203 [B]   81–51142
  ISBN 0–8122–7809–7   AACR2

Printed in the United States of America

CONTENTS

▭

Preface   vii
Acknowledgments   ix
Illustrations   xi

INTRODUCTION   3
EDITORIAL PRINCIPLES   45

DIARIES

PHILADELPHIA, 1902–03   53
SAVANNAH AND THE SOUTH, 1916   115
GREENWICH VILLAGE, 1917–18   147
HOME TO INDIANA, 1919   257
A TRIP TO THE JERSEY SHORE, 1919   269
HELEN, HOLLYWOOD, AND
THE *TRAGEDY,* 1919–24   275
MOTORING TO FLORIDA, 1925–26   415

Appendix: Diary Fragments, 1914–18   445
Textual Apparatus   451
Index   459

PREFACE

▭

Dreiser's careful preservation of his papers bears new fruit with the publication of his personal diaries for the years 1902–26. This volume presents all seven of Dreiser's hitherto unpublished American diaries, the intermittent journals he kept during the most productive years of his literary career. Together they constitute a revealing self-portrait as well as a valuable commentary on the American scene during the first quarter of this century. They offer reflections on turn-of-the-century Philadelphia, the American South and Mid-West, Greenwich Village of the nineteen-teens, and Hollywood of the twenties. The diaries begin in 1902, when Dreiser was at a low point after the "suppression" of *Sister Carrie,* and continue until 1926, when he was enjoying the greatest success of his career with *An American Tragedy.*

This publication constitutes in its entirety a new source for biographical and critical study. This is particularly true of the diaries covering Dreiser's experience in Philadelphia, Greenwich Village, and with Helen Richardson—all of which were not available to previous biographers. The present Introduction by Professor Riggio is the first biographical narrative to make use of these materials. Future biographers will now be able to speak with more assurance of Dreiser's whereabouts, the people he knew, what he was reading, which writings were in progress, and of his fascinating private affairs in general. In addition, these diaries will be of interest to students of Dreiser's literary art, as they reveal subtle aspects of how Dreiser viewed the external world and transmuted it in his daily creative efforts.

The diaries were written usually on half-sheets, often on trains, in parks or hotel lobbies, and were interspersed with postcards, ticket stubs, and rent receipts. Dreiser generally wrote casually, at times hurriedly, posting these "notes," as he called them, to capture an immediate impression, to record fleeting exhilarations or depressing moods, and to note his reactions to literary associates and to various women companions. These materials have been edited in conformity with widely accepted principles and designed to make Dreiser's difficult scripts accessible to contemporary readers.

Thomas P. Riggio, as editor, conceived the volume, wrote the introductory essay, supplied the annotations and identifications, and compiled the index. James L. W. West III, as textual editor, devised the editorial principles, emended the texts, and compiled the apparatus. Neda M. Westlake, as general editor, coordinated these efforts and served as liaison with the publisher. West and Westlake shared equally in transcribing and verifying the diary texts.

Philadelphia   NEDA M. WESTLAKE
November 1981

ACKNOWLEDGMENTS

This volume was made possible with the aid of the following institutions which kindly granted access to their holdings:

The University of Pennsylvania Library, for the manuscripts of the diaries of 1916 and the periods from 1919–26 in the Dreiser Collection.

The Lilly Library, Indiana University, for the diary of 1902–03.

The Manuscripts and Archives Division of the New York Public Library, Astor, Lenox and Tilden Foundations, for the use of the diary of 1917–18, which had been deposited there by H. L. Mencken.

The Clifton Waller Barrett Collection in the Alderman Library at the University of Virginia, for access to Dreiser correspondence in their possession.

The Museum of the City of New York for photographs.

Professor Riggio's debt to the American Council of Learned Societies and Professor West's debt to the National Endowment for the Humanities are acknowledged formally on the copyright page.

Riggio expresses his gratitude to Dean Hugh Clark and the University of Connecticut Research Foundation for their support, and to Milla B. Riggio for her assistance in compiling the index.

West wishes to thank Amy S. Doherty, University Archivist, George Arents Research Library, Syracuse University, and Saundra Taylor, Curator of Manuscripts, the Lilly Library, for help with identifications. He also thanks Melinda W. West, Virginia Polytechnic Institute and State University, for assistance in transcribing the diaries.

Riggio, West, and Westlake wish to thank Ingalill Hjelm, of the University of Pennsylvania Press, for the energy, good counsel, and editorial skills she brought to this project.

ILLUSTRATIONS

—

Theodore Dreiser's prescriptions, inserted in the text of the Philadelphia diary, are by courtesy of The Lilly Library, University of Indiana. The two views of the Brevoort Hotel are by courtesy of the Museum of the City of New York. All other illustrations are from the University of Pennsylvania Library.

1.	Theodore Dreiser	ii
2.	Sara White Dreiser	88
3.	Philadelphia Dispensary	103
4.	Markham–Dreiser "at Home" Card	115
5.	Street Map of Savannah	130
6.	Hotel Savannah Menu	141
7.	Brevoort Hotel	148
8.	Estelle Kubitz	168
9.	Louise Campbell	194
10.	Brevoort Hotel Dining Room	197
11.	"Daimio" Caricature of Dreiser	240
12.	Kosciusko County Court House	257
13.	The Beach at the Esplanade, Asbury Park, New Jersey	269
14.	Helen Richardson in Hollywood	279
15.	Dreiser's Wasserman Report	293
16.	Dreiser and Helen in Hollywood	301
17.	Manuscript Page of Diary	324
18.	Dreiser and Helen in Hollywood	328
19.	Telegram from Helen	344
20.	Helen with the Cat	346
21.	The Note Tied to the Cat's Collar	346
22.	Guest Card for the Bohemian Club	354
23.	Clipping: Poet Upholds Dive in Lake	367
24.	*Sunland, The Magazine of Florida*	416
25.	H. L. Mencken in Baltimore	418
26.	Horace Liveright Telegram Reporting on Early Progress of the *Tragedy*	432

AMERICAN DIARIES
1902-1926

INTRODUCTION

▭

The life of every man is a diary
in which he means to write one story,
and writes another. . . .
J. M. Barrie, *The Little Minister*

When Theodore Dreiser arrived in Philadelphia, sometime in July 1902, he was weary after nine months of travel that had taken him through Virginia, West Virginia, Delaware, Maryland, and to his wife's family in Missouri for a brief Christmas holiday. Sara White Dreiser, called "Jug," had followed her husband from town to town as he tried unsuccessfully to calm his nerves and to write *Jennie Gerhardt,* a second novel which he would not be able to complete for nearly a decade. He was sick: he was suffering from what used to be known as neurasthenia but what today we would call an identity crisis accompanied by nervous prostration. The distinction is worth noting, since the bias of that period led Dreiser to believe that his condition had underlying physical causes. Consequently he sought to explain his weakened state variously as "malaria," "some inherent blood [affliction]," or "mental exhaustion from past excesses both of the sexual passion and mental labor." Unknown to him, the doctor he found in Philadelphia, Louis A. Duhring, was a distinguished professor of dermatology at the University of Pennsylvania who, despite his specialty, took on neurasthenic cases. Duhring himself apparently had a nervous disorder, which may account for the unusual directive he gave Dreiser, along with routine doses of several arsenical preparations.[1] The doctor proposed that his patient keep a daily medical record. On 22 October 1902, Dreiser wrote what was to be the first entry of a diary he would continue intermittently for twenty-five years.

He began the Philadelphia diary under handicaps as serious as any

---

1. Herman Beerman and Emma S. Beerman, "A Meeting of Two Famous Benefactors of the Library of the University of Pennsylvania—Louis Adolphus Duhring and Theodore Dreiser," *Transactions and Studies of the College of Physicians of Philadelphia* 42 (1974): 43–48.

he had faced in his thirty-one years. He was fatigued, down to his last few dollars, and aware that he was developing a resistance to sustained writing. In the two years before he had completed his first novel in 1900, he had published over one hundred articles; *Sister Carrie* had been written in seven months, and he had given over some of that time to short pieces for the magazines. When he began *Jennie Gerhardt* in January 1901, he worked at the same quick pace, completing forty chapters within four months. Then his troubles began. He found that "an error in character analysis" made necessary a wholesale revision of the text. Publishers seemed to shy away from committing themselves to his new work. He spent part of the summer of 1901 with Arthur Henry in Noank, Connecticut, trying to recapture the impetus to write that their summer together in 1899 had provided for *Carrie.* Henry's account of this time in *An Island Cabin* (1902) suggests that Dreiser was already showing signs of strain. In September 1901 the small publishing firm of J. F. Taylor offered him weekly advances to free him to finish *Jennie.* But by November he left New York for Bedford City, Virginia, and there he began the peripatetic routine that lasted until he moved to Philadelphia the following July.

In spite of increasingly severe bouts of anxiety, Dreiser kept doggedly to his task. As late as 2 July 1902, he received a statement from his typist, Miss M. E. Gordinnier, for 110 pages of manuscript he had sent her in June. She was touched by the story of Jennie and regretted not having read earlier chapters. Shortly after, Dreiser moved to 210 Sumac Street in Philadelphia and tried again to write his way out of his impasse. By the time he started the diary in October, however, he was paralyzed in his creative efforts; in December he wrote J. F. Taylor, admitting he could no longer hope to fulfill his commitment in the near future. To himself he said in his journal, "I feel as if I cannot write. [The absence of] lucidity of expression and consecutiveness of ideas is what is bothering me. I cannot write continuously. I lose the thread and forget" (14 February 1903). His state of mind at this juncture is commonly attributed to the poor critical reception of *Sister Carrie* and the shabby treatment he received at the hands of his publisher. To a remarkable degree, the popular legend has displaced the more compelling reality.

It is true that the "failure" of *Sister Carrie* took on excessive symbolic meaning in the young novelist's mind. Partly this stemmed from the change Dreiser underwent in the course of writing the book. Its composition crystallized his burgeoning sense of vocation as he made the transition from a free-lance hack to a writer of serious fiction. He knew now what he wanted to do. Writing of the sort that had made him financially independent in the late 1890s was no longer what he expected of himself. Along with its share of defensive bluster, Dreiser's response to Walter H. Page's attempt to withdraw *Carrie* from publication conveys this sense of maturing purpose and large ambition.

A great book will destroy conditions, unfavorable or indifferent, whether these be due to previous failures or hostile prejudices aroused by previous error. Even if this book should fail, I can either write another important enough in its nature to make its own conditions and be approved of for itself alone, or I can write something unimportant and fail, as the author of a triviality deserves to fail. Therefore I have no fear on this score.[2]

What crippled Dreiser for a time was not his critics but his inability to achieve such resilience in handling the greater demands he began making on himself.

Available evidence indicates he overreacted. He worried that his brand of realism would be hard to place and the reputation of his novel would make him a literary pariah. There was encouragement in 1901–02 from many quarters—the favorable English reviews of the Heinemann edition of *Carrie,* the interest publishers expressed in future books, his election to the Indiana Club of Chicago, his reappearance in *Who's Who* as a prominent editor, poet, author—but nothing helped. His editor at Taylor's, Rutger B. Jewett, tried to get him to reduce the internal pressures that were building up: "Brace up, stop worrying, and rest your head as well as your body. You exaggerate greatly the obligation under which you think you are staggering."[3] Jewett must have sensed that for someone with Dreiser's energy and will, to turn the force of his critical powers inward could only result in massive debilitation.

Dreiser eventually pushed beyond his personal confusion, and out of the turmoil of the moment he left a literary legacy. During the first quarter of the century, as *Sister Carrie* progressively became the rallying point around which American writers denounced genteel standards, he increasingly came to identify his early collapse with the sufferings of the

2. Dreiser to Walter H. Page, 6 August 1900, *Letters of Theodore Dreiser,* ed. Robert H. Elias (Philadelphia: Univ. of Pennsylvania Press, 1959), 1: 61.
3. Jewett to Dreiser, 19 December 1902, Dreiser Collection, University of Pennsylvania Library.

artist in a puritanical society. He succeeded in doing for himself and his generation what Baudelaire had accomplished for Poe. He created a cultural myth, larger than his own experience, which served as a sustaining metaphor of artistic integrity in his time. But in the process, his version of the beleaguered artist-genius established the link between his professional anxieties and his breakdown so rigidly as to obscure equally important dimensions of his story.

This first diary, which does not mention *Sister Carrie* or the Doubledays, suggests that the source of Dreiser's three-year crisis ran deeper than the strain from troubles with a first novel. It points to a pervasive uncertainty about the aims of his writing, accompanied by a disabling anxiety over the possibilities of failure in his career. "Going to work I do not get very far before I question the order and merit of what I am doing and find myself utterly confused as to what is best and interesting" (22 November 1902). The entries alternate between moments of despair and manic feelings of hope when he recalls himself as a promising novelist whose success as an editor and journalist secured him a good living in the literary marketplace. He reads novels ("Since I shall want to be writing another one myself someday"), particularly those of Americans he admires—William Dean Howells, Hamlin Garland, Harold Frederic, Henry B. Fuller. At times their example only ignites his frustration: "Me. Theodore Dreiser. A man who has ideas enough to write and to spare and walking for want of a nickel" (13 February 1903).

It is not easy to know how clearly Dreiser understood his predicament. He was a man of colorful and passionate moods who responded to experience with unusual vividness, but with no knack for incisive self-analysis. This was not due to any shallowness on his part but to a lifelong awkwardness in expressing deep emotions. Moreover, his characteristic habit of studying human behavior within the framework of general ideas often impeded the more directly efficient action required in times of weakness. Other avenues to self-knowledge were closed to him. He had no close friends at hand, and he was too embarrassed to confide in his family. He frequently mentions having "bad dreams," but he had not yet read Freud; so he simply dismisses his nightmares without relating them, as he would in later diaries, to his present needs. Daily in the diary he was able to tell himself only that he feared poverty and failure.

His obsession became part of the novel he was struggling to finish:

"Poverty was driving them," he says of Jennie Gerhardt and her family. Curiously, no attention has been paid to the impact on Dreiser of his second book, which he began at the outset of this troubled period. In *Jennie Gerhardt* he first gave shape to the disquieting memories he associated with his youth in Indiana and Chicago. In the diary, Dreiser's reaction, after listening to the editor Joseph Coates's lukewarm response to his manuscript, underscores the intensity of his emotional ties to this material:

We then went back and sat talking about my novel of ~~Ger~~ Jennie Gerhardt, the manuscript of which I had given him to read and which ~~he consider~~ in parts he considered very good. It was mixed, he thought, and and overwrought in parts, but when I told him the whole story, as I had originally conceived it, he was as moved as everyone else has been and told me it was fine. I could see by his interruptions though that he was even more wrought up than his words would indicate and when we parted for the night, it was with the assurance that he would give the mss some new thought. . . . [10 February 1903]

The "whole story" he told Coates had so strong a hold on his mind that whenever he tried to put it on paper he would exhibit physical symptoms and labor under "a disturbing sense of error." The decision to put aside the novel and restrict himself to articles and short fiction was not the result of his running into technical problems with the longer form. He slowly came to realize this was not the point to open old wounds; he knew he needed greater distance from his subject and time to decipher its meaning for him.

We can only speculate on what elements of the story most affected him. Unlike *Sister Carrie,* Jennie's tale combined the adventures of more than one Dreiser sister. And Mrs. Gerhardt introduced memories of his mother. In later autobiographies, the picture of his mother and sisters generally corresponds to the portrait he drew of the Gerhardts. Jennie, like Carrie, is idealized somewhat, but Dreiser worked that out consciously in several revisions of both novels. The moving but sentimental treatment of Jennie's father, however, may hold a clue to Dreiser's conflicts of the moment. One of his most memorable characters, Old Gerhardt, is modeled on John Paul Dreiser, the German-born father who, as Dreiser emphasized in his memoirs, instilled in him a lifelong fear of failing and of being poor. In *Dawn* John Paul Dreiser is presented as "an illustration of the beaten or at best psychically depressed man."[4] Throughout his life Dreiser associated personal de-

---

4. *A History of Myself: Dawn* (New York: Horace Liveright, 1931), p. 164.

feat with the world of his father, and there is reason to believe he found it difficult to shed the influence of that example. On Christmas Day 1900, shortly before Dreiser began what he would term the "down-hill" phase of his career, John Paul Dreiser died. Twelve days after, on 6 January 1901, Dreiser discarded an autobiographical novel entitled "The Rake" and wrote the first chapter of *Jennie Gerhardt*. [5]

That the elder Dreiser's death stimulated his son to brood on failure and poverty appears likely. Richard Duffy's letter of 30 December 1900 indicates that those closest to Dreiser understood how susceptible to depression he was under the circumstances: "I am very sorry to hear of the bereavement you have suffered in the death of your father. . . . I hope you will force yourself to bear this trial with fortitude, the

---

5. Dreiser mentioned "The Rake" to Dorothy Dudley, who gives round (and vague) figures for *"The Rake* and *Jennie Gerhardt*. Since 1900 he had written thirty chapters of one and ten or twelve of the other" (Dudley, *Forgotten Frontiers: Dreiser and the Land of the Free* [New York: Smith and Haas, 1932], p. 196). Because Dreiser dated the first chapter of *Jennie* on 6 January 1901, and none of the correspondence after this date mentions any other novel but *Jennie,* it is safe to assume "The Rake" was begun first, before the trouble with *Carrie* at Doubleday. Dreiser's letter of 27 November 1923 to Fremont Older suggests this is true. He describes his excitement after *Carrie* was accepted by Doubleday in the spring of 1900: "this so stirred me that I decided to be about the work of another novel—to join the one a year group, which seemed to be what was expected of me. And to this end I scraped together a little cash and returned to the country" (*Letters,* 2: 418). This is clearly not a reference to *Jennie;* and the "country" is the home of Mrs. Dreiser's parents in Montgomery City, Missouri, where early in June 1900 Dreiser went to write his second novel. By mid-July, when Arthur Henry began sending the news of Doubleday's turnabout, he could have completed ten chapters or more, if he was writing at the same pace as he would when he began *Jennie* in January 1901. (The dating on the *Jennie* manuscript shows he completed the first five chapters of the novel in six days.) And certainly he might have finished ten or more chapters between 14 July 1900 and 6 January 1901. As Dreiser wrote to Arthur Henry in late July 1900, he hoped his "forthcoming book," which he meant to complete "this winter," would persuade Doubleday to "publish *Sister Carrie* and preserve my credit" (*Letters,* 1: 53).

"The Rake" of 1900 survives on the small yellow sheets that Robert Elias first noted in the manuscript of *The History of Myself,* vol. 2 (*The Library Chronicle,* University of Pennsylvania [1971], p. 43). Dreiser used these yellow sheets, on which he wrote *Sister Carrie* and the chapters of *Jennie* he finished in 1901–2, only in this period. When he returned to *Jennie* in 1910, he began using the standard-size typewriter paper he would continue to write on for the rest of his career. "The Rake" was obviously an autobiographical novel, dealing in part with Dreiser's experience as a newspaperman. For his main character, he used the name Eugene, as he would for the hero of *The "Genius".* Despite this, one cannot consider "The Rake," as Swanberg does, an early version of *The "Genius"* (W. A. Swanberg, *Dreiser* [New York: Scribners, 1965], p. 543, n. 7), except in the broadest sense of its being an autobiographical novel which *may* have dealt with Dreiser as artist. *The "Genius",* however, by-passes Dreiser's newspaper days and focuses mainly on his life after the publication of *Sister Carrie.*

Dreiser's troubles with Doubleday may have made "The Rake," which was begun in a mood of triumph, hard to complete; or he may have felt, in the light of the criticism of *Carrie,* that a "rakish" theme was unwise; or the death of his father on 25 December 1900, may have pushed him toward material closer to his childhood memories; or he may simply have run into a dead end, technically, with "The Rake." For whatever reason, the story of Jennie entirely displaced "The Rake" by January 1901.

more so, since it has seemed to me that you are lately inclined to ponder sadly."[6] Eventually Dreiser would trace the origin of this inclination. As he confided to Dorothy Dudley, "there is an access of gloom, a brooding in me over long periods, so like him [John Paul Dreiser] that I feel a close relationship."[7] He could admit this without threat in later years, but, as the diary shows, in his early thirties his ego was not strong enough to integrate such an awareness into his consciousness. Perhaps the idealized image of the father in *Jennie Gerhardt* was Dreiser's way of handling repressions and conflicts in other parts of his mind. The implied brutality, early in the novel, of Gerhardt's outraged piety, in the face of Jennie's pregnancy, runs like a dark undercurrent throughout the story and re-emerges years later in the portrait of his father in *Dawn.* Moreover, there is at least unconscious symbolism in the impulse that led Dreiser to mark the end of his crisis—the resignation from his laborer's job and the return to literary work as an editor—on Christmas Eve 1903, instead of when it actually occurred, sometime in early 1904. As far as one can understand such a gesture, the symmetrical framing of his three-year hiatus points as much in the direction of the senior Dreiser as toward *Sister Carrie.* [8]

Dreiser's journal record of regular attendance at church services also points to the inner discord of unresolved emotions he faced after his father's death. Dreiser afterward came to see his parent's defeatism as a by-product of religious fanaticism, and to this aberration he traced his enmity to all versions of orthodoxy, particularly Roman Catholicism. The violence and intensity of his subsequent pronouncements on formal religion are a measure of the distance he had to go in order to free himself from the restraints he carried into his young adulthood. And a gauge of his lasting attraction to the varieties of religious experience is the surprising glimpse we get here of the self-proclaimed foe of organized religion participating in Catholic or Episcopal worship.

I walked to Manayunk and attended mass at the Catholic church there, a spectacle which I enjoyed very much. The church was soothing, the music beautiful and the lights and candles upon the altar a spectacle to behold. I rejoiced enthusiastically in it all and came home feeling as if I were better than ever. [8 February 1903]

6. Dreiser Collection, University of Pennsylvania Library.
7. Quoted in Dudley, *Forgotten Frontiers,* p. 25.
8. Ellen Moers notes the discrepancy, but accounts for it as a "romantic" impulse, in *Two Dreisers* (New York: Viking, 1969), p. 178.

The casualness of such passages indicates that traditional religious ritual remained part of Dreiser's landscape of thought longer than he was later willing to admit. Whether he associated, as he subsequently did, such observance with the figure of his father is hard to know. The diary does, however, push us to re-examine his widely quoted claim that reading Herbert Spencer and Thomas Huxley in 1894 conclusively "took every shred of belief from me" and "destroyed the last remaining traces of Catholicism."[9]

The death of his father and the memories uncovered by the story of Jennie intensified Dreiser's acute sense of passing time, which was to become a permanent theme of the diaries. Although only in his early thirties, he had already started to feel an urgency about the passage of life and certain roads not taken. "Would that I had a vast fund of technical information. That I were twenty five, successful and happy" (11 February 1903). Dreiser was extraordinarily sensitive to the transience of youth. One of the outstanding facts about the portrait of Hurstwood, which is among the finest accounts of mid-life crisis in fiction, is that Dreiser wrote it in his late twenties. Few portions of the Philadelphia journal tell us more about Dreiser's state of mind than those in which he goes through motions reminiscent of Hurstwood's downward spiral: the planning of his day around his last few dollars and then his last few cents, the shame-filled dread of appearing down-and-out at the University of Pennsylvania's Free Dispensary, the outbursts of prideful resentment at his condition, and the registering "as an applicant for a position as a street car conductor" (9 February 1903). In time he came to realize the identification had no basis in reality. The involuntary pull in the direction of Hurstwood was neutralized somewhat by a healthier association with a figure whose example gave Dreiser some comfort.

If light and merriment and love are all so far from me, must I weep alone? Rather I took up my life of Lincoln and read eagerly in it, the story of that man of sorrows having much in it that reminds me of my own. [13 February 1903]

Lincoln, as early as Whitman's great elegy, had displaced earlier revolutionary heroes as the father of his country, and Dreiser's attraction to him throughout this period underscores the depth of his need for a

---

9. Frank Harris, *Contemporary Portraits: Second Series* (New York: Frank Harris, 1919), p. 91; *Letters,* 1: 211.

paternal model. His reaction also suggests, however, the wealth of inner resources he had to call upon in troubled times. Unlike his fictional saloon manager, Dreiser possessed youth, a will to survive, and an underlying faith in his calling.

He also had the support of a wife who seemed willing to clear his life of the bread-and-butter chores that impede writing. The temptation here is to interpret his relation to Mrs. Dreiser in light of the unhappy picture he drew afterward in memoirs and in thinly disguised autobiographical sequences of *The "Genius."* By 1919 he would say to Frank Harris, "In half a year I realized that for me marriage was a disaster. At the end of the first year and a half it had become a torture."[10] But the diary presents a less reductive impression of the Dreisers after four years of marriage. Read objectively, it reflects Dreiser's dependence on Jug—for physical needs, companionship, and the editorial help he came to expect of all the women he knew intimately. When she leaves on 26 January 1903, he panics, and the diary thereafter becomes more introspective and revealing. A genuine sense of loss shows through: "All the desire of my heart is centered on getting well, on getting my wife back, on having a home" (3 February 1903); "I would call on Coates and ask him to give me that balance due me and with it go to Missouri to Jug. I wanted to pack up at once. . . . succeeded in eating something by sheer force. I was so homesick I could have cried" (6 February 1903). Admittedly, the entries before Jug leaves do not reveal much intimacy in their marriage; but the circumstances under which Dreiser recorded his feelings put limits on what he could express. The diary, after all, was begun as a medical record for Dr. Duhring, who seems penurious and closed to personal revelations in the one office visit Dreiser describes in detail. In addition, the fact that Jug had access to the journal, and occasionally served as his amanuensis, surely encouraged Dreiser's reserve.

In connection with Jug, one of the most revealing aspects of Dreiser's dilemma at the turn of the century is the neurosis which led him to ascribe his debility to sexual indulgence.

Suffered a great deal during early morning and previous evening from sexual desire which seems to affect my head. Managed to resist it however in so far as abstaining from copulation, but the effect of the desire was weakening. [15 November 1902]

10. Harris, *Contemporary Portraits,* p. 91.

Have noticed that the contemplation of marital joy of these people [his in-laws] is apt to produce physical passion in me—a thing that delays my mental recovery at this time. [30 November 1902]

Nervous condition rather worse this morning owing to a foolish hour of trifling with Mrs. D. Felt or seemed to feel the effects of it at once and during day suffered from a growing headache. [29 December 1902]

The mixture of naiveté and pathos in such moments may seem contrived, particularly when put beside the figure of the self-styled "varietist" who appears in other parts of the diaries. Yet for Dreiser, the relation between passion and disease is real; it cannot be dismissed entirely as a hangover from Victorian medical lore. As he would explain in other places, he had from his youth internalized a great many sexual taboos. Not surprisingly, the puritan precedes the rake. The aggressiveness with which he pursued women in his middle years seems to be a form of compensation for the fears of the younger man. The record he set down in Philadelphia is the only surviving document that allows us to see this side of him without the various masks he developed in his autobiographies. In the latter, he created a classic embodiment of the adolescent filled with phobic dread of impotence. Together with the counterbalancing image of the roving artist-lover that he self-consciously cultivated, Dreiser all but obliterated the strangely Chaplinesque figure we find in the pages before us.

Being homely and backward, with no art of impressing women, I have always suffered on the side of my affections. Some men have so much. I have had so little.
I came away feeling rather depressed over this again, but I tried not to feel too blue. All men do not have it. There must be thousends like me. There must be thousends more who do not countenance immorality or even flirtation. Anyhow I have not got it and here I am. [14 February 1903]

In the years ahead he would discard the tone of self-pity and get "it," but he would always be mindful of the circumstantial nature of his good fortune.

There is little wonder that such unresolved identity problems— linked as they were to the pressures of a recent marriage—should contribute to Dreiser's general depression. Nor was it unnatural for him to try to explain the sense of creative and physical impotence that pervaded this period by projecting it onto external causes, like a poor constitution—or the unwillingness of a publisher to support a novel. However, even after Dreiser became more secure in his position, he never lost sight of the hidden complexities of this time. An unpublished manuscript at the University of Pennsylvania entitled "Down Hill and Up" shows him struggling to comprehend this critical moment well into the 1920s. The terms "up" and "down hill" represent the inscrutable and precarious poles of human existence; fate and character, he insists, determine whether one strides above the storms of life or succumbs to them. Dreiser isolates the obsessive question of his crisis— "Who was I?"—and its most transparent concern: "my doubt as to whether I should ever be able to write again." The piece shows him looking back as a survivor; yet even then he can analyze his situation only metaphorically:

It is never quite possible, I think, to lay one's finger definitely upon the causes of either success or failure, strength or weakness, under certain circumstances or at certain crucial moments. There is a star, a providence which shapes our ends.

What the end looked like was by no means clear on 17 February 1903, when, for some obscure reason, Dreiser broke off the diary in mid-sentence. He took a train to New York and settled in Brooklyn with a vague idea of reestablishing himself as a free-lance writer. But before long he drifted close to suicide in a manner that made Hurstwood's decline seem like a dress rehearsal for real life. In "Down Hill and Up" he describes the temptation to end it all, as he stood on a Brooklyn pier "looking at the then miniature and unimpressive skyline of New York, the red of a February West beyond it." He recalls his thoughts as fatigue and lack of food slowly began to wear down his resistance.

The sight of the icy cold and splashing waters naturally appealed to me. It would be so easy to drop in. The cold would soon numb me—a few gulps and all would be over. All that was necessary was to slip down into this gulf and rest. No one would know. I would be completely forgotten.

He was saved by his brother Paul, who fed and clothed him and paid his way to Muldoon's health spa in White Plains. The New York episode, the stay at the sanatarium, his subsequent job on a railroad gang—the whole painful experience—found an outlet in "An Amateur Laborer," an unpublished memoir he wrote shortly after he returned to editorial work in 1904.

By 1907, after working his way up through the editorial ranks, Dreiser had become chief editor of the prestigious Butterick publications. Although he made several starts at writing novels—at one point he thought of turning "An Amateur Laborer" into fiction, and he tried to resurrect *Jennie Gerhardt* more than once—he could not devote full time to it. *Sister Carrie* went through a second American publication in 1907, and with this printing the novel became a recognizable factor in American literary history. When Dreiser decided to complete *Jennie Gerhardt* in 1910, he did so with a sense that he had "fought a battle for the right to live" and had emerged the victor. Yet ten years had passed since the publication of *Sister Carrie*. The lost decade haunted his memory for years and provided him a subject and focal point for books as different as *The "Genius," Twelve Men,* and the autobiographies. However volatile his moods thereafter, he would never again feel so completely at the mercy of uncontrollable forces.

Between 1916 and 1926 Dreiser wrote the bulk of the diaries that remain. He seems not to have had a future audience in mind for these daily entries; rather they appear to be part of a day-to-day ritual of rough note-taking he developed in order to impose order on his hectic schedule. In a technical sense, Dreiser did not keep one continuous diary but a series of separate journals that can be thought of as representing three distinct phases of his career. The Philadelphia diary presents the beginning novelist who, however vulnerable emotionally, is forcing himself into a stance that would eventually release him psychologically from limited modes of writing and thought. Dreiser's turbulent and prolific middle years are captured in the records that survive of his trip to Savannah in 1916, of his life in Greenwich Village in the nineteen-teens (which included occasional excursions to fashionable resorts on the New Jersey shore), and of his ambivalent reactions to his native Mid-West in 1919. Finally, there are the early years with Helen Richardson, the chronicle starting with their meeting in the fall of 1919, extending through their time together in California in the 1920s, and culminating in the period during which he wrote *An American Tragedy*. The diary as a whole did not serve Dreiser as a mine for later fictional projects, as did Twain's for him; or as a meditative act, as did Kafka's; nor was it an art form, like Anaïs Nin's. What Dreiser's personal notes offer is something more basic: the record of a man who has committed his vast energies to survival through creative work and intense participation in the life around him.

A trip to Savannah in early 1916 resulted in an extended moment in the diaries. Dreiser was trying to finish *A Hoosier Holiday,* and New York proved uncongenial to the nostalgic mood of his Indiana idyll. He felt distraught over the pending breakup of his affair with Kirah Markham, the actress he had lived with since 1914. On her part, Markham vacillated between fitful attempts to get him to propose marriage and punitive attacks designed to put him on the defensive. "I'm beginning to think you're too old for me," she writes to him in Savannah, deliberately touching a sensitive nerve.[11] To avoid such pressures and to escape the winter cold he dreaded, he headed south alone. At this point in his career he could find prominent citizens who would host him whenever he cared to break the solitude he needed to work. By 1916 his writing had earned him an international reputation. In just five years he had published four long novels and *A Traveler at Forty*; *Plays of the Natural and the Supernatural* appeared during his stay in Savannah; and he records the completion of *A Hoosier Holiday* there on 13 February 1916. Sporadic but time-consuming work on *The Bulwark* and occasional journalism were also part of this amazingly fecund period. What he had not managed to do was to earn a comfortable living with his pen. Financial success would be postponed until ten years later when, during yet another southern tour, he would jot down in his diary the first news of his only bestseller, *An American Tragedy.*

Dreiser was forty-four in 1916 and still straining to balance a tight monthly budget. He lived by what he wrote, and—to his friend Mencken's dismay—he would write in the same week for magazines as diverse as *Masses, Cosmopolitan, The Seven Arts,* and *Saturday Evening Post.* He worked hard. Worry over meeting deadlines triggered regular spells of melancholy and exacted its toll in headaches and stomach disorders. Another type of headache came from unremitting battles with publishers: the Century Company prudishly edited *A Traveler at Forty*; Harper's decided to drop *The Titan* after printing ten thousand copies ("If this were *Sister Carrie* I would now be in the same position I was then,"[12] Dreiser confided to Mencken); soon John Lane Company would force him to fight the ban on *The "Genius"* imposed by the New York Society for the Suppression of Vice. To relieve stress he resorted, in a general way, to practices he associated with his mother. He relied on omens to bolster his trust in the future. Like Sarah Dreiser, he was prone to believe in signs, mystic moments, and psychic phenomena—forms of magic for which his philosophy had no use. In

---

11. 29 March 1916, Dreiser Collection, University of Pennsylvania Library.
12. 6 March 1919, *Letters,* 1:162.

his journal he notices horseshoes, hunchbacks, cross-eyed children, and cripples. Such signs filled his mind the way household saints and charms cluttered his home as a child. The sight of a broken horseshoe and then a whole one is a token that "my spiritual guardian & enemies are fighting" (17 February 1916).

These beliefs were encouraged by the conclusions he came to in the autobiographies he wrote from the early nineteen-teens to the late twenties. *A Hoosier Holiday* uncovered his Indiana boyhood in the form of a travel book; by 1916 he had completed a version of *Dawn,* which dealt with the same material in greater detail and carried the story into his adolescence and to the early Chicago days; and shortly afterward he began *Newspaper Days.* His work in this vein solidified an image of himself that derived in part from the ambivalent identifications he made with his parents. In the process of defining his past, Dreiser turned his back on John Paul Dreiser's moralism and orthodoxy, having found in his father's repressiveness the source of the family's vagaries and his own disturbed personality. His mother he apotheosized as he did Carrie and Jennie—as a poet, a dreamer, a "pagan" who followed nature's way.

Dreiser incorporated his vision of the natural pagan into his life. He enjoyed chronicling his relations with women in his journals. Discreet to the point of squeamishness in his language and public references to sex, he nevertheless was at pains to record each time he bedded down with a woman. He made a habit of incorporating selected love letters into the diaries. Beyond the autoerotic stimulation this practice provided him in his forties and fifties, it was a way of distancing himself from the weighty moralistic tone he had early learned to attach to such activities. Language was a potent weapon in this campaign. His verbal bluntness counterbalanced the softer side of his sensibility and acted as a shield against emotional hurt. Most often he describes the sex act as "fierce" or "richly brutal"; and Nina Wilcox Putnam's reaction to his overtures seems fitting: "You talk like a thug" (15 November 1917).

Detached mechanical description of sexual encounters was another way of protecting himself against the sentimental, more vulnerable parts of his personality. "The Sea" and "Clouds," the prose poems he composed on the boat to Savannah, are transparent examples of the substitutes he found for these impulses.

Pearl Grey and pink and a few thin bars that are as red as hot blood. The sea below is so cool and flat. The clouds in the east reach out like hands. They beckon and signal, like fingers speaking of lands that never were. They talk to

me of dreams that I had in my youth. "Better lands than this," they say, "await you."
"Out! Come forth. Shake off the thing that holds you. Spring up into the blue. . . . Walk over the water to us. Forget all life & come." [26 January 1916]

With such obvious displacements, he allowed himself a freedom to engage the feminine that he resisted in the emotional side of his relations with women. As Dreiser himself recognized, he hardly could be mistaken for a modern Werther:

Bert [Estelle Kubitz] is morbid over love. Tells me how keenly she feels about me. . . . Sometimes she seems almost insane over me. At other times able to leave me. I must be very calloused. The love moods torture me at the moment, yet a little while later I forget them. And I believe it would almost kill me—be absolutely impossible for me to be faithful to one woman. At this date it would be almost the severest strain I have yet endured. [6 June 1917]

There existed an ingenuousness about Dreiser that, as he took stock of his actions, gave the impression of his being half-staggered by his own sense of sinfulness.

Nevertheless, he found consolation and immediate gratification in the company of many women. In this respect he was very much a man of his time and place. Dreiser lived at 165 West Tenth Street and belonged to the group of artists and intellectuals who lived in or near Greenwich Village between 1912 and 1917, challenging the nation to a radical shift in social mores in the name of a higher morality. They were, to paraphrase the title of Hutchins Hapgood's autobiography, Victorians struggling to make a modern world. Dreiser gathered with friends at places like Polly's Restaurant and the Liberal Club where he listened to, among other things, the anarchism of Emma Goldman, Margaret Sanger's theories of birth control, and Henrietta Rodman's free-love program. Harry Kemp, the "Byron of the Village," was perhaps more energetic than most in his bohemianism but no less representative as he declared, "I need women for my body, I need women for my soul, I need women for my poetic inspiration."[13] Kemp's female counterpart, Edna St. Vincent Millay, proclaimed equal rights for her sex to burn the candle at both ends. The new freedoms brought forth manifestoes based on the recent revelations of Freud, Krafft-Ebing, and Havelock Ellis, who showed this generation how the amorous and artistic lives are mutually fruitful and conjoint. Most such declarations were not as thoughtful as Dreiser's "Neurotic America

13. Quoted in Allen Churchill, *The Improper Bohemians: A Re-creation of Greenwich Village in Its Heyday* (New York: Dutton, 1959), p. 46.

and the Sex Impulse," though they tended to be as serious, and often as heady. After the war there was less need for polemics, and the old Villagers could look back wistfully and define themselves more securely in books like Floyd Dell's *Love in Greenwich Village*.

Dreiser found this setting conducive to his temperament and needs. He resorted to sexual intrigues for the same reasons that some people turn to risky sports: to control restlessness and satisfy the desire for adventure and stimulation. His sexual appetite matched his appetite for writing and was as compulsive. Like many of his contemporaries, he looked to libidinous drives to inspire his art—the more so as he concluded that literary creation is as shot through with eros and the will to power as is the sex act. His liaisons offset the problem of "being an intellectual. One is too distant & people do not draw to one" (4 February 1916). The women who filled the vacuum were, predictably, the sort that hang out on the fringes of bohemia: minor performers like Kirah Markham and Lillian Rosenthal, or those like Estelle Kubitz, Louise Campbell, and Anna Tatum who harbored literary ambitions. They belonged to a breed of women who were leaving behind them the stricter codes that determined how men and women mingle, and who, welcoming the secular freedoms of the modern city, were willing to submit themselves, if only for a mid-day fling in a cheap hotel, to the necessities of "genius." Of course numerous affairs did not heal all the old wounds. As Frank Harris noticed when he interviewed Dreiser during this period, he was still preoccupied by his early "shyness with girls and his fear of failure in life."[14] His insecurities were not helped by his understanding of the cult of personality and fame that brought these women to him.

There is a certain magnetism about success or fame or wealth or publicity or personality that tends to draw, often fatally and hopelessly, those who are fascinated by these peculiar attributes.
In my own case I would not be able to say exactly what it has been that a fascinated individual has seen in me. But always, or ever since the publication of my second book—and even before—there has been a stream of these followers. . . .[15]

These followers did little to relieve his loneliness, however, since what he called his "varietism" precluded intimacy.

Dreiser's lovers did foster in him a sense of control over his environ-

---

14. *Contemporary Portraits,* p. 92.
15. Dreiser, "The Story of Elizabeth," *This Madness, Hearst's International-Cosmopolitan* 86, no. 5 (1929): 81.

ment. He had known for years that he was his own worst enemy, and he sought in a variety of mistresses a way of guarding against excessive self-contemplation. He developed strategies to ward off downhill plunges in his life. Besides the diversions of his social life, his chief defence was the street-tough mask he wore to meet the world. No one knows what is behind such facades, but Dreiser clearly was comfortable interpreting experience as struggle, and he developed a knee-jerk reaction to forms of political and social idealism which acted as a safety valve for many of the social pressures he felt. Armed with the idiom of liberal politics, he found a ready-made language to express his disdain for the "horrible American bourgeoisie." At times his ideas got the better of him and led to questionable conclusions. He evolved many views of the world, some of which he could not even pretend were consistent with one another. When, for instance, he writes in the diary "On Niggers" (30 January 1916), his position has little to do with the human side of the Negro question as he showed it in "Nigger Jeff" or his long correspondence with the Negro presser J. E. Bowler. (Bowler and he became friends when Dreiser spent time in Bedford City, Virginia, in 1901; on 3 October 1903, he wrote Dreiser saying, "in all my life you are the first white man I've ever written a letter that was not strictly a business one."[16]) Instead the issue becomes a pretext to attack sanguine concepts of progress and evolutionary theory. So too his remarks about Southern society appear less quirky if we take into account his real complaint—the effect of "sex repression" on that region.

In the end, Dreiser's greatest asset was his amazing capacity for work. He seemingly could write anywhere—aboard ship in New York harbor; in a dreary room in Savannah; on a bench in the "graveyard park" where, by his own account, he averaged more than a chapter a day on *A Hoosier Holiday*; or in his Manhattan studio where, between two trysts, he casually says, "Fall to work on article, America. Do about 2000 words" (29 May 1917). He seems to have derived an almost sensuous pleasure from the act of writing. As George Jean Nathan observed, "Of all the writers whom I knew intimately Dreiser is the only one who actually enjoys the physical business of writing."[17] Whatever the cause, Dreiser taught himself to keep putting words on the page during even the most uninspired phases of his career.

16. Dreiser Collection, University of Pennsylvania Library.
17. Nathan, *The Intimate Notebooks of George Jean Nathan* (New York: Knopf, 1932), p. 48.

Dreiser's diaries after 1916—until the decision to devote full time to *An American Tragedy* in 1924—show him marking time as a novelist. There would be ten years between the publication of *The "Genius"* in 1915 and *An American Tragedy.* Although he continued with *The Bulwark,* the book frustrated him and he found ways of avoiding it, expending his powers on revisions of old stories or on devising plots for quick sales to the magazines. He flirted with the idea of producing his plays and selling the movie rights to his novels. The important writing between 1915 and 1925 has a retrospective quality. Dreiser's energy went into large memoirs; and other books—*Twelve Men* (1919), *Hey Rub-a-Dub-Dub* (1920), *The Color of a Great City* (1923)—reflect both the reordering of past work and its autobiographical cast. New directions came in genres that are not major forms for him: dramatic writing like *The Hand of the Potter* and speculative essays such as those in *Hey Rub-a-Dub-Dub,* all of which helped him define the philosophical views he held until the Depression years. In these pieces he gave new personal status to the principle of mutability (usually as an argument for the necessity of change in human affairs), without discarding the notion he had derived from Herbert Spencer that physical, social, and psychological reality tended toward a mechanistic balance of forces. Characteristically, he raised to the level of philosophical discourse issues in which he had a personal stake: he argued that ethics have a material basis and are therefore contingent, with the corollary that responsibility is not in any ultimate sense individual: "there is but one will, or lack of it, a huge, inescapable compulsion."[18] His answer to Mencken, who was awaiting a novel and impatient with such speculation, underlines the concurrence between Dreiser's ideas and his inner needs: "These things had to be done to release a psychic urge in me. It is useless to say they should not."[19]

Dreiser's diary brings to light the nature of the private concerns that underlie his theoretical positions. The personal record corresponds to a decade of change in American life which is reflected in the alterations brought on by the World War. Along with pre-war writers like Edgar Lee Masters and Edith Wharton, Dreiser had revolted against the rigid formality of American writing. With H. L. Mencken he had conducted

18. "Suggesting the Possible Substructure of Ethics," in Donald Pizer, *Theodore Dreiser: A Selection of Uncollected Prose* (Detroit: Wayne State Univ. Press, 1977), p. 211.
19. Dreiser to Mencken, 3 February 1919, *Letters,* 1: 259.

a frontal assault on the bastions of "puritan" morality. He had earned the respect of his peers if not the general public. Most of the younger group starting out during the war years could agree with Waldo Frank that "In the good old days before the War, Dreiser was the one American novelist whom a self-respecting American radical could take time to read. He towered above the inarticulate flatlands of the Middle West. And there was none beside him."[20] In 1917 the *Seven Arts* published his "Life, Art and America," which Frank called "a creative man's confession of what it is to be an American artist."[21] Although few could claim such authority, the essay marked a watershed in Dreiser's career. It looked more to the past than the future. It was the summary of the goals of a generation of writers who, however rootless and cut off from traditional American pieties, chose to stay at home and redefine American culture. In 1917 many of the issues Dreiser associated with the fight for art in America—the trusts, religious intolerance, sexual prudery—were becoming less crucial to a younger crop of artists and intellectuals who were shaping the literary scene in response to other pressures.

John Dos Passos, Hart Crane, E. E. Cummings, Edmund Wilson, Marianne Moore, and Matthew Josephson were among the men and women who had moved into Greenwich Village by 1916. The new atmosphere they were creating had little in common with the ideals of the artist Dreiser portrayed in *The "Genius."* Even in the old days, as Ludwig Lewisohn recalls, Dreiser had "an amusing passion for Bohemia, but was kept out of it by what he was."[22] This became truer after 1917, when he found himself less comfortable with the new avant-garde which was interested in psychology more than society, in style more than ideas, and in Europe as much as America. Malcolm Cowley points to the cleavage between "those who had lived in the Village before 1917 and those who had first arrived from France or college."

"They" had been rebels: they wanted to change the world, be leaders in the fight for justice and art, help to create a society in which individuals could express themselves. . . . "We" couldn't see much use in crusading against puritanism: it had ceased to interfere with our personal lives. . . .[23]

20. Frank, *Time Exposures* (New York: Boni and Liveright, 1926), p. 159.
21. Frank, *Memoirs of Waldo Frank,* ed. Alan Trachtenberg (Amherst: Univ. of Massachusetts Press, 1973), p. 88.
22. Lewisohn, *Expression in America* (New York: Harper and Bros., 1932), p. 473.
23. Cowley, *Exile's Return* (New York: Viking, 1951), pp. 72–73.

Dreiser represented the old guard, and he reacted to the cultural shifts of the time. His essay "Change," which argued the necessity of staying open to the flux of events, was rooted in the need to confront the dislocations of the period. Little things, Dreiser noted in the piece, reflect a world of change. Once he and Kirah Markham held open house for artists and thinkers on Sunday evenings from November to March; now, with the exception of a few close friends, he kept to himself. His diary note on the author William Salisbury suggests something about his own situation: "Is non-puritanic. Finds himself isolated. Needs some one to talk to" (20 November 1917).

Dreiser's isolation deepened with the war. Anti-German sentiment before and after the war put him—and other German-American intellectuals like Mencken, George Sylvester Viereck, and Ludwig Lewisohn—on the defensive. "I see Germans singing America!," he exclaims acridly (14 October 1917); Fred Booth "is pro-German, as most able Americans are" (17 November 1917). "I am very bitter," he says in reaction to a "new ruling against Germans" (21 November 1917). Recently he had worked on *Dawn,* and his bitterness was exacerbated by the ambivalence he felt as the son of a German immigrant. He wrote the militant "American Idealism and German Frightfulness," but none of the magazines would accept it. In the wartime climate of 1917, a writer or a journal did not have to be German to lose favor with the public. Randolph Bourne's anti-war articles in *Seven Arts* brought charges of pro-German sympathies and spelled the end of an important journal; *Masses* folded after the trial of its staff, including Max Eastman, Floyd Dell, and Art Young, for violating the Sedition Act of 1917. The stigma of his German heritage followed Dreiser into the critical arena, where establishment critics like Paul Elmer More and Stuart Sherman lambasted him for his mixed loyalties. Sherman's famous attack on his "barbaric naturalism" stressed that its roots were in Dreiser's German-American background, and he held up Dreiser's books as representative of "a new note in American literature, coming from the 'ethnic' element of our mixed population."[24] The war-inspired xenophobia accompanied him every place, even into his bedroom, where one of his mistresses casually tells him of her husband's "modified anti-German attitude" (21 February 1918).

24. Sherman, "The Barbaric Naturalism of Mr. Dreiser," *The Nation,* 2 December 1915; reprinted in *The Stature of Theodore Dreiser,* ed. Alfred Kazin and Charles Shapiro (Bloomington: Indiana Univ. Press, 1955), p. 72.

Dreiser's sympathy for Germany was not the only reason for his sense of displacement in the teens. No settlement had yet been reached in early 1918 on the obscenity case brought against *The "Genius"* by John Sumner's Comstock organization. The book itself offered the occasion to link Dreiser to the "Hun menace." "We hope," one reviewer quipped, "that *The 'Genius'* will immediately appear in a German translation. That's how kindly we feel toward the Germans."[25] Mencken, who badgered the Author's League of America into defending Dreiser, had gathered wide support for the cause. Although Dreiser relished the fight, it also reminded him of his uncertain place in literary circles. Many who backed Mencken made a sharp distinction between their principled support of literary freedom and their less than enthusiastic interest in *The "Genius"*. Dorothy Dudley at least suggests what Dreiser felt about his status in those years.

For one to speak of him in the presence of conventional people, at a dinner party for instance, even if they were writers and supposedly interested in our literature, was received as improper; the subject was instantly changed.[26]

In addition, it became clear by 1918 that the struggle for the brand of artistic freedom needed to publish a book like *The "Genius"* was already passé, and the trial was a last hurrah for an issue that had run its course. For Dreiser it climaxed his career as America's leading literary rebel. In the end the case was dismissed on a technicality, and it established no legal precedent to insure against further assaults from the censors.

Dreiser's legal entanglement not only gained him no new friends, it signaled the last major defense of him by Mencken. Mencken too sensed a turning point in their relation, and, to some extent, fostered it in his public statements after 1916. Thoroughly devoted to the novelist's vision from *Sister Carrie* to *The Titan* in 1914, Mencken read almost as a personal affront Dreiser's thematic concerns in more controversial work like *The "Genius"* and *The Hand of the Potter*. Dreiser, on his part, took to heart Mencken's changing opinion of him.

Yewdale calls up, wants me to get proofs of Mencken's <u>Book of Prefaces</u> and persuade him to modify his estimate of me. Asserts it is all unfavorable and untrue, that he dismisses <u>The "Genius"</u> as a mass of piffle and that he states that my first work was the best and that I have steadily deteriorated since. Urges

25. N. P. Dawson, "Books of the Week," New York *Evening Globe,* 30 October 1915. Reprinted in *Theodore Dreiser: The Critical Reception,* ed. Jack Salzman (New York: David Lewis, 1972), p. 226.

26. Dudley, *Forgotten Frontiers,* p. 237.

me to point out Bourne's estimate, which is better, but I tell him I can't influence Mencken. Get the blues from this. Bert adds to them by saying that such a criticism will fix public belief, that it is always anxious to believe the worst. [13 August 1917]

At this time, helped no doubt by the fact that Dreiser and Mencken had mistresses who were sisters, their relationship withstood the strain. But Dreiser's idea of Mencken as "a cautious conventionalist" (2 August 1917) surely stems as much from his sense of Mencken's growing literary conservatism as from his un-Dreiserian discretion with Marion Bloom.

Like his Carrie Meeber, Dreiser was stirred to more intense yearnings of the imagination by success of esteem. "Life is so puzzling. I feel all the time that I am wasting my time, and yet I am not really" (25 May 1917). Dreiser met his growing isolation with a rigorous if erratic schedule of writing. Then there were the women in his life. At points it seems the writing takes second place, that he is spending more time at Lüchow's and the Brevoort than at his desk. The dizzying pace with which he ran from one affair to another may obscure how much he subordinated everything to his work. To every bedroom he carried along a manuscript as well as a change of clothes.

No sooner get in than we begin undressing. Fire in the grate. We play in the rear room before mirror, then go into bedroom. Stay in bed from 2 to 6, playing. Between rounds she reads A Story of Stories and likes it. At 6 she has to dress. . . . Takes first ten chapters of A History of Myself to copy. Wants to marry me. [26 October 1917]

Describing Dreiser in this period, Hutchins Hapgood recalled years later that "he rarely talked about anything except literature," and "the only other absorbing interest he had was sex; and that took decidedly second place . . . for he didn't sacrifice anything important to [his writing]."[27] Hapgood, smarting from an unflattering portrait of him in *A Gallery of Women,* caught only half the truth. One of the startling aspects of Dreiser's diaries is the extent to which they center on the women he knew. The diaries are virtually written *around* them. The daily entries between 1916 and 1926 reveal few male friends, and little socializing beyond a rare evening with John Cowper Powys, George Sterling or Edgar Lee Masters, and an occasional night on the town with Mencken. Women, on the other hand, function as his chief partners in

27. Hapgood, *A Victorian in the Modern World* (New York: Harcourt, Brace, 1939), p. 266.

conversation, his editorial advisors, research assistants, traveling companions, and ultimately as a prime source for his writing.

It is an open question how much Dreiser's writing depended on his expectations of a female audience. Male images dominate our thinking about twentieth-century American literature, which is associated with a revolt against the "damn mob of scribbling women" Hawthorne complained about. In Dreiser's case, women came to be his major prepublication readers; and much of the fiction originating in this period—for instance, "The Second Choice," *This Madness,* and a good portion of *A Gallery of Women*—is written from a woman's point of view. The diaries find Dreiser constantly submitting his writing to the scrutiny of one or another of his close female friends. Many of his intimate and long-term relations—with Louise Campbell, Anna Tatum, Lillian Rosenthal, to name a few—began with letters that soundly criticized one of his books. The best part of the large correspondence he maintained with women, often for years without meeting them or for decades after their intimacies ended, revolves around their consideration of his work. As his writing became less accessible to old friends like Arthur Henry and Mencken, he came to rely more on the talented women he knew to judge his initial drafts. Mencken, trying to persuade Dreiser not to go public with *The Hand of the Potter,* sensed the drift in this direction: "Change your play into something else. Jack the Ripper is an old, old story. . . . Take the advice of men with hair on their chests—not of women."[28] Mencken misunderstood the intent of Dreiser's play, but he judged correctly that his friend, in effect, had surrounded himself with a private coterie whose amorous and editorial capacities were indistinguishable.

Just as the lives of his sisters inspired his first two novels, so other women influenced later fiction. The story Anna Tatum told him about her father led to decades of work on *The Bulwark*; "Chains" came out of long afternoons spent with Louise Campbell; Kirah Markham appears as "Sídonie" and Anna Tatum as "Elizabeth" in *This Madness.* In the midst of diary accounts of erotic scenes, Dreiser will stop to exclaim "What a tale!" (14 November 1917) or "Would make a fine short story" (15 November 1917). He was equally alert to the dramatic potential in the lives of more casual friends. On winter days his neighbor on 10th Street, the actress Mary Pyne, would leave the cold apart-

28. Mencken to Dreiser, 20 December 1916. Quoted in *Letters,* 1: 243.

ment she shared with the improvident Harry Kemp and sit for hours before Dreiser's fireplace. Usually she sat quietly while he worked, but at times he would stop writing and ask her about her life. "The history of Mary Pyne would make a good short story—a bad-good girl" (25 November 1917). Perhaps no male writer of the period—with the exception of Henry James—was as interested in the lives of women. Dreiser wrote Mencken in 1919, "For years I have planned a volume to be entitled *A Gallery of Women.* God, what a work! if I could do it truly—The ghosts of Puritans would rise and gibber in the streets."[29] By 1929 when he published the fifteen long portraits in *Gallery of Women,* the puritans who remained needed a stronger stimulus to anxiety. While some of the writing suffers from Dreiser's overly literal rendering of the careers of his subjects, a number of chapters are among his finest biographical sketches. They are not fully developed or carefully plotted portraits, but loose characterizations depicting unusual personal destinies or responses to the problem of getting on as a woman. Many of these figures appear in the diary: Henrietta Stafford, the maundering fortune-teller; Miriam Taylor, the morphine-addicted nurse who shared rooms with Estelle Kubitz and her sister; Mary Pyne, whose marriage to Harry Kemp, affair with Hutchins Hapgood, and early death of consumption became part of Greenwich Village lore. Other material of this sort Dreiser published in magazines or, like the piece on Estelle Kubitz entitled "Gloom," retained in manuscript.

Dreiser looked upon these women, who belonged to the generation born in the 1880s and 1890s, as the representative types of the day. He tried to define in their lives an emerging class of woman—the offspring of a century of industrialization, of the movement from town and farm to urban center, and of rapid shifts in roles and values. He had, however, no programmatic interest in the woman's movement. In his journals we may observe him talking over the "position of women" with Nita Pearson, or marching off to a suffrage parade with Estelle Kubitz, but he shied away from anything more organized. His attraction was to the drama of the lives, which he understood were at a stage of social transition that affected everyone from the scrubwoman he calls "Bridget Mullanphy" to the political radical "Ernita" (Ruth Kennell). There is nothing ideological about this writing, but as a chronicle of the women who came to maturity just before World War I, it owes some-

29. Dreiser to Mencken, 8 April 1919, *Letters,* 1: 264.

thing to the intellectual climate established by Dreiser's progressive neighbors in New York. The true analogues to Dreiser's work are books like Rheta Childe Dorr's *A Woman at Fifty* and Fannie Hurst's *Anatomy of Me*—studies, that is, of the new freedoms women gained in the modern city, and the price they paid psychologically as traditional roles were abandoned.

The diaries present Dreiser interacting with the originals of his *Gallery* characters. They respond to him as men did under similar circumstances: by identifying with his impulse to conquer the social order, to cast off traditional marital and familial roles, to free himself from sexual and religious taboos. Despite his isolation Dreiser came to be, for his restless contemporaries, the representative writer of the age, a liberating force of great importance for the times. Although often meeting rough treatment at his hands, women revealed themselves to him because they sensed how many of their obsessions and fantasies he shared. Often he seems to act as a kind of guru whose practical function consisted of running a counseling service, particularly on domestic matters. Mrs. Ludwig Lewisohn, who wrote under the pen-name Bosworth Crocker, is typical.

[She came] to complain of her family troubles, how restless and sexy Ludwig is, and to ask my advice whether she had better give him up. I urged her to do so—which she resented, of course. [27 October 1917]

(Years later, Ludwig Lewisohn wrote this episode into *Don Juan,* a roman à clef in which Dreiser, called Blaffka, recounts the incident to a confused Lewisohn, called Lucien.) The letters he includes in the diary read like bintel briefs, with all the pathos of post-Victorian marital crisis:

I think I am willing to risk love outside of marriage . . . although I am not unhappily married. That is one of the things I cannot understand—why I should seek it elsewhere. It is a terrible thing, is it not, to promise to "love, honor and obey" any one man for life?[30]

Of course Dreiser was aware the time was ripe for such revelations. As Douglas Doty reminded him, there was a growing market for stories of "American girls who have emancipated themselves from American home conditions and conventions and succeeded in life" (30 November 1917). In *A Gallery of Women* and other writing, Dreiser typically

30. Bertha Halloran to Dreiser, undated, with entry for 7 August 1917 in diary.

chose to tell about the failures too, and about the desire that remains after success. They became part of the permanent record he created of his time and place.

In the summer of 1919, Dreiser began traveling to ease his restlessness. His preoccupations made writing difficult. "Tired of my various girls and wish I had a new love," he notes in the journal. *The "Genius"* was not yet back in the bookstores, his plays were not being produced as he had hoped, he could not make any progress on *The Bulwark,* and no other novel was coming. He had his usual money worries. In June he boarded a train for Indiana, his first trip back since the tour he had taken with Franklin Booth four years earlier. To Edward H. Smith, he wrote from Culver, Indiana, "New York was getting on my nerves so much that I had to get out for a time."[31]

Dreiser returned to see May Calvert Baker, his seventh-grade teacher in Warsaw, whose early encouragement he never forgot. Indiana was the place he kept coming back to in imagination. The reality was less tractable. In some ways, he felt comfortable there: he found German-Americans like himself, and the local gentry was given to palm reading. Here were hometown intellectuals and artists, like his old editor at the *Chicago Daily Globe,* John M. Maxwell, the Russian theater scholar Oliver Sayler, and the composer Gaylord Yost. In Indianapolis, the *Star* interviewed him, the city remembered its production of *Laughing Gas,* and someone commissioned a local painter, Simon P. Baus, to do his portrait. Yet the uneasiness remained. Dreiser knew he could not compete for the state's attention or affection with the memory of his brother Paul Dresser, much less with cherished Hoosier authors like Booth Tarkington, Meredith Nicholson, and George Ade. The state song, Paul's "On the Banks of the Wabash," had a following that none of his books—not even *A Hoosier Holiday*—had achieved. To this day, visitors to Warsaw are more likely to hear of the periods Ambrose Bierce and James Whitcomb Riley spent there than how Dreiser put the town on the literary map of America. There is pathos in the scene of Dreiser sitting under the stars with Mrs. Baker, discussing his obscurity in the neighborhood. "She talks of forwarding my books & spreading my fame" (18 June 1919). Yet Dreiser knew from her letters over the

31. Dreiser to Edward H. Smith, 19 June 1919, Dreiser Collection, University of Pennsylvania Library.

years that she too would have preferred her most famous pupil to have written more uplifting books.

Northern Indiana carried Dreiser's thoughts back in a special way, though with the exception of brief asides, he is quiet about his feelings. In memoirs, he describes how his family moved in the fall of 1884 from Chicago to Warsaw where some of Sarah Dreiser's relatives lived. At first, the resettlement seemed a blessing to the boy; his overbearing father remained at his job in Terre Haute, the early scandals connected with brother Rome and his sisters were behind him, the older sisters themselves stayed in Chicago—and for the first time, at age thirteen, Dreiser was free of the dreaded parochial schools. In May Calvert's classroom he received the kind of attention—part motherly, part intellectual—that he sought in later affairs with women. The public school also offered him his first contact with the children of "respectable" families. These young people—many of whom he was meeting as adults in 1919—had taught Dreiser something about the social desires and feelings of inadequacy a newcomer experiences. Now, despite his fame, he was still an outsider to the larger community. He must have remembered that earlier time—"Life passes so achingly," he repeats— as he revisited old haunts. In their way, these emotions deepened the writing of the following summer when, in the process of conceptualizing the story of Clyde Griffiths, he started to explore the potential for tragedy in such childhood traumas. In effect, his Indiana travels and autobiographical probings were pushing him toward the last major breakthrough of his career as a novelist. We may imagine that even the fishing and rowing on the lovely lakes around Warsaw, which led to "dreadful dreams," found their way into the dense water imagery and lake scenes of *An American Tragedy*.

The summer of 1919 found Dreiser still groping his way toward the larger theme of his major novel. The stay in Indiana focused his mind once again on the dramatic potential of the Midwest of his youth, providing flesh and bones for the abstractions of his polemical essays, and diverting him from the stories about women. "Thoughts as to how to write 'Her Boy'" came to him (26 June 1919). Dreiser never completed the long narrative in which he studies the early influences on the criminal course of a young Irishman, Eddie Meagher. He placed the action in Philadelphia and used the techniques he learned from Stephen Crane's fictional treatment of lower-class urban Irish. But readers of *Dawn* would recognize Eddie Meagher in Dreiser's childhood neighbor "Red" Sullivan. More importantly, Meagher's emotional make-up and his victimized life look ahead to Clyde Griffiths.[32] For reasons I will return to later, Dreiser increasingly experimented with stories about crime, which was becoming a major factor in his composite idea of America. In the summer of 1920 he would undertake the book that tapped the deepest meaning of what Indiana had taught him about the nature of crime and punishment in America.

In July 1919 Dreiser went, with Estelle Kubitz, to the resort areas at Ocean Grove and Asbury Park, New Jersey. The neighboring communities were dramatic reminders of American society's incomplete transition from a strait-laced, basically fundamentalist morality to more liberalized standards. "The religionists," as Dreiser calls them, ran Ocean Grove's Methodist community. Although the Eighteenth Amendment outlawing alcoholic drinks had only just been passed in June, the town had had its own dry laws since its founding in 1869. The community was, in many ways, a throwback to the seventeenth-century Puritan townships where the church reigned supreme, regulating everything from swimming to the hanging out of clothes on the Sabbath. It was Billy Sunday territory, one of his favorite sites for revival services. In contrast, Dreiser notes, was the wide-open quality of the town down the road, and especially "The girls at Asbury—very beautiful & costumes very daring" (14 July 1919). Asbury Park self-consciously paraded its anti-puritanism, becoming well-known for its nightspots, amusement parks, bars, and other places of entertainment shunned by Ocean Grove residents. Such postwar oppositions, as the nation sped up its retreat from rigid moral principles while at the same time imposing stringent prohibitions on itself, confirmed the linkage in Dreiser's mind between repression and deviant behavior. As was often true, he grappled with the larger social context in terms he derived from the engagements of his personal history. The lessons of the Indiana of his youth—particularly those garnered from the harsh nineteenth-century restrictions on sexual relations—were being put to the test on the national level. Critics often wonder at the indeterminate atmosphere and setting of Dreiser's novel of the twenties, *An American Tragedy.* What is overlooked, however, is the fable-like tenor of the social dis-

---

32. Donald Pizer has the fullest discussion of "Her Boy" in relation to *An American Tragedy,* in *The Novels of Theodore Dreiser: A Critical Study* (Minneapolis: Univ. of Minnesota Press, 1976), pp. 205–07.

ruptions of the postwar era, which Dreiser captured in his book. As we shall see, his move to Hollywood on the threshold of the twenties gave him an almost surreal vision of the times and reinforced his sense of America's living out a vast social and moral allegory.

As the summer of 1919 drew to a close, Dreiser became noticeably more anxious about the lack of progress in his work. He dreamed that he possessed a key that allowed him to fly "up & around & between great buildings and over vast territories much to the admiration of many & myself." He soon realized the key was beginning to lose its powers, that he had a rival who held "a key like mine."

I could not tell from this—waking up at that point as I did, whether my mental & literary soaring days were over—whether I was ever to be permitted to fly again—or whether I was still to fly very high & then lose my power. The thought of the first possible meaning made me very sad. [3 August 1919]

The imagery flows naturally from his private symbolism. The diary is cluttered with the flight of birds—Dreiser had a special fondness for gulls, probably as a result of years spent in lower Manhattan—and mention of them is a sure sign that he is experiencing an earthbound mood. By this point he had read Freud, and so knew something about his nocturnal flights. A more thoroughgoing Freudian might have interpreted the loss of power associated with the key as sexually symbolic, which has some logic to it, since he follows the notice of this dream with a paean to the last important woman in his life. The title he uses is simply "Helen."

"This day I met Helen," Dreiser records on 13 September 1919. Within three days he is convinced "a new chapter in my life is opening which may lead any where" (17 September 1919). He had been, for some time now, keenly aware of the need for such a turning point. He was nearly fifty and, not having completed a novel in over five years, the sense of time wasted was growing upon him. Although there had been productive bursts of activity, he felt an increasing paralysis whenever he turned to longer works of fiction. For years now he had sought and received relief in the company of women receptive to the special demands of his calling. But not since the first years of his marriage had he known the intensity and sense of emotional compatibility that Helen Patges Richardson brought to him. Eventually he would marry Helen, when he was in his seventies and after they had spent a stormy twenty-five years together. In 1919, she seemed to be a spiritual link to his mother—Dreiser's mother and Helen's grandmother were sisters—and he described her as he did Sarah Dreiser: compassionate, unconventional, a "pagan" with an artistic temperament. Although only twenty-five, she had already had a brief engagement in vaudeville and had sustained herself in New York after a failed marriage. She was now planning a move to California to act in films. A month after their meeting, Dreiser abandoned the familiar associations of over two decades and accompanied Helen to Los Angeles.

Helen gave Dreiser good reason to feel euphoric and to throw caution to the winds. She was young and beautiful; and she impressed him with "her simple direct humanity, her large charity and her affection for me" (20 September 1919). The portrait of her he put in the diary indicates she was shrewd enough to know what a man of Dreiser's age and temperament wanted to hear:

Not interested in children, save as a writer would be. Interested in all types and conditions of men. Understanding and sympathizing with their necessities, compulsions and lacks. Disliking strident, aggressive and vain youth. Caring more for age, weight, grey hairs and intelligence and force, when combined in a man. Disliking most women. Exquisite taste in dress. Liking only good books, plays & poems. Loving scenery, the out of doors, to ride, to drive, to dance, to sing.

The intimacies Dreiser describes hint at the source of Helen's hold on him. She injected a new element of play into his demanding daily routine: there are more instances of laughter in the 1919–23 entries than in the previous years taken together. Three years after their first meeting Dreiser could still comment regularly on "the fun of being with Helen." She assumed the burden of stimulating him sexually, though before long she seems to have realized how exhausting a job that was to carry on singly. Understandably, she suffered from fits of fatigue and soon began to exhibit symptoms of hypochondria. Her fantasies suggest the strain under which she labored in her attempts to satisfy Dreiser.

Confesses her desire to see me in transports with other girls. Wants to arrange it with some movie beauty. [24 October 1920]
She outlines her scheme for extracting more bliss out of sex. Is to get me girls & watch me manhandle them. [26 October 1920]

Years later, during a period of separation, Dreiser would write to her commenting on her "incest moods"—an obvious reference to another verbal aphrodisiac based on their blood ties: "Of all people I know you can have the incest moods—when the wind is in the right direction.

And the wind has been in pretty much the right direction ever since I first saw you."[33] Fortunately, Helen was able to alternate such activities with other kinds of stimulation. With her he reread old favorites: in fiction, Balzac, Dostoyevsky, and Poe; in philosophy, Spencer, Haeckel and the naturalists; in science Loeb and Freud. She was a willing student who remained in awe of his genius. He guided her along new intellectual paths—and there are shades of Ames's relation to Carrie in the influence he exerted over the younger woman: "he wanted me to continue with my movie work. . . . But how could I be wholly interested in a field where so much lack of artistic understanding prevailed?"[34]

Life with Helen revitalized Dreiser, but his situation made it hard for him to concentrate on *The Bulwark,* whose story demanded a mood very different from what he now had. Also, away from the familiar distractions of New York, he had more time on his hands; and this intensified his natural inclination toward introspection. "I keep very much to myself as I need to," he wrote Edward Smith.[35] Hoping to earn extra money, Dreiser got up articles dealing with life in the movie industry. For these he absorbed information second-hand from Helen's nightly reports of the goings-on at the studios. He worked on a number of movie scripts; he renewed efforts to sell the film rights to his novels. Although Horace Liveright was sending him monthly advances of $333.33 to free him to complete *The Bulwark,* the writing only frustrated and depressed him. "I tackle Bulwark & finish Chapter 13— terrible hard work. No gayety of soul here" (9 April 1920). Anna Tatum was threatening to sue if the book was published, but his inability to finish the story of a good man defeated by changes in a materialistic world had less to do with external factors than with a shift in the center of his interests. The dualism implicit in *The Bulwark*'s initial theme was giving way to the more complex and darker view of the individual not as simple victim but as partaker and perpetuator of a society's ruling passion. At the beginning of the 1920s Dreiser sought to test this perspective within the framework of a narrative dealing with money and criminality. As we shall see, a certain type of crime came to stand for him as a resolution to the crisis he faced with Helen in Hollywood.

33. Dreiser to Helen Richardson, 17 April 1924, Dreiser Collection, University of Pennsylvania Library.
34. Helen Dreiser, *My Life with Dreiser* (Cleveland and New York: World, 1951), p. 61.
35. 5 January 1920, Dreiser Collection, University of Pennsylvania Library.

Even before he knew Helen, Dreiser's experience had prepared him to write about the potential for tragedy in America's obsession with wealth and its horror of poverty. His personal rebellion, rooted in a childhood burdened by the judgments organized society made on his family, led him to identify imaginatively with criminals in all his writing. He tended to connect criminal action with class conflict, and so he was sensitive to the likelihood of antisocial behavior in what he called the underdog. He believed, as his portrait of the financier Cowperwood dramatized, that the appetite for power was inseparable from the appetites for beauty, money, and sex. He had learned as early as the 1890s that, for the outsider who reaches from the bottom of the social ladder, a sanctioned way to satisfy these drives was through marriage. And from the cases of murder he collected from the turn of the century, he saw how often this route gave birth to destructive impulses.

Dreiser's diary during his years in California reveals how his mind seized upon these themes in his personal life and conditioned his thinking as he moved closer to writing the *Tragedy*. His infatuation with Helen carried home to him what he had been observing at a distance for decades. For the first time in years, the fear of losing a woman pushed him to contemplate marriage: "I would give *you* anything— *anything* in the world that I could. If it is marriage you want, you can have that too."[36] This was not a real possibility until Sara Dreiser's death in 1942, since she was never willing to grant Dreiser a divorce. The journal indicates his anxiety centered not on this obstacle but on his sensitiveness to his lack of means; and Helen's connections with the film world heightened his apprehensions. As he wrote in an unpublished article entitled "An Overcrowded Entryway," Hollywood epitomized the class war in which sex and material goods were the chief weapons on both sides. "She is too beautiful not to have a car & I resent our poverty," Dreiser reflects as he strolls with Helen past the mansion of Douglas Fairbanks and Mary Pickford (18 April 1920). He observes "a kind of debauch" as Helen, in a "wild desperation over not having all the money she wants," pawns her ring to buy clothes: "Her frenzy of delight over her purchases. Wildly describes their beauty. Drunkenness in men & clothes buying in women are kind passions. . . . The gleam in her eyes. . . . Her beauty in one of new hats staggers me" (22 April 1920).

36. Quoted in Helen Dreiser, *My Life,* p. 25.

The hidden drama of this period altered the direction of Dreiser's writing. Seated at the work table in the kitchen cubicle of their Glendale bungalow, he tried to write *The Bulwark,* imagining all the while that Helen inhabited an exotic world—"the sex atmosphere and excitement of the realm"—which his own Spartan existence could hardly challenge. Helen came home escorted by directors in limousines, and she told how young romantic actors, like the new Italian star nicknamed Rudi, flirted with her. Dreiser took to writing thinly disguised autobiographical stories like "Fulfillment," in which the aging artist dies, leaving a beautiful woman behind to ponder the vacuity of wealth without "beauty of mind." But he clearly felt how weak a defense this was in the world he saw before him. As Helen began to receive larger parts at the studios, he became more despondent: "I dont think I can keep her long now that she has work & the work is gayer— & the crowd— than I am" (14 May 1920). For relief he turned to a story line that reflects the way his imagination instinctively grappled with the problem.

I am very lonely. Horribly so. Concieve the story of the jealous clerk who cannot lose his beauty bride to the movies & finally kills her & himself. [18 May 1920]

Dreiser was still a long way from the entanglements of Clyde Griffiths's history, but his experience was pushing him to imagine scenarios that held the germ of that story. His passion for Helen, played out against the glitter and easy money of Hollywood, confirmed his growing sense of the causal links between the lure of beautiful women and the desire for riches in crimes of passion.

Helen's later account of these years inadvertently lends credence to Dreiser's private notes. Initially "impressed to the point of wonder" by the famous author and writing after his death, she tends to overlook Dreiser's vulnerability in their first years together. "I noticed in Dreiser a definite poverty complex,"[37] Helen says, but she seems unaware of her part in exacerbating his normal tendencies. One incident appears to have brought her to the brink of understanding the underlying dynamics of Dreiser's response to her. On 3 July 1923, she accompanied him to the scene where Chester Gillette killed Grace Brown in Cortland, New York, and they rowed in a canoe on Big Moose Lake

37. *Ibid.,* p. 44.

to the exact spot of the murder. In the diary Dreiser notes simply, "We row on the lake and listen to the music and watch the dancers." Helen's version provides the most telling moment in her reminiscences, bringing her face to face with a side of Dreiser (and herself) that she intuited rather than fully comprehended.

Here it was that the girl had met her death, and her unheeded cries had rung out over the waters that closed about her. As we sat there the hypnotic spell of it all frightened me a little. I thought:
  "Maybe Teddie will become completely hypnotized by this idea and even repeat it, here and now."[38]

Whatever gift Dreiser had for imaginatively entering into the mind of a murderer, he found release for conflicting passions in the act of writing. One suspects this account is a projection of Helen's own pent-up aggressions, which are never far from the surface of her memoir. Nevertheless, she touches upon a dimension of their life together that is relevant to our understanding of his work at the time. We can see now, with the aid of the diary, how Helen influenced Dreiser's late masterpiece. Ellen Moers once pointed out that "Sondra Finchley, the debutante who bewitches Clyde through many chapters of the *Tragedy,* was Dreiser's invention," having no counterpart in the Gillette case records.[39] The Helen of the early Hollywood years, however, must be considered a strong candidate for the source of Dreiser's inspiration.

What is the total effect of these years on Dreiser's writing? Pieces like "Fulfillment" and "Reina" (the sketch of Helen's sister Myrtle in *A Gallery of Women*) come directly from events recorded in the diary. Other factors are less easily traceable. Whether, for instance, Dreiser's intense feeling for his "western cousin" encouraged him in his thematic use of the Eastern and Western branches of the Griffiths family—and particularly the symbiotic ties he establishes between Clyde and Gilbert Griffiths—is a matter of speculation. So too with the phrases and incidents sprinkled throughout the journal—the street-corner "Salvation Army singers," the "fabled city" of New Orleans, Helen's Sondra-like baby talk—which prompt us to think of the *Tragedy.* In describing their apartment in Los Angeles, with its Asa Griffiths Bible-quoting landlord, Helen offered perhaps the best way of reading the diary: she said the occasion "supplied the necessary climate for the engendering of the

38. *Ibid.,* p. 85
39. Moers, *Two Dreisers,* p. 201.

soon-to-be-born *An American Tragedy.*"[40] While we now know the novel had deeper and more complex roots, the "climate" had a fructifying effect on the ideas Dreiser had carried around with him for decades.

Dreiser's autobiographical volumes also conditioned his output in the twenties. He records the completion of *Newspaper Days* on 11 May 1920, as well as continuing revisions of what would be *Dawn.* The origins of the early novels—from *Sister Carrie* to the first two Cowperwood books—were biographical, but he became less comfortable with this mode (*The Bulwark* is a prime example of the resistance he had to overcome) and more at ease with the vein he had opened in *The "Genius"* and *A Hoosier Holiday.* As the diaries show, much of the short fiction from the late teens onward is close to the bone of Dreiser's experience. They also reveal how, as he felt his way toward fictional norms for the criminal cases he was studying, he was stimulated by the autobiographical potential of each story. But uncompleted manuscripts of numerous novels suggest that this initial excitement dissipated into frustrated stops and starts precisely because Dreiser's sources—murders involving wealthy or middle-class figures like Roland Molineux, Clarence Richesen, and Harry Thaw—did not easily lend themselves to the emotional pattern of the yearning outsider that he understood best. "Mea Culpa," which Dreiser was struggling with in California, is one example. The manuscript develops three motifs that point toward the *Tragedy*: the conflicting values of father and son, the symbolism of money as a psychological factor, and the negative effects of sexual repression on mental health. The protagonist, the fifty-year-old son of a factory owner, narrates his own history. Dreiser was not able to move the story beyond character definition to a central action, partly because he tried to impose his own childhood memories on a figure with an upper-middle-class background. This sort of psychological mismatch is evident in every version of this theme, going back to the second "Rake" novel he started in 1915. Based on the Roland Molineux trial, this fragment of six chapters comes to a halt with Dreiser unable to solve the problem of how his hero can be at once an outsider and a member of the local country club. Put another way, Dreiser did not gain control of his subject until he switched the focus of his tale from, figuratively speaking, Gilbert Griffiths to his cousin Clyde.

Dreiser had progressed no further than twenty chapters into the

40. Helen Dreiser, *My Life,* p. 37.

novel when he left California and returned to New York in the fall of 1922. He was depressed over his lack of success in working out the narrative. "At the moment see no very clear way out of money troubles or that I am making any real artistic headway with work. The relentless push against the individual on and away into dissolution hangs heavy on me" (11 September 1922). He may have needed the familiar tensions of New York, its harsher sights and sounds, to realize the somber feel of reality his theme demanded. He told reporters in Los Angeles,

I want to be back where there is struggle. . . . I like to walk around the quarters of New York where the toilers are. . . . That's health. I don't care about idlers or tourists, or the humdrum, or artistic pretenders that flock out here. . . . There is no art in Los Angeles and Hollywood. And never will be.[41]

Dreiser had been more isolated in California than anywhere else; with the exception of brief excursions to San Francisco in the company of George Douglas, or George Sterling's group at the Bohemian Club, he lived reclusively. From the diary we learn that, on his return to New York, he tried to revert to his pre-Helen lifestyle. He rented an apartment for Helen on West 50th Street and another for himself at St. Luke's Place in the Village; to these he added a working office in Room 1516 of the Guardian Life Building. He found, however, that New York presented a different face to him after three years: it isn't "interesting at all—an immense, congested, sloppy, smoky, unruly place smeared over by millions of unsignificant people. I never saw such a change in a city."[42]

The change was in Dreiser himself, but clearly New York in the mid-twenties no longer provided him the familiar field he had known before the war. Although he again resorted to the stimulation of a number of women, there remained an emotional dependence on Helen that had no precedent except, perhaps, in his early life with his first wife. When Helen prepares, in an act of estrangement, to return home to Oregon in March 1924, he writes in the journal "I am very much depressed for Helen is the only one I really care for now, anymore. . . . I hold close to Helen all night because I feel so gloomy about her leaving me. It is for the 1st time in 4 years—over four years really . . ." (20 March 1924). During their nine-month separation, the diary

41. Quoted in Dudley, *Forgotten Frontiers,* p. 442.
42. Dreiser to Margaret Johnson, 8 January 1923, Dreiser Collection, University of Pennsylvania Library.

became sporadic, as his correspondence became the vehicle for daily note-taking. His letters may seem double-dealing at times, since he could not do without the company of other women; but there is no reason to think his attachment to Helen was not genuine. To no other woman did he write "I will always love you," or commit himself to "get a divorce and tie up as per your dream."[43] The letters are more important, however, as an index to Dreiser's mental state while writing the *Tragedy.* To Helen he emphasized the love element in his story:

B. & L. [Boni and Liveright] don't like "An American Tragedy" as a title. What do you think of *Orion* or *Icarus* or *Xion?* These are all Greek heroes or fabled characters who were misled by or suffered through love. I have still another —The Love Lost.[44]

Most often he is "having a bad time. I really fiddled 5 whole days over one chapter. Not that I didn't know what to say but just too nervous and wrought up to be able to say it."[45]

Finally, on the first of January 1925, Helen returned to rescue Dreiser from an unusual indulgence in gin and cigarettes. At his request she rented an apartment in Brooklyn, at 1799 Bedford Avenue, where they spent nearly a year while he completed the novel.

Dreiser had tried many times to find relief of some sort, but he could not escape. The story tracked him everywhere he went. He could only return to his desk as helplessly as a man under sentence.

"The dark days of Brooklyn," he once wrote. And so they were. Dark days for all of us.[46]

The book, at last, appeared on 10 December 1925, but Dreiser had already left the shadows behind, and again was heading south.

Dreiser's final journal entries, as if to provide a symmetry to his American diaries, contain a tour of Philadelphia and the South, including Savannah. The man who in 1902 wondered about his ability to write had just finished a novel that, after severe editing, ran to nearly four hundred thousand words. Aware perhaps of his distance from the figure he made twenty-five years earlier, he chooses not to remember that dismal time in Philadelphia—or at least not to record it. True to the philosophy he had lived by in the ensuing years, he dwells on the

---

43. Dreiser to Helen Richardson, 2 May 1924, and 1 June 1924, in *ibid.*
44. Dreiser to Helen Richardson, 22 April 1924, in *ibid.*
45. Dreiser to Helen Richardson, 22 May 1924, in *ibid.*
46. Helen Dreiser, *My Life,* p. 113.

signs of change along the way. In Philadelphia, he comments on the new subway and the growth of the University of Pennsylvania, where he would eventually leave the bulk of his papers; further on, he notes "Life & vigor everywhere. The old south [is] gone" (15 December 1925).

Another cause for change, though Dreiser probably did not recognize it at the time, was the stop in Baltimore to see Mencken at his Hollins Street home. From this visit Mencken dated the break that lasted, despite a superficial reconciliation, until Dreiser's death. Since 1919, the friendship had stood on shaky ground. Mencken had grown more and more intolerant of Dreiser's bluntness, his sexual adventures, his politics and philosophizing; and Dreiser needled Mencken for the conservative turn he took as editor, critic, and political commentator. The two tough guys of American literature had made names for themselves, and they now could afford to put aside the old friendship they had cultivated for professional survival. Neither man made a virtue of tolerance, so there was a tendency to exaggerate personal differences. Mencken, who could write "I can no more understand a man praying than I can understand him carrying a rabbit's foot to bring him luck,"[47] bristled at the novelist who could observe with awe aboard ship in Miami, "I see a meteor fall. A cross-eyed man" (24 January 1926). The ostensible reason for the explosion in 1925 was Dreiser's seeming lack of concern for Mencken's mother, who was ailing at the time of his visit. Dreiser mentions in passing "His mother is very ill," but in his hurry he obviously offended Mencken who, known for his vigils at the sickbeds of even casual acquaintances, read callousness into Dreiser's haste. The death of Mrs. Mencken the following day did not help matters. It would be nine years before he would resume correspondence with Dreiser. (When he wrote to Helen on 30 January 1946, shortly after Dreiser's death, Mencken recalled the incident and registered a more balanced judgment than he could have in 1925.

I remember seeing you in Baltimore at the time the two of you started South together. It was, to be precise, on December 12, 1925, for my mother was desperately ill in hospital and died the next day. I remember how I resented his leaving you sit in a cold car up the street, and how I resented likewise his aloof indifference to my mother's illness. It was a long while afterward before I ever felt close to him again. But I should have known him better. There was

47. Mencken, "Sabbath Meditation," in *A Mencken Chrestomathy* (1949); reprinted in *On Mencken,* ed. John Dorsey (New York: Knopf, 1980), p. 133.

a curiously inarticulate side to him, and it often showed up when he was most moved.)[48]

Helen remembered Dreiser's words as they left Hollins Street that afternoon; if Mencken had overheard them, they might have made some difference: "It doesn't matter what he ever says about me or does to me, he is a great guy and a great friend and I will always love him."[49]

Despite the many notations during the drive to Florida, Dreiser appears to be mentally fatigued. The nervous staccato style of the entries reflects his eye for detail and his usual capacity for wonder, but he was too tired for extended commentary. Although impressed by the signs of industry and progress in the South, he concludes, "No art for soul," and frequently expresses a wish to be back in New York. Little wonder, since the trip soon turned into a minor comedy of errors. The couple had their goods stolen in Georgia, and the Maxwell they were driving broke down almost as often as it ran.

They arrived in Florida at the crest of its historic real estate boom, but its commercial aspects only irritated Dreiser. Both he and Helen were physically run down from the push that had gone into making his big novel, and they could not hide their frayed nerves. Dreiser repaid Helen's mean spirits by cruelly exposing his correspondence with other women. For the first time in over six years, a note of real dejection enters into his response to her: "Wretched days with some-one I really dont care to be with" (11 January 1926). No other segment of the diary contains such a feast of birds—gulls, cranes, pelicans, owls, ducks, and even mud hens—a sure sign he was feeling personally entrapped.

Dreiser fled New York partly to avoid the stress of facing reviews of his novel. The first letters he received boded no good. Sinclair Lewis, he was told, disliked the book, which he had read in proofs, and decided against reviewing it. But three days after, on 8 January, the news of its success began to trickle in; on 12 January Sallie Kusell, who had worked closely with him on editing the million-odd words of the manuscript, wired to announce the *Tragedy* had sold seventeen thousand copies; by 18 January there could be little doubt he would finally make a profit from his writing. There must have been some sense of satisfaction for him, particularly since he had achieved the fame he

48. *Letters of H. L. Mencken,* ed. Guy J. Forgue (New York: Alfred A. Knopf, 1961), p. 494.
49. Quoted in Helen Dreiser, *My Life,* p. 117.

sought without compromise. If anything, he had written a more demanding, somber, ponderous, unyielding book than ever before. He surely savored the moment—a first in the diary—when an assistant cashier in a local bank paused to congratulate him on his contribution to literature. Whatever he felt, he did not dwell on it, logging the moment with no more emotion than a notice of his last meal. A creature of habit, he made notes for an article on Florida, and seems disturbed when the *Saturday Evening Post* refuses to consider it. (*Vanity Fair* published it, as "This Florida Scene," later in the year.) Unwilling to chance another long drive in mid-winter, Dreiser and Helen shipped themselves home, along with the Maxwell, aboard the *Kroonland*—the boat on which he returned from Europe in 1912, after having been scheduled on the *Titanic.* It must have struck Dreiser as another portentous token of change. This time he was right.

After the trip to Florida, Dreiser was to keep only two more extended diaries, both records of overseas travel, one to Scandinavia in the summer and fall of 1926, the other to Russia in 1927, out of which he wrote *Dreiser Looks at Russia* (1928).[50] Like the notebook he used during his tour of Europe in 1911–12, each was written mainly as an *aide-mémoire* for projected magazine pieces or a travel book, not as a private record. Dreiser, then, ended his American diaries after he returned to New York in 1926, to be lionized amid the hoopla surrounding his only commercial triumph. He apparently no longer felt compelled to monitor his daily thoughts and movements. For one thing, he was now a celebrity with ample opportunity to avoid the isolation he once knew. With the money earned from the *Tragedy,* including the sale of the movie rights, Dreiser moved uptown to a posh studio on 57th Street, where, in his own inimitable way, he participated in the whirlwind pace of the late twenties. In the thirties he addressed himself to the social and political challenges of the decade, and he became deeply involved in compiling a massive philo-

---

50. For an analysis of Dreiser's Scandinavian diary, see Rolf Lundén, *Dreiser Looks at Scandinavia* (Uppsala: Almquist and Wiksell International, 1977). Dreiser's diary of his Russian experience begins on 3 October 1927 when he first heard of the invitation to visit Russia from Arthur Pell of Boni and Liveright, and it ends on 13 January 1928 as he boarded a train to leave Russia. By 19 October 1927, he was aboard the S.S. *Mauretania,* and the diary thereafter records his daily activities abroad. This fascinating document, most of which Dreiser dictated to his secretary, Ruth Kennell, records Dreiser's reactions to the social, cultural, and economic conditions that he found in Russia.

sophical study on the nature of things. For these purposes, his public and private lives merged as never before, and the diary became a thing of the past.

Manchester, Connecticut   THOMAS P. RIGGIO
November 1981

EDITORIAL PRINCIPLES

≡

Theodore Dreiser's American diaries are "private" literary documents, written by the author with no thought of immediate publication. An edition of these diaries should therefore attempt to preserve their private character. "Public" documents (novels, short stories, poems, essays) should be presented in "public" texts: grammatical errors, misspellings, and verbal slips should be corrected. But these same mistakes and idiosyncrasies are essential to the flavor of private documents such as letters, diaries, working notes, and trial drafts. These "errors" show the author writing casually, with ideas flowing quickly from pen to paper, with little regard for style, and with minimal attention to grammar and spelling.

In this edition we attempt to recreate Dreiser's actual diaries for the reader, insofar as it is possible to do so in a printed medium. Nearly all misspellings and grammatical errors are reproduced without correction. A few substantive emendations are introduced to clarify confusing passages, and some punctuation is added to assist in readability, but for the most part the diary texts are presented without emendation. Characteristic Dreiser misspellings such as "recieve," "excitment," and "accross" are reproduced. Grammatical slips are also preserved, and the fragmented style of the entries is allowed to stand. Readings are emended only if they are confusing or nonsensical, and significant emendations are reported in the apparatus.

For the most part the diaries are presented in "clear text," with no bracketed emendations or interpolations by the editors.[1] Underlinings are printed as underscores, not as italics; blanks where Dreiser could not recall a word or name are rendered as ⌐   ⌐. The punctuation mark most commonly introduced has been the period. Dreiser nearly always left out the period when it fell at the end of a line, and he frequently omitted it at other points as well. A reader is usually able

---

1. Occasional illegible readings are signaled by "[unreadable word]."

to determine, from the sense of the passage, where the period should fall, but the frequent necessity of doing so is annoying and distracting. Periods are therefore added at the ends of Dreiser's fragmented comments throughout. One feature is regularized: A.M. and P.M. are rendered throughout in small caps.

Place names present a special problem. Dreiser kept many of his diaries while traveling, and he usually recorded the names of towns through which he passed, highways on which he drove, and hotels in which he stayed. He often did not make his diary entries, however, until hours or even days after passing through a town or staying at a hotel, and as a result he sometimes misspelled these names. Whenever possible such names have been checked for accuracy against maps and directories of the period, and misspellings have been corrected. Sometimes it has been impossible to find the name of a town on any available map; in these instances we have simply transcribed Dreiser's handwriting as accurately as possible.

Dates have also demanded special attention. Dreiser nearly always knew the correct day of the week, but sometimes he did not know the correct number of the day. Often he became confused on weekends, adding or dropping a digit on Sunday. He then compounded these errors by his tendency to take a date of a diary entry from the previous day's entry rather than from a calendar. Thus he often made a single error in dating and then repeated it for several days. Certainly these mistakes contribute to the private nature of the diaries, and perhaps they should be preserved. More practically, however, they are potential sources of confusion to biographers and scholars. Dating errors have therefore been corrected by reference to a perpetual calendar, and the emendations have been recorded in a separate section of the apparatus.

The provenance of these diaries is of some interest. With two exceptions—the Philadelphia diary of 1902–3 and the Greenwich Village diary of 1917–18—these journals were saved by Dreiser and came to the University of Pennsylvania Library with his other literary papers after his death. The provenance of the Philadelphia diary is obscure. The late David A. Randall acquired it during his years as a bookdealer and donated it to the Lilly Library in 1966, after he had become Librarian there. From whom he originally secured the diary is not known. Physical evidence in the diary, however, suggests that he acquired it from Dreiser's first wife, Sara White Dreiser. The verso of the final leaf of the document bears this notation in her handwriting:

"Theo's Health Record | Kept for Dr. Duhring." And a reference to sexual intercourse on leaf 26 has been censored in her hand. One may therefore speculate that Randall acquired the diary from Sara Dreiser, or perhaps from a member of her family after her death.

The history of the Greenwich Village diary of 1917–18 is more easily traced. Dreiser kept this diary while he was involved with Estelle Bloom Kubitz—the "Bert" of the diary—and as the entries show she was unhappy over his pursuit of other women. Estelle was Dreiser's secretary and typist, and she probably had access to his papers. At some point she seems to have taken the original handwritten diary and made a typed transcription of it. She then turned this transcript over to H. L. Mencken, her friend and confidant, who was himself involved with her sister Marion. Mencken kept the transcript and bequeathed it, along with his other literary papers, to the New York Public Library at his death. The manuscript of the diary has disappeared and presumably is no longer extant.

Dreiser may also have kept other diaries which have not survived. He was an intermittent diarist, usually producing these journals in periods of emotional turbulence or intellectual ferment, and he often went for days or weeks without making an entry. But the diary "habit" seems to have been fairly well established with him, and it is therefore curious that there are no diaries for the long period from 1903 to 1916. Dreiser may have lost or destroyed these diaries, or they may still survive in unknown collections from which they will eventually surface. For the present, however, this volume includes all known diaries kept by him while he was living or traveling in the United States.

The diaries that survive in manuscript are quite similar in physical appearance. They are inscribed in black pencil on half-sheets of inexpensive paper measuring approximately 220 × 140 mm. None of the diaries is bound; all are inscribed on loose sheets; all writing is on the rectos. Dreiser wrote a few entries in black ink, and he seems to have pecked out several pages in the "Helen" diary of 1919–25 on a typewriter. Some of the handwritten entries have been difficult to transcribe because Dreiser wrote them on his lap while riding in a train or an automobile, but most of his words have been deciphered.

Estelle Kubitz's transcription of the Greenwich Village diary is a 52-page single-spaced ribbon typescript. The leaves measure approximately 300 × 205 mm., with all typing on the rectos. As she typed, Estelle corrected Dreiser's spelling and punctuation, as was her habit.

The text of this diary is therefore more nearly correct, more "finished," than the texts of the handwritten diaries. The manuscript of the Greenwich Village diary undoubtedly contained Dreiser's usual misspellings and verbal idiosyncrasies, and it might therefore be argued that one should introduce these features back into the text in order to create an impression of "authenticity" for the reader. That notion, however, has been rejected here because of its artificiality. The integrity of the surviving document must be respected. In emending the text of the Greenwich Village diary, only typographical errors have been corrected.[2]

Dreiser's diaries often contain other items which he pasted or pinned in, or laid between the leaves. These include drug prescriptions, receipts, photos, picture postcards, newspaper clippings, maps, telegrams, and letters. These materials do contribute to the "look" and flavor of the original diaries, and in the best of all possible worlds one would facsimile each item or give a printed transcription of its text. Space is limited, however, and much of this material is insignificant. In this edition we have facsimiled or transcribed the important and visually interesting items. Other significant materials have been mentioned in the footnotes. The rest—most of it detritus of travel like ticket stubs, train schedules, and picture postcards faded past reproduction—has been silently omitted.

Professor Riggio has provided historical, biographical, and explanatory annotations throughout this volume. Dreiser's relations with many artists, intellectuals, and public figures are covered, and his more intimate friendships are documented. Where appropriate, the compositional and bibliographical history of certain of his writings is traced. Some names appear in more than one diary; in these instances, a descriptive note is given only for the first appearance of the name. In later diaries, the person is identified the first time his or her name appears, and these identifications are then cross-referenced to the original note. For example, Kirah Markham is first mentioned in the notes on p. 117, and a lengthy note on her life and career is printed in a footnote on that page. First appearances of her name in subsequent diaries are cross-referenced to the note on p. 117. In a few cases no annotation appears for a name or title; here the editors have been unable to identify the person or to locate information about the literary work.

2. It is possible, of course, that Estelle made changes or omitted embarrassing passages as she typed, but there is no way to test that speculation.

The textual apparatus for this volume presents only a selective record of emendation. Most of the emendations are so minor that they are unimportant even to the specialist. The published apparatus therefore contains only a table of significant substantive emendations and a list of corrections in Dreiser's dating. A full record of emendation, however, is available for examination at the Rare Book Room of the University of Pennsylvania Library.

Blacksburg, Virginia   JAMES L. W. WEST III
November 1981

DIARIES

PHILADELPHIA, 1902-03

Dreiser began this diary as a medical record at the beginning of the nervous breakdown that followed the publication of *Sister Carrie.* He was living in Philadelphia with his wife (the "Jug" of this diary), and he was being treated by Dr. Louis Adolphus Duhring, a prominent physician who was associated with the University of Pennsylvania. There is a note in Mrs. Dreiser's hand accompanying the manuscript of this diary ("Theo's health record kept for Dr. Duhring") which accounts for Dreiser's careful description of his symptoms and his response to the medications. In the early entries of the diary, Dreiser gives straightforward details of his illness and treatments; when his wife leaves him and returns to Missouri, however, he becomes more personal and revealing. He records himself, then only thirty-one years old, facing a debilitating illness, lack of funds, and inability to work. The diary reflects this strain in its odd syntactical patterns, misspellings, frequent duplication or omission of words, and erratic punctuation.

Medicine Record.

From Wednesday, Oct 22—1902 to[1]
Case taken up by Doctor Duhring[2] after a consultation fee of 5$\underline{00}$
and a prescription fee of 3\underline{00}$. Considered it one of nervous
exhaustion and prescribed as follows:
Had this filled at Evans drug store and paid them sixty cents. Took
it as follows:

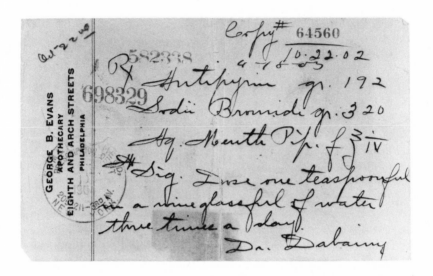

Wednesday Oct 22 —First dose 2 P.M. Noticed soothing sensation
about 5 P.M. Enjoyed supper. Second dose 6:30. Yawning at at
8.30. Bed at 9. Sound sleep to 12 midnight. After that wakeful and
restless. N. B. Mention of meals always presupposes the going out
to them to a boarding house two blocks away.

1. Dreiser left a blank space here, probably meaning to affix an end date for the diary
when he was cured, but he never added that date. The diary breaks off in mid-entry on 17
February 1903.
2. Dr. Louis Adolphus Duhring (1845–1913), physician and distinguished professor of
medicine at the University of Pennsylvania. Dr. Duhring treated Dreiser for neurasthenia, but
his specialty was dermatology, about which he wrote several books. For a fuller discussion of
Duhring's career see Herman Beerman, M.D., and Emma S. Beerman, M.A., "A Meeting of
Two Famous Benefactors of the Library of the University of Pennsylvania—Louis Adolphus
Duhring and Theodore Dreiser," *Transactions & Studies of the College of Physicians of Philadelphia*
42 (July 1974): 43–48.

Thursday Oct 23 —Rose at 7 yawning. Slight headache and with feeling of having rested little. Exercise, bath, breakfast. First dose at nine. Felt no especial symptoms. Muscles pained me a little all morning. Felt as if I would like to sleep but could't. Dinner at 12. Second dose at one. Still weary, increasing to an irritable headachey feeling towards evening. Supper 6:30 which I enjoyed. Medicine 7.30. No especial symptoms, although lack of sleep seems to have set up muscle pains of a curiously indefinite nature. Went to bed 9.30. Felt drowsy and slept until sometime after one, when wakefulness, intermixed by thoughtful and wearisome dreams, kept me busy until 7 A.M. Rose not much refreshed and with a drowsy, vaguely achy sensation in the brain, which exercise and bath did not dispel.

Friday, Oct 24 —Rose 7 A.M. not much refreshed and with a drowsy, vaguely achy sensation in the brain, which exercise and bath did not dispel. Breakfast at eight. Medicine at nine. Felt sensation of mental heaviness as if from past strain until noon. Lunch at twelve. Medicine one. Felt less weariness mentally but more fatigued or inert physically. This state held until about five P.M. when a mental ache set in—a vague throbbing as if the mental fibre itself were worn. This held until dinner, after which a more comfortable physical state ensued. Medicine at seven. Reception to Hall Caine 8 to 10.30.[3] Bed 11:30 with best night's rest since present course begain.

Saturday, Oct 25. Wakeful at 5.30, with wearisome dreams from then on till seven. Exercise, bath, breakfast 8. Medicine nine. No perceptible improvement so far as ability to work is concerned, but suffering no special pains or aches of any kind. Mental sensations those of nervous fatigue. Continued till noon. Enjoyed lunch. Medicine at 1. Read till 4 P.M. Went down town. No particular change of sensations. Dinner 7. Medicine 8. Bed 11. Slept only lightly.

3. Dreiser seems to be responding to something he was reading by or about Hall Caine (1853–1931), English novelist and playwright.

Sunday Oct 26$\underline{^{th}}$—Rose with slight headache and no feeling of having slept well. Ate hearty breakfast. Went to church. Fatigue sense in brain continuous. Dinner 12.30. Enjoyed it very much. Medicine 1:30. Read till five. No particular relief from fatigue sense in brain. Tea 6 P.M. Medicine seven. Very Drowsy by 8.30 and so to bed.

Monday Oct 27$\underline{^{th}}$—Rose with sensation of having slept but little since 3 A.M. or earlier. Wearisome dreams troubled me and my head ached. Exercise. Bath. Breakfast 8—which I enjoyed. Medicine 9 and so to work. No perceptible increase in working ability. Felt when I began as if I had already worked all day. Enjoyed luncheon at noon. Medicine at one. Worked until 3. Several passionate outbreaks weakened me, but enjoyed walk & dinner and felt very drowsy immediately afterward. Went to bed at 8. Slept but brokenly until morning.

Tuesday, Oct 28$\underline{^{th}}$ Rose with a sore sensation in upper half of skull. Enjoyed breakfast at 8. Medicine at nine. Wrote letters until noon. Eat hearty luncheon at 12. Medicine 12.45. Immediately afterward felt comfortable but no interest to work or write. In fact felt exceedingly dull and played out as usual. Went to couch and rested half dozing until five. Rose. Eat dinner. Medicine 7. Went to bed 8.30.

Wednesday Oct 29—Rose feeling pretty good, having slept most of the night. Exercise. Hearty breakfast. Medicine 9. Worked with comfort until noon. Eat hearty lunch. Wrote with some interest until 4. Walked until five feeling tired in brain. Eat dinner six which I enjoyed. Visited Holden.[4] Medicine 8.15. Felt easy and comfortable until bedtime.

Thursday Oct. 30$\underline{^{th}}$ Rose 6:30 after a night full of irritable and wearisome dreams. Had headache or rather that soreness of the

4. Alfred Holden, a professional photographer, lived near Dreiser at 5109 Ridge Avenue. At the University of Pennsylvania there is a letter dated 11 July 1924 in which Holden writes to Dreiser reminding him of their meetings together in Philadelphia during the period covered by this diary.

brain complained of before. Took exercise, cold bath and enjoyed my breakfast. Medicine 9. After breakfast worked at story until noon with no results. Quit despondent at noon and ate hasty lunch. Returned, took medicine and worked with what seemed some success until 4 P.M. when I went for a walk. Returned six, dined. Took medicine. Went to bed at 10.

Friday, Oct. 31 st Rose at 7 after having lain awake from 3 A.M. on. Such sleep as I had was troubled with painful and wearisome dreams. Exercised. Bathed and breakfasted with good appetite. Took medicine at nine. Bowels fairly regular but not quite free enough. Began work at 10, but with little enthusiasm. No imaginative ability whatsoever—no interest. Worked on until noon. Enjoyed lunch. Medicine one. Went down-town during after noon. Had talk with Coates.5 Came home feeling fine and enjoyed supper. Afterward at seven, felt sleepy but went out to see Halloween parades and remained until eleven. Went to bed and slept fairly soundly until 4 A.M. perhaps.

Saturday Nov 1 Rose feeling pretty good. Took Exercise, bath & enjoyed breakfast. Worked at my story with some interest but accomplished little. Went to lunch at noon which I enjoyed. Medicine at one. Returned and worked with pleasure until four when I walked down track of the P & R to The Falls. Enjoyed walk back and tea. Read until 8.30. Went to bed and slept fairly well.

Sunday Nov 2nd Rose feeling good. Exercised, bathed & ate hearty breakfast, after which went to church. Back at 12.45 for dinner. Ate heartily and walked about West Laurel Hill and upper Manayunk until 5 when returned. Tea at 6. Read until 9:30. Retired 10 P.M.

---

5. Joseph Horner Coates, editor, publisher, author. At this time Coates was an editor at *Era,* which was published by his family's firm, H. T. Coates and Co. In 1903 *Era* published two pieces by Dreiser, "A Mayor and His People" 11 (June): 578–85; and "The Problem of the Soil" 12 (September): 239–49. Correspondence at the University of Pennsylvania reveals that Coates and Dreiser remained on friendly terms at least until 1912. Coates later published a literary appreciation (*"Sister Carrie," North American Review* 186 [October 1907]: 288–91), and when Dreiser was writing *The Financier,* Coates supplied him with facts about Charles Yerkes's career in Philadelphia.

<u>Monday Nov 3 rd</u> Rose at 9.15 after a night of practically no sleep. Exercised, bathed, but ate no breakfast. Brain ached or rather felt dull & rather weary all morning. Went to lunch at noon and enjoyed same. Walked to spring for water.[6] Returned and worked with some enthusiasm but the effort wearied the brain and produced heat. Ate hearty supper and read until nine. Sleepy by ten and so to bed.

<u>Tuesday Nov 4</u> Rose 7 A.M. after having been awake since about three. Felt however as if I had some little sleep. Exercised, bathed and enjoyed breakfast, after which I felt drowsy and had a long spell of rumbling in my ears. Wrote letters and worked at my story until noon with some success. Went to dinner and enjoyed it. Rumbling continued. Worked to four with fair interest but felt dizzy. After dinner, which I enjoyed, went down town. On going to bed at eleven noticed old time heat of skin and scratched shins & feet with brush. Arm also had little pimples on it, which opened. Slept until one A.M. Soundly.

<u>Wednesday Nov 5</u> —Rose after having experienced semi consciousness since one. No appetite for breakfast. No sensations of weariness either however. Took no medicine. Went to see Dr. Duhring who gave me attached prescriptions (cost 1.10). Came down town, had them filled. During this time brain was developing a feeling of ache and fatigue. Drank glass beer and ate light lunch. Afterward hearty lecture on Worlds progress to two literary workers. Home at four, head still aching. Took two tablets 4.15. In somewhat over an hour I felt a lifting of the headache and general depression that seemed to follow abstinence from medicine since the night before. Took liquid tonic quarter of six and then ate dinner. After dinner took Phenacitine tablets. Felt sleepy by 8.30. Upon taking night dose of tonic and retiring was troubled by painful itching in feet, by heat in skin and also by subsequent wakefulness. Did not get any sleep to speak of.

6. Walking for spring water is an old Philadelphia custom. As late as the 1940s, Philadelphians were taking bottles to the fresh springs in Fairmount Park to take home spring water as a relief from the ill-smelling and -tasting tap water. The springs have since become contaminated and are no longer usable.

Thursday Nov 6   Rose feeling slightly weary for want of sleep but taking of tonic at 7 A.M. seemed to restore me. Exercised, bathed & ate hearty breakfast at 8 after which I took two tablets. Settled to work at 9.30 feeling rather drowsy and yet exceedingly weary and achy in the brain. Worked until noon making fair progress but feeling rather excitable mentally—as if I might be dizzy. Tonic at 11:20. Haircut. Lunch at twelve which I enjoyed only fairly. Returned and worked until three, when some little thought of doing well with my story and later a detail by Mrs. D. of some injustice done her by Am Express Co. caused me to get greatly excited and subsequently to feel an intense mental fatigue—Laid down from 3 to 5 but could not rest. Head hot. Brain achey and nervous. Rose at 5. Took tonic. Eat dinner at six but did not enjoy it much. Medicine seems to be affecting my appetite. After dinner went down town to see Kauffman whose talk weighed upon me.[7] Came home at eleven still weary and with some brain ache, anxious to rest but uncertain as to get it. Bed 11.20.

7. Reginald W. Kauffman (1878–1959), editor, publisher, author. Kauffman was on the editorial staff that in 1898 had begun *Ainslee's Magazine,* a journal that published Dreiser's poetry and articles and for which he acted as an unofficial consulting editor. Kauffman's connection with Dreiser thus dates back to his early free-lance days in New York.

<u>Friday Nov 7th</u> Rose 7.20 after having had but 3 hours sleep. On first retiring suffered intense itching in feet. Slept by 12.30. Woke at 3.30. So restless after that I took two tablets. These caused me to feel drowsy but did not produce sleep. During and after taking tonic, bathing, breakfasting and work until noon found myself exceedingly drowsy and played out. No especial headache however as on previous day, and took considerable interest in story. Tonic at 11. Dinner at 12. Tablets at one. Laid down at one for two hours feeling extremely weary and exhausted. Rose at three, but not much refreshed as I had no sleep. Worked at reorganizing until 4.30, after which took tonic and then walked until six. No especial appetite for dinner and felt drowsy immediately afterward. Took tablets 6.45. Bed at 8 and so rested until nine when I roused and took last dose of tonic.

<u>Saturday Nov. 8th</u> Rose 7 after a very wretched night. Did not sleep any after three and had not slept soundly before. Bathed, took tonic and so to breakfast but scarcely any appetite. Went to Holdens after that, after which I took tablets. Read newspaper and then went to work feeling rather flat imaginatively but no headache and no sense of that extreme exhaustion endured the afternoon and evening before. Anticipation of Duffys coming put me in fair nervous condition, and his arrival, dining and subsequent visiting about with him kept me from feeling my own state.[8] Saturday evening Preston and Duffy conversation as well as my own lifted me up to a high nervous state, but I settled down a little and slept some, retiring at 11.30.

<u>Sunday, Nov. 9th</u> Rose at 7. Bathed, shaved and breakfasted with good appetite. Walked with Duffy and Preston till noon, feeling the nervous strain of it and yet enjoying it. Find that I suffer from a peculiar illusion as to the necessity of varying the progress of an idea—changing the direction of my thoughts—which is purely a result of mental overwork. Ate hearty dinner Sunday and now find that medicine no longer disagrees with me. In fact I rather like it.

---

8. Richard Duffy, an editor at *Ainslee's Magazine* and a friend of Dreiser since 1898. Correspondence at the University of Pennsylvania suggests that Duffy gave Dreiser moral and financial support during the difficult years of 1902–3.

Talked to Duffy all P.M. and after seeing him off and eating hearty supper went to bed and slept possibly until 5 A.M. At least I did not notice wakefulness.

Monday, Nov. 10<u>th</u>

Rose 8 A.M. after being awake since 5 and longing very much for sleep. Ate and enjoyed my breakfast. Also felt fairly fit for work. My chief complaint at this time concerns a certain nervousness of temper over enthusiasm tending to mental wildness coupled with a permanent and sometimes noticeably disturbing form of brain ache. It seems to move about in the head like flashes of sheet lightning round a summer sky. During the morning wrote letters and at noon ate only fairly well. Afternoon worked on story but failed to do anything. Disturbing sense of error haunted me and I quit at three. During remainder of day felt rather flat, but suffered no especial symptoms of headache or nervousness. To bed at 8.30.

Tuesday Nov. 11<u>th</u> Last night was perhaps as bad as I have had for some time. No sleep to speak of after midnight. Turned fifty times. No headache however and ideas all of the simplest and most commonplace order which is a blessing. Rose at 7.15 with an intense feeling of weariness and if I could have stretched out and slept would gladly have done so for a week. The medicine however seems to be ineffective in this respect. Went to lunch at twelve and enjoyed it fairly well. Lay down from 1.15 to 3 P.M. as directed. Could not sleep but felt exceedingly drowsy. Worked or tried to from 3.15 to 4.30, but with small result. Walked until 6. Enjoyed dinner. Went home and read. Retired at 9.00, but did not sleep much before midnight. In fact slept but little all night.

Wednesday Nov 12 Rose 6.40. Bathed and dined at eight with moderate appetite. Felt no especially depressing results from nights light sleep, but could not work very well. No imagination. No physical buoyancy. Felt utterly flat. Walked down town along the river but suffered greatly from nervous ache in the region of the genito-urinary organs. Found that my tendency to overindulge in thoughts concerning the sexual relation, as well as in the relation itself, has this painful result. Took medicine at noon. Visited

Bulletin. Rode to Mrs. Scott[9] and walked from there up river home but suffered so greatly from nervous ache described that I was almost sick. Went to bed at 10 and slept moderately well until about 5 A.M.

Thursday Nov 13<u>th</u> Rose at 6 feeling somewhat refreshed but no way excellent. Went down at nine and visited Bulletin, Ladies Home Journal, Post Office and Seymour Eaton, returning at five.[10] Condition during this one of comparative fatigue, accompanied by headache. Nervous elation, following talk with Eaton, very hard on my brain.[11] Any excitment of that nature seems to play me out completely. Enjoyed my meals and took medicine regularly. Retired at nine sleeping brokenly and with much nervous thought until 5 A.M.

Friday Nov. 14<u>th</u> Rose seven A.M. after tossing restlessly and longing for more sleep. Breakfasted at 8 and felt exceedingly languid immediately afterward. Sensations being some akin to the achy wretchedness produced by malaria. Worked at medical diary and four hundred word literary contribution until noon when I went to lunch but did not enjoy it. Worked again after dinner but was not very successful.[12] Took walk after four—about 2 miles. Back at 5.30. Medicine and dinner, which I enjoyed. Read until nine when I retired, the desire to sleep being as strong as ever.

9. Mrs. Lillian Fulton Scott lived at 3220 Columbia Avenue, Philadelphia. In a letter at the University of Pennsylvania, dated 2 November 1902, she introduces herself to Mrs. Dreiser as an admirer of *Sister Carrie* and mentions that Dreiser is the writer who should complete Frank Norris's Trilogy of the Wheat. The diary suggests that a literary friendship subsequently developed between the two women.

10. Dreiser visited the offices of various popular publications in order to watch for opportunities in the free-lance market. The *Bulletin* was a local weekly begun in 1876 which dealt with society news, the arts, and amusements. The *Ladies' Home Journal* was a great success at this time; according to Frank Luther Mott, it "made Philadelphia important in the magazine world" (Mott, *A History of American Magazines* [Cambridge: Harvard Univ. Press, 1957], 2:87). Dreiser's efforts did not result in publications in these journals.

11. Seymour Eaton (1858–1916), publisher, editor, author. Eaton owed his popular fame to his creation of the "Teddy Bear," whose adventures he told in verse in the pages of the *New York Times*. He also founded the Booklovers and Tabard Inn Libraries of the United States, an international lending-library system. In January 1903, Eaton founded and edited *Booklovers Magazine.*

12. Dreiser may have been trying to write short essays for Seymour Eaton's *Booklovers Magazine,* which was to begin publication in January 1903; in fact, *Booklovers* printed a short piece (432 words) by Dreiser, "True Art Speaks Plainly," in its first issue (February 1903).

Saturday Nov 15 th —Woke at 4.30 or earlier having had very little real sleep. Suffered a great deal during early morning and previous evening from sexual desire which seems to affect my head. Managed to resist it however in so far as abstaining from copulation, but the effect of the desire was weakening. Rose at seven and bathed, after which ate a hearty breakfast which I enjoyed. Worked at writing 400 word criticism for Eaton. As usual found that consecutive thought and close reasoning is very difficult for me. Found that I could not do it in fact. Gave it up after dinner and rested, drinking bottle of beer at 3 P.M. and lying down till five. Ate tea, came home and read, retiring at eight and being read to sleep by Mrs. Dreiser, which however did not assure me a full nights rest. Medicine taken regularly.

Sunday, Nov. 16 th . Rose at 7 A.M. after having enjoyed a moderate nights rest and seemed to be in good mental and physical condition. Enjoyed breakfast, listened with pleasure to a service at Holy Trinity[13] and ate a hearty dinner. Afterward rested and read, the night bringing me considerable sleep. No headache, no nervous sensations, no especial weariness, but I was resting and taking my medicine regularly.

Monday, Nov. 17 th Woke at five feeling fairly well rested. Rose at 7 A.M. Ate hearty breakfast, felt calm but not energetic or capable of thinking. Began work on 400 word criticism and stayed at it until noon when I felt mentally tired. Ate hearty lunch after which went to city, walking and musing and feeling very good. Returned at six having walked so much that I felt depressed and rather played out. Ate hearty supper and retired at ate feeling quite nervous and flighty, with slight pains in my head until about 10.30 or so when I must have dozed off.

Tuesday Nov 18 th . Waked early as usual and remained so until nearly 7.30 when I arose. Bathed and breakfasted with appetite after which I shaved, read morning paper etc and prepared to go down town. Felt rather weak from walking or brain exertion of

13. Dreiser attended either the Episcopal church at Walnut and S. 19th Sts., or the German Catholic church at 6th and Spruce Sts. These were the only Holy Trinity churches in Philadelphia at the time.

previous day and not as if I could attempt any difficult labor of any sort. Ate two hearty meals and rested from 4 to 5 after down town trip, but did not feel much stronger. Retired at eight and slept moderately well until perhaps 4 A.M.

<u>Wednesday Nov. 19<u>th</u></u> Rose at seven after having foolishly taxed myself by copulating with Mrs. D but I could not control my desire.[14] Took bath, medicine and went to breakfast which I enjoyed. Suffered from nervous weariness during early hours, but toward noon felt better and after hearty lunch walked down through park and out Ridge to Reading tracks where I shuttled to Broad Street and back, reaching home at 5:30. Felt very poetic during latter half of this trip but also taxed myself too much and felt weak, rested lying until 6 when to dinner which meal I enjoyed. Came home 6.30. Retired 8. Slept fairly well until about 6 A.M.

<u>Thursday Nov. 20<u>th</u></u>. Rose feeling fairly well rested and after bathing, exercising some and breakfasting took books and went to library down town. Called on Coates, and 3<u>rd</u> Nat. Bank, and after securing some money visited Dr. Duhring. That gentleman heard what I had to say concerning record previously noted and then prescribed some light form of exercise or labor—driving or store tending together with regular consumption of the following prescription which he thought would do me good.
Visited Evans drugstore and had it filled (60 cents) after which had lunch which I enjoyed and so to library where I secured my books and came home. Felt exceedingly tired when I reached here and after straightening out some paper lay down until five when I had my wife bath my head with cold water. Took dose of old tonic and went to dinner, which I enjoyed, after which visited the spring over the Schuylkill for water. Came home, read Bulletin, wrote up this account and then went to bed at exactly nine oclock.

<u>Friday Nov. 21<u>st</u></u> This day beginning with my waking as usual at about 4 A.M. was not any more satisfactory than the others. Throughout the morning and afternoon I felt that mild mental

14. The words "but I could not control my" are written in Sara White Dreiser's hand; Dreiser's original words were so thoroughly erased that they are now indecipherible.

GEORGE B. EVANS
APOTHECARY
EIGHTH AND ARCH STREETS
PHILADELPHIA

aches which show that my brain is not in good condition. Bathed, breakfasted with appetite, read the morning paper and studied Sir J. Lubbocks Scenery of England until noon.[15] Lunnch was not so satisfactory to me, nor was my walk to spring anything but a proof of my physical inertia and weariness. During P.M. tried to read but found myself becoming nervous and apprehensive and so stopped to rest. Toward evening felt quite flighty and played out in the head, but ate a good dinner and retired at 8 feeling quite drowsy. By ten I was asleep and so rested until 4 A.M.

Saturday, Nov. 22. Much like the preceding days, this passed without any appreciable increase in mental ability. Either I am very much mistaken and am confusing physical opposition to labor with

15. *The Scenery of England* (1902) by Sir John Lubbock Avebury (1834–1913), English scientist and author.

illness or I am in a much depressed mental state. Going to work I do not get very far before I question the order and merit of what I am doing and find myself utterly confused as to what is best and interesting. My mind seems to be in fair working order otherwise. I enjoyed to read—a little. I enjoy to walk and my appetite seems fair. Still I have an unaccountable drowsiness and achyness both in body and mind which reduces me to the necessity of lying down a great deal. Malaria might be a reason for it. Some inherent blood affliction also. I am not sure however that it is not purely mental exhaustion from past excesses both of sexual passion and mental labor. Read comfortably today. Ate and walked some with pleasure, but could not worked. Went with Coates to Berwyn and talk until after midnight with the result that I scarcely obtained three hours sleep.

Sunday Nov. 23$\underline{rd}$. Rose seven, bathed and took breakfast which I enjoyed. Went with Coates and his family to church at St. Davids which I enjoyed.[16] Drove to New Centreville and back, after which a hearty dinner and more philosophy. Walked and talked with Coates from 4.30 until after six when tea followed. Enjoyed that also. Took train back at eight and reached home at ten. Retired at once and slept moderately until seven when I arose not feeling startlingly refreshed. Medicine regularly taken.

Monday Nov. 24$\underline{th}$ Woke at about four as usual. After rising at seven and eating a hearty breakfast felt so weary that I lay down and rested until nearly noon. Rose 11.30 and ate lunch, after which retired again, resting until six. Rose and ate hearty supper. Read afterward until 8. Retired and slept moderately well until morning. During all this time my feeling of being played out was very great and even disturbing. Took medicine regularly.

Tuesday, Nov 25 Rose 7.15 feeling somewhat improved. Being rainy day read all morning in house and during afternoon walked to Falls station and back—about two miles, where I drank a glass of beer. Appetite during three meals extraordinary. Feeling before and after one of extreme languidness causing me to desire to lie down,

---

16. Dreiser visited a church in St. Davids, a suburb of Philadelphia.

which I did upon my return. Head seems to have recovered somewhat from moving pain, but objection to or rather incapacity for working out my novel as great as ever. The mere thought seem to weaken my reasoning capacity and I at once become confused.

Wednesday Nov. 26th Rose at 7 A.M. after waking at 3, and having slept in all perhaps six hours. Feeling of languidness still dominant. Ate hearty breakfast which I enjoyed, after which read "English Scenery" (Lubbock) until noon. Took short walk to lunch and ate heartily, after which went for water to spring across Schuylkill—one mile. Came back and wrote up this diary, after which I rested until about six, feeling rather fagged out. After dinner went to bed early and slept as usual until about 4 A.M.

Thursday, Nov. 27th

Rose at 8—it being Thanksgiving day, and ate a heavy breakfast, after which returned to room and trifled about reading and preparing for dinner which was very good. Ate heartily and then went down town to see Henrietta Crosman in "the Sword of the King."[17] Enjoyed that fairly well also. Came back about 6.45, having failed to secure Jugs muff which she lost, and read, after which retired quite tired. The amusements of the day served to keep my mind off myself but I felt fatigued.

Friday, Nov. 28th

Rose at 7.15 after having slept lightly five or six hours. Went to breakfast and afterward read "Scenery of England," feeling quite interested. Ate luncheon at twelve and left for city at 1.15, visiting library, Academy of Music, Wanamakers and getting a second bottle of last prescription. Went down to Delaware water front and surveyed the boats, after which I came home feeling rather gloomy. On my arrival found Dick (Jugs Brother) and his bride who livened

17. Henrietta Crosman (1861–1944), one of Broadway's leading actresses in the first two decades of the twentieth century. She performed for, among others, Augustin Daly's famous stock company; and in 1902 she was acclaimed as the foremost Rosalind (in *As You Like It*) of her time. Dreiser saw her in *The Sword of The King,* an English play by C. E. Vallance which had a successful run in New York and on the road in 1902.

my mood for me.[18] Spent dinner hour and evening until nine talking to them. Retired 10, but did not sleep so very good. Perhaps due to excitement.

Saturday, Nov. 29th

Change from rainy to clear weather to affect me favorably this morning. Exercised with pleasure and enjoyed my bath. After breakfast took a two mile walk and felt splendid, shaved, read papers and trifled about until noon when I ate a hearty dinner. Afterward saw Jug, Dick and his wife off to football game and then strolled alone down bank of Schuylkill to Dauphin Street and back. Felt lonely and wrote a little poem. Afterward felt drowsy and went to bed early that night feeling quite weary. Slept moderately until three or four A.M. after which I rested without sleeping.

Sunday, Nov. 30th

Rainy weather and no hope of feeling superfine. Talked with Dick and Carlotta all day. Have noticed that the contemplation of marital joy of these people is apt to produce physical passion in me —a thing that delays my mental recovery at this time. Ate heartily at all three meals and took my medicine regularly but did not notice any special improvement.

Monday, Dec. 1st

Rose at 6.30, after a night of restless dreaming and much passional disturbance. Ate light breakfast and escorted Dick & Carlotta to train, after which returned to my work feeling somewhat depressed. Worked at arranging my letters all day, but suffered some from slight headache and other nervous disturbances due to hardly restrained desires the night before. Felt very weary towards evening and laid down for half hour, after which went to dinner. Appetite not so good this time and drowsyness afterward very marked. Went to bed at 8 P.M. but found as usual that I was

---

18. Some information about Mrs. Dreiser's brother is found at the University of Pennsylvania in Dreiser's unpublished autobiographical fragment "An Amateur Laborer." This manuscript recounts Dreiser's experiences in New York after he had left Philadelphia in February 1903. Dreiser there identifies his brother-in-law as a lieutenant in the U.S. Navy who recently was married and who had visited him in Philadelphia. Despite his embarrassment over his appearance, Dreiser was hungry enough to take dinner with him on the battleship *Indiana*.

not sleeping sound. Wake at 4 or thereabouts and rested poorly afterwards.

Tuesday Dec 2nd Sensation of weariness quite strong on this morning. Breakfast nothing to speak of and mental state dull. Wrote letters from 9.30 until noon. Ate hasty lunch which disagreed with me, as did my dinner of the night before. Am noticing a marked falling off in appetite which contrasts strangely with my previous great hunger. Went to city at 1.30 where I looked for a position until 5 P.M., finding nothing. Rode out on Reading after five and ate moderate dinner at six. Came home and retired at eight. Waking at 4 or earlier as usual. Night was troubled with hurrying and crowded scenes which made me feel very much as if I were awake and weary of thinking.

Wednesday, Dec. 3rd Rose at seven after a very restless morning, during which I suffered from headache and a sore and painful scalp. Breakfast was but little enjoyed and feeling afterward anything but exuberant. Went to city at 9.30 and after walking about some, visited P. R. R. Station, office of Drexel Biddle, Times, and Record.[19] Went also to see Coates but without result. Enjoyed luncheon and returned at 6 feeling very tired. Ate a medium sized dinner which I relished. Read paper from 7 to 9. Retired at 9.30.

Thursday, Dec. 4th Woke feeling moderately well rested but was foolish enough to indulge in copulation which put me back a number of days no doubt in my recovery. Ate a moderate breakfast and afterward sat about reading, feel no inspiration or ability to do mental work. Went down at 3.30 and saw Coates. Returned at six feeling hungry and ate well. Retired at 9 but rested badly—in fact got no sleep to speak of at all.

Friday, Dec 5th As a consequence felt weak this morning on rising, but after bathing and breakfasting felt some better. Read Lubbock on Civilization all morning and till late in the afternoon but noted

19. The Drexel Biddle Press is listed in the Philadelphia directory of 1902 at 228 S. 4th St. The *Times* and the *Record* were among the top four or five newspapers in Philadelphia at the time. Dreiser may have been thinking of returning to newspaper work temporarily.

no recrudescence of the literary spirit in myself. Felt an occasional twinge in the brain above each ear and soreness in the upper portion of the brain, but this has continued so long and so regularly that I do not mind it much. Went to dinner at six and ate heartily, after which came home and went early to bed sleeping moderately well until morning.

Saturday, Dec. 6th Rose at seven. Bathed, ate hearty breakfast, and felt excellent until noon or later. Visited Dr. Duhring at 10.30 A.M. Stated case as written above and recieved the two prescriptions herewith attached. He did not seem to think that the headaches and soreness of scalp amounted to much. Said they were a result of my played out physical and mental condition and would pass with the recuperation of my nerve power. Advised light reading and a little exercise, not too much of either.

Had these filled, shopped until three and home at 3.30. Read till six. Ate hearty tea and retired at nine, falling asleep about ten and waking again at two. Rested thereafter brokenly until seven when I arose.

Sunday, Dec 7th Being snowy and cold, I staid in the house most of the day reading. Appetite at the three meals was good. Interest in news normal and general feeling fair. Had some slight pains in my head and some slight tendency to lassitude owing to brevity of sleep. It was not a day marked by any special variation from those preceding.

Monday Dec. 8$\underline{\text{th}}$ Rose at seven having experienced a poor night. The usual wakefulness began at 12 M. with some slight head pains thereafter and a few dreams. Rose at seven and went through usual routine, reading, dining and walking out a little with the result that I felt very tired by night. Indeed I felt very drowsy during the afternoon but did not lie down. Went to bed at nine feeling very weary but slept no later than twelve M, when I awoke and dozed fitfully until morning. My feeling during the day had been about the same as the day before. No marked head pains but some lassitude, no imaginative or initiative powers. Ate normally and with relish.

Tuesday Dec. 9$\underline{\text{th}}$ Feeling on this morning was one of great weariness owing no doubt to lack of sleep. Ate breakfast with appetite but afterward, and before taking any of the sleeping potion, felt very drowsy. Yawned a great deal. Wrote up this record for three days. Read paper. Then endeavored to complete a poem by noon, but failed. Ate luncheon with relish and returned to room to work but felt so weary that I had to lie down. Rested on back till 3.30 when rose and went down town feeling very weary. Saw Kaufmann and returned his books & came home 6. Dined and went to room. Read from seven to eight. Retired at that hour feeling very weary. Took none of the sleeping potion until waking at midnight. Slept wretchedly or not at all after that. All during this day my head had felt heavy and achy, as if it were cramped for space or pressed in upon by a plate. No doubt but that my nights are becoming less and less satisfactory—a thing which is literally wearing me out.

Wednesday, Dec. 10$\underline{\text{th}}$ As stated above this night was most unsatisfactory, perhaps the least restful of any since I have taken treatment of Dr. Duhring. Thoughts seem to flow on in a continuous and wearying chain and I rise so sore in the brain that I fairly ache. Last night as usual I awoke promptly at twelve. Rose and took the teaspoonful as directed but it did me no good. Strange to say my appetite continues good however and I enjoyed a hearty breakfast. Mental ache and physical uncomfortableness immediately reasserted itself and by ten A.M. I was as as tired and indifferent as ever. I tried to work but failed and at noon gave it up and went to lunch. Enjoyed latter, but suffered greatly during the remainder of the day from headache. Walked all afternoon and by night felt worn and very wretched. Ate heary dinner and went to bed immediately afterward falling to sleep possibly by ten. Woke again at four and rose at seven feeling slightly refreshed.

Thursday, Dec 11th. Bathed, breakfasted, shaved and then wrote until noon feeling pretty well. After luncheon, which I enjoyed, went down town to witness rehearsel. Walked home afterward and felt very tired. Thought I would sleep well, but upon retiring found myself wakeful and very restless. Body extremely hot. Took one dose of the soporific at 8.40. Being still awake and more restless at 10.30, rose and took another. Dozed thoughtfully after that, but did not really rouse until 5 A.M.

Friday, Dec. 12<u>th</u> Owing to my slightly better rest of the night I felt better this morning and worked all day, until 3.30 P.M., on a short story. Grew weary by then and a headache developed, whereupon I quit. Walked from 3.30 to 5.30 and ate a good dinner, after which I went to bed very tired. Sleep did not come though until 10 or after and I was awake again at three. This produced a form of headache which was bothering me when I finally arose much against my will at seven. I find that lying in bed does not seem to help me any. Somehow I cannot sleep in the day and every little noise annoys me.

Saturday, Dec. 13<u>th</u> Worked at my story until noon when I ate a hearty dinner. Went to library during P.M. and then read until evening, feeling quite good. Took tea at six and read thereafter until nine when I retired. Feeling during the day was an improvement over that of day before. Appetite as good as usual. Bowels regular. Medicine regular.

Sunday Dec. 14<u>th</u> Woke at 5 A.M. having had about six hours sound sleep I should judge. Bathed, ate hearty breakfast, shaved, Read. Dinner at 12.30. Ate heartily. Walked from three to six taking pills at 6.30 and last dose of coruminative at 9.30. Slept at about ten and did not wake until about five but night was not of best. Too much half wakefulness. Bowels regular. General physical sensations fair.

Monday, Dec. 15th The progress of this day was of the usual order. Writing in the morning, working in library during P.M. and reading in the evening. Appetite for meals was good. Mental state comfortable and rather more sprightly than the day before. Went to bed at nine and slept until 5.30 A.M., waking without a headache. Whether the drift is for the better I am not absolutely sure, but I have felt some better during the past three days.

Tuesday Dec 16th. Feeling during morning one of great drowsiness. Yawned nearly all the time. Wrote up diary. Worked on story. Went to Coroners office and back. Rested 5 to 6. Ate 3 good meals. Felt well till 3 P.M. After that nervous and weary, due to overwork I think. Did not take any of the liquid soporific during day so this must have something to do with it. Retired 9, woke 1 A.M. Took soporific and dozed until 7 A.M. Felt poorly on waking and feel worse this morning. Must see Duhring today.

Wednesday Dec 17th (Day) Went to see Dr. Duhring at 10.30 and stated my case substantially as above when he recommended a continuance of the pills and gave me the following prescription. (See copy of prescription attached.) Had it filled and took it at two. And regularly throughout the day but with no perceptible results. Felt sick at my stomach at five. Took a dyspepsia tablet and so got in shape for dinner. Ate heartily and enjoyed the first hour after it but soon grew drowsy and retired.

   <u>Night</u> Woke at 1.10 feeling very nervous. Rose and took dose of liquid and retired again but was subject to nervous and disturbing dreams, intercolated with wakeful periods. Rose at seven very weary and apparently but little benefited by the night.

Thursday, Dec 18th (Day) Bathed, breakfasted and took a walk during and by which I seemed to be much improved. Took pill at breakfast, liquid at 10.30, and between whiles wrote until noon. Physically felt very weary and ached in muscles and head. During afternoon worked on story until 4. Then walked to Manayunk. Ate supper six, read till 8, went to bed.

Night Slept until two when I woke, slightly nervous and took teaspoonful of panapepton. Dozed thereafter until 7 A.M. but did not feel much relieved.

Friday, Dec 19<u>th</u> (Day) Bathed and breakfasted. Then walked. Read paper till 10. Wrote on story till noon. Lunch. Story work until 4. Walk from 4.30 to 6 and then dinner. Feeling during day one of depression owing to small rest and general nervous state. Night Retired 9. Slept fairly well until 5 A.M.

Saturday, Dec 20<u>th</u> Felt fairly refreshed this morning and wrote on story until eleven A.M. when it was completed (The Investigations of Mr. Buckley, Reporter).[20] Read while Jug corrected it. Ate lunch, went down town. Bought scrap book, pie, etc. Returned at six feeling unstrung by crowd, but general tone of this day was good. Night Went up to Manayunk and walked about from 8 to 9.30. Came back at 10. Retired and slept until 5 A.M.

Sunday, Dec 21<u>st</u> 1902 Rose at 8. Took bath, hearty breakfast and read until noon. Enjoyed dinner and afterward reading until 6. Took no tea, but ate a peice of pie instead. General feeling this day, very good. Night Read from 6.30 to 8. Retired 8.15. Slept by 9, perhaps. Did not rouse thoroughly again until 5 A.M. General feeling good.

Monday Dec. 22 —(Day) After my fair sleep of the night I fancied I was going to have a good day, mentally, but unfortunately it was not to be so. Physically I was apparently well enough, but mentally I was incapable of consecutive thought as a child. Tried to write a story but went entirely to peices, became sick of it, and left at 12 for down town. Hunted about all P.M. for factory information and came home at six weary and rather dispirited mentally. Night—Ate fair dinner and read paper until 8.30. Retired at nine and slept lightly until about 4 when I awoke.

20. "The Investigation of Mr. Buckely, Reporter," did not represent new work: two years earlier, on 28 February 1900, *Harper's* had written Dreiser, rejecting the piece.

Tuesday Dec. 23<u>rd</u> (Day) Went through usual routine so often described and worked at my short story unavailingly till noon. Gave it up quite fatigued and went down town after lunch where I secured typewritten mss of <u>Buckely</u> and came home. General feeling one of mental incapacity resulting from overwork.
Night. Ate good dinner and then entertained company until after nine, when I retired very weary. Seem to have had a fair night up to two or three A.M. but after that rest was broken.

Wedesday, Dec. 24th (Day) Rose 7 and took cold bath. Ate hearty breakfast and trifled until noon, shaving, dressing and getting ready for the holiday. Ate good lunch and worked awhile in my room, after which took a walk about to factories around Midvale getting home at 6. (Night) Ate hearty dinner and then went down town with Jug to buy Christmas toys. Came home about 10 very tired and retired at eleven sleeping lightly until 3 A.M. after which I turned to and fro considerably until 7.

Thursday Dec 25th Day Rose and ate a hearty Christmas breakfast —after which came back to room and watched Christmas visitors until Gray arrived from New York.[21] Greeted him cheerily and spent fine day raking up old times and eating Christmas fare. (Night) Went downtown with him to train and got back at 9, after which I went to bed, sleeping but poorly until 3. Too much nuts and candies I think.

Friday Dec. 26th (Day) Rose up feeling quite badly and after breakfasting tried to work but without much result. Head troubled me and stomach was much disturbed. Took walk after lunch to Overbrook where took car for down town and had rubber heels put on my shoes. Came home at six. (Night) Ate hearty dinner

---

21. Charles N. Gray, a friend of Dreiser and his brother Ed, is known only through his letters to Dreiser at the University of Pennsylvania. The correspondence for 1902 is on the stationery of "The Jewelers Association and Board of Trade," which had offices in New York. Gray states that he is in charge of the "collection department" for the organization. His earliest surviving letter to Dreiser is dated 12 September 1899, and the final one is on 28 August 1931. From first to last there is one recurring theme: the hard times Gray has fallen upon and his need for small sums of money. In a letter dated 14 December 1902, Gray invites himself for the Christmas visit Dreiser records here; he mentions receiving a pay raise and promises to pay back part of a thirty-dollar debt when he comes. In 1931 Dreiser was still sending Gray small loans of five or six dollars.

after which I went to bed feeling very tired. Fell asleep at about ten but was awake again at three or earlier, the condition of my stomach seeming to affect my sleep.

Saturday, Dec. 27<u>th</u> (Day) Bathed, took tonic and tried fasting until noon but it did not seem to benefit me much. Felt better physically but could do nothing with my short story (His Annual Appearence).[22] Went to lunch at noon. Worked until three afterward. Went for walk to Manayunk to look for skates. Found none. Saw and talked with Lieutenant of police though. Came back at six feeling good physically but mentally very dull. (Night) Ate hearty dinner and after reading paper until 8.30. Retired. Slept fairly until 12 perhaps, when I awoke and after that had a bad night.

Sunday, Dec 28<u>th</u> Day Did not attempt to work this day, but read in the morning and rode over to Kensington in the afternoon. Appetite was good and general feeling fair. At night I retired short after nine and slept with some few wakeful moments until six or thereabouts in the morning.

Monday, Dec 29<u>th</u> Day. Nervous condition rather worse this morning owing to a foolish hour of trifling with Mrs. D. Felt or seemed to feel the effects of it at once and during day suffered from a growing headache. Day being rainy and dark may have had something to do with it. Walked out after lunch following Wissahickon to Indian Rock and thence across Roxborough to a hill crest overlooking Manayunk, where I stood in a flurry of snow looking at the city below. Came down and went up to Dr. Fussells office but he was not in.[23] Walked back along Main street enjoying the gloom and slush and reached home by 5.30 where I found the room warm and comfortable as usual. Head was feeling bad by now and I laid down a little while rising at six to eat my dinner which I enjoyed. Night. Afterward I came home and read until eight when I retired. Restless that night and tossed with scarcely more than three hours sleep between that and seven A.M.

22. This title does not appear on any published work by Dreiser or on any of his unpublished manuscripts.
23. There is no listing for a Dr. Fussell in the Philadelphia directory of the period.

Tuesday, Dec. 30<u>th</u> Day. Arose at seven, but seeing I had slept so little and was feeling badly I decided to walk over to Kensington and at eleven oclock began to do so. Roved all about that picturesque region, looking at the mills and brooding over the narrow houses until 2.30 P.M. when I took the car and went down town. Looked in Library for Philadelphia Factory reports and then came home, my head fairly burning with a plan for an article. Mrs. Dreiser bathed my head for me, after which we spent to supper, I enjoying a fairly one.

<u>Night</u> Felt wrought up during remainder of the evening and at 8.30 retired, rolling until about ten and then sleeping until about 2, when I awoke. Dreams were very bad that night and my general feeling next morning one of retrogression.

Wednesday, Dec. 31 — Rose at seven this morning, shaved quickly, and after breakfasting heartily decided to walk across the park to see Doctor Duhring. Struck out and had a fine lot of fun out of it, reaching there in good spirits at 11.45. Told the Doctor just how I had been, how medicine had given out Sunday last and I had decided to try two days without any. Described feelings ensueing upon my visit to Kensington and he seemed surprised to hear that I had flushes of blood in the head at times, accompanied by cold feet and so on. Asked me whether my bowels moved regularly, whether my skin felt moist or dry and whether I had sufficient saliva in my mouth. Learning that I thought that I had not, he wrote out the following prescription telling me to take the tonic 2 or 3 times a day until I noticed a pleasent softness of the skin and a sufficient quantity of saliva. If too much so, I was to reduce the dose. Similarly I was to take one pill every night unless my bowels became to loose when every other night would do. Here are the prescriptions as returned.
Took the first of these at 1.30 and by four noticed soft, damp condition of skin, as well as a steady flow of saliva in my mouth. Not being quite sure whether I was not imagining this, I took another dose just before supper and a pill at bedtime.
<u>Night</u> During night felt this dampness continue. Waked at 12 with noise of bells and whistles greeting the New Year and at 3, not being able to get to sleep again, took a tablet of Stearns headache powder which gave me a little rest before morning but not much.

Copy 256315
12-31-02.

R
Pilocarpine Hydrochlorate
gr ii
ft in Tablear No XXX
Sig. One tablet 2 or 3 times
a day as directed.

Dr. L. A. Duhring

Copy 256316
12-31-02.

R Hydrarg. Chlor. Mitis gr viii
Ext. Colocynth Co gr iv
ft in pil. No viii
M. Sig. One pill nightly
or every other night.
Taletter.

Dr. L. A. Duhring.

81299

Thursday, Jan 1—1903—Day. Rose at seven, feeling pretty fair for all my nights loss of sleep and enjoyed bath and breakfast. Went down town to see Mummers parade,[24] after which came home, the action of the pill taken the night before now first beginning to gripe me. Ate and enjoyed hearty dinner, after which I returned home, going straight to toilet where I excreted a large amount of material. Felt quite comfortable after this and took first dose of Pilocarpin tablets for the day. Wrote, or tried to, during afternoon but did not succeed very well. Ate hearty luncheon at six and retired at nine, waking again at 12 and resting badly from then on till morning. Symptoms during day one of softer skin and slightly richer flow of saliva but not too much so. General feeling fair.

Friday, Jan 2<u>nd</u> 1903—<u>Day.</u> Rose at seven, bathed and went to breakfast where I ate heartily. Came back to room and tried to work, but feeling rather weak and ideas being incoherent could not do so. Gave it up at 12 and after luncheon went for a walk in lower section of city. General symptoms during day one of light

24. The Mummer's Parade is described as follows in Joseph Jackson, *Encyclopedia of Philadelphia* (Harrisburg: National Historical Association, 1932), 3: 918: "Since January 1, 1901, this procession of fantastically costumed New Year's Clubs has been the principal feature of the celebration of New Year's Day in Philadelphia each year." The practice follows the old English custom of Mummers who visited local homes and public places at New Year's. The parade continues in Philadelphia to this day.

headedness, coupled with slight nervous pains in my body as for instance my left heel and big toe. Returned at six feeling quite refreshed and ate a good dinner, after which I came to our room and soon retired.

Night Was not quite as good as I expected. Woke at twelve and slept lightly after that, being much annoyed by dreams.

Saturday, Jan 3<u>rd</u> Day. Feeling this morning one of extreme lassitude and weakness. I feel as if I had worked a great deal and had made my muscles tired enough to ache slightly. Breakfasted at 8 with a moderate appetite and at ten tried to work, but did not succeed. Gave it up and read. Went to dinner at 12, enjoying my meal only fairly. Saturday afternoon remained here at home until 4, when I went for a walk with Jug. Returned at 6 feeling quite light-headed and flighty. Ate light tea and visited Holdens, after which returned home and went to bed.

Night. Slept until 12. Rose and gargled sore throat. Took about a gill of malt extract and retired again but did not sleep much. Too much thinking.

Sunday, Jan 4—Day Feeling this day was dull and wearisome during A.M.—owing to bad night and not so very much better during afternoon. Breakfast was not very appetising to me. Interest in things general not very bright afterward. Read papers and Bryces Commonwealth till noon, also Commonwealth after dinner.[25] Walked about a mile to spring after four, but felt dull and unprofitable just the same. Skipped tea at six and retired at about eight, waking at one out of a prolonged and wearingly thoughtful dream. Gargled sore throat and tried to sleep again, but brain was too much for me. Canvassed a thousend subjects between two and seven and arose dull and unrefreshed.

Monday, January 5<u>rd</u>. Nothing good to report of this day except that my appetite remained fair. Felt very dull from my bad night and after trying to work all morning went down town after lunch and worked in library until 5.15. Came home and ate a good

25. *The American Commonwealth* (1888) by James (Viscount) Bryce (1838–1922). The book is a classic study of institutions in America.

dinner, after which I read papers until 8.30 and then retired. (Night) Sleep was fairly sound and I did not wake until 4 A.M.

Tuesday, Jan 6<u>th</u> Rose this day feeling excellent and after bathing, exercising and so forth went to breakfast where I had buckwheat cakes, honey, sausage and coffee. Came home after securing a paper and tried to work but found that my coffee was disagreeing with me. It grew some worse and caused me to abandon my intention of eating lunch. This help some and by two oclock I was feeling better —by four excellent. Worked with some slight success on my short story and at 5 oclock went for a walk. Got as far as the middle portion of Manayunk and back before six. Dined and came home and read but did not grow sleepy as usual and when at nine I tried to sleep found myself turning and twisting with no end of annoying thoughts. Rolled all night more or less thinking half sensible and half disconnected thoughts, and got no real sound asleep. Was broad awake a score of times and rose at eight feeling stiff and weary, with a kind of sick headache and a general opposition to labor of any sort.

Wednesday, Jan. 7<u>th</u> Worked all morning at story, but without success. Gave it up at noon and went down town where I secured Smith college stories, read in Nicolay Life of Lincoln and saw Coates.[26] Did not feel very well during morning or afternoon but ate a moderate dinner at six and came home to try to read. Grew sleepy by eight and retired at nine, sleeping until four I fancy, when I awoke.

Thursday, Jan 8<u>th</u> Rose at seven suffering from a slight attack of cramp and nausea due to the action of the pill taken the night before—a feeling which these pills seem to regularly produce. Had a strong action of the bowels once in the morning and twice during the afternoon, the color being slightly green. Ate only a light breakfast and a poor dinner, though the lunch was fair. Found

26. *Smith College Stories* by Josephine Dodge Daskan (1876–?). This collection of ten short stories about college women at Smith was published in 1900.

John George Nicolay (1832–1901), journalist, historian, and biographer, became private secretary to Lincoln in 1860; with John Hay he wrote the ten-volume *Abraham Lincoln: A History* (1890). Dreiser probably is reading Nicolay's *A Short Life of Abraham Lincoln* (1902).

myself short of working ideas and inclined to feverishness in the head, a thing which this medicine was supposed to counteract. Took a brisk walk from 5 to 6 and read the evening papers from seven to nine. Retired at that hour and slept lightly during the night, waking several times to adjust the covering and being irritated some by a thread of ideas which my will cannot cut off. Awoke at about four for the last time and so did not get anymore sleep until I arose at seven.

Friday, Jan 9<u>th</u> Feeling this morning a slight improvement over that of yesterday. Body less stiff and brain less weary. Enjoyed my exercise before bathing and my bath also. Took no breakfast, but shaved myself instead and afterwards sat down to write, feeling rather clear in the head. Worked until noon but without success. Ate hearty luncheon and again tried to do something after dinner but my mind remained unproductive. Walked at four, getting back at five and at six ate dinner. After dinner read till nine when I retired, sleeping in a fair way until perhaps four or five.

Saturday Jan 10<u>th</u> 1903.
Ate hearty breakfast. Tried to work on editorial till noon. Still no power of organization. Ate light dinner at 12. Tried to work again. Went to tea at 6. Took warm bath about 8. Retired about 10. Slept very badly. Pill I took Friday night didn't act any more than if I hadn't taken it.

Sunday. Jan. 11.
Felt very good in spite of bad night. Ate hearty breakfast. Read papers until noon. Ate light dinner. Tried to complete an editorial after dinner but without success. Trying to write produced a light nervous headache. Caused the blood to go to the head too. Gave it up at 5.30. Ate light tea. Took breathing exercise. Took pill & retired at 8.30. Waked at 12.30 and slept the least bit afterward. Couldn't stop thinking, and when I did was bothered by annoying dreams. Took Stern's headache tablet, but no effect.

Monday Jan. 12.
Felt very badly. Took breathing exercise. Ate little breakfast. Had headache and sort of stomach trouble. Pill acted at 10.30 about like an action should be without pill. Slightly green passage. Worked

out an editorial, but it was quite a strain.[27] Produced fever in head.
Went to lunch at twelve and ate heartily, after which went down
town to Miss Bradleys who type-wrote my editorial for me.[28]
Carried at once to Seymour Eaton.[29] From there went to Coates
and from there to Evans drug store. Took train at 5.08, feeling not
any to brisk, and arrived in time for dinner which I enjoyed. Came
to room and read until nine when I went to bed. Slept a little
between 10.30 and twelve but after that was restless and could
hardly say that I was ever really sound asleep. Rose at seven,
feeling rather drowsy, and so began the new day.

Tuesday, Jan 13 th. Morning—exercised, bathed, ate hearty
breakfast and worked at story until twelve. Noon, ate hearty lunch.
Afterward worked on editorial concerning sympathy until three
when I felt myself becoming confused and went for a walk. It was
very cold outside. Walked about a mile to Fairmount pumping
station and back. Felt quite quiet while walking but my head was
hot, a thing which rather astonishes me. Ate hearty dinner at 6 and
came to my room where I read until 8.30 P.M. Then retired. Slept
poorly most of the night, being disturbed by dreams. Now that I
look back on it I do not believe I have had one real sound nights
rest since my first going to Duhring. Action of bowels during day
small and of light brown color. State of mind slightly restless. No
power to think consecutively. Tablets gave out at noon. Last pill
taken this night.

27. The portion of the diary from "Ate" at 82.19 to "strain." at 83.1 is inscribed in the
hand of Sara White Dreiser. She might have recopied these sentences in order to censor some
comment by Dreiser, but the leaves of the original diary suggest that this was not so. Her portion
begins at the bottom of leaf 75, immediately after the date in Dreiser's hand, and ends on leaf
77 where Dreiser picks up the inscription. Dreiser often dictated to his wife when he was tired
or indisposed; this passage seems to represent such a dictation.
28. The Philadelphia directory of 1903 lists Anna D. Bradley's stenographic service at
14 S. Broad St.
29. Among the unique features of Eaton's *Booklovers Magazine* was a brief "editorial" of
about five hundred words written by a guest contributor on a subject of his choice. Here Dreiser
is referring to one such piece, "True Art Speaks Plainly," which appeared in the February 1903
issue. Guest contributors included, among others, Hamlin Garland, Brander Matthews, and
Amelia E. Barr. Eaton stated his goal in the introduction to this section of the journal: "We want
short, pungent, vigorous, signed editorials by men and women who have things to say and who
want to say them 'hard'—anything which hits the nail on the head; any nail which needs driving
home or down. We shall pay cash and good prices." After June 1903, however, *Booklovers*
discontinued these essays.

Wednesday, Jan 14th Morning. Exercised, bathed, ate hearty breakfasted. Walked down to stand for paper and came back feeling as though I ought to work but not having much power for it. Had 1st action of bowels from pill taken at bedtime night before at 10.30 A.M. It was not so very heavy and of a light brown color faintly tinged with green. From 10.30 till noon tried to work out an editorial. Did not succeed. Noon ate hearty lunch. Afternoon went down to see typewriter and editor of Book lovers. Came back at 5 and stopped at Gustine lake to skate. Ate hearty dinner at six and from 7.00 to 7.30 skated again on Wissahickon creek. Came home at 8 and after reading went to bed thinking certainly I would sleep but was disappointed. Rolled all night getting little real sleep and awoke next morning with a slight headache.

Thursday, Jan 15th Worked all morning at editorial but without success. Went to lunch at 12 and after dinner skated till 2.30 when I came home and lay down. Rose at 3 and walked to Manayunk where I interviewed an old lock keeper in his lock house. Walked home very tired, and after eating a good dinner returned to my room. There I read until 8.30 and then retired. Owing to my general weariness I felt sure I would sleep but was disappointed again. Rolled the larger portion of the night and awoke early next morning even more wretched than usual.

Friday, Jan 16th Appetite poor this morning. Walked direct from breakfast table down Ridge Ave to 33rd Street and down 33rd to Market, cutting across railroad yards, through the Park etc. Telephoned at 32nd and Girard to Coates and from there went quickly to Dr. Duhring to whom I stated my case. He seemed disturbed over the fact that I did not sleep and said this time I would try a mild narcotic which he would trust me to use with discretion. Said it would cause dryness of the mouth and throat of a morning—also a headache if taken too liberally. I was to follow instructions exactly and stop short of having a dry throat. Also I was to take the drops of the other medicine beginning with three drops a dose and increasing it to six. Walked down town after interview, had prescriptions filled and after dinner called on Coates who gave me my check. Also called on street car ad man and book agent man. Returned at six feeling very tired and took first dose of three drops at dinner. First dose of opiate at bedtime or rather after 3 hours of rolling in which I had tried to go to sleep without it. Was so wrought up by then however that the medicine did not seem to do me much good. I did doze a little but not enough to make me feel good and consequently rose at seven as much in the dumps as ever. Attached is the prescription given.

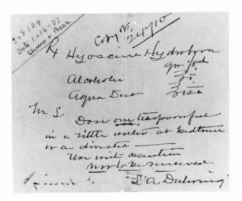

Saturday, Jan 17<u>th</u> Bathed, shaved and breakfasted this morning with considerable freshness. At 10:30 went to city. Drew Frederic's "March Hares" from Library,[30] saw Coates and took lunch with him, after which strolled about streets enjoying the sight of the crowds. Whether medicine helped any or not I felt rather bright and took keen interest in everything. Came home at four and finished reading March Hares. Ate plentifully at tea and afterwards read from 7 to 9. Retired then, taking night medicine and sleeping until morning.

Sunday, Jan. 18<u>th</u> On rising this morning experienced the dryness of mouth which the doctor told me to look out for but no headache or other disagreeable sensations. Found my appetite to be good and general feeling excellent. Dressed and went to church at ten, enjoying the episcopal service, and at 12.45 returned and ate

30. Harold Frederic (1856–98), journalist, novelist. Frederic is remembered for his contribution to the early development of realism in America. He published *March Hares* in 1896.

dinner. During P.M. read and rested until 4 oclock when Lieut. Gleason and wife of navy called. They stayed till 5.30. After that went to tea, then read till 8.30 and so to bed feeling as if I might sleep. Took one and one quarter spoonfuls of the Hydroscin and soon went to sleep, waking though again shortly after two. Did not sleep much after this. Will increase dose to 1 1/2 tonight (Monday).

Monday Jan 19th Went through usual course of reading and eating today without any mental depression or unrest other than that which would flow from a bad night before. A slight cold which I took Sunday afternoon developed into a soreness of the chest and caused me to feel rather dizzy and irritable. Took three grains of quinine in whiskey at noon, another three at six and still another three at bedtime with the result that I felt somewhat better. Incidentally Mrs. Dreiser rubbed my chest with Chicago oil and quinine. About 2.30 in the afternoon I went down to the library and drew several books—"Damnation of Theron Ware," "With the Procession" and "Bryces Commonwealth", reading in the first during the evening.[31] At nine, after taking my quinine, I went to bed and tried to sleep but could not, so at eleven I rose and took a spoonful and a half of hydroscin. Did not notice things thereafter so much, but my rest was not sound and my feeling this morning was not one of chipper healthfulness owing to taking the quinine at 6 P.M. I neglected to take the five drops but will not let it occur again.

Tuesday, Jan 20th Feeling this day was one of irritation due to the cold on my lungs which did not loosen its grip over night. Salts taken night before did not act. Quinine made me feel dizzy. Ate light breakfast and then read until lunch. After lunch went to city with Jug where I visited R. R. ticket offices and saw Coates about ticket. All this time my chest was irritating me and I felt rather gloomy. Came out at 5.30 and ate a not over hearty dinner, after which I read till ten and then prepared to retire. Took glass of salts as well as a spoonful of hydroscin. Lay awake till perhaps eleven, after which I slept until four or later.

31. Harold Frederic, *The Damnation of Theron Ware* (1896), his best-known novel. *With the Procession* (1895) by Henry Blake Fuller (1857–1929), novelist, poet, critic. A forerunner of naturalism in America, Fuller won acclaim for *The Cliff-Dwellers* (1893), one of the first notable American city novels.

Wednesday, Jan. 21<u>st</u> Rose this morning feeling fairly good. Cough seemed slightly looser. Ate moderately at breakfast. Read steadily until noon afterwards. During P.M. read again, still feeling no power to compose. Took medicines regularly but noticed no improvement. Went down at 4.30 and saw Coates about ticket. Came out at 5.30 feeling well, but dull, and ate a moderate dinner. Read afterward until 9, when Jug greased my chest and I went to bed. Half hour later I took the hydroscin and perhaps another half hour later fell into a thinking doze from which I did not arouse clearly until three or four in the morning. Felt only moderately refreshed by it when I got up. This dose of hydroscin I had raised to one and one half spoonsfuls.

Thursday, Jan 22<u>nd</u> Nothing new today. Feelings almost exactly the same. Read till noon. Went to Coates and library afterward. Ate three moderately appetizing meals and retired at nine oclock. Cough no better. Mental state during P.M. Have no power of initiative. Do not really feel wide awake. <u>Night</u> Went to bed at 10. Took 1 1/4 spoonsful Hydroscin. Dozed thoughtfully until 12. Thereafter brokenly until seven. Did not feel a bit good on rising and feel dull now 10.15 A.M.

Friday Jan 23<u>rd</u> Condition throughout this day practically same as that of yesterday. Read without interruption in "With the Procession." Felt moderately clear mentally. Ate three good meals. Friday night took 1 1/2 spoonsful of hydroscin but waked again at 12.30 and did not sleep so well afterwards. Still my rest was not utterly broken and I felt well awaking. Forgot to say that after supper we called on the Scotts. Lungs felt very bad from cold. Jug greased and ironed me at bedtime, and on that account I felt some easier.

Saturday Jan 24<u>th</u> Ate no breakfast today but enjoyed right hearty dinner. Cold was looser, though action of bowels was still clogged. After dinner 3 P.M. went to spring. Ate good tea and visited Holdens, after which came home and read until bedtime. My night was in a measure spoiled for me by my eating some cakes and afterwards drinking two glasses of hot lemonade. Was awake at two and after that some later and really did not get a good nights rest.

Sara White Dreiser

Incidentally my hydroscin gave out with the dose taken at two A.M. Woke feeling rather drowsy and so did not get up till 10. Mental feeling during day had been fair.

<u>Sunday, Jan 25</u>^th This day was much the same as yesterday, the general tone of my feelings being optimistic. Ate, read and

otherwise amused myself until about 8 P.M. when I retired.
Medicine having given out I tried resting without it but was rather
unsuccessful. In fact got scarcely any sleep to speak of.

<u>Monday, Jan. 26</u>th In consequence of loss of sleep last night had
very little appetite today and have been feeling intensely dull and
achy ever since. Jug left this morning at 9 for Missouri and from
now on I will be alone for a time. Went with her to train and
returned, sitting in my room until noon and thinking over my loss.
Lay down at 11.15 and tried to rest until twelve but could not
sleep. Rose and went to lunch but did not enjoy it owing to
stiffness and drowsy condition. Came home and secured Coates mss
which I took down to him. Drew out "Rise of Silas Lapham" and
"Bread Winners."[32] Came home at six aching all over from loss of
sleep. Ate light supper and, after having hydroscin prescription half
refilled, came home and went straight to bed. Took one
teaspoonful. Did not sleep good however. Ached and rolled a good
deal and felt quite badly when I arose again at seven.

<u>Tuesday, Jan 27</u><u>th</u> Spent most of this day in my room. Muscles
ached for want of sleep and otherwise I felt generally depressed.
Read "Silas Lapham" all morning and afternoon. Appetite was not
good owing to sleeplessness. Took 1 1/2 spoonsfuls hydroscin, but
got little sleep. Was restless and rolled a great deal. The whole
question of recovery seems to have narrowed down to one of
sleeplessness.

<u>Wednesday, Jan 28</u>th Owing to my late lingering in bed, because
of sleeplessness, I did not get any bath this morning. Came home
after breakfast and read "Silas Lapham" till noon. At noon ate small
lunch and then, the day being springlike, strolled over toward
Cynwyd and Overbrook. It was very lovely and I felt very fine for
a while. Came home and went for a pitcher of spring water, after
which read Silas Lapham. Ate a light dinner at 6. Bought bottle of

---

32. *The Rise of Silas Lapham* (1885) by William Dean Howells (1837–1920).
   The Bread-Winners by John Hay (1838–1905), lawyer, secretary to President Lincoln, diplomat, secretary of state, author. Hay anonymously published *The Bread-Winners,* in which he sought to defend property against the "dangerous classes"—that is, organized labor. The novel was published serially in *The Century Magazine* from August 1883 to January 1884, and it appeared in book form in 1884. Its authorship was acknowledged only after Hay's death.

panopepton. Read "Silas Lapham" till 10.30. Took dose panopepton. Went to bed and tried to sleep but at 12 rose and took 1 3/4 spoonsfull of hydroscin. Felt slightly more restful thereafter but really did not sleep good and rose this morning feeling very ache and quite awry. Sleep, sleep. If ever I obtain that again, what a precious boon I will have to be grateful for. He giveth his beloved sleep.

Thursday, Jan. 29th Record for this day—no change. Went to breakfast 8. Read from 9 till noon. Lunch 12 to 12.30. Afterward gathered up story and took it to Coates to read. Took "Silas Lapham" to library and drew out "Unleavened Bread".[33] Came home on street car. Ate dinner 6 to 6:30. Read 6:30 to 8. Went to bed after taking 1 1/2 spoonsful hydroscin and drowsed from perhaps eleven to 4 or thereabouts. Sleep was not very refreshing and I did not get up feeling any better than usual.

Friday Jan 30th. Progress of this day was entirely unsatisfactory. My head ached a great deal and I was otherwise distressed and unhappy. Read in Bread winners till noon. Then took walk through Lehigh Ave and 22nd Street region which depressed me even more. Came home at six and ate a light dinner, after which I talked to Kleckner for an hour. Left him and came home to room where I read. Later about 9 I took remaining dose of hydroscin—1 spoonful, and went to bed but did not sleep much. Rose at about 2 A.M. and took a dose of Panopepton but that did not help much either. Felt very restless and weary during remaining hours of night and rose as usual—unrefreshed.

Saturday Jan 31 —Feeling of drowsiness and exhaustion was very marked this morning but could not stay in bed. Rose and ate a light breakfast, after which I walked across park to University of Pa. where I looked for rooms. Abandoned search about noon and walked down to Wanamakers where I had my eyeglasses mended. Then I had lunch for 15 cents and came back through Chestnut

33. *Unleavened Bread* (1900) by Robert Grant (1852–1940), lawyer, judge, novelist, essayist, poet.

street to University Museum where I brooded till 5.[34] Came on from there through Park to room. Ate supper and read until 8.30, after which I retired feeling as if I would sleep. <u>Night</u> As usual I was disappointed however. I did not sleep but only drowsed a little and at midnight rose and took a spoonful of Panopepton together with a raw egg. Did not sleep so very much better after that but it did seem to help me a little and I was rather glad than otherwise that I did it.

<u>Sunday, Feb. 1.</u> Being very weary this A.M. I took another tablespoonful of Panopepton over a raw egg and felt slightly strengthened. Went to breakfasted but ate very little and after that read in room till 12.45. At that hour ate a hearty chicken dinner and felt much refreshed. Took strolled from 1.15 to 2.30. Attended vespers at The Falls 2.30 to 4 and came home after that reading in "Unleavened Bread," without supper until bedtime. Retired at nine, but although sleepy did not sleep. Keep rolling and tossing until 2 when I rose and took another dose of panopepton accompanied with a raw egg. Went to sleep a little after this or rather drowsed but did not get enough to make me feel very good. Indeed I am so drowsy I can scarcely think this morning and yet I cannot sleep. I wonder sometimes how it is all going to end.

<u>Monday Feb 2nd</u> Read in till noon feeling quite good after all my weariness. Ate moderately at breakfast and lunch, not enjoying either very much, and after one oclock I went down town, strolled about trying to make up mind what to look for but couldnt do it. Called on Coates but he had not finished Gerhardt. From there I strolled out Walnut to bridge overlooking the Schuylkill, where the sun came out and the day began to take on a spring-like tone. Hung about dreaming over the river and the sky until 4.30 when I started back, reaching Reading Terminal at 5.30. Took train and came home. Ate hearty dinner. Read in "Unleavened Bread." Went to bed at 9. Strange to say slept moderately well this night and had no medicine either. It is past guessing how insomnia goes.

34. Dreiser is referring to the Free Museum of Science and Art of the University of Pennsylvania, located at the corner of 33d & Spruce Sts. The first section of the building was opened in 1899.

<u>Tuesday Feb 3<u>rd</u></u>. Today like so many others spent in the idleness which I despise and deplore. I have no money, or very little left. I am alone. I am homesick. All the courage I have seems to have gone out of me and I sit in my chair brooding. True I have a novel to cheer me, and I love to read, but I know it's only passing the time that ought to be given to something else. All the desire of my heart is centered on getting well, on getting my wife back, on having a home and yet, but why go on. All I can do apparently is wait, but oh the weariness of it. This morning after breakfast I bought a paper and strolled down to the water works and back reading it. Then I came home the moment I thought my room was made up and sat down in it, a feeling of cowardly content holding me, as if here at least I was safe. Then I read, rocking and dreaming, the interesting life the novel pictured being a sort of a salve to my distress. Afterwards, about noon, I rose up and went out to lunch feeling as if I were doomed to rot, whether I would or no. After lunch I came out and strolled up to Manayunk, the need of having my shoe patched taking me that way. It can be done very cheaply in Manayunk.

I do not know how it is, but although I am ill and really cannot write very well or make my living by my pen as I used to do, I am still subject to the most halcyon and delightful moods. One would fancy now that, being sick and weary as I am, I would have no heart for anything save the wretched contemplation of my mood, but I am not thus steadily afflicted at all. I have no money it is true, or only sufficient to last me until the end of next week, and yet here I am (or was until five oclock) strolling about the warm sunshine of this early February day and delighting in the premontory spring atmosphere. The world seemed young and beautiful to me. I sang as I walked. Every step of the way seemed delightful and as I sat down in the little Italian's shoe shop I felt as if I were not poor, but one in really comfortable circumstances. I examined my shoes and, after trying to persuade to have them half-soled for forty-five cents, agreed to patch the one most in need of repairs for ten. Then he cut and hammered at it for a few minutes and I came out mended again—good for another month or so in that foot at least. I would not be able to wear these shoes much longer if it were not for the patching they would stand.

After leaving the Italian I strolled home again singing. These streets were bright, the miserable old grey mills quaint, the river flowing a broad blue current at my left. All the way I kept indulging in the thought that I was really not so bad off as I thought, and when I neared Wissahickon began to speculate on how I would arrange to leave my room. My board is paid up to Saturday evening, or will be, for I have the money for it, and my room until Saturday noon. Over and above that I have four dollars and forty five cents. If I leave my room on Saturday I will have to get some place to store my trunk, and if I stay I will have only one dollar and forty five cents wherewith to face the difficulties of the next week and to move my trunk which will probably cost fifty cents at the least. Then I will have to have some washing done sometime—a bill which will cost me twenty five cents probably at least. I do not know how it is to come about, but I can only face the future with an unfaltering faith and wait.

Wednesday Feb. 4th After writing the above I read in my chair in my room until six oclock, feeling that I might as well use my time to improve my knowledge of current novels since I shall want to be writing another one myself some day. The enthusiasm which the action of the one I was reading, "Unleavened Bread," aroused in me was very marked and I felt for a time as if much of my own ability and power had returned. I walked down to the nearest drug store to see what time is was, my own watch having stopped, and when I reached there decided to take a glass of beer. All my money was nearly gone as I have stated, but I wanted the beer to stimulate my appetite and quiet my nerves which the book I was reading had excited. I secured it and went on to supper where I ate a hearty meal—coming home feeling very much invigorated. After that I sat and thought awhile, deciding that life could not truly prove a failure at my age, and then arose and shaved and shined my shoes. My purpose in doing this was to get an early start in the morning as I wanted to go and see Dr. Duhring and tell him that I could not pay him any more money now, but that I would like to continue his treatment just the same and settle with him when I secured work. Also I fancied I would look for something to do. When I had finished these two things I retired and slept only poorly, awoke in the morning with a very dull sensation in the brain and no desire to get up. However I did so and went to breakfast at eight where I dined but poorly and then went down town.

My success in the city was not what I hoped it would be. Walked about until noon, drew "The 13$\underline{th}$ District,"[35] bought gas globe and came home. Read all that afternoon and evening, and slept but poorly that night.

Thursday, Feb 5$\underline{th}$. Although feeling badly this day I read eagerly until 1 P.M. when I finished "The 13$\underline{th}$ District" and went down town again, saw Coates and told him I was drawing books from the library on his share and then went home. Ate three good meals this day and on this night slept fairly well from 9 to 3. After that I did not sleep at all.

Friday Feb 6$\underline{th}$ Thought I was getting along finely this day until about 3 P.M. I suddenly suffered a most surprising change in my feelings and felt threatened with a nervous collapse. I never felt more wretched in my life. All the horror of being alone and without work, without money and sick swept over me and I thought I should die. I was trying to work but I gave that up and then in my excitement I thought I would shave to distract my mind but I could not do it. I could not even whet my raszor. I gave up trying and put on my overcoat, feeling sure that on the morrow I would call on Coates and ask him to give me that balance due me and with it go to Missouri to Jug. I wanted to pack up at once and did write a letter to Gray asking him to send me the balance of $15 he owes me. Then I went out to supper, succeeded in eating something by sheer force. I was so homesick I could have cried. I came back after seven and went directly to bed leaving the light burning but did not sleep. Rather I grew more wakeful and wretched and, after spending most of the night, rose this morning feeling utterly played out. I must get something or do something for a change or I will utterly go mad.

Saturday Feb 7$\underline{th}$ For all my wretched night and so on, after I had my bath this morning I did not feel so bad. I went to breakfast and

35. *The 13th District: A Story of a Candidate* (1902) was the first novel of Brand Whitlock (1869–1934), journalist, lawyer, diplomat, author.

---

ate with a fairly good appetite, after which I came back to the room and shaved. This seemed to cheer me up some and I read in "Rose of Dutchers Coolly" until noon when I went to dinner.[36] The meal was not extra good and I did not enjoy it as much as I might have but I made the best of it. After dinner I decided to go down to the University of Pennsylvania, my object being to find the free Dispensary and see if I could not obtain treatment for my nervous trouble free of charge.[37] I walked all the way, feeling for all my previous terrors, as if the world were good and lovely and as if I was getting rapidly well. I reached the University at 3 P.M. and went straight to the Dispensary door but when I got there I could not go in. I was ashamed. I walked to and fro, thinking of what they would and what I would say and then finally I felt as if I had better not try it. Accordingly I started toward the city but when I got as far as the bridge that spans the Schuylkill at Walnut street, I recovered my courage and went back. When I reached the sidewalk opposite however a negro was cleaning the windows. I felt as if he would know what I was coming for and so I strolled by again, visiting the new dormitory building back of the University and walking down around the Free Museum of Science and Art. When I had thought it all over and reasoned with myself once more, I made another effort and this time I succeeded. The negro was still in the window but I walked nervously past. When I reached the hall I found an ambiguous sign which confused me as to the whereabouts of the dispensary, and so I stood about the hall too shamefaced to do anything in particular. Finally I screwed up my courage and went into the drug store and asked.

"It's through that door, out in the courtyard there, but your too late said the clerk. It wont be open until Monday."

Rebuff, in a way, as this was, it was a relief to me. I strolled comfortably if not gaily out. I gave up bothering any more about

---

36. *Rose of Dutcher's Coolly* (1895; rev. ed., 1899), a novel by Hamlin Garland (1860–1940). Dreiser is reading Garland's story of a girl from the Middle West who rebels against farm life, attends the University of Wisconsin, and then goes to Chicago to begin a career as a writer. Garland and Dreiser did not meet until late 1903, but it is worth noting that Garland, four months before this diary entry, read and admired *Sister Carrie,* Dreiser's version of the story of a young midwestern girl come to Chicago.

37. The Free Dispensary was a clinic for the needy at the Hospital of the University of Pennsylvania, located at Spruce St. between 35th and 36th Sts.

the University or about rooms for rent and walked in to the city resolving to use fifty or 60 cents of my little cash left to have one of Dr. Duhrings old prescriptions filled. I had brought them all along to show them to the physician who should take up my case at the Free Dispensary. Now I selected one—the one that had been least repeated, and walked down to Shinn & Baers at Broadway and Spruce streets where I went in and asked them to tell me what 250853 was. My object in doing this was to find out if it cost more than 50 or 60 cents, in which case I could not take it. When they told me it was Phenactine tablets I remembered that at the time I had taken these first they had done me a little good and so I resolved to try them now. In fact I would wait and see if I could not have the prescription put up in liquid form up in Wissahickon. I walked up Broad and down Chestnut through the gay Saturday afternoon crowd and finally reached my dreary, commonplace Ridge Avenue car, which I took to Wissahickon. There I ate a hearty supper and afterward went over to the principal druggist who told me he could not fill the prescription in liquid form and would not tell me the price of it beforehand. This discouraged me a little but I took it to the other druggist who filled it for forty five cents. That night, feeling so strangely buoyant as I did about getting well, I took the dose and shortly afterward went to bed, sleeping soundly until about 3 A.M. About that hour I woke finding the medicine had caused me to pass seamen, almost unconsciously, my gown being quite wet with it. I rose and cleaned myself but did not let it worry me any and soon succeeded in getting a little more sleep. This caused me to feel quite comfortable in spirits Sunday A.M.

Sunday Feb 8<u>th</u> A rainy day this was. Gloomy and wretched but I did not mind it. The fact that I was feeling better and that I had got some sleep was joy enough for me. I went to breakfast feeling quite hungry and ate heartily of beans and eggs. After that I walked to Manayunk and attended mass at the Catholic church there, a spectacle which I enjoyed very much. The church was soothing, the music beautiful and the lights and candles upon the altar a spectacle to behold. I rejoiced enthusiastically in it all and came home feeling as if I were better than ever.

Sunday afternoon I read, getting through almost half of volume

---

one of Ida Tarballs Life of Lincoln.[38] The same I continued Sunday evening feeling quite interested in it. At last retired feeling as if I had spent a very satisfactory day.

Monday Feb. 9$\underline{^{th}}$ My enthusiasm about my recovery had not palled by this morning. Although I only had 52 cents above my board and room rent (seven dollars in all, but due) I was as merry as a lark. I rode down to the car barns of the union traction company at 8$\underline{^{th}}$ and Dauphin street & register as an applicant for a position as a street car conductor but reached there too late. You can only register before nine. After that I walked down tenth, eleventh and Twelfth street to Market and the Reading Terminal where I had two old unused ticket stubs, between Philadelphia and Wissahickon, cashed. These netted me ten cents. From there I took the car and rode out to Dr. Duhrings, having resolved that I would go to him and tell him, not that I wanted another prescription but that I couldnt come anymore as I had no money. I felt to be sure that he might be pleased by this exhibition of frankness and become interested in my case sufficiently to offer to carry me on his credit list for awhile, but whether he did or no I resolved to see him. I walked boldly up and sat down and when it came my turn I went into him and frankly stated that I had no money and had only come to tell him that I was feeling better and that I laid my improvement in so much to him. He did not seem to understand me at first and began to ask me about my case, after which he wrote out a prescription.

"I meant to tell you doctor," I said to him when he had finished this, "that I had no money to pay for a prescription. I cannot pay you now. If you give me this you will have to wait."

He looked at me as if he were puzzled a little and, I felt—though I may have been mistaken, slightly displeased.

"Very well", he said. "You can to me in two or three days."

"I will be glad to do it as soon as I get the money I said.

He turned to discussing my case again, cautioning me about having his old prescriptions refilled, and when I went out the door

38. Ida Tarbell (1857–1944), author, editor, journalist. Tarbell's *Early Life of Abraham Lincoln,* 2 vols. (1900), for which she gathered material from many persons who knew Lincoln, helped create the popular legend of Lincoln as a mystic man of sorrows.

said, "You can send me that money by mail as soon as you get it.

"Oh I will," I said "certainly."

"I trust to your honor to do that."

"I will do just as I say," I replied. Here is the prescription he gave me.

Since I had my other medicine—the refilled prescription of his, still three quarters full—and as I also had some of the old drops he now prescribed anew still in my room, I did not think of having it filled. I did not have the money on hand to do it if I had wanted to. Instead I strolled back toward the city wondering what I should do next. My eye was hurting me a little—my only good eye, and so I decided to go back to the Free dispensary and see if they would prescribe for my eye for me. I turned and walked back, this time going boldly in, but the dispensary was not open. On the door a sign reading 2.30 P.M. was posted.

It being noon now I decided to go down to the city and see if I could screw up my courage to look for something to do. I was in no mood to accept a common wagon or store job of any kind, not because I found such work vile, but simply because I feel or felt that I was cut out and called upon to do literary and socialistic work and that very shortly I would be able to do it. To be sure I only had 52 cents in my pocket, but I was expecting 15$\underline{00}$ due me on an old loan from Gray, an enduring and true friend of mine, and another 35$\underline{00}$ or 40$\underline{00}$ due on an article accepted in July of the previous year by Joseph Coates of H. T. Coates and Company.[39] I have always had a horror of dunning people for money, and this particular claim at this particular time would have, as I thought, required so very much dunning that I was ashamed to try it. Coates is good friend of mine—a man very much after my own temperament, and it has always been very hard for me to say anything to him on these matters. He knows just how I feel about it no doubt, but he is or rather was not in the best of circumstances at the time. So I did not go to him this day.

Instead I walked round wondering whether I had not better go to the Woodyard of the Society for Organized Charities and see if they would not let me saw enough wood for my dinner. I did not really think that in the last step I would go or would really have to go, but I walked down there and took a look at it. It was a fine building four or five stories high, with a broad entrance way and an appearance of prosperity, but it was in a very poverty stricken neighborhood. I did not want to enter it when I reached there. The idea of an appeal was too painful. I walked on a way, rejoicing in my general feeling of returning health and feeling very sure that one of these days I would be on my feet again, writing articles and finishing my story. I felt as if I could almost write on them. I had a number of ideas in my mind.

I went on up 17$\underline{th}$ street and then East on Market to 15$\underline{th}$ when I encountered a Horn and Hardart restaurant. I was hungry and still anxious to pay my own way and so I went in. Here I ordered a bowl of mock turtle soup and some bread, an order which cost me 15 cents. While I was eating, who should come in by R. E. Powell, the head of the Philadelphia Vacant Lots Cultivation Association— an out and out Single Taxer and a man of broad and interesting perceptions.[40] He sat down beside me and as he had just come back from Dover where he had been trying to get a law passed to have real and personal property taxed separately, I asked him how things

---

39. Dreiser is undoubtedly referring here to one of two articles that Coates accepted for *Era* in 1902. The fact that neither article was published until later in 1903 helps explain why Dreiser had not yet been paid in full. The two pieces are "A Mayor and His People," *Era* 11 (June 1903): 578–84, and "The Problem of the Soil," *Era* 12 (September 1903): 239–49.

40. Powell would have subscribed to the ideas of Henry George (1839–97), who argued that a "single tax" on land owned by monopolies and speculators would relieve industry from other taxes. Industry, in turn, would give back to the community its share of the land value it helped create, thus alleviating the poverty that George felt was caused by the accumulation of great wealth by the few.

were getting along in Delaware. This started a conversation which lasted all afternoon—until 20 minutes of six in fact. He knew the ins and out of the main Addicks fight to obtain a seat in the Senate, and as he accused the Pennsylvania Railroad of the main opposition I was greatly interest.[41] We passed from one allied topic to another, finding great interest in the discussion of the ideas which control men, and how they are practically hypnotized by words. After he had explained the entire single tax idea and had told me of the status of the cause in different parts of the country, I persuaded him to help me to obtain material for two articles upon it which I promised to do. After leaving him I hurried over and caught the Ridge Avenue car, the total sum of money lying in my pocket when I reached Wissahickon being fifteen cents. I ate a moderately good dinner and immediately afterward came over to my room where I read the new February Booklovers Magazine sent me until 9.30 P.M.[42] Then I went to bed.

Tuesday, Feb 10ͭͪ My feeling this A.M. was as delightful as ever. I had slept fairly well and now went to breakfast feeling as if I could eat satisfactorily. My eye was hurting me but I thought I would go down to the Free Dispensary again to see if they would not examine it. This I was not very anxious to do—dissatisfied with myself rather, but life is life and I did not see at the moment how I could avoid it. At the breakfast table I paid Mrs. Shoop the 4⁰⁰ due for my meals of week past and coming to my room, after stopping and securing a stamp with the odd two cents I had left. I paid Mrs. McNally my remaining three dollars for room rent. This left me with just fifteen cents in cash. My bills due from Gray and Coates and my room rent paid until Saturday noon. Anything I might to do now, until Grays fifteen dollars should arrive, would have to be done out of the fifteen cents.

I sat down in room and posted up my medical account as written,

41. John Edward Addicks (1841–1919), Delaware financier who ran unsuccessfully for the U.S. Senate for many years. Like Charles Yerkes, Dreiser's original for his character Cowperwood, Addicks was born in Philadelphia, rose from modest beginnings, lived flamboyantly, and had a spectacular series of highs and lows in his financial career.

42. This is the issue of *Booklovers Magazine* in which Dreiser's "True Art Speaks Plainly" appeared (reprinted in Donald Pizer, ed., *Theodore Dreiser A Selection of Uncollected Prose* [Detroit: Wayne State Univ. Press, 1977], pp. 155–56.

after which I got out pen and paper and wrote Mrs. Dreiser. This & another letter I concluded by noon and then went to lunch. After lunch I strolled down toward the city, the idea being to save carfare as well as to enjoy myself. I reached the university grounds at 2.30 after a most delightful walk and made bold to go right to the eye dispensary, though I was rather ashamed to enter. An old man came up just as I reached the door, and as he was going in I had to follow. I did so, shocked to find myself confronted by a larger company of waiting patients to whom I felt as if I must look out of place. I went into an adjoining room where I sat, observed as I fancied by many and feeling very strange. While I was thinking however a young doctor motioned to me and when I went to him began to take my name and address as well as the details of my difficulty. When he had finished he gave me a card which I took and waited, another young young physician coming eventually to examine me. He placed me upon a chair near a light and looked into my eyes. Later he took me into a dark room and placed me before a revolving machine. Here he looked into my eye again and then, coming out, gave me a printed prescription calling for drops to enlarge the pupil of eye, which I was to use that night. He also cautioned me to buy a pair of smoked glasses, both of which I knew I could not do. I went out and as I passed the hospital drug store I fancied they might filled the prescription free, but on inquiry I discovered this was not so. He wanted 45 cents and I had to back out simply saying I would get it down town.

"You wont get in any cheaper than that anywhere else", he said.

"I know," I replied, "but I would rather buy it down town".

Here I was then with my eye hurting me, a prescription to heal it with and no money. I walked down town thinking of the lot of the poor who sometimes under such circumstances have no resource in their own intellect, and speculating on how hard it must be. Going to Coates I told him I was thinking of going to New York and asked him if he would not wind up my account and pay me the balance due this week. To my delight he told me that he thought he could. We then went back and sat talking about my novel of Jennie Gerhardt, the manuscript of which I had given him to read and which in parts he considered very good. It was mixed, he thought, and overwrought in parts, but when I told him the whole story, as I had originally concieved it, he was as moved as everyone else has been and told me it was fine. I could see by his interruptions though that he was even more wrought up than his words would indicate and when we parted for the night, it was with the assurance that he would give the mss some new thought and see if he could not suggest a way of improving it. "We will hear more of you yet," he exclaimed when we parted and I could not help smiling.

Going up to Ridge Avenue I spent another five of my remaining fifteen cents and so reached home safely. Dinner was waiting and I ate heartily. After dinner I read in Tarbells "Life of Lincoln" till about 10 when I retired quite sleepy. I thought a little while over my plans for the future and then fell asleep, enjoying another such a nights rest as I have not had in months.

<u>Wednesday, Feb 11</u>th Raining this morning and very gloomy but I am not feeling badly at all. Read awhile in Tarbells Life of Lincoln until noon in fact and then went out to luncheon. It was still raining when I got through with that meal, but I decided to go for a walk, so I strolled up to Manayunk along Manayunk Avenue and went across and came down the Schuylkill on the other side. It was raining very hard. The great mills of Manayunk and Pencoyd look like faint outlines in a solid foreground of gray. The river was running muddy and deep, the smoke of the factories and engines hanging low. All was sombre and dark to me and yet it had color and was not without beauty. It seemed to me that if I were an artist I could paint a thousend pictures of Manayunk. It so squalid, so poor, so suggestive of all that is artistic and grim in toil.

Coming down through the yards of the Pencoyd Iron works I was finally stopped by an Irish Policemen and had to go over to hill road to get down. He was of the usual Hibernian order—stout, self-assured, preemptory.

"Where do you want to go"

"I want to get to the city avenue Bridge."

"If you want to go this way you will have to get a pass."

"Allright. I'll go to the office and get a pass."

We were both rather savage in our manner and I turned on my heel sneeringly, but he followed with a more conciliatory air.

"Do you want to go down through the yard," he inquired.

Philadelphia Dispensary

"I want to get to the city Ave bridge. It doesnt matter how I get there."

"It doesnt matter how you get there," he repeated half humorously.

"No", I said.

"Well you can go across here to those house and go around the lane there."

I walked away without thanking him, angry at the assured air of fellow, and yet I could not quite make out why. I was sorry that I had spoken so and yet I was joyfully conscious of hating the type. How I would like to have the authority to take him down, I thought, and then—oh then all the thoughts about the inexplicable conflicts of life, the uselessness and wretched of temper, the floods of wrath and pain. Why, Why? Why not always, as Christ said, gentle and kind. "If any man compel thee to go with him a mile, go with him twain."

I returned home via the City Ave bridge, wet and rather glum. Took off my cloths and dried them, reading the while in the Life of Lincoln. About six I took medicine and went to dinner, returning and bringing Mr Bebber with me. He was very much interested in my exposition of single Tax and the value of life in general and left at nine, declaring he wished he knew as much of the theory of life as I. It made me laugh. The uselessness of speculation. Would that I had a vast fund of technical information. That I were twenty five, successful and happy. Ah me—Ah me, who is it that tells the truth and is happy.

Thursday, Feb 12 . This day being so beautiful and I feeling so good, I might have gone down town but I had no money. As suggested previously my money has been dwindling until the paying of my fare home on Tuesday night left me but ten cents. With this, in case no other money came, I had decided to pay my fare back from down town on Friday to see Coates, and if he did not give me the money as promised to use the other five cents on Saturday to carry my grip to the station where I could check it for nothing. I had no real anticipation that Coates would fail to pay me, but I thought he might and if he did it would leave me without means to pay my room rent, providing Grays fifteen did not come. Consequently I would have to leave my room and loaf about the city or put myself in jeopardy for another weeks rent, and that I did not choose to do. As it was, Saturday night would see me owing Mrs. Shoop four dollars for board and unless I could pay it by the Tuesday following I would be in danger of being disgraced. At least I would have to confess that I had no money to pay her with or leave without saying a word. As I did not want to do this I was hoping Coates would pay or Gray would write and was hanging on to my ten cents to see me safely to the depot where I could deposit my grip anyhow.

As it happened however a letter came from The Outlook asking if I would accept 10$\underline{00}$ for a portion of my article on "The Problem of Distribution,"[43] and as I was anxious to get the money as well as greatly elated to think that anything of mine should be accepted at all—you know how it is when you are going down hill temporarily, nothing seems to go right—I went at once to the drug store and bought a couple of stamps. With one of these I mailed a letter to the Outlook saying I would accept the offered mentioned and with the other posted a letter to Jewett of J. F. Taylor & Co, in answer to one I had recieved this same morning, asking how I was, in which I told him I was getting better and was coming back to New York.[44] This left me 6 cents. Then I read in "The Cliff Dwellers" until noon and so went to lunch.

During the afternoon I took a walk. It was a beautiful afternoon, warm and sunshiny with a perfect flood light upon the hills about and a general throb of spring in the air. I strolled up through Roxborough and along the banks of the Wissahickon to Shawmont lane, where I crossed back and came home along Ridge Avenue again. Truly it was beautiful. I do not know how I can feel so when

43. "The Problem of Distribution," rejected by *Ainslee's* earlier in 1902, survives in a ten-page typescript among Dreiser's papers at the University of Pennsylvania. The article deals with the problems of distributing fruit and vegetables at the marketplace, and the need for a central organization to protect the growers. The weekly *Outlook* was a miscellany of biography, national affairs, fiction, and literary criticism published by the Outlook Company in New York. Although during this period, nothing appears in its pages under Dreiser's name, the *Outlook* may still have used Dreiser's material, since at least half its space was given to short, unsigned features and brief book reviews. The low fee and Dreiser's willingness to sell a "portion" of the piece suggests that he settled for an unsigned publication.

44. Rutger B. Jewett (1867–1935), editor and head of the trade department at J. F. Taylor & Co., which had contracted with Dreiser to publish *Jennie Gerhardt.* An admirer of *Sister Carrie,* Jewett supported Dreiser emotionally with letters of encouragement—and financially with advances on *Jennie Gerhardt.*

Jug is away and I am not quite well and almost entirely without money, but somehow the contemplation of nature is sufficient for me. I looked at the trees and the river murmuring along over the stones and my heart was glad. I sang, as I always sing when I am walking, a half dozen different melodies of a minor or plaintive note and at last came to feel as if life were delicious. I was not to remain poor always, I fancied. I was to recover and grow strong and be able to write again. Love was to come back and play its part in my life again. Life, love, sunlight—so I sang and dreamed.

It is not without a pang, though, that I face the evenings. Somehow after a beautiful day of this kind their is always a revulsion. It is too beautiful. We dream to deeply. I came home, wondering as the twilight fell whether my dreams were to come true and then I found as I always do that I was expecting them too soon. Not now. Not now. Somehow now is almost always commonplace. We see when we return that we have to wait. To be alone, to live alone, to wait, wait, wait, that is the lot accorded us, and only the dreams are real. The substance of them is never with us—never attainable.

I sat down after supper and read again—read the Cliff Dwellers— an interesting but rather unfinished book, and finally went to bed. This night I did not sleep so well and yet I cannot say that I slept badly. It was only medium.

Friday, Feb 13<u>th</u> This has proved a somewhat unlucky or perhaps I had rather say slightly discouraging day. I had hoped that it would bring me the money I had asked for of Coates but it did not. I wrote and read all morning, getting off a cheering letter to Mrs. Dreiser which I had no stamp to send, however, and then walking all the way along the river, and through Ridge Avenue down into heart of the city where I called upon Coates. I had thought some of walking down in the morning, the idea being to give myself a rest before walking back in the afternoon, but when I realized that I had no money wherewith to buy myself a lunch, I did not try it. Mrs. Shoop would furnish her regular lunch at noon, and as I could eat that quickly at 12 oclock I fancied I could down and back in time for dinner and not be too much ⌊　⌋ by it. Anyhow I considered this better than going without my lunch and tried it.

Walking down to the city is not such an easy matter as some

might imagine from the casual mention of it I have made from time to time. It is a good five mile if not more and is not quite level walking. I have made it in as little time as two hours and twenty minutes (one way) but I did not expect to be over two hours above this time. Anyhow I started at 12.30 and arrived there at 2.10, a fairly rapid walk I fancied.

It is one thing to walk a distance like this for pleasure and another to be compelled to walk it for the saving of five cents, or the want of it. I was not anxious to do it. Lovely as the day was, the thought of being compelled to do it was a little painful. I was anxious to shut out of my heart any complaining against it, but sickness and poverty are horrible things. Profess as I may and draw myself up to the full stature of my courage, there is nothing but sorrow for me in thinking of what I might have. The beauty, the comfort, the affection of the world. How the sign of it or its semblance pricks the soul in want.

As I say I reached Coates at 2.10 but I was not successful in obtaining the money. He was busy at first and then, when I did get him, he turned the conversation off on Napoleon, which I was too timid or too good natured to interrupt. We talked on that till half past four and then, realizing that I must get or walk back, I asked him.

"Did you manage to straighten out that little matter of the balance due me."

"Oh yes that balance. Well no. Mr. Stoddard isnt here today.[45] Could you come in Monday."

"Yes, I said "I can come in Monday."

"He will be back then and we can fix it up then I guess".

I left him after a few of the bland pleasantries of a situation like this. I hurried away knowing that if I did not I would not get back in time for supper. I had a long way to walk. My feet were slightly sore, but I walked. All the way I hurried so that I did not have much time to grieve and yet I did. Me. Theodore Dreiser. A man who has ideas enough to write and to spare and walking for want of a nickel.

I reached home or rather the boarding house at just twenty

45. This may be Joseph Stoddard, Jr., an editor at *Era* at the time.

minutes of seven having covered the distance in an hour and twenty. Weary, panting, I sat down to supper. I was hungry and yet glad that I was hungry and that I had a place to eat. After, I came out thinking how I would write all this. What a peculiar story my life would make if all were told, and so sat down in my room alone to read. I was lonely. I was homesick. All the wretchedness of situation was pressing upon me but I fell to reading. If I cannot have things, must I eat my heart out thinking of them? If light and merriment and love are all so far from me, must I weep alone? Rather I took up my life of Lincoln and read eagerly in it, the story of that man of sorrows having much in it that reminds me of my own. That night I slept a little better than usual.

Saturday Feb 14th Well this as fruitless but not so unhappy a day. It was bright as the day preceding, not so warm but beautifully bright. All morning, after I had wandered about a little and waited for my room to be fixed, I sat in it and read of Lincoln or wrote on this diary. I was not thinking of writing on my story or doing an article, although I feel as though I ought to. I have need of money, heavens knows, and yet I feel as if I cannot write. Lucidity of expression and consecutiveness of ideas is what is bothering me. I cannot write continuously. I lose the thread and forget.

After I had read until noon however I went dinner (we always have dinner on Saturday) and then I heard how Darrow had closed up the miners case.[46] It was powerful speech, some thought. The lady next to me, however, the only one present who seemed to consider herself somebody, expressed the feeling that she would liked to have slapped Darrow. The miners were such wretches in her estimation.

I do not know why, but this had a most depressing effect on me. Men, working men, a mass of any men desiring something and not being able to get it is always depressing to me. I feel so sorry for them. They seem so deserving of my pity. Poor, ignorant, leading grimy, narrow lives—oh I know how they fight and quarrel among

---

46. Clarence Darrow (1857–1938), lawyer, reformer, lecturer, writer. Darrow's major practice was in labor law, and when President Theodore Roosevelt set up a commission to arbitrate the Pennsylvania anthracite coal strike of 1902, Darrow was chief counsel for the miners. Dreiser here is referring to Darrow's closing speech on behalf of the miners.

---

themselves. I know too full well that they drink and carouse and are like other men, low and corrupt and mean. Are they not like other men? Are they not like the men who oppress them? Is Morgan pure, is Baer clean?[47] Have they tender hearts, noble souls, fine and beautiful lives? They have money and fine clothes and a pleasant atmosphere of comforts and refinements to move in, but some men are born to degradation and the fault is not theirs after all.

Anyhow it grieved me and I went out after dinner and walked about to think of these things. I walked down Ridge Ave to School Lane and across School to some street in Germantown and along that I walked north until I reached a branch of the Wissahickon along which I walked toward the section called Wissahickon in which I live. It was very, very beautiful, not warm and not exactly cold. Everybody seemed to be enjoying, and I met a crowd of children playing in the water as well as group of old men gabbling in the sun. I tried to think of my story after a time and wondered how I should ever finish it but did not reach any conclusions. Later I came to negro fishing by the stream and fell to talking with him. He seemed to be a happy go lucky creature and told me he had place as chief cook at Capon Springs in season and waiting for the season to open. He also told me the society people were very bad at that resort and the women were all immoral. I wondered at this a little but said nothing as I not wish to appear curious or condemnatory of the whites with him. Still I could not think of all that gayety and license without worrying over my own condition. Being homely and backward, with no art of impressing women, I have always suffered on the side of my affections. Some men have so much. I have had so little.

I came away feeling rather depressed over this again, but I tried not to feel too blue. All men do not have it. There must be thousends like me. There must be thousands more who do not countenance immorality or even flirtation. Anyhow I have not got it and here I am.

I came up along the hillside and saw a funeral taking place in my

<hr />

47. John Pierpont Morgan (1837–1913), banker, financier. Dreiser is probably referring to George F. Baer (1842–1914), lawyer for J. P. Morgan; in 1901 Baer became president of the Reading Coal & Iron Company in Pennsylvania.

street. It was from a house just a few doors above mine and one in front of which I saw a curious thing take place the day before. I saw a black dog come down to the cross or lane opposite the morning before and after he reached the middle of the street he lifted up his head and howled most mournfully three times. I was dressing at my window at the time and noticed him doing it but was not sure what it meant. I had heard my mother say it was a sign of death. I do not like to believe in such things and I have a vein of superstition in me. When the dog turned and trotted slowly away, back in the direction from which he had come, I fancied it might mean death. When I saw the crepe on the door today, right opposite where he had stood, I felt maybe that he had howled for that.

The rest of the day was not very eventful after that. I sat in my room and read until six, went to tea from 6 to 6:30 and read again from 6.30 or seven till nine. Slept very comfortably during the night and rose the next morning, Sunday, feeling very good.

Sunday, Feb. 15<u>th</u>. My life this day was not even as varied as that of the day before. Rose, bathed and shaved before 8. Eat breakfast at that hour and at nine came back and read my life of Lincoln till twelve when I finished it. At 12.30 I went to dinner and after that came home and read the Cliff Dwellers till four when I finished that. No striking mental thoughts or feelings occurred to me. Lincolns life moved me deeply as any such tragedy as that always moves me. Lincoln and Christ—somehow these two are naturally associated in my mind. They were both so kind, so tender, so true. Oh that we could all be great, noble and altogether lovely. It not possible that any but a few should be so, however—conspicuously so, perhaps.

My sleep this night was not so good owing to my wrought up mental state, the tragedy of his life staying with me until late. I rolled and turned a great deal and suffered one of those periods of physical depression during which I felt as if my heart were beating too light. I had bad dreams also but came out of it sufficiently rested not to feel entirely bad. It was not a good night however by any means.

Monday, Feb 16<u>th</u> This day I could call an excellent commentary on the want of money. Being without a penny—I spent my last six cents Sunday night for three stamps, I found myself constrained to walk down to the city hall again, a distance of 7 miles I find, as I had Friday, to collect my money due from Coats. At first I felt that I did not want to walk, but being so much in need of it I started anyhow. It had been raining and sleeting Sunday and all throughout the night and as consequence the trees were covered with ice. There was some little ice on the ground also in spots, and on the whole many would have called it a disagreeable but I did not mind. I took my Life of Lincoln, The Cliff Dwellers and Thomas Love Peacocks Maid Marion and started out.[48] At first I grieved a little at being compelled to do it, but after I got started I did not mind. I'm a good walker and soon reached Mrs Scotts house, 3322 Columbia,[49] where I delivered Maid Marian from whom Mrs Dreiser had borrowed it. Then I was East on Columbia to Ridge Ave again and so down to Coates office where I arrived at almost noon. Running across the street I returned my 2<u>nd</u> volume of Lincoln to the Free Library and then intruded myself on Coates who invited me to sit down. As usual we fell into a conversation, this time a very enjoyable one, concerning my new novel. When we had finished that I ask for my mss of Jennie and received it. Then I asked for my check. "I'm sorry", he said, "but Stoddard isnt here again today, and as I dont know how much your account is I cant pay it."

"The transportation couldn't be more than fifteen" I said, meaning the transportation he had given me on Mrs Dreisers behalf.

"Oh well in that case I can pay you," he said. Just sit down a minute and I'll go out in front and get it."

As fate would have it I didnt get my check, though. Although he went front he came back to say the man who signs the checks wasn't present just then.

---

48. *Maid Marian* (1822), a novel by Thomas Love Peacock (1785–1866), English poet and novelist.

49. Mrs. Scott's letters at the University of Pennsylvannia indicate that she in fact lived at 3220 Columbia Avenue.

"Come out and take lunch with me and you can get it as you come back."

We went to lunch at the Franklin Inn, the chief authors club of the city.[50] It is a bizarre affair got up after the old English Inn style, very well decorated of course, but rather trite. I sat down speculating on how, had he not invited me, I would have secured any dinner at all. Here we talk, a company of local editors and newspaper men being present, until 2.30 when we went back. Coates was in a pleasent humor and immediately went to get my check for me but came back to say that the man was still out. He would mail it to me. I said very well and came away, but oh me it was not very well. To walk so far, not to be sure of getting it after all, to have to face a weekly room rent and board overdue and probably very much expected. I decided I could only wait however and if the money did not come, I could still eat my breakfast and possibly my lunch at the old place, pack my things and leave them in my rooming place until Friday or Saturday and then go out into the streets where I could subsist, say at the wayfarers lodge, until some word should come, either from Coates, or Gray or the Outlook—all three debtors of mine, and I could pay up my dues and go to New York. I felt as if I could curse heaven and earth for the moment. Instead I went over to the Book Lovers and left another editorial which I had written Saturday in the hopes they would buy it. Also went to Phila Lib. Co and drew out a Life of Grant.[51] With this and my big story mss and an umbrella, I trapsed way out here to Wissahickon—seven miles again. It was sleeting, the wind was blowing and I was tired, but on I walked. When I did finally get here I was tired and hungry but I was not despondent. Much adversity has taught not to despair. I can still live. Though one has neither houses nor lands, nor affection nor companionship, he can still live. It isn't pleasent I'll admit but it can be done. How I am trying to tell you.

Tuesday, Feb 17 th Fortune seemed to smile on me at first today. I rose after a somewhat broken nights sleep and found my check

50. The Franklin Inn Club, founded in 1902, was Philadelphia's most exclusive literary club. It was located at 1218 Chancellor St. at the time, but is now at Camac and St. James Sts.
51. Dreiser is probably reading Hamlin Garland's *Ulysses S. Grant: His Life and Character* (1898).

waiting. Coates had really sent it. Now I'll go down and get it cashed. It was snowing and there was seven inches of the white stuff on the ground but I decided to go. Accordingly after breakfast I tramped down only to find that it was election day—a legal holiday and all the banks were closed. Then I tramped back again.

I wish those who are doubtful about the[52]

52. The diary breaks off here. Dreiser began this sentence, but did not complete the thought, leaving the rest of the page blank. He never returned to the diary to finish the entry.

SAVANNAH AND THE SOUTH, 1916

In late January 1916, Dreiser traveled south to Savannah, Georgia, to escape the northern winter and find a quiet place to work. He had visited the South before and had always found its pace and atmosphere restorative. In January 1900, for instance, stalled at a troublesome spot in the manuscript of *Sister Carrie,* he had gone south to gather material for free-lance magazine articles. The trip refreshed him, and when he returned he was able to push ahead with *Sister Carrie* and finish it in late March. In January 1916 Dreiser again had problems, but of a different nature. His work was going relatively well, but he was troubled by the impending breakup of his long-term affair with Kirah Markham. The trip to Savannah gave him a chance to relax, observe, reflect, and write.

Friends can always find
Kirah Markham
and
Theodore Dreiser
at home on Sunday evenings
November — March.

165 West 10th St.   Chelsea 7755

Markham-Dreiser "at Home" Card

Jan 26—1916 (Wednesday) Gray & foggy. Horns & bells in rivers about N.Y. quite noisy. Kirah and I stay in bed until about 10:30 although we had planned to rise early.[1] Mrs. White present, cleaning up. I do not feel extra good. Shave with sexto blade and old shaving brush rather than unpack my bag. No letters. A bill— (R. Thomas & Sons—London.[2] 1 notice of "Old Ragpicker.)[3] We hurry because we have to go to bank. Udell phones—wants me to see dummy of "Plays of the Natural & the Supernatural."[4] Promise to get there by 12:30. Am worried over L——.[5] She did not meet me night before as agreed. Am afraid she will appear at boat and K—— will see her. We go to Brevoort for breakfast.[6] Eggs Benedictine & coffee for us both. I get angry because waiter insists on reserving two best tables at front, though no one comes to sit in them before we are through. From here take 5th Ave. Bus to Astor

1. Kirah Markham was an art student and actress who took part in the little theater movement of the nineteen-teens in Chicago and New York. She met Dreiser in 1913 when she was acting with the Chicago Little Theatre and living with Floyd Dell. She moved to New York, and by early 1914 she and Dreiser were living together at 165 West 10th St., where they often held a weekly open house for artists and intellectuals. Their invitation card, preserved among the Dreiser papers at the University of Pennsylvania, reads: "Friends can always find Kirah Markham and Theodore Dreiser at home on Sunday evenings, November–March"—along with their address and telephone number. Their intimacy ended shortly after Dreiser returned to New York from Savannah in April 1916. Miss Markham had traveled to Savannah in early March 1916 in an attempt to save an already unsettled relationship. But by early summer of that year she had left Dreiser and joined the theater group led by George Cram Cook and Eugene O'Neill that became the Provincetown Players. As later diaries reveal, she and Dreiser afterwards maintained a distant but genial friendship. Many years later, Professor Robert H. Elias spoke to her after she had become Mrs. Kyra Markham Gaither, the wife of a teacher and painter at Marlboro College in Vermont. Elias notes, on a card in the Dreiser Collection, his impression that she thought of herself as "the second Mrs. Dreiser."

2. Correspondence at the University of Pennsylvania shows that Dreiser owed R. Thomas & Son, Ltd., £5 7s. 6d. for boots he bought in London in 1911. He paid the bill, finally, on 26 June 1916.

3. Dreiser's play "Old Ragpicker" was first published in *Plays of the Natural and the Supernatural* (1916).

4. The British firm of John Lane Co. published *Plays of the Natural and the Supernatural* on 18 February 1916. The firm sent Dreiser for inspection a dummy—a pattern volume of the book with blank pages and pasted-in examples of type or illustration to indicate its general appearance and dimensions.

Udell is Merton S. Yewdale, an editor at John Lane.

5. Dreiser took to concealing the names of his mistresses at this time, probably fearing that the diary might fall into the hands of one of the women. K—— is Kirah Markham; L—— is Lillian Rosenthal (see p. 150, n. 8).

6. The Brevoort Hotel, on the northeast corner of Fifth Ave. and 8th St. Allen Churchill notes that the hotel, "since 1845, had brought the flavor of la belle France to lower Fifth Avenue" (*The Improper Bohemians* [New York: E. P. Dutton & Co., 1959], p. 15). Its basement cafe was a gathering place of Greenwich Village's artists and intellectuals.

Trust Bank where I draw $35. From here to Jones (John Lane Co) where Udell shows me model of book.[7] It is very pleasing. K——— then leaves me to go to 42nd Street to buy me a health belt. In her absence I try to get Mrs. S——— on the phone to tell her I am leaving town but she is out. I try to think of some way of reaching L——— but cannot. Too dangerous to phone her at her family. It is raining. New York seems stuffy and sicky—an unhealthy season. I go to house—165 W. 10th—change my coat for rain coat & finish packing. While doing so K——— arrives with belt. At last moment I discover that brown suit I intend to wear is still accross street at tailors being pressed. K——— runs over and gets it. She is as beautiful as ever to me with her long body & beautiful head. We start at 2 P.M. for boat thinking it will take longer than it really does. Arrive at 2:30. Much to my releif L——— is not present but two books (Homo Sapiens and Taras Bulbos) and a box of candy from her are.[8] I see them through the pursers window but do not take them. Forgot to say that previous to going to boat I phoned Purser not to put anything in my berth (stateroom) until after ship has sailed.

K——— and I visit cabin & put in bags. Stand up in front & admire river & boats. Owing to heavy cargo, boat does not sail at 3. K——— has to leave to act in "The Weavers" (Garden theatre) there being a matinee.[9] Promises to come back at 5:30 to see if ship has gone yet. I know she feels that there may be some other woman in the offing but she says nothing. She goes & I loaf about watching cargo being put aboard. 5:30 comes & we are still here. It is dark & breesy but warm. Also very foggy & the bells & horns of the river make a great uproar. We stand & look at the lights appearing & disappearing in mist until whistle sounds all ashore. It is then 6 P.M. K——— goes & they remove the gang plank but we lie here just the same. It is too foggy to leave. I eat dinner—6:15—

---

7. J. Jefferson Jones (1880–1941), the American director of the British publishing house of John Lane Co., which had published *The Titan* (1914) and *The "Genius"* (1915), and would publish *Plays of the Natural and the Supernatural* and *A Hoosier Holiday* later in 1916.

8. *Homo Sapiens* by Stanislaw Przybyszewski (1868–1927); Dreiser probably has Thomas Seltzer's 1915 translation of the Polish novel.

Taras Bulbos by Nicholas Gogol (1809–52), probably in Isabel F. Hapgood's 1915 translation.

9. Gerhart Hauptmann's "The Weavers" opened at the Garden Theatre on 27th St. and Madison Ave. on 14 December 1915 and ran for eighty-seven performances.

a poor dinner in a dull dining room. The travelers on this line are a scrubby lot. I must say—horrible American bourgeoisie. For relief I get out "The Village" by Crabbe and read in it.[10] Also write Claire Uecke at Honolulu.[11] Finally go in and lie down in berth, reading Hutchins Hapgoods "An Anarchistic Woman."[12] Leaving my berth door open I can see the upper portion of the Woolworth Bldg tower, beautifully lighted. Also top of Singer building. Get sleepy finally & put out lights. We do not sail before morning, that is plain. It is odd to sleep in a boat in a slip in New York harbor with all the noise of the city & the river about.

Awakened about 4 A.M. by roar of whistle & trembling of boat. We are just moving out. (From Pier 35 North River.) Lights in many buildings of lower Manhattan are still burning—a jewelled scene. We go out into dark of upper bay. Stop at Quarantine (I think) & I fall asleep. Awake to see eastern sky streaked with red and boat clear of city—just a smooth flow of water on every hand. Read "An Anarchistic Woman" fall asleep & awake again at 7:30—breakfast bell ringing. Get up & take a deck walk. I have a good cabin—55 on Hurricane deck. Eat but the food is bad—a wretched ships cook. Go to my state room, get my notes & go to writing room to work. A fairly sunny day so far. Should note the two women—one the "Brood Sow" as I have named her, in blue velvet & cream lace—the other, the other, "the young pig" in the pink velvet lounging jacket. The Brood Sow is nervous, sensuous, self-conscious & very uncertain of herself. The other is bumptious, noisy, froward. Sings very well & is fairly clever. She is obviously the most attractive bit to the weak minded male and knows it. Sings in parlor until about 10 P.M.

10. "The Village" by George Crabbe (1754–1832), English poet. Dreiser may have found "relief," much as Thomas Hardy did, in Crabbe's realism and his tough-minded portrait of the tragic ironies in life.

11. Clare H. Uecke's relation with Dreiser began with a letter dated 9 October 1915, written from Oahu College, Honolulu. She introduced herself and expressed her admiration for *Jennie Gerhardt* and *The Financier*. Later she moved to Greenwich Village, became a writer, and maintained a friendship with Dreiser.

12. *An Anarchistic Woman* by Hutchins Hapgood (1869–1944), journalist, social commentator, novelist. Hapgood, one of the more notable Greenwich Village intellectuals of the day, became part of Dreiser's circle; his autobiography, *A Victorian in the Modern World* (1939), contains a portrait of Dreiser during these years.

Gulls

8 A.M. About this hour I watched the gulls. There were about 24 of them—grey white, trailing the ship. They had a rusty squeak and kept craning their necks & looking from side to side and up & down, watching each other. Some seemed old—wise old hawks that hung close to the ship in easy positions doing nothing to trouble themselves. Others younger or more active were constantly moving from side to side in wide sweeps, dropping back, coming forward, dropping to the water for food—a restless crew. What brooding spirit of life generated them? What thing is it, in nature, which wants to be a gull, haunting the grey sea. Or is it a curse—but I do not see any form of life as a curse. I never did, not in my darkest, most unhappy hours. Change in life, not less life or no life was what I craved.

The sea

The sea, the sea, the crinkling sea. Here in my chair with a book and the sssh of the water in my ears. Dull people go by. ¶ My ears are troubled with inanities. ¶ I hear clatter concerning ghastly trivialities. ¶ But the sum of all life is not trivial or it does not appear so. The integral atoms of the sea may be nothing.
But the sea!
Just now in the clear glistering foreground—above the blue floor, a white gull goes by.
I love the sea! I love the sea!

Clouds

Pearl Grey and pink and a few thin bars that are as red as hot blood. The sea below is so cool and flat. The clouds in the east reach out like hands. They beckon and signal, like fingers speaking of lands that never were. They talk to me of dreams that I had in my youth. "Better lands than this," they say, "await you."
"Out! Come forth. Shake off the thing that holds you. Spring up into the blue. Be spirit not matter. These pearly and pink fields are real. They hold as real the dreams that still are dreams to you. Out and away. Walk over the water to us. Forget all life & come.
Little done this day except read "The Anarchistic Woman" which I finished—an excellent book—ate two meals which I shouldn't have and looked at the sea, which because of a slightly trouble stomach seems not as nice as otherwise. In the parlor after dinner "Mme. Aria" or "Little Pig" as I called her played & sang as usual, same

---

songs as the night before. "The Brood Sow" posed as usual. Horrible food. It couldn't be worse.

Life Moods

Nothing is more interesting to me than just the silent passing of moods in the mind, hour after hour, day after day, year after year though nothing is said. A man draws near—you dislike him. He goes again and is forgotten. The sun comes out. You say silently to yourself—how beautiful. Life is good. In its light colorful dreams and moods rise and fall like the waves of the sea—all in silence. The sun goes under a cloud. Life is not so pleasing any more. You begin to recall difficulties that have assailed you at one time or another—errors.

On this boat sitting alone I have noticed this—dwelt on it. I have watched my moods shift chameleon like from grave to pleasant but with never a word to me from anyone. The sea has facinated me. I have smiled. My stomach has felt a little upset—immediately I have become disgusted with life. On everybody present I have passed judgement, weighing them lightly—perhaps most unfairly—in my hand. This man is a fool, this woman a silly, that one a strumpet, this other man a wolf or a dull materialist. Scarcely a person have I approved of in my mind and yet I know that coming in contact with them I would more or less like them all. That is the way with me. In silence I condemn and contemn in verbal contact. I explain away my dislikes and take them as they are and as life is—with a shrug and a smile, making the best of a world that I cannot improve upon. I know it to be more or less of a perfect scheme of things (as good as well can be) as bad as I know it to be.

Friday, Jan. 28, 1916   Savannah Trip

Still enroute. Had good night's rest. Read "The Spirit of Labor" (Hutchins Hapgood) which I like.[13] He is an earnest seeker after fact and to be commended. At 3:30 A.M. I awoke and saw a waning but still nearly full moon rising out of the sea in the East. The sea had a strangely dismal aspect—pearly black, like pictures of dismal swamp I have seen. It was interesting.

Closed the window, read awhile, then fell asleep and woke to

13. *The Spirit of Labor* (1907) by Hutchins Hapgood.

hear the first breakfast bell clanging. A negro goes about on this ship ringing a hand bell. Open my window & looked out. A soft south wind was blowing—very summery & gay. The sun was out too—lovely. All the cold and drearyness of N.Y. gone. Dressed quickly, washing my hair & body & went down to breakfast— hominy & cream, steak & bacon, toast & coffee. Only fair. Went out in front afterward & stood in the very prow of the boat watching the ship's nose cut the water forty feet below, feeling the cool air blowing over me, alluring dreams of a new heaven & new earth to sway me. I thought how wonderful it would be to create a new world out of a pathless sea. The water to my right in the shade of the boat was black like coal or black glass. Sometimes it seemed to take on a dark—very dark green—hue. Sea weed was about. I thought of what Columbus saw days before he discovered land. The air on my face & hands was wonderful. I was so glad to be leaving New York for awhile anyhow. I would not mind if it were for years or for good. It feels wonderful to be alone—and to be warm again. Winters in N.Y. make me sick. A youth comes forward and stands beside me—a mama's boy with money. He is very handsome, very gay, very vacuous and sings all the while. I notice that his clothes are intended to be the best—and are—after their fashion. We exchange a few words. Sailors are rubbing down the brass & wood work. Everybody is feeling relieved at the end of the bite in the air. After a time I go to my room, get my book (Spirit of Labor) and read. Then post notes till noon. Have a brandy & soda. The Scotch on this boat is horrible.

The people who are on this boat—several groups at least— interest me. One group seems sporty—and now from odd bits of conversation dropped here & there I learn we have a prize fighter on board, "Andy" Cortez, and a trainer Phil alias "Chicken" Cox of New Haven, Ct. They are both here in the writing room now, writing, joshing each other & desiring to play poker. A dull crude lot. "If your writing say that your here with Phil, better know as Chicken Cox of New Haven"
"Give 'em my love"
"Andys gone around here like a chicken with his head off wantin' to play poker etc."

The blonde girl who is thick with them but apparently not of them sings "Mother McCree" "My Little Grey Home in the West"

"You Never Believe Me" etc. etc. continually. She fancies herself absolutely destructive in the matter of charm.

"Bring my chair"

"What's the number?"

"17—just my age—ha! ha"

There's another man who looks exactly like the late John W. Gates[14]—very aggressive & commercial—is lead around by a wizened, anemic wife who commands him like a child.

There is still another young man—quite young, who looks like a cross between Harry Thaw & Roland Burke Molineux.[15] He has an auto on board & horses and is going to Georgia to shoot. The blond beast of a woman who I have called "the brood sow" is either his wife or mistress. Her fingers are crowded with jewels & she has a maid. He has a manager with him.

There are other groups of Southerners, so refined that they rarely come out of their state rooms.

But the sea. It's so wonderful today. No driving wind, no bite in the air. Most of the gulls that were with us out of N.Y. have gone. Only 10 or 12 left. Ships are occasionally seen in the distance. The waves are very small. We cut on, mile after mile. I walk, read, lie down, read, walk & all the time marvel at the sea. It thrills me. It is so immense, so floor like. I read that the Atlantic and the Indian Ocean are the same size & that the Pacific is nearly as big as the two of them combined. And terrafirma is only 1/4 of the world. What ancient mysteries do not the seas contain. What puzzles might they not unravel if we could search their beds!

---

14. John W. Gates (1855–1911), financier.

15. Harry K. Thaw (1871–1947), the central figure in one of the great criminal causes célèbres in America. The heir to millions, Thaw was a wealthy playboy who shot and killed the architect Stanford White on the roof of the old Madison Square Garden on 25 June 1906. Thaw was acquitted on grounds of insanity and then sent to a hospital for the criminally insane, from which he escaped to Canada. Brought back to the United States, he was acquitted of the crime after a jury declared him sane in 1915. His later years followed a pattern of commitment and release from asylums.

Roland Burke Molineux (1866–1917) was at the center of a famous murder trial in New York. The son of a wealthy family, Molineux was a chemist who was convicted of the murder of Mrs. K. J. Adams in 1899. He was sent to the death house in Sing Sing for twenty months, and then he was acquitted in 1902. He wrote in prison, including a play called "The Man Inside," which David Belasco produced. Molineux had a nervous breakdown and spent the last four years of his life in the New York State Hospital for the Insane at King's Park, Long Island. In 1915 Dreiser began a novel, "The Rake," based on Molineux's career; he completed only six chapters before he abandoned the project.

Saturday, Jan. 29, 1916—Savannah Trip

I wake again at 2:30 or thereabouts and see a full moon over the sea just rising. The water has an olive greenish look, tinged in the moon's pathway with silver. Go to sleep and dream. Wake at dawn. The charm of being at sea in this balmy weather is delightful. The state rooms being equipped with lattices (windows & door—there are two windows in my room) a sense of light and air, delicately subdued, pervades my bed. Opening one lattice wide I can look out over the sea—already pearly & blue in the morning light. The constant roll of the boat & the swish of the water along the ship's side is now pleasent to me.

I get up wondering how soon we are to land. At seven the rising bell is rung. I lounge till 8—when breakfast bell is rung, then sponge with towel, wash my face, brush & comb my hair, brush my teeth & go down to breakfast. I know my near neighbors at the Captain's table, where I have been put, take me for a boor because I have not spoken and cannot speak. Bashfulness and an easily roused sense of superiority and indifference make it hard. They talk of such trivial things. "If I had money" etc.

It is plain, though, immediately after breakfast that we are nearing Savannah. The rougher sea dies down and we are nosing along through a silky, crinkly world of water, so safe and soothing that one could never suspect it of storms and smashing brutalities. Here are scores of gulls now where awhile back, or at least the night before, there was scarcely a baker's dozen. They probably camp outside the mouth of the Savannah River where ships are always coming & going. They are scavengers but such beautiful ones. I have never seen a more beautiful sight than that in which a pail of slops having been cast over board they all circle and quarrel, nudging each other, lighting in each other's way, floundering and fluttering. They seem to love to tease each other with food, for one having found a crust, will fly with it in its bill, hither and yon, where gulls are thickest, stirring up desires, enmities and contest. Do not people with wealth or treasures do the same? (A dull remark, really.)

But the air today and the sky in this harbor—although we are out of sight of land. I have just asked the wireless man & he tells me we should get to Savannah by eleven. A pearly mist encircles us at a distance, landwards, I think. Immediately beyond the prow of the boat, say a thousand yards, is a rainbow of mist, very pale and diaphanous but a rainbow still. I stand at the prow of the boat and note a rainbow about my head—a fact which pleases me. I wish and would like to believe it a favorable omen.

Presently we drop anchor & idle here. There is a whistling buoy near at hand, a thing which we have been approaching for some time. Also there are two small steamers here, both white, anchored & waiting to go in, too. Everybody is in the best of spirits. It is so warm. I talk to the ship's pilot, a fat, jovial Norwegian, who tells me that always south of Hatteras it is warmer—no matter how bitter cold it may be in N.Y., it is fairly comfortable south of Hatteras. Tells me entrance to Savannah via river is very difficult— "Like a snek (snake) it winds."

I learn now from one remark & another that the little dark haired broad shouldered youth with the stubbed face whom I have seen in tow of "Phil—alias "Chicken" Cox of New Haven is a prize fighter & and that he is going to Savannah to fight. He has been dancing around with the girl who sang so much—a bold, rather attractive tomboy. He and another girl, who looks like a third or fourth rate actress—but not physically unattractive, hold the following conversation in my presence.

A Ship Conversation

Your a graduate, aintcha?

No. I'm a quituate.

You know the toast what it is for a graduate?

What.

You know the toast

Well, what is it?

Heres to the girl whats a graduate.

She's prettier than nearly anyone else and she don't use no slang & she don't chew no gum. Ha! ha!

Well I'm not a graduate. I told you, I'm a quituate. I'll chew gum if I want to.

Silence

Say Andy. Your as funny as a crutch.

Your as funny as a cry for help.

The dropping of the anchor. The man in charge of the poor scummy deck hands. The man who went down to straighten the anchor Truly for me at least, the sea breeds illusions—the most wonderful

of dreams. It is neither land nor life as we commonly know it—this
wonder world of the water but some chemic intermediate, the
significance of which has not yet, perhaps, dawned upon us.
Looking in to these pearls and grays and pinks and blues of sky and
water I get a faint suggesting of the spawning power of the ancient
world. Out of so fluid and perfect an atmosphere what might not
arise? To me it is supremely generative in its mood and
suggestiveness. It lifts me up, fecundates my mind, throws off the
years. I am young, malleable, pliable. Nothing has happened to me.
I am virgin soil and in me any strange new, wonderful, brilliant
ideas can take root and grow. Here comes poetry to me—out of no
known experience. I want to sing in colors! Novels such as I have
planned seem old, unimportant, of a condition and a state of things
which is unimportant. The things which the sea itself has down thus
far—its fishes and birds, from which have come so much else, is
unimportant. What this pearly, silky roseate, cloudy world suggests
is something new—a perfection, a beauty, a music, a harmony
hitherto unknown. And what is that? And of what frail material
shall it be built? How shall the soul divest itself of materialities and
acquire this—this diaphanous wonderful.

Or is it full of souls. And do they marvel at our heavy materiality
as we, staring at fish and shiny eels and snakes and crabs, wonder at
theirs?

! – ! – !

The wall of white mist. Clouds above it. The buoys! Land at last.
Tybee light house and the entrance to the Savannah river. We
enter. The dinner bell. From my table I watch the land go by,
thinking of rice & cotton fields & wild ducks. My wealthy friends of
the automobile (she of the rings) are going duck hunting. She is a
horrible type—the very worst. We finish eating. On deck again.
Savannah in the distance—a delicate penciling of buildings and
chimneys over a flat waste of brown marsh grass. The redness of
the Savannah—red looking west, pink as you look back. Gulls.
Small light houses. The first wharves—cotton & oil. It is very hot in
the river. The girls talk about New York & Savannah ("I just love
Savannah"). The little girl's scepticism.

We make the wharf in town. No bridges. Negroes. The river
front is like that of New York—lumber yards, oil yards, coal
packets ware houses. Negroes fighting for money. I check my

baggage. Forget my rubbers. Pay my waiter ($1). Go ashore. Buses and small Fords. Negro town. Every house a porch or covered doorstep. Shanties. Yellow, red & white head peices. "Rub-my-tism" (A Rheumatism cure!) The idling negro—five to one of white. Great dudes. Rather trivial street car lines. Old low square brick houses with fretted iron balconies and open doors & windows. Canary birds hung out in cages. Palm trees—yes real ones. All trees still green & the grass. I feel very hot & wish I had on a lighter suit & underwear. Find P.O. & get letters (Hale, Dodge, Anderson,[16] L——) None from K——. Disappointed. Go to newspaper—"News" & consult furnished room advs. No good ones. Walk about & see how town is laid out. Streets run like this.

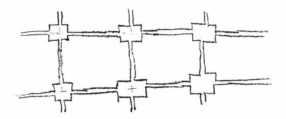

Walks go through center of these squares. Wagons go round. Squares set with palm trees and ⌐ ⌐. There are jay birds here. You can here them call. In some yards I saw flowers. A slow town. Fruit is not as numerous in kinds & not nearly so attractive as in N.Y. and no less expensive—Rather more so. And this is the South. Visit rooms in Oglethorpe Street. Very poor. Call up 636. Room offered 2.50 per for a week. Bath on same floor. I go there & see Mrs. Harms. Husband has grocery store on corner. 320 East Liberty. Big room—pink & gray paper. Light yellow matting on floor. White iron bed. Cheap bureau, washstand table & two chairs. Corner partitioned off by scrim for clothes. Car line going east &

---

16. Ralph T. Hale, editor at Small, Maynard & Co., a Boston publishing firm that was interested in Dreiser.
Ben W. Dodge's friendship with Dreiser dated back to 1907 when Dodge's publishing firm reissued *Sister Carrie*. Dodge's private and public fortunes collapsed in the following decade; and his last letters to Dreiser, dated shortly before his death in 1916, show him working on a chicken farm in New Jersey, searching for a way back into "the book world." It remains unclear whether his drowning in the East River was a suicide or an accident resulting from a drinking spree.
"Anderson" is author Sherwood Anderson (1876–1941).

west on Liberty between Palm & L ⌐ . Car line going north and south on Habersham. Not very annoying as they don't run often. Habersham car line goes to Thunderbolt.

I take room, pay in advance, leave 75 cents for my bags. Go out & take car to Thunderbolt. Latter mostly negroes. A charming view of the Savannah River there. Also Savannah yacht club. Walk under trees, see negroes hang about store and argue. Character of Southerners—a thin, aneamic, prejudiced people. Negroes ignored —and rightly. Negro with white child must sit with negroes. Wonderful sunset. Wonderful sky. Meet boy who came to me in prow of boat. His family stopping here.

Take crowded car back. Walk principal street & examine all stores. Put adv. in paper. Pawn shop. Negro conversations. Auction bell. I buy paper. Find "The Genius"—3 copies. Buy "Life of Sam Johnson," "Voyage of H. M. S. Beagle," "Crime & Punishment" at old book store. See adv. of fight between "Andy" Cortez and L ⌐ . Buy red hat. Come Home. Very tired. Unpack trunk. Straight to bed.

Sunday—Jan. 30th 1916—Savannah

Not up until 9 really. Write up notes. Gray & foggy. Negro boy calling papers in streets. Dress, unpack trunk, bath—cold bath—eat two tangerines. Go to breakfast "New Manhatten Lunch." As bad as Oxford Lunches of N.Y. Greek proprietor. Savannah on Sunday. Church bells. Negroes idling. Police station just back of this house. Palms look so inviting. Cant believe they are native to this region but afterwards find them growing wild. Walk to Tybee depot (Central of Georgia). Its character. Walk to two other depots— Union & Central of Georgia—at west end of Liberty Street. Segregation of blacks an odd but necessary custom. Character of Southerners—peaked, whiny, suspicious, jealous, touchy—an offensive company. All this is due to the perversion of naturalness following upon a promoralistic atmosphere. The result of sex suppression is jealousy, suspicion, envy, false witness, false pretense, a better than thou viewpoint. Women going about like saints craving subconsciously what they sniff at openly—sex. It is a horrible case of race or national perversion which will end in disaster. The south as it stands today will be destroyed. It will pass away.

On Niggers

Actually in relation to negros it would seem as if nature intended a laughing commentary on the self importance and constructive determinism of man. In the negros blood—sui generis—there is no desire apparently to progress. Unless explained climatically, black Africa is standing commentary on civilization so called, and yet the negro is not to be bemoaned any more than any other wondrous animal. Do we bemoan the lepard or the tiger or the donkey or the ibis? Then why the negro? Because he is a man you answer and must progress and because progress is admirable.

To the latter I agree. At least the mental and mechanical development of man is interesting to me—but that he must or even ought to—save developed instinct might urge me to say that, but at that it is largely a matter of faith or unintelligible race impulse. I cannot explain to myself why we should progress because I do not know where—or to what—we are progressing.

To a wider knowledge of life, says one.

To the alleviation of suffering

To greater happiness

I would not start an argument on all those subjects here for anything. A Darwin or a Spencer or a Haeckel might take them seriatum and introduce all the evidence pro and con—but seriously I doubt whether he would venture a conclusion.[17] Seemingly progressive and at least astonishing movements have seized upon and agitated races and peoples over vast periods of time but that these things have spelled greater intelligence or progress is a question.

All nature is supremely intelligent. It expresses itself amazingly without the aid of man—in the construction of animals for instance and sideral systems. That it needs man's aid to get anywhere—is doubtful. It created him. That it may be using him as it uses certain other types of animals for a purpose or no purpose (just idle self-expression) is entirely possible and even likely. No one knows for instance why coral insects build reefs. It may have a cosmic purpose or it may not. No one knows why the great auk or ten

17. Dreiser is referring to three pioneers in naturalism who influenced his thinking early in his career: Charles Darwin (1809–82), the English evolutionist; Herbert Spencer (1820–1903), the English philosopher; Ernst Heinrich Haeckel (1834–1919), the German biologist.

million other animals (races of animals) for that matter, appeared and disappeared. They may have been necessary to civilization or evolution & and they may not have. Not even Darwin would insist that they tended toward or are essential to greater civilization. Nature is supremely intelligent in a large way. How could evolution, so called, aid here. Why should it.

But away with these abstrusities and let me dwell on the negro as such. Here in the south when you see them— thousands of them, breeding like flies, living under the most haphazard and ⌐   ⌐ circumstances, indifferent to appearances, indifferent or unconscious to morals, laughing, good natured, joyous; grilled and yet smiling—it would seem as though nature were intending a jest at the seriousness of the whites, and the negro was this cosmic smile of disdain—a God's gargantuan laughter. For look you—

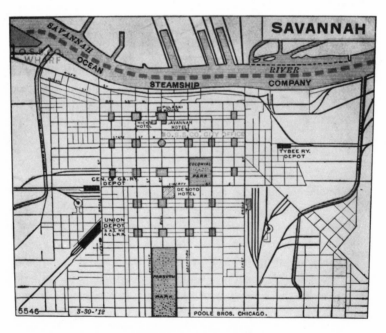

Street Map of Savannah

Monday, Jan. 31—1916—Savannah[18]

309 W. President St.

19 W. Perry St. 2506—J

228 W. Liberty—Phone 4796

19 W.   "

116 West Harris Street

131 Liberty—West

Fair 115 West Oglethorpe—8.50

107 West Jones St.—Phone 1072

126 West Oglethorpe—Phone 4534

408 West Gaston St.

1 West Jones (cor. Bull) Phone 3778

203 West Liberty

In addition to visiting all these places haunted P.O. Pain in groin.
Greatly wrought Masters up. Breakfast at Geigers 1 egg—2 peices
bacon—orange. Tea. Couldnt eat. Dinner at Hicks—regular—50
cents. Couldn't eat. Lovely Evening cool. Read in Crime &
Punishment. To bed early.

Phone 2183—285 York West—250

   "   4796—2nd and Liberty—25.00

   "   3999—20 Gannett St. 10 per Mo.

x "   1951 J.—Mrs. T. P. Keck—103 W. Fagler

x "   5080—[unreadable word] 34—West Sutton

   "   3087—[unreadable word] E. Liberty

   "   4221 J—

                 238 Bull

                 965 Whitaker phone 4424

                 1210 Montgomery St.

                 Harris & Drayton Sts.

118 East State—Phone 3122

Good 304 Oglethorpe—6.00

204 E. State—Corner Abercorn—243 Abercorn

Speaking of these places—304 Oglethorpe was interesting.
"Everybody in Savannah knows me.

126 W. Oglethorpe was fat blonde who looked very lusty and
suggestive

18. Dreiser made the following list of addresses as he searched for a room.

1. Jones was the clean old negro & beautiful room on second floor. 126 West Liberty was typical southern woman. Girl taking out biscuits. Furniture horrible.

Tuesday, Feb. 1—1916—Savannah

Rose at seven. Bathed. Went early to P.O. No letter. Breakfasted at Geigers. Couldn't eat. 1 egg. 2 peices bacon—Tea. Went into park & wrote chapter 48—Hoosier Holiday.[19] Again to P.O. about noon. No letter. Back to park. Wrote 19 pages of Chapter 49— Went for walk to west Savannah. End of car line. German store keeper. Government Revenue inspector on a motor cycle. Back to P.O. No letters. To movie. Poor films. To Hicks. Dinner 50. Much cooler outside. To room. Read Crime & Punishment. Very lonely. Feeling very bad. To bed early & didn't sleep well. Beautiful day out—warm & clear. But altogether a bad one for me. Children going to school a pretty sight in this warm climate.

Wednesday, Feb. 2nd 1916

Almost sick with worry. Arise—headache, sick stomach. Pain in vitals. Bathe, shave, dress. Write to Mame to see K——.[20] Also to A. P. T., B. H. M. & several others.[21] Go to P.O. No letters. Cant eat. 1 1/2 crullers. Cup of tea in Plaza Restaurant. Go to Postal Telegraph send message. "Are you sick—or dont you want to write. Reply, collect—Postal—Tel. Savannah." Come to grave yard

---

19. John Lane published *A Hoosier Holiday*, Dreiser's account of his motor trip to Indiana in 1915, on 17 November 1916. One of the reasons for this trip to Savannah in early 1916 was to give Dreiser a chance to work on this book without the usual distractions of the New York scene.

20. "Mame" is Dreiser's sister Mary Frances (1861–1944).

21. "A. P. T." is Anna P. Tatum (1882–1950). Anna Tatum was a bright graduate of Wellesley living at home in Fallsington, Pennsylvania, when she wrote to Dreiser on 7 November 1911, telling him of the impact on her of *Jennie Gerhardt* and "The Almighty Burke." In the fall of 1912, after many letters had passed between them, Miss Tatum and Dreiser met in New York for the first time. She told him about her Quaker ancestors—and particularly about her devout father's personal career, which moved Dreiser to begin planning a novel based on this story. Thirty-odd years later that novel was published as *The Bulwark* (1945). According to Dreiser, he and Miss Tatum lived together from 1 May 1912 to 1 January 1913 (see below, the diary entry for 14 November 1917). She worked with him closely on *The Titan* (1914), and later correspondence at the University of Pennsylvania shows that in the 1930s she began again to type and edit his work. She initially objected to the writing of *The Bulwark*, but in later years when she felt her family no longer needed to be protected from what she imagined Dreiser would write, she encouraged him to finish the novel. Dreiser turned his relationship with Miss Tatum into a fictional account in "This Madness: The Story of Elizabeth," *Hearst's International —Cosmopolitan* 86 (April 1929): 81–85, 117–20; and 86 (May 1929): 80–83, 146–54. "B.H.M." has not been identified.

park—begin to write. It begins to rain. Go home. Try to write. Cant. Try to read cant. Noon, sit & think of K—— making an appeal. Message comes. See message—next page. Intense relief. Headache subsides. Pain goes. Take message. Go to P.O. See chief clerk. He get me two letters—one from K——. One from L——. K——s letter ok. Feel much better. Come to room. Write K—— long letter—also L—— also B. H. M. Go down stairs in rain & mail em. Come up. Work on Chapter 49 & finish it. Start on 50. Work till 5:30. Feel tired. Get up. Go to P.O. No letter. Dont mind. Go & buy clips. Poor town for stationary stores. No "Genius" in principal book store. Get clips—10 cents. Go to hotel Savannah. Dinner $1.00. A fine dinner. Man & wife opposite. Woman with glasses commenting on War & Wilson's preparedness tour. He is enroute in West. Germans have just brought liner Affam into old Point Comfort. Buy postals—30 cents & come to room. Paste 'em up. Write these notes. Very tired but feel much better. Go to bed.

Newyork Feby 2nd 1916
Theodore Dreiser
320 East Liberty St. Savannah Ga
Sweetheart have written every day since Friday love.
                                            Kirah

Thursday, Feb. 3—1916—Savannah

A bad day. Not very warm but bright. Breakfast at Plaza. Chicken Liver Omelet. Go to bank. Check hasn't come. No letters at P.O. Come home. Several here. Go out to Public Library, Whitaker & Gaston. Work until 4 P.M. Boy who stuck his head in door and said "is this the way into the Library." Then address an old woman. Cross eyed boy. Whole horse shoe. Go to P.O. at 6:30. Letter from L——. Eat at Geigers. Young man who wanted to make train. 30 cents too much for pie, sandwich and milk. Downs the Greek restaurants. They are filthy he says. Talks to me —quite preoccupied with himself—but when I talk to him doesn't answer. I come to room. Write several letters. This is a dull life for me. I despise life without a woman. Bed at ten P.M. Very cold in room. Put overcoat on bed & wear old gray coat in bed. Still can't

keep warm. [unreadable word]—fate—for—At 4 P.M. was west to
Estill Ave. Out Estill Ave. to end. One road to city line & canal.
Along canal a wild grapevine. Numerous cars. Pleasant spring
evening. Red setting sun—people riding out just to motor. Girl
sitting on running board of auto. Very pretty. Walk back to Estill
Ave. Then north and west to car line. Boys riding about on
bicycles. People waiting for car. Evening lamps. Evening voices.
First stars. The stars in this region seem wondrously lucent—the sky
blue. I am cold and put on coat. Feel lonely & wish for company,
male or female. See how I live, day after day, with scarcely a word
with anyone. The curse of life is loneliness.

Friday, Feb. 4—1916—Savannah
Very cold today. Lit stove in bath. Fortunately there was hot water.
Went down town after recieving three letters here—and found four
more at P.O.—telephone bill, Masses adv. Letter from Willard
Dillman, Minneapolis, Minn. etc.[22] Go to bank. Check has not
come back from N.Y. Try to find blue shirt. Cant. Try to find map
of Georgia. Fail. Look for seals. Can only get red ones! Decide to
visit Walter Hartridge.[23] Change mind & mail introductions. Write
nine letters L——, K——, Hale, Dillman—Lewisohn[24]—Hartridge,
Jonas—Telephone Co—N.Y.P.O. Go to P.O. & mail them. Kick on
mail being sent to 320 E. Liberty. Pack trunk bag ready to leave.
Phone express co. Post notes and at 4 P.M. only am ready to write.
A wasted day. Room is cold and am lonely in spirit. It is a bad thing
being an intellectual. One is too distant & people do not draw to one.
This came today, advertising Masses ball.[25]

22. Willard Dillman was a businessman and partner in the printing firm of Brooks-
Dillman of Minneapolis. He first wrote to Dreiser on 28 January 1916, giving him a sympathetic
and careful response to his novels. Over the years he became a source of critical opinion that
Dreiser seemed to appreciate. By 1918 they had developed an epistolary friendship to the point
that Dillman offered his home as "an old manse" for Dreiser to write in, and they planned a
boat trip down the Mississippi together.
23. Dreiser's introduction to Walter C. Hartridge, a prominent Savannah businessman,
came through Clifford W. Hartridge, Walter's brother and a lawyer who had given up his
practice in New York in order to write. At the University of Pennsylvania there survives a
complimentary pass to Savannah's Oglethorpe Club for 5 February 1916, made out to Dreiser
courtesy of Walter C. Hartridge.
24. Ludwig Lewisohn (1883–1955), author, editor, teacher, critic.
25. The *Masses* staff sponsored what was to become the most famous Greenwich Village
ball. Held annually at Webster Hall, this dance-till-dawn and costume ball was the center of
Village party life. Pasted into Dreiser's diary at this point is an invitation to the ball.

Saturday, Feb. 5—1916—Savannah

This was moving day from 320 East Liberty to 103 W. Taylor. A cool morning, too, but promising a fine day. Lighted blue heater in bath room & took hot bath. Had slept in my brown coat it was so cold. Wrote several letters, packed remaining belongings—then went to P.O. Four or five letters. One from Belgian Professors relief. One from L—— (Imagine I am there and —— me good & hard) One from K—— much more loving. One from Nayan Little enclosing reprint of "Of Human Bondage" review.[26] Go to National Bank of Savannah—draw $100. Go to Mr. Smith—345 Abercorn to see about a cottage at Tybee. Can rent one furnished for $15 per mo. Go to 320 East Liberty and get my bag. Trunk was gone. Walk to Taylor and begin unpacking. Fire in grate. Like this room much better. Take lunch here. Meet one legged son and two men. We talk of Savannah life. Girl who was too bashful to come down. After lunch return to my room & work. Then go down town, looking for hat, blue tie, blue shirt—find nothing. Get very lonely. Return to house at 5:30 (Do buy paper & socks) Eat dinner at house. About 8:30 Walter Hartridge calls up. Wants to know if I've eaten. Calls round. I hurry & change clothes. We go to Oglethorpe Club.[27] Stories of Gen. Gordon—cut on face—cut on ass.[28] "Going to Atlanta to earn an honest living. Go on young man, you'll have no competition." Frank case comes up. Young Mangam comes in. Talk of celebrated cases. Webster-Howard case. We drink Scotch high balls, then go down in grill & have club sandwishes & coffee. At 12:30 lights are blinked on us. Few people in club. Talk of an auto tour next day. To Hermitage[29]—also where fine trees are. Mangam & Hartridge bring me home. I sit & rock for an hour.

26. Letters at the University of Virginia indicate that Nayan Little worked for Dreiser as his secretary and typist.

Dreiser is referring to his review of W. Somerset Maugham's *Of Human Bondage*, "As a Realist Sees It," *New Republic* 5 (25 December 1915): 202–4.

27. The Oglethorpe Club at 450 Bull Street was the former residence of General Henry R. Jackson. It had been turned into an exclusive men's club.

28. Brig. Gen. William Washington Gordon (1796–1842), lawyer and soldier, who played a prominent part in Savannah's history.

29. The Hermitage was the name given to the Henry McAlpin plantation, located three miles north of Savannah, where the celebrated "Savannah Grey" brick were manufactured. Known for their distinctive color, the bricks were used in the construction of many notable Savannah houses.

Sunday—Feb. 6th   Savannah

Gray & not very promising but charming room. Have cold bath.
Go down to breakfast. Little Tom is getting ready to go to Sunday
school. Boarders spik & span. I go to P.O. no letters. Come home.
Special delivery from K——— roasting me. Am in blue funk and
compose a letter to her but do not mail it—calling whole thing off.
Write on Hoosier Holiday & letters till lunch. Eat. Expecting call
from Hartridge. None comes till 2:30. Wants to know if 4:30 is ok.
I work till then. Car comes. Wife & Ethel are in it. Ethel—We
speed out to Hermitage. Very interesting. The river—long line of
trees. Northern girl who tried to fix it up. Negros scrambling for
pennys. Back through town. Cotton in front of Exchange. Out
Abercorn and Bull to new addition. Out wonderful avenue of live
oaks to Work House. Great roads. I see a rice field being made
ready. Also a cotton field. Around & on to Yacht Club. A Judas
Tree. Origin of weeping willow. Ethel & I became friendly.
Beautiful leg. Sensuous neck. She declares herself a pagan—wishes
to be like Lucrezia Borgia. Drinks, smokes, plays golf. Has money.
Rides. Hales from New England. We drink at club. On to banker
OByrne. His wife & her sister. Baby in house. More Hartridge
stories. Irwin Cobb was here for six weeks.[30] Sam Blythe.[31] Talk of
Ince, Griffiths, movies. More drinks. Wife finally comes down. On
to club. Patridges drinks & champagne. Story of trip to Pacifico.
Genneau Governor. "Herr Colleague." Being arrested in N.Y.
Clifford Hartridge & Walter. Negro who always called him
"Quer." Admires Harry Leon Wilson base ball stories.[32] How he
got admitted to N.Y. dock. How he got trunks out without duty,
talking base ball. Mrs. OByrne tells of her trip to New Orelans.
Cold. I stand it till 11:30 rather bored. Finally home, dying to
urenate—Think of Ethel.

Monday—Feb. 7—1916   Savannah
Rise 9:30. Feel punk. Cold bath. No breakfast. Letter from K———
to house here, much more friendly. Wants to come here. Weavers a

30. Irvin S. Cobb (1876–1944), humorist, writer, actor.
31. Samuel G. Blythe (1868–1947), newspaperman, memoirist.
    32. Harry Leon Wilson (1867–1939), humorist, novelist, playwright, short-story writer,
editor.

frost. No money. I write her. Go down town. Mail letter to her, Willard Dillon & De Casseres.[33] Buy pills & go & get razor strop. Perfect day. Wonderful. Come back—write till one. Eat lunch nearly alone. Work till 5:15 writing Terre Haute—Sullivan chapters in Hoosier Holiday. Change clothes. Put on blue suit. Go down to P.O. No mail. Thence to Thunderbolt on 6:02 car. Beautiful bay. Red sky. Order a scotch. Then a fish dinner. Eat it all alone. Inquire price for dinner of five. Stay till eight. Catch 8 P.M. car back. Go to Bull St. & P.O. No letters. Walk out. Small co. of soldiers drilling. Southern boy quarreling with girl over rival caller. (Why does he call without an invitation. I dont know.) Home. Post these notes for Sat. Sun. & today. Read Crime & Punishment. Bed.

Tuesday, Feb. 8—1916
Can't remember a thing about this day.
Wrote a chapter. Ate two meals in house. P.M. was down town. Went to P.O. Watched Isle of Hope car go up street. Came home —saw attractive woman over way. Sat on porch 20 minutes. Came down, walked out to 40th waiting for Isle of Hope car. Got it. Isle of Hope.[34] Interesting. Barbees zoo & pavilion. Eat dinner—egg & oyster sandwich—cake. Watch German Eagle, Wild cats, etc. White mice bite my cane. Home. Very dreary—sleepy. Go to bed. Probably wrote L—— & K——.

Wednesday—Feb 9—1916
Rose 8:30 Hot bath. Breakfast in house. To P.O. Find horse shoe. Letter from Murrel, L——, K——, Nayan Little—all favorable. Go along Bull Street. Into 1st Presbyterian church.[35] Very Beautiful. Read M's letter there. Walk on out home. Write Murrel K——

33. Benjamin De Casseres (1873–1945), newspaperman, drama critic, poet, biographer. De Casseres was a prolific writer with radical political leanings whose career Dreiser tried for years to advance with editors. Letters to Dreiser during 1915–16 show that De Casseres had not yet gained an audience for his writing, and, as he says, "I am reading proof on the Herald at nothing a night, and my eyes will no longer stand it." In later years, however, he found a market for his many books.
34. The Isle of Hope is a small village ten miles from Savannah on a high shell bluff. Its oak-lined avenue is one of the area's noted drives.
35. The Independent Presbyterian Church, on the corner of Oglethorpe Ave. and Bull St., was built in 1815–19 and is one of the outstanding examples of Georgian architecture in Savannah. It was here in 1885 that Woodrow Wilson married Ellen Nixon, the granddaughter of the church's pastor.

L——. Then work on A Hoosier Holiday. Do part of 54 & 55. Havent any cards to send Murrel. Go out at noon & buy. Lunch in house. Beautiful day. Work all P.M. 5:30 go down town. Buy jug Kintore, black bow tie, whisk broom. Go to Barbers & get shaved & haircut. Home. Deposit broom & old brown tie. Go over to 2 or 3 East Charlton. Meet Hartridge's cousin. Dine—talk till 11 P.M. Then to Oglethorpe. 3 Kintore high balls. Talk of south & changing conditions. Home & to bed. Happy over M——.

Wednesday—Feb. 9—1916—Savannah
Independent Presbyterian Church
A church very nearly square. Pale cream grey walls & snow white wood work. Wide, high oval topped window set with plain glass but shaded with delicate white lattices throughout. A three sided white gallery supported by eight small doric columns aided by four large ones supporting the roof—an oval triumph of carved white wood work. The benches, long & of cherry. A parqueted stone floor and a lovely rostrum or lecture platform of cherry. It was a dream.

Thursday, Feb. 10—1916—Savannah
A rather dull day today. Hot bath. Breakfast 9:30. Came upstairs. Wrote L—— K——. Mencken. Went to P.O. Had letter from two people who wanted to rent rooms and Winifred Bush—908 W. Broad St. Went out to look for picture cards to send Anna, Murrel & others. Met Mr. Mangan. To drug store for butter milk. To book store for cards with him. He shows me dead Indian chief's monument. Came home. Sort cards & address them. Write chapters 57 and half of 58—of A Hoosier Holiday. Had to quit at 5:30 fingers ached. Walked to 908. Looked at house. Shabby neighborhood. Walked out West Broadway to 40th & back on Barnard Ave. Change socks. Dinner at 7. To P.O. Letters from Mencken & Hersey.[36] Mencken says he was here in 1902. Wrote these notes. Very sleepy. To bed.

---

36. Harold Hersey (1893–1956), editor, poet. During the period of this diary Hersey played a large part, as head of the Authors' League of America, in defending *The "Genius"* against its hostile press.

Dear Dreiser,

Let the poetry matter go over for a couple of weeks; I want to consult my spiritual adviser.

What are you doing in Savannah? Be careful. The presence of barbarian Germans in any American seaport provokes grave suspicion and you may find yourself in jail on the charge of trying to mine the forts in the harbor.

Down at Tybee Island, 6 or 8 miles below Savannah, I came very near being drowned in the year 1902. Perhaps you will care to go to the spot and throw a beer keg overboard in memory of that historical event. The water, I dare say, is still dirty.

The Appan overfilled me with such mirth that I was quite unable to work for two days. Two or three more such jocosities and even Lansing will be forced to snicker.

Sincerely yours,
HLM

[This letter from H.L. Mencken was inserted here by Dreiser.]

Friday, Feb. 11—1916—Savannah

Rise 8:30. Hot bath. Nervous over dinner. Breakfast 9. Go down town. Letters from L & K. Go to Savannah Hotel. Get dinner cards. See headwaiter. Home. Write L—— K—— Mencken & others. Make out menu. Put in pocket. Write till 2 P.M. Chapter 59 —Hoosier Holiday. Shave. Go to 908 W. Broad. See Winifred Bush. Queer old maid. Literary type—but unschooled & homely. Find horse shoe on road there. Back and write until 5:30. Dress. Go down town for mail. Don't recall that I got any. Back to house. Phone for auto. (In A.M. had called up after visiting a garage.) Rate listed at 1.00. Get car for 7:10 arrives 7:18. Mrs. H—— calls at 7 to say husband may not be home till late. I drive in car till 7:30. Then to H's. Wait 5 minutes. Then to her sister's. Wait five more minutes. Then to hotel. Fare 2.85 (with tip). In to dinner. See menu next page. Bill 14.65. Tip 1.35. Total expenditures 19.00. We walk to De Soto grill. Nothing there.
Over to sisters in Hull St. Fine old house. Scotch & soda. From there home. Very tired. Massage Pr——.[37] Don't sleep very well.

37. Prostate.

Friday, Feb. 11—1916—Savannah[38]
4 Bronx Cocktails
4 Soups
  Broiled mushrooms
4 Lemon Ice
1 Whole Chicken Caserole
2 Summer Squash
2 Stuffed Tomotoes
2 Asparagus (Roquefort Cheese Dressing)
4 Cafe Parfait
4 Iced Coffee (in glasses)

                          1 Bottle Champagne
                          (with the Roast.)
Dinner to Mr. & Mrs. Walter Hartridge and Ethel

Friday—Feb 11—1916—Savannah

Bronx Cocktails—	4 @ 20	.80
Cream of Tomatoe—	4 @ 20	.80
Broiled Fresh Mushrooms	4 @ 60	2.40
Lemon Ice	4 @ 15	.60
Whole Chicken Casserole	4 – –	1.75
Summer Squash	2 @ 20	.40
Stuffed Tomatoes	2 @ 35	.70
Asparagus	2 @ 40	.80
Cafe Parfaits	4 @ 25	1.00
Iced Coffee (glass)	4 @ 10	.40
		8.85
Champagne		5.00
		$13.85
Auto (to—1.00)		
(from—1.00)		2.00
		$15.85

38. Dreiser is listing the menu items and the price of dinner for four. The total bill for the dinner was $9.25 instead of $8.85.

Hotel Savannah Menu

Friday—Feb. 11—1916—Savannah
Bronx Cocktails—4
    &
Cream of Tomatoes
Onions au Gratin
Mock Turtle
Chicken Okra
    &
Broiled Mushrooms on Toast
    &
Lemon Ice
    &
1 Whole Chicken—Casserole
or
Porter house for 4
or
Filet Mignon—Garni (4)
    &
Summer Squash—Stuffed Tomatoes
Asparagus—Roquefort Cheese Dressing—4
Cafe Parfaits—4
Black Coffee—4

Friday—Feb 11—1916—Savannah
Called
This is walking distance S. of Union depots.

Savannah Ga.
Feb. 9/16

P.O. Box 282

     If you will call Friday afternoon or Saturday morning or either nights of this week, I will show you what I have to offer.

     If you would like a plain neat cottage life and a companion literary inclined (and now alone) shall be glad to have you call on a visit even if I cannot please you in regard to room.

Sincerely

908 West Broad St.   Winifred Bush[39]

39. Dreiser had advertised for a room and received this response.

Saturday, Feb. 12—1916   Savannah

Up at 8:30. Massaged Prostate. Hot bath. Breakfast in house. To P.O. Letter from L—— Walked back to house. Wrote L—— K—— Jones. Went out & posted them. Back and to work. Did chapters 60–61—Hoosier Holiday. Tired at 6 P.M. Quit. Went down town. Article from Mencken. Pictures from Kirah. Went and bought 3 Valentines—1 to K—— 1 to L—— 1 to C——. Bought bar candy for Tom. Walked out Bull Street. Sat on De Soto Veranda till eight. Back to Schwartz Restaurant Club Sandwich. Coffee (The goodness of Durkees Salad Dressing) queer Georgia Harpist. Playing for collection. Went out & to P.O. Letter from Beppie Rykens-Culp.[40] Sends back clippings. I sit on porch. Paste up views. Address envelopes to Hale, Hersey, Greil Postmaster General, Beppie R-C & picture cards to Mrs. Roberts,[41] Claire H. Uecke, Mame, Moe Powys,[42] Mr. & Mrs. S—— Pagany. Post notes. To bed.

Sunday Feb—13—1916—Savannah

Warm & bright. In bed to 8:30. Bath up & to breakfast. Go to P.O. No letters. Broken horse shoes—several. Back, work on Hoosier Holiday to dinner time & finish it. Dinner. Mrs. Kecks daughter & her husband. We discuss prohibition in Georgia. Back up stairs. Write K—— & L—— & Jones—Hartridge, Nayan Little— seven letters all told. Sit on back porch. Rain comes up—a summer shower. After is over go to P.O. & mail letters. In a fine philosophic mood all day. Glad book is done. Walk about down town, look up Restaurant. Sit on De Soto side porch listening to Savannah church bells—7 to 8—very musical. Walk again, finally go to Oglethorpe Club. Young bloods drinking & telling of wealthy marriages. Tell of Franklin's letter to his nephew on women.[43]

40. In Amsterdam, during his 1912 trip to Europe, Dreiser met Mevrouw Julia Rykens-Culp, a friend of the British publisher Grant Richards. She and Dreiser corresponded for many years after.

41. Mary Fanton Roberts, editor. Dreiser met her in 1898 when she was an editor on *Demorest's Family Magazine.* Throughout the long years of their friendship, Dreiser often turned to her for critical advice on his writing.

42. Marion "Moe" Powys is the sister of Dreiser's friend, the English author and lecturer John Cowper Powys.

43. Dreiser is referring to the letter commonly known as Benjamin Franklin's "Advice to a Young Man on Choosing a Mistress."

Home. Sit on back porch. Throw coal at a noisy cat. Bed. Wishes for magnetism.

Thursday—Feb 17—1916—Savannah
Much colder after rain of yesterday—quite wintry, bell clear. No hot water. I bathe & wash my hair. Breakfast here. Off to P.O. Only a letter from Mencken wanting to know about Jones—and one room reply. Off to police court—Oglethorpe Ave & Habersham. Mostly negro cases—quarrels and drunkenness. One white man given three months for cohabiting with a negro girl. It grows dull though & I leave. Back to P.O. No letter. Out to 102 East Jones. Don't like room offered, not as good as this. Price 25.00. Come home, get out Bulwark & start cleaning it up. Make good progress with revision of Chapter 1.[44] Down town for paper—3 P.M. (500 sheets—60 cents) Find whole horse shoe after seeing two half ones. Go to P.O. Two letters from L—— and one more room adv. None from K—— Gloomy over that. Out along Whitaker Street. See 1 more broken horse shoe. Then whole one again. My spiritual guardian & enemies are fighting. Meet old broken down hunch backed cripple on crutches. Give him 1 dollar. To room. Start copying chapter 1. Work to 6 P.M.
Down to P.O. Mail letters to Mencken, osteopath & Madame Rykens-Culp. Go to Drug store. 1 glass malted milk with egg. Walk. Phone N. L. Monroe. She isnt in. Out to a dance. Walk to 25 York to see about a room. A dizzy place. Walk out to house. Sausage, hominy, yeast biscuit, tea, strawberries, fried potatoes, molasses, small cakes, etc. etc. Content with tea & cakes. Up to room. Meditate on reason for K——'s indifference. Write her a short note & L——. Post notes. Mail letters. To bed.

Friday—Feb 18—1916—Savannah
Rose 8:30. Heavy night. Warm. All windows open. Bath. Wash hair. Breakfast in house. Go to P.O. One letter from Wash. D.C.

44. According to Donald Pizer, who has made the most complete study of the evolution of *The Bulwark,* Dreiser started the novel in the fall of 1914. He expected "to complete the novel during the winter of 1915–16, and in response to this expectation John Lane prepared a salesman's dummy of the book which specified a 1916 publication" (*The Novels of Theodore Dreiser* [Minneapolis: Univ. of Minnesota Press, 1976], p. 302). Dreiser worked sporadically on the novel until 1920 when he put it aside to undertake *An American Tragedy.* He did not return to the project in any sustained way until 1942 and finally finished it in 1945.

about British censor opening Mme Culp's letter. Seeing rooms—see list next page. Girl in Charlton Street, where man was delivering package. Rear room—upper room. The house at 23 West Jones. Also corner Jones & Barnard. (Woman a writer—she says.) To house. Endless broken horse shoes. Find 6 copies "Plays of Natural & Supernatural." 1 to Mencken, 1 to Masters,[45] 1 to Anna, 1 to L——. Write K—— and send check to Durrell's Press Clippings & Collectors in N.Y. Dinner before going down town. Then to P.O. Letters from K—— & L——. K—— says is sure coming. Go out to 18 Oglethorpe East. Fine old colonial house. Room & board for 1 —$15 per. Out to 1811 W. Broad on telegram. Amazing house— Room 2 per week! Back to room. Picked up by Mrs. OByrne in her car. Go back to 612 Barnard. N.G. Back to room. Change clothes. To [unreadable word]. Stop & get egg malted milk. Go to P.O. No letter. To house. Read rest of plays. "Old Ragpicker" N.Y. Prepare copy for Mme Rykens-Culp.

Write notes. Work on story.

411 East 36 – 1250 G. A. Mercer & Co.[46]
12 West Bull
23 Jones – West
18 Oglethorpe West
612 Barnard
101 Taylor East
16 East 39
905 Whitaker
126 Waldburg
609 Barnard
8 West Liberty
243 Abercorn
119 W. Oglethorpe
1415 Habersham—supper rooms furnished
124 East Jones
109 W. Gordon
14 West Liberty—a flat furnished
235 Jefferson (Ca Perry) 2 rooms

45. Edgar Lee Masters (1869–1951), lawyer, poet. Dreiser met Masters in Chicago in 1912 and began a friendship that lasted for over three decades.
46. Dreiser made this list of addresses as he searched for a room.

117 W. Charlton
32 East Liberty
123 Gordon West
223 Whitaker

Friday, Mch 18, 1916—Savannah[47]

47. The diary ends at this point; there is no entry for March 18.

This diary gives an intimate picture of Dreiser's daily life while he was living in New York City, working on a variety of literary projects and participating in the social and intellectual life of Greenwich Village. The diary also records the story of his liaison with Estelle Bloom Kubitz, his mistress and secretary. Though Estelle was Dreiser's constant partner, she played a subordinate role to many other women, particularly those like Louise Campbell who helped him with his writing. The diary underscores the links between Dreiser's work and his sexual encounters, and therefore is important for an understanding of his entire career.

Dreiser met Estelle in August 1916 through H. L. Mencken, who was an intimate friend of her sister Marion Bloom. Between 1917 and 1919 Mencken and Estelle carried on a lengthy correspondence that focused on the difficulties of her relationship with Dreiser. Mencken lent a sympathetic ear to her problems, which is probably why she typed this diary and gave it to him. (She practiced a form of emotional masochism, even typing copies of old love letters to Dreiser and erotic documents written to him by his former mistresses.) Attached to the typescript is a note by Mencken dated 14 October 1938, which reads in part:

This curious document was handed to me in 1920 or thereabout by Dreiser's secretary. Whether she gave it to me because she was then on bad terms with Dreiser and eager to make him look foolish or because she thought that the diary would aid me in my writings about him I don't know. I put it aside and forgot it completely, and it was only the other day that I disinterred it.

It seems to me that it may be of interest to someone writing about Dreiser in the future. It at least reveals his state of mind at a critical point in his career.

Mencken eventually deposited the transcript at the New York Public Library with his correspondence and some other literary materials. The original diary has disappeared; the text survives only in Estelle's transcription.

Brevoort Hotel

May 15, 1917.

Little Bill cold to me.[1] We have argument in bed as to how many women I have watched suffer under my indifference.

Wednesday, May 16.

Argument this morning over Kirah's picture, and house being full of her things.[2] To soothe her I take it down, but she could scarcely speak at breakfast. Dinner tonight at her sister's flat.[3]

Thursday, May 17.

Little Bill depressed and silent. Last night she lay apart from me in bed. My nerves hurt. Didn't sleep well. Tension of opposition— who is to control? Walk to French restaurant. Bill doesn't speak. Reads American. I buy her four cinnamon buns. Walk across to 11th Street, and stop at Greenwich. "Well, Bill, I guess it's about all over isn't it?" "I don't want to talk. I want to think." Leaves me. Thursday night, for first time, I fail to call her up. She doesn't call me. Same night I write. I write her a note enclosing check for $15.00, say I know she needs money. I walk up 6th Avenue to 42d Street and home.

Friday, May 18.

Marion calls me up. Wants to bring down my stuff ("Kismet") that Little Bill has been working on.[4] She comes and returns check I sent Little Bill. Marion shows me her torn shoes. I offer her three dollars cash. Takes one dollar. Takes check back to Bill. Mencken is coming to dinner, and she asks me too. I take lilacs and butter-dish. Charming dinner, steak, fried mush, spinach, spoon bread, chocolate pie. Mencken witty. Nathan comes. Kidding about "Orf'cer Boy."[5]

1. Dreiser's nicknames for Estelle Bloom Kubitz (1886–1954) included "Little Bill," "Bert," "Gloom," and "Bo."
2. Kirah Markham was an art student and actress who had lived with Dreiser for a time in Greenwich Village. See p. 117, n. 1.
3. Marion Bloom (1888–?), the sister of Estelle Bloom Kubitz. She and H. L. Mencken met in 1914 and later developed a close relationship. Mencken encouraged her in her writing career and published her work in the *Smart Set* in 1917. Mencken often visited her in New York; as Dreiser's diary shows, the sisters created an extraliterary link between the two writers.
4. "Kismet" was first published in *Esquire* 3 (January 1935): 29, 175–76.
5. A satirical poem by Mencken, first published in his *Ventures into Verse* (New York: Marshall, Beek & Gordon, 1903).

Little Bill sits on my knee. We all go over to Lüchow's.[6] I want Bill
to come home with me. She won't. Leave her at door.

Saturday, May 19.
No word from Bill. Very lonely. Letter from Louise.[7] Visit from
Lill.[8] 2 P.M. I call up Bill and want her to go out in country to
work on <u>Kismet.</u> She won't, is washing hair. Wants to know if I
will come to dinner. No. To breakfast? No. Lill comes. We go up
to Far East Garden and sit looking out over park. Home on 6th
Ave. L. No word. Write, Read. Lill calls up 8:30. I go to bed, Very
tired. Bell rings. It's the janitor, locked herself out. To sleep—
wishing.

Sunday, May 20.
Clear day. I get up. Water flowers. Write these notes. Wish to hear
from Bill. No word. No engagements. Must go out alone and eat.
Feel depressed. Play "Poor Butterfly," Bill's favorite. Wake up
feeling relieved and yet sad that Bert was not with me. Now I
could live my life uninterrupted, and yet I was lonely. Dressed—
with that wretched feeling of tug at my solar plexus (some call it a
gone feeling). No place to go, no friends, albeit I have plenty, I
suppose. Wondering if Bert has really quit me, whether she will
call me up. Incidentally I had a lonely thought to think that Louise
had gone to Baltimore over Sunday instead of coming to New
York. Incidentally, I thought of Lill on her trip to Brooklyn.

6. Located at 110 East 14th St. One of Greenwich Village's most famous restaurants,
Lüchow's is a New York landmark with a history of association with prominent editors and
writers.
7. Louise Campbell. From 1917, Louise Campbell acted variously throughout Dreiser's
life as his lover, literary advisor, typist, researcher, and editor. She began working for Dreiser
in October 1917 when she edited and typed the manuscript of his autobiographies, later
published as *A Book about Myself* (1922) and *Dawn* (1931). In 1945 she was helping to edit the
ailing Dreiser's last novel, *The Bulwark* (1946). She published a selection of Dreiser's letters
to her, together with valuable biographical introductions, in *Letters to Louise* (Philadelphia: Univ.
of Pennsylvania Press, 1959).
8. Lillian Rosenthal (1890–?) was the daughter of a prominent New York attorney and
patron of the arts, Elias Rosenthal. Dreiser attended Rosenthal's literary evenings and became
a family friend. Lillian read a typescript of *Jennie Gerhardt* in January 1911, and her criticism
influenced the final form of the novel, encouraging Dreiser to revise his initial "happy ending"
which had Jennie and Lester Kane marry. As the diary shows, she became Dreiser's lover. She
was trained as a singer, and after her marriage to attorney Mark Goodman in 1922, she became
a well-known vocal teacher under the name Lillian Rosedale Goodman.

Beautiful Lill. And of Mrs. Armstrong leaving me all of a sudden,[9] and of Kirah in California wanting to come back—and I not wanting her. Went to Brevoort for breakfast in basement.[10] Home through 9th Street on chance of meeting Margaret Mower.[11] Beautiful Margaret. Lill called up to tell me how much she loved me. Worked on till 5:30. Very lonely. Got up, went round to see if Miss Little was in. Out.[12] Came back, played Victrola. Went out to Em's.[13] Not in. To cheap restaurant in Broadway. Waitress smiles at me. Home on 6th Avenue L. To bed, wishing Bert would call up. She doesn't. In night I can't sleep for thinking of her.

Monday, May 21.

Wake up after a short doze, feeling wretched because I haven't slept. Wonder what is to become of me in my old age. A short note from Louise in Baltimore. Shave, dress. Decide to call up Bert and ask her to breakfast. If she turns me down I propose to cut her. May leave New York and go to Philadelphia to be near Louise. Do call up Bert. She comes. Blue suit, little blue straw hat. Wants to know what she is to do. Declares she loves me. We go to French restaurant. Bert does love me. It's so plain. In spite of other women. We make up. Return to studio. She is so sweet. We kiss and fondle each other till noon. Bert takes story to do over and two letter files full of personal mention. I take two books, one to Louise (Plays), one to Decima Vivian.[14] Go to Bert's door, then to P.O. on 18th Street. Lill calls up and comes down. Looks beautiful.

---

9. The surviving correspondence between Rella Abell Armstrong and Dreiser indicates that they collaborated on "The Financier," a dramatization of *The Financier* and *The Titan*. Although completed by 1926, "The Financier" was never produced, probably because it was too long. In a letter to Mencken, dated 21 December 1916, Dreiser suggests that he had for years relied on Mrs. Armstrong's critical judgment of his writing (see *Letters of Theodore Dreiser*, ed. Robert H. Elias, 3 vols. [Philadelphia: Univ. of Pennsylvania Press, 1959], 1:244).

10. The Brevoort Hotel (see p. 117, n. 6).

11. Margaret Mower was an actress in New York at this time.

12. Letters at the University of Virginia indicate that Nayan Little worked for Dreiser as secretary and typist.

13. Dreiser's sister Emma (?–1937).

14. *Plays of the Natural and Supernatural* (New York: John Lane, 1916).

Decima Vivian first met Dreiser in 1911 after she wrote him seeking employment as a typist. She prepared much of the copy from manuscript for *The "Genius"* (1915) and *The Titan* (1914).

Wants me to go with her and Clare to dinner, theatre and supper. I
have made dinner engagement with Bert, so can't, but fix it to meet
afterward at 8:15 at Moulin Rouge. She goes, and calls up me later,
5:30 to make it 10:30 at Moulin Rouge. I agree. Go to Bert's to
dinner. Wonderful dinner. I help her get it. We read Arabian
Nights afterwards. Bert decides to come down here to sleep, while
I go up to meet Lill and Clare. Do so. They are waiting. Clare in
fine form. Very sensuous. We sit down. Clare tells me of her new
country place, $60,000, 60 acres. Hastings-on-Hudson. Her
bedroom next to guest room. Shows me she has discarded wedding
ring. Take them up in taxi. She asks me how I would like to have
her and Lill in same bed. Lill laughs. Go up to apartment and stay
little while. Kiss Lill goodnight. Then home 1:30. Bert in bed.
Hold her close and go to sleep.

Tuesday, May 22.
Lie awake and tease Bert, kissing her awake, then dress. Go to
breakfast. Bert says she is going to theatre with some one. Won't
be down to eat or sleep. I go to studio. Lill calls up. Wants to come
down at once. I let her. No word from Louise. Disappointed.
Buckle down to my story (Kismet). Work from 11 (after Lill
leaves) to 5:30. Very tired. Bert calls up to say she will come down
to sleep. Glad. And yet I am slightly troubled lest she make
sleeping here a regular thing again. I want Louise to come. Finally
go out to dinner. Mouquin's.[15] Back to house because I'm very
tired. Retire early. Run cards.[16] Hang keys outside for Bert.
Restless till 12, when she calls up to say she isn't coming, that she
has been in bed for an hour. Liar. She has been with somebody
else, who brought her roses—and did what else?

Wednesday, May 23.
Had agreed to breakfast with Bert at 9:30, so did. At breakfast I
was sore because of her conduct. Left at 11 and came home. Lill
called up, wanted to know whether she had better come down.
Told her no, not until late. Worked hard on Kismet. Lill called up

15. Located at 38th St. and Sixth Ave., Mouquin's was a favorite dining place for writers
and artists, who referred to it as "Mook's."
16. Dreiser is trying to read his future in the cards.

saying she couldn't come down but would meet me at the
Samuelses. Called up Bert. Took story up to her to do. She was in
a kidding mood. Makes fun of my dress suit. Clare kisses me in
coatroom. Lill squeezes my hand. Lill sings some of her songs.
Clare tells me she will positively give herself to me during the
summer, after she gets to her country place. Will come to town to
see me. Lill comes home with me. We have one round, and then
she takes taxi to her home. I call up Bert and want her to come
down, 12:30, but she won't.

Thursday, May 24.
Rise at 8:30. Up to Bert's. She is up, starting my breakfast. I take
her wilted pansies home with me and plant them. Lill comes. Can't
stay long, but we go to bed for little while. A hearty screw. Return
to my book. Finish chapter 16 and part of 17.[17] Call up Bert at 5
to know about dinner. Tells me to bring calves' liver and bacon.
[Here follows long list of what he bought, with price.][18] Up to
Bert's. We have fine meal. I dictate part of an article on America.
Read Arabian Nights. Take a hot bath and go to bed there. One
hour or so of wonderful copulation, then to sleep. Bert is such a
gay, laughing girl, and so wise.

Friday, May 25.
Got up, began to dress, persuading her to sleep instead of getting
up and getting breakfast. My real object was to get down to my
studio by 9 or 9:15 anyhow, to see if there was any mail from
Louise. I had written her, asking her to meet me in Trenton at
11:30. There was a note, but it said she couldn't come, but would
be over Tuesday sure for all week. Disappointed, and yet pleased

17. Dreiser was trying to complete *The Bulwark,* publication of which John Lane had
announced for the spring of 1917. Dreiser had begun the novel in 1914, and after a number of fitful starts, turned to it again in late 1916. He continued working on the book until
the fall of 1917, when the conflict surrounding *The "Genius"* caused a rupture in his relations
with John Lane. Dreiser eventually finished the novel in 1945, over thirty years after he began it.
18. All bracketed comments in the text of this diary were added by Estelle Kubitz as she
typed. She also added a scattering of superscript footnote numbers, apparently planning to
identify some of the persons mentioned by Dreiser. She never did so—at least no notes survive
with the typescript she gave Mencken. These superscript numbers have therefore been silently
deleted. The bracketed comments, however, have been retained.

that her letter was so loving. Sent me a Dinah pincushion.[19] 11:30 Louise called up from Philadelphia saying she couldn't come next week, but I am to meet her in Trenton Monday. She thinks she is going to Europe. Lill comes. Is about to get into vaudeville with singing act. Will get $300 a week. Wants me to come along on road. Wants to get a studio next winter and a cottage by the sea next summer. Full of plans for living her life with me. Life is so puzzling. I feel all the time that I am wasting my time, and yet I am not really. Cards predict a new bed, a long journey over sea, and money. Instead of calling up Lill and going to her home for dinner went to Bert's, taking along chapter 16 of The Bulwark. We had a fine dinner. Afterwards corrected Kismet. Left it for Bert to do. Took hot bath. To bed. Bert sore, thinking I don't care for her. Pushes me away from her.

Saturday, May 26.
Bert in same mood on rising. She is tired imagining she is loved and trying to be happy. We have left-over steak, etc. [long list of breakfast]. Midway in getting breakfast I persuade her to make up, and we have long lusty screw across bed. Bert is enthusiastic for me —for a little while. She has such a soft enticing body. After breakfast I return to studio, about 11:30. Lill calls up. Wants to come down. Make her wait till 3. Finish chapter 17. Lill comes. I change clothes and we go for a walk. Lill and Vivian Holt to go on road in vaudeville next week, singing. She is very beautiful. Come back here, get my brown shoes shined, get chapter. Go up to Bert's to dinner. We decide to go to East Side for live chickens. Take L to Port Arthur and eat there. Go in Chinese shop below, then through Pell Street to Clinton. Buy Bert a pink Chinese bracelet (15¢). Home. Bath. Almost quarrel over love. Go to bed. Bert in fussy mood.

Sunday, May 27.
Bert and I fuss because she does not want to screw on waking. I take cold bath, shave and dress, leaving Bert to herself. When she is dressed she comes in and wants to make up. I do. We walk up

19. A pincushion given the shape and the name of the popular stereotype figure of the Negro "mammy."

Waverley Place. I stop and get milk and cream and strawberries (48¢). Bert makes waffles, kidney and bacon, etc. Marion is at home and tells of operation on Miriam.[20] Her career and Jake's would make a book. While we eat, or just after, a man calls up Bert. Her philandering talk makes me sore. I leave as she talks, half resolving to break with her. It will come to that anyhow in the end. All my love affairs these days are so casual. I like her, and yet— well, I could do without her. Come down here, work on short story, "Love."[21] Do 18 pages. At 4:30 Lill calls up. Wants to come down. Does so, 4:45. Lies in my arms a while in big chair. Says she feels nervous. Just had one of her songs sung before Allies Relief Fund concert, and had been much applauded. Wanted to walk in Central Park. We stay till 6, then I take her to Broadway car. Come down on 8th Avenue L. Tell her I'm going to Louis Wilkinson's for dinner,[22] when as a matter of fact I am going to Bert's. Have promised to be there at 7, but have to come home to get a bag to take to P.R.R. station so I can leave at 10:08 A.M. for Trenton to meet Louise. Expect Bert to stay all night here and won't be able to get out with bag in A.M. unless I arrange it in this way. Last time she missed small bag's absence. Hence her leaving me, really. This time I take a large one belonging to Mrs. Harris Merton Lyon, containing some of her husband's mss.[23] Take it to station on 7th Avenue car. It is raining hard. Get there 6:45. Put it in package room, go out to 8th Avenue entrance. Bert meets me at door, says she was about to give me up. Marion announces slyly that Bert has

20. Miriam Taylor, Marion Bloom's friend and roommate at the time. Unpublished letters in the Mencken Collection at the New York Public Library suggest that Miriam was contemplating marriage with the "Jake" of this passage, who was a medical doctor. In addition, in a letter dated 18 December 1929, Mencken mentions to Estelle Kubitz Williams that Dreiser's *A Gallery of Women* contains a "long chapter in it on poor Miriam Taylor." This chapter is the "Regina C——" section of the book. Dreiser's portrait, which includes Marion and Estelle Bloom as the Redmond sisters, shows that Miriam Taylor ("Regina") was a nurse who became a morphine addict and degenerated physically and pschologically in an attempt to support her habit. Dreiser calls Jake "Walter La Grange" and describes him as a surgeon who tries to help Regina.

21. "Love" first appeared in the New York *Tribune,* 18 May 1919, pt. 7, pp. 2–3; it was reprinted as "Chains" in *Chains: Lesser Novels and Stories* (1927).

22. Louis Umfreville Wilkinson (1881–1966), English author.

23. Widow of the writer and drama critic Harris Merton Lyon (1883–1916). When Dreiser was editing *Broadway* in 1906, he met and hired Lyon. Dreiser believed that Lyon's early death owing to a kidney ailment was a genuine if minor loss to literature, and for years he sought a publisher for Lyon's manuscripts. He wrote a sketch of Lyon called "De Maupassant, Jr." which appeared in *Twelve Men* (1919).

to go to hospital to see Miriam. I don't believe it. Think it a hoax
to get out and see man who called her up at 11 A.M. I say nothing.
Marion talks as though Bert were to come back to 274 to sleep. I
say nothing except how soon she starts. Bert invites me to go along.
Can't make out whether it is a bluff or not. Get to hospital about 9.
Nurse says not to stay long. Miriam very pale and thin. I suppose
Bert had arranged to go this far if necessary, then excuse herself
quickly and beat it, or in case I didn't go all the way to go directly
to her lover. I think yet that was what was done. Don't want to
spoil her scheme, so leave at 9:30. Get off at 9th Street and walk
through in hope of possibly encountering Margaret Mower who
lives in this street. It begins to rain. See no one. Arrive home
10:30, undress, play Victrola, bring these notes to date. Am
wondering if Bert will show up and whether she is still at Flower
Hospital or not. Am very uncertain in my mind whether I will quit
her or no. If I had the right girl for a substitute, I would—and yet
I am very fond of Bert really. It will hurt me very much to leave
her but she couldn't behave herself any more than I can. And
should I ask her to? I think not—and yet I do! Go to bed at 12.
Bert shows up and we go to sleep.

Monday, May 28.
I wake up early feeling that I must hurry up and get to the bank
and make the 10:08 train for Trenton. Tell Bert that I have an
appointment with Arthur Hopkins at 10, and so get her up.[24]
Shave, bathe, have coffee and rolls at French place and walk with
Bert to Woolworth's where she buys some glass plates (I give her
$2 to do it). Get on L there and go to 38th and 6th Avenue.
Jewish girl who spread her legs so wide apart. Was heavy and
sensuous, but beautiful in a coarse, vulgar way. Draw $25.00 at
bank. Go to Liggett's at 34th and 6th Avenue and get bottle of
B.K. [a disinfectant]. Go to Macy's to buy a large black comb for
Louise. Go to station, get out my bag and get on train. A pleasant
ride to Trenton. Am thinking Louise may not come, it's raining so.

24. Arthur Hopkins (1878–1950), producer. Robert H. Elias says of Hopkins that "in
May of 1917 he had regarded *The Hand of the Potter* seriously enough as worthy of production
to ask Dreiser, on May 23, to delay its publication" (Elias, ed., *Letters of Theodore Dreiser*, 1:302).
Hopkins later decided not to produce the play, a decision that Dreiser believed Mencken and
Nathan had influenced.

Arrive there in downpour. Go to northbound tracks and wait for her. She steps down smiling, in a downpour. Is as pretty as ever, and very coquettish and mincy. Says she didn't know till last minute whether she would come. Has qualms about husband. Feels she is doing wrong. Conscience troubles her and she is watched. Reputation at stake. Will not come any more. I get a little angry, but conceal it, and I tell her very well, that I think so too. We go to the Sterling this time. A fierce hotel, but as good as any in Trenton. Register as Mr. and Mrs. of Newark. Shown to a fierce room and bath on 3d floor. It is raining cats and dogs. Louise has torn her coat and wants to mend it. Feels she doesn't want to go with me—but———. We undress, and she is as pretty as ever. A wonderful form. I lay her across the bed and feel her hips and breasts, then get in with her and we begin. She is so very passionate, a perfect little cormorant of lust. We stay so, busy except for odd moments, until 4:45, having entered the room at 12 M. Then she thinks we ought to eat. I have promised Bert to dine with her at 7. There is a train at 5:51, which will get me in New York at 7:23 if on time. I tell Louise I have a dinner engagement with Auerbach, my lawyer.[25] She thinks we can get a little something anyhow. Go down to inquire. There is a restaurant in the hotel. The dinner food is ready. We eat in a hurry. Bill $2.05. I pay room, $2.50, taxi to depot 70 cents. Had to smile at landlord who, knowing we were using the room for immoral purposes, was so courteous and helpful. At station I have barely time to make train. Buy Louise a ticket to Philadelphia, 85 cents, my own to New York $1.40. Give Louise ten for stockings. She has changed her mind during afternoon and now begs me to write her. Says she can't live without me. It is raining something wonderful. The train is almost dark for clouds. Enormous flashes of lightning. Arrive 32d Street at 7:30. Rush to parcel room, put up bag and hurry to 8th Avenue and take car. Arrive at Bert's at 7:40. She meets me at door very glum. Suspects something. Silent at table. I demand to know of Bert what she is cross about. She won't

25. Joseph S. Auerbach (1855–1944), the attorney who aided Dreiser in his attempt to stop the suppression of *The "Genius"* by the Society for the Suppression of Vice, led by John S. Summer. Auerbach pled the case for Dreiser in May 1918 and published the argument he made before the Appellate Division of the New York Supreme Court in *Essays and Miscellanies*, 3 vols. (New York: Harper & Brothers, 1922), 3: 130–65.

say. I tease her about being a crosspatch, and she cries. Marion goes uptown. We lie on bed awhile, and she weeps still more, and finally we fall to screwing. Work at this almost an hour. During afternoon I come four times, Louise seven or eight. We finally come down to studio and go to bed. Letter from Arthur Hopkins, and some girl in St. Louis, who wants to get in with me, I think. Go to bed, and after an hour of tossing about get excited and have one more long fierce round. Then am able to sleep.

Tuesday, May 29.

Get up at 8 to let Sarah in to clean. Tease Bert about her laziness and her dark lover, a cellist aged 25 who threatens to kill me and her if she don't marry him. I tell her to tell him not to shoot but to call a conference. This enrages her and she won't speak. Get up at 8:30 and have hot bath. Go to French place for breakfast. Walk with Bert across 11th Street and leave her at 7th. Pretend to turn home but catch car and go to 32d Street and get my bag. Bring it down. Sarah lets me in. Gave Bert keys so she can get in tonight, since I am going out to dinner with Harriman and Fuessle.[26] Fall to work on article, <u>America</u>.[27] Do about 2000 words. Lill phones. Wants to come down. I let her. Arrives with blues. Manager who was to sign contract for her road tour has gone to Chicago till Monday. I cheer her up. Send her out to get Italian pork-sausage and rolls. She comes back, makes tea, fries sausage and serves light lunch. Mrs. Jarmuth calls up.[28] Wants me to auto to Long Branch in the morning with a Mrs. Prof. —— of Columbia, to attend a peace conference. I refuse. This woman professor has been hounding me through Mrs. Jarmuth for six months. Wants to meet me and has

26. These references are to Raymond Lee Harriman, an editor of Butterick's *Designer,* and Newton A. Fuessle, a writer. Both championed Dreiser's cause in the case of *The "Genius."*

27. Dreiser never published "America"; it survives in four pages of typescript in the Estelle Kubitz Williams file at the University of Pennsylvania. Subtitled "A Chain of Phylacteries," it is a list of epigrammatic statements which satirize various aspects of American life and character.

28. Mrs. Edith De Long Jarmuth. A correspondence among the Dreiser papers at the University of Pennsylvania reveals that Mrs. Jarmuth came to New York from Colorado and became active in avant-garde and radical circles. She was intensely interested in Dreiser's work and enjoyed discussing ideas and literature with him. Mrs. Jarmuth divorced her husband in 1918 and married Dreiser's good friend Edward H. Smith. In June 1919 she died unexpectedly after being hospitalized for what was thought to be influenza. Later Dreiser wrote about her as "Olive Brand" in *A Gallery of Women.*

got up all sorts of plots, which so far I have succeeded in frustrating. After lunch Lill and I fall to petting and we go in back room. She is always anxious to screw, and we have a fierce round, first on her back, then on her knees. Lill is sensuous and beautifully formed, an ideal shape for a stoutish girl. Afterward she leaves and I return to work. She reminds me that tomorrow (May 30, 1917) is her birthday. She will be 27, and I decide to go up to Brentano's and get her Lawrence Hope's <u>India's Love Lyrics.</u>[29] It may inspire her to more songs. Return 5:30. Buy bottle of milk on way and drink it. Also one dozen very large envelopes [itemized list of what he bought]. Write several letters. Bring these notes up to date. Go to dinner with Harriman and Fuessle at Brevoort. I get very drunk and can hardly walk. Find long love letter from Bert on mantle. She is in bed and helps to undress me. Pets me and tells me how much she loves me till I fall asleep.

Wednesday, May 30.
Very bright and warm. Wake up with headache. Get up, have cold bath. Bert and I have a delicious round. Go to French place for coffee. I have promised Lill to call her at 9, but can't on account of Bert. Buy Bert 100 Helmars[30] and promise to come to dinner at 7. Leave her at 10th and Greenwich. She lends me $3 at corner. Get home. Clara calls up. Says Lill is coming there (45 East 82d St) at 12:30 and I am to come. I call up Lill at her home. Tell her I have a book for her and will bring it to Clara's. Lill is 27 today. Get there. Clara and Lill in fine mood. We lunch, decide to go up to Clara's new country place for afternoon. Samuels, her husband, is up there, has car. We take taxi to Grand Central, train to Harrison. En route Lill reads my short story <u>Kismet.</u> Thinks it too long. Clara reads start of <u>Love.</u> We talk of trouble in different families. We get in her car at Harrison and go out to her new place. Beautiful, 60 acres. Lill falls on wobbly stone by river. I cut weeds. The Robert S's arrive. Back at 5:30 all the way to New York in car, driving along Pelham Bay road. Wonderful evening. Thousands of cars. Arrive at Lill's at 7. Big dinner on, but owing to agreement with Bert, I can't stay. Tell Lill I feel bad, and leave. Call up Bert at

29. Lawrence Hope (Mrs. Malcolm Nicolson) (1865–1904), English poet.
30. "100 Helmars"—cigarettes came 100 to a flat box.

corner. She is angry because I'm late again. Tells me to come down, though, and to bring loaf of bread. Arrive at 8. Bert is very gloomy. We eat, then come down here. She plays Victrola. We go to bed. Wake up. Have exquisite round. Go to sleep. Bert very depressed.

Thursday, May 31.
Up at 8:30. Bert in fussy mood. Wants to work. We decide to take up files of clippings of Jennie Gerhardt and The Financier, to be gone over by her. Also the full penwritten copy of A Traveler at Forty, which she is to re-copy in order that it may be left intact when I die.[31] We leave at 9:30. Go to her place for breakfast. Bert very gloomy. I wash dishes. Take her up to McCreery's to buy her two pairs of silk stockings. She needs them very much. Then to bank. Draw $25.00. Down on 5th Avenue bus. A gay, crowded morning. Mrs. Jarmuth calls up. Wants me to go to conference at Long Branch with Mrs. Shepard. Lill calls up. Wants to come at 3. O.K. Work on story Love. Gertie calls.[32] Wants to borrow money. I give her a little, and some sage advice. Get her out by feigning engagement. Leave her at 10th and 6th Avenue. Return. Bring these notes to date. Go to work on story. Am very gloomy today— blue. Don't seem to be able to get anywhere. In little while Lill calls up, wants to come down. Does so. I put her to work editing Kismet. She stays till 5:30, when Frank Shay, one of my various publishers, now publishing the sixth version of Sister Carrie, phones he is coming over.[33] Lill debates whether she will sit in back room until he goes or go now. Decides to go now. I am glad, for I wanted to get her out by 6. Shay comes. Agrees to arrange with Jewish paper, The New World, for the serial publication of The Financier, on condition that they run an adv. for all my books. He

31. In 1913 the Century Company published *A Traveler at Forty,* Dreiser's book describing his European travels. The Century editors refused to print many chapters which contained scenes of explicit sexual encounters or of lower-class urban life. Dreiser often expressed his desire to have the unexpurgated text published after his death. The manuscript has not been recovered. The extant version closest to Dreiser's original is a typescript at the University of Pennsylvania which contains 103 chapters. The printed book has 53 chapters.
32. "Gertie" is Gertrude Nelson, the daughter of Dreiser's sister Emma.
33. Frank Shay (1888–1954), a Washington Square bookseller who entered into an agreement with Dreiser to publish a thousand-copy edition of *Sister Carrie.* Dreiser was to receive a 25% royalty and retain ownership of the plates. Dreiser means to say here that Shay would be the sixth publisher to issue the book. The deal collapsed when the Army drafted Shay (see p. 173, n. 51).

also agrees to publish <u>The Hand of the Potter</u> in the fall if I wish. I call up Bert. She tells me that because I didn't say I was coming up to dinner she has invited an American Frenchman just returned from France, one of her lovers before she knew me, to dinner. This makes me sore and I hang up receiver. Instantly I feel a psychic wave of distress coming from somewhere. I assume her. Work on till 7:30. Start Victrola—it busts. Dress and go uptown to see the Winter Garden show. A leggy-leggy-girly-girly thing, but amusing in spots. The girls are the cutest and most sensuous things I have seen in I don't know when. Return at 11:30. Go to bed. Expect Bert to call up. She doesn't. Fall to sleep for a minute, but am troubled. Am aroused at 4:30 by ringing of doorbell. It is Bert. She couldn't stay away. Hurries and gets in bed with me. A fierce round follows—richly brutal—then sleep.

Friday, June 1.
Wake up at 8:30. Bert very tired. Get her up at 9 and we dress and go to French restaurant for breakfast. She leaves, very happy. Wants me to come up to dinner. Buy her three ears of corn and give her back the $3 I borrowed. Return to house. Letter from Louise begging me not to throw her. I write her to come Tuesday. Phone call from Lill. Wants to come down. I let her. Lill argues that she has been a good wife to me and as faithful as one for seven years, in spite of all my other girls, and it's true. Tells me she will do anything for me—take in washing, shine my shoes—but will she? Leaves. Buys tickets for <u>Peter Ibbetson</u>.[34] I agree to go to theatre with her tomorrow and to her house for dinner at 6:30 (611 West 114th Street). Work an hour, then go to five-and-ten-cent store for red lamp. Go to Bert's. She is getting dinner, liver and bacon, noodles in chicken broth, green corn, apple pie with cream, coffee. During dinner we have long discussion of prostitution—Lilly of London (see <u>A Traveler at Forty</u>), the Everleigh Club of Chicago, etc. etc.[35] Bert gets sick at stomach listening to prostitution stuff.

34. *Peter Ibbetson,* John N. Raphael's dramatization of George du Maurier's novel, opened at the Republic Theatre on 17 April 1919 and ran for seventy-one performances.
35. Chapter 13 of *A Traveler at Forty,* "Lilly: A Girl of the Streets," describes a streetwalker Dreiser picked up in London. The title echoes Stephen Crane's *Maggie: A Girl of the Streets.* The piece also appeared as "Lilly Edwards: An Episode" in *Smart Set* 50 (June 1913): 81–86.
The Everleigh Club of Chicago was a famous house of prostitution.

Lies on bed. Has on new hot socks I bought her. I sit and feel her legs and talk. We get up and come down here. Bath. I finish these notes, then to bed.

Saturday, June 2.

Bert is very sleepy and sicky. Looks very cute and sweet, naked and rubbing her eyes and playing baby. I get her to dress and we go to French restaurant. Take along last half of A Traveler at Forty to copy. Leave package at Bert's, then to McCrory's to exchange red lamp and get three new ones. Go to bank, after trying to get Lill in drugstore. Get Eleanor. Ask her to tell Lill I have two tickets for Peter Ibbetson and will she go. To bank. Deposit $75.00 I received for The Dream from the Seven Arts.[36] Draw $25.00. Come home. Letter from Bertha Halloran in Daytona, Kentucky.[37] She is married, yet running with a doctor and trying to get in with me at the same time. Go to Bert's. Find her and her Washington Friend (a girl) together. Bert is very down at my going out to dinner without her but says nothing. Walk to 23d Street to get shoes shined (10¢). Go to Lill's. Find her father, mother, Uncle Vasily, Eleanor and her intended, a young doctor, there. Lill is distressed because I didn't call up at 10 as she planned—her mother thinks now we fixed up an outside deal to go. Lill is so girlish and colorful. Rose leaves on floor and window. We eat—soup, roast, salad, strawberries and cake, coffee. Rosenthal (her father) is very gay because I praise his stones. Eleanor wants me to get her in movies as a star. Leave at 7:45 for Peter Ibbetson, playing at New Republic, 42d Street and 7th Avenue. A middleweight play. Lill gets much wrought up about love, and whether I will always love her. Snuggles close like a calf. She is so beautiful it is a shame. We go to Murray's and have a long cool drink. Watch dancing, then take Broadway car home. Lill keeps talking about wanting to sleep with me, but there is no chance. Leave her at door and go home. Bert in bed. Cries when I get in bed with her, and cries during the

36. Dreiser's play, The Dream, was first published in Seven Arts 2 (July 1917): 319–33; it was later included in Hey Rub-a-Dub-Dub (1920).

37. Bertha Halloran's letters to Dreiser at the University of Pennsylvania reveal that she first wrote Dreiser on 1 May 1917, commenting favorably on The Financier and A Hoosier Holiday. This letter began an exchange that lasted for more than a year. The correspondence shows that Dreiser visited her briefly sometime in October 1917.

night in her sleep. I promise to take her to the country in the
morning if she feels up to it. Bert has a beautiful figure.

Sunday, June 3.
Bert too tired to get up. Cries all morning, although we screw
nearly an hour in between. Feels too sick to go to country or public
restaurant. Wants to go to apartment. We go. Bert makes waffles,
ham and eggs, creamed potatoes and coffee. I eat heartily. We sit
about. Bert cries still more, and lies down. I join her. We kiss and
then fall to screwing—very wonderful—for all of an hour. We sleep
a little, then screw some more. Finally, 3 P.M., we get up. She
makes some coffee. I drink some and come down here. Go over
chapters 18 and 19 of The Bulwark, and at 5 call her up. We
decide to go to Coney Island. Bert very gay. Dine at Henderson's,
a wretched yet expensive place—one plate roast ham, $1.25. Go
over the way to Luna Park. Ride on various things. 11:30 we leave.
To bed at once. Very tired.

Monday, June 4.
Bert and I go to French place for breakfast. Lill comes in afternoon,
and we go to little restaurant at 7th Avenue and 14th Street for
sandwich. Lill full of schemes for future. Very loving. Had a card
from Louise this morning saying she would arrive Tuesday noon.
Worked all of P.M. and arrange in my mind how to get rid of Bert
and Lill so I can have day with Louise. 6 P.M. I go up to Bert's.
She has cooked a nice dinner. Tell her I have an appointment in
morning which would necessitate my leaving the studio early.
Immediately her face falls, manner changes. I urge her not to feel
bad. She cries. We go to Central Park. Full moon. Bert is horribly
depressed. Has headache. Go to drugstore for Bromo. Bus to
Washington Square, and so home to bed. Bert sick because of her
feeling about me.

Tuesday, June 5.
Bert very gloomy and weepy. She is weepy because she thinks I am
going to spend the day with some woman. I am expecting a phone
call from Louise and want to get Bert out before it arrives. Have
one round. Try to make her gay, but can't. Get up and take cold

bath and leave her here while I go out to Wanamaker's to look for new pen (she wants this one). I buy three neckties, 25¢ each. Can't get pen. Go down Broadway to Waterman's for one. Can't get it. Eat at Child's. Rolls and coffee. Buy can of bedbug fluid. Come home. Ask Sarah about towels. She denies taking any. Lill calls up. Wants to come down. I let her. After Lill calls Louise calls. Is at Penna Station. Wants to come down. I invite her, but suggest lunch at Brevoort first so as to get rid of Lill. Lill comes. Stays until I leave for Brevoort. Louise is in entrance. Go upstairs. She looks very sweet in new English suit. Have light lunch, $1.00. Come back here. I hold her on my lap till I get her to undress. We go in back room. We embrace and screw for three hours. She tells me bits about her home life, husband, mother, sister. Is here stopping at Waldorf. Husband expects her to arrive at 5 P.M., and she will pretend to. Is very fond of me. I can see that. While Louise was here Gertie called. We wouldn't let her in. While Louise and I were playing, bell rang often. Finally she dresses and leaves. Will call me up tomorrow. No sooner is she gone than I call up Bert. She is sick in bed, she says. Too sick to get dinner. I go up. She looks bad. I feel her a little while, then make her dress and come up as far as Gertie's house so I can give Gertie a little money. I hand her five. Say this is to help her on her great career and that I don't want it back. She bursts into tears, thinking I'm making fun of her. Bert and I walk to Broadway and up to 96th Street to a Chinese restaurant, then take Riverside bus for home. Get here 8:45. Hutch has already been here and gone.[38] Don't know whether Wilkinson has. We sit down. They come. A fine gay talk about Germany and England. Bert makes lemonade. They go at 11. I finish these notes. Bert is now in her bath. I'm going.

Wednesday, June 6.
Bert and I eat at French place. She is in good humor, but tired. I buy her a peony. Dictionary of sex terms arrives. Louise calls up. Is going to New Rochelle today to play tennis. Will come down tomorrow. I post these notes. Lill calls up. Wants to come down. Does so in half hour. Is very gay. Has closed contract for

38. Hutchins Hapgood (see p. 119, n. 12)

vaudeville engagement until March next at $300 per. I let her look at new dictionary of venery which just came. She gets excited. Wants to copulate. We do, in back room. Lill leaves. I go to bank, 2:45. Return. Get bottle of milk and box of Sanatogen. Make myself drink. At 5:15 call up Bert. She is sick in bed. Can't cook dinner. Doesn't want to go out. I get mad, thinking she doesn't want to come down here. Decide not to go up, but change my mind. Feel intensely drawn to and sad for Bert. She is lying in her little room in a suit of pajamas, a hot water bottle on her stomach. Marion is very grouchy, principally because they are broke, I think. I go out, get a steak (2 lbs. 70¢), 2 boxes strawberries (25¢), one bottle milk (quart, 11¢), half pound butter (23¢), 3 oranges (6¢). Return. Make cocktail. Bert broils steak, makes biscuit, prepares green peas, coffee and strawberries. We eat, read papers, talk of war. After dinner I want Bert to come on down here. She teases to make me say I want her to come very much. I won't do it. Threaten to leave and stay away until Sunday. She gets hard, then frightened. I can see it. I finally say I want her and she comes—a little bit irritated by my being such a poor lover. Once here I mail Gertie ten. It starts to rain while I'm out. Bert plays Poor Butterfly. That's her. We start to go to bed. I undress, post these notes, sitting in a knee-length union suit. In bed we can't sleep very well. Bert is morbid over love. Tells me how keenly she feels about me. Says she is all shot to pieces emotionally. Wants to work with me. Do I remember the toast she made over the new tea set I gave her —that I was to love her as long as a single piece remained unbroken, and so far only one saucer was broken? Sometimes she seems almost insane over me. At other times able to leave me. I must be very calloused. The love moods torture me at the moment, yet a little while later I forget them. And I believe it would almost kill me—be absolutely impossible for me to be faithful to one woman. At this date it would be almost the severest strain I have yet endured.

Thursday, June 7.
Bert in a slightly fussy mood this A.M. We go to French place for breakfast. We go to Woolworth's. 1 spool thread, a pink comb, 6 lamp candles. Bert wants me to knock off this afternoon and go to a movie, but since Louise is coming down I can't. Home. Boy brings

cut version of <u>The Genius</u> from Hearst's. They don't want it.[39] Lill calls. Wants to come down at 3:30. Is menstruating. Hutch calls up. Wants to bring his book at 5:30. Louise calls up. Wants to come at 1. Ed calls up.[40] Louise arrives at 2. Looks very pretty. Brings me a bunch of sweet peas. Claims she just wants to sit and talk today. Is unhappy with her husband. He wants her to live at Forest Hills, L.I. She wants to live in New York, somewhere on 5th Avenue. He claims she has a common streak in her because she likes tango teas and won't pose in sedate society. Says she wants to retire and write a book. Claims to be a good pianist. After awhile, in order to get me to make love to her, she says she has to go. Comes around near my chair. I fondle her awhile and urge her to copulate, but I am not very much interested and neither is she. We lie on couch and play, feeling and kissing each other. Play her several pieces on the Victrola. She decides to go. Says she is going back to Philadelphia tomorrow, but will see me before she goes. Can't stand to live with her husband. Prefers to live at home with mother and sister. Leaves. I work awhile. Lill comes. Very fussy because I wouldn't let her come down at once. Is worrying because she has to go on road June 24th and leave me. Wants to know if I will travel with her or meet her in different places. I promise. Wants me to go to Reno and get a divorce so we can live together. Says she will get a car, etc. Goes out and buys a silver cake. Comes back and makes tea. Hutch comes. Lill leaves. I call up Bert, tell her to come down. We fall into a heavy philosophic discussion about different things. I think Bert likes Hutch very much. We go up to Budweiser Garden and sit there till 9:30 discussing Loti, Goethe, barbarism, the war, etc., etc., etc. Bert says there is one good thing about men: they can go so far and no farther. We go to a bowling alley and play a few games. I win (cost 40¢ a game, tips extra). Come out. Go to Riverside Drive at 96th Street to get a bus. Hutch leaves. Bert and I walk along river to 86th Street. Beautiful night very soft, warm,

39. Unpublished correspondence at the University of Pennsylvania helps explain this incident. On 14 April 1917, Sewell Haggard, an editor at *Hearst's Magazine,* wrote to Dreiser expressing interest in running a shortened version of *The "Genius"* in serial form. Dreiser provided Haggard with an abbreviated text of the novel, but in a letter dated 6 June 1917, Haggard sent his regrets at being unable to use it, citing the publicity surrounding the attempt to ban the novel by the Society for the Suppression of Vice: "It would look too much like taking advantage of the situation and would react upon both of us."

40. Probably Dreiser's brother Ed Dreiser (1873–1957).

hazy. Ride to Washington Square. See big festival in MacDougal Alley. All lights, color, etc. Return and enter. 5¢ each. Meet Dorothy Cheston. She has a job now with <u>Cheating Cheaters.</u>[41] Also several others. Bert gets down on society airs. Wants to go home. Arrive home at 12. Bert fussy and certainly not very affectionate. I sleep. Have irritable dreams.

Friday, June 8.
Bert and I wish to be alone a little, I think. No particular attraction for each other this A.M. Have a little fun jesting, and I get up and take cold bath. Want Bert to make coffee and get rolls and serve here, but she isn't very enthusiastic. Wants to go out. Get her to water plants. We go to French restaurant, then to Woolworth's for (1) a bottle of ink (5¢), (2) a ribbon for Bert's watch (3¢), (3) a tube of mucilage (10¢), (4) one dozen yellow roses for Bert (50¢), (5) 2 lids for her stewpans (20¢), (6) 1 earthenware plate for pies (10¢). Go over to Greenhut's to look for big tin pan to cook ham in. They are too expensive. I make Bert sore by saying that the dozen roses will get her a beau at the Rialto Theatre. She wants me to come to dinner. I say her sister doesn't like me. She says her sister says the same thing of me. The truth is we have nothing in common. Return here, agreeing to call her up later. Post these notes. Clip items from papers concerning the war.[42]

.   .   .   .

Thursday, August 2.
Hot, muggy, Rise at 8. Bath. Too hot to eat. Girl downstairs brings up geraniums I ordered. I plant them in window boxes (14 of them). Letter from Petronelle in St. Louis.[43] Wants my advice. Is coming in September. Plainly in love. I write her. Go out and get milk punch. Return and re-edit war article to send to her.[44] Call up

41. Cheating Cheaters was a theatrical company located at 263 West 42d St.
42. The four spaced periods which follow this entry were typed by Estelle Kubitz to indicate a chronological break in the diary. It is possible that she deliberately omitted Dreiser's entries but more likely that he simply did not keep notes for these days. Estelle indicated other chronological breaks throughout the diary in the same fashion.
43. Petronelle Sombart was a professional dancer whose studio at 303 West 4th St. Dreiser frequented during this period. Their relationship continued until she returned to St. Louis in 1919, after which they corresponded frequently.
44. Dreiser is probably referring to his pro-German article "American Idealism and German Frightfulness," which he was never able to get published.

Estelle Kubitz

Yewdale for statement.[45] At 5 call up Bert and tell her I can't come to dinner. Lill is to be here at 5:30, but at 6 calls up. Is to call up again at 6:30. It is now seven. Post these notes. Hot! Sicky, disagreeable day. Wait till 7:30. Lill does not call again. I suspect she has a date with some one else. Call up Bert. Ask her if she doesn't want to come down, that I am tired of the bunch I am with. She comes, bringing several chapters she has done for me. We decide to go up to the Far East Garden, 59th and 8th. Ride up on 8th Avenue car. Dine, then walk down Broadway to 42d. It sprinkles. We stop in Palace Theatre and view portraits. Stop at Gertner's and get ice cream. Walk down to 19th and 6th. Bert wants to come down but is uncertain whether I want her. I am not particular. In the main would rather not, but say yes. We walk to 7th Avenue and 19th. She is still uncertain. Wants to go home and change her dress. Mencken is there with her sister and likes to have her stay there nights when he is there, "for looks." The cautious conventionalist! Because I am uncertain Bert feels it. Says she will come if she can. I come on down to my house. Find this letter from Lill in mailbox.

My darling

Oh, if you knew what this meant to me tonight you would be kind, honey. I've been praying all day that things would be alright and then—an idiotic message which my mother took saying Vivian won't be down for rehearsal. She is staying in Scarsdale. That meant I couldn't use her. So I immediately went out and phoned some one I knew and said to please do me a great favor and come to get me at 5:30 sharp. Also asked that I receive a telephone to that effect. That was all arranged so I phoned you at one saying I would be down, depending on the 5:30 appointment.

I was dressed, hat on, no one turns up. Thought surely in a half hour, then I again phoned you.

No one came and I was choking with rage and disappointment. I was frantic. I had counted on being with you. It meant so much and I was so sure I could do it. Well, honey, that's my luck. I always have to depend on some one else and then get left. Ah, what a life. I couldn't eat dinner and at 7:30 the bell rings—two hours late, and the answer was that it was 7:30 and not 5:30. Well, anyway there was a chance for me to get out. So here I am. Said goodbye to the miserable creature who misunderstood me and came down in the Broadway car. It's now, 8:45—and I'm so upset I could scream. I don't imagine you're in just now but honey please let me see you tonight if only for a second—I shall phone you to see if I can get you in—and if you'll let me come down for one minute I'll feel better—I must have you tell me that you see I've done my best—But I get tired trying. It all goes wrong. I'm just damned unlucky. There's absolutely no

45. Merton S. Yewdale was an editor at the John Lane Co.

other way out. I must get a place of my own. No more people I can't depend on.

Am going to wait till I can get you on phone. Please honey—understand how this is for me and if I don't see you tonight I don't know what I'll do —but phone at 10, 10:30, 11, 11:30.

L.

A moment later she calls up. Wants to come down. Is weeping over phone. I won't let her. Too tired. Tell her to come tomorrow. She hangs up. I go to bed. Expect Bert to come for a long time but she doesn't. The fact that Bert can let me alone at times lends her more charm in my eyes. This letter from Bertha H.

My dear D.

Don't you suppose I felt what an inanimate thing that letter was? I always start out to write you just what I feel and think, and then change and write the conventional thing. As to my being afraid of the world . . . I don't know. I try not to be, but it is so hard to stand out against all the rest. I always say "I do not care what people say," but maybe that is because nothing has ever been said against me. Oh—but I want to live and not be tied down to this conventional life. It is so hard for a woman to do as she wants or desires. I am all at sea at times (when I try to figure this problem). I think I must be morally bad, and yet I'm not. I do want the friendship of other men besides my husband.

Now write and tell me what you think. You do not know how I look forward to your letters.

Bertha H.

Friday, August 3.

Bright and warm, but cooler than preceding hot days. Get up. Shave. Bathe. Take crosstown car to 3d Avenue, L to 59th. Going to Bloomingdale's for geraniums. Go to nursery and get two. Walk across 59th to Madison Avenue. Breakfast in a restaurant called Plaza Lunch. Get home and put flowers in window box. Kirah calls up. Is at 7 Fifth Avenue. Wants me to come over. Go. She is downstairs when I get there. Haven't seen her in over a year, when we lived together. Cries and hugs me. Tells me of her life in Los Angeles as star of Little Theatre. The attitude of Ordynski the director toward her.[46] Played two leading rôles. Didn't like her because she wasn't his style of beauty. Now is Mrs. Frank Lloyd Wright, jr. Character of her father-in-law, the architect. His opposition to her because he thought she wanted to return to me.

---

46. Richard Ordynski (1878–1953), director. At this time, Ordynski was most frequently associated with the Metropolitan Opera Company, though he also directed in various other theaters in New York and California.

Her father also in opposition—same reason. Wright's great estate in Wisconsin. His mistress. Housekeeper steals letters and publishes them. He takes his discarded mistress back. Kirah wants me to meet her occasionally when she is with her husband and pretend not to have seen her before. I leave, agreeing to meet her somewhere soon. Return here. Work on book. Bert calls up. Wants to know if I'm coming to dinner with Mencken and Nathan. Since Marion wouldn't speak to me the night before, I decline. Think Bert had better come out to dinner. She is doubtful. Wants me to call up in an hour to say what I will do. I agree. Work again. Boy brings letter from Marion, asking me to join the party. Decide to Go. Call up Bert, who seems a little bit surprised. Lill comes down. Is greatly upset about the day before. Looks wretched. Weeps. We agree that it is all right now, and have a round. Go to 7th Avenue and 14th Street for a sandwich. She goes uptown. Return and work until 6:10. Bert calls up, says crowd is waiting. Go up. Mencken, Nathan, Marion and Bert are there. Cocktails. Dinner. We discuss publishers, books, the war. After dinner Mencken, Nathan and I go to Lüchow's ahead of the girls (they wash dishes). Very heavy from over-eating. Drink only iced tea. The practical joke concerning me appearing in the movies as a celebrity. Bert and Marion come at 9:30. At 10:30 we go to the Brevoort. Very hot and crowded there. Taxi to my studio. Menck and myself, Menck and Nathan, and Menck and Bert work the Ouija board. Afterwards Menck admits he was pushing it. A long discussion of the war, until 1 A.M. Some feeling between Bert and Menck because she will not stay at 274 while he is there. Bert and I go to bed.

Saturday, August 4.
Beautiful day, clear and cool. Letters from Louise and Hapgood. Bert and I go to restaurant at 14th Street and 7th Avenue. I return here, work on chapter 20, Newspaper Days. Sarah fails to come. Lill comes down at 2:30. Reads Newspaper Days to chapter 16. Likes it very much. We go to restaurant at 7th Avenue and 14th Street. Lill wants me to come up tomorrow at 3. I return here. Work till 4:30. It is so beautiful I want to walk. Phone Bert, and she comes. We go to Newark on tube. Walk out Broad Street to park, return to Nankin Garden and eat and watch dancing. Afterwards to market to see crowd. Then to old book shop. Buy

<u>Julian the Apostate.</u>[47] Get sundaes at drugstore. Return home. The theatrical troupe and the little girl who flirted with me. Both very tired. Go to bed at once.

Sunday, August 5.
Beautiful today. Sleep till 9:30. Bert and I indulge. We dress and go to breakfast at L & C, 81st Street and Broadway. Walk down Broadway to 65th. Buy the <u>Seven Arts</u> with Mencken's article about me. Take 6th Avenue L home and read it en route.[48] Bert gets off at 19th. I try to work. Lill calls up. Wants to come down. Is lonely. I let her. Wants to screw but I won't. Reads Menck's article and likes it. Leaves to go to Clara's at Harrison. Has a plan for an auto ride Wednesday. Leaves for Louisville on 19th. I post these notes to date. Write Louise, then phone Bert, who comes down. We decide to go to Chinese restaurant, but en route change our minds and go to her place in 19th Street. Buy cheese, butter, ice cream, bananas, etc. Make welsh rabbit and dine. Bert gets sick. We read Arabian Nights. Play with cat. Finally come down home here and go to bed. No copulation, as Bert is sick.

Monday, August 6.
Bright and clear, but a slow day. No letters to speak of. Work on <u>Newspaper Days.</u> Also send out 55 notices to literary editors of article on "What's the Matter With the Newspapers."[49] Call up <u>The Mail</u> and order 25 copies of Saturday issue, containing history of <u>Sister Carrie.</u>[50] Lill comes down. Is in blue funk. I am getting very sick of her really. At 5:30 call up Bert, who comes down. We

47. *Julian The Apostate* by Gaetano Negri (1838–1904). Dreiser has the 1905 translation by Duchess Litta Visconti-Arese. Negri was a rationalist fascinated by figures like Julian whose energies, despite his apostasy, were essentially religious. Julian's move from orthodoxy to paganism attracted Dreiser and many of his contemporaries, as it spoke to their own spiritual needs.
48. Mencken's article in *Seven Arts* 2 (August 1917): 507–17, is entitled "The Dreiser Bugaboo." The essay is at once a defense of Dreiser against academic, genteel criticism and a balanced assessment of his literary strengths and limitations.
49. Unpublished manuscript at the University of Pennsylvania, in which Dreiser attempts to encourage American newspapers to print higher quality items. His argument is not so much with editorial policies as with the average American's low standards, which he sees as the determining factor in this situation.
50. H. L. Mencken, *"Sister Carrie's* History," *New York Evening Mail,* 4 August 1917, p. 7. Mencken's article emphasizes Arthur Henry's importance, the novel's "suppression" by Doubleday, and the irony of Harper's original rejection of the manuscript in light of its later publication of the book.

go to Turkish restaurant at 24th and Madison. Stop to hear speech of exconvict. After dinner go to public library. Work two hours with Bert copying addresses of bankers and doctors. Then to Mirror Candy store for ice cream for Bert. Then down Broadway and 6th to home and bed. Bert a fine companion.

Tuesday, August 7.
Bright and warm. Bert puts new rule of getting up early into effect. Up at 8. Cold bath. Shave. Bert goes for rolls and coffee, which we have here. Then she leaves. Yewdale calls up, says Boni & Liveright are issuing <u>Sister Carrie</u> without my consent. I call up Boni & Liveright, then Shay. Go round to Shay's. Without my consent he has sold his edition to Boni & Liveright. Shay gives me an order on Vail-Ballou Company for the plates. Boni wants to take over all my books.[51] Return here. Begin on <u>Newspaper Days.</u> Work till 3:30. Lill comes down. Am horribly bored by her today. Nevertheless we screw. She is leaving for Edgemere to sing. I fold 40 American Newspaper articles and use old addressed envelopes of editors to send them out. Am anxious to hear from Petronelle and Bertha H., but no letters. One from Louise wanting to come over Thursday. Finish chapter 21 <u>Newspaper Days.</u> Post these notes. Dress and go to Bert's for dinner. Hot as blazes inside her place when I get there. Ham and dumplings à la the Smith's in Maryland.[52] I want to go up to Lill's after dinner, in accordance

51. Correspondence at the University of Pennsylvania shows that as late as 24 July 1917, Frank Shay was prepared to publish *Sister Carrie* under his name. Shay wrote then that the novel "is all printed and ready to go to the binders." A summer 1917 advertisement for "Frank Shay & Company" lists among its publications *Sister Carrie* at $1.50 a copy. Dreiser's diary entry suggests that Shay unexpectedly and secretly sold the printed sheets of *Sister Carrie* to Boni & Liveright, and that firm did in fact issue the book shortly after Shay was drafted. Dreiser's corespondence confirms that by 7 August 1917, *Sister Carrie* was being sold through Boni & Liveright. Boni & Liveright had the initial gathering of the book reprinted with its own title page. These first gatherings were then bound up in a Boni & Liveright binding with the remaining gatherings of Shay's printing.

The printer, the Vail-Ballou Company, was located at 200 Fifth Ave. Since Dreiser retained ownership of the plates of *Sister Carrie,* Shay was obliged to have them returned to Dreiser. (See p. 160, n. 33.)

52. Dreiser and Estelle spend most of June and part of July 1917 at the farmhouse of the Bloom family relative Harry Baile Smith in Westminster, Maryland. Dreiser worked on his autobiography and *The Bulwark* and was visited by Mencken in early July. The Mencken Collection at the New York Public Library contains a series of scenes written by Estelle that are based on their weeks there together. Dreiser is called "Old SOB" and she is "Miss Damn Phool." The thinly disguised complaint beneath the humorous dialogue was written for Mencken's perusal, a token of intimacy on the subject of Dreiser that provides background to Estelle's later gift of this diary to him. See Fragment 3, p. 449.

with her request, so as to make all safe for Wednesday, but Bert doesn't want to stay alone. Says she wants to go to bed right away. "How would you like to lie down and rest and let me go for a walk? Then I'll come back and get you." Her face drops. A change in atmosphere. "I don't want to keep you in if you want to go. You'll get the notion I'm keeping you in when I don't want to." Finally we go. I am tired, and with no chance of seeing Lill, steer her down here. She is glum because she feels that I resent it. Gets sick at her stomach. I fancy there is something seriously wrong with Bert. We get three lemons to make some lemon and soda for her. To sleep, after a bath, holding Bert close. I always feel so sorry for her—her wonderful mind and her dreams—that can never be realized, I fear—those about me anyhow.

Bertha's letter:

My dear man
    Why should I be shocked? It was just as I would have you write. I have been irresistably drawn to you since your first letter . . . even before that. While reading your books I felt and liked the man behind . . . the man whose mind was capable of producing such characters as Cowperwood. The miracle is that you could be interested in me, and I want you to be. If I were with you I would want you to do the very things you said you should like to do. As to my responding—I am sure I could not resist you. Nor would I want to. Of one thing I am sure, I could be very sweet to you, if you desired it. Would you?
    I think I am willing to risk love outside of marriage . . . although I am not unhappily married. That is one of the things I cannot understand—why I should seek it elsewhere. It is a terrible thing, is it not, to promise to "love, honor and obey" any one man for life?
    Of one thing you can be certain, if you should come here, or see me there (which is out of the question) and all resistance was put aside . . . I would not hold you responsible for corrupting me, as I know I would not be corrupted by any contact with you and I would never regret it.
    My one fear is—that you would not find me as sweet as you expect. Would that not be a catastrophe? So do not expect too much—just an ordinary home-loving girl, who is mightily attracted to you. Can I hope to see you?
                                                                                    Bertha.

Louise's letter:

Dearest
    Thanks for your charming letter, it was so interesting. You're not an incident to me—you're a big event—a gosh darn lot to me—you don't seem to want to believe it—I'm sorry—
    I'd love to spend the day with you—I can hardly wait at present—I can't

stay away at night—I'd love to see you—say Thursday—but I'm poor—my whole allowance has vanished—and it's some time to the next one—so lack of carfare is the only thing keeps me away from you.

I'd like to work on your book—because I'm through gadding about for a little while, I guess. Rather fed up with it—had a wonderful time at the shore, but I'm "off it" for the rest of the summer. I'd like to do something serious—see you—for instance—ha!

You're so wonderful and say such brilliant things—I love to be with you —and I hope I shall be <u>very soon</u>—

Louise.

XXXXXX—kisses for you.

Wednesday, August 8.

Get up at 8:30. Sitting on side of bed, look at Bert lying on her tum and cannot resist her. Pull her over and indulge in a long round. There is this about copulation and affection: it is the one thing that convinces a woman that you still care for her. I always notice that Bert, Lill, Kirah are alike in this. It dispels their heaviest moods. Lill is to call up some time this A.M. to explain about train. I am anxious to get Bert off, as I have a lot to do. We dress and go to Child's for breakfast. Then I return, finish folding and enveloping "What's the Matter With the American Newspapers". Write note to Sarah not to come Thursday. Want to write Louise and Bertha Halloran, but haven't time. Finish work. About 1:35 Lill calls and says train leaves at 2:15. Go to bank at 42d and 5th Avenue to draw $30. Go to Grand Central, meet Lill on lower level. She is very cheerful. Made a hit the night before at Edgemere Club, she and Vivian. We have a soda, then take train. Lill full of plans for road tour. Is leaving for St. Louis one week from date. A little angry because I didn't call up family and come up last night. "Now if they call up Clara's and find you up there it will give the whole thing away." We ride to Harrison. Lill smoothing my hand. Arthur is there with car. Quick run to "The Oasis." Clara upstairs dressing. Call to her, then sit in wooden swing with Lill and talk of her admirers, the one who tried to get in with her. Clara comes down and gets in swing too. Has a long tale of woe about the servants. 60 acres of ground, 30 planted, five men to take care of them, and no vegetables or fruit. Weeds taking everything. 3 cars. One always out of order. Arthur complaining he is overworked. Lill goes and gets peach brandy and cake. Jerry, the Airedale pup, and Flossie, the terrier bitch. Lill and I go for a walk.

Sit down by stream and talk of the farm and its poor managment. Flossie comes down and tries to kill a duck. I give her a good beating. We walk on under trees to a hill slope. When we get behind it Lill wants to screw, so we look about and then go to it, I leaning back against some rocks, Lill bending over before me. Her groans of delight! Afterward we walk back, sit by water and go up to house. Once more the swing and brandy. Arthur mows the lawn with an electric mower. We wait for Samuels till 7, then dine. He phones he will arrive at 7:30, and does. Talk of farm, F. W. Woolworth, Fale, etc. After dinner Lill plays a while. I lie on porch hammock. She comes out and sits beside me. We examine Vicaya, Deering's new home at Miami. Chaflin, who built it, is coming to dinner tomorrow after we leave. Clara afraid of burglars. I go up to my room. Lill comes up and says she will slip in if she can in the night. I really don't want her. Kisses me and leaves. I am very tired and undress at once. Hear Clara in closet next to me, but make no noise. Lie down. The bed is so wretchedly soft and stuffy that I can scarcely sleep. Feel that I must give up so much screwing or I will break down. At same time think of Louise, who wanted to come Thursday for the day, and Bertha H who wants me to come to Louisville. I feel a stormy sex period brewing there. A heavy rainstorm in the night. Cooler. No mosquitoes or flies here—a large airy country house, beautifully furnished.

Thursday, August 9.
Awake in the bed at "The Oasis." Hear Clara and the children with their ward in the next room. Lill did not come in, thank goodness. Bathe, dress, and go down. Lill comes down. Breakfast on porch. Samuels is supposed to leave for New York at 9 but doesn't. Lill and I plan to stay and go for a swim at Rye, then leave in afternoon. It begins to rain. Lill plays on piano—"Deep River" and songs of the North. Her exquisite voice! The quality of her music! Looks beautiful and I feel that I can go on with her—only I have so many girls now compared with my one-time luck. Will I ever have money, I wonder, to contrast with my poverty? Sit in swing. Pick golden glow. Idle till 1 P.M., when lunch is served. Lill and I decide to leave at 2. Clara's story of Mitchell's indifference. Sides with servants. Their laziness and secret complaints. At 2 Arthur takes us to Mamaroneck. I get tickets. We talk of Lill's leaving.

Wants me to come on tour with her. Gets off at 125th. I ride down 4th and across 8th. As I get here Louise calls up from Philadelphia. Wants to come over Monday. Is very humble and loving now. I agree. Letter from Fannie Hurst congratulating me on "Married," the story in the <u>Cosmopolitan</u> just out.[53] Letter from Boni, offering to take over my books.[54] I work on letters. Call up Bert, who is angry at my going away without telling her, but she comes down. Has three chapters done. Looks very bad. Plays Victrola. We go to Allaire's at 3d and 17th. En route see Kirah and her husband in distance on 5th Avenue. We turn back to avoid contact. Bert very dour. Makes me unhappy. My nerves on edge. At restaurant "la Paloma" is played. Bert won't talk. Walk out to 3d. Start to take car to Fort George, but change our minds and go to movies at Academy. "Under Two Flags," with Theda Bara, a horrible show. Home at 10:30. Bert very ill at tum. I get lemons and make her a soda. We go to bed. Her mood, silent and sad and dour, tears me to bits. Can't sleep and feel wretched.

Friday, August 10.
Rise at 8:30, feeling fine. Bert still sick and heavy in mood. Fix her more medicine. Want her to go to breakfast but she won't, then changes her mind—a sardonic type. She leaves. I return here. Stuff envelopes. Write Louise and Fanny Hurst. Post these notes. Buy 100 ones and 50 twos. Meet Kleinschmidt of Butterick's, learn all about Wilder.[55] A queer German type, this. Makes $10,000 a year drawing "fashion pictures." Return here and go to work on <u>Newspaper Days.</u> Lill comes down, stays a few minutes. Blue because she sees traces of Bert. Leaves. At 5:30 I call up Bert, who

53. Fannie Hurst (1889–1968), author. Her autobiography, *Anatomy of Me* (1958), contains a striking portrait of her first meeting with Dreiser, when he was editor of *The Delineator.* They were neighbors in Greenwich Village, but she seems to have had little personal contact with Dreiser in 1917–18.
    Dreiser published "Married" in *Cosmopolitan* 63 (August 1917): 31–35, 112–15. The story was later reprinted in *Free and Other Stories* (1918).
    54. Albert Boni (1892–?) of Boni & Liveright had just published a reprint of *Sister Carrie.* He was contemplating the possibility of being Dreiser's sole publisher.
    55. Carl Kleinschmidt, an illustrator at the Butterick Publishing Co., which produced dress patterns and published magazines that specialized in women's fashions. Dreiser worked as chief editor for Butterick from 1907 to 1910, during which period he met Kleinschmidt. George W. Wilder, as president of the Butterick Publishing Company, hired Dreiser as chief editor in 1907.

comes down. She wants to go to Kloster Glocke, but changes her mind. We go to Far East Garden. Omelettes and chow main. See Vivian Holt and her family. Bert and I walk up Broadway to 87th. The drunken man in street. Ride down to 6th and 42d. I see Gerald Brooks and his wife.[56] Three years since I saw them last! Avoid them. Bert and I take 6th Avenue L and so home. She feels better tonight and sleeps better. Reads me a part of Hajji Baba before we go to sleep.

Saturday, August 11.
Bright and clear. Up at 8:30. Bert and I have breakfast at Halloran's, 6th and 14th. She goes to her house. I return here. Work without interruption until 2, when Lill comes and talks awhile. Then she goes. At 4 I call up Bert. Can't work any longer. Decide to go to City Island. I dress, walk up 7th to 14th. Stop at Slevin's saloon and get a milk punch. El Bart quoted at $2, Bushmill at $2. A lovely afternoon. Stroll on to Bert's. She is dressed and we walk across 19th to 7th Avenue. No cars running. This line is always broke down on account of subway building. Stroll on to 6th. No car in sight. I curse the car companies. We walk to 23d. Get a crosstown and transfer to 4th Avenue. Get off at Grand Central and inquire. No trains running to City Island on this line. Never were any. Go to R.R. lunch and have sandwich and coffee (70¢). Go out and take 3d Avenue L to 133d Street. Walk to depot of Westchester Short Line and get tickets to City Island Station. Bert in gay mood but discouraged over sick stomach and loss of weight. We ride out and get off at City Island. Might have had a car over if I had only looked, but not seeing any we walked. The Jewish tent city. Hundreds of Jews returning from bathing, a stodgy, sicky crowd. We finally arrive at City Island. Beautiful clouds and water effects. Get a table at a restaurant overlooking water. Bert moved by scene. Food not very good but music pleasant. We stay until 9 P.M., then walk to end of island and sit on dock outside Chateau Laurier. The many cars that came down to stand and view the scene. Girls dancing on pier. We finally take

56. When Dreiser first met Gerald Brooks in 1907, Brooks was assistant treasurer of the newly established publishing firm of B. W. Dodge & Co. Dreiser was one of the initial investors and officers at Dodge, which reissued *Sister Carrie* in 1907. During Dreiser's years as Butterick's editor, Brooks worked with him on various publishing projects. At this time, Brooks was employed on the New York Stock Exchange.

street car from here to City Island depot and train to 129th and 3d Avenue L to 8th. Crosstown to door. Bert very tired but happy. Reads Hajji Baba to me, after which we have a round, then go to sleep.

Sunday, August 12.
Clear, bright, warm. Wake at 7, very tired, and pull down blinds. Bert has been weeping and moaning in sleep much during night. Am depressed by her loss of weight (10 pounds since Christmas) and the fact that she cannot retain anything on her stomach. We play about, finally winding up in a long copulation period. For all her thinness Bert retains her perfect figure. We bathe, dress. Tease her about bringing an orchid to her grave. She makes coffee. We play "Lead, Kindly Light," "Holy, Holy, Holy," "The Lord's Prayer," "Mother Moscow," "O, Sole Mio" on Victrola. Go out and walk up 4th to 8th at 14th.

I have promised Lill to come to dinner at 1:30, and it is now 11:30. Take car to 81st. I show Bert where I lived (225 Central Park West, top floor right) when I finished The "Genius". (Those lovely days!) Walk across 81st to Broadway to C & L restaurant. Bert goes in while I get an American. We order cantaloupes, waffles and coffee. Bert can't eat much. Leave at 1:30. Put her on car at 81st and Broadway and after the car is out of sight I take Broadway car north to 114th. Arrive at 1:50. Lill comes to door. Evidently Vivian didn't tell her she saw me the night before with Bert. Sit down to dinner. Rosenthal crazy for America to get out of war.[57] After dinner Lill plays. Puts on her new stage dress. A beautiful thing, and she looks beautiful—a typical Broadway beauty. Afterward we come downtown, supposedly to catch 5:30 train at Penna. Instead we ride on here, undress and have a round. Lill surprises me by her animality and yet her sweetness and loving weakness. Gas so strong in bathroom that we call up Gas Company to come and fix it. At 6:30 Lill has to run for her train. I call up Bert to come down. Start posting these notes. Gas men come with big red wagon and finally find leak downstairs. Bert comes. Brings some finished chapters. Plays Victrola while I post these notes to

57. Elias Rosenthal, a wealthy lawyer who held open house for artists and intellectuals at his apartment at 608 Riverside Dr. Dreiser attended these functions and even rented a room there in 1910 when the Thelma Cudlipp scandal forced a seperation from Mrs. Dreiser. Rosenthal's daughter, Lillian, is the "Lill" of the diary.

date. We go out to the Monopole at 2d Avenue and 9th Street and sit outside, having soup and cottage cheese, cream and onions. Bert is so fearful of her stomach that she scarcely eats. We read the Evening Telegram and discuss Marion, Mencken and Wright,[58] then take 3d Avenue car to 42d and public library. Bert defiant of conductor. Is so crazy about me that she whimpers of love all the way. At library we copy addresses from 9 to 10. Come out and go to Gertner's for French ice cream, but they haven't any. Bert eats peach ice cream, and I wait to try the store below. They haven't it either. We walk down Broadway to 3d. At 33d fall to discussing Spafford and her fortune telling.[59] I say what she told me came true —thinking of Mary Smith and the desk under the trees.[60] Bert wants to know what came true and I avoid telling her. (She heard the fortune.) At once her mood changes to one of intense depression since Spafford said I was to fall in love with some one else. She becomes so self-centered and remote that we quarrel. I urge her not to spoil this night. A long argument about love and the fact that I don't care. She falls to crying and keeps up till 1 A.M. When feeling better we indulge in a long seige. At 2 we get to sleep, but I have a bad night. Dreams and unhappy thoughts of failure.

Monday, August 13.
Warm, mixed clear and gray. This being the 13th I expect a lucky day but have an unlucky one. My nerves are upset and I am tired. Expected a letter from Petronelle but none comes—due of course to my having foolishly made advances to her. A letter from

58. Willard Huntington Wright (1888–1939), author, journalist, editor. Wright was a close associate of Mencken and Nathan, a past editor of *Smart Set,* and, at this time, the literary critic of the *New York Evening Mail.* Later, as S. S. Van Dine, he wrote the popular Philo Vance detective novels.

59. Jessie Spafford was a fortune teller living in New York to whom Dreiser, Mencken, Nathan, the Bloom sisters, and their friends went for amusement and counsel. She appears as "Giff" in *A Gallery of Women,* where Dreiser seems open to the possibility that she is clairvoyant. Mencken's letters to Estelle Kubitz at the New York Public Library suggests that he was more skeptical than Dreiser about Mrs. Spafford's powers. On 15 April 1937, he wrote: "The news that old Spafford is still alive really amazes me. The next time you see her please ask her to give me a dollar's worth of counsel on the Irish Sweepstakes."

60. Dreiser's letters at the University of Pennsylvania indicate that he had visited a Mary Smith in Westminster, Maryland. The context of this diary reference leads one to believe that Dreiser had a brief flirtation with Mary Smith when he and Estelle Kubitz visited her relatives in June and July 1917. Estelle's letters to Mencken at the New York Public Library also suggest this possibility, though Mary Smith is not mentioned by name.

Mencken praising Bourne's estimate of me in The Dial.[61] Yewdale calls up, wants me to get proofs of Mencken's Book of Prefaces and persuade him to modify his estimate of me.[62] Asserts it is all unfavorable and untrue, that he dismisses The "Genius" as a mass of piffle and that he states that my first work was the best and that I have steadily deteriorated since. Urges me to point out Bourne's estimate, which is better, but I tell him I can't influence Mencken. Get the blues from this. Bert adds to them by saying that such a criticism will fix public belief, that it is always anxious to believe the worst. We go to Child's. Then I come here and get out some old notes and start a short story called The Return, in the hope of selling it.[63] Note from Mame,[64] saying she is moving from 135 West 13th Street and wants to see me tonight. Phone from Lill, who is doing her act for soldiers downtown, a recruiting station. Have fierce case of blues all day. At 4 P.M. am sick at stomach. Lill calls up. I meet her in restaurant at 14th and 7th. We talk over story, which she likes. Tells me of hypnotizing methods practiced at recruiting station. Notices my blues. I return here. Work on story. Post these notes. 35 Mails come from downtown. I call up Bert, who says she will come right down. Lill calls up to ask how I feel. I am horribly blue and sad, feeling eventual failure staring me in face. Bert comes. Plays a few records while I work. We go to Kenelly's at 111th and Broadway. Have excellent meal. Walk down to Drive to get bus and up Drive to 135th. There get bus to Washington Square, riding on top. Bert very sweet. We reach here at 11. She reads Hajji Baba until I am too tired to stay awake.

Tuesday, August 14.
Bright and clear. Louise is to come today at 12:30. In order to get clear way, I told Lill I would not be in after 12. She is coming at 11. Bert and I go to breakfast at Halloran's, after which she goes uptown carrying paper and list of books to address. Return here,

61. Randolph Bourne (1886–1918), critic, journalist. The reference is to Bourne's short, perceptive essay, "The Art of Theodore Dreiser," *Dial* 62 (14 June 1917): 507–9.
62. Mencken's essay "Theodore Dreiser" appeared in *A Book of Prefaces* (1917), pp. 67–148. Mencken defended Dreiser against genteel criticism, but he also took the opportunity to dwell on his literary faults. Dreiser's *The "Genius,"* for which Dreiser had a special affection and Mencken a special distaste, received extended attention as a sample of Dreiser at his worst.
63. This title does not appear on any published work by Dreiser or any of his unpublished manuscripts.
64. Dreiser's sister Mary Frances Dreiser (1861–1944).

begin cutting editorials from papers. Lill calls up. Wants to come down. Has only a minute or two with me before she leaves, and I with her. Am going to Mame's to tell her Lill will try to get her a place as caretaker. Mame and her troubles. Conscription has taken all her men roomers and she has to give up her place. Go on to Brevoort to meet Louise. Avoid 8th and 5th, the SE corner, because Kirah is there. Go upstairs. Louise smiling and dressed like a society bud. We go below. Crab Ravigote, sloe gins and dessert ($2.25). As usual, Louise is full of delicious tales of people, happy or in distress. Her charm is really great. She quarrels with me because I do not care for her. Is coming to live here in October on account of me. We stroll back here and begin playing. It is so warm that clothes are a distress. I undress her. We get in bed at 1:30 and don't get up until 5. The delicious animality of it all! Louise talks wild in her transports. We bathe and dress and I take her to Penna Station. Buy her her ticket and parlor seat. We have sandwiches and coffee. She tells me why I ought to like her and of how much help she could be. Wants to write. If she had $300 a week she would forget all men. Wants to know if I would marry her if I could. She would marry me today. Leaves at 6:60. I jump on 8th Avenue car and meet Bert at Far East Garden door at 7:10. Phoned her at 6:30 while Louise was buying magazines. We eat, then walk down Broadway to Gertner's for ice cream. Thence home. We read and I fall asleep. My nerves are pretty much beaten up by this afternoon. Louise gets more thirsty each time.

Wednesday, August 15.
Bright, warm. Up at 8:30. Bathe and dress. Coffee and rolls at Halloran's (60¢). Bert leaves me. Is sicky again, her stomach, and a little blue. I return here. Sarah is cleaning. Tear out and mail 70 sheets of Mencken articles on <u>Sister Carrie.</u> Lill comes at 12:15. Tells me she is leaving Friday at 8:30 A.M. I hope so. Wants me to come up to her house tomorrow or meet her at train. I agree to come up. Finally she leaves and I work on short story. Correct chapter 21 of <u>Newspaper Days.</u> Call up Hoyns of Harper's to get two copies of <u>Jennie Gerhardt.</u>[65] He suggests that Harpers become

65. Henry Hoyns (1868–1945), an editor at Harper and Brothers who in 1918 became the firm's vice-president and a member of its board of directors; in 1931 Hoyns became chairman of the board at Harpers.

my publishers again. I make an appointment to meet him and Wells Monday at 3 P.M.[66] Call up Jones to get statement of book sales to date.[67] Says he will send it down by Yewdale, who is coming Thursday P.M. John Cowper Powys calls up.[68] Wants me to come there at 8:30 Thursday. I agree. Work on love story till 5. Lill calls up. Wants to come down. I let her. Is very unhappy at leaving. Wants me to travel with her later. I take her to corner. Return, call up Bert, who comes down. We go to Scheffel Hall, 18th and 3d Avenue, because of music.[69] A pleasant dinner. A little German girl next to me tries to flirt with me. Bert freezes her. We take Broadway car to South Ferry and walk along Battery Wall. Bert wants to know what I would do if she jumped in and drowned herself. I say "Nothing." An argument follows. She gets very angry. Won't talk. We return, on surface car. Because she is so silly I get angry. Lie on my side of the bed and let her alone.

.   .   .   .

Sunday, October 14.
Clear and warm. A charming day. Bert and I sleep until 9:30, then get up and go to Lafayette for breakfast ($1.90). From there we walk up University Place and Broadway to 19th and across. She is happy now because she thinks I love her. Leave her at 7th. Return here and write letters and work on story. At 1:30 Mr. Ramsey calls up and wants to come down.[70] I fear he is a bore. Let him come at 3. 3 to 6 I have to talk to him. He is an intense admirer of mine, but a little dull. He is a botanist and ornithologist. Tells me of biologists in American colleges who can't teach truth for fear of losing their jobs. At 6 he calls up some actress and invites her to come along to dinner. I call up Bert, feeling sure I am to be bored stiff by them. Dinner at Lüchow's. A dull affair. I see Germans singing America! At 9:30 we go to Sunshine Coffee House on East Side. I plan to get in with one of the pretty

66. Thomas Bucklin Wells (1875–1941), editor of *Harper's Monthly Magazine* and later chairman of the board of Harper and Brothers until his retirement in 1931.
67. J. Jefferson Jones (see p. 118, n. 7)
68. John Cowper Powys (1872–1963), English author and lecturer. At this time Powys was one of the most vocal protesters against the suppression of *The "Genius."*
69. Scheffel Hall is a famous beer hall which O. Henry described in "The Halberdier of the Little Rheinschloss." It is now called Tuesday's.
70. C. T. Ramsey, a botanist from Allentown, Pennsylvania, began a correspondence with Dreiser in 1917 about the proper management of his books. Letters at the University of Pennsylvania indicate that the two met for discussions at least into the 1920s.

waitresses there. Walk along 2d Avenue and see Socialist parade demanding a free press and free speech. They are likely to get it—here! Yes. At 11 plead that I have work to do and come home. Bert feels sicky. We go to bed. She is very restless. We finally screw and then go to sleep.

Monday, October 15.
Clear and gray by turns. Pleasantly warm. Both Bert and I were troubled by wild dreams. Hers apparently very disturbing. I dreamed Mame had killed herself. Also that I was being haunted by a dope fiend. We get up at 9:20. Go to Child's at 34th and 7th for breakfast. Thence to Macy's for a suit for Bert. See several but they are no good. I tease Bert about her new sunshine program and how hard it is to keep it up. The negro elevator man who loved to slam the gate. We go to Arnold, Constable at 40th and 5th. Find just what Bert wants at $25. Also a pair of silk stockings. The superiority of the service here! Go to Bankers Trust Company and deposit unused portion of travel checks. $350. Take 6th Avenue L. down. Bert gets off at 18th. Come home and begin work. The present political and war situation makes me sick. The canting fol de rol of American politicians! Am revising a short story called A Story of Stories.[71] Go to Jefferson Market for milk. Kirah calls up. Wants me to see her tomorrow instead of today. Yewdale calls up. Offers me 5000 cheap white envelopes for $5., 10,000 yellow ones for $7.80. I order him to send them down. At 3 Hutch calls for a little visit. Is going to Vermont for a week. Work till 5:10, then shave, post these notes, write Bertha and call up Bert. Two letters from Lill today, enthusiastic over love being made to her by so many. Bert comes. We walk over to the Constantinople and eat. Waiter thinks I have only put down a dime, when it is twenty cents, and lets it lie. We walk back along Madison Square, 23d, and down 6th to 10th. See Hersey.[72] At home we read Haremlik, which I think is very bad.[73] In bed by 11.

71. Published in *Free and Other Stories (1918)*; also incorporated into *A Book about Myself* (1922), chapters 44–56.
72. Harold Hersey (see, p. 138, n. 36).
73. *Haremlik: Some Pages from the Life of Turkish Women* (1909) by Demetra Vaka Brown (1877–?).

Tuesday, October 16.

Clear and cool. Nothing very important today. We rise at 9, after a round, and go to Child's. Afterwards we walk to 15th and 7th. I return here, get milk, and work. Mrs. Pearson (Nita) calls. Wants some one to love her. Tells me the history of her relations with a married man in Frisco. Wants him with her all the time, but if she had him would leave him. When there he supports her, but not here. Has written 33 sonnets, in a series of a hundred. Recites me one on death. I tell her of 150 I have begun. Wants to give me outlines of her life and let me make a book of it. Has no one to comfort her here. Is tired of jewels, clothes, automobiles and smart people. Is bored. I half indicate that I will take her the next time she comes. She goes at 5:30. At 4 Ludwig Lewisohn calls up. Is coming down tomorrow to get data or part of it for a book on me.[74] I write Lill. Letters from Louise and Bertha. At 4:30 I carry over pictures and books belonging to Kirah. Find her packing to leave for Chicago. Is going back to her husband. "What's the good of a freedom I don't want and can't use?" Considers her stage efforts a failure. Shows me wonderful embroideries she is doing, also an evening gown she has made. Puts it on for me. Would let me screw her, but I don't insist. We talk of the stage, Greenwich Village, Jack's operation, Hersey, etc. Says that Hersey told her he had to come over here to keep Mrs. K (Bert) and myself from boring each other—a silly taunt on her part. Wants me to keep certain of her pictures, which I do. At 6 I leave and come here. Find envelopes from Lane Company.[75] Also that Bert's suit has come and gone. I call her up. She comes down. We go to C. & L. at 81st and Broadway. The young girl who made eyes at me—and just the type I could like. This makes the presence of Bert irritating. We go over the way to a movie, "Baby Mine." It is very clever. Come out at 11. Home on 6th Avenue L and to bed at once. Very tired, and I feel irritated with Bert because of the girl I

<hr>

74. Ludwig Lewisohn (1883–1955), author, editor, teacher, critic. Lewisohn never wrote an entire book about Dreiser: his *Expression in America* (1932) contains a long chapter on Dreiser; and Dreiser enters as a major figure in Lewisohn's autobiographies, *Up Stream: An American Chronicle* (1922) and *Mid-Channel: An American Chronicle* (1929), and in *Cities and Men* (1927). In addition, the character of Blaffka in Lewisohn's novel *Don Juan* (1923) is based on Dreiser.

75. The John Lane Co., the British publisher of a number of Dreiser's books.

saw. She was so much like Thelma, and looked at me so
seekingly.[76]

Wednesday, October 17.
Clear and cool. A beautiful day. Sarah comes at 8. One letter from
Lill. We go to breakfast at Child's, and from there to 7th and 15th,
then down here because we forgot mss, and to get Bert's suit if it
has arrived. Find the suit and Bert puts it on. She looks fine. Is
irritated because on answering the phone for me she finds it's a
woman's voice. I try to reassure her, but she is very sad. She leaves.
I go for milk. Work on A Story of Stories, the name of which I am
going to change to Force.[77] Lengel calls up.[78] Wants to come down
at 1:30, and I let him. Elias Tobenkin, author of Witte Arrives, calls
up.[79] Wants to visit me some day. I set Friday P.M. Arthur Henry
calls up.[80] Wants me to see a certain actress in a play at the
Riverside. Wants me to do a one-act play for her. I say if I have
time. Work on story until Lengel arrives. Is full of his own efforts
at short-story writing and his success. Wants me to come up to
dinner Sunday but I refuse. He goes. Kirah having said she is
coming at 3 or 4, I put away the things that might irritate her or
bring up old memories, photos, etc. It is so hard for me to
completely rid myself of old loves. I am always letting myself in for
new difficulties. I really do not want to see her, but still she is
coming. Lengel tells of seeing her in September and how she burst

76. This is probably a reference to Thelma Cudlipp, with whom Dreiser fell in love in
1909. She is the original for Suzanne Dale in The "Genius".
77. Dreiser retained the title "A Story of Stories" in the published version.
78. William C. Lengel (1888–1965). Trained as a lawyer, Lengel came to New York in
1910 from Kansas City to pursue an acting career. He was deeply impressed by Dreiser,
however, and took a job as his private secretary at Butterick's. (See his account of Dreiser during
that period in "The 'Genius' Himself," Esquire 10 [September 1938]: 55, 120, 124, 126.) Thus
began a lifelong relationship between the two men, reinforced by Lengel's many years of faithful
service and companionship. He ultimately became senior editor at Fawcett Publications.
79. Elias Tobenkin (1882–1963), author, journalist; Witte Arrives was published in 1916.
80. Arthur Henry (1867–1934), editor, journalist, author. An intimate friend since 1894
when, as city editor of the Toledo Blade, he offered Dreiser a job reporting local news. Henry
admired Dreiser and encouraged him to write his early fiction. Dreiser spent the summer of
1899 at Henry's house in Maumee, Ohio, and he later recalled that their time together resulted
in a literary pact that led him to begin Sister Carrie in the fall of 1899. In 1899 and 1900, Henry
helped Dreiser prepare Sister Carrie for publication, and the first printing of the novel is
dedicated to Henry. After Dreiser read an uncomplimentary portrait of himself in Henry's An
Island Cabin (1902), their friendship lost much of its early intensity. Henry is the Winnie Vlasto
of the sketch "Rona Murtha" in A Gallery of Women. The portrait reveals Dreiser's strong
attachment to his friend as well as his growing awareness of Henry's personal limitations. In later
printings of Sister Carrie, Dreisier had the dedication to Henry removed.

into tears at mention of me. Write Lill, Bertha and Louise. Work until 4:30, but she does not come. Phones she can't. Shave. Change to new blue suit. At 6 call up Bert and agree to walk up Greenwich and 8th meet her. We meet at 13th and Greenwich and decide to go to Colonial at 63d to see a vaudeville show. Go to L at 14th and 9th and get off at 66th. Walk back to theatre and get tickets, two in 1st balcony. Then down to Far East Garden for dinner. Back to theatre, which is fair. Out at 11, and stop for a highball at 59th. Then home and to bed.

Thursday, October 18.
Clear and pleasant, a fine fall day. Bert and I get up at 9. She looks very smart in her new suit. Getting along fine for the present. Claims she has turned over a new leaf and proposes to be cheerful from now on! We go to Child's and from there across 14th. I return here and work on A Story of Stories. Finish first version by 1:30. Go for milk. Then decide to go up and see Sarah Padden's act.[81] Imagine she may become interested in me. (Hope springs eternal, etc.) Get in wrong theatre by mistake (Riverside movie next door) and don't find out my mistake until it is too late to see her act. Return here. Work on 2d revision of A Story of Stories. In going up to theatre I stopped at Bert's and gave her first revision to type. We agree to have home dinner at her place. After working on 2d revise I go out and get a steak and take it up to Bert's. We have a fine dinner—potato pancakes, peas, steak, muffins, pudding. Bert is a good sport. At 7:30 we hurry off to Riverside to see the Padden act. It is fine. The show is good also, although Eva Tanquay is the headliner.[82] At 11 we go to Nickells' at 97th Street. 4 Scotch highballs cost us $1.40! Home on 6th Avenue L and to bed.

Friday, October 19.
A clear, warm, springlike day. Air balmy. Have a cold bath and feel fine. No letters. Bert and I cool but still friendly. Go to Child's and then back here. Put away the 15,000 envelopes in closets. Go for milk, 3 quarts. Henry calls up, wants me to take Miss Padden book

81. Sarah Padden, popular vaudeville performer of the day.
82. Eva Tanguay (1878–1947) actress, singer. In the early nineteen-teens, Eva Tanguay was considered the queen of American vaudeville and musical comedy. Famous as something of an exhibitionist, her popular act included freakish costumes, madcap humor, risque jokes, and bawdy songs, all of which kept the censors attending her performances.

of my plays, but I refuse. Wants me to call her up and talk to her, but I refuse. She must see me or nothing. Louis Wilkinson calls up and wants to drop around at 4. I agree. Kirah calls up, says she is coming at same time. Tobenkin calls. Announces he is coming. Water flowers with warm water and write Lill and Bertha, then settle down to revise story. Am rather cheerful these days because my money problems are not pressing. Work until 4:30, when Tobenkin comes. Has just finished a novel and wants advice as to what to do next—work on a paper or a magazine. Thinks he'll return to Chicago. Then Kirah comes. Is leaving for Chicago Sunday night. Is irritated, I think, because Tobenkin is here. Then Wilkinson arrives—long, lank, English. We discuss food, the cost of living, my portrait, Heinz, Wrigley (the gum man), Carnegie, Rockefeller, etc. Kirah gets very gay. Then Mr. Trimble, a young actor who played Demyaphon in the Indianapolis production of Laughing Gas, arrives.[83] Wants information of theatres in New York. I turn him over to Kirah. We discuss the war until 6:30. Kirah leaves. Kisses me goodbye and promises to write. Then Tobenkin and the others go. I call up Bert. We go to Pezzo's (Italian, in 34th Street near 7th Avenue). A good dinner. Then to Gertner's (41st and Broadway) for coffee and pastry. Walk to 44th and Broadway. Put Bert on car for home. Go to Hudson Theatre and meet Arthur Henry, whose wife (Clare Kummer) has a play there.[84] A fair play, largely spoiled by a poor company. Henry wants me to do a tragedy for Sarah Padden. Leave at 11. Come home. Find Bert working on a short story. We go to bed, very tired.

Saturday, October 20.
Raining at first. Clear and cool later. A fine day. We don't get up till 9:30. Then return and play one hour. I do it because I feel Bert wants it. Go to Child's for breakfast. A dear letter from Louise.

---

83. On 7 November 1916, Carl Berhardt wrote Dreiser asking permission to produce "Laughing Gas" for the Little Theatre Society of Indiana, an experimental group based in Indianapolis which tried to give exposure to native playwrights. Dreiser wrote back on 21 November giving Bernhardt the right to stage and direct the play which opened at the Masonic Temple on 7 December 1916 and ran a limited engagement of three performances. (See p. 265, n. 20.)

84. Clare Kummer (neé Clare Rodman Bacher) (1873–1958), playwright. Dreiser knew her as early as 1909 when he published her work in his *Bohemian Magazine.* She later married Dreiser's old friend Arthur Henry, and she remained close to Dreiser into his last years.

Give revised copy of <u>A Story of Stories</u> to Bert to do. Return here, pay Sarah, who is leaving, take winter suit to tailor's and get my overcoat back. Then go to American News Company for 2500 red seals ($1.88). Return here. Work on <u>Newspaper Days</u> till 5:30. Write Louise, Yewdale, Liveright, Knopf, and Bertha H. Post these notes. Call up Bert, ask her to come. While she is en route Dorothy Cheston blows in looking sweeter than I have ever seen her, a black velvet cap on her yellow curls.[85] Wants to stay and make tea, but since Bert is coming I have to get her out and pretend I am leaving at once for appointment. She walks to L with me. I see new moon over right shoulder. Tells me of her engagement with Mrs. Fiske, and how sure Mrs. Fiske is that she is a great actress.[86] I go up steps of L. She leaves. Come down. Return here. Bert comes and we go at once to Monopole for dinner. Not very good. Then to Chinatown for two glass bracelets to make a handle for a new purse for Bert. Then up through East Side looking in shop windows. I tease Bert about using windows as a trick to get things, and she gets very sad. We return here, make lemonade, read <u>Haremlik,</u> take hot bath and go to bed. Fall to screwing and continue until tired out.

Sunday, October 21.
Clear and warm. Bert and I get up at 9. She is very cheerful and we have a gay time kidding and singing. She is working on <u>A Story of Stories,</u> cutting it down, and thinks it's fine. Go over to Lafayette for breakfast ($1.85). Then I walk up to 19th Street with her. Return here and finish correcting chapters 36, 38, 39 of <u>Newspaper Days.</u> Also start <u>Irrepressible Edward.</u>[87] Do ten pages. Call up Bert, who suggests that I walk up there for her. Two special delivery notices in box. Go to P.O. to get them. One a letter from Lill, other a small box from Bertha containing a jar of grape preserve and four small cakes. Take it back to house. Then to Bert's, who is all alone. We decide to go to Grand Central Station for dinner. An excellent meal, wonderful codfish saute. Go from there to library

85. Dorothy Cheston, actress and casual acquaintance of Dreiser.
86. Minnie Maddern Fiske (1865–1932), prominent actress, stage manager, producer.
87. Dreiser never finished "Irrepressible Edward," but twenty-six pages of typescript remain at the University of Pennsylvania. It is the story of a young man's rise from obscurity to riches by means of dubious banking practices, the morality of which the authorial voice questions.

with Bert and we copy names of bankers and doctors until 10. Then to Mirror for hot chocolate. En route buy a box of Orange Blossom talcum powder. Bert and I jest over it. Take hot baths, Bert reads Haremlik. Almost quarrel over arguments for a harem advanced in book. But we make up. Then to bed. Lust seizes me and we fall to. A heavy round. Finally at about 1 we quit, tired out.

Monday, October 22.

Wake at 8. Clear and cool. Bert not anxious to get up. I tease her about her great bluff about rising every day at 7. We dress and go to Child's. Food bad this A.M. Then to 5-and-10-cent store for a pail for Bert to get milk in. Can't find anything. Go to Greenhut's. Nothing under $1. Walk with Bert to 7th; and then I come home alone. On way read letters from Lill and Bertha, the latter explaining how her husband caught her receiving a book from me. Settle down to work after going for milk, but no sooner do I do so than Nita Pearson arrives, bringing me her book of poems. Looks very charming in gray, with black furs. Tells me she is leaving for Frisco. Cannot stand to be alone. Her lover wants her back, but when she gets there he will lead no open life with her. Afraid of exposure. Will never go to a theatre or restaurant with her. We talk about the position of women, and the meaninglessness of democracy. She does not believe in independence of women. Sure it leads to unhappiness. I advocate Mormonism and prove that she already accepts it in fact while denying it in theory.

As we talk I pull her over to me and feel her breasts. She kisses me, and in a few minutes I persuade her to undress. From 11 to 1, although she has an appointment, we screw in back room. She has a charming figure, very soft and rounded, lovely thighs and arms. We finally get up and she agrees to return tomorrow at 10:30, her last day here. Wants to make a tour of the Rockies with me, roughing it. After she goes I work on story till 2:30. Check arrives from Frisco for $25. for two performances of The Girl in the Coffin.[88] Take it to bank and cash it. Pass three kid girls who flirt with me.

88. Dreiser's play *The Girl in the Coffin*, written in 1913, first appeared in *Smart Set* 41 (October 1913): 127–40. The production referred to here opened on 9 October 1917, at the Colony Ball Room, Saint Francis Hotel, San Francisco. It was produced by the Saint Francis Little Theatre Club and directed by Arthur Maitland.

Once here I begin on story and stick to it. Letter from Mrs. Dreiser saying she has lost her place on <u>Delineator</u> and demanding that I support her.[89] Also one from collection agency wanting to compromise on Hill Brothers bill. Kirah calls up. Is not going to leave. Wants me to come and see her. I beg off. Clara calls up. Wants me to come to lunch and go the Grand Opera in Brooklyn with Madame Keller. Ask her to invite me another day. About 5 the attached letter from Dorothy Cheston arrived [no letter attached]. Since I really wasn't seeking her in any way the thing has humor. There is an element of pathos in it, too. I go to barber in 8th Street and get my hair cut. Then up to Bert's, carrying her milk pail and the 1500 cards I want her to address. Meet young Leeds there, a friend of Wright's, who was bounced from <u>The Mail</u> at the same time. Bert and I go to a Chinese restaurant at 34th and 8th. Not very good. Bert in splendid spirits and very entertaining. We try to find a good movie but can't. I buy her a box of Murads and some milk and we come home, paste up folders to be sent out (600 tonight) and make cocoa. Finally to bed, and wind up with another fierce go.

Tuesday, October 23.
Clear and cool. Up at 9. Bert teasing as usual about early rising. Take milk pail and leave it at Jefferson Market until I return. We try to get in new French restaurant at 8th Street and 6th Avenue but it isn't open yet. We go to Child's. I send back bad piece of melon. We cross to 7th and I leave Bert and walk down for milk. Hurry back in time to receive Nita Pearson, but she phones that she can't make it. Is leaving at 2:30 on Chicago limited. Hopes to come back. Glad she's not coming for I am sexually tired. Work on <u>Irrepressible Edward</u> until 4:30. No one calls. At 4:45 I go to rubber stamp store in 23d and get a stamp made for 80 cents. It is to be delivered tomorrow. Return here. Write letters and checks. Call up Bert, who wants to come down here. Shave, and when she

89. Although Dreiser and Sara White Dreiser had not lived together since 1910, they were not legally divorced. In 1914, Mrs. Dreiser wrote an agreement for Dreiser, giving up support payments for eighteen months, beginning 1 February 1915. The letter is at the University of Pennsylvania and is published in W. A. Swanberg, *Dreiser* (New York: Charles Scribner's Sons, 1965), p. 186. With the loss of her job at the *Delineator*, Mrs. Dreiser once again requested support from Dreiser.

comes we go to Kloster Glocke. Breakdown on 6th Avenue line. My great rage at rotten street car service. Meal at Kloster Glocke not very good. We return here, go to work on folders, clearing up the whole 2000. At 11 we are done, and go to bed.

Wednesday, October 24.
Raining cats and dogs. Bert in a bad mood and won't talk. We go to Child's in silence. It's pouring and I get my feet soaked. Return here and start correcting Bert's clean copy of A Story of Stories, or rather Force, its new name. Get it done by 1. Lewisohn calls up. Can't come tonight. Makes it Saturday. Louise writes that she wants to copy my book for me, Vol. 1 of A History of Myself.[90] Kirah calls up. Wants me to give her typewriting to do. I write Dorothy Cheston, the Duffield Company, Louise, Bertha, Lill, etc. Go for milk, three quarts. Post these notes. No news from any one. A box of cake from Bertha. At 5:30 I call up Bert and we go to the Kloster Glocke. Then to Academy of Music. See Douglas Fairbanks and Charlie Chaplin. Then here. Work on cards and make chocolate and go to bed. No sex.

Thursday, October 25.
Cold and gray. Bert and I eat at Child's. Then I go to bank and draw $35. Then to P.O. in Grand Central. Buy 2500 one-cent stamps. Then to bag company in South Street. Buy 12 250-pound bags for 25¢ apiece. Carry them up here. Get milk. Try to buy a ton of coal and can't. Try to get Jones to sell me 50 copies of The "Genius" but he won't. "Must get consent of board of directors."[91] Work on Irrepressible Edward. At 5 shave, call up rubber stamp company about my stamp. Out with boy. It doesn't come. At 6 I get Bert and go up there. Then we go to Allaire's. For some reason I feel very dour. Bert tries to cheer me up. We come here afterwards. Expect Paul Halley at 9, but we decide to shut him out

90. Louise Campbell did most of the editing and typing of vol. 1 of *A History of Myself,* which deals with Dreiser's first twenty years in Indiana and Chicago. The first volume did not appear until 1931 when it was published under the title *Dawn.* Dreiser had finished a first version by 1917, but he continued revising the book, particularly in the periods 1919–22 and 1929–30. Louise Campbell worked with him on this project from beginning to end.

91. The John Lane Co. was under a court injunction not to distribute *The "Genius"* until the suit brought against it was settled.

and work. Get a great deal done. He rings and rings. At 12 we quit and go to bed.

Friday, October 26.
A clear but cool day. Louise is coming at 12:45, over from Philadelphia, especially. Her lust is that driving. Cold bath. No letters. Bert and I go to Child's. Then we walk up to P.O. at 18th, where I have my postcard circulars vised. Get 1000 one-cent stamps. Come home. Work on A Story of Stories to get it in shape for mailing. Call up Bert and tell her I have to go out for dinner. Will see her at 9 or thereabouts. Go over to Brevoort. Find Louise waiting. We have lunch. More of her history. Her husband's fondness for her illegitimate baby. The kid's vanity. Tells me of people who try to flirt with her and shows me letters. The man who threw the note out of the parlor car window after her ("Wire me collect your name and address"). Her sister's affair, a man of 47 spending thousands on her. A cold, intellectual girl. We return here. She teases me about wanting to go to movie instead. No sooner get in than we begin undressing. Fire in the grate. We play in the rear room before mirror, then go into bedroom. Stay in bed from 2 to 6, playing. Between rounds she reads A Story of Stories and likes it. At 6 she has to dress. We go to Penna Station and have dinner. She tells me of the ridiculous associate editor of the Home Journal. Has to leave at 8. Takes first ten chapters of A History of Myself to copy. Wants to marry me. Will get a divorce if I will. She goes, and I read two letters from Lill in men's waiting room. Then go to Bert's, get her to re-copy last page of story and mail it as we come down. Bert sore because she suspects something. We arrive here at 9 and work till 11 on postcards. Bert quarrels until I threaten to leave her. She won't talk. Cries in her sleep. Claims she finds evidences of presence of another woman here.

Saturday, October 27.
Bright and clear. A delicious day. Bert distant and weeping. I try to make friends with her. She denounces me for never giving her a place here, no position. Wants to know if I won't at least refrain from bringing other women to this particular bed. "I would like one room in which I would not always be finding traces of other women." I want to know if she won't cease quarreling. She

Louise Campbell

demands to know if I propose to keep this up. I reply that I can't say—very likely—yes. Then I add: "Why quarrel? Why not just quit?" Get up. Take cold bath and dress. Sarah comes. No mail. Start out for breakfast and there are tears in Bert's eyes. I try to console her. On way see tailor about coat. To Child's, but Bert doesn't eat. Big tears in both eyes. I want her to ride in bus with me to bank but she won't. Leave her at 14th. Go to bank and draw $50. This is the last day of 2d Liberty Loan Drive. Go to Dodd,

Mead and Company. Get 6 copies of September <u>Bookman</u> containing poem about me.[92] Take car to Wanamaker's. Find a piece of silk at 85¢ a yard which would make curtains. Return here, carry out 2000 postcards to P.O. at corner, bibliography. Receive package of 50 Literary Supplements of Chicago <u>American</u> containing poem and picture of me. Address 100 blotters advertising Mencken's book. Take these out and mail them. Go to American News Company in Park Place for 1000 red lawyers' seals. They haven't them. Go to P.O. at Park Place and get 1000 one-cent stamps. (The leisurely effrontery of Government mail clerks. The public be damned, is their motto.) Next to Tower Mfg. Company, Broadway and Worth, where I get 1200 red seals for six cents a box. Take 8th Avenue L home. Boil some milk. Post these notes. Get ready to take Bert to Suffrage Parade. 20,000 women walking in Fifth Avenue today. We go to the Alps restaurant afterward (57th at 6th) and get Bert a bowl of soup and a cocktail. Walk down 6th to 50th. En route I buy her some flowers—the first I ever bought her. She is pleased beyond words. Then to 6th Avenue L at 50th Street, and home. En route I tell her of Mrs. Lewisohn's visit to me last March, to complain of her family troubles, how restless and sexy Ludwig is, and to ask my advice whether she had better give him up. I urged her to do so—which she resented, of course. At 6:30 Ludwig comes without wifie. She was afraid to face me, I fancy. He says she is sick. We walk across 11th to 5th Avenue and up. Ludwig tells Bert all about his experiences as professor of Germanic Literature and Language at the University of Ohio. The narrow college life. Hirsch, who is

---

92. The poem in the September 1917 *Bookman,* p. 28, is by Richard Butler Glaenzer:

> Dreiser
> You, at least, have provoked
> Opinion.
> How many, how many,
> Have done more than sneak along
> The groove of tradition?
>
> You, at least, have created
> Two women and one man
> Who cannot die.
> How many, How many
> Can preserve their own puny souls
> From daily living death?

very unhappy and admires my work. The latter's wife said " 'The "Genius" ' ought not to be given to young men over 18 or old men under 70." It was too unsettling!

We go to the Koster Glocke. A fair meal. Conversation excellent. Literature, the war, New York publishers, American newspapers, etc. If the Germans win he believes things will be a little better intellectually, a little freer. I predict the eventual breakdown of monogamy, the handmaiden of Christianity. We leave at 9. Bert and I go to the East Side to buy her a hat. It begins to rain. We quit in Grand Street. Wait at Bowery in rain for a car. The drunken man who kept saying: "Our flag and the love of Jesus Christ!" Get home and make some tea. Then to bed. We indulge in a terrific round, one of the worst since we met. Very exhausting. Bert very loving since I threatened to leave her.

Sunday, October 28.

Clear and bright, a stunning day. Bert and I get up at 9. Both in fine spirits, kidding each other about love. Decide to go to Hotel Albert for breakfast, but change our minds and go up to her place instead. Buy eggs, bacon and butter en route. Bert makes waffles, creamed eggs and bacon. Marion and Miriam in bed. I leave at 11, come down here and work. Mrs. Armstrong calls up. I wanted to tell her to go to, but she promised to do better in future. Is coming down to see me Wednesday or Thursday. Says it is my mind she can't stay away from. It is her driving lust which brings her. Work on till 6:05, then call up Bert, who comes down. We go to Albert for dinner. I tell her full story of my experiences as editor-in-chief of the Butterick publications. We discuss the war. Germans have won big victory over the Italians on the Isonzo. I hope they get a draw out of the war anyhow. It would never do to let England win. We return here and clear up the circular stuff—2500 cards, all told. At 11:30 go to bed. Bert is a brick for work.

.   .   .   .

Thursday, November 1.

Cold and gray. Bert and I go to Child's as usual. Because I brought my milk can along and left it at the market I return via 6th Avenue. A dull day. Little mail and no visitor. Saturday Evening Post returns A Story of Stories. I put it in another envelope and decide to take it to Hearst's. Finish revising The Door of the

Brevoort Hotel Dining Room

Butcher Rogaum for my book of short stories, and take it up to
Bert to copy.[93] Call at Duffield's because Mr. Laurie wants to see
me. He's not in. Go to Hearst's. Meet Mabel Daggett in
doorway.[94] She tells me of her trip to England and France, the
wretched condition of both countries. Endless one-armed,
one-legged or foot-less or hand-less or eye-less people. Rank and
file afraid to talk for fear of spies. Thinks French and English as bad
as Germans. Leave story and return via 6th Avenue. Stop at Macy's
and buy a small rug ($8.00). Come home and go to work. Revise
The Cruise of the Idlewild, a short story for the book.[95] At 5:30
call up Bert and suggest having dinner up there. Go out and get

93. "Butcher Rogaum's Door" was first published in *Reedy's Mirror* 11 (12 December
1901): 15–17. Here Dreiser is revising it for inclusion as "Old Rogaum and His Theresa" in
Free and Other Stories (1918).

94. Mabel Potter Daggett (1871–1927), editor, author. Letters at the University of
Pennsylvania indicate that Dreiser had known her since 1907 when she worked under his
editorship at the *Delineator.* She remained on friendly terms with Dreiser for years, often inviting
him to social events with her and her husband.

95. "The Cruise of the 'Idlewild' " was first published in *Bohemian* 17 (October 1909):
441–47. Here Dreiser is revising it for inclusion in *Free and Other Stories* (1918).

steak, some French pastry, half pound of butter, three pounds of flour, one can spinach, and at 6:30 take it up there. Bert prepares a dandy meal. Marion tells of the young writer who calls and tells her he can write better than I can anyhow (she is a literary agent and the writer was talking about me while I was dining in next room. Has no idea she even knows me.) Bert and I leave at 8:30 for a movie. See a horrible claptrap affair called <u>The Scarlet Pimpernel</u> at the Academy. Laugh at its high asinine romance. Home at 11:30. Read Sindbad in the Arabian Nights and then to sleep.

Friday, November 2.
Cold and clear. First day of new three-cent stamps, theatre ticket taxes, etc. Bert and I get up at 8:30. Go to French place at 11th. See Randolph Bourne and the manager of the Washington Square Players, whom I turned down. Am restless and irritated because I can't finish this latest short story. Also because <u>The Saturday Evening Post</u> turned down <u>A Story of Stories.</u> Return here and work. Letters from Lill and Louise. I send checks to New York Telephone Company, Kent and Macy. Small rug comes from Macy's. At 2:30 I go up to bank at 42d and 5th Avenue. Draw $30. Walk up 5th to 47th, then back along 5th to Macy's to buy another small rug. Return and go to work on story. Tired of my various girls and wish I had a new love. Work on here uninterrupted until 5, when doorbell rings. I open it. Petronelle is there. Has stayed away a month without a word. I can tell by her manner that she is nervous over her intrusion—a confession. I invite her in. She sits down and soon regains her composure. I ask her if she likes me better now. She admits it. We talk of St. Louis, the war, the fact that German Opera has been barred from the Metropolitan. Finally I take her hand, then put my arm about her waist and kiss her. She explains about her Italian lover. Has never yet been with any man. Doesn't object to. Wonders if she likes me enough. Invites me around to her studio—303 West 4th. We go. A charming place. Her dancing protege is there. We have tea and I admire the decorations. A gay conversation about Italy and grafters. Then up to Bert's, who is slightly peeved at my being late. We walk to Kloster Glocke and have an excellent meal. Decide to see a movie and go to Broadway at 42d. Finally find one at 44th and 8th.

Very poor. Home at 10:30. Read Sindibad. Indulge in a long round, then sleep.

Tuesday, November 6.
Election day. Clear and warm. Like spring, and beautiful day. Feel like walking in woods. Letter from Lill, the faithful. Letter from Hearst's, rejecting A Story of Stories. Bert and I decide to eat at her place. I buy Aunt Jemima's pancake flour (10¢), small jar Beechnut bacon, half pound of butter, and go up to her house. She makes cakes and serves bacon and fresh eggs from her home. Return here at 11:30. Work on chapter 41 Newspaper Days, and finish it. Cold is so bad I go out and buy one bottle Vinol ($1.00) and take that. Also boiled milk. Do up chapters 20 to 40 of Dawn and express to Louise. No phone calls. Call up Petronelle at 5 and tell her I haven't been able to get cider yet. Advise her where to see election crowds. Call up Bert and arrange to go up there. Shave and dress. Get her and we go to Taj Mahal (Hindoo) restaurant in 42d Street. Afterwards stroll out and watch crowds. It has changed now and is cold. My mood changes. Hylan wins.[96] We return here. I revise a part of Rogaum story. Then we undress. I grease myself and put on sweater to sleep. In bed Bert reads final Sindibad story, very dull. So stuffy with cold I can't sleep and feel wretched. A wretched night.

Wednesday, November 7.
The morning after election. Mitchell got a good drubbing. So much for rampant American patriotism. Cold and clear. I have a hell of a cold. Kept me awake all night. Sore throat, etc. We go to Child's, then to Wanamaker's for paper for Bert. I look at cloth for a cape for Bert. The only thing worth having is $12.00 a yard! Leave and take car to bank. Bert gets off at 14th. I give her a quarter for fare. Stop in saloon at 42d and 6th and have a gin rickey—for my cold. (The best cure I know.) Draw $40. Take 6th Avenue L home. Mrs. Stanton is cleaning. Gives me telegram from Lill. I have to go for a floor brush, ink, etc. Return. Settle down to work. Revise A Story

96. On 6 November 1917, John F. Hylan was elected mayor of New York City with the largest plurality ever registered in New York. He carried the entire Democratic/Tammany ticket with him, beating the incumbent mayor, John Purroy Mitchell, who ran on the Fusion ticket.

of Stories and mail to <u>Red Book</u> of Chicago.[97] Revise <u>Will You Walk Into My Parlor?</u> and mail to <u>Cosmopolitan.</u>[98] Revise <u>Old Rogaum's Door</u> and lay it aside for Bert to copy. Looking at Mrs. Stanton gives me an idea for a one-act play. At 1 Jessie Spafford (a story in herself) arrives to tell my fortune, via tea leaves and my palm. She was once in an insane asylum in Canada. Now plays a harp, reads palms and sings in M.E. Church for a living. Gets 25¢ an evening for singing. Tells me she sees success for me. I make three wishes, all of which are supposed to come true—money, success in work, beautiful women. Sees money for me by November 15th. Also a great triumph with some book, one of three. I give her a dollar and she departs. Work till 4. Lewisohn is due by now, but I have to get cider for Petronelle and her roast ham dinner tomorrow night. Go to corner and mail letters. Take 6th Avenue L to 53d and 8th and get off and walk to 518 West 52d (Day and Company). They sell me one gallon cider for 50¢. Take 10th Avenue car to 42d and 10th and walk over to 9th and 42d. Take 9th Avenue L to 14th. Get off and carry jug to Petronelle at 303 West 4th. She is out. Stop in saloon and have one more gin rickey (25¢). Come here. Find note in mailbox from Lewisohn saying he's been here. Write him and say I couldn't be here. Post these notes. Cold is making me feel wretched. Call up Bert. We decide to meet at Kloster Glocke. I go over on 8th Street car. Meet Bert going in. Upstairs we run into Lewisohn and his wife. Have to invite them to our table. We talk of books and plays. She congratulates me on <u>The Hand of the Potter.</u> A mess of a woman. A Western, narrow, puritan turned semi-liberal and trying to seem worthy of her husband. Finally they leave. Bert and I return here and meet Paul Halley, who comes at 9:30. A once down-and-out drunkard, of good family, who has now partially recovered and is working on <u>The Times.</u> Full of quaint stories of the Irish and of life, but Bert doesn't like him. Says he's a tufthunter. At 11 he goes. We go to bed. I have no more sex interest in her at the present time than in a wooden table.

<hr />

97. The *Red Book* did not accept "A Story of Stories." It first appeared in *Free and Other Stories* (1918).

98. *Cosmopolitan* did not accept "Will You Walk into My Parlor?" It first appeared in *Free and Other Stories* (1918).

<hr />

Thursday, November 8.

Clear and cold. Bert and I have round on waking. Hot bath. Letters from Louise, Carolyn Lawrence (Ernest Shipman) wanting to contract for movie rights of my novels,[99] Madame Courton, etc. We go to Child's. Then across 7th, where I leave Bert. She keeps insisting these days that I am soon to throw her off and that all my interest in her is dead. Return here and go to work revising Will You Walk Into My Parlor? and A Story of Stories. Find both in good shape and mail. Take up rough-typed chapter 39 and correct it for Bert. Then begin work on chapter 42.[100] Do 10 pages by 5, when I decide to go to Woolworth's for soap and take the various revisions to Bert before going to Petronelle's for dinner. Get soap. Drunken soldier in store assuring a small group that he is sure to come back from France alive. Walk over to Bert's. Stop en route and have a gin rickey on 7th Avenue (25¢). Used to be 15¢. Go on to Bert. She has forgotten I am going out and is a little glum. While I am there Marion mashes her thumb under window. Weeps over her hard lot. I have to console her. Leave finally at 6:20 and walk down to Petronelle's. "Ducky" Cady lets me in.[101] ("Ducky" is a dancer). Find Petronelle in kitchen in evening gown, with long earrings, baking the ham, according to instructions. When Ducky isn't looking I kiss her and bite her neck. A most delightful dinner, the ham first soaked and boiled in cider, then baked. Candied sweets, brussel sprouts, carrots done in a new way, a salad, pumpkin pie and coffee. I indulge in a cigarette for a change. We talk of the war, the American workingman, the need of autocracy to put the rank and file in order. Also dancing. Petronelle sings, and I find that she has a lovely voice. Ducky wants to dance but can't get up the courage yet. I propose that we go to Lüchow's but they would rather stay here. At midnight I leave. Come here. Bert not in yet. Think she isn't coming, and go to bed. At 12:15 she comes, fussing

99. Carolyn Lawrence was a New York "dramatic agent" who attempted to sell *Sister Carrie* and other books to the motion picture studios. She received Dreiser's power of attorney in 1915 to act as his movie agent. "Ernest Shipman" is the name of the agency for which Carolyn Lawrence worked.

100. Dreiser is working on *Newspaper Days* (1922), the first of his autobiographical volumes to be published.

101. This reference is to Agnes Cady, the companion of Petronelle Sombart (see p. 167, n. 43). Both women were professional dancers.

because I didn't call her up on arriving. Undresses and gets in. Bert cries in her sleep at night.

Friday, November 9.

Clear and cool. Bert in a heavy frame of mind over her future. No anchor to the windward. Her life wasted. I will soon throw her off, and then what? Letters from Louise saying she received the 2d twenty chapters. Also one from Lill in Chicago, glowing with excitement. Italians still retiring before Germans in Italy. News from Russia that Bolsheviki have overthrown Kerensky. Good.[102]

Bert and I go to Child's. Sugar so scarce now that they sweeten the coffee before bringing it in. The great thing is to continue to pay eight and ten per cent. on endless watered stock, whatever happens. Bert goes up 6th, I return here. Prepare bin downstairs and corner in kitchen for this precious ton of coal I'm going to get some time or other. Revise <u>When the Old Century Was New.</u>[103] Also chapters 40 and 41 of <u>Newspaper Days.</u> Do up twenty more chapters of <u>Dawn</u> for Louise. Around 2 P.M. go up to Macy's. Buy an attractive small rug for $12. Also a step ladder for $2.50. Return here. Go out and get three quarts of milk. Start on chapter 42 once more and almost finish it. Mrs. Jarmuth calls up. Wants to bring an old schoolmate here tomorrow at 4 P.M. to see me. Mr. Edwin Goodwin (Eddy, no less) of the Washington Square Players calls up to know if I won't take $100 down and $50 per week for eight weeks for <u>The Girl in the Coffin.</u>[104] I offer it at $200 cash and $50 per week for six weeks. Says he may accept.[105] Albert Mordell, the critic, of Philadelphia, calls up.[106] Wants to come tomorrow between 5 and 6. At 5, having got stuck on chapter, stop and play the second Hungarian Rhapsody. Post these notes, then

102. Alexander Kerensky (1881–1970). One of the early leaders of the Russian revolution, Kerensky was ousted from power in 1917. He settled in the United States in 1940.
103. "When the Old Century Was New" was first published in *Pearson's,* 11 (January 1901): 131–40. Here Dreiser is revising it for inclusion in *Free and Other Stories* (1918).
104. Dreiser is referring to Edward Goodman (1888–1962), director, playwright. In 1915, Goodman helped found the Washington Square Players, which later became the Theatre Guild. In 1917 he was managing the company and directing many of their productions.
105. The Washington Square Players produced *The Girl in the Coffin;* it opened on 3 December 1917 at the Comedy Theatre in New York, under the direction of Edward Goodman.
106. Albert Mordell (1885–1965), lawyer, author, critic.

call up Bert. Am getting bored by regularity of this thing. She asks me to come up there. Go, leaving a revised chapter. We get on 8th Avenue car. Decide to go to Hotel Endicott, then to a vaudeville show at Riverside (96th and Broadway). Lovely night. We have a fair meal. See Will. N. Harben, the author, and his wife at dinner.[107] Walk over to Broadway, catch car and get to the theatre at 8:10. A very fair show. Too many song acts. "The Forest Fire" a fine spectacle. Come out. Stop for soda in 6th Avenue and get stung. Take L, come home and get straight in bed. Very tired. I meditate on whether I had best continue this home life or no.

Saturday, November 10.
Clear and cool. Bert and I go to Child's. Then across 14th, and I leave her. Come back here and work on Newspaper Days. Stop at carpenter's to get him to put knocker on door, but he refuses because I haven't proper bolts. Mrs. Stanton is here cleaning. The slowest ever. Finally finished at 1:30. I continue until 4, when Mrs. Jarmuth and her friend call (Miss Stewart, ex-chair of English Literature in Montana University).[108] A very interesting and attractive old maid of thirty-five. Looks as though she had been thirsting for passion and never had it. Hopes that I will pull her out, I am sure. This might be called "sex charity" or "relief," but she is attractive and as brilliant mentally as Anna Tatum.[109] Does her best to show off. Mrs. Jarmuth tells of Mrs. Behr and how she tried to meet me. Also we discuss mental conditions throughout America. At 5 Mordell comes, as dull and faithful as ever. Brings me clippings about my work. I introduce him to the others. Finally Mrs. Jarmuth and her friend make tea and I send Mordell for cake. He stays until 6, they until 6:30. Miss Stewart wants to know if she can't come back. I tell her yes. Call up Bert, then go up there. We decide to go to Kaiserhof, now Café New York, at Broadway and 39th Street. An excellent meal. Good music. I smoke cigarettes for a change. Later we walk down Broadway and I have Bert's photo taken, 3 for $1.50, in a little store. Proofs ready Monday. Go into

107. William Nathaniel Harben (1858–1919), novelist, short-story writer.
108. Mary Stewart had left her academic position to settle in Greenwich Village. The brief correspondence at the University of Pennsylvania suggests that she was somewhat in awe of Dreiser and that he did not return the compliment.
109. Anna P. Tatum (see p. 132, n. 21).

Liggett's, Broadway and 34th, for an electric lamp for Bert to work by. They have none. A peach of a girl in there in a soldier's suit. We go across 34th to 5th Avenue and up to 42d, looking in windows. Wonderful display. We walk across 42d to 6th, and because I stop to look at picture of a lot of ballet girls of "Oh, Boy!" she flies into a rage. I never look at her—only others. I'm tired of her, etc. We walk without speaking to 38th, then take L to house. She still won't talk, and I get angry. To bed in silence. This episode so angers me that I decide a break or change is near. And yet it's all love on her part.

Sunday, November 11.
A beautiful, clear day, delightful. I am very sore over Bert's anger of the night before and do not talk to her. She makes various efforts but finally lets go. We go over to Lafayette. That angers me, because I proposed going up to her place for breakfast, but she won't. Cost $1.55, with tip, for coffee and rolls for two, a bowl of oatmeal for her and one egg Benedict for me. Refuse to walk up to her place. Return here. Want to post these notes and write Lill and Bertha before going up Lengel's, but don't get time. Work on McEwen of the Shining Slave Makers until 1 P.M.,[110] then scribble letters to Lill and Bertha. Go out and take 6th Avenue L to 155th and Ogden Avenue car to Lengel's place. Find Lengel and wife and baby as usual, an adoring group. This apartment, overlooking High Bridge, reminds me of the one I lived in in 123d overlooking park. The old days of suffering and unrest come back so strong. An excellent dinner. We discuss the war, how Lengel is to get a new job, the recent election, how to promote Socialism, etc. Little baby amuses me greatly. Mrs. Lengel tells me of efforts to cultivate her voice, but she has none to speak of. Sings, and evade complimenting it as best I may. She is very much like Mrs. Dreiser, savage in her opposition to being no one, and yet without any real ability to be some one.

I leave at 7. Invite them down to dinner any evening. Take train at High Bridge for Grand Central. Bring away two books by Dr.

---

110. "McEwen of the Shining Slave Makers" was first published (as "The Shining Slave Makers") in *Ainslee's* 7 (June 1901): 445–50. Here Dreiser is revising it for inclusion in *Free and Other Stories* (1918).

George M. Gould, which he brought Lengel for me.[111] Arrived at
42d, I debate whether to call up Bert or not. A new order must be
put into effect, or I must break with her. Finally call her up. Get
her to come to 8th and 42d. Tell her I have had dinner with Gould
at the Belmont, and she flares up. I refuse to explain. We reach
Café New York (formerly Kaiserhof) and order. Then I announce
that unless she wants to change her manner I am through. She must
accept me as I am. I am to come or go as I choose. I refuse to dine
with her or sleep with her every night unless I want to.

She cries. Stops her meal and goes to retiring room. I feel
dreadful. She returns and says she'll go and leave me there. I say
"If you do I'll run a knife through you." "But you want me to
go." "If you go and leave me here before all these people I'll kill
you. They've all seen you crying." "Yes, every restaurant in New
York has seen that, thanks to you." She stays, but weeps. After a
time we leave and I take her to a movie, a rather charming
interpretation of one of Chambers's books.[112] At 11 we come
round to the Automat and get cup of coffee. Then home. Bert is
very sad. I feel it absolutely necessary to break with her in order to
prevent her from running me.

Monday, November 12.
Clear and warm. A fine fall day. Rotten groggy from last night's
argument. Bert tearful, but soft in mood. We get up at 9. Letters
from <u>Cosmopolitan,</u> sending proofs of <u>The Second Choice;</u>[113] from
Hapgood, saying he is in Norwich, Vermont; from Knopf, saying
he can't furnish any more slips anent Mencken's book.[114] From Lill,
also Davis, making a lunch engagement at Union League at 12:30

111. George Milbrey Gould (1848–1922), physician, author. Gould was known for his
medical dictionary and his encyclopedic collection of rare and abnormal medical cases (*Anomalies
and Curiosities of Medicine* [New York: Julian Press, 1896]), both of which might have been
useful to Dreiser. Gould also wrote *Concerning Lafcadio Hearn* (Philadelphia: George W. Jacobs
& Co., 1908). Hearn's early death and his streak of anti-Catholicism would have interested
Dreiser, as would have Gould's genetic bias in his unsympathetic interpretation of Hearn. In
addition, Dreiser may have had a personal interest in Gould: a letter at the University of
Pennsylvania indicates that Dreiser was under Dr. Gould's care in 1919. Clearly, at the time
of this diary Dreiser knew Gould on a social basis.

112. Probably Robert W. Chambers (1865–1933), painter, novelist, writer, poet.

113. "The Second Choice" was published in *Cosmopolitan* 64 (February 1918): 53–58,
104, 106–7. It was reprinted in *Free and Other Stories* (1918).

114. Alfred A. Knopf, publisher.

tomorrow.[115] Pet Bert as she fixes her hair before mirror. We go to French restaurant. See no one I know. Then down to 8th for milk (I left can going out.) We stand at 7th, I trying to cheer Bert up. Agrees to meet me for dinner as usual. I come back here and settle down to work. Paste up proofs of St. Columba and the River[116] and The Second Choice for book set. Then complete revision of McEwen of the Shining Slave Makers. Louise calls up from Philadelphia. Is coming to stay with me Wednesday. "Eddie" Goodman of the Washington Square Players calls up to say he will pay $200 cash and $50 per week for six weeks for The Girl in the Coffin. Contract and check to come tomorrow. Post these notes. At 6:30 call up Bert. We agree to meet at Far East Garden. After dinner we walk down Broadway to Rialto. Uncertain whether to go for Bert's pictures first. Buy candy. See Elsie Ferguson in The Rise of Jennie Cushing. Saw her once before in Barbary Sheep and The Song of Songs. Have a feeling that she and I are some day to live together for a little while.[117] Feel more or less indifferent to Bert. Come home and she makes lemonade. Go to bed. I screw her, but without much joy in it.

Tuesday, November 13.
Fair and warm. Another lovely fall day. We get up at 8:30. Dress and go to the French restaurant. Same old Village crowd. News from Italy still looks promising for Germans. Walk over to 7th with Bert, then down here. Start on chapter, but Goodman of Washington Square Players arrives with his contract and check. I refuse the typewritten contract and make him write me a letter here. Then accept his check for $200 in advance. He goes. Work until 2, when I decide to take check up to bank. Do so, draw $40. Return here and work until 6. Call up Bert and go with her to Kloster Glocke. From there up 5th and Broadway to get her pictures at small photographer. They are poor, and I get into a row with him. Call him names and make a scene. Finally leave, and Bert

---

115. Probably Robert Davis, editor at *Munsey's* and Dreiser's old friend.
116. "St. Columba and the River" was first published (as "Glory Be! McGlathery") in *Pictorial Review* 26 (January 1925): 5–7, 51–52, 54, 71. It was collected in *Chains* (1927).
117. Elsie Louise Ferguson (1885–1961), actress. Known for her stage performances, Elsie Ferguson made her first silent film, *Barbary Sheep,* in 1917. She and Dreiser never lived together.

and I cross 38th to 8th. Then up to the Ideal, where we see two horrible films on which thousands have been wasted to no purpose. Return afterward and go to bed. This is getting to be a dull game.

Wednesday, November 14.

A beautiful day. Bert in excellent humor. I wonder what she would think if she knew Louise were coming at 12. Mrs. Tanner arrives and begins cleaning. Rug arrives from Macy's and completes my floor scheme. Place looks well, except that it needs an artistic lamp and new curtains. We go to French place. Then across 11th to 7th, and I return to see Mame. She has a scheme to get me to take a small country place with her (at $12 a month), I to pay the rent. Knows a judge who will get me a divorce for $150 and will arrange it. [Mame is his sister.] I agree. Said she visited Ed's wife and that she told her all about Anna Tatum.[118] (I lived with Anna Tatum from May 1, 1912, to January 1, 1913, when I met Kirah Markham.) According to her, I had seduced Anna, an innocent girl, and then threw her out on the street. Also, according to the same tale, Anna took to drink, and sank to death through poverty and disgrace. The facts are these. Anna was the daughter of well-to-do Quakers living at Fallsingham, Pa. They subsequently died and left her about $30,000. She was a graduate of Wellesley and the mistress (Lesbian) of a woman doctor (the head of the Women's Hospital at 15th and 2d Avenue). Anna came to me, by writing first and sending her picture. She was beautiful, a virgin except for being a Lesbian, and absolutely sophisticated. Fell in love with me, urged me to take her, which I did. She insisted on it, against my advice. After six months I tired of her. Very brilliant, but I tired, and I told her so. She started drinking the second month I knew her, but never to excess. Was addicted to cigarettes before I knew her—forty a day. I went to Chicago and met Kirah, who was leading woman of The Little Theatre. I liked her, she gave herself to me, and we began living together the following June. In between, I returned to New York. Anna met and fell in love with a man named Don ———. I met him. He was charming. She began

118. Dreiser's brother Ed's wife, Mai Dreiser, who severely disapproved of Dreiser (see her daughter's account of their relation in Vera Dreiser, *My Uncle Theodore* [New York: Nash Publishing, 1976], pp. 167, 176).

going with him, sleeping with him, and I dropped out. She was still drawn to me, and when I quit drank and indulged herself in a debauch of romanticism. Later she quit Don and took up with young Englishman in Philadelphia, who eventually left her. I saw her twice afterwards, and we stayed together. Anna did not care for me at this time, and laughed over her old infatuation. She got angry because I suggested putting her and her family in a novel, and left me. She is still alive at this writing, attractive, doesn't drink, and has a new love.

I laughed Mame's story to scorn. Ed's wife is an intimate of Mrs. Dreiser, who used to despise her, but now, since she can use her, is friendly. Mrs. Dreiser and Mai predict my public disgrace, arrest, etc. I want to record here that I never seduced a virgin in my life. The first one urged me to screw her, and I didn't.

Return here. Revise <u>Will You Walk Into My Parlor?</u>. At 12:30 Louise calls up. Has arrived at Penna Station. Has first 30 chapters of <u>Dawn</u> for me. Takes a taxi and comes here. I tell Mrs. Stanton she must be out by 1:30. Louise looks charming, the smartest girl I know. Full of stories of country club life, automobiling, dancing, etc. Her sister is the mistress of a millionaire. Has made a pumpkin pie and brought it—the best I ever tasted. We eat a piece. Then go over to Brevoort for lunch. I see Nina Wilcox Putnam and Rheta Childe Dorr together.[119] Nina nods. After lunch we return here. Louise tells me all the news to date. We return here. Mrs. Stanton has gone. Louise is crazy about the place. We undress and remain in large studio, naked. Throw all pillows from couch and lie in front of fire on the floor. Such loving. Louise is delicious. A perfect body. We screw and talk until 6, when I am flat. Dress and take car to Penna Station. Buy her her ticket and chair car seat to Philadelphia. 22¢ war tax on the two. We dine afterwards in station restaurant ($2.00), and Louise recounts full story of her life. It must

---

119. Nina Wilcox Putnam (1888–1962), author, social activist. A Greenwich Village regular, she was a disciple of Henrietta Rodman, an ardent advocate of free love and social reform for women. Her marriage to the publisher Robert F. Putnam ended with his death in 1918. In the nineteen-twenties Mrs. Putnam was one of the most successful woman writers in America.

Rheta Childe Dorr (1872–1948), journalist, author, leader in the woman's movement of her day. In 1917–18, she was the war correspondent for the *New York Evening Mail.* In her autobiography, *A Woman of Fifty* (1924), she mentions that Dreiser occasionally was a guest in her East 31st St. apartment.

be true, for it is the same each time. What a tale! At 8:34 she leaves, very loving and urging that we get divorces and marry. I leave her. Walk down to 303 West 4th and call on Petronelle and Ducky, who are singing when I come in. They give me cake and cider. At 10 I leave. Call up Bert. She is not in. Went out at 7:30. I leave word for her to call me up. Return here. Write Lill and Bertha, and mail them. As I come in door from this, phone bell is ringing. It is Bert. Is coming down. I get in bed. Begin reading History of Chinese Literature, sent by Davis. Bert comes. Very angry that I didn't call her up. Cries and moans all night. Claims she has no friends now and cannot leave me. I try to cheer her up, but no use. She lies beside me all curled up and weeping. Of such is the tragedy of desire.

Thursday, November 15.
Rise at 8:45. Beautiful clear day. Springlike. Letters from Claire H. Uecke, on here from Hawaii;[120] Boni & Liveright, enclosing check for $100 for Sister Carrie royalties—a complete surprise. The Red Book, returning A Story of Stories, and William Salisbury, an admirer.[121] Bert in a contentious mood. She won't talk. We go to French place. I see Frank Shay and Randolph Bourne. Italian line on Piave holding, according to papers. Bert fights with yellow-haired waitress over order. We leave at 10, and walk to 7th. I tell Bert she treats me like a dog, which cheers her up. Come down here. Find memo from Carolyn Lawrence and go up to see her at 17 West 44th. Shipman a character. Wants to try to sell Sister Carrie and Jennie Gerhardt for movies. I suggest several actresses, tell him about Madame Kalisch and come away.[122] Go to Bankers Trust Company at 42d and 5th Avenue and deposit the $100. Come on down home. Revise McEwen of the Shining Slave Makers. As I work, Nina Wilcox Putnam calls me up. Wants to see me. Saw me in Brevoort yesterday with Louise. Why don't I come to see her? Nina is a married prostitute, 27 years old, the wife of a publisher. She is gross, but attractive. Beautiful in her way. I tease

120. Clare H. Uecke (see p. 119, n. 11).
121. William Salisbury (1875–?), journalist, author.
122. Madame Bertha Kalich (1875–1939), prominent actress on the Yiddish and English stage in America who had come to the United States in 1894 after a successful acting career in Rumania.

her about her last visit and say I will look her up. Later decide that I will go around yet today. The mere thought of her makes me feel sensual. Look up names of new editors of Century, American and Collier's and send stories to two latter. Take them to box, then walk around to 161 West 13th. Nina comes to door. Says she is dictating to a stenographer. I ask: "Is that his cane?" She laughs. We go in and she dismisses the girl. Then we sit on couch and talk about her recent work, since she had the baby in June. Her child is by an artist lover or paramour. Claims she has written four novelettes, five one-act plays, some poems and essays. (Her stuff is above the average.) I compliment her on her looks. We talk of Rheta Childe Dorr and the Russian radicals.[123] Ask her, banteringly, why she sent for me. She says she feels drawn to me, that I stimulate her and that she feels the need of a sexual anchor, sufficient to hold her for six months, that unless she gets enough that way she can't work. Few men are good. They look strong, but they have no sexual force. Imagines that I have, but isn't sure. Tells me of some of her affairs—a big brute whom she took on, just to get enough. The poet she seduced, "for charity's sake," her present lover and his affairs. Saved his life from a mistress, and that when she was eight months gone herself. Has only written poor stuff heretofore. Now proposes to write real stuff.

As we talk I feel her legs and breasts. She has large hips and legs, well-formed, and big breasts. Says she likes the feel of my hand, but doesn't know that she wants me—yet. Will tell me, fast enough. Refers to my living with Kirah as a mistake. Doesn't want any binding affair. Wants to be free, and is willing to grant freedom, but must have plenty of sex to work.

We talk of masquerade costume at Village Ball. She went as a nun. I saw her in Brevoort—a nun with painted cheeks. Underneath had on pink panties, etc. "I created a sensation."

We almost quarrel before I leave, because she is so aggressive— wants everything her own way. I bite her neck and feel her thighs, but tell her that unless she is just so she may not get a chance. "You talk like a thug."

---

123. As war correspondent for the *New York Evening Mail,* Rheta Childe Dorr spent time in Russia, sympathized with the Revolution of 1916, and wrote *Inside the Russian Revolution* (1917).

Come back here and post these notes. Write Claire H. Uecke. Work on chapter 43, then call up Bert and agree to meet her at Kloster Glocke. Over there the same little girl who eyed me before comes in. Does as before. I try to throw her a note but cannot avoid her lover's eye. Bert and I leave and go to Colonial Vaudeville (62d and Broadway). Nanette, the gypsy violinist, particularly appeals to me as suggesting the spirit of youth. Lust and romance written all over her charming young body. Bert and I come home. I find her more appealing. We indulge in a long round, then fall to sleep. [This is undated scrap, probably in re the fair Nina]:

. . . is plain her desire is for a man. I listen to her long story of why she and the president of university were fired. Would make a fine short story. Has a Greek profile and charming figure. Highly romantic and emotional. When she finishes I take her arm and soon feel her breasts and thighs. She leans back against me. We get ready to screw, but because I am languid about it she begins a long talk about the lack of enchantment in her for me and what she ought to have. I let her go and listen to stories of her books, poems and adventures until 5 P.M., when once more she seems ready. Feel her breasts and thighs and get between her legs, but once more she pleads non-interest. Begs to be let go, and I do. We talk more and she tries to get the mastery of the situation but fails. At 6:15 I dismiss her for good, unless she should change.

Call up Bert and go to Cavanaugh's with her. She has retyped The Lost Phoebe and McEwen of the Shining Slave Makers. Tell her of Jack Powys and his Western friend, who are coming to see me, some admirer. She decides not to come down. Return at 8 and light candles. At 8:15 Jack and his friend, a Detroit newspaper man, arrive. We discuss Russia, the American puritanic spirit, the South, negroes, the New York World, Comstock, Sumner, a long list of things.[124] At 11 they leave. I call up Bert. Ask her to come down, but she decides not. Post these notes. Write Bertha Holloran and retire, very sleepy. Take letters to mail. A wonderfully clear sky.

---

124. Anthony Comstock (1844–1915), literary censor who founded the Society for the Suppression of Vice, an organization that conducted campaigns against what it considered obscenity in art. John S. Sumner (1876–1971) inherited the leadership of the society from Comstock and led the attack on The "Genius" in 1916.

Orion's belt directly overhead. It takes me back to my youth. How short is a life, with that thing comparatively eternal!

.   .   .   .   .

Oh, darling—as usual after I've seen you—such a hazy, indefinite feeling—don't know what time it is and don't care—my mind is filled with you—no room for anything else.

The house was quiet when I got home—everybody in bed—

I tumbled in bed with thoughts of you—asleep in one second—woke up this morning at 9:30—and breakfast at 10. It was so lovely, wasn't it? You and your rooms and the candles and everything—Oh, dear—I wish it could only last longer.

I was so sleepy in the train I couldn't finish reading your story—I'll finish it tonight and write you tomorrow what I think of it. Also will mail it back to you tomorrow morning—I've written some more of the History—it's good to have something around me belonging to you—and I love doing it —Today is another beautiful day—I'd love to be with you today—And from now on you're to be very busy, aren't you, dear—rehearsing your play—won't I get some thoughts then, I wonder.

Perhaps some time when you're all alone you might look in that famous mirror and see a vision—of beauty?—Maybe—some people have such peculiar ideas of beauty, don't they?

But, truly, dear—I'm thinking of you—and longing for you—Oh, so much—I keep thinking of how wonderful it is to be together—on the street, in the car, at dinner, in your studio—all of it is lovely—there seems to be so much to all of it—does it to you?

Louise

Saturday, November 17.

Clear and pleasant. A delightful day. Get up at 8. Bathe, shave. Call up Bert at 9:15. She is just up. Comes down and we have a reconciliation. A note from Mame in my box says she has no food for over Sunday. Stop by and give her $5. Then Bert and I go to Child's at 17th Street. A bad breakfast. War profits are reducing food quality here. Afterward we go to Greenhut's to look for cloth for her cape. Nothing decent to be had. Women elevator men and captains amuse me. We walk up to Macy's and look there. Nothing. Then to McCreery's. Nothing there. I want Bert to select silk for two pillows for my couch. She refuses on the ground that since other women are going to lie on it she will not exercise her judgment in the matter. We quarrel, and I leave her there, outside door. Come down here via 6th Avenue L. Go for milk—3 quarts. Settle down to work here and finish chapter 43 Newspaper Days, as well as part of 44. Letter from Bertha and one from Harpers enclosing a royalty check for $47.71. At 5 I am tired and quit. Bell

rings, and Fred Booth, Franklin's brother, arrives.[125] Has been out
to see Krog at Central Izlip asylum. (Krog was once one of my
editorial assistants and pets who went insane.) Tells me he is better,
but still crazy.[126] We discuss news of old friends—Amick,
Cowan.[127] In discussing war find he is pro-German, as most able
Americans are. Invite him to stay for dinner. We discuss dreams,
mind-reading, hypnotism, etc., and I tell him of my strange cases.
At 6:15 we walk up to Bert's, then across 19th to 3d Avenue and
down in 3d Avenue L to The Oriental, Chinatown, corner 3d and
Pell. A fine dinner for three, $2. Go out and walk along Division
Street to Allen, and up that. Booth has never seen either. We look
in old brass shops and I buy a seven-branched candlestick. In Bert's
favorite Russian store she gets two ounces of special tobacco for
cigarettes. Walk through Rivington, for Booth's sake, then on 8th
Street car home. Get a Drake's gold cake and make tea. Light a fire
in grate and smoke and talk. I tell them of my walk with Duffy up
the Hudson four days in 1904.[128] We talk of winter tramp for six
in snow, camping out as best we may. Also discuss war, the rise of
the Bolsheviki, American puritanism, etc. At 11:15 Booth goes.
Bert and I to bed.

Sunday, November 18.
Clear and pleasant. Special delivery from Lill. Also an offer for the
movie rights of <u>The Titan.</u> Bert and I are on fairly easy terms.
Nothing extraordinary. We go to Hotel Albert, University Place
and 11th, for breakfast, (Steak, potatoes and coffee), and afterward

---

125. Franklin Booth (1874–1948), artist. Like Dreiser, Booth was born in Indiana and
came to New York to work as an artist. The two old friends took a motor trip back to Indiana
in 1915 and published *A Hoosier Holiday* (1916), for which Dreiser provided the text and Booth
the illustrations.

126. Fritz Krog, editor, writer. An associate since Dreiser's Butterick days, Krog had
been the nominal head of Dreiser's *Bohemian Magazine* in 1909. Krog's letters at the University
of Pennsylvania suggest that his mental instability was intensified by lack of success in his literary
career. At various points after 1909 Dreiser came to Krog's aid with both financial and moral
support. In 1916 Krog entered the mental hospital at Central Islip, New York, where Dreiser
often wrote and at times visited him.

127. Robert Amick (1879–?) and Percy Cowan, artists. Dreiser, the Booths, Krog,
Amick, and Cowan made up a Greenwich Village group whose relationship began in 1907. The
correspondence at the University of Pennsylvania indicates that the men shared lively parties
as well as professional interests. During this period, Amick and Cowan rented a studio together
at 36 Washington St.

128. Richard Duffy, editor (see p. 61, n. 8).

walk across 11th to 7th. I come down here. Read and work until 2:30, then start out to find Claire H. Uecke, who is in New York from Hawaii. Call at 114 Morningside Drive. She is out. Walk along to opposite 423 West 123d Street, where I used to live with Jug. Those sad, beautiful days. [Jug is Mrs. D.] Looking at old apartment window gives me an idea for a short story, The Victim.[129] Am anxious to write it. Walk across 122d to Broadway and down to 114th to see Rosenthal. He is out. My mind is full of loneliness and need for color and life. Take Broadway car down to 42d and 8th. Change to 6th Avenue L. Stop in at Automat for a cup of coffee. Come here and work until 6. Call up Bert, who comes down. We go to the Monopole for dinner, then to a movie in 14th Street, where we see Clara Kimball Young in Magda, a good film. Excellent. No false ending. Afterward across 14th and down 5th and across 10th to here. Have tea and cake. Then to bed. Bert desires sex, but is distant and we fall to sleep without doing anything.

Monday, November 19.
Clear and cold. Bert lies to one side all curled up and refuses to talk. Get up, take bath, dress, and we go to French coffee house. Afterward walk up to Woolworth's and get shoe strings (two pairs) and 12 boxes of matches in a package. On to Bankers Trust Co at 42d. Draw $40. Deposit Harpers check. Return via Macy's and try to get silk for windows. Nothing doing. Return here. Fix candles in new seven-branched candelabra. Write for new house cleaner. Last one left on account of Louise. Mr. Boone, an agent, calls up. Wants to know if I'll take $3,000 for movie rights to The Titan.[130] I hesitate, and he suggests $5,000. Tell him to see what he can do. Edith Jarmuth calls up. Wants me to attend a concert of the Music League of America with her Friday night. I agree. C. T. Ramsey, of Allentown, Pa, drops in. Wants to talk war. I get him out as soon as possible. Louis Wilkinson calls up. Wants to come and see me at 5:30. I agree. Shave. Work on new story, The Victim. At 5:15

129. This title does not appear on any published work by Dreiser or on any of his unpublished manuscripts.
130. J. Allen Boone, movie agent. Boone was head of J. Allen Boone Agency, 730 Aeolian Hall, New York City. He did not succeed in selling the movie rights to *The Titan.*

Wilkinson comes. Has a clipping from N.Y. Tribune denouncing his new novel, The Chaste Man.[131] This clipping practically charges him with describing a pervert and of being one. Wants me to name a lawyer who will sue on spec. I don't know any.

We discuss American self-righteousness, the war, and what not. Call up Bert and tell her to come down. He wants to wait for her, but in so doing eventually misses his dinner. She comes at 6:45. We go to Kloster Glocke, leaving Wilkinson at 23d. In restaurant we encounter Lewisohn and his wife, and arrange to meet them Wednesday night for dinner. Eat scallops and bacon. Then we come down to the Academy of Music and see Geraldine Farrar in The Woman God Forgot, a story based on Gen. Lew Wallace's The Fair God but no credit given.[132] An old-fashioned swash-buckling romance. Bert and I come home, make tea and play four games of casino, and go to bed. We screw, but without much zest. The original passion has petered out.

Tuesday, November 20.
A cold, gray day. Left eye twitching, bad dreams the night before. Feel wretched all the while. For one thing, new coal won't burn, and I have no maid to clean the place. Letters from Lill, Miss Uecke, some school in California that wants to do The Girl in the Coffin, and Jones, who refuses to sell me 50 copies of The "Genius". Write Davis and Miss Uecke during day. Bert and I go to French coffee house. See the girl waiter who is like a duchess. I leave her afterwards and go to Hearn's looking for silk for curtains. Can't find. Then go to Wanamaker's. Ditto. Buy silk for two pillows, one green, one cerise. Build up fire and start working. Story don't go very well. Make a "paper log" according to newspaper instructions and find it burns exceedingly well. At noon Mr. Salisbury calls up and wants to come down at 5:15. I agree. Work on alone, feeling vile, until 5:15, when he comes. Recalls meeting me at Economic Club.[133] Was once on Associated Magazines. Is non-puritanic. Finds himself isolated. Needs some one

---

131. *A Chaste Man* (1917) by Louis Wilkinson.
132. Geraldine Farrar (1882–1967), opera singer, actress.
The Fair God (1873) by Lew Wallace (1827–1905); Indiana writer, lawyer, statesman, soldier.
133. The Economic Club of New York, of which Dreiser had been a member since 1907, was located at 23 West 44th St.

to talk to. Has book of short stories, a la de Maupassant, which no one will publish. Believes I have forced public recognition by now and can help him. I recommend Knopf and Huebsch.[134] We discuss Ben Dodge and his death in East River.[135] Also old Taylor, once editor of Associated Magazines.[136] Wants me to visit him and his wife in New Rochelle. She paints. At 6:10 he goes. I post these notes, then call up Bert, who comes down.

Wednesday, November 21.
Have an appointment at 10 this A.M. at Borough Hall, Brooklyn, to meet a so-called "Judge" Seamen who can get me a divorce for $150. (One of Mame's grand will-o'-the-wisps.) Have trouble getting Bert up. Too late for breakfast. I go past Mame's to tell her to come over here and watch while new colored girl cleans. She does. At corner, before I leave, Bert hands me attached letter, which explains itself.[137] I know it is a plan to stay away nights. Feel very sad to think affection is always jealous and painful, in myself and every one. Go over to Borough Hall platform, but no one to meet me. Wait half hour. Then go to phone in reporters' room and call up Mame. She isn't there. Call up my place. She hasn't arrived. Go to buffet lunch for breakfast. Then call up again. No answer. Take subway back. Here she tells me woman is still waiting. Wants me to come to library of Borough Hall at 12. I return. There is no library in Borough Hall. I am directed to law library in County Court House, further up street. Go over there and find damned old fool. She is nothing at all, a silly old Mother Goose. The judge is a down-and-out disbarred lawyer. He has no standing and knows no speedy way of getting a divorce. I must live two years in Jersey. Return here fighting mad, but you can't row with Mame. She is too big a fool. Let her fix up place—wash curtains, etc. I have appointed 2:30 to rehearse <u>The Girl in the Coffin</u> at Comedy Theatre. Go up at 2:45. Find Goodman in charge. Actors on stage.

134. Benjamin W. Huebsch (1876–1964), publisher.
135. B. W. Dodge (see p. 127, n. 16).
136. Joseph F. Taylor (1874–1956), editor, publisher. With Rutger B. Jewett as editor, Taylor's publishing firm supported Dreiser during the difficult period after the publication of *Sister Carrie.* In 1901 the company thought of reissuing *Sister Carrie,* and it supplied Dreiser with cash advances as he attempted to write *Jennie Gerhardt* in 1901–3.
137. Estelle Kubitz did not copy this letter into her transcription of the diary.

Am introduced. Take seat in front and watch fairly capable first reading. I think these actors may do. Come out at 4:30. Meet Norah Donna on 6th. Same old Norah. Rags and tatters. Her steady income of $100 a month. Her recital of poem. I tell her how to get a one-act play, and leave her greatly cheered. Come down here. Go to work on The Mighty Rourke.[138] Work till 6:30, then dress and go up and get Bert and go to 110 East 22d for the Lewisohns. I give him the ms. of my new book of short stories to examine. We discuss war and new ruling against Germans. I am very bitter. Mrs. Lewisohn is duller than ever. A horrible bore. We go to the Oriental, at Pell and 3d, and have a splendid Chinese meal. Lewisohn in great form. Has just been made instructor in French and Greek in some Brooklyn school. We talk of the foibles of the human race. Leave at 9:30 for the Lafayette, but change mind and come here instead. Mrs. L wants to work Ouija board with Bert. I buy a bottle of cocktails, then build fire, which goes out before morning. Ouija brings Mrs. L's mother, who tells her not to worry and to be happy, etc. (I suspect Lewisohn of working it.) At 12 they leave. Bert and I go to bed. Bert must have a lover on the side. She has so little interest in sex now.

Thursday, November 22.
Bert angry over nothing—rain and having to get up. At 8 negro girl comes for wash—two dozen pieces. Letters from Lill complaining of no word from me, and Bertha insisting on her love. Take two razors to be sharpened, one spoiled by heating it over gas jet. Bert and I go to French coffee house. The Austrian owner of it fears being sent to 150 miles west of coast, under the new government order. We leave and go to razor place. I buy a new Cranford razor for $2.50. Walk across 13th with Bert. Then down here and go to work. Mame comes to clean, bringing a picture. I do up twenty chapters of Dawn for Louise and send it by express. Buy green, pink and white silk thread and needles for Mame to sew two new pillows. Call up Petronelle, Miss Lawrence about sale of Sister Carrie. Edith Jarmuth calls up and wants to include ———. I refuse. Finish editing The Mighty Rourke and take it up to Bert.

138. "The Mighty Rourke" first appeared (as "The Mighty Burke") in McClure's 37 (May 1911): 40–50; it was reprinted in Twelve Men (1919).

She begins explaining that she is expecting her brother-in-law Fritz, who promised to bring her 200 cigarettes. I stay for lunch, and as I am leaving he comes. "I've been expecting you all day, Fritz." (A stall) I scent a liaison and get angry, but say nothing. Come down here, write Lill and post these notes. Am uncertain whether I'll call up Bert tonight or no. She's such a bluff. Finally, after contemplating being alone, call up and get her to meet me at 42d and 8th. I go up on 6th Avenue L. She is excited about a man who stopped and asked her if she wanted a drink—a bluff, I think, to get my sympathy. Says I am always late and make a target of her for such things. We go to a Chinese restaurant, then to the Rialto to see Douglas Fairbanks in Reaching For the Moon. Afterward to Gertner's for ice cream and coffee. Then we walk home. I am distant all evening. Bert lies on couch. I ignore her for a time, but finally go over and we have a heavy union.

Friday, November 23.
Clear and cool. Bert in pretty fair spirits. We go to French place for coffee. I reflect that I have engagements with Claire Uecke, Mrs. Jarmuth and Petronelle, and hurry home. Work on letters and story until 12. Hutch comes. Is going to Washington. Is willing to try to revive the Seven Arts. Says I am like "a beetling crag with moss on it." Leaves. I shave with new razor. It isn't bad. Take 6th Avenue L to bank. Cash Century royalty check for $27.60.[139] Then take subway to 129th and walk back along Amsterdam to 114 Morningside Drive. Ask for Miss Uecke. She asks me to come to phone. Wants to hear my voice. Is so afraid of me—hardly wants to come down. When she does is so ashamed of her old age and looks that she makes me unhappy. A terrible example of the neglected old maid, but a wonderful mind just the same. And the hat! We walk down Morningside to 110th. Take L at my suggestion and go to hear rehearsal of The Girl in the Coffin. It goes well. Coming out I am bored by her and want to leave, but invite her to have tea (pity stuff). She suggests that I come back to 114 and have tea with her. Curiosity impels me. Go. Find her room charming—she with an air of distinction and a kind of faded beauty, once her hat is off.

139. Dreiser was receiving royalties from the Century Company for *A Traveler at Forty* (1913).

Her books—delightful Pater, Frazer, Loti, Hauptmann. We have excellent tea and cakes. Talk of chemistry, Hawaii, President Dole, Mrs. Fahnestock, fortune telling, Chicago, New York. At 5:15 I leave. Hurry for L across 123d and get home at 6. Put away letters and papers, lock desk, hang out keys for Bert, and go around to Petronelle. She is looking charming but is mad at Ducky for something. Dinner is nearly ready. Petronelle shows me all her pictures. Is trying to get in movies. I motion her over when Ducky is out of room and kiss her and feel her breasts. Brown toast for Ducky, then we sit down—a wonderful meal, vegetarian. Talk of everything under the sun. At 8 we start for Carnegie Hall. Wait for Mrs. Jarmuth at wrong entrance, but Petronelle discovers mistake in time. Find Mrs. Jarmuth and get in. Mary Stewart and some professor is there. I avoid her eye. Like programme very much. At 10 it is over, and Petronelle, Ducky and I go to The Alps and have drinks and a sweet. We talk of Emma Goldman,[140] the types of lovers of music, St. Louis, Petronelle's mother, dancing, etc. At 12 we leave. I ask Petronelle why she doesn't come over with me. Says she is afraid. Return here at 12:45. Find Bert in bed. Wants to know if I'm glad to find her here. Crawl in beside her and sleep soundly.

Saturday, November 24.
Clear and cold. Colored girl doesn't come. Collier's return A Story of Stories. Letters from Lill, Louise, Carolyn Lawrence and several lawyers. Bert and I have round before getting up, then dress and go to French place. I try to get her to agree to take a cape from me. Doesn't want to. Complains that I don't care for her. Return here and go to work. Correct The Mighty Rourke. Also chapter 43 of Newspaper Days. Write Lill, Bertha, Louise. Mss. from Hutch arrives with letter. Go for milk at 4:30. Quit at 6:30 and call up Bert. We agree to meet at Kloster Glocke, where I have a good meal. It has blown up cold. Bert has no coat save the one she refuses to wear. We agree to go Monday and look for one. Walk down 4th Avenue to the Academy of Music and see All For a Husband, with a girl in the title rôle who is trying to imitate Theda

---

140. Emma Goldman (1869–1940), anarchist, social activist, author.

Bara. The cat that walked across the stage while the tenor was singing. Home at 11:30. Have a hard time heating the house. Soon to bed.

Sunday, November 25.

Being Sunday, we sleep till nearly 10. Have a long round. Then get up. Cold and clear. We decide to eat at the Brevoort. Meet Hapgood and Mary Pyne together. The history of Mary Pyne would make a good short story—a bad-good girl.[141] Hutch comes over and wants to come around at 9 P.M. He bores me a little, but I agree. Bert has recently read his An Anarchist Woman and now is very much interested in him. Would like to get up an affair. We return here. Meet Gus Myers on the way (author of The History of the Supreme Court, The Great American Fortunes, etc.).[142] He is on his way here. Tells me of his troubles with different organizations that employ him to gather facts. Has recently quit his latest in Washington. Quit another in Minneapolis (too many Socialists). We leave Bert at Greenwich Avenue, then come here. He tells me of Mr. Price who made eight millions in rubber and is now regretful of the methods by which he made it. Wants me to put him in a short story. Wants me to get the magazines to buy articles from him (!). Leaves at 2:30. I work till 4:30, then, restless, take L and go to 104th. The pretty girl with the skates. Walk up Broadway to 114th. Call on the Rosenthals. Only Eleanor and her beau are there. Show me the clippings about Lill. Leave at 6:30. Coming down to 110th two girls flirt with me. Call up Bert at 110th. Arrange to meet her at Far East Garden. Take subway down. Am carried to 50th and walk back. A cold night. We dine until 8:30. Then walk down Broadway to 34th. I buy toilet paper at

141. Dreiser eventually did write about the actress Mary Pyne (1894–1919). In *A Gallery of Women,* she appears as the delicate and fated "Esther Norn," her poet-husband Harry Kemp as "Doane," and Hutchins Hapgood as "J. J." At this time, Mary Pyne and Kemp lived on 10th St., a block away from Dreiser. Kemp was improvident, and Mary, who died young of a combination of tuberculosis and heart trouble, often stopped by Dreiser's flat to warm herself by one of his fireplaces. In 1917 she was acting in several plays with the Provincetown Players, and there she met Hapgood. Dreiser wrote disparagingly of their love affair in "Esther Norn," particularly of Hapgood's motives and character; Hapgood attempted to defend himself in *A Victorian in the Modern World* (1939), pp. 429–31. In 1919 Mary Pyne died in a sanatorium at age twenty-five.

142. Gustavus Myers (1872–1942), socialist historian whose ideas about American capitalism influenced Dreiser's writing and political views.

Liggett's. Price on that has risen. We take L here, come home and play cards, half-expecting Hutch, but he doesn't come. At 10:30 I build fire in grate and we go to bed.

Monday, November 26.
Very cold, but clear. So cold I insist on Bert coming to look for a coat. We visit Arnold, Constable, Franklin, Simon & Company, Lord and Taylor, and Macy. Then give up. En route in 6th Avenue above 36th have breakfast. Buy Bert half-pound of face cream in Macy's. Come down on 7th Avenue car. Go to work fixing up fire. Mame comes. Wants money, and wants me to get her a job. Wants to sell Paul's piano for $100.[143] Is talking of moving out into country. I give her $2. Then go to work on <u>Free</u> (a short story).[144] Work till 4:30, a hard job. Think of silk needed for windows and go up to Macy's. No silk there a yard wide like sample. Go to McCreary's. Nothing there. It is getting colder. These great stores are so fascinating in winter. Go on to Altman's. Find it one yard wide at 85¢. Take eleven yards and give my check. Come out, walk to 34th Street L station. Am thinking of youth and health and love all the way. See many hunchbacks, the symbol of love. Get home at 5:30. Work some more. Then call up Bert. We agree to meet at Kloster Glocke. Arrive. Find Lewisohn and his wife. She has been reading my short stories for him. Leave at 9:30. I give him a revised version of <u>The Mighty Rourke.</u> Bert and I walk back here. Play cards. Take hot bath. It is very cold. And so to bed.

Tuesday, November 27.
Very cold. Letters from Lill and Louise. Mame comes before we get out and meets Bert. We go to French place. I buy four crullers (8¢). Return here and talk to Mame of curtains. We measure them. I agree to take Paul's piano at $10 per week for ten weeks. After she goes I work till 2:30 on story. Left eye twitches all day. Go to bank. Draw $40. Return here. More hunchbacks. White petals on

143. This is a reference to the piano of Dreiser's brother, the songwriter Paul Dresser (1857–1906). Dreiser never sold his brother's piano, but had its top converted into the desk table on which he did his writing.

144. "Free" was first published in the *Saturday Evening Post* 190 (16 March 1918): 13–15, 81–89; it was later included in *Free and Other Stories* (1918).

sidewalk. At 4 Bert calls up. Wants me to come up there for dinner and bring one pound of steak. I go out and buy it. Turkeys 44¢ a pound. At 5 Claire H. Uecke calls, bringing a horrible theosophist propagandist, a terrible Christ-like philosophic type. They make me sick. Wants me to re-christen her Sanchia Hewlett, which I do. We get a small goblet, light candles in front of mirror and perform this right [his spelling]. Finally they go. Work on The Mighty Rourke revision till 7. Then go up to Bert's, taking steak. She gets me a fine dinner. She reads Turgenev's The Jew to me.[145] Afterward Marion comes home, and we go. Walk down here. Delicious night air. I want to work a bit. This angers Bert, who goes in and apparently to bed. I finish, play six records on Victrola, then go in and find her standing in that cold room, waiting for me to come. Wouldn't get in without me. I fuss at her, but feel sorry just the same. The arts of women! To sleep about 12.

Wednesday, November 28.
Cloudy and snowing, a delicious day. Bert gets mad because I get up ahead of her a little and won't talk. Negro girl who failed to come last Saturday comes and I can her. We go around to French place and have coffee. Meet Fred Booth and he agrees to come to rehearsal at Comedy theatre at 11. I return here. Call up Lengel and ask him to come. He agrees. Finish correcting new insert into The Mighty Rourke, and take whole revise up to Bert. Stop at Mame's and give her key. She is out. Take 7th Avenue car and go to Bert's. Her machine won't work, and she agrees to come along to rehearsal, leaving her machine en route to be fixed. I get off at 41st and walk over. Meet Lengel there. Booth comes next. Then Bert. Some other one-act play is being rehearsed so we have to go over to 131 West 41st and rehearse there. A very good performance. Booth, Lengel and Bert make excellent suggestions. In trying to make one actress get the idea of Mrs. Shafer I make her cry and have to let her go for day. Bert roasts me for my "brutality." Mr. Hohl, who is playing Ferguson, tells me the same scheme for doing In the Dark that I had worked out.[146] He is a

145. "The Jew" by Ivan Sergeyevich Turgenev (1818–83).
146. Dreiser's play *In the Dark* was first published in *Smart Set* 45 (January 1915): 419–25; it was later included in *Plays of the Natural and the Supernatural* (1916).

pretty good actor. Take Bert and Booth for coffee at Automat. Then come down here. Build fires. Work on Free and revise chapter 43 of Newspaper Days. Mame calls up. Says she is coming tomorrow. Lengel calls up. Says he thinks play is great. Made him cry. Salisbury (author of The Career of a Journalist) calls up. Wants to know if he should pay Knopf $300 to produce his book of short stories. I advise not, but he wants to do it—so—. At 6 stop and write Lill and post these notes. Letters today from Doty (editor Cosmopolitan) wanting me to call there Friday at 10;[147] from Fort (author of X, Y and Z, as well as The Outcast Manufacturers) saying Thanksgiving dinner is at 6;[148] also one from some woman in Texas wanting a copy of Sister Carrie. Call up Bert at 6:45. We decide to go uptown to see Lincoln Square Vaudeville show. I call for her. No cars on 8th. Take 9th Avenue L at 23d. Get off at 66th, walk down and get tickets, then back to Jameson's at 67th. Excellent dinner. Bert begins to hurry at 8, and I say that whenever it is anything she is interested in she is right on the job to rush things. She begins to cry and I have hard time bracing her up. We go to the theatre. A poor show. Audience rises at some ham actor singing the Marseillaise in an act! And because Bert and I refuse to rise, we are glared at! More American patriotism—and heavy thought! Home at 12. We have tea, and to bed.

Thursday, Thanksgiving Day.
Cold and gray. Looks snowy. To French place for breakfast. Mame is to come today to hang curtains, but doesn't show up. I work on Free till 2:30, then go out and get a drink. No letters, no messages.

147. Douglas Z. Doty (1874–1935), editor, publisher. Doty was the editor of *Cosmopolitan* in 1917–18. He published Dreiser's writing of this period as he had when he was editor of *Century Magazine* in 1914–17. Their relationship began when Doty, as an editor at the Century Company, handled the publication of *A Traveler at Forty* (1913). Doty had a romantic interest in Estelle Kubitz, according to a letter written by Mencken to her on 23 January 1918 (at the New York Public Library in the Mencken Collection). She evidently did not respond to his affection and chose to remain with Dreiser.
148. Charles H. Fort (1874–1932), journalist, author. Fort was an eccentric mystic who waged a private war against modern science. Dreiser first met him in 1905 when, as editor at *Smith's*, he accepted Fort's writing for the magazine. At the time of this diary entry, Fort was living at West 43th St., and Dreiser was championing his cause with publishers, trying to get his books into print. In 1931 a number of Fort's admirers, including Dreiser, Booth Tarkington, and Alexander Woollcott, supported the founding of the Fortean Society, which in 1937 published the journal *Doubt*.

At 5:30 quit and go up for Bert. Find her charmingly dressed in Marion's dress. We take 8th Avenue car to 43d and then walk across to Fort's. I show her tenement in which he used to live (rear). We find his bell by aid of matches and go up. Charming apartment. Learn that a Mr. and Mrs. Charles Bizozer are expected. He is a Frenchman and is working out a new language like Esperanto. Has it nearly done, but no name. Fort suggests BUNK as a good name. Dinner at 7. A wonderful turkey. Fort has a new preserve which he has named "Topeacho" made of tomatoes and peaches. I suggest "Topeaka." It is very good. Long discussion as to moral or immoral character of Nature—or unmoral. Also importance of man. Also Futurists, American puritanism, the war, Fort's work, Bizozer's, etc. Bizozer is very jealous of his wife, who is a pretty young English girl. At 11 they leave. At 11:15 Bert and I leave. She is uncertain whether I want her to come down, but I bring her along. Much loving and a long screw follow. To sleep about 1:30.

Friday, November 30.
Cold and gray. Letters from Lill, Louise and Bertha. Louise is coming over Tuesday to stay with me. French coffee house for breakfast. Bert and I walk up to 18th, where I buy toilet paper and candles. Then take L to 38th. Have an appointment with Doty at 10, but he isn't in. Walk up to 47th and back, then find him. Tells me why he dropped out of Century Magazine. Wants me to send him another short story and to get up three or four autobiographies of American girls who have emancipated themselves from American home conditions and conventions and succeeded in life—mentally at least. Is willing to pay $1500 each. I agree to try. Wants me to find a secretary (woman). I suggest Bert and he wants to see her. I go down to Bert's and try to persuade her to take the job. She is not anxious. I also try to get her to furnish the data for one of the autobiographies, which she agrees to do after some persuasion. Return here and work on Free. Mrs. Jarmuth calls up. Wants me to go and see a Mrs. Cox, 11 West 37th, very rich, who likes my work. I refuse—for today anyhow. Bert calls up. Wants me to come up there for dinner. Her mother has sent her a chicken. At 5:30 Hutch comes. Brings a one-act play for Bert to do. Wants me to

revive <u>Seven Arts</u>[149] and start my society for Certification and
Endorsement (a society to get good books before the public).[150] I
agree to see Mrs. Behr and get her to raise the money. At 6:15 go
up to Bert's, carrying a can of Heinz mince meat for a pie. It is
raining. Bert in gay spirits, preparing an excellent meal. I tell her of
Mrs. Behr, and she has no objection. Marion and her cat. At 8:30 I
leave and go up to see Mrs. Behr. Anxious to know what I want
and to help. Tells me story of her married life, how she won over
step-children. Her first husband. Her objection to being unfaithful.
Willing to be—now. Wants to call a taxi for me. I refuse. Come
down to Bert's, get remainder of pie, and we come down here. She
is very much pleased with <u>Free</u> so far. We make tea, then go to
bed.

Saturday, December 1.
Clear and cool. Bert in fine humor. We go to French coffee house.
Leave her at 11th and 7th, but return to 6th Avenue to buy record
of "Me and My Gal." The stunning girl who urged me with her
eyes. Sit here and play this for an hour. Work here. Mame comes
to clean. By 5 I have nearly finished <u>Free</u> (1st pen copy). Mrs.
Jarmuth comes while I am shaving. Wants me to go and meet Mrs.
Cox. Mrs. Shepard is enraged because I declined to meet her. We
go to Mrs. Cox's, 11 East 38th. Gauche middle-class wealth. A
more or less pretty and young but sensuous and dull woman. Wants
to be a great figure somehow. Is a pacifist! Mr. Hedrich, a sort of
Drouet of the advertising business. The tea tires me. We leave. I
suggest to Mrs. Jarmuth that she write her history. She seems much
interested so to do. Walk over to Broadway. Call up Bert and walk
down there along 8th. Delightful evening. She is alone. We decide

149. *The Seven Arts,* a journal edited by James Oppenheim, Van Wyck Brooks, and Waldo
Frank, appeared in 1917 and proved a shortlived but noteworthy example of the Greenwich
Village art scene of its day. Its emphasis was on new American art, and within its one-year span,
it published the first of Sherwood Anderson's Winesburg stories, Dreiser's "Life, Art, and
America" and his play "The Dream," a number of O'Neill's early plays, and essays by Mencken,
Brooks, Frank, Randolph Bourne, and others. Controversy over its pacifistic position at the
outset of World War I resulted in the withdrawal of its financial backing.
150. Dreiser's idea was to subsidize works of merit which would not otherwise be
published because they would offend the general public's taste and moralistic standards. He
proposed forming a board of notable critics to decide what works deserved such support.
Despite encouragement from influential writers and editors—and a number of spirited meetings
in 1918—the project never got beyond the stage of discussion.

to go to Lüchow's, where we dine and smoke till nearly 10. The way this restaurant has accomodated itself to American patriotism! We return here. Play cards and the Victrola, then to bed.

Sunday, December 2.

Clear and cool. Forget I have an appointment with Hutch at 10 and sleep until ten of. Look and think it says twenty after, and get Bert to call him up at Brevoort and say I'll be twenty minutes late. He thinks it's Mary Pyne and begins "Hello, Mary." Bert kids him. She didn't want to come along at first because she was sore, I am sure, that instead of falling for her and carrying her off he fell for Mary. I tease her and she denies it vehemently, but it's true—Bert couldn't be faithful to any one. Lill can. We dress and go over. Get there at 10:30. Find Hutch eating. Wants to help revive <u>Seven Arts.</u> Also create Society for Certification and Endorsement. Is going to Mexico at once for two months, but will be back living at Brevoort and ready to devote his time to this. Great talk about his hiring Bert as secretary. I describe him as a vulture circling in sky over my head. We leave. Come back here. Bert goes on up to her house. I build fires. Then work on <u>Free</u> till 2, when I call up Eddie Goodman (manager of Washington Square Players) and find that dress rehearsal of <u>The Girl in the Coffin</u> begins at 3. Go up to Bert's and want her to go along, but she wants to finish <u>The Mighty Rourke.</u> I go alone. At entrance meet Dorothy Cheston, who is coming to see it. She acts as though she were my sweetheart. We sit together. Rehearsal very bad. I don't like size of coffin, too small and too obscure. Stage setting not bad. Mr. Hohl doesn't look the part of Ferguson, somehow. I feel disgusted, but it goes big. Much applause. Helen Westley, Marion Powys and several others come down to where I am, crying.[151] Dorothy Cheston is wet-eyed also. They thought it fine. Sure it will go. I leave. Come down to <u>Herald</u> office and get 25 copies of <u>Evening Telegram,</u> from which I cut notices. These latter I mail to those who I am sure will want to know.[152] Come on here. Kirah calls up.

---

151. Helen Westley (1879–1942), actress. One of Greenwich Village's leading personalities, she helped organize the Washington Square Players in 1915 and helped found the Theatre Guild in 1919.
Marion Powys was the sister of Dreiser's friend John Cowper Powys.
152. Dreiser here is referring to notices of the Washington Square Players' production of "The Girl in the Coffin," which opened the following day at the Comedy Theatre in New York.

Wants to know how it came out. She is living with the Ben Allens, 177 West 77th,[153] and designing the next big Village Ball.[154] Wants me to see her. But her husband is coming Wednesday and I can't before then. Says she will call me up again. Work till 7. Then call up Bert, who comes down. We go to Italian place in Bleecker Street ($1.75). Leave there at 9:30. Come home. Play cards. A very cold wind out. She beats me at rum. Once more we talk of separation. Insists I am trying to throw her off because I get her a job with Doty. I deny it. We undress and go to bed. Affection returns. We indulge in a long round.

Monday, December 3.

Today is the opening of The Girl in the Coffin in New York. It has succeeded elsewhere, but I feel a little nervous about it here. Letters from Lill and Bertha, also from Carolyn Lawrence in re Sister Carrie and The Titan. Bert tries to be cheerful, but it goes hard with her. I can't make out whether she is anxious to get the Doty-Cosmopolitan job or not. Denies that she is, but I think she is. This may be the beginning of the end between us. I think it is. Her extreme grief and lovingness toward me would indicate that she contemplates changing. We dress and go to French place. I take along 5-gallon oil can and my 3-quart milk can. Leave both to be filled. Stop at corner and get the Williams Express to go to Mame's and get Paul's piano and deliver it here. ($5 to bring a piano two blocks!) They agree to have it here by noon. Bert and I go to restaurant and see Helen Freeman, who I expect will some day give herself to me.[155] She is a chestnut beauty, very plump and fair. Bert and I walk back to Jefferson Market and I get my milk can. She gets on car. Come down here and shave. Clara calls up. Wants me to go to The Girl in the Coffin with her. I refuse. Agree to meet her at 10:30 at Knickerbocker to hear how it comes out. Dress and take car for Kloster Glocke, where I am to meet Bert. Stop at

153. The correspondence at the University of Pennsylvania shows that Ben Allen was an acquaintance of Dreiser and that by 1934 he was a union official in Washington, D.C. No earlier letters survive to indicate the nature of their relationship in 1917.

154. This is probably a reference to one of the famous Greenwich Village Balls sponsored by Masses at Webster Hall. These costume balls and dances-till-dawn were the center of Village party life.

155. Helen Freeman was an actress connected with the little theatre movement of the period.

Lewisohn's en route and leave <u>The Mighty Rourke</u> for him. Go on
to restaurant. Find Bert and Mr. and Mrs. Lewisohn there. Tell
them of leaving story. He tells me Professor Stewart P. Sherman
(right-hand critic of <u>Evening Post</u> and <u>Nation</u> here) has published a
book in which he has an essay entitled <u>Theodore Dreiser,</u> in which
he denounces me.[156] (Lewisohn's book won't come out till next
year.) Bert and I go on to theatre. I walk up 5th Avenue to 41st
with her, where Comedy Theatre is. See first fire-sign ever carrying
the name of a play of mine. It is on a building overlooking library
(Bryant Park). Bert and I stand and look at it and she wants to
know if I get a thrill out of it. I don't—alas! Return here. She goes
on to theatre with Marion to see how it comes out. Post these
notes. Then go up to Knickerbocker to meet Clara and some friend
of hers, Mrs. Grueshlau. Have to wait until 11 before she comes.
She saw the first production of <u>The Girl in the Coffin.</u> It had 18
curtain calls and many cries for the author. We go to the Claridge
and watch the dancing. At 12 I return here and find Bert waiting.
Tells me the same story, 18 curtain calls and loud cries for the
author. Glad I wasn't there. In spite of her common sense I can see
that Bert is influenced by this latest success. Much more warm and
tender. We have some tea, then go to bed. Pleads she doesn't want
to go and be secretary to Doty but wants to stay with me.

Tuesday, December 4.
Clear and cool. A wonderful fall. Louise is coming today. I have to
call up Bert later and say I am going out this evening. We go to
French place for breakfast. Then I go to bank and draw $40. Walk
down 6th Avenue to Macy's and buy two pounds of cold cream for
the hands. Arrive here at 12. Want to change piano, but it is too
late. Call up Bert and tell her I have to go out to dinner. Louise
calls at 12:25. Have to ask Mame to leave. Louise arrives just after
Mame leaves. Has a fine pumpkin pie for me. Talks of going
skating and back before 8. I get angry and she admits she is joking.
We undress and lie all afternoon on rugs and pillows before the

---

156. Stuart P. Sherman (1881–1927), educator, author. In *On Contemporary Literature*
(New York: Holt, 1917), Sherman republished his famous attack on Dreiser, "The Naturalism
of Mr. Dreiser," which first appeared in *Nation* 101 (2 December 1915): 648–50. Sherman was
a spokesman for the conservative academic view of naturalism in modern art.

fire. Louise's wonderful body. Her experience with her ex-husband, who is now in love with her again, also Tony, also some old millionaire. Tells me of "Kitty Wiggles'" house in Philadelphia and the mirror ceilings. The mayor of Philadelphia is her friend. We copulate in various ways—standing, on her back, on her side, knees, etc—until we are exhausted. She is to leave at 8:34, but we don't begin to dress till 7:30. Take car to station. She buys ticket while I get chair car reserved. Time only for a sandwich. Wants to come once more before Christmas. At 7 Mrs. Jarmuth had called up and I appointed this station at 8:45. Find her and buy coffee and dessert. Wants to know more of story she is to attempt (a history of herself). Explains that she wants all rights, at least $600, etc. Her very great desire to seize everything after I have given her the idea and found the market irritates me and I decide to drop out and tell her so. We part smiling but irritated. At station I buy 6 <u>Globes</u> and 6 <u>Suns</u> containing notices of <u>The Girl in the Coffin.</u>[157] Call up Bert and go down there. Together we walk down here. Because Bert is thirsty I manage one more round, but feel bum.

Wednesday, December 5.
Bright and clear. Bert in excellent humor. We discuss the play and some books. Go to French place. Take tea instead of coffee. Can't get enough sugar to sweeten it. Learn from Bert that people coming from England are bringing sugar back here from there— and we are going without so England can have sugar! Come back here and straighten up. Mame comes and puts up new half curtain in front windows. Is fascinated by news of play. I work all afternoon steadily on <u>Free,</u> and get it finally revised. Bert still likes it. Call her up. She comes down here. We go to Chinatown, expecting to dine at Oriental, but change our minds and go to Chinese Tuxedo. Get stung. Food very bad. Used to be fine. Walk through Chinatown to 4th Avenue car and buy rice cakes on way. Come home, play rum until 11:30, then bed. Bert is going to her home town in Maryland for a week beginning Friday.

157. Among the first reviews of this production were Louis Sherwin, "The New Play: Theodore Dreiser and Others at the Comedy," *New York Globe and Commercial Advertiser,* 4 December 1917, p. 12; and "Three New Plays Given at Comedy," *New York Sun,* 4 December 1917, p. 5.

Thursday, December 6.

Clear and cold. This street outside (new 7th Avenue extension) is being put in good shape now. Bert and I go to French place. She is mad because I say Mame is coming with woman to clean. Thinks I am merely hurrying her out because some woman is coming to see me! Letters from Lill, Mrs. <u>Something</u> in Texas, Davis, and several others. At French coffee house we encounter Kirah and her husband. He looks very interesting (son of Frank Lloyd Wright, the Chicago architect). Bert accuses me of being embarrassed, which I was not. We walk across 11th and I return here. Various phone calls. Mr. Hedrich calls up. Wants to aid in helping re-establish the <u>Seven Arts.</u> I agree. Some girl calls up asking for "the author and playwright". Wants to come and see me at 2:30. I agree. 120 copies of the article on myself in Chicago <u>American</u> arrive. I clip and mark them and file for future use. Go to Brevoort at 1 to meet Mr. Hedrich. He proves a dull sort, of no intellectual significance, and I get rid of him as best I may. Meet Hutch, who is going to Vermont for two days. Come back here and clean up, filing letters, etc. The girl who called up fails to come. I build fires and work on <u>The Father</u> until 6.[158] Call up Bert, who wants me to come up there at 6:30. Have a premonition of evil of some sort. Don't know what. Go up there. She has just finished a 2d rough draught of <u>Free.</u> She likes it very much. We go over to Kloster Glocke. Leave at 9 and walk back here. Bert reads me <u>Magdalen,</u> by J. S. Machar, but we don't like it and quit.[159] Play some cards. Then quit and go to bed.

(Letter)

Another day after—
I really should have made carbon copies of the letter written the first day after we were together, shouldn't I? Because I could rave on today in the same way—only—still that wouldn't do either, because each time is more wonderful than the last—and yesterday I really believe was the best of all—Oh, Really, darling, wasn't it?
And do you know what you are to me? Besides all the other things—a

---

158. Dreiser never completed his story "The Father," but a thirty-two-page typescript with holograph revisions survives at the University of Pennsylvania. The character of the "father" follows the outline that Anna Tatum's story suggested to Dreiser, and that he was trying to incorporate into the central figure of *The Bulwark*: the successful, religious man for whom the shock of the modern secular world is conveyed through the character of his children.

159. *Magdalen* by J. S. Machar (1864–1942), Czech writer.

real inspiration because you make me feel I want to do big things and maybe can do them—It's so wonderful to have some one like you believe in one's ability—And then when you are such a glorious worth-while thing to me—I'd be a dub if I didn't feel impelled to make a try anyhow—so I'm going to. First I shall get the History finished—which may take just another week. In the meantime, too, I'll start something—the autobiography—I've "wirelessed" to you all sorts of lovely thoughts, sweetest longings—a really deliciously sad sense of missing you—do you get them, dear?

Louise.

And I smile at the picture you made carrying those big fat lumps of coal without any clothes on.

.   .   .   .

Sunday, December 16, 1917.
Very cold and clear. It's so cold we stay in bed till 10:30. Then get up. I make fires and dust rugs while Bert cleans up. At 11:30 we go to Brevoort. Same old crowd. I come back here and settle down to work revising <u>A Country Doctor</u>.[160] At 5:30 take a copy of <u>Free</u> over to Lewisohn's and leave it. Then to Bert's, where instead of going out we have a welsh rabbit. At 10:30 we come down here and go to bed. No news of any kind.

Monday, December 17.
Cloudy. Snowing. Very cold in back room. Negro comes at 8 to inquire about doing housework. Bert irritated by my not coming back. Always life is no good, a horrible nothing. We go to French place, then walk to 14th. I take 6th Avenue L to Globe Square. Buy 30 copies <u>Globe</u> of Saturday with N.P.D's attack to send to some friends.[161] Return here and mail these. Letters from Bertha, Masters, Lill, Mrs. Behr and others. Masters is coming this week.[162] At 3 I go out for a drink and a sandwich. Walk up to 14th. Buy two imitation mahogany candlesticks and some Xmas tree decorations for tree. Return here. Write Bertha, Lill, Arthur Hopkins, and some others. At 6:30 call up Bert, who wants me to come up there. She has made a steak-and-kidney pie. Go via 4th and 8th. Buy 3 papers which announce sinking of 14 English ships.

160. "The Country Doctor" first appeared in *Harper's Monthly* 13 (July 1918): 193–202; it was reprinted in *Twelve Men* (1919).

161. The *New York Globe and Commercial Advertiser* of 15 December 1917 published a review by "N.P.D." of Mencken's *A Book of Prefaces* (p. 8). Under the title "Dreiser and Mencken," it attacks Dreiser as a novelist and Mencken as his literary advocate.

162. Edgar Lee Masters (see p. 145, n. 45).

Marion is going out but eats part of meal with us. After dinner Bert
and I come down here. A fine frosty night. Snow like powder
under foot. Post these notes. To bed.

Tuesday, December 18.
Gray and muggy. Bert in a cheerful frame of mind. A good fire in
the back room. We go to the French place. I return here. Letters
from Lill, Lengel and others. Work till 12:30 on letters, then go
over to Brevoort to meet Louise. She is there, wearing a new set of
chinchilla (?) furs. We go to downstairs restaurant. I have a copy of
Stewart P. Sherman's book with its chapter on me, which amuses
her. She has just read the attack in the Globe. Tells me more about
her husband and her beaus. A short story covering him and her
occurs to me. I propose to call it Love.[163] She announces that she
has to be back at Waldorf at 7. Also that she can't stay. I say that is
all right—which enrages her. We walk across 8th to the L station
and she goes up saying goodbye. I wave her a farewell and come
on here. In two minutes the doorbell rings and it is Louise. She
complains that I don't care, but she can't help coming. We sit
before the fire, then undress and spread rugs and pillows on the
floor. A long delicious afternoon of sex. At 7 she dresses and
hurries away. I call up Bert, who is sick over the arrival of some
girl she knew in Baltimore, pregnant and in need of help. We meet
at Kloster Glocke and talk it over, then go to East Side, where I
buy her some silk underwear. At 10 we return here, have tea and
go to bed. Bert poses about in her new things to see how she
looks. I think up a plot for a new play—The Nobody, a story of a
poor drab of a woman who never gets anything.[164]

Wednesday, December 19.
Gray and muggy. New darkie cleaner comes, a crusty soul who
looks as though she took hop. Thinks four hours too short a time in
which to do work. Objects to cleaning windows. Bert weeping
because of girl friend who descends on her for support. I advise
getting a room for her elsewhere. Letter from Haggard of Hearst's
wanting to talk over serializing The Bulwark. Call up Goodman and

163. "Love" first appeared in the *New York Tribune,* 18 May 1919 (see n. 21, above).
164. This title does not appear on any published work by Dreiser or on any of his
unpublished manuscripts.

demand my correct check for $50. Call up Arthur Hopkins about The Hand of the Potter. Can't get him. Bert and I go to French place. Walk across 11th to 7th. She weeps at corner over her troubles. I return here. Hutch calls up about his mss. which hasn't arrived. Work on revising chapters 44 and 45 of Newspaper Days. At 5 I shave and dress and go to S. L. Rothapfel's for dinner.[165] He is a clever Jew who has become managing director of three great movie houses in New York. I am to meet Carlo Edwards (a musician) at the Knickerbocker at 6:15.[166] Stop by Bert's, hand her keys and work I have brought. She is not very cheerful, because I am going out. Take 8th Avenue line to 42d. Heavy blockade on account of snow. 8th Avenue is the street of trucks. Reach Knickerbocker at 6:30. Edwards is there and his faithful satellite. We go across to the Rialto, where I meet Rothapfel again. Plainly I have made a great impression on him for some reason. He is ridiculously impressed. He has some surgeon from the navy there, also his brother, and we pick up a Mr. Jacobs at the Friars Club. Get in his auto and ride to 450 Riverside Drive. That apartment! And his wife! Former kikes all, raised to ridiculous heights by wealth. He wants to play the pianola! Some owner of the Universal Film, a director whom I have never seen, and others. We talk of gambling, cargoes, life in the navy. I must say that Rothapfel in his way shows more tact than any. After dinner more friends—a sister-in-law, aged 19, and very pretty. The men start a gambling game, $1 ante, out of which I stay. A typical American parlor evening—puritanism, until all are thawed out and sure of their ground, then an eager seeking for freedom and pleasure! What a trashy land! Rothapfel has to return to his theatre (the Rialto) at 10. I seize the occasion to escape—as does the navy surgeon and Edwards. We talk of conscription and examinations, the surgeon and I. To Edwards' room in Rothapfel's car, after he leaves. Edwards plays me parts of Strauss's "Rosenkavalier," a rich, colorful work. I leave at 11:30. Find Bert in bed, looking very cute and sucking her thumb as usual. To bed and to sleep at about 12:30.

165. Samuel L. Rothapfel (1882–1936), motion picture and radio manager. Known as "Roxy," he gave this nickname to a chain of movie houses. During this period, he managed the Regent Theatre in New York.
166. Carlo Edwards (1891–1948), musician. At this time, Edwards was a conductor at the Metropolitan Opera House.

Thursday, December 20.

Grey and threatening snow. Bert and I eat at the French place.
Meet Fred Booth, whom I engage to look over The Hand of the
Potter before it goes on in January. Return here, work all day on
chapter 46 of Newspaper Days, which I finish. Also revise chapters
45 and 46. At 6:15 I call up Bert, who has arranged with Mrs.
Lewisohn to dine with us at the Kloster Glocke. She has a copy of
The Hand of the Potter, concerning which she says she has some
suggestions. Also Free. At 7 we meet. I believe the woman has
talent, but she bores me stiff. Makes several good suggestions
and several poor ones. Thinks it a better play than Hauptmann's
————.[167] At 9 we get out and come back here. Bert is bored. We
play cards. I suggest leaving for three months, and she gets terribly
wrought up and looks tortured. I tell her I'm teasing. We go to
bed. She cries in her sleep. The slavery of love!

Friday, December 21.

Clear and warmish, an April day. Bert and I have a long round
before getting up. Afterwards—because of last night, I suppose—
she speaks of us as being drawn together because both of us are "in
the gutter," which leads to a long argument based on what she
means. Jealousy is at the base of it, a desire to impregnate me with
the idea that I should stick to her. I entangle her in contradictions
and she becomes frightened. Finally we go to breakfast. Meet Jack
Powys and his Helen Robins at the French place. She is playing the
Virgin in the old English mystery play at the Greenwich Village.
We laugh and kid and accept invitations to join them Christmas
Eve. Bert and I go uptown afterward, to Woolworth's first for
candles and toys. Then I to the bank. Draw $50. Return here and
to work. Revise A Mayor and His People, also A True Patriarch.[168]
This takes til 5. Then I go to saloon at 8th and 6th and have a gin
rickey and a sandwich. Return here. Post these notes. Letters from
Lill, Louise, Mrs. Heyworth Campbell and others. Call up Bert at
6:15. We agree to meet at the Kloster Glocke. There is a coolness
between us because of her remark about both of us being in the

---

167. Dreiser here cannot think of the name of a play by Gerhardt Hauptmann (1862–
1946), German poet and dramatist who received the 1912 Nobel Prize in literature.
168. "A Mayor and His People" first appeared in Era 11 (June 1903): 578–84; "A True
Patriarch" first appeared in McClure's 18 (December 1901): 136–44. Both pieces were reprinted in Twelve Men (1919).

gutter. When we meet she is very anxious to make peace in some way. Crossing 23d Street I see 6 van-loads of wounded Canadians, landed at some dock here, I suppose. After dinner we walk down to the Academy of Music, but find W. B. Hart playing there and go on. At 14th and Broadway we go into a 5-cent place to see a Charlie Chaplin film, The New Janitor. Very good. On here, make tea and play cards. Then to bed.

Saturday, December 22.
Clear and warm. Give Bert $3 for dinner for the Forts tonight. We stop at French delicatessen and get two cans of mincemeat for pies, then to French place. Then to Woolworth's for four plates for tonight. Then to P.O. to mail Mrs. Campbell's books (Sister Carrie and the Plays). Then to 7th, where I leave Bert and take car to Wanamaker's. Buy two pr. bronze silk stockings for Bert, 1 pr. gloves, and 1 pr. "foot cozys" for myself. Can't get a shirt to suit. Return here. Revise various articles. Work till 6. Then go up to Bert's and get 12 bottles of beer en route. The Forts are already there. Fort presents To-pruno, his tomato and prune preserve. Very good. Bert presents a wonderful steak-and-kidney pie, spinach with eggs, hearts of lettuce salad, beer, wine, coffee and mince pie. Swell! We dine and talk till 11. Fort describes tenement life. His experiments in psychics. The impression of red and gold in the dark room and the dream of the two birds! The snowy bird emerging from filth! At 11 they go. Bert and I take hot baths. Then to bed here. Wade is away, Marion in Washington. A long heavy round—one of the worst. At 1 we sleep, or thereabouts.

Sunday, December 23.
A clear, sunny day. Wake in Bert's place feeling fine and we indulge in another gross feast. Then up to a hot bath and breakfast. Bert produces a fine breakfast of pancakes and creamed eggs and coffee. At 12 I come down here and go to work on Love. At 1 Mrs. Armstrong calls up. Wants me to come up to see her. She has an actual Stradivarius (1735), value $20,000, to show me.[169] Belongs to an old Southern family. Forced sale. I call up Bert and tell her. Then work till 5:30, shave and dress, go up and leave Bert

169. A violin by Antonio Stradivari (1644–1737), Italian violin-maker whose craftsmanship brought fame to his native Cremona.

the keys, then on to Mrs. Armstrong's. Meet the oldest daughter, who always hangs around me. (Very pretty.) Misfortune is pulling this family down. These girls, all in fashionable boarding schools once, are now looking for practical positions. Mrs. Armstrong, as pretty as ever, keeps up her spirits. Dinner at 7. The Sunday baked beans have been forgotten. We make the best of cold lamb and salad. Stories of war and transports. Upstairs at 8. Mrs. Armstrong and I sit apart and gossip. She wants to come and see me soon. An awful stuff of a politician arrives to court the cousin. At 10:30 I leave. Take Madison Avenue car to 59th and across down 7th. Find a small torn purse with nine coppers in it! Arrive here, find Bert reading and drinking tea. Tell her all sorts of stuff about the play Hopkins is going to put on. (Have told her I was dining with Hopkins.) At 12 we go to bed.

Monday, December 24.
Gray and snowy-looking. Warmish. Letters from various people, including one from the New York Santa Claus Association wanting me to buy presents for a little girl, Madeleine Sullivan, 432 West 58th. I show it to Bert and she is very enthusiastic about it, until I suggest that she do it alone, and then she carries on dreadful. Always when Bert gets mad or she doesn't want to do anything, she comments on her sad past life and weeps. I agree to go along, also to get the Christmas tree and take it up to her place, whereupon she cheers up. We go to breakfast at the French place. By chance meet Fred Booth and give him a copy of The Hand of the Potter to read. He comments on the old idea I had years ago for a national mausoleum a thousand feet high to be built in the centre of the U.S., (Kansas or Nebraska) on a flat plain ten miles square. Four diagonal "Avenues of the States" to approach it, lined or studded with steles (a la Washington Monument), 800 feet high. The mausoleum itself to be absolutely square, 1000 feet each way and 1000 feet high. The centre to contain pyramidal platforms for the tombs of the great dead, each platform a class or order. The floor space to be devoted to special tombs. The walls to memorial tablets. No one to be buried permanently until after 100 years have passed. Temporary entombments by order of act of Congress. An electric pipe organ distributed so that sounds are equalized to all parts of mausoleum at once. Music in this hall never to cease until

nation ceases. Booth wants his brother Franklin to draw a
double-page spread of it for Collier's, and me to write the
description of my idea (text). I agree. Take check for $15 to
Mame. Bert and I go to Hearn's at 14th Street to buy Madeleine
Sullivan a doll ($1.50), a baby carriage ($1.75), a purse (60¢), and
a train of cars ($1.30). Have them all wrapped up and take along
ready for delivery later in day. We walk over 14th to 8th and down
8th and 4th to 10th across to Bleecker, looking for a small tree.
Finally find one for 75 cents. I hire a boy to carry it and my
package to Bert's and leave her at Charles and Bleecker. Her face
falls. I agree to come up early.

Return here, answer notes and work on Love until 4:30, when I
call up Bert. Go up there and help her trim the tree, which puts
her in a good mood. Then we go up to Madeleine Sullivan's,
arriving at 6. A filthy Irish tenement. Madeleine a sweet dirty kid.
We leave Santa's gifts and come away. Go to Pabst's (58th) for a
highball, then to Far East for dinner. No sugar there, and I get into
a row with the management. We leave at 8:10, come down
Broadway and watch demonstration of new railway lock system.
They are selling stock. Then on to 42d across to 5th. Take bus
down. The three showy, hard-faced society women, one especially.
Get off at 12th and go up to see Jack Powys. Marion in bed with a
cold. Helen Robins there. She is playing the Virgin in The Chester
Mysteries being given at the Greenwich Village Theatre at 11:45
this same evening. Odd to see the Virgin, her arms and shoulders
bare, skirts pulled up to her knees, smoking a cigarette—or many—
but so it is. She agrees to give me a bottle of Gordon gin she has
in the A.M. because she don't want it. Jack reads some of his verse.
At 10:30 Helen takes a taxi to the theatre. Bert, Jack and I go
around to the Purple Cat (W. Washington Square), where two or
three shabby girls are dancing with young boys. The usual
atmosphere of college boys trying to be devilish and finding it
difficult. Jack tells us of his youth in England. Also of his father and
mother. Also of John Ashurst, librarian of Philadelphia, who has a
great pornographic and demoniac collection.[170] At 11:25 we go
around to the Greenwich Village Theatre to see the Mysteries

---

170. John Ashhurst, Librarian of the Free Library of Philadelphia, 1916–32, who
donated his collection of pornography to the Free Library.

performed. Nothing to them much. Old-fashioned churchly processional stuff, the Adoration of the Magi, etc. Crowded house. 300 turned away. They could make thousands out of this by going on with it and distributing handbills to the churches. (And this was the best the Middle Ages could do after Sophocles, Euripides and Aeschylus!) At 1:15 Bert and I return here, build up the fires and have some tea. Then to bed.

Tuesday, December 25.

Christmas. It is raining. Letters and postcards from a score of people—Lill, Bertha, Louise, etc. Bert inclined to be fussy but changes when she receives a dozen pairs of silk stockings. We indulge. Letter from <u>The Saturday Evening Post</u> accepting <u>Free</u> $750.[171] Weekly check from Washington Square Players for $50. This makes $350 paid so far. $150 still due for this twelve weeks engagement. Bert and I decide to eat at her house. She is very angry over the presence of Wade, who lives on her without compensation. We dress. I shave while Bert goes on up and prepares breakfast. Go to drugstore and mail her letter. Think of going to Helen Robins for the gin, but haven't time. Bert's place looks spick and span. We light the Christmas tree. Have breakfast. Bert reads the letter from the enthusiastic patriot in Washington D.C. to Marion. He helps the government in the war by not having new clothes made. Leave and walk across 19th down 6th to Helen's. Meet her at the door (37 West 10th). She is just going over to take dinner with Jack, Dorothy Cheston and Ralph Roeder.[172] Wants me to come to tea some day and meet Frank Conroy, her director.[173] He may want to put on my plays. Return here. Send telegram to Lill and receive one, two minutes later. Package of candy and handkerchiefs from Bertha, and I sent her nothing! Fall to work on answering and filing letters and working on <u>Love</u>—or trying to. No interruption of any kind. At 6 I dress, call up Bert. We agree to go to the Beaux Arts. Meets me at 18th Street L. We get a fine table. The crowd of men next to us, bankers

171. "Free" appeared in the *Saturday Evening Post* 190 (16 March 1918): 13–15, 81–89.
172. Ralph L. Roeder (1890–1970), journalist, author, actor.
173. Frank Conroy (1891–1964), actor, director. Conroy was born in England and came to America in 1915. In 1916 he arranged for the construction of the Greenwich Village Theater and directed it for the next three years as a repertory theater.

and movie promoters. The young brunette who was popular with them all. Bert wants to drink at the women's bar. The man who looked like ex-Governor Francis of Missouri,[174] who eyes Bert trying to flirt with her. At 9:30 we leave. Come down here and read Chekhov. Bert's gift to me. At 12 we go to bed.

Wednesday, December 26.
A grand round. Bert looks odd in her smart Christmas togs this A.M. We go to French place, then take picture (Peter's of me as a Daimio) around to Rotherberg's to be framed.[175] We mistake Rotherberg's for Hearn's. Leave, walk across 14th to 7th. I return here. Petronelle calls up. Wants me to take dinner with her and Ducky Cady tomorrow. I agree. Kirah calls up. Tells me of her married life and the ball she is getting up. Wants me to come down some afternoon next week. I wish she wouldn't, really. Letter from Eveanna (Bertha), complaining of bad treatment. Also from Mary Stewart, wanting me to come and see her. Work on Love till 4:30, then to corner saloon, 8th and 6th, for a gin rickey. Return here. Call up Bert. She suggests getting a steak and coming up there. I buy one, also a can of mincemeat and several frankfurters, and go up. Wade is there, a dull creature. Bert prepares a fine meal. After dinner Spafford comes in and tells my fortune. An amazing fortune really, the new woman to come into my life, travel, money. I am to enter national affairs. Describes the story I am writing, accurately too. Predicts America will not win the war. She leaves at 10. Bert and I come down here. Have tea. Bert beats me at rum. We go to bed.

Thursday, December 27.
Cold and clear. Bert and I have breakfast at French place. Same old routine. I have a dinner invitation with Petronelle. Work on Love (a hard story to write). At noon call up Bert and say I have to go out and suggest she use the two seats at the new Rivoli. Find her at Miriam's (128 & Madison). Says she will stay up there instead. At 4

174. David Rowland Francis (1850–1927), governor of Missouri (1889–93).
175. A daimio is an hereditary feudal nobleman of Japan. The drawing Dreiser is referring to is by P. B. McCord (the "Peter" of *Twelve Men*); it appeared in the *New York Evening Post*, 2 December 1916, and is reproduced on the following page.

"Daimio" Caricature of Dreiser

go to a saloon at 8th and 6th for a gin rickey. Lunch is on yet and I wait for it. Come back here and work till 5:30. Then shave and dress. At 6:30 go around. Petronelle is as cute as ever. Reminds me of Kirah. Has same art tastes. She is roasting the chicken in the gas stove. Ducky Cady is helping. Petronelle and I make love by snatches. They both tell me of their experiences working for ????? Company, just before the Christmas holidays, painting Christmas cards at $6 per day, 9 to 5. The manager! Union labor! Their Christmas tree! I make a mess of carving the chicken, which isn't done. And no sharp knife. Their songs afterward. We talk of food cost, St. Louis, the St. Louis girl who is coming on to capture me (but I don't like her picture). Return here at 11:30. Find Bert playing solitaire. We have some tea, then go to bed.

Friday, December 28.
Warmish and pleasant. Bert in the dumps. Will take no interest in anything. At 8 the plumber comes to fix the toilet flush, which has been running all night. We lie in bed while he works. Afterward get up and go to French restaurant. Then I walk with Bert to 14th and take L to 42d. Draw $50 on Washington Square Players check. Return here, get fur coat and take it to the furrier (30 East 10th). New otter collar is to cost $30. Taking out and repairing lining, $25. Return here. Ramsey calls up. Wants to come at 5. I let him. Mordell calls up. Wants to come at 5. Ditto. Work on Love till 4:30. Seem to get along fairly well. Go to saloon at 8th and 6th for a gin rickey. (That world of buzzing politicians!) Return here. Ramsey comes. Has been to see The Girl in the Coffin. Very excited about it. Thinks I ought to do plays only. Has a copy of "Plays of the Natural, etc." which he wants me to autograph. Mordell comes. Is looking more prosperous these days. Tells me of a roast on me by Professor Paul Elmer More in a book called The Supernatural in Modern Literature.[176] At 6 they go. I am taking a

176. Paul Elmer More (1864–1937), critic, philosopher, editor. Along with Irving Babbitt and Norman Foerster, More was a leading spokesman for the so-called New Humanists who attacked the artistic and philosophic basis of modern literary naturalism. For an example of his thoughts about Dreiser, see More's *The Demon of the Absolute* (Princeton: Princeton Univ. Press, 1928), pp. 64–69. Here Dreiser may be confusing something written by More with Dorothy Scarborough's *The Supernatural in Modern English Fiction* (1917), which devotes some space to Dreiser's *Plays of the Natural and the Supernatural* (see pp. 208; 278–79).

bad cold, nose running and throat sore. Call up Bert, who wants me to come by for her. She has revised Change[177] and chapter 44 of Newspaper Days. Letter from Louise. We go to Kloster Glocke. It's becoming very much better. A good dinner. We then return here, via car. Stand at 8th Street a long time in Wanamaker's door to keep out of icy wind. Make tea. Bert reads me two of Chekhov's stories. We bring down bed from rear room and put it in front of fire. The flickering light and Bert's voice, after we go to bed, soon puts me to sleep.

Saturday, December 29.
Very icy. At 6 Bert gets up and lights gas and oil stoves. At 8:30 we get up and dress. Hot baths. Mailman comes at 8, bringing me a letter from young Robinson, editor the Medical Review of Reviews, who is enthusiastic about The Hand of the Potter. Wants to help Hopkins put it on. Bert and I tease as usual. I try to cheer her up but she is down on life in general. We go to French place. See Randolph Bourne. I go round to Washington Square Bookshop and get a copy of Mrs. Lewisohn's (Bosworth Crocker) The Last Straw.[178] A cheap imitation of Hauptmann (the end of The Teamster especially). Return here. Meet Elise Green, my colored woman, coming away in the snow. We return. She cleans up, mailman comes, bringing Japanese ivory from Lill. Representative of the Theatre Magazine calls up and makes a number of flashlights of me at my desk. He leaves. Card to Lambs' Club from Rothapfel.[179] Post these notes. Go to work on Love. Elise leaves. Uncertain if she can come any more. About 3:30 I go up to Rotherberg's to see if drawing is framed yet. Also stop at National Lunch for a sandwich. A biting day. Priced red box plant (dyed) for my window box. Return here. Work on Love until 5, when Fred Booth comes, bringing his copy of The Hand of the Potter.

177. Two paragraphs of "Change" were published in *Pagan* 1 (September 1916): 27–28. The full essay first appeared in the *New York Call*, 26 January 1918 (*Call Magazine*, p. 1); it was reprinted in *Hey Rub-a-Dub-Dub* (1920).

178. Mary Arnold Crocker Lewisohn (?–1946), author. Under the pen name "Bosworth Crocker" she wrote, among other things, *The Last Straw*, a play performed by the Washington Square Players.

179. Dreiser is probably referring to The Lambs Club at 130 West 44th St.

Thinks it's fine. Wants a few minor changes made. Tells of home life around Carmel, Indiana. Leaves at 6. I call up Bert, who has received a basket from home. She invites me up there. Going up I find a young cat freezing. Take it along. The row between Marion's cat and this one, which I name Blizzie because of the blizzard. We watch them and keep them apart all during dinner and after. Later Bert and I bring Blizzie down here. A dreadful night. 6 below. All water pipes frozen, very little coal. We shut off all but middle rear room and read Chekhov until 12, then sleep.

.　　.　　.　　.

Sunday, February 17, 1918.
Clear and crisp. Bert and I get up by 9:30. Decide to have breakfast up at her place. Dress and walk up Greenwich Avenue. Stop in Italian delicatessen for sausage and peppers. I forget my molasses. Before we leave bell rings. It's a boy with a telegram from Louise, but we think it is some one else and won't let him in. Before going up to her house I go round to the telegraph office at 14th and 7th to get my telegram. It is closed. Go on to Bert's. A wonderful breakfast. Marion gets up and joins in. Leave at 12. Come down here and go to work. Lengel calls up. Wants me to come up there to dinner. His wife's father has just died and she is in Chicago. Decide to go because the day is so fine. 6th Avenue L to 115th, then car. His queer sister-in-law. The baby. We go for a walk up the Grand Concourse. Changes in that street. New subway to Van Cortlandt now open from Mott Haven to the park. He wants the loan of my studio from 8 to 10 Tuesday. I object. Discussion as to faithfulness, divorce, etc. His attitude toward his wife. Agrees that she may do as she chooses and he wouldn't leave her. Must have a little love in his life outside of her. We take L back. Dinner is ready. Discussion of critical papers and room for new critics. His eagerness for sex is so great it is contagious. Recaptures strange, lost emotions for me. Leave at 6. Call up Bert and meet her at 7 at the Far East. We decide to go to Reisenweher's grill and do so. Excellent meal for her, $1.50. Afterward come down to her place for a hot bath (my pipes are still frozen). She reads me a Strindberg story. Leave and come down here and go to bed. I feel a little tied to her, hence restless and bored.

Monday, February 18.

Bert and I get up at 8:30. Nice and crisp. Letters from Lill and some secretary of some bedding company in Milwaukee, who likes my books. Lots of joshing, and we go around to the French place. I get Bert up on plea that I am on jury duty. Leave her at 10. Return here and go to work. No letter from Louise, which angers me. Work on Love revision till 6. Am going to call Bert when Benson calls up (Arthur Benson) and reminds me that I have an appointment with him at the Breslin. Call up Bert and get her to come along. We go to the Russian Inn. Much talk of socialism, prohibition, the Germans, the English, Wilson, the Bolsheviki, etc. A good dinner. Leave and walk down 5th Avenue to the Brevoort. Bert is a little bored by Benson. While we are in Brevoort Mrs. Putnam (Nina Wilcox Putnam) comes in and hails me. I avoid her eye. Bert gets jealous. When she comes over and talks to me Bert is furious and wants to fight. I calm her. Mrs. Putnam makes some remark about Benson which angers him. Wants me to help Harry Kemp and his Thimble Theatre, in which she is interested.[180] Has new serial story starting in Saturday Evening Post.[181] Party breaks up with bad feeling. Bert accuses me of having relations with or pursuing Mrs. Putnam. Come back and quarrel until bedtime. It is all so silly. She is insanely jealous and furious over nothing.

Tuesday, February 19.

Gray and damp. Begins to sprinkle at 9. Bert still in gloomy mood over Mrs. Putnam. We decide to have breakfast up at her place. I shave while she goes up and gets things ready. Get up there by 10. Excellent cakes and chops. At 11 I come down here. Call up Gleason. No answer. Get to work on Love. It's a slow job. Build fires. So many interruptions. Hutch calls. Has Abraham Cahan (author of The Rise of David Levinsky) over at Gonfarone's. Wants

---

180. Harry Kemp (1883–1960), novelist, poet, editor, dramatist, biographer. Called the "Byron of the Village," Kemp was a romantic bohemian who, at this time, was married to the actress Mary Pyne. He appears in Dreiser's writing as Doane in "Esther Norn" (A Gallery of Women). Kemp took over the management of the Thimble Theatre from Thomas Edison, Jr., and he used it to produce his plays and those of his Greenwich Village associates.

181. Nina Wilcox Putnam and Norman Jacobson co-authored "Every Little Bit Helps," which ran serially in the Saturday Evening Post, 16 February 1918, pp. 5–7, 78, 81; 25 February 1918, pp. 17–19, 60, 62, 65.

to bring him around. I agree. They come in 15 minutes. Cahan is also editor of The Jewish Forward, leading East Side paper.[182] I try to get Bert, to ask her to come, since she admires him so. Can't get her on phone. A charming type. Very simple and interesting. We talk till 4. Make an appointment for Friday evening here. Smith calls up. Has ticket for The Master. We agree to meet Thursday at 6 at Jack's. I return to the short story. Call up Bert and go up there. Take along a steak. She is preparing dinner. Tell her of Hutch and Cahan. Marion eats with us. After dinner she goes out and we decide to sleep up there. Bert continues reading A King Lear of the Steppes, by Turgenev. We lie in back room. Marion comes back. At 11 I decide to come down here alone, and so tell Bert. She wants to come along but doesn't insist. At 11:30 I walk down here. Sleep in back room. Very pleasant for a change.

Wednesday, February 20.
Get up at 8:30. Beautiful day. Warm up the place and call up Bert, who wants me to come up there. Do so. A fine breakfast.
Afterward I return here. Mame comes to clean up. At 12 Louise calls up. Is at Penna Station. Wants to come down. To give Mame time to get out I agree to meet her at Brevoort. I am angry at Louise for not writing, and abuse her shamefully. She threatens to leave, but doesn't. Has a pie for me. Reminds me a good deal of Lill. Afterward we walk over here. Talks of leaving at 2. Has appointment. Monthly reds prevent rutting. I get angry and tell her to go and stay. She starts, but comes back, throws herself on lounge and weeps. Start to console her, which ends in the usual thing. We undress and lie on the floor until 5, when she has to go. I call up Bert. Say it is so fine out. We decide to walk up 8th to Reisenweber's. En route we change our minds and come back and have dinner at her place. Finish reading A King Lear of the Steppes, then turn in and have a long round. Afterwards sleep.

---

182. Abraham Cahan (1860–1951), novelist, journalist, editor. Cahan came to the United States from Russia in 1882; by 1897 he had become the first editor of the socialist daily *Vorwaerts* ("*Forward*"), the leading Yiddish journal in America. Cahan deeply impressed Dreiser, who said of him, "I don't believe in saints, but there's one man on this earth who strikes me as being one, and he's Abraham Cahan." (Quoted in George Jean Nathan, *The Intimate Notebooks of George Jean Nathan* [1932], p. 52.)

Thursday, February 21.

Wake up at Bert's. A fine springlike morning. Sun pouring in Marion's office window. We get up at 8:30. Cold bath. Bert goes out for ham. Excellent breakfast. Try to make out my fortune in coffee grounds but can't. Come down here and build fires. Old De Mucci comes for his coal-bag. Take up revision of <u>Love</u> and complete it. At 12:10 Louise calls up and says she wants to see me. Is at Waldorf with her husband. I tell her to come down. She comes and we play about, finally retiring to couch for a fierce round. She is very delightful, so simple in her moods and frank, a beautiful girl. Tells me the story of the daughter of the street preacher led astray by the traveling salesman. Her husband's modified anti-German attitude. Leaves at 2:30. I work on <u>Love.</u> At 5:30 Irwin Granich comes but I am shaving and dressing to meet Bert and Smith.[183] He tells me of the state of the I.W.W. in New York. We walk to L station together. Ride up 6th Avenue L to 42d and walk to Jack's. Find Bert inside waiting, also Smith. Sit down and have a meal. Smith's account of Aleister Crowley, the English pederasts, life in the Village. Seems to know of Crowley and Vierick.[184] At 8:10 we leave for the theatre (meal $7.10). Go round to the Hudson to see <u>The Master,</u> with Arnold Daly.[185] An excellent play. The ideas accord much with my own. The after-piece, by Daly, a most asinine thing. Leave and go to the Claridge. I am sore because of Lengel's trying to borrow my studio. Have hot ryes with rum. A soldier collection follows. Every one asked to take a chance at $5 on a hundred-dollar bill. At 12:30 we leave. Bert and I walk down here. Decide to go to her place, but the janitor is in at the switchboard, and I walk on down here to get my keys, intending to return. Meet Bert, running and out of breath, at 11th and Greenwich. She has decided we had better not stay at her place. We turn in at 1 or 1:45.

---

183. Irwin Granich (pen name, Mike Gold) (1893–1967), journalist, novelist, editor. Gold helped define the term "proletarian literature," and his novel *Jews without Money* (1933) is a model of the type.

184. Aleister Crowley (Edward Alexander Crowley) (1875–1947), author, poet.

George Sylvester Viereck (1884–1962), journalist, author, poet. Viereck's pro-German sympathies during World War I caused him the type of trouble that Dreiser and Mencken always feared for themselves. In fact, when Viereck approached Dreiser to allow him to publish *The "Genius"* in his pro-German journal *The International,* Dreiser refused.

185. Arnold Daly (neé Peter Christopher Arnold Daly) (1875–1927), actor.

Friday, February 22.

Washington's birthday. Gray and cold. Bert a little angry because I wouldn't pay much attention to her the night before. Won't have anything to do with me. I get up and build fires. Decide to let her go up to her house alone and eat, but she refuses. We go to the French place. Letters from Louise and Masters. I return home and call up Smith and arrange for submitting to Arnold Daly mss. of The Hand of the Potter. Call up Harpers but they are closed. Mame calls up and wants to come over and clean up. I let her. Almost faints here. Weeps over her down and out state. Her fine relatives now refuse to do anything for her. I loan her five. We talk of the coal situation, still so acute. She leaves at 2. I write various letters due, then turn to revising Phantasmagoria, which pleases me a good deal.[186] It is much better than I thought when I laid it aside last year. Kirah calls up. Tells me she has left her husband. Is now with Lola May. Wants me to come and see her. Work on without interruption until 5:45, when Hutch comes. Wants to know if Bert is coming. He is stuck on her. At 6 Cahan comes, and Bert a minute later. We discuss Russia, the Bolsheviki, Dostoevsky, and the East Side. I make drinks for the crowd and we decide to go over to Allaire's. We walk. En route Cahan tells me his plan for a new magazine to be more human than the Seven Arts. We reach Allaire's and find Bert and Hutch seated. A fine meal. Long talk of life on the East Side, the work of Cahan as an editor, work of Russian nihilists, Berkman,[187] Emma Goldman, Kropotkin,[188] East Side literary characters. Cahan tells of his early years. Plots for stories.

186. "Phantasmagoria" first appeared in *Hey Rub-a-Dub-Dub* (1920); it was later added to a limited edition of *Plays of the Natural and the Supernatural* (1926).

187. Alexander Berkman (1870–1936), anarchist, author. Born in Vilna, Russia, Berkman came to the United States in 1887 and became involved in the radical labor movement in New York City. During the Homestead Steel strike in 1892, he attempted to kill Henry C. Frick, general manager of the Carnegie Steel Company. As a result, he served fourteen years in prison and wrote of his experience in *Prison Memoirs of an Anarchist* (1912). In 1916 Berkman began a campaign on behalf of the imprisoned labor leader Tom Mooney, a cause Dreiser took up years later. In 1917, Berkman opposed American entry into World War I, an activity that led to his and Emma Goldman's arrest in the summer of 1917, their imprisonment for two years, and eventual deportation to Russia in 1919.

188. Peter Kropotkin (1842–1921), geographer, founder of the Russian and English anarchist movements, author, Russian revolutionary. Kropotkin was the foremost theorist of the anarchist movement.

Saturday, February 23.

Wake up at 8. Severe pain in back relaxing. Am nervously
somewhat wrought up over amount of work on hand and need of
cash. Bert rather sensuously inclined and we come together. A cool
bath afterwards. She goes out and gets pork chops and makes cakes.
We talk of Russia and Hutch and Cahan. Tells me of Hutch's desire
to seduce her. Wanted to know if she really loved me. Her high
opinion of Cahan. I leave and come down here. Letters from Lill
and the Pullman Company. Phone calls from Clara, the translator,
Karsner,[189] Lengel, Louise. Louise is just leaving for Philadelphia.
Lengel wants Masters to help his wife with her estate. Karsner to
call here Monday, etc. Build fires. Call up Wells of Harpers. He
offers me $275 for The Country Doctor, which I refuse. Feel very
much depressed. Start in revising Love, a story of which by now I
am sick. Am troubled by Bert's attitude. Her psychic distress over
leaving me reflects itself in me. Call her up at 5:30 and she comes
down. Long session with her in my arms. She makes me feel that if
she leaves me I will go to bits. Her psychic depression is immense.
We finally go to Mouquin's. I take only oysters. Bert a full meal.
Stay there until 10:45, when I leave for the Russian Inn. Lie to
Bert about whom I am going to see. Meet Clara and Mrs.
Grushlau, Mr. and Mrs. Rosenthal come later. We have a dandy
meal. Mrs. G. and I get to flirting. Looks and reminds me of Anna.
She tells me funny stories. Finally she tells me she likes me and that
we will come together if I wish. "All good things come slowly."
Holds my hand. Promises to call me up Monday and will come and
see me. Gives me a sense of great animality. Very cute and pretty
she is, very. (The doctor sitting alongside never discovers what is
going on.) I return here at 1. Bert is up reading. We go to bed.
Her psychic ache is gone and I feel better also—almost bored!

Sunday, February 24.

A trying, psychic day. Very clear out and warm. Bert very
affectionate but a little depressed over her determination to leave
me. Is going to Washington. Shows me offer made by a former

189. David Karsner (1889–1941), author, editor, journalist. At the time Karsner was
editor of the socialist New York Call. Among other books, Karsner wrote a biography of Eugene
Debs and Sixteen Authors to One (1928), which contains a chapter on Dreiser as "America's
greatest living novelist."

employer to put her in charge of bureau. Can't stay because I won't
be faithful to her, won't introduce her to all my friends. Goes on
up to house ahead of me to get breakfast. I stay here and shave.
Then stop in at Schmeelk's for some ham. Walk up Greenwich and
get seven eggs and a jar of Beechnut bacon. Enraged over delay
caused me by Schmeelk. After breakfast Bert and I discuss her
leaving. She irritates me by her queer logic. Is going to nothing
better. I come back here ready to give her up. Start revising
Phantasmagoria. Day is too fine. Can't work. Call up Bert. Invite
her for a walk. Very lonely for her. Go up to her place. We take
8th Avenue car to 59th subway to 149th (Mott Haven), L to
Kingsbridge Road. Get off and walk back along Grand Concourse
to Mott Haven and 125th Street and 8th Avenue. Our loving
mood. Amazing feeling I have for her. Almost the wildest kind of
romantic love. Can't explain it. Intensely happy in her company.
We discuss love, books, Col. Hersey. I tell her of my past life in
Mott Haven, also proposed stories of Lola and The Mystic Hand,
also The Old Neighborhood.¹⁹⁰ Buy her a bunch of sweet peas.
We take L to 59th. The young Cuban girl with the big teeth and
her two American girl friends. Go to Reisenweber's. We come out,
walk down Broadway to 7th Avenue, then take car home. Smarty
girl in the Mrs. Vernon Castle get-up who got off down here.¹⁹¹
Her father and mother! We buy oranges and lemons and come
here and go to bed. I think I feel only what Bert feels—no more.

Monday, February 25.
Clear and warm. Am due at Court of General Sessions at 10:30.
Jury duty. Letter from Louise saying she is coming Thursday. Lill
and Bertha also. Papers declare Germany, via V on Hertling, has
accepted Wilson's peace terms. But will that end the war? Does
England want it ended peaceably? Bert and I in best spirits, get up
and go to Child's at Broadway and 8th. Immediately after I hurry
away to court. Wrong car. Walk from Canal Street on. Row with
court clerk over unsigned summons. Dismissed till March 4th.

---

190. The titles "Lola" and "The Mystic Hand" do not appear among either Dreiser's
published work or his unpublished manuscripts. "The Old Neighborhood" first appeared in
Metropolitan 49 (December 1918): 27–30, 46, 48–50; it was reprinted in Chains (1927).
    191. A style made popular by Mr. and Mrs. Vernon Blythe Castle, a popular dance team
for a decade before Vernon Castle's death in an airplane accident in 1918. Irene Castle made
fashionable the bobbed-hair, short-skirted "getup" that Dreiser refers to.

Return here via Broadway and 8th. Stop at an expressman's and get him to call at Mame's for the bookcase I am buying. Meet Mary Pyne. Walk back with her to 5th. Meet Hutch, whom she is going to meet. He wants to call a meeting to discuss the Society for Certification and Endorsement. Return here. Meet young Ernest Rowan, the actor, outside.[192] Tells me draft stories. Return here and settle down to work. Revise Phantasmagoria and finish it. At 4 Belle Grushlau calls up. Wants to meet me somewhere tomorrow. I agree. D. F. Karsner, editor of The Call, calls. Wants me to give him an essay. I give him The Right to Kill. Is publishing a sketch of me next Saturday.[193] Mame comes and cleans up. He goes at 5:30. She goes at 6. Call up Bert. Wants me to come up there to dinner. I go. Excellent. Steak and other things. We finish reading A King Lear of the Steppes, then come down here and start reading The Bible in Spain, a delightful book.[194] At 12 we turn in. Bad night, for some reason. Can't sleep.

Tuesday, February 26.
Bright but cold and very windy. Bert and I in pretty good spirits. I take an ice-cold bath. No letters. I am debating all the time in my mind whether to take the offer of Harpers ($300) for The Country Doctor or turn it down. Decide to turn it down. Also to turn down the request of the Evening Mail to write an introduction to Miss Beckley's novel to be run serially.[195] Bert and I go to the G. Washington restaurant, 104 Sixth Avenue. Buy our own butter and take it along. Bert still brooding over whether to leave me or no. Can't make up her mind and is very unhappy. Doesn't want to. Has

192. At the University of Pennsylvania, there is a letter from Ernest Rowan to Dreiser, dated 7 March 1917. Rowan tells Dreiser that he is tired of acting and wants to do newspaper work. This diary entry suggests that he is still acting nearly a year after writing the letter.
193. "The Right to Kill" was published in the New York Call, 16 March 1918 (Call Magazine, pp. 1, 12–13). On Saturday, 2 March 1918, the New York Call published a sketch by David Karsner which praised Dreiser as a writer and an advocate of literary freedom (pp. 20; 16).
194. The Bible in Spain; or, The Journeys, Adventures, and Imprisonments of an Englishman in an Attempt to Circulate the Scriptures in the Peninsula (1842) by George Borrow (1803–81). Borrow was an English scholar whose missionary project for the Bible Society was to promote Anglican Bible studies in Spain. Dreiser's interest in The Bible in Spain may have stemmed from Borrow's attack on the Roman Catholic Church's influence in that country.
195. Zoë Beckley (1875–1961), journalist, author. Beckley worked for the New York Evening Mail in 1917–18 and published A Chance to Live in its pages.

made up her mind that the woman character in Love is Louise and that I am hopelessly in love with her! I don't seem able to disabuse her mind of this. We buy 1 1/2 pounds of mincemeat for a pie and she leaves. I return here and go to work. Call up Haggard and offer him Old Rogaum and His Theresa, which he wants to see at once. I proceed to read it over and revise it. Yewdale comes with some pages he wants me to inscribe for a French War Book, to be raffled off. Has news of Jones, and plays on the piano. I go to Farrel & Son and order a ton of coal. No check in advance no coal! Return here. Mrs. Grushlau calls up. Wants to meet me at the Samovar at 4. I agree. Letters from Lill, Abraham Cahan wanting a picture, Smith wanting to get up a dinner to me in case The "Genius" case is decided in my favor, Edith Jarmuth describing a lecture on The Girl in the Coffin at Columbia! Fall to work again and finish Old Rogaum. First proofs of The Hand of the Potter arrive from Boni & Liveright. Proofs of the Zoë Beckley story from The Mail. At 3:10 I shave. Then take all of them and carry them up to Bert for examination. Leave and go on to the Samovar, 6 East 36th. Bella is there, very pink and gay. Reminds me of Bertha. Wants plenty of time to think. Hartridge comes by and joins us for a while.[196] Won't say whether she'll come here or not. At 5:45 we take bus and ride up to 86th. Her little plump hands! Her ambitions! We get off at 86th and cross to the park. I take 8th Avenue car down. Her great fear of her husband. Go to Bert's. Dinner is quite ready—steak-and-kidney pie. Marion is there and irritates me greatly. Leave at 7:45 and come down here to work, write letters, post these notes, mail letters. At 10:30 Bert shows up. We read The Bible in Spain, a delicious if religious book.

Wednesday, February 27.
Clear and warm. A lovely day. Who says pleasant experiences don't go in spells? Get up at 8:30. Decide to go to French pastry place. Letters from Lill, Louise and Bertha. Also from Karsner, Cahan, Salisbury—all pleasant. Cahan is writing an article. Karsner sends copy of his. Salisbury wants me to organize American literary

196. Correspondence at the University of Pennsylvania reveals a friendship between Dreiser and Clifford W. Hartridge (1867–1937), a prominent lawyer who gave up his New York practice in 1914 and spent the second half of his career writing fiction and history.

radicals. Go with Bert to breakfast. She is in a fine mood. Then up
to 18th with her, where I take L to bank. Draw $40. Return here
and write letters. Go over to coal man and pay for a ton of coal to
be delivered. Take car from there and go to P.O. at 9th and 13th.
Cash old stamps. Go from there to Bramhall Players, 138 East 27th,
to see Kirah in The Silent Assertion.[197] She was fine. Came back
here. Meet Benson at 27th and 6th. Stop at Park & Tilford's and
get a bottle of Gordon gin. They sell it 55¢ cheaper.

Thursday, February 28.
Very bright and pleasant. Owing to being up so late the night
before don't get up till 10. Call up Bert and arrange to go up there
for breakfast, taking up ham and pancake flour. Have a devil of a
time finding the latter. Walk up and finally get it. The wonderful
car service on 7th and 8th Avenues! Owing to the fact that Louise
is coming and that I was out the night before I feel I ought to say
something about not coming to dinner, but don't. Return here and
build fires. Mame comes, but I send her away. Mrs. Grady
downstairs tells me the coal man came and dumped my coal in the
cellar in spite of anything she could do. I call up Farrell & Son and
demand a man to change it. Bella Grushlau calls up. Wants to
discuss our future relationship, but I haven't time. Karsner calls up.
Is coming Saturday with his wife. At 12:30 Louise calls up. Has just
arrived and is coming down. I write some notes while she is en
route. Comes, as sweet as ever, a hoyden who loves only success.
Has a new hat. We talk over new developments, stories she has
read, her sister, her husband, etc. By degrees we sink into the
carnal mood and undress, spending a vigorous afternoon in each
other's arms. At 6 a last round in front of the mirror, standing.
We dress and go to Mouquin's. She has to leave at 9. I give her
Claire H. Uecke's mss. to examine for me. We take 6th Avenue car
up and have a happy meal. Outlines the psychology of her married
state exactly. Her husband's point of view. Hers. His prayers. His
lectures on her "carnal nature." She leaves at 9. Is going to leave
him. Wants to come and live with me. I think it would be
advantageous, since she is really brilliant. I go down to Bert's. She
is almost in a state of collapse over my neglect. We come down

197. Kirah Markham was appearing in "The Silent Assertion" by Butler Davenport,
which had opened at the Bramhall Playhouse on 15 December 1917.

here. I quiet her down. We read George Borrow's <u>The Bible in Spain.</u> Then to bed.

Oh, how tired!!

Friday, March 1.
Bad morning again with Bert. She is unhappy and distant. It is very gray outside and heavy. Day begins well for such a day with the return by Haggard of <u>Old Rogaum</u> as having no dramatic interest. Criticism from the <u>Dial</u> (Chicago) and other papers point out how foolish Professor Sherman as well as Mencken are to include any one so insignificant as myself in any volume of criticism, even though they do denounce me. Certain days! Certain days! The plumber comes to fix a leak. Says he called here twice yesterday but I was out—which might help a little with Bert. We dress in silence and go to French pastry place. According to the papers, Britain and the other Allies scornfully reject the German peace offer, only to be drubbed some more later, no doubt. Pecksniffery on the one hand, moralistic Christian tosh on the other. The British carry greed on the one hand, religion on the other. After breakfast I return here, depressed by the weather. Insist on Bert's taking the photo today to Cahan, also the mss. of <u>The Country Doctor</u> to Harper's. Mame comes and cleans up. Borrows five. Letters from Lill and Bessie Jones.[198] Boring, both. The rent collector comes. I revise the galley proofs of <u>The Hand of the Potter,</u> completing it at 4:30. Make out various checks, gas, telephone, laundry bill, and write Auerbach, Lengel, Yewdale. Call up Yewdale and inform him papers from <u>Sun</u> have not come. The Washington Square Players call up, wanting to sell four performances of <u>The Girl in the Coffin</u> to some little theatre in Detroit. I miss Louise much, the scamp. In the evening Bert and I dine at Reisenweber's, then go to Colonial vaudeville. A poor show. Back here at midnight via 9th Avenue L. To bed.

Saturday, March 2.
Warm and clear. Owing to having sent Smith's letter to Auerbach he calls up, wants to arrange to see Smith about the proposed dinner to me. I need a second set of proofs for Arnold Daly and

198. Bessie Jones carried on a correspondence with Dreiser from 1917 to 1919. She seems to have been an eccentric who believed that the American Indians were the original ancestors of all mankind. Beyond the fact that she lived in California, the letters reveal nothing about her; her occupation or whether she ever met Dreiser remains unknown.

call up Boni & Liveright to see if I can get them. Call up Smith and arrange for a lunch at Auerbach's at 1:30. Arrange to call for proofs at Little & Ives (423 East 24th) before noon. Bert and I go to 42d Street for breakfast. She is in a gay mood. Porkless day. Leave her outside and go to bank. Draw $50. Go to Little & Ives and get the proofs. Then here just in time to get Smith, who is waiting. We talk over the dinner. Then to Auerbach's, who is August Belmont's attorney.[199] He is very enthusiastic over the dinner idea. Wants Col. Harvey to preside. Excellent lunch. Tales of Pulitzer and Yerkes.[200] It is arranged that Auerbach and one ———— are to get together and arrange things. We leave at 3:30. I return here to work on The Weavers until 5:30,[201] but Karsner and his wife call. Bring copies of the article about me in the Call. Want to discuss life. Get rid of them at 4:10. Then work on The Weavers until 5:30. Call up Bert and we arrange to go to Newark. She comes here and we start, walking to Christopher Street subway. Arrive at Newark at 6:10. Walk and see things. Bert in a gay mood. Then to the market, where she eats fifteen oysters standing at a stand. We then go to dinner, but her appetite is gone. Walk about, buy soap, shac, garters, lemons, a steak for breakfast, and return here. Read The Bible in Spain. Then to sleep.

Sunday, March 3.
We rise at 9:30. Having brought stuff from the Newark Market, Bert decides to cook it here—steak, bacon and pancakes. I have The Hand of the Potter proofs to revise for Arnold Daly, an extra set. Get Bert to help me, and by 2 we have them cleaned up. Clara calls and wants me to come up. Mrs. Grushlau and Mme. Keller are to be there for lunch.[202] I refuse. Walk with Bert to 19th. Take proofs to Daly (22 East 62d). Ride up on bus. His very exclusive

---

199. Major August Belmont (1853–1924), financier, son of the banker August Belmont (1816–90).

200. Joseph Pulitzer (1847–1911), newspaper editor and publisher, sponsor of the famous Pulitzer Prizes.

Charles Tyson Yerkes (1837–1905), financier. Yerkes was the model for Dreiser's Frank Cowperwood in *The Financier* (1912), *The Titan* (1914), and *The Stoic* (1947).

201. Dreiser never completed "The Weavers," a play written in the mode of Gerhart Hauptmann's play of the same name and concerned, like Hauptmann's, with the influence of modern mechanistic labor on the human spirit. It remains at the University of Pennsylvania in an eighteen-page typescript.

202. Dreiser may be referring to Helen Keller (1880–1968), the famous counselor on international relations for the American Foundation of the Blind, memoirist, essayist.

apartment. Come down on Madison Avenue line. A lovely day.
Work on letters and correcting <u>Phantasmagoria.</u> At 6 call up Bert.
We go up to Reisenweber's, dine and stay there till 9. Walk down
Broadway and 7th, then car home. Drinks, a bath, <u>The Bible in
Spain,</u> then to bed.

Monday, March 4.
Wake at 7:30. Have a cold and am not feeling quite as well as I
should. The necessity of cleaning up many tasks presses on me.
Also the intense craving for a wider life. Sometimes I think my life
is intensely full—but still—
    Bert in a clinging mood. Her possible loss of me weighs on her.
We get together physically, although this phase of her is no longer
of any great importance to me. Due in court at 10:30. No gin in
the house, and I feel the need of a drink. We go out. Haven't
time to eat. Leave Bert at 8th. Take crosstown to 4th, stop in at
St. Regis quick lunch for a cup of coffee. The girl managers eating!
Hurry on to court. In time for roll-call. Excused till 2. Come up to
Park & Tilford, via new Broadway subway, and buy a bottle of
London Dry Gin. Then home in 6th Avenue car. Mame here and
cleaning up. Make her out a check for $4. Write letters to Cahan,
Davis, etc. Get old newspapers ready to roll. At 1:30 leave for
court. Get there in time for roll call. More explanations of the Rose
case. I am not chosen as a jury and allowed to go. Off for two years
now. Come up to Wanamaker's. Buy bookcase shelf-pegs. Come
here. Mame still here. A phone call from John Williams, mgr (the
man who produced <u>Justice</u>) wanting to see <u>The Hand of the
Potter.</u>[203] I agree to get him a copy. Return to my work. Clean up
more letters. Phone from Salisbury (author of <u>The Career of a
Journalist</u>) wanting to call. Messages from Bella Grushlau and
Yewdale. His cuts her off, and she doesn't call again! He wants to
do another article. At 5:15 Salisbury calls. Wants to organize a
magazine and club or society to further letters (I am to do it!). At 6
he leaves. At 6:15 Rolland comes (ex-star in <u>Youth</u>).[204] We are to
go to dinner together and afterwards to the Greenwich Village

<hr>

203. John D. Williams (1882–1941), producer. Williams's production of "Justice," with
John Barrymore in the lead role, opened at the Candler Theatre in New York on 13 April 1916.
    204. Dreiser is referring to the Washington Square Players' production of Miles
Malleson's "Youth," which opened at the Comedy Theatre on 20 February 1918 and ran for
twenty-one performances.

Theatre. Before this I call up Bert saying I can't come up. Angry as usual. We have a drink, then go around to Broad's in 3d Street between Sullivan and West Broadway, and have a fine meal. The people who greet me. Rolland is reading <u>A Traveler at Forty</u> for the first time. Mr. and Mrs. Williams announce that they are reading it aloud to each other. Rolland describes his early life, his father and mother, etc. We go to the Greenwich Village Theatre. See <u>Karen.</u> The obsequious Gallant.[205] A fair play. Too propagandistic. Leave at 11 and come here. Drinks and a fire. More of Rolland's Canadian life. His one-night stands. The blazing train at Emporia, Kansas. The prairies in North Dakota. No salary. Thirteen rôles to master. The great West's love of Shakespeare.

He leaves at 12:30. I call up Bert. She won't come down. Angry.

Undated:

She gives me her letter to read in my absence. It being a classic, I append it here.[206] It does not make me angry. In a way it is true— only Bert is bluffing also. Return to her apartment and give her her choice of leaving or behaving. Her manner changes at once. Doesn't want to leave me. Will try and do better. I am very tired. Bert is really not self-sufficient. She needs a man—must have one. I feel sorry for her, truly, but what can you do in this world, which is so unbalanced, all running after the few successful, all ignoring the hopelessly poor or unsuccessful or defective. Life is made for the strong. There is no mercy in it for the weak—none.

205. Dreiser may be referring to Barney Gallant, the co-owner and host of the Greenwich Village Inn on Sheridan Square, one of the most popular night spots in the Village.
206. Estelle Kubitz did not copy this letter into her transcription of the diary.

HOME TO INDIA NA, 1919

▭

Dreiser's most memorable visit to Indiana occurred in 1915 when he and artist Franklin Booth took an automobile trip together through their native state. From that tour came Dreiser's autobiographical volume *A Hoosier Holiday,* for which Booth did the illustrations. Four years later Dreiser again visited Indiana, and he kept this diary during his trip. He received a cordial reception from childhood friends and from his grade-school teacher May Calvert Baker, but the memories and dreams called up by the visit were disquieting.

Kosciusko Court House, Warsaw, Ind. 1-WL.

Kosciusko County Court House

A Trip to Indiana
June 15th to July 3nd
1919

A Trip to Indiana

Sunday—June 15—1919— Breakfasted with Bo.[1] Took Subway to
23nd, then crosstown to Erie Ferry. Got my bags out, having
packed & put them here Saturday P.M. Had my ticket & Pullman.
Crossed over to Hoboken & found train partially ready. Put in
bags. Saw baggage cars & engine attached. We pull out at 10:30.
The Meadows. Uninteresting run to Congers—then beauty begins.
Charming marvelous scenery beyond Tuxedo. Grows more
impressive all the way to Port Jervis. The blonde girl in my car
who looked liked Mrs. Sweeney. I dine & read The Crimes of Jared
Flagg—an impressive book.[2] The beauty of The Delaware
River, North West of Port Jervis. Finally we hit the Susquehanna &
follow it to Elmira. I see a rainbow. Then comes the Canisteo.
Wonderful Scenery to Hornell. I dine & retire. The summer life
about the station in Hornell. I think of my trip with Booth.[3]

+

Monday— June 16— 1919—
Awake at Mansfield. Old Soldiers at Lima. Due in Huntington at
12:10 (noon) & arrive on time. Charles Arnold—Wholesale
Drygoods & May C. are at Station.[4] We drive out to Glen Elm—
Mrs. Craig—Virginia—Calvert. Her children—I lunch. Unpack.
Rest under trees—then cut weeds under the peach trees until Dress
& Arnold arrives with his car. We see Huntington. Visit his mother
in his large home. Then see where aviation field is to be placed!

1. "Bo" is one of the nicknames Dreiser used for Estelle Bloom Kubitz.
2. *The Crimes of Jared Flagg* by Jared Flagg (1857–1926). Originally published in 1904
as *Flagg's Flats,* the book is an exposé of the New York police department that stemmed from
Flagg's treatment by the police while he was having housing difficulties in New York City.
3. Franklin Booth, Dreiser's collaborator on *A Hoosier Holiday* (see p. 213, n. 25).
4. May Calvert Baker (1864–?) was Dreiser's seventh-grade teacher at the West Ward
school in Warsaw, Indiana. Dreiser's memory of her kind encouragement is recorded in *A
Hoosier Holiday* and *Dawn.* At the time of Dreiser's 1919 visit, she was teaching at Huntington,
Indiana.

The Wabash & Little Wabash here. New Bridge. We arrive at
Country Club. Prohibition, but drinks in basement. I meet Mr &
Mrs J. Wallace Caswell & their daughter. She has lived in
Greenwich village. He mfgs. Cedar chests. They are rich, many
others—men, women. We dine. Then bowl on lawn. Then swing.
The dancing & bright talk. A 9:30 I leave for a second meeting at
the home of the Supt of Public Schools. A great crowd. We talk
until midnight. The talk. Then home. Mrs. Baker announces plans
for next day. I fall asleep listening to distant trains on the Wabash
R.R.

Tuesday, June 17—1919
    Up at 10 and breakfast then. Sit on lawn. The attentions of
May C. B. The flowers. Wood doves. At 11—Mrs Caswell &
daughter come to drive us around town & see husbands factory.
We do so. His history. Once a drunkard. Made grills—now cedar
chests. Government War work. $600.00 a month useless now. Mrs.
C— is 1$\underline{st}$ Reader in the C. S. Church. We return home at one. I
idle about & read. Much mail arrives. I hear of Oliver Sayler & a
dinner being given for me that night.[5] Beautiful day. My yellow tie.
Crowd arrives. We sit on lawn. Dinner afterwards. The talk.
Snakes, flowers. Whiskey, travel, books, summer resorts. After
dinner a reporter from Times arrives for interview. He gets it—
What his editor told him to get.[6] More talk. The new C. S. church.
The great tree to be cut down.[7] Argument. Crowd leaves at 11.
May C & I sit out & talk until 1 A.M. about old Warsaw people.

Wednesday—June 18—1919.
J. L. Sunhart & wife arrive at 10 & we start for Warsaw Ind. He is
supervisor of music in the schools of Huntington, Ind. We go via

    5. Oliver M. Sayler, drama critic, author. At the time of this visit, Sayler was the dramatic
editor of *The Indianapolis News.* By 1920 he had moved to New York where he built a career
on his writing, specializing in books on the Russian theater.
    6. This interview was printed as "Dreiser Favors Federal Control; Hits Financiers," *The
Huntington Press,* 18 June 1919, p. 4.
    7. An undated clipping, apparently from *The Huntington Press,* is laid into Dreiser's diary
at this point. Entitled "Large Elm to be Saved," it tells of plans to preserve a giant elm tree that
was to have been destroyed so that a Christian Science church might be built on a particular lot
in Huntington. The citizens of Huntington, led by their mayor, decided to raise money to help
the Christian Scientists relocate their church. The elm was to remain and "stand as a memorial
to Huntington county's soldiers in the war."

Bippus, Servia, Bolivar, N. Manchester, & Silver Lake into Warsaw.
The scenery! The fields of grain! Western prosperity. We stop at
Silver Lake. Its present condition. Talk of Dunkards. The Dunkard
with the Honey Colored beard. I read of Dunkards abandoning
beards & hats! Bedsteads made into lawn benches. We arrive
Warsaw. The Catholic church. Our old house gone. We visit Center
Lake. Have a soda in Buffalo St. Meet Mr. Funk. Jud Morris is in
town. Go get him & take him to Eagle Lake (Winona). The feast
on the grass. Jud. The McClung Co. The Firemans parade—The
firemen! We go back to Warsaw. Call on Walter Chipman, now
Treas. of Syracuse (N.Y.) University.[8] Then we go and see John
Shoup in the bank. Then meet old Orren who ran wagon works—
an old man. We then visit Pike lake. The Lillies. An old ache. Take
Jud home. Then we go out through Whitley County to So. Whitley.
The bad roads. A bluebird. We reach Collamer—a mill & dam. We
get coffee in S. Whitley. The old man. Dine by the falls. The
excellent smoked ham. Mrs. Sunhart tells me of her life. Taught
school. Is trying to get up socially. Playing the ideal mother stuff. A
kind of fool. Back to S. Whitley. A band concert is on. We stop.
The village band stand ("Presented by business mens association").
The Little Dog that wanted to be taken along. The boy bandmaster.
We start for home at 10—18 miles to do. There by 11:30. The old
days of the farm. We stop for all. The sweet air. Life passes so
achingly. God! May & I sit out under the stars & talk till one. She
talks of forwarding my books & spreading my fame. I tell her what
I think of Huntington.

Thursday—June 19—1919. We are to go to Lake Maxinkuckee this
A.M. Are to start at 9:30 with the Caswells who are going to
Chicago. I get up very early & am very tired. Breakfast at 9—.
Caswells arrive at 10:30. A great machine. We pack in many bags.
Off accross country—Bippus, Servia, N. Manchester, Akron,
Athens, Rochester (Lake ——), Lake Maxinkuckee. (Culver Ind.)
The Lakeview hotel. Mr & Mrs. Charles Short. Mrs. Short used to
sit behind me in school. Dinner. The black servants. Short—his
history. We sit out on the balcony. Maxinkuckee. The boy twins

8. According to the Syracuse directory of this period, Walter W. Chipman was a cashier
at the university.

Charles & Calvert. It begins to rain. I go to barber shop for a shave. Later row on Lake. Later still—dinner. The dead fish. Small pox in Culver. I take May C. rowing & fishing. The sky—the wind. Get back at nine. To bed very tired & have dreadful dreams.

Friday— June 20— 1919

Up at 10. No breakfast. Loaf around until noon. It is gray. After dinner we go over to visit Culver Military Institute. The Gymnasium & swimming pool. The dining hall! The Office! The riding academy. The uniforms. Type of boy that goes there. We sit on lake shore & talk. Come back & sit on porch. Then we go swimming. Then dinner. Then boating. The wonder of the lake. Home at nine. Talk on porch. We go to bed at 11. P.M.

From a bronze tablet on a Rock at the Culver
Military Institute, Culver, Ind.

Lest We Forget

That out of wild nature we are come, that our instincts are great, our wisdoms little, that the main current of our will is still like the green moving waters & our reasoned choices like the flutter of foam on its surface, that we became citizens but yesterday & were bred in the wilderness.

Saturday June 21—1919. Breakfast at 9. May C & I walk to Something Pier—on the lake. The porches of the houses, swings. Histories of people. Whats wrong with the middle west. What right. Back at 3 P.M. by boat. The horse shoes. I go for sandwiches. Send Bo 25$\underline{00}$. The village restaurants. The dance hall. The boys show us tricks. We decide to return to Huntington by train. Dinner. Auto to some station (De Long). Story of Pat Chapman— her husband & Charline. Her death. We arrive in Huntington at 10:30. Home & sit on stone balcony.

Sunday—June 22— 1919 All day at home. The Craigs are not about. Breakfast at 10. Read. Sit in shade. Go to P.O. to get special deliveries—1 from Lill[9]— 1 from Addison Parry. Walk through

9. "Lill" is Lillian Rosenthal (see p. 150, n. 8).

town. See the life. Return & dine. Too much to eat. The birds. We loaf about till 6:30. Then order a taxi & go to Oliver Saylers. Western courtesy. His garden. Sick father. Look at Russian Revolution & Russian Theatre & Art pictures until 11:30. The Craigs come by & pick us up.

Monday, June 23— 1919 Am supposed to be up by 8:30 but dont make it. The Eben Leshes are coming. He is a lawyer & oil promoter. We are to go to Webster Lake in Kosciusko County to fish. Leave at 10. Mrs. Lesh. Lesh. Gray & rainy at start. Clear at Webster Lake. The Yellow Banks. Dinner. We fish. Lesh alone in boat with me. A long talk. No fish. Others in other boats catch plenty. The Sapps (Mr & Mrs).[10] Mrs. Sapp sings. Mr & Mrs Glenn Brown. The Joker. The meal in the cottage. We start for home at 9— Arrive at 11. Wonderful ride. The Lights. The spot light. I am due to leave in the A.M. at 10:30 for Indianapolis.

Tuesday, June 24nd 1919
Up at 8 A.M. to pack. Horribly tired. Breakfast at 9. May C is greatly greived at my going. Her offers of a home. I am to go by Interurban. Car Leaves at 10:50. Arnold comes at 10:20 for me. We talk of life here. He knew Paul[11] & Pete Darty in N.Y. Invites me back. The ride to Peru. To Indianapolis. Muriel gets on at Carmel.[12] I recognize her. Some friend rides with her. Indianapolis. The Interurban Terminal. Then Union Station. I get hat cleaned, buy an umberella. It rains. Take a taxi to Golden Hill. 3$\underline{00}$ for 5 miles. The great storm. The great house. Mrs. Parry. Miss Elizabeth Parry, Addison Parry. Dinner. We take until 10:30. Miss Brown— Addisons fiancee, comes over. I go to bed. A wonderful room.

---

10. Arthur H. Sapp, an attorney at Huntington, Indiana, who avidly read Dreiser's books and corresponded with him into the 1930s.

11. Dreiser's brother Paul Dresser (1857–1906), the songwriter who composed the Indiana State song, "On the Banks of the Wabash."

12. Muriel Cain, whose correspondence with Dreiser survives at the University of Pennsylvania. In 1919 she wrote him from three places: Fort Wayne, Indiana; Carmel, Indiana (where Dreiser sees her on the train); and Grand Rapids, Michigan. Her letters always return to the same theme, her need for money. One dated 17 July 1919, is at once desperate ("I haven't eaten since yesterday and I can't go to work because the only dress I had fit to wear has given out.") and apologetic for not meeting Dreiser during his visit to Indiana. The correspondence does not reveal how long or under what circumstances they knew each other.

Once occupied by Maxwell Parry. The literary pride of the family. He was killed in the war—an aviator.[13] Am very very tired. Rest but don't sleep much.

Wednesday, June 25th 1919
Am about to call up Maxwell at 10 A.M. when I get up but am informed he is arriving at noon with letters, etc.[14] Mrs. Parry & I discuss the history of C. M. Post—his wife & daughter & her attitude toward Mrs. Post. Maxwell arrives. His age. Letters from Lill & Muriel & a telegram & special delivery from Muriel. We have lunch. Maxwells old smile. He relates the history of his discovery of who Shakespeare was. We walk around the grounds. The decayed formal garden— weeds— and a weeks wash. The fountain. History of the woman doctor who was murdered—and the spirit. We discuss a future life. Sit about until 5—Then I go down with him, meet City Editor, Managing Editor—indeed all editors—and Anna Nicholas.[15] My picture in file. Another letter from Muriel. At 6 P.M. I leave John & walk about city. Visit a cafeteria. Then go into Circle theatre. The singer. Leave at 10—on account of dog out at Golden Hill. The blind & deaf man teaching the boy how to signal him the time. Arrive home at 11. House silent. Answer various letters. To bed at 1 A.M.

Thursday June 26th—1919
Breakfast early with Mrs. Parry. Read & write some letters. Decide to fish a little in stream at foot of garden. No luck. Walk back & find Elizabeth playing. We become friendly & she

13. Dreiser knew the Parry family through John M. Maxwell. Mrs. Hessie Daisy Parry of Indianapolis was Maxwell's sister; Addison Parry was a son of Mrs. Parry who was in business in Indianapolis. He wrote Dreiser on 21 June 1919 asking him to stay with his family when he came to Indianapolis. Addison Parry's daughter Isabell met Dreiser after she moved to New York City to teach school there; Elizabeth Parry was another daughter who remained at home in Indianapolis.

14. John Milo Maxwell (1866–1929), editor, author. In 1892 Dreiser met Maxwell, who was a copy editor for the *Chicago Daily Globe.* Dreiser, at the time not yet twenty-one, was impressed by the veteran editor who helped smooth the way for him on the big city newspaper (see *Newspaper Days,* chapts. 7–14). Maxwell left Chicago in 1901 and returned to his native Indianapolis. In 1919 he was working for the *Indianapolis Star,* which ran an article on Dreiser during his visit. Maxwell was also at work on a long study, "The Man behind the Mask," which tried to prove that Shakespeare's plays had been written by Robert Cecil, first Earl of Salisbury. Dreiser encouraged him in this undertaking, and tried for years to find Maxwell a publisher.

15. Anna Nicholas was an editor on *The Indianapolis Star.*

telephones for me to the Heineys. I go down at one to mail letters. Stop in & see H. P. Lieber. He shows me his store & theatre. His war attitude. Leave there & walk out South to the end of a car line. Thoughts as to how to write "Her Boy".[16] Return. By a pair of shoes, a razor strop & drink & take car to Golden Hill. Letters from Gaylord Yost[17] & Mrs. Baker. Messages from Lieber, Heiney & others. We dine, sit out on porch. A long talk with Addison Parry. He tells me about his business career. At 11 P.M. to bed.

Friday, June 27—1919 — I have a dinner engagement with the Yosts—an afternoon call to pay at the Heineys. Interview with me in A.M. Star.[18] Message from Maxwell to come down & have my picture took. Breakfast at 9 with Mrs Parry & Elizabeth. Mrs. Parry tells me of Max Parry & her husband. Elizabeth plays on piano. I walk with her on the lawn. Take car down to P.O. Send Bo 25. Then to Star. Have photo taken. Buy 100 copies of paper. Take car out to Coliseum Ave (College Ave Car—marked Fair Grounds). The boy in the cowboy outfit. Our talk. His history. The Heineys. They warm up. Heiney's History. The alledged American Book Trust. Our Schools. His boy who wants to write. We & the boy ride down town together. I advise him. Go back & buy my papers. Wrap & leave at Interurban Parcel room. Go to Claypool, set about & study crowd. Get a shave. The blues. Take car to 2735 & meet Yost. I like him. George Chambers Calvert is present.[19] The Yost Apt. His wife. "The Shades of Death," "Turkey Run". We fall to talking. I hear of Laughing Gas[20] & Miss ———. The excitement it

16. "Her Boy" is a long, uncompleted story which survives in holograph and typescript in the Dreiser Collection at the University of Pennsylvania. It tells the story of a lower-class Irishman, Eddie Meagher, who turns to crime after a hard childhood. It resembles Stephen Crane's slum stories and is partly based on the career of one of Dreiser's Irish neighbors in Indiana. It is one of Dreiser's numerous experiments with criminal narrative in the years before he began writing *An American Tragedy*.

17. Gaylord Yost (1888–1958), composer, violinist, author. In 1919, Yost was teaching at the Indiana College of Music in Indianapolis. He was the son of Charles E. Yost, who founded the Ohio newspaper *The Fayette Review*. Gaylord Yost gave up his career in music and became the paper's editor and publisher in 1951.

18. "Noted Novelist Visits In City," *The Indianapolis Star*, 27 June 1919, p. 5.

19. George Chambers Calvert's correspondence with Dreiser indicates that he did free-lance writing.

20. Dreiser's "Laughing Gas" was produced in 1916 by the Little Theatre Society of Indiana, a group based in Indianapolis. The play opened at the Masonic Temple on 7 December 1916 and ran for three performances (see p. 188, n. 83).

caused. Talk of the Middle West. Addison Parry comes but they want me to stay on. At 11:30 the younger Parry arrives & carries me up in his car. They have arranged to have me painted by L. S. Baus—a fine portrait painter their.[21] First sitting at 9:30 A.M.

Saturday, June 28—1919 Up early. No breakfast. Meet Gaylord Yost in Claypool at 9:30. We stop in Cafeteria for a cup of coffee. To Baus studio in the Union Trust Bldg. Baus. The pose. He makes a fine start. Is a German by descent. I pose until noon. Calvert arrives. I leave & visit local art museum. Some fine things. Go down town. Into Catholic Cathedral. Get my papers, envelopes & a marker. Return to Golden hill, fold & stuff all the papers. Dress in light shirt. Go down & wait for Stuart Walker & His Mother who are coming to dinner. The Walkers— a dull posy pair.[22] Learn that Margaret Mower is in town.[23] Am invited to his theatre. Elizabeth & I go with Walker & his mother. We see "Milestones"—poorly done. Afterwards I take E. to The Athenaeum. Then Taxi home. We go to kitchen for food. Love stuff until 1 A.M. To bed.

Sunday, June 29—1919 Up early to sit for portrait. Get down town at 10. Baus waiting. Finishes picture by noon. Yost comes. Also Calvert. Also Maxwell. Elizabeth has promised to have lunch with me & Maxwell. All consider portrait a success. Baus recits his history. Maxwell & I go to Claypool & wait for Elizabeth who comes at 1:30. At 3 we walk north to the Blocherue—Calverts Home. Maxwell leaves us. A reception in my honor. Yost plays— Also Elizabeth— We leave at 6 & walk out Meridian St. She shows me their old home. Tells me of her fathers life & attitude. At 7 we arrive at Athenaem. Another dinner in my honor. The Liebers. Talk until 10. Mrs. Parry & Elizabeth are taken home. I stay with the crowd till 12:30 & am taken home. The German cause. I make a number of friends.

---

21. Simon P. Baus was a local painter who later exhibited his painting of Dreiser in Indianapolis. On 13 July 1919, Baus wrote Dreiser, sending "3 photoes of the portrait I painted of you" and asking him to show one to Franklin Booth, the noted illustrator from Indiana.
22. Stuart Walker produced Dreiser's "Laughing Gas" in Indianapolis in 1916.
23. Margaret Mower was an actress who knew Dreiser in New York.

<u>Monday, June 30—1919</u> I am leaving Tuesday A.M. at 7. Breakfast at 9. Elizabeth not about. John comes out at noon. Stays all P.M. I address & stamp all letters. We visit Mrs. ＿＿ ＿＿ Meiers. She reads my palm. Future looks good. Am to live to be 80. At 5:30 John & I go down town. We go to Union Station & I buy a ticket to Toledo. Then to Star office. Meet Prof ⌞   ⌟, once of University of Illinois. Then we go to Dinner. (Chinese) Then to Circle theate. We meet the Liebers. Then to two reformed saloons. Then to Star. I talk to Anna Nicholas & win her over slightly. Then to Prof again. Then to another saloon. The decay of youth. Then to Golden Hill. I pack my bag. At 1 A.M. bid John good by. To bed.

<u>Tuesday, July 1—1919</u> Up at 5:30. Dressed by 6:10. Go down to breakfast. Young ⌞   ⌟ Parry gets up & gets his car out. I am raced to station. Just make train. The girl who flirts with me until we reach Bellefontaine. The hot ride to Toledo. The thin traveling salesmen. His joke "Arrive Wednesday night God willing. Thursday whether he is willing or not." I lunch in Toledo. Take interurban car to Fayette. The country. The big Dempsey-Willard fight on.[24] Arrive at Fayette at six. Yosts father.[25] The home. Mrs. Yost. The superintendant of schools! Talk until 11. Ice cream & cake. To bed in the Blue Bird room.

<u>Wednesday, July 2—1919</u>
   All about the Yost family. A fat land. The barns. The fields. The dull farmer. His interest in my books. An automobile ride. Breakfast. Elbert Hubbard.[26] The "Genius". Take Eleven A.M. car for Toledo. Read Loebs Physiology of the Brain.[27] Toledo by 2 P.M. Buy ticket. Go out & see the fight Coliseum. The Hunchbacks.

---

24. The heavyweight championship fight between Jack Dempsey and the then champion Jess Willard took place in Toledo on 4 July 1919. Dreiser's diary entry for 2 July suggests that he saw one of the pre-fight events in which the two men sparred to make extra money.
   25. Dreiser went to Fayette, Ohio, to visit Gaylord Yost's father, Charles E. Yost. The elder Yost had read Dreiser and had written him, praising his books. Their correspondence began in 1917 and continued into the 1940s.
   26. Elbert Hubbard (1856–1915), businessman, printer, editor, writer. Among Hubbard's other successful ventures, his series of "Little Journeys" to the homes of notable men and women made him one of the most famous literary entrepreneurs in America.
   27. Jacques Loeb (1859–1924), biologist. Loeb's theory of animal tropism was an early influence on Dreiser's thought. Dreiser is reading Loeb's *Comparative Physiology of the Brain and Comparative Psychology* (1900).

Return. Go to train. The hot car. My berth partner. She tries to make friends. I refuse. Read my book. Dinner on train. The advertising man at Cleveland. The wreck at Dunkirk. I sleep in an up berth. The four school teachers over the way.

A TRIP TO
THE JERSEY SHORE, 1919

◻

During the nineteen-teens and twenties, Dreiser occasionally took short holidays at resorts on the Jersey coast. This brief diary records a weekend trip that he took in July 1919 to Ocean Grove and Asbury Park. This interlude suggests the tenor of his life-style in the years before he met Helen Patges Richardson.

ON THE BEACH AT ESPLANADE.   ASBURY PARK, N. J.

The Beach at the Esplanade, Asbury Park, New Jersey

A Little Trip to Ocean
Grove & Asbury Park

Saturday to Monday—July 12 to 14
inc. 1919—

Saturday—July 12, 1919— Spent night with Bo.[1] Up at 9 & went
down to Studio for bag. Packed it. Letters from Maxwell, Muriel
Cain, Isabel Parry—Burton Rascoe—C. T. Ramsey & others.[2] Cant
read all. Beautiful day. Leave at 11:30. Stop off at 36$\underline{th}$ (Ellinge &
Picking) & get my new glasses. Price 10$\underline{60}$. Make out a check for.
Go round into 42$\underline{nd}$ to R. R. Administration office & get tickets
for Belmar. (Two—6$\underline{30}$) Go out & forget tickets. Return & get
them. Then take cross town car to West 42$\underline{nd}$ Ferry. Bo is waiting
& we go on C. R. R. of N. J. Pier & wait for boat. Big crowd. It
arrives at 12:30. Delightful ride down the bay to Navesink,
Atlantic Highlands. Bo's gaiety—showing how little real joy shes
had in life. We change to cars at Atlantic H & ride down to
Belmar. The beautiful towns— At Belmar take bus to New
Columbia Hotel. Charming position but wants 18 per day for rear
room. No salt baths. I object. Offers a front room but it is little
better. We leave bags & walk over to Bradley Beach. Only one
room left there—no bath—at 15$\underline{00}$ per day. Go on to several small
hotel in Ocean Grove— Majestic, Sea Spray. Each wants 8$\underline{00}$ per
day for a room without bath! No elevator. No restaurant or food.
Leave & go to North End hotel. Get excellent room—hot & cold
salt baths with board for 15\underline{00}$ per day for two. Take it. Send back
for bags at New Columbia. We find this hotel very beautiful. Great
palors, lounging rooms over sea & dining room. Excellent food.
We dine & return to room to rest. I fall over bag & sprain my

1. "Bo" is Estelle Bloom Kubitz.
2. John Milo Maxwell (1866–1929), editor, author. Dresier's relation with Maxwell,
who had been copy editor of the *Chicago Daily Globe* during Dreiser's early newspaper days, was
revived when Dreiser visited him in Indiana in June 1919 (see p. 264, n. 14).
Muriel Cain (see p. 263, n. 12).
Isabel Parry (see p. 264, n. 13).
Burton Rascoe (1892–1957) was an editor, critic, historian, and memoirist who wrote one
of the first studies of Dreiser, *Theodore Dreiser* (1925).
C. T. Ramsey (see p. 183, n. 70).

ankle so that I cannot walk. Nervous chill follows. Bo baths it &
we stay in for the night.

Sunday, July 13—1919— Ankle some better but very swollen,
have to get a cane from hotel. Breakfast 9$\underline{30}$. We rest in big sun
parlor over sea. It is grey & foggy. Bo get Sunday papers & reads.
We go out for a walk about noon. It clears up. Dinner at one. The
grand waiters. At 2:30 we sit out on back balcony overlooking
Ocean Grove & sea & enjoy it hugely. The dresses. The
religionists.[3] At 6:15 we dine. Then take a rolling chair & ride to
end of Board Walk. Very beautiful. From there go into parlor
awhile, then to bed. Bo delighted with the day.

Monday, July 14—1919 — Awoke in North End at 8:30. Ankle
much better. Breakfast at 9. Wonderful day— Flowers. Sunlight,
blue sea. Great crowds. Bo tremendously interested. The girls at
Asbury—very beautiful & costumes very daring. The Stout one in
red. The slender one in green. We lounge along until noon. Then
watch them from hotel pavilion.[4] Buy post cards. Lunch at one.
Pack bags & decide to leave at 3:50. I pay bill. Watch the crowds
again from South End balcony. Bo's gaiety. Leave at 3:30 thinking
we're making a boat train, but it goes round via Perth Amboy &
Elizabethport. The great factories. The dreary towns. Arrive at
Communipaw, at six. Big ship building plants on Newark Bay—
Ride up to 23$\underline{rd}$ St in ferry. 14$\underline{th}$ St car to 14$\underline{th}$ St Express station.
Bo goes up town. I go to Studio & unpack bag. Letters from half
dozen people. At 7:15 go up town & meet Bo & Marian.[5] Says
Menck[6] is coming at 8:30. Bo & I go out to dinner. Then return.
Menck & Marian are still there. We go in. I pretend ankle hurts
since I dont want to go out again. Menck goes for beer but cant get
it. Bo & Marian try to interest him in the Jersey Coast so he will

3. Since Ocean Grove was a community governed by the Methodist Camp Meeting
Association, one of its points of interest for Dreiser was its strictly enforced Sunday blue laws
which prohibited bathing, driving, or any form of unnecessary labor. As a church-ruled town,
it was famous for a religious atmosphere that recalled older American traditions in a period
defined by modern secular mores.
    4. Asbury Park, known as a center for amusement parks, bars, and other forms of
entertainment, thrived on the activities shunned by its neighbor Ocean Grove.
    5. Marion Bloom (see p. 149, n. 3).
    6. "Menck" is H. L. Mencken.

join a party sometime but he isn't much interested. Tells of his plans for the future—a book on American literary conditions. What he does to Irwin Cobb[7] & the American Academy of Immortals. At 11:45 he goes. Very tired we sleep.

7. Irvin S. Cobb (1876–1944), humorist, writer, actor.

HELEN, HOLLYWOOD, AND THE *TRAGEDY*, 1919-24

▭

This lengthy diary covers the early years of Dreiser's relationship with Helen Richardson, who eventually became his second wife. Dreiser and Helen met in September 1919 and soon afterward traveled together to Hollywood where Helen pursued a career in the movies. Throughout these early years with Helen, Dreiser recorded his strong emotional reaction to her, and how his writing was conditioned by their tumultuous life together. This diary also captures the historical context of the years in California, especially the account of Dreiser's friendships with George Sterling, George Douglas, and the San Francisco literati. Dreiser attempted to write in Hollywood—he worked on many projects, including some movie scripts—but for a variety of reasons he did not find the atmosphere congenial. He did, however, begin *An American Tragedy* in Hollywood and completed the early chapters there. By January 1923 he and Helen had returned to New York, and late in 1925 he finally completed the *Tragedy*.

Saturday, July 19—1919

At 3 P.M. Bo[1] & I met at the Pennsylvania Station & took the train to Babylon, L.I. —walking down to the ferry that goes to Oak Beach. Watching the crowd eating & the little hotel there & watching a fisherman catch crabs. At 7:44 we took the train back Home (Lenox Ave). At 11 P.M. We had mushmelon & ice cream & read in Grote's Greece.[2]

Friday, Aug 1—1919   At Lillian Rosanoffs[3] request I went up to her apartment 648 W. 160th at 8 P.M. Had to tell Bo I had business. Her brother a professor of chemistry in Pittsburgh & some female professor of history was there. They went out to dinner. She sat on my lap & told me of her proposed marriage to some wealthy adv. man. Wants to pension me—afterwards. I laughed. At 10:30 we went for a walk along Riverside Drive. Stunning night. At 12 I went to Bo's, who let me in in spite of the fact she said she wouldnt.

Sunday—Aug 3rd 1919.

Last night being worried about my work & income asked my pychic control what my future was—to show it forth if possibly—symbolically in a dream. Accordingly at 4 A.M. I awoke from a dream which seemed to have a symbolic significence & related to me. It appeared that I was possessed of a key by the aid of which I was able to fly—much to my delight. It was a fair sized Yale Lock key to which was attached some sort of a rope—a handle. By hanging on to this & holding up the key—I could rise & fly & did so—up & around & between great buildings and over vast territories much to the admiration of many & myself. And there seemed one with a key like mine who imitated me. Nevertheless, after a time I was on some high place—a landing & departing stand preparatory to flying & was holding up my key, but was compelled to stand & wait for the reason that at that time it seemed to lack power. I could not tell from this—waking up at that point as I did,

1. "Bo" is Estelle Bloom Kubitz.
2. *A History of Greece*, 12 vols. (1846–56) by George Grote (1794–1871).
3. Lillian Rosanoff began a correspondence with Dreiser in 1919 that lasted until 1922. Her letters are adulatory, but they suggest that Dreiser never took the relationship beyond the point of responding with an occasional letter.

whether my mental & literary soaring days were over—whether I
was ever to be permitted to fly again—or whether I was still to fly
very high & then lose my power. The thought of the first possible
meaning made me very sad. I tried to have the psychic control
further elucidate the symbol in a dream, but nothing came though I
slept.

Helen.

To give her history will no more account for her than the process
of manufacture explains the most delicate of scents. Poise, quick
deduction, natural intuition. A ravishing smile. The look and
gestures of a girl of eighteen. Sympathies quick and warm.
Intolerant of cruelty or unfairness in others. Liking to work. Liking
to battle for success. Realizing that life cannot be other than a
struggle for all. Sensual to a degree at times. Astonishingly
suggestive of youthful innocence and inexperience at others.
Delicate features. A dazzling skin with the natural bloom of youth
upon it. A perfect and sensual form,—soft, yeilding and rounded,—
horribly provocative to all men. Full of delightful and innocent
dreams of beauty and peace under simple circumstances. Not
interested in children, save as a writer would be. Interested in all
types and conditions of men. Understanding and sympathyzing with
their necessities, compulsions and lacks. Disliking strident,
aggressive and vain youth. Caring more for age, weight, grey hairs
and intelligence and force, when combined in a man. Disliking
most women. Exquisite taste in dress. Liking only good books, plays
and poems. Loving scenery, the out of doors, to ride, to drive, to
dance, to sing. A pretty emotional and moving voice, carrying with
it a sense of youth, summer and happiness. Graceful in movement.
Her hair a half way shade between gold and brown, changing color
in changing lights. Beautiful hands. Small graceful feet. A light,
girlish, healthy step.

Saturday, Sept 13—1919 This day I met Helen. Dont remember
much about the morning. Was reading at 11 A.M. when door bell
rang. Slipped on my blue Chinese coat & went out. Saw a young
girl of about 19 or 20, I thought, hiding behind the door. She
came out. Wanted to know if I was T.D. Then asked if I could give

---

Helen Richardson in Hollywood

her the address of Ed Dresser.[4] So fascinated I invited her in. Looked very much like my sister Theresa.[5] We sit & talk. Am able to tell by her look that she is as sensual as she is beautiful. Tells me she is my cousin—a 2nd cousin rather distantly removed.[6] I learn that she is married and 20 years of age. Give her Eds address. Then ask her for hers. She trembles as she writes it. The message of my right eye. I am tempted to take her in my arms & kiss her.

Sunday. Sept. 14—1919 Spent this entire night thinking of Helen. Very restless. At 2 A.M. was about to call her up. In a perfect fever of desire. Bathed & dressed at 8:30. Could scarcely wait for 10:30 to come so I could call her up with seeming propriety. Did so & she seemed glad. Told me afterward she danced about her room & upon her bed. I invited her to breakfast at the Pennsylvania. Although suffering menstrual pains was determined to come. Agreed to meet me at one. Read, worked on essays and then at 12:30 walked up 7th Ave. Dying to see her. At 1:10 she arrived. Her vivid beauty & elastic step quite fevered me. We went to roof garden. Asking what she had been thinking she evaded me by saying her thoughts were wild. A kind of lymphatic sensuality, so radiant that it permeated me and combined with my own made me feel as though I had taken an aphrodisiac. Some disturbing perfume she used helped in this. We talked of The Hand of the Potter, a copy of which I had given her.[7] She liked it—much. We talked of life & her work and her experiences. Began to tell me a little about herself. She had all the sensuous-sexy charm of a Zigfeld Follies girl & was quite as beautiful as any. At the end of breakfast I suggested going down to the studio & she agreed. The day before I had invited her to come to dinner Tuesday eve at 6:30 & she had agreed. In the lobby she asked to me to excuse her a moment. On

4. "Ed Dresser" was the stage name of Dreiser's brother, Edward M. Dreiser (1873–1957).

5. Mary Theresa Dreiser (1864–97), who was killed in a train accident in Chicago.

6. Helen Parks Patges (1894–1955), Dreiser's second cousin. She was the granddaughter of Esther Schänäb Parks, who was the sister of Dreiser's mother (Sarah Schänäb Dreiser). At the time of this meeting with Dreiser, Helen was married to an actor named Frank Richardson, and she went by the name of Helen Patges Richardson.

7. *The Hand of the Potter* was printed by Boni & Liveright in 1918, but it was not formally published until 20 September 1919 because of the possibility of a stage production. Dreiser therefore must have given Helen a prepublication copy of the play.

her return she announced that she didn't believe she would "go down today" & my spirits fell. Felt as though she had changed her mind about me. Talked more about her friends & said she had a religious bias at times. I laughed. We decided to walk & did so—accross 32nd to 5th & up 5th to 56th where we waited for a bus. Told me of her visits to see Ed & what she thought of May—and her early interest in Paul & the Dreiser family.[8] I was in great gloom feeling I was losing the most beautiful girl I had ever known. No bus coming we went to 6th Ave L at 58th where I parted with her. Walked accross 59th to subway. Never felt more depressed in my life. In my gloom took road to Canal Street By mistake. Although she had agreed to come down Wednesday I didnt believe she'd come. Walked up 7th to 10th from Canal. Deep depression. As I was entering Kirah & Howard called.[9] I entertained them but was glad when they went. Walked out to dinner at 7 but couldn't eat. Walked up to Reisenwebers to el subway & went home & too bed. Very sad.

Wednesday. Sept 17—1919. This day Helen was scheduled to come down to dinner with me at 6:30. Didnt expect her really & was still sad—depressed at my inability to capture the most attractive woman I ever knew. Forget how I spent the day—writing perhaps. After 12 P.M. expected a call constantly telling me she wont come. Letter from Louise saying she will be over Friday to stay with me doesn't interest me at all.[10] Lills arrival in N.Y. & her success in "Hello, Alexander", merely bores me.[11] I go up & see Bo (Mrs. K) but my interest in her is so dead that I merely wonder how I can get away—once & for all. At 5:30 & 6—expect every telephone call is from her—saying she cant come. But at 6:30 she comes & her attitude is so collie like & warm that I take her in my arms and kiss her and she responds as though she passionately

8. May is Mai Skelly Dreiser, Ed Dreiser's wife. Paul is Dreiser's brother, the song writer Paul Dresser (1857–1906).
9. Kirah Markham (see p. 117, n. 1).
Howard is Howard Scott, at the time chief engineer of the Technical Alliance in New York and a writer on technical subjects for *The Nation*. Scott later founded the Technocracy group, which influenced Dreiser's social thinking in the thirties by impressing him with the significance of technology in achieving a more equitable form of society.
10. Louise is Louise Campbell (see p. 150, n. 7).
11. Lill is Lillian Rosenthal (see p. 150, n. 8).

loved me. You would have thought this was the culmination of a long courtship. The dinner at Pollys. How she hung on my arm. The ice cream at the Brevoort. We walk back to studio & she sits on my couch. I kiss & press her, but when I try to feel her breasts and thighs she with draws & we begin a long argument which ends at midnight by her threatening to leave. Doesn't want to give herself to me. I feel sick—almost defeated. Call her back & tell her she must yeild—there can be no mere simple friendship between us —that it is impossible for me. Finally she yeilds & agrees solemnly to come Friday night & I can tell by her manner that she will. We walk out & I ride up with her on the Subway, feeling positively that a new chapter in my life is opening which made lead any where.

Friday, Sept. 19—1919 Helen is scheduled to come down & sleep with me for the first time tonight. I am in a fever heat for her to come.

Saturday. Sept 20th 1919. After more delicious morning hours with Helen we finally get up at 10:30—in time for her to get to her bank before noon. She tells me more of her past life—her life in Seattle, her life in Charleston—her husband—her employer—mere bits that make a delicious world of interest to me. Sex satisfaction & agreement have brought us close together. She is satisfied with me & I with her. Tells me of the only affairs she has had outside her husband—the one with a young engineer in Omaha—the other with a society man in Charleston. I am anxious to stay with her & she agrees to come back at 4 or 5—going up to 111th Street to change her clothes. We breakfast at the ⌞   ⌟—and then I take her to the Subway at Christopher & see her off. Return to studio & try to work but cant do much. My life seems torn up by the roots. Feel that I am due for a long period with her, maybe years. She appeals to me so much—gay—good natured, animal, clever, attractive. I feel I should go up & see Bo, but wait hoping she will come. At 3:30 much to my surprise & delight, she does return, bringing pictures of her husband, mother, father—her fathers people in Norway—her aunt and what not—also seventeen victrola records. I am engrossed by her simple direct humanity, her large charity and her affection for me. We think of going out but finally go to bed instead & do not get out to get anything to eat before midnight. She planned to go up to her room for looks sake but by 12:30

agreed she could not bring herself to leave me and we made a mavelous wakeful night of it. I never saw a more beautiful body. No painter ever painted a more beautiful girl.

Sunday—Sept 21—1919 Helen & I breakfast at Cavanaughs & go to Newark via Christopher Street ferry & the Hudson tube. The park. The little boat ride. The new cathedral. The woman who nearly fell in the water. The small boy who tried to get us our boat. "You got me into this". Home via Cortlandt Street & 6th Ave L. I buy Helen Bell-Aus. We go to bed & play until 11 P.M.—then to the Crows Nest in Christopher Street for dinner & back to bed. All the joy in the world in sleeping with Helen.

Sunday. Sept 28—1919 A beautiful day. Helen & I decide to go to Pleasant Plains on Staten Island for an outing. We have breakfast at[12]

Oct 8—1919—Wednesday. Helen & I are to leave today for New Orleans. I have to go to bank & get $1,000 in A.B.A. checks. She has to go to Wanamakers. The boat (The Momus) (God of Ridicule & Censure) leaves foot of W. 11th Street at noon. We eat in a dirty little restaurant on 6th Ave. near 9th St. I take L to 42nd, get A.B.A. checks. Helen & I hardly get bags packed before taxi comes. I leave my grey hat & dressing gown by mistake. Letter from Louise begging me to see her before I go. In taxi & rush to dock. The crowd. Boat really doesnt leave till 6 P.M. Our trunks not there. Helens not sent from Hotel. Is finally sent down in a taxi. Lill comes after Helen has gone to our berth—Helen & I lunch after Lill goes & I get trunks straightened out. We go about deck & see the ship. It is very raw—though clear. Then retire & lie in our berth until 5—when the boat sails. The river, the bay, the narrow. Helen & I see a new moon over our right shoulder. The dark waters. Bay Ridge, Coney Island. Then the chill of the sea. We go to dinner. The guests at our table. The tall New Orleans youth. The general & intense interest in Helens beauty. After dinner on the deck for a little while. To our berth & we sleep close in one—waking, kissing & playing all night long.

---

12. The entry breaks off at this point; Dreiser never finished it.

<u>Sunday, Oct. 12--1919.</u> On board the Momus & off Key West. At noon this day we see it lying like a fabled city over the water. And the waters of the sea here—blue & green. It is hot & clear & yet the moisture in the air makes it muggy. Helen & I get up about 9. & make the breakfast table. She is as wonderful as ever in her gold glacé skirt & pale cream beaded shirt waist. The usual band of admirers follow her with envious eyes. We read in our chairs at the rear of the 1<u>st</u> class cabin. Meet the young prospecter from Desdemona Texas who butts in on her account. A full story of life in Desdemona. We pay 60 <u>cents</u> for two bottles of pop on this sweet ship. The Southerner & how he looked when he found he could only get "pop". Dinner as usual—a poor one. The coffee! The poor chicken. The young gentleman from New Orleans—as grand as ever. P.M. we spend in our berth—I looking at Helens naked body. The beauty of it is simply maddening to me—unbelievable. I can hardly trust that she is as insane over me as she seems. It seems as though some one must have hypnotized her & told her that she was in love with me. From one to 2:30 we write in the writing room. I write Lill, Bo, Louise & four or five others. Being as crazy about Helen as I am makes it hard to write them at all. At four we come on deck again & walk. Then dinner at 6—and the wonderful starry sky & late moon. Helen never leaves me. We whisper & dream of New Orleans & Los Angeles & what the west will bring us. Such dreams. Helen wants a bungalow & a car & flowers and a pet lion & what not. It is a fairy tale come true.

<u>Wednesday—Oct—15th 1919</u>

Hot afternoon in New Orleans. Mailed Bo—P.O. order as below.[13] Man in window said: "I was just wondering what had become of you." From there went to St. Charles Hotel for Helen. Found her talking to the young prospecter from Desdemona Texas. It made me as sore as hell & I cut him. Afterwards at 1417 St. Charles Ave. I had it out with Helen. She was not to speak with men she didnt know. Nor to pretend to a vague interest in me.

---

13. At this point in the diary Dreiser pasted in a receipt for a postal money order for $25.00.

Oct 27—1919

Last day in N.O. Pack—call Taxi. Go to St. Charles—then to I.S.
station. Then back to Blascos, Helen solemn. We breakfast. Look
for cheese cloth. Hot N.O. cfe. I lose The Moon & Sixpence.[14] We
go to station. Observation car. [Four unreadable words] Forrests
hung with moss. Sugar Plantation. A Lake or Gulf. More cabins &
swamps (Ruddock). Cabins in water, (Manchoe—an arm of the
Gulf or River (Magnolia). See my 1st cotton field & pickers.[15]

Oct 28—1919—

Awake with Helen in berth. Enroute from New Orleans to St.
Louis. Flat country with trees showing brown leaves. Helen warm
& sensuous grumbles because men are looking when she wants to
go to bath. We dress. I wash as we pass through East St. Louis. She
is ready as we near station. St. Louis once more. Cant remember
quite when I was here last. We arrange about berths to Denver.
Check bags & walk down town. New Court House. I revisit 10th &
Market. The Shop still there. We go to Pine & along it to
Globe-Democrat office. Then accross Broadway to Washington Ave.
See—Barrs & Nugents. Nugents a copy of Wanamakers in N.Y.
We walk out Olive again to 12th. Breakfast at the Jefferson. I write
Lill & Mrs. K. Send rent to Crist & Herrick. After we go to old
Exposition car—sixth & Olive. New Library & Park ala Bryant
Park. Then to Catholic Cathedral. (Maryland Ave Car.) Then down
town for overcoat. Visit 5 stores. Finally get one. Price 40. The
man who had been to Los Angeles. Then we walk down Olive,
Pine & Market to old Republic Bldg. Visit levee. Then back. Have
cup of coffee. Walk out to Union Station. Buy Papto, Mangan &
White Vasalene. We get to depot—get out bags & board train.
Different type of people. More western. Helen suffering from cold.
We chat & read. Leave St. L 2:15—Go north along Missouri to
Clarksville, Louisiana & Hannibal. I think of Rose. Evening at
Hannibal. Beautiful coloring of foliage enroute. Simple houses &
farms. The constant distrust of Helens beauty & how it may make
me suffer tortures me. Dinner in diner. She looks so charming.
Seats in drawing room afterward. The typical middle west father &

---

14. *The Moon and Sixpence* (1919) by W. Somerset Maugham.
15. This entry is written, nearly illegibly, on the back of an envelope.

---

mother & their two boys. The club dressy middle west girl mother
& her baby. She gets fooled about where to get off. Early to bed. I
fuck Helen a long time in our berth. She has to go back to ladies
toilet.

Wed. Oct. 29—1919. Awake in berth with Helen 200 miles west
of Lincoln Neb. On the C. B & Q en route to Denver. Helens
sweet body. She is like a young Aurora or Hebe. We play until 9.
Last call for breakfast doesnt disturb us & we get it anyhow at
10:30. The young priest who has the berth overhead. How I dislike
him. Dress finally & after breakfast we rest in drawing room. Helen
& I quarrel over her past loves—the boys & men she has flirted
with on trains to everywhere. I tease her & she leaves & wont talk
but comes back. Am interested in this Nebraska country. So flat &
dry & homely. God what a country. Significant when sad perhaps
but vile when dull & prosperous.

Saturday, Nov. 1st—1919 —Enroute from Salt Lake to Los
Angeles. Awake at dawn in berth with Helen. I insist on rutting
here. She protests but kisses me & lets me. A darling cutey who
swears when she looks out & sees people all ready up—and she has
to pass them. The long sandy deserts of this route. Wonderful bare
mountains around Santa Fe (Arizona?) The areas in which only cacti
& sagebrush grow: Oro del Grande I see my first Pampas Grass
(Pompous grass one woman called it) Barstow (2 P.M.) The
beautiful Station. Summit (4 P.M.) where we start down into the
green part of California. The good roads. Machines. Flowers. We
arrive at ⌊   ⌋ California. Then at Riverside. Then at Pasadena.
The Orange Groves. Helen & I on the back platform. Her joy in
beauty. We reach Los Ange. 7 P.M. Helens efficiency. Phones. The
incident of the boys. We get off at the wrong corner. Finally reach
the Stillwell at 9th & Grand Ave. Room 523. The nice service. We
dress & go to a restaurant in Spring Street. Not much. Then back
to hotel & spend a delicious night together. I am crazy about her.

Sunday, Nov. 2—1919 Awake in Stillwell in Los Angeles—with
Helen. A wonderful sunny day. We play in bed until nearly noon.
Then dress & go out looking for a Restaurant. Find a poor one in
Spring St. We like L.A., the sunlight & flowers. Decide to take a

Seeing Los Angeles car & do—making the trip to Hollywood, Beverley Heights, the Studio, Santa Monica & Venice. Start at 1 P.M. Are delighted with the trip. View East Lake Park & the house of Griffith, Lasky & others.[16] The Sea at Santa Monica. Helens interest in the seal & the gulls. I see live Octopi & Skate. Back by 5:30 & we go to hotel to clean up. Then to dinner. Another Sweetie night with one of the prettiest girls I have ever known— and as sweet.

Tuesday, Nov. 4<u>th</u> —Helen & I decide we must find a place to live. Get up after a customary night of delight & breakfast at Gabes (corner 8<u>th</u> & Grand). Then stop in several bungalow agencies but find nothing. L.A. is over run with incoming residents. No houses, no flats, no furnished apartments, no rooms even. We start out Hope & Grand & Flower Aves or streets & examine every apartment house en route. The L.A. idea of an apartment is one room & bath in what might be called a 2<u>nd</u> rate rooming hotel. Prices 30 to 60—per month for room & bath! We walk out as far as 30<u>th</u> St. Beautiful homes—hotels—flowers. The aisle of Palms near 22<u>nd</u>! It gave me an idea for a colonade, each column to be 200 feet high with branching bronze limbs & leaves at the top—like a palm. By one P.M. we get discouraged. A lean man in a shabby house offers us 1 one room without connecting bath for $17 per. That ended it.

Back to hotel in despair. Helen examines papers. Her lusty image "You cant tell there are any rooms or flats in this town because I know there are—and I'm going to find em". There are just lots of em".

Looks & finds an add for room in a private residence. Calls up the lady & asks her to describe it. The description is so pleasing that we decide to go out at 2:30. Take West 1<u>st</u> Street car to Alvardo Street near West Lake Park. The Oil wells in the city! The Alvardo hotel. The queer little woman who met us. The great palm in front of the door. The open porch from our room with flowers & curtains. Her compliment to Helen—"You have a pretty young wife". We decide to take it at 30 per. I pay $10 down in advance.

16. David Wark Griffith (1875–1948), director.
Jesse L. Lasky (1880–1958), director, producer.

We then go to West Lake Park. Helens moods. The day we were out to West Park (338 Alvarado Street) the sudden change in West Park. Reminds me of Kirah in this—that her ideals outrun life & when life fails her, as in the matter of an instant bungalow by the sea, a cave, flowers etc, she becomes moody. Wouldn't talk in park until I threatened to leave her alone until dinner. Offered her money to go home with and she changed instantly. But later took it out on a "Sun" Drug clerk who tried to offer her a "Sun" gargle in place of "Liquicide" which she wanted. Her throat was still troubling her. "I don't want that junk"! We came to hotel. Later went to The Saddle Rack, one of the worst of LAs rotten restaurants. On the way home Helen reexamines the hat in the N.Y. Store. Decides she must have it. To bed & wonderful screwing with her.

Thursday Nov 6—1919 —We go to Pasadena in the afternoon via the Pacific Electric. Before that I had gone in the early morning out to breakfast alone. Then to a Japanese Laundry in 8th Street to get Helens Teddy Bears ironed. The peculiarity of the Jap in LA. So numerous. So industrious. Just at this time there is agitation here to prevent them from holding property. Stopped at restaurant & sent Helen waffles & coffee. Then to P.O. via Grand Ave car. Check from B & L. $333.33.[17] Letter from Bo saying she is getting along well. See the oldest mission church in L.A. Also Mexican—Spanish —Chinese quarter (Foot of Los Angeles Street). Find a wooden table for 2.50. Go to Woolworths & get buttons & safety pins. Then to Bullocks—a fine store—for 6 hdkfs. Cash a A.B.A. check for 50. Then deposit the B & L Check at the Hellman Night & Day bank & open an account. Back to the Stillwell & find Helen dressed. We decide to go to Pasadena. At 1 we start, stopping for a sandwich & coffee en route. Cars leave 6th & Main. The East Side of LA.— Mexicans & Japanese. Some big studio. The bungalows—hills— flowers out Pasadena way. Orange Groves. We stop at the Pign-Whistle in Pasadena. The Green Hotel. The ⌐   ⌐ Hotel. Hotels everywhere in this region. Their character. Poor coffee. H's interest in fineries. The belts, stockings, shoes & hats of Pasadena.

17. Boni & Liveright, Dreiser's publisher at the time. Horace Liveright had agreed to pay Dreiser $333.33 per month for a year as an advance toward the completion of *The Bulwark.*

We walk about—Go out to the Busch Gardens. The sunny rich life of this world— & still the poor appear to be about as poor as they are anywhere. One of Helens moods. I ignore her. She soon changes. Back to hotel. Then to McKees—another bum restaurant. Dreadful. I am offered another mans check—3.35 in the hope that I will pay it by mistake. Old book store. I encounter Branns Iconoclast—2 vols—$4^{00}.[18] We come back. Helen is sick—monthly dues, but we indulge in two of the worst rounds yet. No sleep until about 3 A.M.

Friday Nov. 7$\underline{th}$ 1919 We are too pack trunks today & go out to 338 tomorrow. Helens Sweetie ways. Cant sleep after I get up. Gets up. Her Teddy bears re-ribboned the night before. Her interest in all things seductive. Licks my P & A—Cant let my roger alone. Always getting it out & feeling it. Comes off with me now very quickly. Didn't at first. We dress. I start keeping these notes. Her expressions. "Honey." Boy-eh-bile. Sweet heart. Repeats all the bad things I say to her—just like a little copy cat. Tells me of the time she wouldnt go to school if she didnt get fried potatoes for lunch.

Saturday, Nov. 8—1919 Awake with Helen in Stillwell at 8:30 but do not get up. We are due to leave here at 6. Trunks must go by noon. Helen has a dress to leave at cleaners. We have laundry to get & some dress goods to buy. After doing the smaller errands we go to breakfast at Holsts in 8th St. Then on to an old 2nd hand store in Main Street where I pay for a table—$2^{50}. Then on to P.O. No mail. Then on through the Mexican quater. I show Helen the old mission & the little Park at the foot of Los Angeles Street. We go though the Chinese quarter—the most charming I've seen— then back to the big stores—Bullocks, Coulters, Robinsons, Hamburgers—looking for Lavender Chiffon velvet. Finally get 3 1/2 yds at the Poppy-Shop at 7^{50} per yard. The nature of LAs stores. Their richness. The high prices. Back to hotel. Pack laundry & at 5:30 leave. R.R. Co. charges me $3.33—for excess baggage,

---

18. Dreiser is referring to W. C. Brann's journal *Iconoclast.* In 1892, when Dreiser was working at the *Globe-Democrat* in Chicago, he was given the "Heard in the Corridors" column after Brann left the newspaper to edit the *Iconoclast.*

---

sneaky swindle. Helen is furious. We come out to 338 Alvarado. Unpack. Then back down town to the Pign & Whistle for dinner. A poor place. Afterward we shop a little—buy apples & flowers & come out to 338. A lovely night in a charming room with Helen.

Sunday, Nov. 9—1919 Awake with Helen at 338 Alvarado—after first night there. Beautiful, sunny yard with flowers outside. We go to little restaurant in 7th Street at Alvarado. The waitress who said "you betcha" when I asked for a cup of coffee. Good T bone steaks here. We go from there into West Lake Park. The gulls, black birds, ducks. The playful dog—the girl & the sailors. The new apartment house we look into. Rents $3000 per for 4 rooms & bath! We come back home—unpack & I straighten out my papers. Blues toward evening over work. Helen tries to advise. We play in bed till 7—then to dinner at the Chocolate Shop—7th & Alvarado (A poor meal). The spider walks on the table. We were talking of the spider on the Sands at Charleston, S.C. Go over in Park & sit in wooden swing. Discuss society & what people would think. Helen is for me—once & for all—whatever happens. Back to bed. Wonderful moonlight—I seem never to weary of her.

Tuesday Nov. 11—1919 Armistice day. Holiday commemorating the armistice with the Germans—Nov. 11—1919. I was with Bo last year & walked down through Central Park—watching the wild joy of the people. Today baby & I wake in our room at 338 Alvarado. Every day sunshine here. I had a dream last night that I got off a train & that it started without me but I ran after it & with difficulty made it. Helen & I indulge in a delightful round, as usual. She has the most teasing methods. Talks all the time & tortures me into an orgasm by her sweet brutalities & descriptions. Up at 9:30 & go to the little restaurant in 7th St near Alvarado. A tea bone steak as usual. Then to the Park & we watch the ducks & black birds. See a fat moving picture actor. Then out & to the West Park Hospital to get the address of a doctor—as Helens neck hurts. Then home (338). Miss Cobbe (Virginia) our landlady here has discovered who I am. She refused me a chair, curtly enough, Sunday but now talks of "entertaining angels unawares"! Worked for Bobbs-Merrill in Indianapolis. Hails from Richmond, Va. I hear that Meredith Nicholsen is wont to speak of me familiarly as "Ted

Dresser"!¹⁹ I am now to have the chair & a waste basket. Helen is
amused & pleased by the adoration. I caution Miss Cobbe to tell no
one. Afterward read "The Chemical Origin & Regulation of Life"
by Leonard Thompson Troland.²⁰ Am sure he only has hold of a
part of the facts. Loeb is nearer & better.²¹ Later baby & I get to
playing in the bed. Her beauty just knocks me. It is unbelievable—
a dream of fair women. She looks like an angel or a classic figure &
yet is sensuality to the core. We indulge in a long suck & then I
put her on her knees. A wild finish. Return to my work. The palms
& flowers here seem in no wise affected by the sharp coolness
which begins at about 5. A wonderful climate. We go down town
at 6:30 to the B & M Cafeteria—a very large affair. A very fair
diner for 90 cents each but no atmosphere. Afterwards we try to
find a theatre but cant. Go to Grunwalds Movie—a large house
where we see Charles Ray in a crook play. The usher girls who
danced on the stage. Home at 11 & Helen & I talk in bed until 3.
Another delicious round with her. Has the full forward, lavender
lids & bluish white eye lids of a sex extremist. Uses the most
coaxing & grossly enervating words of any girl I know. (Theo &
Helen are between the sheets & no one sees what they are doing.
No one, No one. Oh— oh— no one. Theo is between Helens
thighs—Helens soft white thighs. Theo is fucking Helens cunt. Yes
—he is—yes—yes—oh. Theo is fucking her and Helen is taking it—
giving herself to him—her belly—her tittys—her thighs—oh—oh).
So on to orgasm.

<u>Wednesday. Nov. 12, 1919</u> Very little sleep. Very tired. Up at
10:30 but no energy. Walk a little. Take suit to cleaners. Helen & I
go to restaurant at 7th & Alvarado. Cant get cakes or waffles &
leave & go down town. Eat at Holsts. Helen glum. No sex vitality.
Get laundry from Jap, shirt from Jap & then I go to Express office
to see after my packages. Get one. Go to bank (Hellmans) and
deposit $45.93. Go to P.O. & get a cross letter from Bo. None
from Lill. Then home on West 1st street car—reading mail—
Glorious clear warm day as usual.

19. Meredith Nicholson (1866–1947), Indiana novelist, diplomat.
20. *The Chemical Origin and Regulation of Life* (1914) by Leonard Thompson Troland
(1889–1932).
21. Jacques Loeb (1859–1924), German-born biologist.

<u>Friday, Nov. 14—1919</u> The usual pleasures with Helen. I have a
bad cold. We get up at 9:30 & go to the T bone restaurant in 7th
St. Then back to room. Helen has an appointment with her grafting
specialist. Incident of the blood test man not being able to find a
vein in her arm. I decide to visit the Lasky Studios in Hollywood.
Go down town first. Telegram from Liveright saying Lane threatens
suit as to infringement of rights in The Bulwark. I wire Liveright to
demand right to see contract.[22] Go out to Famous Players. Cant
even get in. Dont know me. Return down town to Express Office.
Cant get my boxes. Come out 7th to tailor. Cant get my suit.
Wonderful skies & twilight here impress me. Come home & find
Helen in Pink on bed reading Mark Twains what is man.[23] We
dress & go down to a French Restaurant in 1st Street. But its no
good. The old book man who had a sign recommending all books
on that shelf—and on it were Pollyanna & The Moon & Sixpence.[24]
I asked why & he said both were good.

Home on West 1st Street car. I write Liveright. Then turn in
with Helen. A long delightful hour.
Auditorium. Walter Henry Rothwell, Conductor.[25] The German
who sat beside me tells me Rothwell is a Hollander. 90 pieces to
orchestra. We have Strass, Wagner, Bizet & Grieg. German music
coming back. My German friend comments on it. Afterward Helen
& I walk down Broadway & get a chocolate ice cream soda. Then
out here & play about until 9 when we go to the Chocolate Den
for tea. At 10 we sit in Park—then home & indulge in a long
delicious round. Its all the more delightful because we know we aut
to quit. Helen looks back over her shoulder & talks about her own
beauty. Before this in the evening we discuss May & Ed—our work

22. In August 1916, the John Lane Co. had paid Dreiser $2,000 in advances on *The
Bulwark*. By 1919, when Dreiser was in process of transferring book rights to Boni & Liveright,
Lane agreed to accept either repayment of the money or the completed manuscript of the novel.
The money was not repaid. When Boni & Liveright advertised its plans to publish *The Bulwark*
in 1919, John Lane therefore threatened to sue, holding up publication and demanding payment
of damages for infringement of its rights to the book. Eventually the issue died a natural death;
the novel was published posthumously in 1946. See Jack Salzman, "The Curious History of
Dreiser's *The Bulwark*," *Proof 3* (1973): 21–61.
23. *What Is Man* (1906) by Mark Twain.
24. *Pollyanna* (1913), a sentimental children's novel by Eleanor Hodgman Porter (1868–
1920). Dreiser is interested in the juxtaposition of such a book on the same shelf with W.
Somerset Maugham's brutally realistic *The Moon and Sixpence.*
25. Walter Henry Rothwell (1872–1927), British-American conductor.

—the delight of having a bungalow here, Paul & her aunt Myrtle. Of more happy days together. We return & talk. Helen puts on her Teddy bare & sits on my knees. Finally to bed & the most delicious sensual play follows—Helen finally working me off. The Sweetest, Prettiest, Grossest girl I ever knew—positively Electric in her power.

Dreiser's Wasserman Report

Thursday, Nov 20—1919 Los Angeles. Day spent with Helen in getting two tests made, one by the Pacific-Wasserman Co—the other by Messrs Brein & Zeiler as to her blood. Both tests later proved negative. Helen not so nervous. We meet the insurance agent who was on the Momus. Later leave Helen at B. H. Dyer & Co (Big dry goods store) & return to 338. Work on Movie

Scenario—"The Long, Long Trail."[26] Helen returns about 4 and
we get to playing as usual ending in a long orgy. Helen develops
the traits of some fine breeds of animals. She desires to wallow.
Return to work at 5:50 & continue until 8. Then we go downtown
to a good hotel & dine. Take West 6th St car to Hollywood & walk
back part way under the stars. Then home to bed. Helens high heel
shoes. Wont even wear low ones for walking. Best she will do is
"Cuban" heels! Powders her nose & paints her cheeks even on
going to bed.

Friday—November 21—1919 —Los Angeles. More idling with
H— which worries me—however delightful. We go to "Billies" in
7th St. Then buy a box of Uneeda biscuit & feed the Gulls, ducks
& black birds in West Lake Park. Their greed. Then get some
apples—25 cents a pound—(5 apples) & come home. I shave. Then
go down to meet Caroline Dudley—Mrs ——— H's sister.[27]
Brunch at Moralles $3.35. We go to Chinatown. I do not care for
her as much as I do Dorothy D—— not as bright. The Dudley
family—She tells me of Santa Fe & Nordfeldt. She buys a coat in
Chinatown. Get rid of her at 3:30. Call up Brein & Zeiler & The
Pacific-W. Co. Both return a Negative on Helens blood. Come
home. Find H waiting on porch. We walk—then over to West Lake
Park & watch the red sky at dusk & listen to the ducks. Return &
Helen produces an unused cape. Go down 7th & find a new
restaurant—Very good. The box of candy with the naked girl on it
which interests Helen. Back to room & play until sleep time.

Sunday. Nov. 23rd 1919. Los Angeles. Helen sets clock for 7:30—
but at 6:30 wake & in the dawn indulge in one of the lovliest
rounds ever—she lying on her side one arm up. We laugh & dress
& at 8 leave for Pacific Station En route to Santa Catalina. Down
town on West 1st street. Breakfast in a Cafeteria Quick Lunch—a
new proposition to me—Get our own steak & waffles. Then to
Station & take 3 car trolley to San Pedro. The mountains in the

---

26. "The Long, Long Trail," one of the numerous film scenarios Dreiser wrote in this
period, is among the Dreiser papers at the University of Pennsylvania. The main character,
whose name is Giffen, is wrongly accused of a crime and spends many years on the road trying
to elude his pursuers before he is finally vindicated.
27. Caroline Dudley was a dancer and the sister of Dorothy Dudley, who later wrote
Forgotten Frontiers: Dreiser and the Land of the Free (1932).

distance—small towns—Cattle, oil wells etc. Arrive at San Pedro at 10 A.M. & take boat for Santa Catalina. Helen looks too sweet in her light grey gorgette & grey hat. Seats on side of boat. The man who threw the candy, selling it. The negro porters. Blue sea, gulls & a lovely sky. Gulls sitting on all the little launches in San Pedro harbor. Santa Catalina in sight from San Pedro—but takes 2 hours to get there. Helen tells me of Lucille—her probable insanity. Also of how she peed on the school floor at 6 years of age. Also how male & female teachers regarded her. The gulls on the upper deck. We whisper love stuff all the time. Arrive at 12:30. Walk along Maine Street. Lunch in a cheap restaurant. Santa Catalina doesnt impress us much. The glass bottomed boat. We leave at one thirty. See perch & sea gold fish in their native haunts. The diver after Abalone Shells. Back to dock. Aeroplane takes passenger at 1$\underline{^{00}}$ per minute for a 10 minute flight. Then onto boat again. The blue sea. Rainbow. A whale. The old woman who roasted the girl piano player. Near beer in the bar at 25 $\underline{cents}$ a bottle. Helen gets cold. Wishes she could get drunk. Feels a kick from near beer! We take trolley train at San Pedro. Back to 6$\underline{th}$ & Main by 7 P.M. Eat at the hotel Hayward. The sexy atmosphere. Girls all crooked Helen thinks. A poor meal for 2\underline{^{10}}$. We come home & go straight to bed. Very tired but before long we pull a heavy screw, finally getting down on the floor on pillows to avoid the squeaking of the bed.

Babes <u>Cute</u> Ways

Coming out of bath room I meet her. She touches my hand. "Next".

———

It does yah—just lots a good.
(This refers to nearly everything.)

———

Wants her beauty eaten by a big rough brute.

<u>Friday, Nov 28—1919—Los Angeles</u> Helen & I being depressed by two days of cold & rain here & no adequate heat in this room decide to move. I cannot work. Our thin little Southern mistress of this house gives us neither heat nor hot water & one can never get in the bath room. After breakfast at "Billys" in 7th St. Helen goes to look up certain advs. I return here & go to work. At 1$\underline{^{30}}$ she calls up from "Highlands"—having found a place. I am to go to

Ave 60—on the So. Pasadena car & meet her. Go at once. She is
on the corner. We walk along a road & accross a bridge into a
valley surrounded by hills. Find a charming place—light on all sides
—no other houses nearing. Dining room, Library, two bed rooms—
kitchen & bath. Gas heated throughout. Rent $55<u>00</u>—Wood $28—a
ton. Decide to take it. Pay a deposit & leave. Helen says I have a
pompous manner with people. We learn there has been & is a
strike on this line. Cars uncertain. Still we take it. Come back
roasting the L.A. social atmosphere—the way they blow about the
climate when it is really not as perfect as they say. Stop at a
Cafeteria in 4th St & serve ourselves. Helens democratic way of
studying things out. Afterward go to P.O. & get <u>one</u> letter from
adv. for rooms put in Examiner. Then return home & to bed.
Room very cold. We read—I, "Pragmatism" by Prof. Paul Carus;[28]
Helen—The "Genius"—She quits crying over Angela. The
description of the Ceasarian operation frightens her. After a while I
soothe her & we indulge in a long round & laugh at her fright.

Friday, Dec 5—1919— Los Angeles. Rains all day—damp & chilly.
I work on the South Sea Scenario. In the even Helen & I go down
town & dine at Hoffmans (2nd & Spring)—a new, and the first
decent medium priced restaurant I have found. Afterward to the
Auditorium theatre where we see <u>Woman.</u> A trashy attempt at
something grand by one Maurice Tourneur.[29] Home in disgust &
in the rain. I am depressed because Helen recieved a letter from
Hess. I recieved letters from Mencken, Ida Goldman.[30] The
modernist group etc. Read <u>Modernist</u> which has three excerpts
from books of mine & an editorial.[31] To bed & I am cold which
worries Helen greatly. Finally she wins me round to—the usual
seance. We do not get to sleep before 3:30.

28. Paul Carus (1852–1919) was a German-born philosopher who settled in America.
Carus was an insistent rationalist who believed that philosophy could be reduced to an objective
science. He was a prolific author but published no volume entitled *Pragmatism;* Dreiser is
probably reading one of the several hundred articles Carus wrote during his career.
  29. Maurice Tourneur (1876–1961), producer, director.
  30. Ida Goldman was a young stenographer working in New York who began writing
complimentary letters to Dreiser on 18 September 1919.
  31. Dreiser's "True Art Speaks Plainly" appeared in the first issue of *The Modernist,*
November 1919, p. 21. Subsequent issues of the magazine, which seems to have had only a brief
run, have not survived.

Sunday, Dec—7—1919 (Highland Park LA.) Helen & I get up late
—Breakfast here—She has a pork roast for dinner. We climb the
hill at the East End of Walnut Hill Ave. The hills that looked liked
people lying down. We find a fine place for a hammock. The queer
whose windows the boys daubed. "Whoever put this paint on these
windows had better come & rub it off. The jail awaits such as you".
Wonderful dinner & evening—We read & go to bed early.

Dec   1919—L-A.
The Mexican Theatre in Spring St Los Angeles. The tearful play
————the simple audience. Mexican romance & American.

Thursday—Dec 18—1919 Los Angeles. At 4 Helen & I knock off
& walk East along 60th Ave into the hills. The Jap farm. The Jap
picture bride in mens clothes singing & picking white geraniums for
the market. The wonderful cups in the hills. Somehow brings back
my youth & my mother. We climb the rise & then down—picking
up a little wood for a fire. Helens beauty—almost unbelievable.
Work some more—then down to stores. Aspargus 45 cents a can.
Bread 14 cents a loaf. Eggs 75 cents a dozen. Butter 78^{cts} a pound.
We dine at Cowans—then home & work until 10. Then to bed.
Helens moods. Most ugly in character. Her indifference to public
opinion. Her playfulness. She likes to torture the cat. Hours before
the mirror. Her brutal lust.
  "He's got me down & he's putting it to me"
  "He's putting it to me now. He's putting it to me now"
  Her love of clouds, flowers, sunsets, beautiful views & homes.
  "Doesn't need to read—she claims—gets all life direct & knows
as much as anyone. Optomistic. Her letter to Mary Pickford.[32]

Wednesday—Dec. 24—1919— Los Angeles. A Hot day. Sky clear
as usual. Being the day before Christmas we think we ought to go
somewhere but do not. I go over to S. Pasadena Ave & get stamps,
bananas & toilet paper. Send telegram to Mencken & Lill. The dull
girl sending the message. Return & at four Helen wants to go
down town. We decide to go together. Ride to P.O. on Garvanza

32. Mary Pickford (1893–1979), actress. Helen's letter has not survived.

---

car. New moon. Beautiful sky. We get off at P.O. Letters from
McCardell & Jones.[33] A silk shirt from Lill. We walk up Spring to
4th—looking for Fig Pudding. Go to a place in 4th near Hill. Get
2 puddings, a pumpkin pie & a fruit cake. Take dinner afterwards
at the cafeteria next door. Excellent ham with champagne sauce &
spinach. Afterward we take a car & come directly home. Sound of
Christmas festivities upstairs. Helen & I have some tea & go to bed.
She is as delicious as usual. It is amazing how her charm wears.
Each new view of her is as fascinating as the first.

Millicent Dolores Blaha	Williamina Patricia Shellshock
Herman Majolica Dillwine	Rollin Otto Peddlecord
Leguma Sittenstriker Katznoratz	Maurice Littleribbon
Roscoe Skunkwiller	Fraschhouser
John Groan	Bettina Fishbone
Rhondda St. Cyres Nethercut	Gloria Schimmelflug
Katinka Rarehide	Harry Riviera Spotcash
	Axel Goldenrod[34]

Dec. 25—1919 — (Thursday—Christmas Day—Los Angeles.) It is
as bright & warm as yesterday. Helen & I decide to take a trip
somewhere—to Santa Barbara possibly. We dress & go down town
without breakfast. Stop in & have cakes & coffee. Then hunt for
car. No cars ever on any holiday in L.A. We find one—at 3\frac{00}{}$ per
hour. But the trip is too long. Decide on Mt Lowe. The trip out
there. Leave at 1:30 P.M. Fare 2\frac{32}{}$. The delightful mountain views.
Echo canyon. The incline (1300 feet). The 3 1/2 mile trolley ride
around cliff edges! The Inn. Inspiration Point. A christmas dinner
without roast turkey. Fierce roast suckling Pig. Car leaves at 7:15.
The lights of L.A. & all the other places. View of sea going up. We
get off at Pasadena & get some Magnesia water. Take S. Pasadena
car & get off at our place. Helen does a little clog. The cards on
the bushes on Mt Lowe. The observatory. Cappella in the
Constellation of Sagittarus. 40 light years away. A double Sun.
Light travels at 186,000 miles per second.

---

33. Roy L. McCardell, author, journalist, editor. McCardell did a brief biographical
sketch of Dreiser that appeared in the *New York Sunday Telegraph* of 28 December 1919.
J. Jefferson Jones (see p. 118, n. 7).
34. This list of comic names may be an exercise in imitation of Mencken, who often
invented similar characters in his letters.

Friday. Dec 26—1919. Los Angeles. Beautiful day. Something wrong with my stomach. Work until 4 P.M. on The Bulwark—then walk with Helen.[35] Do the two little hills up the road. Then walk along St. L & LA back to Ostrich farm. Gather Pepper tree branches. Then along S. Pasadena ave to store. Helen in a gay mood—most beautiful. We have dinner. The incident of the <u>veal loaf</u>. I get sick. Wind up with a long delightful hour in our bed.

Wed. Dec 31—1919—Los Angeles. Gray-bright day. Get up at 8 A.M. & walk to S. Pasadena—Mission St. See a small barn covered with palm leaves. See a man using a palm leaf as a brush or broom. Buy 2 dozen oranges off the trees at 30 cents a dozen. Am offered fresh cleaned rabbits. This is the day after my turn down by Mr Lasky & I am feeling rather glum. Also the early death of Frank Pixley (Pixley & Luders) depresses me.[36] Life seems so futile—a mere nothing. Return & Helen is just starting breakfast. I build a fire in the grate. After breakfast write letters—to Lill, Liveright.
    This was sent over fastened under the cats neck ribbon*

Sunday, Jan 4—1920. L.A. Worked at home in A.M.   P.M. (about 2) went down to P.O. Letters from Lill & several others. Helen & I walk up Spring to 4th. See hot crawfish from Seattle. $1<u>20</u> a dozen! Have chocolate in a Pig & whistle place—then take West 11<u>th</u> St. car to end. Beautiful new residence section out Hollywood way. Delightful evening. Warm. A moon. Our search for a public comfort station. None! Back to hotel Stillwell. Then to Pign Whistle—or one like it. Dinner 1<u>00</u> each. Small booths. The dutch costumes. No real service.

Sunday Jan 11—1920 (Los Angeles)
Trip to Long Beach. Beautiful day. Helen & I rise early & take Pasadena Ave (Red Car) down town to P.E. Station—(6th & Main). There buy tickets for Long Beach & then having 1/2 hour to wait walk South in Main to an old bookstore. Life of U.S. Grant!

35. Dreiser continued to work sporadically on *The Bulwark* until he began *An American Tragedy* in the summer of 1920.
    36. Frank Pixley (1867–1919), teacher, writer, editor, dramatist. Pixley belonged to The Lambs Club in New York and the Bohemian Club in San Francisco, both of which Dreiser attended.
    *See the facsimile on p. 346 of this volume.

Mrs. Sigourneys Poems![37] Look at some young puppies in a dog store. Dogs are so emotional. Back to car & ride out to Long Beach. Great speed. Helen looking charming in her maroon velvet. Flat, open country between L.A. & Long B. The goat "service" for sale. Santa Catalina in distance. We arrive at LB: Cottages. The search for a restaurant. So many closed on Sunday. The beach. The gulls. We walk out & back along an avenue on the cliff facing sea. Rare flowers. Charming houses. No flats for rent. The red conical flowers on a tall stalk. Helen says they remind her of dogs——. The sea. Her natural artistry. Back to Virginia hotel where we rest. The palm rooms, flying machines, lawn, tennis courts. A battle ship fleet comes into view. At Sunset we walk toward it to end of walk. Ocean ave. All property for sale. At dusk take car to Los Ange & dine at[38]

Helen to the cat
"Is a itty bitty skookoo
Whas matter? Eeh?
Dos like at? No?
Oh, dare! Yaas. Was itty bitty skookoo

<u>Los Angeles—Sat Jan 17—1920.</u> A hot clear, bright day. Helen & I rise at 7$\frac{30}{}$. Easy enough to get her up when we're going somewhere (San Diego). She gets breakfast—("hominy & chops) & sees Mrs. Meuler about care of cat in our absence. Leave at 9:30 for Motor Bus Station (5th & Los Angeles Streets) to San Diego. Grand. We check grip. Walk up to old book store. Book on Arizona with picture of National Boundery Line in heart of Nogales. Also painted desert. I buy "Terminology of the Vedas" by Pandit Gura Datta Vidyarthi, M.A. Prof. Physical Science, Government College, Lahore.[39] Read in Huckleberry Finn. Back to Motor Bus. Our grip is lost—then found. In car & we're off through Anaheim ∟　　　∟ Fullerton, ∟　　　∟ to San Capistrano & San Diego. The smooth road. Oranges. Lemons. "Sunkist" ranches.

37. Lydia Howard Huntley Sigourney (1791–1865), a poet whose sentimental verse won her the title "Sweet Singer of Hartford."
38. The entry breaks off at this point; Dreiser never finished it.
39. *The Terminology of the Vedas and European Scholars* (1893) by Guru Datta Vidyarthi (1864–90).

Dreiser and Helen in Hollywood

Our speed. Our companions. Beautiful eucalyptus trees. "Pompous" Grass. The smudge pots under trees. Drain pipes at ends of rows. Heavy traffic. Mountains in distance. Helen very loving en route. Arrive at San Capistrano Lunch. Buen Chicken ala King. The old monastery. We speed on. A touch of desert. The road by the sea. The different towns L   ,   ⌐ . Sunshine all the way. Great views. Great climbs. Country that suggests Stevensons Scotland. Into San "Deego." Poorer looking town. The Hotel U.S. Grant. Room without bath $4 & $5. With bath 8\underline{^{00}}$ per day (no borad) for two. We register & then indulge in delicious screw. At 5$\underline{^{30}}$ go out & sit on balcony. At 7 go to Palace restaurant. Order three things which we don't get & leave. Then to Maryland. Fried chicken & corn. At 8 walk about & look at town. Learn we cant go to Tia Juana on Sunday. Helen rages against American puritanism.

Tell her story of Mrs. Springer of N.Y. We return to hotel. Sit on balcony. To bed at 11—very tired.

Sunday, Jan 18—1920 San Diego.
Gray at first—clearer later—but misty at night. Up at 8—expecting to go to Tia Juana. Breakfast in hotel ("Little Pig" Sausages & wheat cakes) This hotel. Officers—Navy & Army. The usual solemn, homely family groups. We go round to the Hotel Botsford (6th near Broadway) & try to get tickets. No tickets on Sunday. Government officers not on duty! We go to Balboa Park. Our surprise. The chicken & cat show. Accidental. The pool & arborium. Japanese garden. I describe the ideal hotel. We sit near the pool. Discuss the Japanese. Visit ethnological museum. Early Indians—Choctaws, Chicasaws, Cliff Dwellers. Then primary skulls of men Nieanderthal Man, ⌐ , ⌐. We leave & go into gardens again. The beautiful colored church (California Bldg.) We here an organ. Find it. Scripp out of door organ. Helen steals flowers. To car & on out to end of line. Soldiers & sailors! Our comments. Mission Ridge View of Distent Mountains. Back to hotel & rest. Then out & hire a car to take us to Cliff Rocks 3\underline{00}$. Chauffeur is like Williard Huntington Wright & tries to do us.[40] I sting him. To hotel, wash & dine. Excellent Sole Marguery, tomatoes fried & a salad. We sit in lobby after & Helen tells me of Ned Weyburn & Gus Edwards—their attitude toward her.[41] Up to balcony & we discuss Alice Joyce & Mary Miles Minter who is in hotel.[42] Her white car: She is appearing at a movie house. Has a maid, secretary & chauffeur. At 10$\underline{30}$ up to room. No screw. To bed. Very tired.

Monday. Jan 19—1920—San Diego. Up at 8. Go to "Bean Pot" for breakfast. Get stung. Then to another restaurant. Then to Botsford House & get auto tickets for Tia Juana. Gray day. The two characters we take on at the Union Station. National City. Sweet Water Valley. San Diego & Arizona railroad. Chula Vista

---

40. Willard Huntington Wright (1888–1939), author, journalist, editor.
41. Ned Weyburn and Gus Edwards were well-known vaudevillian actors and songwriters with whom Helen was associated for a brief time.
42. Alice Joyce (1890–1955), actress; Mary Miles Minter, motion picture actress.

region. All lemons. Tia Juana Valley. Poor houses. The border. Our American inspector. The Mexican Inspector. New Casino & hotel. Tia Juana. The little low wooden houses. Mexican soldiers. Bull ring.   The two saloons. "Ladies Welcome." The Gamblers. Helen gambles. I win 10-to-1. The men who broke the bank at the 21-table. Leave at 1:20. Up Silver strand to Coronado. We get off. That hotel. The town of Coronado. We have lunch. Car to ferry. The bay. Flying machines. War vessels. Back to hotel. Dinner at 7 in hotel. We take a walk. Then back. Helens interest in dancing. Her practice.

Tuesday. Jan 20—1920 San Diego Up at 8. We breakfast in hotel. Then to Mission Gardens where we see a beautiful view of a deep valley. The sheep being turned out. Flowers. Old men pitching horse shoes. Back down town. The little Italian girl who giggled so. It is gray & dull. We sit in hotel till 12:30. Then out for a magazine & some candy. Then to Union Auto Station. Get our old seats & same driver to L.A. The fine beaches. Stratford, Cardiff. The story of Mary Cardiff—told by Helen——Oceanside. The sharp curves. Our reckless driver. The husband who came late to the car & the nervous wife. San Capistrano. The wretched guide. Oranges, Walnut trees, Cypress. Eucalyptus. We go over same rout—Tustin, Orange, Anaheim, Fullerton. Dusk as we enter Fullerton. In via Stephensen Ave. We arrive at 6. "Back to the United States". To P.O. Various letters—Smith, Rodick, Miss Haviland, Lill, etc.[43] We dine at 4th St. Cafeteria. Water affects my stomach queerly. We come out to Herman on Garvanza car. Helens apprehension as to cat. We go to bed about 10.

Thursday—Jan 22$^{\underline{nd}}$—1920 L.A. Rain all day. Work on & all but finish A Summer in Arcady.[44] (Clara) Helen goes out to Culver City to see Ince.[45] We meet at 7—Rosslyn Hotel to dine. I draw

43. Edward H. Smith, journalist and close friend of Dreiser. Smith is the original for "Jethro" in "Olive Brand," in *A Gallery of Women* (see p. 158, n. 28).
   Florence Earle Haviland wrote to Dreiser on 12 January 1920 expressing her appreciation of *Twelve Men.*
44. This title does not appear on any published work by Dreiser or on any of his unpublished manuscripts.
45. Alexander Ince (1892–1966), director, producer, publisher.

$40^{\underline{00}}$ at Hellman Bank. We eat at Levys—a bad one. See a girl who looks like Louise.

Tuesday, Feb. 24—1920   Los Angeles. This is the ninth day of gray or raining weather (5 straight days of rain here) & cool all the time. Helen sick with tonsilities & cold. From 10 to twelve I work on mss. Two to 4:30 play with Helen. We copulate 3 times. At 5 return to work & at 7 get dinner. 9 P.M. to bed. This day I began again on the Bulwark trying to go ahead with it after having laid it aside for some weeks.

Thursday. Mch. 4—1920. Los Angeles
A glorious day. P.M. I write on porch but stop to go with Helen up to the top of the hill. We take the cat which puffs with its tongue out & climbs trees. The wonderful lavender shaded hills—the letter T over back of Pasadena. We come down at 4 & indulge in long round in the bedroom. Then I return to work & Helen goes down town to the store. At six she comes back wildly enthusiastic because of the moonlight & after toast & tea we walk over toward Garvanza car line. Find a College of some kind—yellow stone—rich in the moonlight. The voices of the boys—singing! We study quaint streets in the dark. Finally arrive home at eleven. Helen so beautiful. Her physical lovliness makes me sad at times.

Friday, March 5—1920— Bright & clear. A wonderful day. Helen & I worrying over Wrights proposition to take us to Frisco decide that we have to notify him without giving him our address or telephone number. We start to dress at 2. The day is so fine. Helen cleans house & presses my suit. Our gay trip down. She wears her new sport coat & pink hat. Go to P.O. & mail income tax form & check. Then Walk over to Hollywood line. Get shine. Call up Ferdinand Pinney Earle, who invites me out to his studio in Hollywood & says he will have Wright here.[46] Helen insists on walking back to Red electric line Station at 4th & Hill to get a seat. This makes me angry but we go & fail to get a seat. Dont speak but finally make up. The Earle Studio at dusk. The beautiful bungalow

46. Ferdinand Earle, motion picture director.

done—adobe-cliff dweller style. We rave. Earle explains his scheme. Wright is there. He is doing The Rubaiyat. Invites me to stay & meet his wife & children. We do. At 8 he takes us to car line in his car. I tell Helen that I told Wright that we were going to Santa Barbara together & she gets angry—cries & wont speak. We quarrel. To McKees where she eats & demands cigarettes. Finally tries to make up & we do, but quarrel again on way home. She finally leaves bed & sleeps in back room with cat but we cant stay away from each other long & I go & get her & we make up.

Saturday March 6—1920   Los Angeles We get up early as we are off to Santa Barbara. It is bright & clear. I pack bag. Helen takes cat upstairs for girl to keep. We go to car & then to P.O. & then to bank where I draw $50<u>00</u> and then to breakfast in the Pullman Lunch in 6th Street, then to the Pickwick Stage. Our companions! Harold Lincoln Palmer—the aviator! Auto goes out through Hollywood. New types of bungalows suggesting Mayen-on-the-Moselle. Santa Susansa Moorpark. Camarillo. Oxnard. Ventura Sea Cliff.
The beauty of the day—pearly gray. Suggests an English spring. "When Shepherds pipe on oaten straws". The fine homes. We rave over the delights of travel. The wonder of the ranges of hills. We cross a valley 6 miles wide. Fine schools. Sugar beet fields. The range of hills this side Moorpark. The machine ahead & its dust. Palmer gets gay of drinks that are supposed to be had at Santa Barbara. (A psychic jag) The history of the Lima bean (The Lewis Lima Bean). Palmers history. The man who gave the church to Camarillo. Why Palmer is riding. Broke his flying machine at Paso Robles. We drink (near beer) at Oxnard. More gay talk. The men at Ruicon. Palmers idea of an ideal trip— ("From Seattle to Alaska in a 30 ft Motor Boat") We pass Ventura, Strike Sea. The largest grape vine in the world. We blow out a tire. Arrive finally at Santa Barbara—3:10. Old English Coaching days. We get a taxi & go to the Arlington—No rooms. None at any hotel. We phone. In dispair appeal to a real estate man. The Rainey. Our room. Bath & dress. Go down Main Street to the Ambassador. The grill—or Palm Room. I am over awed. Return & eat at the Rowes—then back to the Ambassador. Palmers grand grill is closed. The Ambassadorians. Helen & I sit outside & watch them. Walk by sea. The full moon.

Her gayety. Home at 11 & to bed. For once I am really happy with a woman. H's talk about herself. Her keen insight into life. Not envious. Her moral brutality. "I have the —— & I know how to use it, don't I? Don't I? (etc)

<u>Sunday March 7—1920—Santa Barbara</u> Cloudy but warm. We bath & dress by 10:30. Then go to breakfast at the State Café. Excellent country sausage & cakes. I have a better appetite than when in L.A. Afterward we return toward room & price autos by the hour. They are $3<u>00</u>. At the hotel I get Mrs. Huston to call up the same garage & they want $4 & $5—$3<u>00</u> for a Ford—thinking she is speaking for tourists. Roses in my path. We clean up in room—I shave. Then go out & hire a machine—2 hours for 5<u>00</u>. Visit the old mission & listen to the history of that institution by a monk who looks as though the love of God didnt agree with him. The indian decorations, the vaults & graves—the cross in the trees. Deadly night shade. Out & into machine. We pass the home of Prince Hopkins & his mother—Also El Mirasol, the hotel. Also the tourists hotel on the hill. A lovely view of Santa Barbara. Then down & accross to Boyland—Prince Hopkins School. The map of the world in concrete & water. The lovely rooms. We stay nearly an hour. Helens joy. Then down & start up a hill to the North of the town but a tire blows out & we limp back to the Main Street. The smallness of Santa Barbara—the beauty—the lovely Moorish & Spanish houses here & there. A bottle of ginger ale "with capsicum." Afterwards we start for room. More roses. The "niceness" of the section in which we live. By accident we come upon El Mirasol again. The perfect hotel. Its rugs, silk hangings. Its interior! Sit in its chairs & on its lawn till 3. Helen plans a trip to Frisco & smokes. The robin on the lawn. Her appetite for granduer. Decide to return here to dinner. We go to room & dress & read. At 6:45 walk over through park. Miss Armour & her table for 6. The dinner. Afterward walk over to Arlington. The crowd there, listening to a lecture. We then go down to the Ambssader. The gross woman singer. The crowd. At 10:30 take car home. Get a gingerale—"with capsicum". More fun in room. Helens love. Asleep about midnight. We like Santa Barbara.

<u>Monday, March 8—1920, Santa Barbara</u> It is very cloudy & this decides me to return to L.A. this day. Why stay when it looks like

rain. I Go to the barbers for a haircut & then meet Helen at the State cafe. The English according to the papers are just trying to grab Constantinople & the Sweet French to distroy the Bolshiviki. We walk down "Main" street & register for the 4 P.M. bus back. Then walk along Sea Shore north, past The Ambassador. Sea weed. I eat some. Sea gulls. A Sandpiper. Rocks & cliffs. The King wave! A "hell diver" or Northern loon. Back by a road known as Alta Vista. The naked Eucalyptus trees. The house so Moorish—a silk rug over a balcony! We come down by the road our driver meant to take. The small houses below. Helens dreams of ours— & what it would be like. We steal some roses. The neighborhood children "skipping the rope." Back & buy a veil. Rest awhile. Dress & go to the auto stage line office. 4 P.M. leave for L.A. The gray clouds. The different kind of crowd. The heavy handsome fellow who wanted to flirt with Helen. Montecito, Ventura etc. Arrive at Moorpark by dusk. The lights on the road—like long antennae. The danger. We enter L.A. at 8. At stage office at 8:15. We dine at the Pullman café. Then to P.O. I get little but books & complaints. Lills three letters swearing eternal fealty! Home & I tease the cat, then play with Helen & finally go to sleep.

Tuesday, March 9—1920. Los Angeles. Very grey & rainy—a horrible day. Work on letters all day. Helen goes down town in a sour mood. I follow at 6. Dinner at the Lankershim. Checks from Liveright & ⌊ ⌋ totaling $433.00. Deposit them at bank. Helen gets letter from her sister. She wants to leave her husband & come & live with her. Cries because her sister said she neednt let anyone know that she was her sister. Her sobbing, moving method of crying—most wonderful. I pet her & get her out of it. A sweety girl this.

Friday, March 12, 1920 Los Angeles

Work all day at Newspaper Days & succeed very well.[47] It is charming out of doors. At night go down to meet Helen who has gone on ahead. She is all excited about selling Mary Pickford a movie I wrote with her in mind called Lady Bountiful—Jr—pure

47. Dreiser was trying to complete *Newspaper Days,* which Boni & Liveright published on 15 December 1922, as *A Book About Myself.* In 1931, when Dreiser published *Dawn,* Liveright reissued the book and added "Newspaper Days" to the title.

hoakum— & sweet morale optimism prepared for movie sale.[48] The
agent thought it was so good. Favorable letters from many quarters
including Liveright. So, for an hour, occasionally the winds die
down, the sun shines & all is well. Even the evening is spring like.
We dine in the Alexandria Grill. Helen is simply stunning—like a
pansy for beauty. We leave at 9:30 & come home still gay & after
much love making go to bed. A successful day—one.

+

Sunday, March 14—1920, Los Angeles A nice, clear day but
windy. Helen & I start for Pasadena to see the big hotels—
Raymond, Green, The Maryland, etc. On my advice we go via
Eagle Rock car to Eagle Rock Park & look for a bus. There is a bus
line, but we miss one. Helen becomes pettish & we fight. I call her
a "god damned sour dough." She gets nervous after a time &
attempts to make up. Along this road which is beautiful we see the
Annandale Country Club, a handsome thing. Soon enter Pasadena
via a wondrous viaduct. Then to a restaurant, then to the Hotel
Green which is a huge barn, badly furnished. From there we go to
the Hotel Maryland, a very different place—almost as good as El
Mirasol at Santa Barbara. The hat shop. The Italian & his monkey. I
give up 10 cents. We stay till 7 P.M. Then to Renee's in the Hotel
Green where we dine. I see a stunning girl there & attract her
attention. Helen becomes conscious of it, but says nothing. We
walk to the So. Pasadena car & then home. Helen dances naked &
in a small tight fitting chemisette which ends in the usual way.

Tuesday. March 16—1920. Los Angeles
Work all day in Public Library on Pittsburgh.[49] At 6:30 meet
Helen at the Lankershim. We eat at the Chocolate Shop. Then go
to see "Into the Light" one of the worst movies I have ever seen &

48. "Lady Bountiful, Jr.," which Dreiser called "a film adaptation of a proposed novel,"
is among his papers at the University of Pennsylvania. In twenty pages of typescript, Dreiser
tells a convoluted, improbable story of disinheritance, class conflict, and romantic intrigue. The
climax occurs when the heroine, a young singer who is set adrift in the world after being cheated
out of her money by her stepfather, is rescued by her real father whom she has never met. Her
father, an internationally known opera star, reunites her with her lover and takes them both to
Europe with him.
49. For the Pittsburgh chapters of *Newspaper Days*, Dreiser is here supplementing his
recollections with research into the city he visited as a younger man.

I have seen some fierce movies. Home in the rain. All of a dozen letters this day.

Wednesday, Mch. 17—1920. Los Angeles. St. Patricks day. Helen & I get up early & go down to Public Library—5th & Brdwy. I am looking up data about Pittsburgh for Newspaper Days. (To refresh my memory) We have breakfast at the King George. Cakes & country sausage. The waiter's mistake. "Yes—cunt". We see a parade of the Al. G. Barnes Circus along Broadway & I see how tame the old lurid show wagons have become along side the modern auto moving van, etc. Work 2 hours in Library. Then go out into West Lake region looking for rooms. The beauty of the day. West Lake Ave. Hoover Street. At 3 come down town & go to bank. Then to Times office & put in an adve. Then to P.O. & meet Helen. We come out on Garvanza car line & stop & get some ham. Cross the little bridge at foot of 57th & see the young kids. Go to work at 5:30 & work without stop until 9 P.M. Then eat & to bed.

+

Sunday, April 4—1920, Los Angeles
(588 N. Larchmont). A wonderful day. Clear & warm. Helen & I walk to Hollywood for Breakfast. Enroute find Metro Plant & the Hollywood Studios (Film). The latter very graceful & old Spanishy. We walk out streets north of Hollywood Boul & see splendid homes. Helens hopeful dreams of a place for us. Stay in Hollywood Hotel & rest on porch. Types of movie actors & actresses here. The cars! The riding costumes for women! At 3 P.M. we go down town to P.O.—then home on West 6th St car. That night we dine again in Hollywood—(Franks) & meet Wright & Claire Burke who has come on from N.Y. City. Her history. Home & to bed. I am depressed about Bulwark.

Monday— April 5— 1920 Los Angeles Beautiful, warm day. Helen in her new black & white striped dress essays the Christie & Metro Studios. She makes an impression. An actor follows her. Christie personally promises her work. She is very much excited & looks wonderful. I never saw her look better.
　　Christie "Can you wear a bathing suit."
　　H — Yes. I can wear a bathing suit, all right.

<u>Christie</u> You may hear from me sooner than you think.
We find a dandy little restaurant opposite Hollywood Hotel—cor.
Highland Ave & eat there Monday night.

<u>Friday—April 9—1920. Los Angeles</u> Living at 588 N. Larchmont
Street. We breakfast at a little place in Santa Monica Boul for 1<u>st</u>
time. View a charming new, Frenchy Studio in ⌐　 ⌐ . Return
home & I tackle <u>Bulwark</u> & finish chapter 13—terrible hard work.
No gayety of soul here. It rains. Helen goes down town. Bring
futile mail—a letter from Maguerite Lopez for one thing promising
me a new girl if I will meet her![50] At one, in rain we go to the
Cafe Beaux Arts opposite Metro—in Romaine Street. A wretched
little place. Home & to bed—very tired. I read a pamphlet on Sex
Hygiene before sleeping. Also in La Peau de Chagrin.[51]

<u>Saturday, April 10<u>th</u> 1920. Los Angeles</u>
Clear & cool but windy—after a rainy day on Friday. We go to
little place opposite Metro Studio in Romaine Street for breakfast.
Poor food. We watch actors & actresses arriving in cars for work. I
get a sense of great animal activity & joy in life in those whom we
see here. Walk back to room & I go to work on Porch. Too windy.
Work in small room till 4—finish chapter 14 (new version) of
Bulwark. Then we go down town to P.O. Get monthly check of
$50 from Miss ONeill for studio.[52] Helen gets hopeful letter from
Mary Pickford as to "Lady Bountiful, Jr" the film story we
submitted to her. Take car out to Hollywood & dine at Franks.
Walk around before & enjoy beauty of a spring evening. In
restaurant meet Ferdinand Earle (once known in East as 'Affinity
Earle') who is now a moving picture director in Highland Ave. &
doing <u>Omar.</u> We talk of Wright. Come out & walk along
Hollywood Boul. Buy fish for cat & a jar of blackberry jam. Then

50. Marguerite Lopez was a young woman living in Fresno, California, who began a
correspondence with Dreiser in April 1918. Over the years their letters resulted in a casual
intimacy in which Miss Lopez often brought her emotional problems to Dreiser's attention.
51. *La Peau de Chagrin* by Honoré de Balzac (1799–1850).
52. Dreiser sublet his New York studio apartment to Eleanora R. O'Neill, an old friend
whose literary judgement he trusted. Their correspondence begins in 1911 when, as an editor
at the *Boston Transcript*, she wrote Dreiser to praise *Jennie Gerhardt.* By 1913, he was showing
her the manuscript of The *"Genius"* for editorial suggestions.

home across Vine Street. Stop in charming new cottage which is open, to see it. An idea for a start of a movie comes to me. Farther on—an idea for a short story comes to me which someday I hope to do, title, "Fulfillment"[53]—Helen is reading The Riddle of the Universe by Haeckel—and enjoying it very much.[54]

+

Sunday. April 11th—1920—Los Angeles (Living at 588 N. Larchmont Street—near Brunton & Metro Studios. Studios in neighborhood are—National, Reelart (Both on Santa Monica Boul.) Brunton is on Melrose Ave, near Western. We are near Gower & Vine Streets, leading directly into Hollywood. Radium-Sulpher Bath House at end of our street.) We get up at 8:30. Helen plays with cat. I give it some fish. At 9:30 we start down town. Helen in her dark purple velvet & little black hat. She finds a cat over the way with a broken leg. We then have to go for enough chloroform to kill it—Price 35 cents for a small phial. Chloroform turned over to woman who has taken cat in. The owner arrives & offers to return the .35^{cts} to Helen. We finally go down town on the West 6th Street car. Helen complains of pains in her kidneys. I recommed a little sweet spirits of nitre in hot water. We go to the Gates Hotel Dining Room—6th & Flower for breakfast. At table Helen faints. Cashier & I lay her out on floor. She comes too, sits up & finally lies down on a couch in lobby. We try for a doctor—none to be had on Sunday. All motoring here. I then call a taxi & take her home—fare $2^{50} for a ten minute run! Once in bed she feels better. Eats blackberry jam & crackers. Finally goes to sleep. Believes it is due to menstrual period coming on. I return to work at my desk at 2 P.M.

Sunday April 18—1920 Los Angeles Helen & I rise late. Breakfast at Franks in Hollywood Boul. Then go out to Beverly Hills. Our long talks about a cottage here. We plan one—a beauty. The beauty

53. "Fulfillment" was published in *Holland's Magazine* 43 (February 1924): 7–9, 31. It was later reprinted in *Chains* (1927).
54. *The Riddle of the Universe at the Close of the Nineteenth Century* (1900) by Ernst Haeckel (1834–1919).

of Beverly Hills. The Park near the station. Red water lillys in the pond there. The Beverly Hills Hotel. The tea pagoda. Tea for two 1$\underline{^{00}}$. We sit on the verandah. The women playing tennis. Their affected voices. The many high priced cars. We take a walk. The beautiful houses. That of Douglas Fairbanks & Mary Pickford interests Helen most. Her dreams. Mocks my singing. She is too beautiful not to have a car & I resent our poverty. Back on Santa Monica line to El Centro Street. Then over to house. We ride down to Alvarado Street & eat in the Chocolate Shop. The outrageous prices. I get sore over the whole gouging system & swear never to eat there again. Home & to bed. Reading "Conflict Between Science & Religion" by Draper.[55]

Wednesday. April 21$\underline{^{st}}$ 1920. Los Angeles Breakfast in Cohens Santa Monica Boul. Helen dresses & goes to look up movie work. I work all day on Newspaper Days. Complete Chapter 15 & get 5 ready to send on East. At 5 Helen returns. We dress & walk over to Hollywood. The incident of the black starving cat. We buy it meat. The dog chases it. Helens mood. We go down town to P.O. A delightful ride. I get various letters including a $300 check from E.R.O.[56] Also many favorable reviews of Hey, Rub-a-Dub Dub.[57] Read them on way out. Laugh over Menckens characterization of the character of American newspapers—anent Upton Sinclairs—The Brass Check.[58] Finish last chapter of Drapers Conflict of Science & Religion. Then to bed & soon to sleep. My heart is bothering me a good deal these days.

Thursday. April 22$\underline{^{nd}}$ 1920. Los Angeles. Up at 7:30. Hot bath & shave. Instead of going over to Santa Monica Boulevard for breakfast (Cohens Cafeteria) we go down town. After walking into a Greek Restaurant & finding it empty we go on to our favorite place at 8th & Grand—near the Stillwell. Deliver laundry to the

---

55. *History of the Conflict between Science and Religion* (1875) by John William Draper (1811–1882).
56. "E.R.O." is Eleanora R. O'Neill (see p. 310, n. 52).
57. *Hey Rub-a-Dub-Dub: A Book of the Mystery and Wonder and Terror of Life* was published on 15 January 1920.
58. *The Brass Check: A Study of American Journalism* (1919) by Upton Sinclair (1878–1968).

Japs in 8th Street. I get mad at Helen because she failed to put in a silk shirt of mine & call her the most infernally lazy creature I ever knew. She gets angry & freezes up. In restaurant afterward can hardly eat. On way out she cries & I try to console her. She is truly sensitive & so easily wounded that a much less rough comment would make her cry. Leaves me at Hill Street & I go into Hamburgers Dept Store to find a P.O. Branch. There mail Chapters 61–65 of Newspaper Days to Mrs. Kubitz to be copied. Register same. Go accross to Main Street & down to Hellman Bank where I deposit $300—loaned me by E. ONeill. Walk on down to 5th for a car. Get a shoe shine. Now that the tourist crowd has gone L.A. shines are 10 cents. Enquire & learn of an auto trip to the top of Mt. Wilson for 3⁵⁰ round trip. Take car. On entering drop a quarter which supposedly rolls into street. Conductor tells me to go get it & without thinking I obey. Find it on step. Felt confused & ashamed at so easily being made to obey. Read of failure of morphine clinic in L.A. Also of Lloyd Georges contempt for Wilson & the League of Nations. Once home (588 N. Larchmont) write various letters & finally work on Newspaper Days. At 4 Helen comes. In a kind of wild desperation over not having all the money she wants she has pawned her ring & bought two hats, 1 dress, a pair of shoes & some stockings. Her frenzy of delight over her purchases. Wildly describes their beauty. Drunkeness in men & clothes buying in women are kind passions. It is a kind of debauch. The gleam in her eyes. I cannot complain for the ring is her own. Her beauty in one of new hats staggers me. We fool around & finally indulge in a fierce round after which I return to work. Am working on the porch this day in the sun. It is bright—very—but not exactly warm. We are going over to Hollywood to dinner.

Saturday, April 24—1920. Los Angeles Troubled with heart pains. Worked part of day on Newspaper Days. Then took bath in Radium Sulpher Springs bath house. Heart pains leave in sweat box. I am assured by the doctor that I have heart trouble. Helen who has just visited Christie Comedy Studios returns with news that she has captivated leading man & he will get her a part. (How he saw her—waiting in lobby) We return to room & go down town. I buy 2 pr. white flannel trousers. Price has jumped to $15⁰⁰ per pair. Go to P.O. Letter from Liveright saying Anna T. has called on him & threatens to sue if I publish Bulwark.[59] 4 long reviews of Hey Rub-a-Dub-Dub from Detroit. A letter from Arthur Maitland —Frisco, saying he owes me 100\underline{\underline{00}}$ on The Girl in the Coffin—a windfall.[60] We dine at Blue Bird Cafe—go to see ⌞   ⌟, at Magestic Theatre—Then home.

Sunday—April 25—1920—Los Angeles Another clear, warm Sunday. Get up late. Breakfast at Franks in Hollywood. Walk out Highland Ave & look at new type of bungalows—best seen in America so far. (Most chic) Return to Hollywood Boul & take car to Beverly Hills & Beverly Hills hotel where we spend day. See Owen Moore—Mary Pickfords 1st husband. Have tea in summer tea-house. Remain till 6:30—then home. Dinner at Franks. Sit on porch afterward—jot these notes & then to bed.

May 11—1920, Los Angeles—588 N. Larchmont Finished Newspaper Days at 11 A.M. Breakfasted as usual at Cohens in Santa Monica Boul. near Vine Street. Helen & I are taking Tanlac & feel much better. Two reviews of Hey, Rub-a-Dub-Dub, one in Pearsons (Frank Harris) & one in The Review—New York amuse me.[61] My 10$\underline{\underline{00}}$ Nettleton Shoes crack & I decide to return them to the sellers & demand a new pair. Gasoline in New York goes to 33 cents. Carranza being crushed in Mexico. Wilson reported crazy— bars at his window in White House.

Wednesday. May 12—1920 Los Angeles. Mostly cloudy, as usual. I continue to work on a short story called Fulfilment. A fairly interesting day this. Helen & I had planned to go down early in the A.M. to new store just opening in order that she might buy a green waist that I saw in a window for 5$\underline{\underline{00}}$. We get up at 7:30 in order to

---

59. Anna P. Tatum, who in 1912 had told Dreiser the story of her Quaker father which gave him the idea for *The Bulwark* (see p. 132, n. 21). In 1920 she strenuously objected to his using her family in his novel. In later years, after deciding that her family no longer needed protection from publicity, she encouraged Dreiser to finish the book.

60. Arthur Maitland had directed a production by the St. Francis Little Theatre of Dreiser's "The Girl in the Coffin." The play opened on 9 October 1917, at the Colony Ball Room, St. Francis Hotel, San Francisco.

61. Dreiser is referring to Frank Harris, "A Word to Dreiser," *Pearson's Magazine* 45 (May 1920): 902–4, and to an anonymous review, "Brave Mr. Dreiser," *New York Review*, 24 April 1920.

---

get there before anyone else. Owing to a call from the Charles Ray studio & see if they want her at once. This is her first day in the movies. She stays to dress & I go down town. Get waist, send last of <u>Newspaper Days</u> chapters to Bo—then take shoes sold me by the Nettleton Co. in 5<u>th</u> Street back. They refuse to change them & we have a quarrel. Go down to P.O. No letters. Back to 4th Street & have breakfast in a small waffle joint. Pick up a May Smart Set & find Menckens Review of <u>Hey, Rub-a-Dub-Dub,</u> a silly business— but clever.[62] Then come out home (Larchmont 588. North) & fall to work on story. Work all P.M. until at 5:30 Helen calls up & wants me to meet her at Santa Monica Boul & Gower Street. I do. She is full of her experiences as a super —— & the great stir made by her beauty. Ordered to action tomorrow. We walk home & I make some coffee. Then to Cohens for dinner. She turns over 7$\underline{50}$ first days wages for me to keep. Afterward she presses her gown for tomorrow & then takes a bath & then to bed. We stage an orgie— so delightful that it knocks me out. Copulation is beginning to effect my heart.

<u>Friday, May 14</u>—1920 Los Angeles. Helen working over at Charles Ray Studio. Greatly depressed now that she is away all day. Am thinking of returning East. She has made so great a hit that I am slightly jealous. The Studio Photographer comes & gets her in his car & brings her home. Reports all sorts of civilities & approaches from Storm the director— & Ray—down— & I know they are true. Taken to lunch by the group of principals in their car. How they cut out the girl she was with. Al Kaufman the ex prize fighter dances with her & offers to get her work under Raff—at the Brunton. The little "greenie" from Cincinnati. The Yid drummer girl. The extra who wants her to go to the theatre & dinner. Sore because she wont & cuts her on dancing. Storm compliments her on her dress. The old woman who tells her everyone is talking of her. So it goes. I dont think I can keep her long now that she has work & the work is gayer— & the crowd—than I am. Go down to P.O. in A.M. Get insurance blank from N.Y. & fill it out before a docter in the Merchants National.

62. H. L. Mencken, "More Notes from a Diary," *Smart Set* 62 (May 1920): 138–40. The "silly business" is Mencken's analysis of Dreiser's lack of ability in philosophical discourse.

Tuesday, May 18—1920—Los Ange Helen working over at
Charles Ray Studio—43rd & Sunset Boul. Leaves at 7:30 A.M. I am
very lonely. Horribly so. Concieve the story of the jealous clerk
who cannot lose his beauty bride to the movies & finally kills her &
himself. (Bleeding Hearts)[63] Return home & work on Fulfillment.
At noon go over & get a little sausage to eat. At 6:30 Helen
returns—brought home by the Studio camera director in his car. I
feel a little jealous. Helen tells me she's been worrying about me &
shows me the attached letter written to me at the studio which she
didnt get a chance to mail. We go to dinner over in Hollywood.
The poor kid. The work is very trying I know.

9 A.M.
Tuesday.
May 18—1920

Dearest Sweetheart:
  Just finished making up and want to say Hello Honey. I can't think of
anything else but you this morning "seepin in his little beddie". I wish I
could be with you right this minute.
  Honey I love you more than anything in the world. You are wonderful.
My darling baby Teddie boy.
  They are calling "on the set" so I will have to run. I love you, love you,
love you. Wish I could kiss you a million times. The day is so long. I wish
it was 6.30.

Sweetheart.!

Bank Bldg. Am told heart, lungs etc ar o.k. Go down in A.M.—
then again in P.M. Between times cut out all data in relation to
"Blue Beard Watson". Then work on Fulfillment—a short story.
Helen returns at nearly seven—brought by her photographer. I am
made sore by delay, but say nothing. We go to Franks in
Hollywood. I suggest returning to N.Y. in June. She cries. Still I
think it will work out so. We ride down on Hollywood car to Santa
Monica line—then Back on that to Gower Street.

Sunday, May 23rd 1920—Los Angeles.
588 N. Larchmont. We get up at 9 and go to Cohens for breakfast.
Arranged last night for two horses. Helen has bought riding
trousers & puttees in which to ride. Return to room. I work some

---

63. Dreiser never completed "Bleeding Hearts," a short story that survives in twenty-one
handwritten pages at the University of Pennsylvania. In it Dreiser tried to show the erosion of
a young couple's relationship after they are exposed to the pressures of Hollywood. The young
woman's beauty and her ability to earn a larger salary than her husband are the sources of tension
in their marriage.

on chapters 61–64—of Newspaper Days—which Bo sent on. We
then go over & get the horses, riding back across North El Centro
to get the keys & lock things up for fear Mrs. W——will go into
our things. Then out Melrose Ave. to Sawtelle, & up past the
Doheny Estate to a beautiful view. Then on to Beverley Hills &
some canyon, up which we ride. Back along Boulevard which runs
in from Beverley to Melrose Ave & so back. Very tired & sore.
This is the first time I've ridden since Muldoons—1904.[64] Stand
it very well. We eat at Cohens & so to bed. Helen very tired &
sore.

<u>Monday, May 24—1920—Los Angeles</u> Work all day on <u>Fulfillment,</u>
cleaning it up before sending it on to Bo for typing. At 4:30 stop &
go over to office of Camera to see if adv. for a scenario editor has
been put in. It hasnt. Has even been lost. (4513 Sunset Boul). I
raise h—— & upset things generally. Go down to P.O. Letter from
Lillian Rosanoff wanting to will me her savings.[65] One from E. R.
O'N—telling of moving from 165 W. 10 to her new place in
Stuyvesant Sq. Letter from Smith throwing cold water on Hey-Rub-.
One from Kenneth Miller praising <u>The Hand of the Potter.</u>[66] One
from Sam Knoop, a relative inviting me to go back to the 100<u>th</u>
Anniversary of the Univ. of Indiana! (Haven't heard from him
since 1888!)[67] One from Literary Productions Co N.Y. wanting
to know my Price for <u>The Financier.</u> I propose to quote
$10,000.

Go on to the Lankershim to meet Helen. She is all keyed up.
Another director (this time of the Goldwyn Co) very much taken
with her. Promises a part Thursday. She can only talk films,
stardom, a car, a cottage, trips to N.Y. love & what not. Her youth
& beauty & force & ambition are always exhilarating. I never knew
a child more intense or loving. We go to Pettifils ⌐   ⌐, for
dinner. Then to the Stillwell to see her dressmaker. She isnt in.

64. William Muldoon, a professional wrestler who ran a clinic in Westchester, New
York, for alcoholics and victims of nervous disorders. In 1903 Dreiser's brother Paul Dresser
sent him to Muldoon's to cure his neurasthenia.
65. Lillian Rosanoff (see p. 277, n. 3).
66. Kenneth Hayes Miller (1877–1952), painter and teacher who lived near Dreiser in
Greenwich Village.
67. Dreiser evidently forgot that he had received a letter from Sam Knoop on 10 April
1902 inviting him to dinner in New York.

Then to get the cat some fish. Then to 6th St. Car. More talk of stardom. Home & to bed. She loves me always to suffocation.

Tuesday, May 25—1920—Los Angeles Work all day on Fulfillment, cleaning it up. Write various letters. Post these notes. Down town at 5:30 to meet Helen at Lankershim.

Sunday, May 30—Decoration Day 1920 Helen & I very tired. Lie about most of the day. At 5 P.M. we go to the Riding Stables in Santa Monica & get two horses & ride out Laurel Canyon. The pretty hills & houses. Back at 7. Dinner at Cohens. Then home. Helen is such a genuine lover of beauty & rides so well.

Friday June 4—1920. Los Angeles. Helen get up early—5:30 to be able to arrange make up & get to Culver City by 8. I make coffee. Taxi comes at 7:30 & we ride over & get there at 8. She looks very sweet. I ride down town & go to P.O. No mail. Get a bottle of Pierces Golden Medical Dis—— then home. Work all day on Bulwark. At 6:30 she calls up from down town. Test made but she cant tell how it came out & wont know till Tuesday. Is greatly fussed up but thinks she did all right. Frets terribly until following Wednesday when she learns she is ok.

Sunday, June 6—1920—Los Angeles—588 N. Larch We get up fairly early, go down town to 7th Street (Boos Bros) Cafeteria & get breakfast. I eat $1.12 worth—mushmelons, fried chicken, iced coffee, strawberry short cake. Too much. Then we go round to P.E. Electric & get tickets to Long Beach. Train not due till 1:15. We wait in Alexandria. Fine bright ride. The sea. We sit on lawn & look at battle ships. The gulls. The girl in the yellow bathing suit— at 6:30 we go to the Ocean Spray cafe & have an excellent meal. Beautiful costumes of those on the lawn at the hotel. I get very sad as I think how life slips on. Back at 8:45 & take car home. The old man & the car who makes up with the middleaged woman & takes her home.

Tuesday, June 8—1920 Los Angeles 588 N. Larchmont We breakfast at Cohens. Helen reviews story of her youth. Mother kept an actors hotel down town. Vaudeville Theatre backed up on her mothers hotel. A Stock Theatre was over the way. Helen at 6 years wrote part in school theatricals. Wore velvet pants as Little Lord Fauntleroy & they were so tight she couldnt climb on stage at time curtain was going up & she was supposed to be there. Was lifted up. At 8 & 10 various Vaudeville teams stopping in her Mothers house fascinated her & she wanted to go along. Mother frightened lest she would. The little girl who was a dancer & having her legs whipped by her father to make her dance. Always hung around stage door of theatre back of her home & was given run of stage & parts. Had a dog & a pony & loaned them to the stage people. To part of Queen of Danes in the Pot-latch Parade (like Veiled Prophets Ball) To other parts—Queen of Night. Also Elks organized three short seasons of Amatuer Theatricals & she had a good part in each—at 14 years of age. Need to stand & admire leading lady of the local stock. Thought she was more than human. Was crazy about The Two Orphans—Under Two Flags—Camille, Zola. Got job in artists supply store at 10 years & tapped the till for as much as a dollar a day. The boss crazy about her. Got a two weeks job as wrapper in retail dry goods store & made 8 per. Took sick though & was in bed two weeks. The "cowboys club" & her beau who got boys admitted by giving her a bracelet set with a diamond chip. The boy who tried to rape her on an island. The stables for which she broke horses & was allowed to ride them. How she would bring her troop in front of her mothers window & yell for her to come & see. The old man who gave—or from whom she borrowed a dollar—ever so often. He fondled her. Also the business man who fingered her & gave her a dollar each time. The "Exhibitionists" who "showed off" in front of certain girls. How she met Frank,[68] then also older man. Old Weaver kept a car for her & gave her money, but got nothing. He bought her a ring. She gets married at 16—gets into Vaudeville at 17. Her trip to Tonapoli & Montana. Her smart clothes. How she left old Weaver to rebuke Frank who was with a girl—when she was with W—only he did not know it. The old Scotchman who sold her & cared for her pony.

We walk home accross Vine. She is sick (menstruating) & has cramps in room. I write letters to Stevens—Mrs. Kubitz—Lill—

68. Frank Richardson, an actor and Helen's first husband.

Huebsch, & others.[69] Figure I only have enough to stay here until July 1. We talk it over. Helen goes down town. She begins with the Golwyn Players Tomorrow in <u>The Great Lover.</u> Is to appear in 11 different scenes. I am to meet her at the Stillwell at 7 P.M.

<u>Wednesday. June 9th</u>—1920—Los Angeles 588 N.L. Helen up at 6. Has engagement & must be at Chevas at 8:30. Makes up from 6 to 7.30. I make coffee. The pink dress in the grip. "God all Ceaser"—her Expression. At 7$\underline{^{45}}$ we take car. She arrives on time. I go to The Broadway Store & buy a white shirt—size 16 1/2 for 2$\underline{^{50}}$. Then to P.O. No mail worth while. Back to house & use all day to revise <u>Fulfillment.</u> At 5 Helen comes. Brought in a car by a Mrs. Aldis. Divorcée. In movies. Has been to Lasky Studio & seen Cecil B. DeMille.[70] Tells how she worked it—worked other woman to go. Her estimate of Mrs. Aldis. May get work from DeMille. Tells of movie day. The crowd of super—700—at 7$\underline{^{50}}$ per! Principals extra. They are doing The Great Lover. We go over to Cohens. The movie mutts eating there. It is warm. On way home Helen talks of _____ how she will—etc. A baddie girl. We take papers down in lot & burn them. The toads in the back yard. 500 snails killed by Mrs. Wood. At 8:30 to bed. Helen & I have a hot round. Then to sleep.
I dis wuv uh.
Do seepy
Oll dat!
Stay wiss me

<u>Thursday, June 10</u>—1920—Los Angeles—588 N. Larchm
H & I get up at 7. She is working at Clunes Auditorium with the Goldwyn Films. Has to be down at 9:30. The "girl friend with the machine" didnt call. We take car & stops at the Cafe Louis—next to the theatre. I quarrel with the French waiter & don't eat. Leave Helen & take car to P.O. Letter from Liveright enclosing 333$\underline{^{33}}$. One from Literary Productions Co—calling for synop—— of

---

69. Harold W. Stevens, owner of the Stevens Yarn Company in New York City, wrote to Dreiser throughout 1920 after reading *Hey Rub-a-Dub-Dub.* The two men exchanged long philosophical letters about the nature and meaning of existence.
   Benjamin W. Huebsch (1876–1964), publisher.
   70. Cecil B. DeMille (1881–1959), director, producer, playwright.

Financier. One from Yewdale about L'Humanite of Paris & translation rights of Jennie G—— for same.[71] Write Lill, Mrs. ONiell, Yewdale etc. Send out 81 <u>Notice</u> pamphlets to literary editors. At 4 Helen comes home. Let off early. Is making 15\frac{00}{}$ a day now. Has letter from her Frank turning her down on a $50 loan. That letter. She composes a 10 page reply. I go up to corner for a sandwich & coffee & some gum drops. Send mss. of Financier Synop to Literary Productions.

<u>Monday, June 21—1920—Los Angeles Cal.</u>

This day at 6:48 P.M. Helen & I being in Boos Brothers Cafeteria 723 Broadway we feel our first real Earthquake. The floor & walls rock. I have a sense of the mystery & terror of it. A sense of huge merciless forces supersedes that of life. There is hush—a slight sense of nausea—then a babel of voices. I am like one in a dream—standing tray in hand ready to pick up an order of string beans. Helen is white & shaking. Since it is a long way to the door & there is a crowd—we wait instead of trying to run out. No one leaves—no panic—but there is a sense of possible death imminent. It all very wonderful & different, so remote from the mood of ordinary life. I have a hard time quieting Helen & her mood remains nervous for days. She is busy arranging to have a photographer named Witzel take special poses of her next Sunday in order that she may use the photos to get work. Is getting together hats, costumes & furs from wherever she can in order to make a good showing—have a great variety of costumes. I cannot help admiring her energy, resourcefulness & ingenuity.

<u>Tuesday, June 22—1920</u> <u>Los Angeles</u>. Another slight Earthquake jolt this noon. Helen almost in a panic. I rock her in my arms. Before this & after breakfast at Cohens we go to Mrs. <u>Wonders</u>— Santa Monica Boul to look up costumes for her pictures. Mrs. Wonders daughter directs us to Mme M<u>u</u>la, farther west (1/2 block) who rents costumes—8\frac{00}{}$ per day—for the first day. 4\frac{00}{}$ the second & 4$\frac{00}{}$ from then on. We learn from her of Schlanks in Sunset Boul & another place in Hollywood Boul to which Helen

71. Merton S. Yewdale, an editor at the John Lane Co. who handled such matters as translation rights for Dreiser's books.

goes later. This day she visits several studios in Hollywood & one agent who promises her work. We take Temple Street car to Hollywood from Downtown where I have gone (Silverwoods) to try on my suit & dine at the Hollywood Cafeteria. Cost $1.80. Walk home—this night especially very much in love with each other & dreaming of a possibly happy bungalow life out here.

Wednesday, June 23—1920 Helen still working on her photo costumes. The Jew who wanted to loan her furs in exchange for—a Sunday visit. We dine at the restaurant 8th & Grand—Cakes. Walk out 8th. Earthquakes still in Helen's mind. I worked all P.M. on Ambling Sam.[72] No luck. Very discouraged. Go down to P.O. before seeing Helen—no mail worth while. Beautiful P.M. Wonderful skies. I think of a thousand tales. The Street Car—1331 —and all the 13ths rung up while I aborad—91st fare rung up just as I leave at 7th & Hill.

Home about 9 & to bed. I give Expressman order to deliver box from N.Y. The burglar who had a trunk built & himself put in it & stored in a storage house silver vault. My expressman knew him. The policeman in the small 7th Street restaurant talking to the waitress who looked like Gertie[73] about the kids fishing in West Lake Park "against the law."

Thursday, June 24—1920 Work all P.M. on Nemesis.[74] Not so very much luck. Box with books arrives from N.Y. Row with Expressman over charges. Coffee & sandwich at 4 P.M. at Melrose & El Centro. 5:45 P.M. go down town to meet Helen.

Sunday June 27—1920—Los Angeles. Helen & I spend the morning at Witzels, having some photographs of her made. Her care as to her mouth & eyes. The arrangement with the furrier &

72. "Ambling Sam," an uncompleted short story, is among the Dreiser papers at the University of Pennsylvania. It is the story of Sam Candless, a Negro from New Orleans who works on Mississippi steamboats. The description of river life owes much to Mark Twain's *Life on the Mississippi*. Dreiser never found a suitable action or plot for the character of Sam, who resembles Dreiser in his emotional makeup.

73. Gertrude Nelson, daughter of Dreiser's sister Emma.

74. "Nemesis," an uncompleted short story, is among the Dreiser papers at the University of Pennsylvania. It tells of a man pursued by criminals who had been sent to prison as a result of information he supplied to the police. After years of psychological torment, he meets his death at their hands.

Hollywood dressmaker. How she bought scraps of lace to make $10 stockings. Two dresses in a bag & two hats in a band box. Twenty poses. Before this we have breakfast at Boos Brothers. The kid who filled a tray so full he couldnt eat it. The small kids in the cafeterias here with large trays of food—spindle legged little creatures carrying 80 pounds of food. After the Photos we come home & then walk down Melrose to the Heliotrope drive car. The beautiful houses. See some desirable lots at 1275$\underline{00}$. Dinner at Boos in Broadway. That night we see the Idol Dancer by D. W. Griffith in a small theatre in Alvarado Street. The best film I have seen in a long time. Shows what may be done. The work of the actor Richard Barthelmes. He was the one who did Huckleberry Finn. Home & to bed.

June 28, 1920, Los Angeles, Calif. Monday We breakfast at Cohens for the first time in a number of days. Cohen asks Helen— "Do you want sugar "to" your coffee" and she laughingly says to me "I ought to say—Yes—Put it to it." Feel very punk until noon —when Helen & I _____, then I feel better. Decide to go to Bimini Baths at Vermont & First for a hot sweat.

Wednesday, June 30—1920 Los Angeles. Work all day on revising Chapters 64 to 78—inc of Newspaper Days. It is now ready to file or publish. Also working on "Her Boy".[75] Helen goes out to see certain studio people. Five P.M. returns with proofs of her pictures. A ten strike these. Wonderful photos. She is very much elated & sees herself getting work. We go down town at 6 to a Cafeteria— then to the P.O. Letters from Yewdale & Donald McCord.[76] Telegram from Lill. Afterwards see Clara Kimball Young in some trashy film. Leave before it is over. Home & to bed. Helen forces me to _____.

Sunday. July 4—1920. Los Angeles. (588 N. Larchmont) Helen & I get up about 10. She is greiving because I said, the night before, that I was "as fond of " her, "as ever". How often that complaint from others. Looks very beautiful & by eleven we make up &

75. "Her Boy" is an uncompleted story (see p. 265, n. 16).
76. Donald McCord was a medical doctor and the younger brother of Dreiser's old friend Peter McCord, the illustrator (and "Peter" of Twelve Men).

Saturday. Sep. 11 - 1919 This day I met Helen. Don't remember much about the morning. Was reading at 11 A.m. when door bell rang. Slipped on my blue Chinese coat & went out. Saw a young girl of about 19 a 20 I thought hiding behind the door. She came out. Wanted to know if I were ?.) Then ~~said~~ asked if I could give her the address of Ed Dresser. So fascinated I invited her in. looked very much like ~~Ser~~ my sister Theresa. We sit + talk. Am able to tell by her looks that she was

Manuscript Page of Diary

indulge in a lusty bout—on her knees. Afterwards, while she dresses I play various records on the Phonagraph downstairs. "E Lucivan Stella". "Because." Sextette from La Boheme, "You'll Be Surprised.

Finally she is ready in grey dress & grey hat. We go down to Boos Brothers for breakfast—then take Pacific Electric to Long Beach. Visit at the Virginia—see programme![77]—then to see the wave power plant on the pier. Finally take a boat ride to San Pedro. The docks their. Group of Japanese fishing boats. A lighter loading baggage for a Japanese steamer making a call at this port. This river at San Pedro reminds me of the Chicago river—save that it is open to the sea at both Ends ⌣ . The beautiful silver & yellow sky after sunset. A cloud that looks like a whale. Gulls flying landward into the yellow light. Helen touched by the poetry of it cries.

We reach Long Beach & stand out on long dock looking at the shore fire works & lights. Go in finally to dinner in an excellent cafeteria—then back on dock till 9:30. Sitting on a bench. Helens loving mood. Finally we go in and get a seat in a waiting train. Downtown stop for coffee & a sandwich. Helens comments on two women leading on a drunken man to get a little money out of him. She reads character & understands life so well.

Monday, July 5—1920, Los Angeles. Bright beautiful weather— everyday— & cool. We get up at 10 & decide to go down town to dinner. Helens cat has 4 kittens—taken care of by others of course. Democratic convention at Frisco is tied, against McAdoo.[78] We breakfast at Boos Brothers—then walk round to Hill Street & see Charles Ray in a movie called The Egg Crate Wallop. Are Planning to go to Van Nuys—but instead go to the house to take the cat some ham (!) then to the Bimini baths. The delightful water there. A black haired girl flirts with me & Helen cries & wants to leave. Delightful walk across Vermont Avenue to Hollywood Boul.

77. On the next page of the diary Dreiser pasted a program for a Fourth of July Pageant entitled "Americanization" and presented at the Hotel Virginia. At the top of the program he wrote "The amazingly vapid crowd—"

78. William Gibbs McAdoo (1863–1941), the unsuccessful candidate for the Democratic nomination for President in 1920. Mencken attended this convention and wrote about it in the essay "Romantic Intermezzo," in *Heathen Days* (1943).

(Helen in Green Jersey waist & white silk skirt & green hat.)
Coffee & salad at Franks. The Greenwichy-Village-y crowd. We
walk home accross Vine Street—then sit out on porch for a time.
Finally to bed & another delicious round. Helens body is as
graceful & plump & yeilding as one of Raphaels nudes.

Wednesday. July—7—1920. Los Angeles. We breakfast at The
Welcome Inn—at Melrose & El Centro. Helen restless because of
no work. At noon gets a call from The Famous Players Lasky. They
claim they tried to reach her the night before so that she lost a days
work. She is almost sick. Prepares during P.M. for work which
begins at 6:30. I decide to remain here & do, working on "Her
Boy". At 5:30 she leaves & at 7 P.M. I knock off & go down town.
No mail. Get my five silk shirts from the Jap. Eat at Boos Bros—3
vegetables. Greatly wrought up in my nerves because of fruitless
results of my efforts to write & impending separation from Helen
owing to no money. Come home at nine. Call from Helen at
midnight saying she will have to work till 3 A.M. maybe & I am to
leave keys outside. I go to bed, leaving out keys. She arrives at 3
A.M. sent home by company in a car.

Thursday July 8, 1920—Los Angeles Another Perfect day. We
breakfast at Beaux Arts—opposite Metro Pictures Corp. Helen full
of her experiences of the night before—Mr. Goodstal—the casting
director, Mr. Franklin, Beebe Daniels director, Beebe Daniels
herself & the twelve manikins, of whom she is one in the new
Beebe Daniels production.[79] The property man who got her a glass
of water, a telephone booth & had a bench built for her. The new
old gold dress! How she got herself in the picture although she was
an odd girl—no 13— & really out on account of her failure to
show up the night before. The dress making parlor scene. The
woman who said she looked tired. Story of the actor who stared at
the girl when her bathing costume came off & how the others froze
him out. Beebe Daniels says that she, Helen, looks like Elsie
Ferguson & others that she looks like Katharine MacDonald.[80]
    I work on Her Boy, during day. At 5 P.M. we leave to eat. Walk

79. Bebe Daniels (1901–71), actress.
80. Elsie Ferguson (1885–1961), actress; Katherine MacDonald (1894–1956), actress.

to Hollywood Boul. Wonderful P.M. Dine in Cafeteria. Flowers on ground—before Helen. I walk with her to door of studio then down Sunset Boul to street below Gower & accross. The pretty homes. Marvellous pearly sky above blue mountains. The cars. The open doors. I wish so that we could stay & live here. Money helps so much. Helen does not get in till 7 A.M.

Friday, July 9—1920—Los Angeles (Correct Date) Helen gets in about 7 A.M.—delivered by auto. Has made a big impression. Tells me all about Beebe Daniels—her mother, maid & sister & their flattery of her. How she orders a closed car to go home in. They take pictures of her in costume—(as a mannikin). Then undressing —behind a screen—a shadow of her taking off her stockings etc. Then a picture of her in a "Teddybear", in tight pajamas, in bed, getting into bed—etc. This sex struck country. Helen has her pearl necklace stolen by a hair dresser—A policeman called: She gets it back. Reporting the loss to Mrs. Chapin "the mistress of wardrobe causes her to be seen in full costume by him—an advantage. She is called back after all "stills" are taken, by the director—Mr. Franklin, to have a special still taken of her. The envy of the other girls. They hate her she says. The "freshness" of new girl— employed as a page in the play—giving advice & orders to everyone else. She is very worn. Goes to sleep & stays until 1. P.M. I go to breakfast at The Welcome Inn. See row between owner & his wife. I suspect he plans to kill her. He tells me that she is so home sick for England that she wont do anything. Lies in bed while he slaves. 14 hours a day etc. Get cake, blackberries & a ham sandwich for Helen & come on home.

Saturday, July 10—1920—Los Angeles. We get up at 9. Helen is going over to Laskys to cash her checks. We decide to breakfast at the Metro-Restaurant. Then she is going down to Willis & Inglis to talk about The Choice for ⌊   ⌋.[81] Enroute she stops in at Metro

81. Willis & Inglis Motion Picture and Theatrical Enterprises was located at the Wright & Callender Building in Los Angeles. On 11 October 1919, the firm wrote Dreiser, offering to be his western agent to sell the motion picture rights to his work. "The Choice" is a screenplay now among the Dreiser papers at the University of Pennsylvania. It tells the story of a young girl who comes from the West to New York City and is falsely convicted on a vice charge. After prison and years of concealment, she becomes a movie actress and finds herself romantically involved with the judge who had originally sentenced her.

& is asked to come back after lunch. In restaurant we see Mme Nazimova who is working at Metro[82]—Also her vamp companion— Helen returns to Metro & at 5 comes home with news that she is working Monday. Is to dance on a table in a café—a society girl who gets a little wild with excitement. This is her fourth good part. We stay here until 6 P.M. then walk across Gower & Gordon to Sunset & down Sunset to Hollywood Boul. The Firenze Court— beautiful little homes. The Fox Films Dinè—9 P.M. at Boos Brothers. Helen very loving. At 11 P.M. we return with cherries, some fish for the cat & some candy. To bed.

Helens letter from her Mother. Sister unhappy with husband. She wires her to come here & arranges a job for her at the Pign-Whistle. Wants her to live with us but I fear any Knowledge which her husband may gain.

Dreiser and Helen in Hollywood

82. Alla Nazimova (1879–1945), Russian-born stage and screen actress.

<u>Sunday, July 11—1920</u> <u>Los Angeles</u> Helen sleeps till 1 P.M. I work on circulars to libraries & literary editors. At 2 we ride down to Boos Brothers & breakfast—then out Stephenson avenue—(1st time) for a ride. Down to P.O. A few letters—all pointless. Home & we play victrola till bed time. Wonderful sunset & silver-orange Sky. A Walk before Bed time—We stop at the Welcome Inn for a sandwich. The keeper shows us his album of English relatives and his ex girls in various places. A talkative, equivocal person. I really dont care for him. Fear that some day he may injure his wife. He tells us of a three room cottage for rent which turns out to be a lemon.

<u>Wednesday, July 14—1920, Los Angeles</u> Helen & I breakfast near Metro. I return here & get things to mail. Then down town to P.O. She is rejoicing over her big hit at Metro working with May Allison, a star. At P.O. I get a letter from Donald McCord who is at Hotel Webster—259–East 6<u>th.</u> Go there & wait an hour. Fall in with an old prospecter who tells me how prospecting for gold is done. Would make a story. At 1 P.M. McCord comes. A small, brown, waspish man. We go to Boos Brothers for lunch & talk of Peter.[83] Then he gets his car & drives me out here. We come via Hollywood & Sunset Bouls. The bright day. Beauties making for different studios. Sit on porch here until 4:30. Then take car & go across Melrose to Hollywood. I leave him at Highland Ave—after buying a drink. Go to Bornlei Place & see Doty.[84] Tell him plots of <u>The Choice</u> and <u>The Door of the Trap.</u>[85] He is very much enthused. Thinks Universal will be interested. I leave to meet Helen & McCord at Lankershim at 8<u>00</u>. Ride down Hollywood Boul feeling fine. The thought of Helen is a perpetual joy. Get there & wait. She comes. McCord is sitting there all time but dont see us. We go to <u>The Blue Bird.</u> Helen doesnt like him but we enjoy watching the dancers. See a girl who looks like Peters wife. At 10 we leave—cost of meal 7<u>25</u>. Leave McCord at 7<u>th</u> & Brdwy & ride home. Helen pleased with her work. Tells all sort of

83. Peter McCord, illustrator and the model for "Peter" in *Twelve Men.*
84. Douglas Z. Doty (1874–1935), editor, publisher.
85. "The Door of the Trap" is a movie script now among the Dreiser papers at the University of Pennsylvania. It recounts the story of a girl falsely convicted of theft who falls in love with a respectable man of means. Love triumphs over her past reputation, and they are united at the end.

incidents about movie actors, actresses, directors, calling directors, camera men etc. The acter with the $8,000 dollar car always talking about his wife Della. The girl who steals Helens place at the table before the camera. The young bolshevik who is crazy about her & jealous when he hears she is in love, etc. She is in a hectic mood & forces a heavy round on me.

Thursday, July—15—1920. Los Angeles Take breakfast with Helen near Metro. Santa Monica car down to P.O. Letters from Liveright & some man who has written a book of poems. Go to hotel Webster—(259 East 6th) and listen to a long story by Donald McCord of how he was robbed of his right to be a major. I can only feel that he was fairly dealt with. Tells me of Mrs. Van Poole —the woman he was in with and Mrs. Watts, who exposed him. He suggests lunch but I decline. Gets his car & invites me to ride to San Diego—but I decline—agree to ride to Santa Ana. His search for gasoline—there being a "shortage" while they put up the price. Final start out Stephenson Ave. I cant like him. He is a small man —though Peters brother. We stop at Fullerton for a bite to eat— then on to Santa Ana. Get there at 3:50. Train back at 4. Flat country. I feel lonely for Helen. Call up the house twice—once from Santa Fe Station—once from Drugstore at 7th & Broadway. Get a Coco Cola. It is 5:30. Then take car & get out here at 6:15. Helen not yet here but comes in a minute crying because she only got 7$\underline{50}$ instead of 10$\underline{00}$ per day. The cheap tactics of Mr. Singer, casting director, Mr. Rosen, director, & Mr. Funch, the assistant director. "Passing the buck" as she says. I soothe her & we go up to Ye Welcome Inn. Soup, bread, tea & cake. Then walk a little & get early to bed. Some local lion hunter calls up & assures Mrs. Wood he is my second best friend & must see me.

Friday, July 16—1920. Los Angeles. Helen not working today. Is going down town to look at & get her photos from Witzel. Total cost 48$\underline{00}$. Morning American is not delivered & it makes me angry.

Saturday, July 17—1920—Los Angeles.— We go to French Restaurant <u>Metro</u> for breakfast. Helen calls up Lasky & Goldwyn. Is advised to come out to Goldwyn. Goes later in P.M. & is promised a weeks work at $10 per—Very gay at evening. We go down town to dinner. I work all day on Her Boy.

Sunday, July 18—1920—Los Angeles Hot & Clear. We get up at 10. Go down town to breakfast. No place to go. Return to house & I take 24 nudes of Helen using Mrs. Woods 3 1/2 × 5 1/2 Camera. The lovely sensual picture she makes. At 7 we walk over to Hollywood. Looking for the monkey she saw. Dinner at Chinese Restaurant & an ice cream parler afterwads. She calls me out before going to view an Umbrian sky. New moon directly ahead. We dream of a cottage, a car etc. Walk home past Metro. At 10:30 we are in bed.

Monday. July 19—1920—Expenses

Helen—	.75
Carfare to Vermont — — — —	10
" " 588 — — — — — —	05
Breakfast—self — — — — — — —	.40
Carfare down town — — — — — —	05
Dinner H & self — — — — — —	1.45
Song — — — — —	.40
Peroxide — — — — —	.11^{cts}
Cuticura — — — — —	.26
Bottle water — — — — —	10
Carfare home — — — — —	.10
	$3.77

Friday, July 30—1920—Los Angeles Helen goes to Metro & some other companies to look for work. Rousing reception at Metro. Mr. Singers enthusiasm for "that Picture." "I want you to look just like that." "Let Helen Richardson come in." Agrees to give her $12.50 a day—highest yet. "I'll shoot you for twelve-fifty." She goes to Lady Jane Lewis & orders white dress. We meet at Stillwell—at 7— where she tells me all this. Dinner at Boos Brothers. We ride out to Fountain Ave & walk because the night is so beautiful.

Saturday, July 31—1920—Los Angeles Helen & I go down town at 1 P.M. to look for a white scarf. Finds a beauty at 7^{50}. We save 7^{50}. Then home & a little later Hollywood Boul to get a white silk sport hat. After browsing in 6 shops find one beyond Highland Ave. Helen charmed with hat—a bargain. We stop for sandwiches & tea. Then on to Venice—at dusk. The little old man who was a "wrastler" in his day. The young kid that "was like I was" in

Sullivan. Noisy Venice. The <u>Ship Café,</u> where we get charged .50 cents for bread & butter. Plus a cover charge of fifty cents. The walk between Ocean Park & Venice. Helen looks so beautiful. Back at midnight & to bed.

<u>Monday, Aug 2nd</u>—1920—Los Angeles Work all day on Newspaper Days. Meet Helen at Stillwell at 7. Dine at Boos & go to P.O. Temple Street car to Fountain Ave & walk. We see Lieutenant Lockdear (See clipping) fall from sky in his plane.[86] I thought his plane was a star. Helen & I very much stirred up by it. Whenever I say anything in criticism Helen throws herself on the bed & seems to go all to peices. "When I think you don't like what I do or your not satisfied—I cant do anything at all."

<u>Thursday. Aug 5</u>—1920, Los Angeles
Helen & I dine at the big Pign Whistle. Then walk out 7<u>th</u> to West Lake & go out on the small lake in a boat. Hang around the pavilion in the water where the negroes sing. Her pathetic "You weren't bored last year." Her type of baby talk. "Dis puts little ear on pillow an covers up eyes".
"Dis looks out window at sun on leaves."
"Dis likes lots o nice syrup & sugar ons cakes" etc.

<u>Monday, Aug. 9</u>—1920—Los Angeles Helen still sick in bed. Very weak.

<u>Tuesday, Aug 10</u>—1920 Los Angeles
Helen feeling better. We have breakfast in the room. I go for milk, potatoe chips, crullers, cinnamon buns and a "grandma cake." I am feeling good because of <u>Newspaper Days</u> completed & sent off finally. Also because of the check for "Love" from <u>Live Stories.</u>[87] Write Lengel,[88] McQuade about the "Genius", Mrs. Croft &

---

86. No clipping is included in the diary at this point; "Lieutenant Lockdear" has not been identified.

87. "Love" was published in the *New York Tribune,* 18 May 1919, pt. 7, pp. 2–3. Dreiser is referring here to money received for its second publication in *Live Stories* 25 (December 1920): 3–19.

88. William C. Lengel (see p. 186, n. 78).

several others. Then work over <u>The Choice</u> for a while. Then walk with Helen to Metro for her check for last Wednesday. Then we take a car down Santa Monica. Meet Robertson of Goldwyn. Dine in Fifth Street Cafeteria. Get 50 cents worth of candy. Then home. Helen comments on the conventional gayetie of all movie offices—which means nothing—all forced. She is reading the Life of Neitche by his sister and her comments on him & Wagner interest me very much—very sound.[89]

Wednesday, Aug. 11—1920—Los Angeles.
Helen feeling ok this A.M. for the first time since Thursday—when she broke down. Now says she is going out to see the Rose Singer Co. to see about a part. She began the day with a rousing assault on me.

Saturday, Aug 14—1920, Los Angeles
Decide to meet M. Lopez and her Goddess ⌞   ⌟. Go down town to library at 12. Reach Alexandria at one. Meet this 8<u>th</u> Part Malay. Her one time charm—now fading. Tells us of her husband who is a Swiss & a Christian. Her past relation to me. How she "broke in" her husband. Prayed with her—the first night. Made her put on pajamas when she came naked to breakfast. She is largely Pagan as I can see. Wants me to visit her & get data for a novel. I doubt if it will ever come to pass.

Sunday, Aug. 15—1920—Los Angeles
Up at 6:30 and off to Camp Bonita—San Gabriel Canyon—at Cattle Canyon. 6th St. Line to Pacific Electric Station. Red Line to Azusa —Motor Bus to Woodford—4 horse stage to Bonita. The heat! We cross the San Gabriel 32 times. The dog. Ice being hauled. I hold an umbrella over Helen all the way. The tent. The purling water. Snakes. For one week we sleep out of doors. The Dougherties? The night Editor of The Times & his two daughters. The store. The dance hall & records. The restaurant. Our tall, lank, red headed maid! Wantd to learn to play the saxophone. Wood gathering, fire building, cooking, water carrying. The yellow horned toads, rattlesnakes & spiders. The driver of the donkeys. On Friday we

89. *The Young Nietzsche* (1912) by Elizabeth Forster-Nietzsche (1846–1935).

make one donkey trip. Helen reads Menckens Philosophy of Neitche.[90] I read Parmelees—the Science of Human Behavior.[91] We idle one whole week. No birds much—only house martins in the sky between 5 and 7 P.M. The stars. Moonlight in the Cayon. The ranger & his horse.

Sunday—Aug 22nd 1920—Los Angeles

We return down San Gabriel Canyon—leaving at 3:30. The night Editors daughters. His talk of roasting, editorially, Maurice Tourneurs picturization of Treasure Island, his favorite book. Frank Danby— a Jew——! agent of the Shuberts. We ride in from Azusa in his car. Stop at P.O. I am worn out. Many letters. One from Constable & Co of London—the 1st.[92]

Monday, Aug 23—1920—Los Angeles

We search for a room. Find one with Mrs. Ringstrom—1553 Curran St. City—Beautiful view. Convenient for Helen. Pay $5 down & take it to Oct 1st next.

Sunday. Aug 29—1920—Los Angeles

Preparing to leave 588 N. Larchmont tomorrow. Get up at 10—go down to the Hotel Savoy restaurant at 6th & Grand for breakfast. Helen likes it because it is "pretty". Afterwards we go round to the Public Library—5th & Broadway to find that it is just about to open —1 P.M. But the newspaper room only. No books extended. We to go to the Alhambra Theatre to view the Universal Film Pictures of Cannibals in the South Seas (Kia-Kias.) Rather good stuff—reminds one of Typee but doctored up for movie use as usual.[93] Fake attacks & fake rescues shown. The killing of a tiger was quite realistic—but might have been staged in any southern woods. We come out. Get a box of Squibbs Talcum & another of Rice powder

90. *The Philosophy of Friedrich Nietzsche* (1908) by H. L. Mencken.
91. *The Science of Human Behavior: Biological and Psychological Foundations* (1913) by Maurice Farr Parmelee.
92. In 1920 Dreiser was trying, through his literary agent, Curtis Brown, to interest the British publisher Constable & Co. in issuing his books in a uniform edition. The company wanted to publish not only his earlier work but all forthcoming books, and they had a particular interest in *The Bulwark.* Dreiser was not disposed to make such a commitment in 1920, nor was the firm pleased with his demand for advance royalties. In the late 1920s Constable became Dreiser's English publisher, though it never printed a complete set of his books.
93. *Typee: A Peep at Polynesian Life* (1846) by Herman Melville.

at a Sun Drug Store and come home. Pack trunks & various boxes. In leaving here to go to 1553 Curran we will have two trunks, six wooden soap boxes, 1 table, 3 bags, two hat boxes & 4 packs. The two trunks and six boxes & one table cost 3^50. The taxi costs $2.50 & in it we expect to take 4 packages, 3 bags & 2 hat boxes— 9 all told. We are done packing at 7. At 7^{10} by saying "Gee—what a vaudeville wail" when she is singing—I throw her in a pathetic state of blues. She cries. It takes until 8 to bring her out of that. At 8 we start to walk accross Larchmont to 3rd. Cat follows & Helen wont let me drive it back—but carries it back—staying 1/2 hour. When she comes I fly into a rage & call her a dam fool. She cries. The cat follows & I drive it back by rocks. A chilly atmosphere all the way down to the Mission Inn. There she cries, saying I wouldn't have talked so a year ago. We get some candy & come home. At the house she wants to go round & see the cat. I refuse until she says that tomorrow shes leaving & its the little kitty we bought together at Highland Park. Then I come round. In the room another argument starts as to efficiency. I claim that H—— is slack in all things except those which relate to her looks & her movie & stage connections. She gets angry, takes blanket & sleeps on floor till 3 A.M.—then comes to bed.

Monday, August 30—1920—Los Angeles Leaving 588—today. Breakfast in the little restaurant at Vine & St. Monica. Order the Hollywood to come before 4 P.M. for laundry. Order the express man for 4:30 & a taxi for 5 P.M. Finishing odds & ends of packing & post these notes. The trouble with the expressman. Calls up & wants $6 instead of three—calls up from Mrs. Woods—after we have arrived at 1553 Curran. Trouble with the Taxi man—wants 4^{00} instead of 2^{50}. I give him 2^{50}. We straighten out our things at 1553 & go down town to dinner. First impressions of this place & Mrs. Ringstrom favorable—an elastic, volatile Swede.

Monday, Sept 6th 1920. Labor Day.
Get a check for $400 from Live Stories for Phantom Gold.[94] Also the promise of the sale of a short version of The "Genius" for $3,000. In the morning Helen & I walk over the hills above Echo

---

94. "Phantom Gold" was published in *Live Stories* 26 (February 1921): 3–23. It was reprinted in *Chains* (1927).

Park Ave. into Alessandro Street. The woman on the Hill who looked like Mrs. Dreiser. "Getting so much iron in my blood". Living in a tent. The two tow headed children. The little pup. We pass Garson & Sennett studios on the way home. I work on "An American Tragedy till 4 P.M.[95] We see ⌐ ⌐ at night.

Tuesday, Sept 7<u>th</u> —1920—Los Angeles —
1553 Curran Street. Because I have a check for $400 from Live Stories for Phantom Gold—Helen goes down town to look for 3 1/2 yards of silk for a black silk costume. I go to P.O. & mail short mss of The "Genius" which Lengel expects to sell for $3,000 to <u>Live Stories</u>.[96] Send wire to Lengel, concerning it. Put check in Bank. Buy a can opener, a jar of Marmalade, two cans of condensed milk, one of theatrical cold cream & two black marking pencils & return home. Fox Studio calls up & wants Helen to report for a part—1<u>st</u> call of this kind. I work on "<u>An American Tragedy</u>". The manager of The Denver Transfer Co who tried to swindle me on hauling my trunks (820 W. 3<u>rd</u>) calls up & wants to smooth things over. I stall him off. Helen calls up. Wants me to meet her at the Stillwell. I do—at 7 P.M. We dine at Boos Brothers —in Hill St. Helen brings home her pretty last years blue dress, lined with fur. I dont like it. She gets very fussed up & depressed.

Wed. Sept 8—1920—Los Angeles— 1553 <u>Curran</u> St—just East of Echo Park Ave.

Mrs. Ringstrom:
   The Shickens yust skratz up de yard
   It don't make good yam (Jam)
   I toll him he mustn't touch em.
   Skeese (Chese)
   In the morning, at breakfast she tells me about Sweden. The Strange Green paroquet, that flew near me for protection. I pile up all the stones in the yard. Helen goes to the Fox Studio.

---

95. This is the first mention of *An American Tragedy* in the diary. Dreiser began the novel sometime during this period—probably August 1920—but by the time he returned to New York in the fall of 1922, he had completed only twenty chapters. Although he was constantly researching the novel, he did not begin writing in earnest again until the summer of 1923.
   96. *Live Stories* never published a condensed version of *The "Genius"*.

Takes a check for 26⁵⁰ for silk for a new dress. Mrs. Ringstrom & neighbors try to catch the green parroquet.

Friday, Sept—10—1920—Los Angeles.
—1553 Curran St. Weather or something causes both of us to feel wretched. I trim the back hedge—before breakfast for Mrs. Ringstrom. Finish Chapter 4—of <u>An American Tragedy.</u> At 4:15 we go out to Glendale. Fare 30 cents—round trip—a Southern Pacific graft. Walk about & see the place. Dinner at what was once a beautiful road house—now "run" by typical Americans. The long boarding house tables. The babys high chair at one & the high priced undertaker places in this region. Much cash in burying people here. We read of Olive Thomase's death in Paris. Helen hopes for a start in the movies. We return at 9. She breaks down walking up the hill & refuses to move until rested. In bed by 9:30.

Saturday—Sept 11—1920—Los Angeles
Helen has 2<u>nd</u> call from Laskys—She is to leave at 7 to go to Pasadena with a lot of bathing girls to do stunts. Is very much elated of course.

Sunday, Sept 12—1920—Los Angeles
1553 Curran St. Beautiful clear day. We spend it in bed—after breakfast down stairs. At night go down to Boos Bros Cafeteria. Curious condition of L.A. Every Boos place has a long waiting line reaching out into street. Movies same. Afterwards we go to the new Pantages. Wait in line 1 hour. Inside galley seats only— I get into fight with ushers & management & compel return of money. Home & very sore.

Monday. Sept 13—1920.
Helens way. I try to make her get up at 8:30. "Now you hush. Just be still. Go to sleep. I know what Im doing"
   In cafeteria last night, when I was thinking of the folly or injustice of leaving one woman for another—she—telepathically I presume, began to brood & cry—thinking I might leave her. The rank materialist would say coincidence. I say attuned chemisms— one highly responsive to the other.

Monday. Sept 20th to Sat. 25th— inc
(Los Angeles) Helen works at the Metro under Rex Ingram in The
Four Horsemen of the Apocalypse & scores a great hit.[97] The white
dress, the black dress—the black lace afternoon dress—the sport
costume. The different people she meets—Rudi—an actor—who
comes around on a black horse when not working. The German
director—the French director. (Cry Miss Richardson—Cry) Ingrams
overtures to her. The Ex-Mack Sennett bathing beauty who playing
the part of a German girl parting from her soldier lover & making
everybody cry. Mme. De Dion comes on the scene. The small Jew
assistant—who gets her the film, then hangs about her dressing
room to say good morning. The vamp-beauty who takes a fancy to
her. The young beginner who becomes hysteric because she has no
clothes to get on with & denounces Helen. A very brilliant week.
She earns $90.

Sunday. Sept. 26—1920. Los Angeles
Lounge about the rooms most of the day—writing & reading. At
4:30 Helen & I walk down Echo Park Ave past Echo Park & look
at the little lake & boats. First ducks from the North. At 6 we enter
Boos Brothers for dinner. At seven go to see Mme X—2nd time—
At Millers Theatre in Main St. Then we walk down Main to P.O.
& home. Two letters from Lill—arranging for a week in S.F
together.

Monday, Sept 27—1920. Los Angeles
   Helen has no pep—but the blues. Lies around worrying over
whether I care for Kirah anymore or not. (Due to Rex Ingram) I
work on novel. Then at 2 P.M. keep an appointment at the L.A.
Athletic Club—with Wesley Ruggles a director. He wants to do
The Hand of the Potter and offers me $12,000—if—he can get the
screen right out of it.[98] I give him a thirty day option. Letters from
Maxwell, Paul Elder, a man in New Orleans etc.[99] I write George

97. Helen obtained a supporting role in Rudolf Valentino's first American film, "The
Four Horsemen of the Apocalypse." Rex Ingram (1893–1956) directed the film.
   98. Wesley Ruggles wrote Dreiser on 24 September 1920 identifying himself as a
director who was producing his own films and gathering screen scripts. Although he negotiated
with Dreiser about a film version of "The Hand of the Potter," he never produced it.
   99. Paul Elder was a San Francisco bookseller who admired Dreiser's work.

Sterling, The Abdys & George Douglas at S.F. that I am
coming.[100]

Tuesday. Sept 28—1920—Los Angeles.
This day Helen gets a long five page typewritten letter from
Woodward—Praising her & depreciating me slightly.[101] Says that I
"drag truth forth by the hair of head". Of himself to her he adds—
"but I can be comforting dear". This starts me thinking & I compel
her to confess—walking beside Echo Lake at 9 at night—that she
had an affair with him once. The reason. Also that meeting me—
staying with me—she went down to his office & dilated on my
physical efficiency. The naivette and unconscious cruelty of it all
astound me. It all winds up, as usual in a gust of sensuality between
us. She appears to be wrought up by memories of those first days
together.

Sunday. Oct 3—1920—Los Angeles
  Helen & I visit Live Stock Show on the South side. See races.
Prize horses, cows, sheep, pigs—boars, stallions, bulls etc. Helens
interest in & comment on the latter. Her delight in seeing perfect
specimens.

Sunday. Oct. 10—1920—Los Angeles
  Breakfast down town at Petifils—Eggs Benedictine & coffee.
Afterwards interview at Alexandria with F. B. Warren.[102] Offers

100. George Sterling (1869–1926) was a poet, dramatist, and critic. H. Bennett Abdy
and Rowenta Meeks Abdy were artists who lived in San Juan Bautista, California. George
Douglas, Australian-born journalist and critic, was literary editor of the *San Francisco Bulletin* in
1920. Dreiser is responding to a proposal for a reception in his honor in San Francisco in
mid-October 1919. He had previously encountered Sterling in New York and admired his work
and his program to combat literary puritanism. Dreiser first met Douglas in 1919 and their
friendship grew over the years, culminating in Douglas's support of Dreiser's scientific and
philosophic studies in the thirties.
    101. William E. Woodward (1874–1950), businessman, novelist, historian. Woodward
was the publicity director of the Industrial Finance Co., which hired Helen when she first arrived
in New York. Later in life he turned to writing fiction and history; among other things, he is
noted for introducing the word "debunk" into English.
    102. Frederick Blount Warren, journalist. Warren began corresponding with Dreiser in
1911. An early admirer of *Sister Carrie,* he reviewed *Jennie Gerhardt* ("Reviews of Some of the
Season's New Books," *New York Morning Telegraph,* 5 November 1911) and later was interested
in promoting the novels for film production. In 1920 he was managing editor of the *New York
Morning Telegraph.*

$20,000 each for Financier & Titan. Helen & I discuss what can be done—how to produce etc—We go home—then walk back—about 4 miles—along Skyline road in Elysian Park. The lights, stars, etc. Anent Louise Glaun, H—— says it is all right for a mediocre woman to be compelled to pay with her body for promotion & favors in movie realm. Wrong if a refined woman has so to do etc.

Monday, Oct 11—1920. Los Angeles
Heart Trouble all night compels taking Radium Springs Bath & sweat. How the Robertson-Cab Co. grows. Down town to see about F. B. Warrens rating. Buy a good union suit for 2⁰⁰. Silk shirts to drop to $6 so Mullen & Bluett say. No letters of import. Helen reading George Moores The Lake & rejoicing.[103] I feel poorly.

Tuesday, Oct. 12—1920—Los Angeles
Cold but clear morning. No gas fire here— & trouble with Mrs. Ringstrom over the rent. See letter herewith attached.[104] I go with Helen to Fox Studio gate. She says of the queer old movie men floating about L.A. that they are "little whiskered goats"—so descriptive. Go out to Radium Springs Bath & get a bottle of Olaxo —then down to Bible Institute looking for someone who knows of little cheap missions. The man in the big mission on Main Street— the "Asst Supt"—a horrible janitor type preaching God & being saved. On home. Mrs. Ringstrom hands me the letter. Work all day on novel. Helen works till midnight. Blows in at five for some money to get the white dress. Her hit with Director Mitchell, Actor McCullagh & others. The sex atmosphere & excitement of the realm. The man who described how "refinedly" a nude scene was posed—so "So careful"—"so respectable"—everything "so ladylike"! Her little actor ⌐   ⌐ still follows her. I dine at Pettifils. Then home early & to bed. Read in George Moores The Lake. Moore seems bent on instructing his readers in art & letters.

103. *The Lake* (1905) by George Moore (1852–1935), English novelist.
104. At this point in the diary Dreiser included a letter from his landlady complaining about the extra bed-linens and towels used by him and Helen. She raised the rent to $50.00 per month effective 1 November 1920.

Wednesday. Oct 13—1920. Los Angeles

2nd day for Helen at Fox Studio. Does not need to get there until 10. I go out with her. Mrs. Ringstrom remorseful over her letter. School girls on Hollywood car. Some so pretty & inexperienced & wondering. Leave H—— Then go for her old hat. —7000 Holly Boul. Back to P.O. Letters from Mrs. Karner & Marion Latour.[105] Home & work on Poe all P.M.[106] Helen comes at 7:30. We go to dinner—5th Street Cafe. Tells me of Mitchell (director) & his antics. Christian Science & sex horribly mixed. Describes his proposed pictures to her.—the cheapest of cheap melodrama. Thinks the line—"Tin I tum in"—a great caption for a little sex struck cutie knocking at a rich bounders door. Grows sentimental over sex. Calls ⌐   ⌐ for talking to Helen. Tries to "queer" her in her work because as she says "she wont fall for him." Finally she wins out & compels him to approve of her. Got her first real chance at lead work this day.

At 10 we come back. Helen sensually wrought up over her own beauty. Poses & stretches about. Finally sinks into heavy, savage sensuality. Takes striking positions, suggestive of her intense lust.

Wednesday, Oct. 13—1920 Los Angeles

Letter to me from Helen—written "on the set"

LA
10³⁰ A.M.
Oct 13—1920[107]

Dearest Teddie,

I have just finished my make-up and am on the set waiting to work. I have started to read but find myself thinking of you continually—so much so that I cannot concentrate on the book at all—anyway not until I have written you a note.

I keep thinking of you and how wonderfully sweet and kind and dorable you always are and how I simply long to be with you every minute. I feel so happy today when I think of how inspiring it was last night to lie in your arms and feel the love and strength emanating from your very being and entering mine. God! how I do love you, my dearest darling Teddy. It is all so wonderful that when I think of you like this I could weep my heart out—the beauty of it is ideal—to me it is almost too beautiful to be true in this old commonplace world.

Honey a cute little old bull pup came over here in the corner to see me

---

105. Marion Latour lived in Burlington, Iowa, and wrote Dreiser frequently to register her response to his books.

106. Dreiser considered Poe "our first and greatest literary genius" (*Letters of Theodore Dreiser*, ed. Robert H. Elias, 3 vols. [Philadelphia: Univ. of Pennsylvania Press, 1959], 1:371). In 1920 Dreiser began rereading Poe and looking into critical and biographical studies of him.

107. "LA" and the date are written in Dreiser's hand, the remainder in Helen's hand.

and is sniffing all around looking for trouble. He is a darling. I wish you could see him.

I hope nothing will disturb your thoughts today and that you will be able to work in peace. I loathe these people and regret every minute of my time that I am not with you. The more I see of them the more intense becomes my longing to come to you and remain with you. I hope you will always let me stay. Will you Teddie?

Old Mother Grouch's conscience is no doubt troubling her. I hope it tortures the soul out of her—if she possesses one. Will now count the minutes until tonight. Darling—

Friday, Oct 15—1920, Los Angeles

Preparing to leave in A.M. for San Fran. Have an appointment at 8 P.M. with Walter Ruggles, Metro Director at L.A. Athletic club. Give Helen ideas for three evening dresses & get her greatly excited—fawn grey—two tone flamingo and light jade—for colors. We spend a delightful afternoon in the shops downtown. Return home—then back to dinner at Petifils. At 8.15 leave & meet Ruggles & his wife at the Athletic Club. She is an "all star cast" type of movie actress. Very interested in me. Tells me of her interest in The "Genius" and Jennie Gerhardt. I hear more about tough actress life in L.A. The Hand of the Potter is not to be done. Leave at 9:30. See a whole host of showy movie girls in extreme decollete at the Club. Out & meet Helen at Library. We get a book on Poe—walk down to P.O. & so home.

Saturday, Oct 16—1920—Los Angeles

Starting for San Francisco via Pickwick Stage at 9 A.M. Helen accompanies me to the stage office. The stout man, who stopped from entering the Anaheim bus before it was ready muttered "demons"—anent the two gaurds who stopped him! Helen very blue—or seemingly so & nervous. We start. Same route as before to Santa Barbara—but not so pleasent as with her, not nearly. I feel lonely. Beautiful day. The "detour" beyond Universal City, and the stalled "Waugh" Laundry Wagon—and its jumpy rediculous exertions to get through—all in the car roar. The route—Quiet passengers. Arrive at Santa Barbara at one. Nice Italian Restaurant there has failed. Write Helen. At 1 leave for San Luis Obispo. Scenery not so nice. Listen to two men who have been to Alaska talk of winters there. Moose killing, Etc. Rear axle of car takes fire, but is put out. We arrive at San Luis at 6:30. I check bag & eat. The busy best restaurant. Standard American types. Spanish names give only touch of romance to these towns that they can boast. Veedersburg would be more appropriate. The two crazy young girls walking around flirting & dying for a good time. How a small town lives on its imagination principally—there is so little to do. The Salvation Army singers. At 9 P.M. return. As usual I am soaked 1⁵⁰ for a room that another man would get for 1⁰⁰ because I look like 1⁵⁰. Sign over door said rooms 75 and 1⁰⁰.

Sunday. Oct 17—1920—San Luis Obispo
Stopped all night at the Travelers Hotel—a poor dump but as good as any in town. Rose 6:45—too early to want breakfast—but took a cup of coffee at the one brisk Restaurant. Then down to bus office. The man who was a gate keeper at Yosemite. People would not pay an admission fee of 25 cents to see the big trees. Stories of the trappers up north. How much was made out of one moose—600 pounds at 25 cents (150⁰⁰). How a hunter goes out alone. We start at 8. The old mission. The old woman who wouldnt sit outside or in & wanted my place finally. Hill road north of San Luis Obispo. The quick & reckless curves. Santa Marguerita Paso Robles. We race a train & beat it. The Valley of the Salinas river. I speculate on how interesting these spanish names make the towns sound. If they were in Indiana or Illinois & called Veedersburgh—or Murphysboro no one would give them a second thought. But the valley of the Salinas River! The mountains, the tawny sands. The upturned hips of hills. Great corrals of cattle. Fields of pumpkins. Sugary refineries. Vast fields of sugar beets & trucks loaded with them. The fine roads. The flowers, bungalows, little walled in ranch homes. Mexicans, Japs & Americans. The fine stores in the little towns. Lemons. Oranges, grapes, walnut groves, fig trees—a world of fine products. And yet the people so raw, brash, talkative, inexperienced, prejudiced even. We arrive (noon) Salinas where I lunch. The very excellent restaurant—scores of fine automobiles: A show in town—circus. Chicken liver omelette. Then on to San Juan, Gilroy. Morgan Hill, San Jose & S.F. It rains. The fine hills & valleys north of Salinas. The car skids. The two chauffers—One gets on at San Juan. A mission here as usual. We see many cars upset. Arrive 3:40 at San José. The large stage station. Due S.F. 5:10. Wander in at 6 because of rain. First impressions of the city. The bay. Fine country places beyond the city—near Palo Alto. The

crowds of cars rushing cityward. I feel a little lost. Call up Club. Sterling not in but has reserved room & there is a telegram. Unpack. Bath. Walk out. Get a sense of delicious life. See Market Street. Then dine. Back to club at Eleven & go at once to bed very tired. See announcement of Curran Theatre show. Send telegram to Helen. Angry because of no word from her.

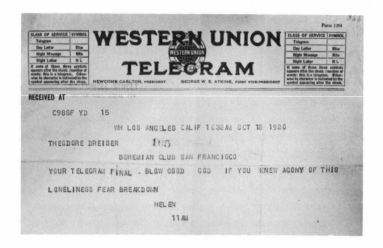

Telegram from Helen

San Francisco, Monday, Oct 18—1920

Up at 8:30—No word from Sterling. Have to look about. Breakfast at Ruffieuxs. Excellent food. Leave word at theatre that I am in town. She has not arrived yet. Go & look at rooms. The Worth Hotel. The Cartwright. Decide on it. Return to Club. Sterling returns. Has plans.—an evening somewhere. L. wants to stay in room.[108] Move her from Turpin & stay there. We have dinner later at The Golden Pheasent. & go down to here some new sings. Vivian Holt & the Rennick Music Co. L's new song. Its worth. At 8 leave & go round to the Club. Sterling & I visit Mrs. ———. Her music—doves—books—drinks. Get drunk & a little wild. We empty

108. L. is Lillian Rosenthal.

a hamper of rose leaves on the floor & put our heads in it. At 1:30 carried home in a taxi. L. waiting. She is very cheerful. After a round—we sleep. Letter from Helen at Club at 6—

1 A.M.
Tuesday

Dearest Teddie:

Tonight I came home in a fever after having walked <u>all</u> day in the rain without an umbrella and I was drenched when I got in, was hysterical, feverish and altogether tortured. When I read your telegram I brightened up considerably for your previous message hurt so and I could not do a thing today but walk to & from P.O. in search of God only knows what. Word from you—and more word I guess but your telegram prayed on my mind so that I sat down, in desperation and wrote that horrid message to you. You know Teddie that I do not mean it.

When I went down stairs tonight to phone a reply to your message, after waiting until Mrs. Ringstrom had retired, the phone was out of order so I went to town and sent it from there and just got back [12.30], and now I am in bed and feel a little quieter.

You think I am exaggerating and that perhaps I am writing these things to you to bring you back but you don't understand. I do want you to stay there until reception is over but you will never know how I have suffered this week. Tonight I thought sure I would collapse on the car. Teddie you must not leave me again. I cannot stand it. You have taught me to love you with my whole heart and if you are not careful you will kill me. I have not been eating, sleeping. I cannot read or work. Can only walk and think. I knew I would suffer but did not dream how intensely. Please come back as soon as reception is over if I am of any value to you whatsoever. I wonder if you are sorry because I cling to you and love you so. I wonder what will happen to me. It is so easy for you to make me suffer and would soon kill me. This is the actual truth. I look like I have been ill.

Teddie dont be too hard on me. I cannot control these feelings. I want you back. Oh so much. Wont you hurry?

Please dont stay any longer, unless you don't want to come.

Goodnight my darling soul mate. Dont you love your baby that simply worships you? A million kisses and a big heart full of love for my big Teddie.

Have nice little stove to keep Teddie warm.

Teddie I am so eager to see you. Hurry, hurry hurry.

Teddie I am at work & am nervous again. Have been talking to girl that just returned from Frisco. I can't stand the agony of being away from you knowing S.F. For Gods sake wire or phone me. I will go crazy without you.[109]

Sunday, Oct 24—1920— Los Angeles

Late breakfast at Petifils. Helen looks wonderful. Stage trip to San Fernando. The base, gaunt, bony mountains. Mexicans. Sunday base ball game. We get back at 6:30. Stop in at Alexandria—then to little restaurant in Hill Street. Then home. More loving. Helen in orgiastic mood. No sleep till 2 A.M. Confesses her desire to see me

---

109. Omitted at this point are two more such letters from Helen.

Helen with the Cat

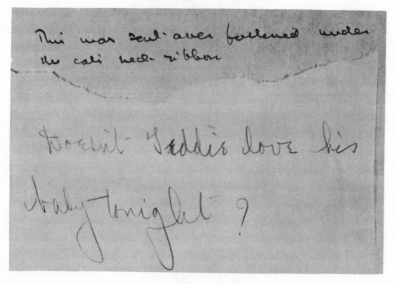

The Note Tied to
the Cat's Collar

in transports with other girls. Wants to arrange it with some movie beauty.

Monday. Oct. 25—1920—Los Angeles

Work on An American Tragedy & letters. Helen collects \$35$\frac{00}{}$ from Metro & gives it to me. Wonderful session in evening—after dinner at Petifils. Helen has a streak of perversion in her. Makes me promise never to teach any other girl to osculate my penus as she does! Her plans for private orgies in Hollywood. Playing continues till one A.M.—then exhausted we sleep.

Tuesday, Oct. 26—1920—Los Angeles

Breakfast with Helen—1553—Staid home all day & worked. She went out about noon to see agents. At 4:10 go down town to look after mail, matches, ink & developer for Helens pictures. Go to Library & look up stuff about Denver. Meet Helen at Lankershim— 6:30. She has check for 25 from her husband which I cash for her at the bank & she gives me the money. We dine at Petifils—then to library where I read till 9. Then home. The beauty of Helen—lying on the bed—nude—like blue veined alabaster. She outlines her scheme for extracting more bliss out of sex. Is to get me girls & watch me manhandle them. We have a wonderful session— exhausting—ending later in a quarrel but I wonder how she would feel—supposing some other woman fascinated me. Bad night on account of this. No sleep till 4 A.M. Storms, cries, fights, curses. Finally makes up & sleeps—the most dangerously jealous beauty I have ever had.[110]

L.A Oct. 27—1920

Found under my writing pad

My darling—
Have gone to Dorothy's and will phone later.
I love you—love you—<u>love</u> you.

Your own baby.

Sunday, Nov. 7—1920—Los Angeles

Helen & I get up at 10 & go down to Petifils. Lill is in town with the <u>Hello, Alexander Co</u> & I am nervous about meeting her. We

---

110. Omitted here are letters to Dreiser from Mabel Eastman and Florence Deshon (see entry for Nov. 29).

dine in back part of room. Afterwards go to see Gloria Swanson in "Her Decision." Not so bad for a movie. We walk out Hope & Flower Streets to about 2800 then take Central Ave Car back & dine at the little restaurant in Hill Street. Finally go home. Helen nervous about going under Ether & arranges everything so I can handle them without publicity. Turns over ring, bank account, trunk etc. We have one long round & then sleep.

Monday. Nov 8—1920—Los Angeles

Up at 6 & dress & take car to Methodist Hospital. No breakfast as Helen is not allowed to eat any. Arrive at Hospital 2826 So. Hope St at 7. Immediately engage room 321—at $8 Per Day. Helen very nervous. Nurses & doctor arrives. She is prepared for table & taken up. I hold her hands while she goes under ether. Her babbling about "Teddy". First operation on nose—(shaving down bridge under the skin) very interesting. 2nd & 3rd —tonsils & adenoids very bloody. So much blood lost that it makes me a little sick—more from fear for her—than anything. Help hold & turn her over. Then watch her for 2 hours while she comes to. The vomiting of blood! Stay all day—till 9 P.M. Only cracked ice allowed her. By then she is feeling better & they give her a hypodermic & I go home—stopping for dinner & and at P.O. Arrive home at 11. Read Menckens new book which just came—Prejudices II.[111] Also finish life of Edgar Allen Poe by Prof Harrison (Univ. of Virginia) and "Erewhon" by Samuel Butler.[112] Very tired but dont sleep well. Nervous about Helen.

Tuesday. Nov. 9th 1920—Los Angeles

Up at 6 and off to Hospital by seven. Stop at a little beanery in 8th St for coffee & cakes. Arrive Hospital at 8:30. Helen some better. Throat very sore. Stay all day, reading Erewhon. At 4 she decides she wants to go home. No service here really—at $8 a day— nothing. At 5 I consult doctor over phone (Dr. Simon Jesberg) & he agrees that she may. Call a taxi & take her—stopping at a Sun Drug Co for a syringe (nose) Peroxide—talcum. After I get Helen

111. Mencken's *Prejudices: Second Series* (1920).
112. *Life of Edgar Allan Poe* (1902) by James A. Harrison (1848–1911). *Erewhon; or, Over the Range* (1872) by Samuel Butler (1835–1902).

in bed go back to store for milk, eggs & canned Bouillon &
Consomme. Give her a glass of milk & consomme & she feels
better. Very tired myself so retire at once. Up a dozen times in
night to wait on her.[113]

Monday, Nov. 29, 1920. Los Angeles.

Get up at six with Helen. She is beginning a new engagement at
the Fox Film Corp., at $12.50 a day. We get a hurried and poor
breakfast here. Car to Hollywood and Western Ave. I dislike the
thought of this day some, because of my agreement to visit and talk
with Florence Deshon.[114] Go down town after leaving H at
Vineyard and draw some money at the bank. Then go to P.O. No
mail except some "Genius" letters returned by Stanchfield and
Levy.[115] Take Temple Street car to Fountain Ave. Then Hollywood
car to Vine. Walk to DeLongpre and down. Find her expecting me.
The usual summery moving picture actress get up. We begin talking
at once of L.A. Max Eastman (her former lover) at New York.
Tells me of her life with Eastman.[116] His literary and artistic
temperament. His poems. How he made money. Got sixty per from
the Liberator, then borrowed for the Socialist cause occasionally.
Could always get money from the rich, sometimes as much as ten
thousand. She made as high as three hundred per, and helped him.
How they quarreled and why. Too strong for each other. She calls
him a slick gin gink. Says that his work was always important and
had to be put first, hers never. The visit of Norman B. Angell, and
the hit she made.[117] The visit of Thorsten Veblin and the second
hit she made, on account of her beauty I presume.[118] She then
throws it up to them that they have been trying to keep her
intellectually in the shade, that they have been ashamed of her
intellectual poverty before their high brow friends when as a matter

113. Omitted at this point are letters Dreiser included in the diary from Louise Campbell,
Rose Korgues, and Florence Deshon.
114. Florence Deshon began corresponding with Dreiser in 1920.
115. John B. Stanchfield and Louis Levy were the attorneys who represented Dreiser in
the legal case connected with the suppression of The "Genius".
116. Max Eastman (1883–1969) poet, critic, editor, teacher. Dreiser knew Eastman in
New York when Eastman was editing Masses and The Liberator and living in Greenwich Village.
117. Norman Angell (1873–1967), British author, journalist, winner of Nobel Peace
Prize in 1933.
118. Thorstein Veblen (1857–1929), economist, social philosopher.

of fact their high brow friends are more interested in her than than they are in the Eastmans. Crystal Eastman drops out of the fight. The book of poems. How she kept it from being dedicated to Lenin. The poems in it to her—some of them very beautiful. How she left Eastman. His distress. Visits her but cannot make her reform. Becomes the mistress of Charlie Chaplin. Tells me of his peculiarities. Likes him but cannot love him. Really craves, as I can see, another literary celebrity. Is angling for me as her letters show. We go to lunch at the <u>Come-On-Inn,</u> a Gower Street Movie restaurant. The movie queens in there. F.Ds vanity. After lunch we return to her place and talk until four. Her life with Chaplin. The character of Mildred Harris Chaplin. How she got him. Became his mistress, then got with child, then made him marry her. Her mother aided her in this. Previously they had tried to ensnare D. W. Griffiths, and after him Maurice Touneur. Neither of these would fall for her. Is very small, very babydollish, with blue eyes and light hair. Threatened to shoot Chaplin and had him frightened, so much so that he ran away. Paid her 200,999 to quit.

I leave at four admiring the apartment, but little more. Wants me to meet Chaplin and Mme. Nazimova. I do not promise. Return to room and go to work. Working on An American Tragedy. Work till 5.30 when Helen comes. Tells me of her day. The lady with the Chinese Mandarin coat which she rents with herself in it for 25 per day. Her crazy inexperienced director. Has made a new actress friend—a friend of Betty Blythe. We go down to Petifils. All the gossip of the movie world. I here it every night. Tell her of F.D. and she gets very jealous but I smooth it over.[119] Home and to bed. I rarely weary of H. She has a perpetual physical appeal for me. I still think she is the most beautiful girl I ever saw.

<u>Tuesday, Jan. 25, 1921. Los Angeles, Cal. 6309 Sunset</u>
Helen working at Morosco Studio. Bebe Daniels picture. Her new director, an ex-army colonel, struck on her,—her usual experience. We breakfast at the little French place, Vine at Selma. Take Hollywood car to Virgel. The Temple Street car to Occidental Boul and Council Street. Helen carries a thrmos bottle with two cups of

119. F.D. is Florence Deshon.

hot coffee in it. Is angry with Miss Hallett, the casting director, for give her a $12.50 a day check after she agreed to pay her $75.00 per. I leave and return via Heliotrope Drive car line. Am working on <u>Mirage</u> (An American Tragedy)[120] and incidentally reading <u>The Inside of the Cup,</u> by Winston Churchill, a dull, mistaken book, typical of American ignorance and American smugness.[121] Work till noon. Lunch at the little French place. Go to Holly P.O. immediatly afterward and mail one hundred of the writers club notice.[122] Return. Read and work until six. Write a poem,—<u>Geddo street.</u>[123]

Tuesday—April 19—1921—1515 Detroit—Hollywood—10:15 P.M. —Helen leaves for S. F. Before that, taxi ride—from 8:15 to 10. We take Myrtle[124] to her new address— —she having been ordered out the day before by Helen. Previous to taking taxi we have dinner at house & Helen plays victrola till eight. Row between us & taxi driver at 10—over agreed upon charge. It was to be 2$\underline{^{00}}$ instead of 2$\underline{^{50}}$. I wander up 5$\underline{^{th}}$ Street after she has gone—have a Coca-cola & then ride home—Hollywood. (Gardner Junction car) to La Brea. Feel rather lost without her & go straight to bed. Her plans before leaving. Hoped to get 10,000 out of Frank.

Thursday—April—21, 1921—Hollywood—1515—Detroit. We have lived here since March 8$\underline{th}$. Previous to that 6309 Sunset with Mr & Mrs. D. H. McDonald. On Tuesday April 17—Helen left for S. F. to meet Frank. Wires on Wednesday. Told me of her arriving safely & registering at Palno. Wires me same day to leave at 10:15 —arrive S.F. Friday—1 P.M. I do. Was working on novel. Go down at once & buy ticket & berth. Return home & pack. Play records till 8. Wonderful spring night. Eclipse—with blood on moon due. Debate over giving away pumpkin pie. Go to station. Sit there. Girl

---

120. "Mirage" was one of the titles Dreiser considered for *An American Tragedy*. He also wrote a poem called "Mirage" which is printed in *Moods: Cadenced and Declaimed* (1926).

121. *The Inside of the Cup* (1912) by Winston Churchill (1871–1947).

122. Dreiser belonged to a club called The Writers, which was organized in 1917. The group issued notices of the new work of its members, held social functions, and held meetings to discuss literary matters.

123. "Geddo Street" was published in *Vanity Fair* 26 (August 1926): 61; it was included in *Moods: Cadenced and Declaimed* (1926).

124. Helen's sister Myrtle.

at Western Union counter. She poses for me. Very young. I get in car. Italians. The old couple going to Santa Barbara. To bed. See only a bit of the Eclipse.

Friday, April 22nd—1921 —En route from L.A. to S.F. in Pullman. (Old Pullman. No lights in berth.) I get up about as we were leaving San Luis Obispo. Same country I saw going up on bus in October. Paso Robles—Salinas. Mountains. St. Francis baths. I breakfast with the Port Warden of L.A. He draws me a map of the State. Jelousy of S.F. The beautiful girl on diner who looked like Helen. Her family. The two brothers. The Italians in my car. The noisy kid in the A.M. The fat woman—like Mrs. Wood—who tried to flirt with me. Arrive at S.F. on time. New moving picture place. Helen waiting. Taxi ride. News about Frank. Only $200. Wants to stay in S.F. a week—Wants to go to St. Francis. We ride out to ocean & back. How we manage. Story of Franks is in Chi—— 5 Grand. The State Senator who came. "Young man—big job. Thought maybe you might need a little money." Irish Catholics in charge. Gun men. Brewers pay 5000 to be allowed to run two days or three. Warehousemen came to be able to cart out stuff between 6 & 8 in A.M. Women come to get in with him. One woman comes to him to plead with him to frame her husband & then falls in love. Wants to prevent F—— from sending Helen anything. Politicians who think diamond pins & rings are marvellous—also golf clubs. Made 100,000 in 3 months. Brother Yeeling aided him. How he tried to persuade Helen. Buys her a 55$\underline{00}$ bag. Gives her 300$\underline{00}$. Quarrels with her clothes. Takes her to Taits. Isn't moved by thoughts of time he walked the streets hungry. # We go to Palace & get bags & trunk. Send trunk to SP. Station. Go to St. Francis & register. Get room 967. Bath. I listen to story of Franks life. We go out Golden Pheasent. Dinner 2$\underline{50}$. Talk of grip of love & children. Take car up Nob Hill—Jackson Car—to Park. Return & walk down.

Saturday—April 23rd—1921. S.F. (St. Francis Hotel) We get up about 10:30. Breakfast at little place in Market Street. Trunk hasnt come. We phone about it. Go to Oakland & see sights. Beauty of Bay. Oakland Hotel. We stop for tea. Take car to Berkeley & see College & Greek Theatre. The Shakespeare contest. A Jap wins it.

Back to S.F. to Golden Pheasent. Then to hotel. Then car ride to little park. To bed—very tired. More talk of Frank. His girl. Helen decides to go to Portland & Seattle. I decide to go along.

Sunday—April 24—1921—S.F. (St. Francis Room 967)—We go to Palo Alto & look at the University there. Leave at 10 A.M. back at 4:30. Cold, windy ride back. Pleasent ride out. See civic centre & auditorium. The Warwick—theatre where Helen & Frank danced. She tells me of Benny Speck. How Frank & Benny & two other boys in Portland used to do a quartette stunt around saloons for drinks. This gave Frank idea for stage act for himself & Helen. They got $90^{00} a week "whirling each other around." The town of Daly & the Daly public library. Beautiful Hill Country. List of towns between S.F. & Palo Alto. The nice Barker. Graveyards. Small road houses (P of Singders). Eucalyptus trees come from Australia. H says they look like Australia—Why Bungalow towns were built south of S.F. The 20 local trains in & out of S.F in this one line. ¶ Palo Alto. The 75 cent dinner. History of the Stanfords. Leland died first. (boy) Then father. Then Mrs. L. Father gave 8,000 acres & $40,000,000 to University—4500 boys—500 girls. David Starr Jordan. The Angel of Grief. The Moseleum. He was "torn". A brother gave an art gallery and an administration bldg. The bum "art" he had collected. The wife placed the church in the centre & filled it full of cheap Christian maxims with a slam at science. The new dormitorys. The "houses" of the students. The 12 Apostles thrown down. Also the new library bldg—1/2 mile away. Also the church tower. Nothing else. Flowers kept before Moseleum. Helen & I fight over tea when served because there was no salt. Later we walk down Market, make up & go out to Townsends restaurant. Oysters, coffee & salad for me. We have long talks about old S.F. The girls etc. Helen orders tickets. To bed at 1 A.M. after a long round. Helen tells of the young student she met on ferry. "People of L.A. don't seem to know what its all about". When told she was married "Well, now thats too bad. Well —Perhaps you'll be coming through S.F. again sometime & youll give me a ring". Gave her address of Spanish Club where booze could be had. He gave a sailer a drink. "Wouldnt you like to go to Iroquois (in Oakland) for dinner? Wouldnt you like to join a party?"

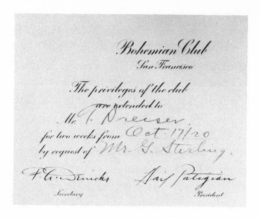

Guest Card for the Bohemian Club

Monday—April 25—1921—San Francisco Awake in St. Francis—
Room 967—We leave today at 4 P.M. for Portland—so I try to get
Helen up. Up at 8:30. Cold bath. We go to Ruffieuxs Sutter Street
—for breakfast. Buck wheat cakes—Bacon—toasted Brioche &
coffee. Helen laughs because I propose to show them how to run a
restaurant. Afterward we go to The Emporium—foot of Sutter St
steep & I buy 4 bordered Hdkfs. Helen buys an under slip & a
new leather handbag—Shirt 2.75. Bag—5⁵⁰. We then take the little
car up Sutter street Jackson Street line—Nob Hill to the Park at the
end of the line. The remains of doorway step & foundations of
houses shaken down by the quake of 1906—Something pathetic
about it. Nurse maids & babys in the park. The difference between
the plain wooden flats of S.F. (built to replace—quickly—brick
homes I presume) & the ornate & smug bungalows of LA. The
smugness & security of L.A. as opposed to the natural humanity &
variety of S.F. We ride back to Mason St. Helen met some Stanford
college youth on the ferry going to Oakland Tuesday who told her
where to get booze.—(Spanish Club—1553—Mason St.) We go
there. An Italian looks out the window. Admits that this is Spanish
Club. We start argument for booze. By using name of George
Sterling I get two bottles of cocktails for $9.50. Also two drinks for
$1⁰⁰. Two men come in while we are there. The Italians daughter
says I must have seen her playing the violin at ⌐   ⌙. Back to St.

Francis. We have three more drinks each. Get lit up & have a round. Pack trunk. At 2 it leaves for station. At 2:30 we leave. Stop for short cake & coffee. Then to Palace Hotel for telegram there from Myrtle. Then Martha Wash Candy Co for Candy. Then to station. We have to wait for St. Francis bus to bring out two bags. Due at 3:30. The life about the ferries. Beauty of the bay. Shasta Limited. Car 43—Lower 6. We leave on time. We sit in lower 8 by mistake. The woman who looks like a vice crusader. We cross a bay at Benicia on a ferry. I dont even know it till Helen tells me. Love bayside ride to Benicia. Flat country between bay & mountain until sunset. Elmira Calif.

Tuesday

Ashland, Phoenix, Medford. A snow white peak, seen over green ones. The dull American on the observation platform spouting what he has read in the papers—Wrigley—Baseball—Chicago etc—Medford—"the gate way to Crater Lake— | Central point | a cloudless day. Fruit trees in blossom | Seven Oaks— | The best view of the Peak. Raygold California-Oregon Power Co. A river, a falls, a view of the Peak over the falls | Gold Hill on Rogue River | Town of Rogue River | Town of Grants Pass. Bluish green hills all the way with tall pines on them. Salem Oregon. Shaving in smoke room at time. Hear—Spring comes first here—1st roses strawberries vegatables. Ect. Country is very green & well watered. Helen in a sensual mood. Most of P.M. spent in observation car. I read bible (Psalms & Proverbs). Eugene—Irving—Swann.

Wednesday—April 27—1921—Portland Hotel Seward—Room 402 —a fierce room—Dusty curtain over bath room transom. Old clothes press standing in room. The very cold water in the faucet. Helen says it comes from Mt. H. The beauty of Helen really makes up for any lack. We go to Olds Wortman & King to buy a tie for me. Also to see if Mr. Skiff is there. Then to Hazelwood for breakfast. Eggs 20 cents a dozen but a chicken liver omelette is still 65.$\underline{cts}$. Helen tries at C. H. Baker & Co for a pair of shoes. Tells me this is same store Frank & his friend ⌞ ⌟ clerked as shoe clerks—getting 35$\underline{00}$ & knocking down 15 more.
She leaves me & I go to Imperial, Benson & Multnomah to look for a room. Decide on Benson—Room 910—6$\underline{50}$. Much the nicest.

Then go to Olds W & King. Skiff in N.Y. Go for a walk. The
beautiful green spring trees at 6th & Salmon. Bridges over
Willamette. South Portland.

River Bridge. West Ivan—loaded with lumber
("Labor Row"—2nd at Couch Streets)
Resaw—lineup man—$3⁶⁰
Door Clamper—$5⁵⁰
Stock Cutter—5⁵⁰
Yardman—driver one horse truck 3⁶⁰
"Jack Tate—Section Boss—Please call "Huddleston—High Climber.
   Please call
Camp Cook—100⁰⁰
Flunkey—45⁰⁰
Marker for resaw—4⁰⁰
Lady dishwasher—50⁰⁰ & Bd
Trimmer man—small mill 3⁶⁰
Teamster for nursery—30 cents an hour—can work 9–10 hours
Down River farm hand $40⁰⁰
       Must have own blankets
Head Pole Roadman 7⁰⁰
Car Tallyman—4⁸⁰
Head Loader—6⁵⁰
Square Deal Hotel—Card Room
   Papers—
   Svenska Kurien—
       "   Tribunen
       "   Amerikanaren
   Svensk Amerkanska
The Toiler
Svenska Socialisten
Skandinaven
Police Gazette
Sporting News
Tyomies (Tyomies)
The Weekly People
The Gaelic American
Aebetaran
Finska-Amerkanaren
Riggs Sled Builder wanted

1 Sniper—4$\underline{^{50}}$
1 Choker Setter 4$\underline{^{80}}$
1 Gas Sawman 4$\underline{^{00}}$
2 Shingle Sawmen 4—
1 Whistle Punk 3$\underline{^{75}}$
1 Rachette Setter 4$\underline{^{00}}$
1 Signal Punk 3$\underline{^{60}}$
1 Wood Bucker 3$\underline{^{60}}$
1 Rigging Rustler—6$\underline{^{00}}$
1 Chaser—5$\underline{^{00}}$
1 Man to Buck 4$\underline{^{40}}$
2 P.M. A flow of rain. A rather poor city I think. Go to Hotel
Oregon.
Built like this

Porch with Rockers
Porch with Rockers

Said Loyal Laura with smile so sweet
Oregon products are hard to beat
Thats why my broom must be a Zan
Its made at home by an Oregon man

+

Advs in Cars—
Wrigleys—Gold Crest Butter
Nealin Soles—Arrow Collar
Lux— | Zan Brooms | Del Monte
Peaches—Autos without Drivers—
Royal White Soap—5 cts—Joto—
E. C. Corn Flakes Blue Ribbon Soda
Wafers—Day & Nite Davenport
Fels Naptha Rinso—G.P. Mayonaise
Jimmy Dawn Tailor
See city from Council Crest. Very rainy. Wait 1/2 hour or more in
rain. The large shed completely covered with closely pencilled
names. Down in rain. Go to the Seward. Have drink. Helen
Comes. Tells of her Mother & Myrtle. Myrtle has wired for money
to come north. Helens Mothers new man or lover. How fine he is.

More details of Helens early life. We move to Benson. She sees a man she knows. Room 910. Dinner at Hazelwood. We get a list of restaurants. Walk. Good Samaritan Hospital. The great ice rink. It rains. I am very tired & quarrelsome. We go to a drug store & I get some pepsin. Then to room. A drink. A hot bath. Helen & I have a round. She remains as sweet to me as ever.

Thursday. April 28—1921—Portland. Benson hotel. Room 910. Helen very talkative about her mother & her youth & how happy— she—Helen—is. We have a swell game in bed. Then to a near by restaurant. I have fried mush & bacon—We then investigate cost of Columbia River Drive trip. East 80$\underline{th}$ at East Stark. Out by <u>Mt. Tabor Car.</u> Back by <u>Montavilla Car.</u> I go into Sweatlands for a Coco Cola. Take North Broadway car to Mason— & E. 31<u>st.</u> Fine city. Encounter a beautiful grove of pine trees. Crows in it. Think of a new kind of Treasure Island—to be built on false coin makers. The queer man on the car who suggested a doctor—also a counterfieter. Cor. E. 33rd & Fremont. Wonderful View of City. Back along Fremont to river. Wonderful river scene. Reminds me of Cincinnati, Evansville & Germany (Herlinghe). Pidgeons. Car foundries. Svensk Boarding Houses. I see clerks bending over desks in great railway freight offices. Back along river to Broadway Bridge. Albers Milling Co. Albers just freed by Government (Attorney General Daugherty). Walk to Portland P.O. & through it. Then East (?) to 15<u>th</u> where I get a N & S. Portland car to end of line. See great big bldg 29<u>th</u> & Thurman. Great viaduct— Beautiful residence road with charming, flower covered homes. View of flying field from viaduct & road, with a flying machine making short trips. The afternoon reception at one house with all the cars about. So much lovely dogwood everywhere. I never saw such beautiful dogwood trees. <u>One man</u> car—the latest corporation money saver—back to town. I go to markets. Very clean & cute. Materials very fresh. I get 1 dozen eggs, 1 dozen oranges and a small bottle of olive oil. To the Bean Pot where I have a pot of excellent beans—2 slices of brown bread & 2 cups of coffee. (30 cents—should have been—I paid 20.) To the Portland Hotel where I sit on the delightful porch once more. Three Hindoos—Green Coats (Purple lined). Yellow Pants—Coral colored caps blue shirts & tan sashes. Very Picturesque. They enter a public lavatory. Two girls in Portland Hotel flirt with me. Two young town sports sit around & smoke in a grand manner. I go to hotel. Helen has been with Mother all P.M.—getting news. She is in a very sensual mood. We lie around & talk until too late for dinner. Then order something from over the way. Hotel grill closes at nine. Helen tips boy 50 cts. He charges her 4⁰⁰ for what could be had outside for 1.²⁵. To bed.

Friday, April 29—1921—Portland—Hotel Benson. Helen has agreed to spend day with mother. I get up early & beat it to Tyrill Auto Sightseeing Co. 125—6th St. Have breakfast first. The cook who was being grilled for stealing some bacon. His thin— bedticking pants. I go & buy my ticket—$5⁴⁰. A handsome silver grey—Pierce Arrow Car—Red T on it. We finally pick up seven passengers—mostly clowns. The Jew from the Hotel Hoyt. We go out through East Portland, Laurel Park, Beaumont to a place called Troutville. Thence to the Sandy River. The water falls. Then to Columbia River Highway. The granduer of it. Shepherds Dell— Bridal veil falls & the lumber co. Benson Park & Wa-Kee-Nah-falls. Multnomah Falls—Horsetail falls. The spray—Bonneville. Hatchery, Tyrill Inn. Upper rapids & locks ⵖⵖⵖⵖⵖⵖ . A set of pictures 1⁰⁰, bunch $1⁵⁰. I see a copy of The "Genius" & want to steal it. Cold wind. Long ride back. Hotel at 5³⁰. Helens Mother just gone. We lie around. Hot bath—Screw. To dinner at 8:15 at the Multnomah. Helen looks stunning—She tells of Myrtle trying to graft on her mother & we roast Myrtle until 10 P.M. Home & to bed.

Saturday—April 30—1921 Portland—Hotel Benson—Gray day. Write 8 letters—To—Sterling, Geo. Douglas, Ethel Kelley, Horace B. Liveright, Margaret Johnson, Louise & Herrick.[125] Postmaster at Los Angeles, Mabel Eastman. Before this long fierce screw with Helen. She dresses & leaves. I take hot bath. Then out & walk out Washington Street to Park (City Park). The green spring leaves. Fine view. Birds in cages. The best bear cage I ever saw. Two

125. Ethel M. Kelley, editor. An old friend of Dreiser, Ethel Kelley had been on the staff of *Broadway* when he edited it in 1906, and she helped Dreiser in his efforts to reissue *Sister Carrie* in 1907.

Margaret Johnson's correspondence reveals a distant, mainly epistolary relationship of twenty years which began in 1919 when she, then a young drama teacher, first met Dreiser in New York.

statues <u>1. Coming of the White Man</u> presented by The Thompson family to Portland 1. Sago ke wa—first white woman—or woman pioneer in Oregon.[126] Think all the time of novel to be based on Leon Dix—His idling, his views of such a city as this etc.[127] The children who are admiring the monkeys. Their chatter. The Lewis & Clark Statue. The dream houses. Mt. Hood at last. I walk out South along the Willamette. Then take car back. Portland burns wood—Wait for Oregon City Car. The man who thought Portland ought to have the movies. The Hoosierlike characters here. I get a car. <u>The New Rodeo.</u> The boat houses on the Willamette. The fine golf course. Fare 25 cts. <u>Island.</u> The man who had half clap-boarded his house & then ran out of money. <u>St. Theresa.</u> Apple trees in full bloom. <u>Concord Oregon City.</u> A young girl greets me. The small town restaurant & pool room. The <u>blow hard</u> keeper. Sex & oaths the chief characteristics. Apricot pie made of apricots and tapioca. I take car back. The dogwood trees. <u>Scotch Broom.</u> Arrive—5 P.M. Look for a map in the Mier-Frank Co. Also a silk shirt. The girl who said she wouldnt let the fellow come out anymore. He had nice eyes but he didnt interest her. I go to Portland & sit down. Then to hotel. Helen not there. She arrives at 7. We quarrel a little. Finally dress & go to Portland for dinner. Service like old Southern Hotel. We discuss her mother & Myrtle. Myrtle divides her mothers last quarter! Back to hotel. To bed.

Sunday, May 1—1921—Portland. Hotel Benson. Room 910— Raining. Helen & I have a lovely affectionate union. Dress about noon. Go to the new Hazelwood—the old <u>Rainbow Grill</u> where as a kid Helen used to meet the wealthy manufacturers. I can see that it is full of delightful memories for her. We have muffins (40 cents) & steaks. From there go to Vancouver Wash. Portland comes to river bank opposite. We see theatre in which Helen played for $25<u>00</u> per. Soldiers. The small park & squirrels. She laughs over my saying that I'll have a <u>dish</u> of ice cream instead of a plate. She is in very gay spirits. Old brewery she went through. Car back. Then to

---

126. Dreiser means Sacagawea, the young Shoshone Indian woman who was the interpreter for the Lewis and Clark expedition in 1805.
127. One piece of correspondence between Leon Dix and Dreiser survives at the University of Pennsylvania. It is dated 1911 and suggests that Dix, who resided at 126 E. 22d St., had the means to live elegantly.

Hazelwood for coffee. The four kids who were frozen by its granduer. We go to the Multnomah & sit there till 6. A House.

Monday—May 2nd 1921—Portland. Hotel Benson. Up at 7:30. Leaving today for Tacoma & Seattle. Call porter to get trunk at 8:30. We go to a small restaurant. Helen decides not to go to Seattle. Pair in restaurant she thinks have spent night together. She goes to Ladd & Tilton Bank for $200. I wait for her in Imperial. A purely commercial Hotel. The best dressed girl I have seen. Dark clothes. Helen comes. We call a black & white taxi. I go over to Benson. Find trunk & bags downstairs. 25 cents to Porter. 25 cents to hall boy. Black & white charges 90 cents to depot—about 6 blocks. Jap porters at station. Helen nervous. Plans to wire Frank for 50 more. Wants me to wire her today. Get on Northern Pacific Train. It is raining. The typical christian moralizing Americans. Cracked over Pecksniffery. Big iron works. North Portland—Swift & Co. & Waxed Paper Co. The many large plants for lumber & shipbuilding. Vancouver proves larger than I thought. Very much water along this route. Woman who looks 50—Says she is 36—own to her one child—bad boy—a kind of Huck Finn who is nosing into everything and encouraged by her "You had your bounteous breakfast." "No it was bumteous." Learn that Post-Intelligencer is controlled by Hearst. All one gets in the morning papers these days is pleas for optimism & doing your duty. A stuffed car—mine. The one in front much better. This is due to the fact that the porters steered all the people into one car—nearly. A rainy, flat—watery country all the way. See stations attached.[128] Chehalis showed the stump from which McKinley spoke in 1901 and Roosevelt—of course—in 1903. 8 feet wide at top—12 at bottom. 300 feet high. Had 30,000 feet of lumber. All towns rather poor, Tacoma little better—a sort of Western Bridgeport Conn. I eat at a beanry. View the Sound. The lovely, glassy, olive green hue of the water. Red & black bridges. Slate & white pidgeons & white gulls. I think all the time of the story about Leon Dix. Red signs along waterside at landing place in Tacoma reflected as a crinkly smeer in the water.

128. Dreiser apparently meant to include a train schedule in the diary at this point but did not do so.

Tacoma-Seattle service—9, 11—1$\underline{00}$ 3—5—Both ways. Fare 1 way
40 cents—Round Trip 80 <u>cts.</u>

Tuesday. May 3<u>rd</u> 1921—Seattle
Hotel St. Regis—2<u>nd</u> Ave & Stewart Sts.—Opposite Washington
Hotel & The New Washington. This hotel is 8 stories high—
<u>Hollywood Gardens</u>—Florists just over the way in the Old
Washington. I walk along Stewart St to 4<u>th</u> Ave—down which I go
to Boulevard Cafe—1422 4<u>th</u> Ave. where I have breakfast—45
cents. At 4<u>th</u> Ave & Spring find Public Library—smoky—and BPOE
Bldg—bright & clean. View of bay—to my right—at every corner.
In these days the Public Library looks like the P.O. The P.O. Like
the City Hall. the City Hall like the County Court House. The
county court house Like the Customs House & so on in a never
ending circle. At Marion St—where I came in & 4<u>th</u> The Hotel
Congress & a really cute brown brick & ivory trimmed hotel—
Colonial motif—The Hotel Pennington. 4<u>th</u> and—Yesler Way.
Small triangular park. King county Court House. Hotel Frye—L. C.
Smith Bldg—a fairly interesting square. Facing bay & looking to my
left—typical smoky—Chicagoesque scene with Great Northern—
N. Pacific depot in foreground—a very scubby specimen of depot.
Right back of me Police department, Emergency Hos. etc. Yesler
Way—I go out that. Horrible street climbing Hill. Silly to permit it
to lead out from so fine a Square. Many, many chinks & Japs
driving autos. Yesler Way car to Lak—13 minutes. Beautiful Park.
Snow topped mountains, ⌐   ⌐ Park & Leschi Boat House. Leschi
ferry. I sit in a wooden swing & look over the lake to the snow
crested peaks. A white ferry boat with a red smoke stack. The
Leschi boat house is white with a green roof. Right before me an
octagonal blue-green band stand. To my left a green lawn dotted
with spear pines. The grip car came direct to a long drab building
containing ice cream parlor, restaurant, peanut stand, etc. A Jap
comes along—We talk. He has a camera. Is in the fishing &
canning business. Saghalian. I walk West? Past small house boats on
shore to a sign at a foot of a stair—King Street. See Mt. Rainier—
once called Yohoma. A huge obtuse mass towering above all else |
King County Ferry System, Mercer Island Boats. Lake Shore Drive.
I find another Park with swings & swing. Pass car line end labelled
Madrona. Lake Shore Boul becomes Blaine Boul. Blaine Boul

becomes Stixrud Drive. Then changes at once to McGilvray Drive. The grand manor by the Waterside. Come to E. Madison Car. Kirkland Ferry. Take car for down town. A poorish region Groceteria—Drugeteria—Marketeria. I go to Chamber of Commerce. Mr. Mady Cake—Ice Cream Coffee—35 cents. University Car to Washington Univer. Eastlake Ave. All the government ships tied up. Up here its the Swift Drug Stores. Car goes out University Ave to end of line. A graveyard Union Bay. I take it back to University of Wash. 800 acres. The Jew woman traveler—Tells me of petrified forrest out of Oakland 4 hours. Los Ange—"the city of folded arms". I go through the forrestry bldg. Its wondrous charm. Alaska Wood wolf. Back to Minor Ave— North neighborhood. I get off & walk—Thomas St Buren Ave north. I come to Westlake Ave N. & walk north on it. A main car route. Take Green Lake car at City, edge of Lake, & ride round it to N. 68th Street. Go West on that to Greenwood Ave. At 21st Ave. North & W. 70th St. I come to a little park. Very green— Wind sighing in pines. Boys swinging in swings. A public comfort station. Walk on. Delightful open common where children play ball at the end of the city. Reach West 70th St N.W. at 33rd Ave. N.W. over looking Puget Sound. Look it up on map. All Seattle children look so healthy & play so naturally. Ball, racing, swinging, pulling wagons. It is 6:15 when I quit & return via Ballard Ave. Car line. Fare ten cents. Funny little dime shaped coins "tokens" sold—3 for 25. All smokestacks have big wire protectors making them look like smoky observatories. Due—very likely—to lumber as fuel. Dexter Ave—Along side Union Lake—48 Goverment ships in a row. A new thing. Dental surgery in a fine grey Electric car— nearly all windows. Get off near hotel—never do go in Seattle Natatorium. Go to hotel & take a hot bath. Very lonely. Decide to wind up by Wednesday night & get back to Portland Thursday in time to go on to S.F. Go across street to New Washington & wire Helen—16 words. Then write her a letter—also Jim Tully.[129] Also

---

129. Jim Tully (1891–1947), novelist, actor, playwright. Beginning as a hobo, prize-fighter, and circus roustabout, Tully turned to writing in the early 1920s. On 25 March 1921, he first wrote Dreiser, telling him of his desire to write ("My ambition is to be the combination of Dreiser and Sherwood Anderson"), after which Dreiser encouraged him and followed his career. Tully wrote a review of *An American Tragedy,* "Mr. Dreiser Writes An American Tragedy," *Literary Digest International Book Review* 4 (February 1926): 167, 169.

Von Sobern.[130] Lose a 5$\underline{00}$ fountain pen. Music in lobby. Walk the Street. Pine Street. Pike Street. The new P-I bldg. The two girls like Helen was—chippies—out for a catch. I get the old chasy longings but argue myself out of it. Eat—scones & coffee. Back to hotel & to bed—very tired.

Wednesday, May 4—1921—Hotel St. Regis Seattle—Room 620—Very lonely for Helen. Thoughts of and suspicions about her grieve me no little. Walk streets from 8 to 9:30—Seeing downtown & getting breakfast. Spanish Omelette & coffee. Look for Picture Cards. Inquire train time. Berth to Portland 4:20. No bus line to Portland. Get cards & walk to hotel—no word. Take Alki car for Alki Beach. Helens home neighborhood. Marvellous view of mountains on way out. Old Street cars fastened together to make a house. Steamer Exact—63rd Ave. S.W. The little colony—1851 Denny—that developed into Seattle—Nov. 13—Fish Crows I never saw them before. "Blends Male Friend"—a flap-jack flour. South Seattle—The home of Carl Dies—2200 Alki Boul.[131] The two kids.

Thursday, May 5—1921—Portland—
Multnomah—Room 636—These notes made at 12:30 noon—top of sight tower—council Crest. Sunshine—A magnificent view of all Portland. Boot blacks sign in Multnomah—"It shines in Portland some of the time. We shine here all of the time." I meet Helens mother. Breakfast—The Broadway Hazelwood. Mt. St Helens very clear. A cloud reflected on its snowy side. "For you a rose in Portland grows." These western "slogans"! Up at 10. Helen telephones at 9:30 to meet her & her mother at the Hazelwood— The poor finish of these Multnomah rooms. Such lumpish, oafish furniture. Helens room 343. I meditate on swiping some lights. To the Hazelwood. Helens mother. She looks much more forceful than I thought. I hear of some trouble over rent & how Helen straightened it out. English muffins, tea & ham. They leave & I go up on Council Crest for a last look. Clear today & warm, a

---

130. Henry Von Sabern was a German-born sculptor living in San Francisco. He and Dreiser carried on an extensive correspondence for more than twenty years after their meeting in San Francisco.
131. Carl Dies, Dreiser's (and Helen's) second cousin. Dies's grandmother was the sister of Dreiser's mother and the sister of Helen's grandmother.

---

beautiful view. Back to town. The woman who was telling where she was born, where her father owned property—the widow of a dead rich man who was now in a poor house. <u>Meier & Frank.</u> I buy to shirts. Back to hotel. Helen waiting. We lunch in a different restaurant in the hotel—very graceful—The Jap girl in trousers who acts as page. At 3.30 we take taxi to station. Helen in fine feather because she has straightened out her mothers affairs. We check trunk. Car 40—labelled Pasha—Lower 9. Very few people on board. We view charming, peaceful, homey scenery out of Portland. Observation platform Salem, Indiana country. The block signals closing behind us. Dinner. A girl who looks like Mrs. Harvey. 8 P.M. Berth is made up. Helen retires first. We have a long grand round before sleep—but a hard night.

Friday—May 6—1921 On board Shasta limited—Car 40—<u>Pasha</u>—Lower 9. Wake up about 8 & soon get up. Helen to tired to talk. We are in the gorge of the Sacramento River south of Medford. Wonderful stream—jade in color—tumbling & foaming. Shasta, Castle Crags. The drummer telling stories. The German—the Irishman & the two cocks. Hills nearer—S-F a study for a painter—golden—lavender, pink and gold.—blue-grey & pink—also bright wheat color—<u>Gerber.</u> We walk 10 minutes. What a dreary station. They take on ice. On. We come out in to the Sacramento Valley—not unlike the valleys farther South. All the big trees gone. The tumbling green rivers—the tall crags. Helens sensuality emphasized by the ennui of car riding. Dock. The ferry at ⌞　⌟. Oakland. A salty ride over the bay. The swarm of cabbys at the ferry. To the Clift Hotel. Room 625. The mirrors. Helen likes it at first very much. A hot bath. Then close the day ala Turkish delight.

+

Saturday, May 7<u>th</u> 1921—San Francisco
Hotel Clift—Room 625. We sleep late. Didnt send up trunk & Helen has no dresses. She takes an intense dislike to the room. I go out to get some liquor. 1553—Mason—The Spanish Inn—3 men setting there. Buy 2/5<u>th</u> at 6.50—per 1/5<u>th.</u> Back to Bohemian Club. 51 letters mostly junk. See Sterling who agrees to come to dinner. Back to hotel. Helen & I go out for breakfast—Ruffieux's—

and candy—Martha Washington. Then to several hotels to look at room. Find one at the Chancellor & take it. Room 50—3$\frac{50}{}$ per. But cant get in till—2. Take room on 9th floor. Go round to Clift, get bags & return. Taxi—3 blocks—80 cents. Deposit bags. Helen dances about. We go for a walk through China-town. The long tunnel. Chink life. Helen wants to take broilers back to L.A. The pictures of nudes for sale—ala Paris. To hotel. We plan to lie down & go out again but Helen feels so bad we stay in bed rest of night.

Sunday—May 8—1921 Chanceller Hotel—S.F. Room 50. Get up at about 10—Free Sunday paper—We dress & go into dining room below for breakfast. No muffins. Then we go to Cliff house & the Sutro Gardens & baths. Their delapitated condition. Grey & cold. We go into the baths. Back on car. Helens stomach troubling her. Into Townsends. Muffins 75 cents. We return to hotel & Helen lies down. I stay with her till 3:45. Then to 1601 Tayler—Home of Erskine Scott Wood & Sarah Bard Field.[132] The young radical lawyer. Wood looks like Bryant. A solid radical. I like Sarah Bard Field. Gives me a rose for Helen. Wood recommends Dr. Terry for operation for Helen. We dicuss Los Angeles life—vice crusader, etc. Powys[133] & his brother Llewellyn come. I like Lewellyn—but not as much as Jack. Cake & cheese & Scotch—I leave at 5:30. We are due to go to George Douglas for dinner. Von Sabern is to call at 6—He comes. Bus to Burlingame. Von Sabern reminds me of Smith. Talks of sculpture. Wants to do my head. Coming to L.A. Aggressive & a little boring. Helen first dislikes & then likes him. Burlingame. The George Douglas Personal Studio addition to S.F. The ⌐ ⌐ Von Saberns Wife, René Bennett, Pianist. A fine meal. Recitations. Back in Bennetts car. A break down. I speculate on whether to look up the lady in the pink hat or not.

Monday—May 9th—Chancellor Room 50—The fresh Jap elevator men—"Beautiful wife. Wonderful." We get up about 10. Breakfast at Hallwigs—a poor breakfast. Walk out to S.F. civic centre. Very

132. Charles Erskine Scott Wood (1852–1944), soldier, lawyer, writer. He lived in California and wrote about its history. Sarah Bard Field (1882– ?), poet and wife of Charles E. S. Wood. She had met Dreiser in 1917 while she was writing a biography of Mrs. Belmont.
133. John Cowper Powys (1872–1963), English author and lecturer.

Clipping: Poet Upholds Dive in Lake

windy. Helen troubled about her stomach. Sterling calls—says he
has made an appointment for three & will take us. 2:40 comes. We
go. Dr. Ernst Abrams.[134] Helen has _____. My depression. We
walk home. The bright evening. I go to see if bus carries trunks—It
doesnt. Call up San Anselmo. Drive with Sterling & Mrs. Warwick
in the Bohemian section of S.F. Helen cheers up. Dances. The
excellent food at Julius's. Bill $8.70. We walk from there to Boglies.
Dancing as before. The girl who sold me the booze at the Spanish
club is fiddling. Helen dances with Geo. Sterling.

O'Day. I met him once before. He comes over & invites me to
lunch at the Family club—Wednesday noon I agree. We go from

---

134. Dr. Ernst Abrams was a friend of George Sterling who treated Dreiser and Helen
with a device he invented called the oscilloclast. Dreiser and Helen continued their treatments
after returning to Los Angeles.

---

there. Reason couldnt get in. From there to Colombo. Orangeade only. Music. A base fiddle—a Dutch Pull Out—Saxaphone. On to another place. Helen dances some more. We walk home through China-town. Leave them at Chancellor. To bed.

Tuesday, May 10—1921—Hotel Chancellor—S.F. Room 50—I go over to Sausilito. Feel very depressed because of Helen. The beauty of the bay. A flock of gulls. Seven 4 masted ships in the quiet little harbor. Jack & Lewellyn Powys waiting for me. Jacks tanned face. We go up to the Alta Mira—hotel where they have a room. The room. We talk on the porch in the sun. Lewellyn reads <u>Black Gods,</u> a fine study of Africa. We return to wharf. I go to Yolanda station. The dusty road. The red tank. 9:45. A long talk. Mr. Herbert, the engineer. Art. Leave at 3:00. Back to ferry at 3:30 and S.F. Market Street at 4. The cranes standing in the water. Mt. Tamalpais. The gulls flying about the bay like bits of white paper.—Car to hotel, Helen in bed. She doesn't want to meet Jack & Lewellyn but I bring Lewellyn up. Then Jack calls & I go down. A talk with Jessica Colbert, the agent. $500 for a single lecture. Wants to sell my books. I send Jack up to Helen. Go up myself. The hit Helen makes. Dinner in the room. I kid young Powys about wanting to take her away from me. Jack recites poetry. Lewellyn recites Kubla Khan. They go. To bed. Helen rapes me.

<u>Wednesday—May 11—1921</u> —Hotel Chancellor—S.F. Room 50. We get up late. I go out & buy Helen a box of Harlem Oil—Gold Seal—"Dutch Drops." To breakfast at Ruffieux's. Into the shops. Helen buys a hat box. I go to the Family Club with George Sterling, George Douglas, Newbegin, the book seller,[135] ODay & myself. All the drinks we want. "Pink Garter" Cocktails—We talk of the limitations of art. I defend freedom. A grand fest till 5 P.M. Back to hotel & finish packing. To Townsends for a muffin. To Golden Gate Park with Helen. Back to Ruffiuex's. We go to hotel & take taxi to train. A box of Townsends candy. Very bad. Car 6—lower 15—The Lark. We get in. To bed. Helen has to be served as usual.

135. John J. Newbegin, a San Francisco book dealer.

Saturday, May 28, 1921. Los Angeles, Cal. 1515 Detroit Street. Up at 6:45. Worried over Helen who complains of more of those cancer pains in the pit of her stomach. Get a little frightened thinking of what I would do in case she died. Decide to rake Leadsworth over the coals for not giving her longer doses of the ocillaclast.[136] No appointment this A.M. At breakfast we discuss going out to the Long Beach Hotel—Virginia, over Sunday. We had previously been wishing that Grell and Myrtle would get over their rowing and come round and take us out in their car. After breakfast I settle down to the novel on which I am working—Mea Culpa.[137] Work steadily until twelve. Myrtle calls up and wants to know what we are doing. She and Grell are going out in the car and want to know whether we don't want to go along. She and Helen fix it up that instead of us going to Long Beach the four of us are to motor out to Riverside and stop at The Mission Inn. Helen get quite excited and goes down town to meet Myrtle. I work on until four when they return. Have fair luck with the story. They are all excited choosing the dresses they are going to wear. At five Myrtle phones and discovers that Grell has gone to Santa Ana and may not get back soon enough. We cant go to Riverside this night. At six Grell calls up and we decide to meet him at the Hollywood Hotel. I am Mr. Bellett. We go, carrying Myrtles bag. It is fixed now though, that we are to go to Riverside in the morning. At seven Grell arrives at the Hotel and we start off. First stop P.O. No word from Frank for Helen. She is trying to make him send her five hundred. I get letters from Van Nosdall proposing an autographed bibliography.[138] Also one from McQuaid, trying to squeeze me a little on the rent.[139] Also letters

136. In Los Angeles Dr. Leadsworth continued the ocilloclast treatments begun by Dr. Abrams in San Francisco.

137. Dreiser never completed "Mea Culpa"; it survives at the University of Pennsylvania as a 175-page typescript with holograph revisions. The story is told by a fifty-year-old narrator and focuses on three themes: the conflict between father and son, the symbolism of money as a psychological factor in character development, and the effects of sexual repression on individuals. Dreiser was not able to move his story beyond character definition to a central action, partly because he attempted to impose his own childhood memories and feelings onto a character from a middle-class, commercial background.

138. George A. Van Nosdall was an amateur book collector in New York who saw Dreiser's books as important for his collection. On 3 May 1921, Van Nosdall wrote Dreiser suggesting that he put together a bibliography of his writing to date. Dreiser gave tentative consent to the proposition, but Van Nosdall never completed the project.

139. Mr. McQuaid was married to Eleanora O'Neill and with her was subletting Dreiser's New York apartment (see p. 310, n. 52).

from several admirers. We drive on to Long Beach. Go out Main to Huntington Park. Then to Walnut Park. On to Long Beach. The freshness of the air. The sea wind. We drive on to end of Beach Drive. Then back and park the car. Go to one of the best places and have sundaes, lemonades, etc. At ten-thirty start back. Delightful air. How far flung L.A. seems. So plain that one could enjoy life here with a car. Back via Main, West 8th, West 7th, West 6th. Vermont, 3rd., Western and Sunset to Detroit. 11:30. We discuss the fun we had. To bed. Helen and I laugh at Myrtle & Grell. A fine, delicious round. To sleep.

Sunday, May 29, 1921. Los Angeles, Cal. 1515 Detroit Street, Hollywood. I wake at 6.45. Try to get Helen up. We are due at Sunset and La Brea—next corner— at 8 sharp. We are going to Riverside. Grell and Myrtle on time. Helen wears her grey dress with the flying streamers. Always looks wonderful. The way to Riverside. I look it up in the Blue Book. Beautiful morning. Bright sunshine. We go out the valley road. The lovely fields and hills. Pomona. The Salt Lake tracks. The mountains on either hand. The fountain on the outskirts of Riverside. The Inn. We stop at the depot. Then to breakfast. $3.50. Then for a drive. Looking for fine houses of Riverside. There are none. I read from the Blue Book an account of the wonders of Riverside. Kid it. Back to Inn and see its wonders. The beauty of the open court dining room. The summery costumes and garden hats. Pink and white and blue squared gingham with a tan and burnt orange hat. We explore the art caves and passges. The chapel. The organ. The art objects and books. The hundreds of guests. Luncheon two dollars. We sit on the lawn and admire the parrots, the flowers and the swings and fountains. Go for a drink. The cashier cheats himself. Out for another Drive. The high hill. The mexican boys bathing in the irrigation ditch. Helen admires them so. On to the Inn. Dinner $2 each. We dine. What we have. Grell tells the story of the man who missed it by four feet. The quarrel between Myrtle and Grell due to his assertion that he would not give ten cents for all the Art objects in the Mission Inn. Myrtle: "Do you know what that there is? That there's ignorance. Grell: Stop now. Don't try to improve on it. You've said enough." The lady who wanted to know if she could walk through the "<u>chapel.</u>" It was merely a concert hall. We drive

---

back. The fresh wind. Helen in a very loving mood. We sing.
Arrive in city about eleven. Home, 11.30. To bed. Riverside, as a
city of homes, was a disappointment to me. I thought it contained
many wonderful mansions.

Friday, June 3, 1921. Los Angeles.—Hollywood.—1515 Detroit
Street. Gray in A.M. Bright later. Up at seven. Helen and I make
our usual visit to Dr. Leadsworth's office. Helen worried over
cancer pain in her stomach. Afterward she stays down town to look
for a coat. I am reading a life of Socrates by R. Nicoll Cross,
M.A.[140] Go to P.O. Then to the POINSETTIA cafeteria with Helen
and Myrtle for breakfast. Helen is reading Balzacs Beatrix[141] and is
all excited over the life of George Sand. At La Brea I stop and get
several things for the house—milk,—rolls, etc. Work until five on
Mea Culpa. Helen comes. Meanwhile The Goldwyn Co has called
up and wants to get hold of her. I try for her at Myrtle's flat. When
she comes she calls up and gets work with Marshall Neilan at
fifteen a day.[142] Is very much pleased by that. Is to begin in the
A.M. Myrtle and Grell are to come at seven with the car. They
really arrive at six-thirty. We motor through Griffith Park. The high
mountain road. The two dead rattle snakes—one still slightly alive.
The many, many rabbits. The blue-bird. The great green mountain
gullies. We come out on the other side—San Fernando valley.
Motor back past golf links and the deer park to Vermont Avenue.
Then out Holly Boul to Cahuenga. We go to The Coffee Pot, the
new Greenwich Village style inn. Myrtle and Grell's interest. The
barracuda tastes of the oil that is in the sea water here. I think of
how much Hollywood is getting to be like Greenwich Village, only
on a finer scale—more truly charming. Afterward we motor out to
the Speedway to look at the work on the big benefit which is to
occur tomorrow. Its really very interesting to see. We go in the
enclosure. Motor back via Santa Monica Boul to La Brea and over.
A delightful night. I wish that Helen and I had a machine.

140. *Socrates: The Man and His Mission* (1914) by R. Nicoll Cross (1883–).
141. *Beátrix* by Honoré de Balzac (1799–1850).
142. Marshall Neilan (1891–1958), actor, producer, director.

Saturday, June 4, 1921. Los Angeles, —Hollywood—. 1515 Detroit Street. Gray in the A.M. but clears up soon. Helen working for Marshall Neilan at the Goldwyn Studio. We are scheduled to go with Myrtle and Grell in their car to the Beverly Speedway—Actors Benefit—at six. I ride with Helen to 16th and Vermont and put her on the Culver City car. Go down town on the Washington Avenue line to P.O. Telegram from Shadowland, Mr. Burton, wanting to buy "Hollywood Now" for $250.[143] I wire a refusal. Go to Dr. Leadsworth's office for my treatment. (Infection of left lung. Also of left antrum. Diagnosis by Albert Abrams of San Frisco.) The ocilloclast. The character of Leadsworth. I have been going now, every morning at nine, for two weeks. And his girl assistant. She is plainly his mistress. His various electric instruements. The type of patient he treats. McFee—the old newspaperman. Has syphilis. The several nuns with cancer. A country doctor, etc. The electronic method of diagnosis. Get twenty minutes this A.M. Go from there to the bank and draw five. Find a purse and turn it in. The reason. Go over to Broadway Store to meet Myrtle. She is going to show me the coat Helen wants. See it. A white one. Buy it. Price fifty. Myrtle not able to get tickets for the Speedway from the B. H. Dyas store. I send her out to the grounds, since she is here with Grell and they have the car. I take Gardiner Jct. car home. Eat remainder of strawberry short cake and the cold stake. Write till four. Helen returns early, brought home by Marshall Neilan, no less, in his great grey car. Like every other director who has ever known her, he wants her to "go out with him." Her phrase. She uses her old excuse—that she is trying to get a divorce and that her husband is watching her. The great thing is not to offend. Tries on her coat and is delighted. Dresses all in white for the evening. We eat at home. A scrap meal. At six Myrtle and Grell appear. We go out to meet them. The ride to Beverly, along the Hill road. The crowd of cars. The various side shows. The movie girls in startling costumes, selling cigarettes, candies, etc. Myrtle is angry because Helen got the white coat away from her but gets over it after a time. The pageant on the big stage. They try to sting the public $3.50 for a seat, after it has already paid $1.50 to get in. The

---

143. "Hollywood Now" was published in *McCall's* 48 (September 1921): 8, 18, 54.

dodge fails. All seats finally thrown open free. We get in. Before that, Helen watching for stars at one of the side entrances. Her curiosity. Very simple, natural and democrat. Not one as pretty as she is. Ted Shawn and his dancers. Bebe Daniels. Mary Pickford and her dog. Douglas Fairbanks. The beautiful Russian wolf-hound that peed on the stage. And the shudder of offended propriety that went of the good American audience. Dozens of stars appear. Fire works afterward. The genial audience yelling "who", when it couldn't catch the names. We go around the outside of the big grandstand looking for the car. Grell goes off to try to find it. Helen and Myrtle quarrling because they have to wait. I finally shut them up with a few hard words. Back to town, by the Hill road. The lights. The cool night air. L.A. always looks like a huge valley of diamonds at night—twinkling orange diamonds. We decide to go to Franks for chocalate. A long wait to be served because of the crowd. We get angry. Served at one A.M. Back to house and to bed. Helen twitters about how happy she is to be with me and how much she loves me.

Sunday, June 5, 1921. Los Angeles, Cal. 1515 Detroit Street, Hollywood. Clear and warm, all day. Helen working for Marshall Neilan at Goldwyn. She gets up at six to make a train at the Santa Fe station. I feel too drowsy from the night before—Actors Benefit, at the Speedway—, and stay in bed. Have a headache. Stay in bed till eleven. Get up and start breakfast but feel too sick to eat. Take a dose of epsom salts. Also drink some hot water. No relief. Try to write. Can't make it. Give up at last and lie down. Telegram sometime during afternoon from Helen saying special train has been taken for Barstow and that she wont be back before nine fifteen. I am to meet her at the Santa Fe station. Suffer from lonliness. Get up about six, dress and walk down Sunset to Vine. Then over to De Longpre and on down to Western, at Santa Monica. Down S.M. to Vermont and accross to First, where I take the car for the P.O. The three young couples taking car for Pantages. "I don't like to go to the Burbank because there are always so many sailors there." "Here she comes." "That car isnt a she. It's a mail car." "I never saw any mail bags on this line." But both boys and girls knew what they were talking about and never blinked an eye. The little girl who looked like Lilian Gish, riding with the old woman. A pathetic smile. Letters in P.O. from Mencken, Mary Louise Ott,[144] Margaret Johnson and Gaston Gallimard in Paris. He is willing to take my books on my terms. Telegram from Liveright, wanting to know about the fall book. Go on up Spring. Buy a bottle of witch hazel at a Sun drug store. Also a box of celery headache powders. Take a bromo-seltzer for my headache. It relieves it. Car for Santa Fe Station. Wait about in the dusk. I listen to two negros babbling about their troubles. Reread my letters sitting outside. Near train time a cloud of taxis descend on the little station. The silent yard. The palm trees. 9:15. Train on time. Helen arrives. She tells me of Marshall Neilan and how he wasted $2,500 taking twenty-five people out to Barstow and not making a shot. We go to a Chinese restaurant in Second Street. Many negroes come in and Helen is offended. We finish our meal and leave. Almost quarrel over the alleged cleverness of directors. Hollywood car. Home and to bed. Helen looks like a young Diana walking about naked.

Thursday, June 9, 1921. Los Angeles. Hollywood. 1515 Detroit Street. To Leadsworths as usual. Afterwards Helen goes with Myrtle to get some prints of stills. I go to the P.O. then home. No mail worth talking about. Work on story till four. Then go with Helen to the Jap cleaning place at Cahuenga and Sunset. Get a jap promised for the morrow. Beautiful afternoon. The kempt green lawns with their flowers. The perfect sunshine. We are looking for peas, spinach, rolls, a cake and some other things. Buy them along the Boul. Meet, of all men, Julius Hilder, of Samstag and Hilder Brothers. He is one of my good luck signs. Met him at Muldoons, when I was there. Met him on the train, the time I was going down to Asheville to Thelma. Met him just before I went to Europe with Richards and before I took charge of Hamptons.[145] His attitude is

---

144. Mary Louise Ott first wrote Dreiser on 13 February 1921 asking for advice on her projected literary career.

145. Dreiser is referring to certain key events in his life. Muldoon's is the health clinic in Westchester, New York, where his brother Paul sent him in 1903 to recover from his nervous disorder. Dreiser had a love affair with Thelma Cudlipp, the original for Susanne Dale in *The "Genius,"* that led to his losing his position as chief editor of Butterick Publications. Grant Richards was the British publisher who financed Dreiser's first trip to Europe in 1912. Dreiser edited Benjamin B. Hampton's *Broadway Magazine* in 1906, his first important job after his breakdown at the turn of the century.

always the same—friendly. Wants to walk with me. Has important connections with Goldwyn. I wonder what new change is approaching now. We return home. Get a scrum dinner. At meal Helen taken with a violent attack of gastritis. We try milk of magnesia. Then joto, in hot water. Then I think of the electric vibrator and that relieves her. Very much relieved myself. Such fierce onslaughts make me very sad. To bed and I read for awhile in Old College Towns.[146]

Friday, June 10, 1921. Los Angeles. (Hollywood.) 1515 Detroit Street. Up at seven. Helen and I go to Dr. Leadsworths office. He takes a drop of blood from the ear of each of us to send to Abrams, at S.F. Myrtle arrives. She wants to know if Helen and I will accompany her and Grell to Bakersfield or to some place over Sunday. She and the Drs. girl assistant come into the small back room where Helen and I are being treated — (the ocilloclast) and we jest a good deal. As Helen and I go out later I find McFee, the local newspaper man, reading Twelve men. He is enthusiastic in his praise. Helen and I go to the Fifth Street, Boos Brothers cafeteria for breakfast. It isnt as good as the Poinsettia we decide. Talk of Myrtle and her attitude toward G. To the library where Helen takes out a card for herself. I get Pluriverse, by Benjamin Paul Blood.[147] His style is much too complex for the import of what he has to say. Also get and read, Rambles in Old College Towns, by Hildegarde Hawthorne. Not a bad book. We go to the bank. Then to the P.O. On the way stop in at the Rosslyn Hotel. A telegram from Burton Rascoe of McCalls, offering $250 for Hollywood Now, which I decide to refuse.[148] Return home. At twelve the jap comes to clean the rooms and everything is in disorder. Myrtle comes and she and Helen palaver till three. Subject, alimony from husbands and how to get it. I work till five, then go to the store for Helen to get some of the things for the trip in the A.M. We rig up a meal and then I work on my story until about ten when we go to bed. Helen is feeling much better since her gastritis attack of the night before.

146. *Rambles in Old College Towns* (1917) by Hildegarde Hawthorne.
147. *Pluriverse* (1920) by Benjamin Paul Blood (1832–1919).
148. Burton Rascoe (see p. 271, n. 2). In 1921 Rascoe was editing *McCall's,* to which Dreiser eventually did sell "Hollywood Now."

Saturday, June 11, 1921. Los Angeles, Cal. Hollywood. 1515
Detroit Street. Awake at 6.30. We are scheduled to go with Myrtle
and Grell to Big Bear Lake. Myrtle is to arrive at nine or ten to
help Helen prepare things. We play about in a most delicious
fashion before getting up. Helen beats me with one of her pink
wool slippers and I finally spank her. French toast, blackberry jam
and coffee for breakfast. I go to the market—Morrisons—at La Brea
and Holly Boul for groceries for the trip. Two bottles of stuffed
olives. Two loaves of sandwich bread. One dozen eggs. One head
of lettuce. Six pounds of potatoes. One half pound of boiled ham.
One half pound of peanut butter. One package cheddar cheese.
One can Carnation milk. One dozen bananas. One bottle milk.
Return and we make sandwiches, deviled eggs, a cake, etc. About
eleven Myrtle arrives with the news that Grell will be along about
noon. She has a cherry pie. I pack the large black bag with all the
things and change to old outing clothes. Then shave. Helen dresses
also. Myrtle calls up to see if Grell has started. Then the telephone
bell rings. His car has been hit by a Hollywood Street car at 3500
Sunset and smashed almost to bits. His own back hurt. Myrtle calls
a taxi and we ride down to the scene. Find him standing alone, the
car having been hauled away. Myrtles attitude toward it all. She is
not very sorry for him. I think that possibly we may have been
saved by this accident from something worse. The broken fender of
the street car that hit him is lying beside the road. I have Grell
photograph it as evidence. We stand about awhile, then cross the
street and eat some sandwiches that Myrtle has in a bag, discussing
the possibility of making the company repair the damage. At two
we cease talking and Helen and I come back. She is very glum.
Thinks such things are spiritual slaps at me on the part of
something that is inimical to me. I am sometimes inclined to think
so—so many things have happened to me at one time and another.
In the rooms we clear away all the debris and I settle down to my
book, the ideal outing off, for good, I presume. The pretty crowd
of hiking girls we saw coming out on the car. They got off at
Highland, evidently planning to go to the mountains beyond
Burbank.

Friday, June 17, 1921. Los Angeles. 1515 Detroit Street,
Hollywood. Usual nine oclock visit to the office of Leadsworth.
Have decided to visit Dr. Burrows, a friend of Leadsworth in the

Consolidated reality building to see about my nose. L says he'll call up and speak to him. Breakfast at the Poinsettia. Helen then goes up to Hamburgers to look for a corset. I go to the Hellman Bank and draw some money. Then to P.O. No mail. A copy of The Freeman. Meet Helen on Hollywood car at Temple and Hill. Home. Stop and buy some groceries. Work on Mea Culpa till three. Clean up chapters 20 and 21. Myrtle comes out. She has all the small kodak pictures that we took the day before of the three of us. Some of them are very good. I go down town at two. Find I have to wait an hour and walk about. Find a malt extract in cans advertised as easy to make, but on seeing the method find it too difficult and do not buy it. Go to Dinty Moores for a glass of beer and a corned beef sandwich. Return to Dr. Burrows office. Find him the usual small, dried-up slicker doctor of the west coast. I do not believe that there is one decent physician in this whole area. He finds that he cannot do much for me but that it will cost seventy-five to have it done. Finds pus in tonsils but decides later that that is not important. I leave disgusted. Return home and read Santayana's estimate of Shelley.[149] Helen writing a long letter to Frank and she is in a bad mood. I about decide to go out to dinner alone. Myrtle calls up and wants to come out. Helen decides to get dinner. Asparagus, hominy, potatoes, chocalate and ice-cream. I eat too much and feel heavy after dinner. Lie about until ten and then go to bed. Myrtle tells how she and another girl watched a crowd of loggers giving a party and how they made the man with the longest roger show it because, ostensibly, he had failed to entertain them properly by playing the fandango. Each was to do a stunt and he who failed had to produce his jock-peice. They had all decided beforehand to vote everything that this poor fish did n.g. in order to make him the goat and joke of the party. Then they all piled on him and led him about exhibiting him. Wonderful moon-light night but I am too loggy to go out.

Saturday, June 18, 1921. Los Angeles, Cal. 1515 Detroit Street, Hollywood. Hot and bright. A typical Los Angeles Sunday. We bemoan the fact that we haven't a car. Lie about until about ten before we have breakfast. Then read. I work a little while. We

149. *Shelley: or, The Poetic Value of Revolutionary Principles* (1913) by George Santayana (1863–1952).

think of hiring a car for about five hours. Helen too loggy because of heat to act. About one I call up the Virginia at Long Beach and get the rate on a room and bath by the day. We are thinking of going down. Nineteen per day, for two. We give that up. Have been reading Balzac's Beatrice and we discuss that. I point out his incurable idealism—the literary and impossible character of his conversations. About five we decide to dine on Hollywood Boul. Go down to the Blue Front. The movie queens and actors. Helen looks charming. We finally get a seat after waiting. Then we take the car down town to the P.O. Also the bank. Walk north on Main and buy plums, some peas and cherries. Then over and take the car home. The delicious quality of the night air. We promise ourselves that we will go to Long Beach in the A.M.

Sunday, June 19, 1921. Los Angeles. 1515 Detroit St Hollywood. Another warm, perfect day. As usual, everyone is getting ready to go off in their cars. The beauty of the sunlight and open windows in this little apartment. I play various records on the Victrola— Whispering, Avalon, The Crazy Blues, Cherie, On Miami Shore, Cuban Moon, That Naughty Waltz, Venetian Moon, etc. Helen lies about and I read. About eleven we have breakfast. About four we decide to take the Red Line to Venice. A delightful ride. The Windermere Hotel at Santa Monica. The Sunset Inn. Endless palaver about a hundred things. We arrive at Venice. The crowd. We stop for a hot dog. The walk to the beach. The vast number of people in bathing. The striped umberellas. We walk to Ocean City and sit outside the dance hall, facing the sea. Helen tells of how, when at Portland, she used to go down to the sea, 100 miles away to stay and dance. Then we go inside to watch the kid dancers. They are all so young and so sexy. Afterward we walk out on the pier. The various Coney Island shows. The beauty of the sea. We watch the racing metal ponies, the fellows slugging the weight, the people watching the sunset over the sea and the mountains. Then we dine in the Chinese restaurant, overlooking the water. The blue black water and the stars. We stop to see the chimpanzees running little motor cars on a track. I laugh to see how they grab hold of each the other's car and hold each other back. Then we ride on the merry-go-round. Then walk to Venice and ride on the giant racer. The big dips make Helen a little sick. Then we get on the car and come home—but not before listening to the singers before the racer place. They are so very town-dandyish, so American wise-heim and patronizing and blase. It is amusing. The little bungalow looks fine and we crawl in with a sigh of content.

Monday, June 20, 1921. 1515 Detroit Street, Hollywood
Los Angeles. Up at seven, as usual, and to Dr. Leadsworths office. The usual treatment. Then to the Poinsettia. Then to the P.O. and for me, home. I work on Mea Culpa all day. Helen has gone to join Myrtle. Later on, from her, I learn that Grell has a new loaned car from the repair co. and that at about 5:30 he and Myrtle want to come out and take us for a drive. Myrtle has made a pie and some sandwiches and we are to go to one of the beaches. I work on until about five. Helen makes coffee and tea and puts them in the thermos bottles. At 5:30 they show up and in the delicious cool of the afternoon we drive out through Beverly and Sawtelle to Santa Monica. The delicious drive along the sea toward Redondo. The waves and blue water. About dusk we find a lone spot and park the car in the sand. I and Grell gather wood and we build a fire. The fine meal. The fishermen. We are disturbed by some sand bees. Then we dance on the shore. The stars come out and the moon over the hills to the east. Helen spreads out a blanket near the fire and we all lie down and sing. Grell draws faces in the sand —that of an indian for one. Helen sings all the old popular songs in her clear, sympathetic and sweet voice. At 9:30 we leave for Venice. Park the car and ride "the old mill stream", then twice on the giant racer. Then we listen to the songs in front. The ride on the little storage electric walk car to Ocean city. The swimming pool is closed. Also the monkey racers which Helen wanted to show Myrtle. But we watch the dancers in the big pavilion, have coco-colas and finally walk back to Venice. Helen tries to outwalk nearly everyone else and about does it. We get the car and drive back through Beverly and along Sunset. Myrtle is very tired and falls asleep. I tell what Coney Island is like. We tell of clever legerdemain with cards and other things. At Detroit Helen and I get out and we vote we have had a splendid time. I shall always think of the sea and the fire and Helen singing and dancing—near Redondo.

Thursday, June 23rd, 1921. Hollywood. 1515 Detroit Street. Up at seven. Usual visit to Leadsworth. Then home. But back again early, with Helen to look for a car. We spend all of the time from four on looking at different makes. The smooth liars who sell used cars and new ones. Have about fixed on a used Nash when we see a used closed Chandler and so the looking begins all over again. Dine at Petifils, very tired, and then go out to Myrtle's,—3823 Moneta. She is alone and sick with her regular monthly trouble. Grell supposed not to get home before nine. We wait but he doesn't show up. Finally, at ten, we leave. Home at near twelve. Nothing much accomplished this day.

Friday, June 24, 1921. 1515 Detroit Street. Los Angeles. This is the day Grell disappears. We learn of it at the office of Dr. Leadsworth. He is telling me about how something is always wrong with his auto-mobile and how much it costs him to keep to keep it. Myrtle phones Helen. We were at her place the night before. We go first to the Pacific Finance Building in Sixth Street and Helen goes up to see what she can find out. No news. Then we go to the Poinsettia and discuss Grell and Myrtle and what she will do. I go to P.O. A letter from Dr. Robertson.[150] Then home and work on my book till evening. Helen calls up to tell me about two cars that she has seen, either one of which would do. I advise her to take the new Overland—for the present. Work on. At six I quit. Seven comes and I begin to worry. Then she and Myrtle show up. Myrtle is a little full. They have been to see some girl friend and have had a few drinks. But Helen is all right. No news of Grell. He has gone. Turned in his car the night before and beat it. Contracted to pay $2300 for that Hudson instead of twelve hundred. Also gave a note for three hundred. Left Myrtle no money so she will be on our hands now for a while. She does not feel bad however. They wouldn't have staid together anyhow. Dinner. Cars, cars, cars. Nothing but car talk. I hope to heaven we get one soon and have done with it. Helen and I walk down to Cahuenga so that I can

150. Dr. John W. Robertson, a practicing psychiatrist with an appetite for literary scholarship. He sent Dreiser a copy of his two-part psychological and bibliographical account of Edgar Allan Poe called *Poe: A Study,* which he printed privately.

send a message to James A. Ettinge in N.Y.[151] He is
superintending the moving of all of my things into storage there.
They will all be moved in the morning and I wire final instructions.
Come home and find Myrtle still asleep on the bed. We get her to
the couch and then retire ourselves. A rather troublesome day.

Saturday, June 25, 1921. Hollywood. 1515 Detroit St. No visit to
Leadsworth on Saturday. We get up late. Helen decides to go down
and buy a used Overland chummy roadster which she saw. I give
her a check for two hundred on account. Settle down to work
revising An American Tragedy. About four she returns with the
car,—she and Myrtle, who is now to live with us, and they try to
start it up. No go. It wont work. I finally leave them and return to
the house. After a time they get it started. Then we go for a trial
spin out to Beverly and back. A delightful ride. Then we take
Myrtle over to Moneta to get her belongings. The packing. $7.50
worth of groceries. We return. The trouble starting and stopping
the car at different places, but we get through. Almost wreck the
garage getting the car into it. The laughter—after it is all over
Helen is very pleased with her purchase and is already planning all
sorts of trips.

Sunday, June 26. Hollywood. 1515 Detroit. We breakfast late.
Then go for a drive. To Sawtelle first to look at some little houses
advertised. Then on to the ocean at Santa Monica, via Wilshire
Boulevard. Helen practices running the car in some of the quiet
streets there. We view the sea at the palisades. Then back and
down town to the P.O. We park the car in Beaudry street and I go
on down for my mail. Various letters—from Smith, Robin, Mame,
Liveright, L etc.[152] Afterwards drive out Echo Park Ave to Holly

---

151. James A. Ettinge was a dedicated admirer of Dreiser who volunteered to move
Dreiser's belongings in New York when he was forced to move out of his apartment at 165
West 10th Street. Ettinge later moved to Los Angeles and served as a general factotum to
Dreiser for years.
152. James G. Robin, businessman, editor, playwright. Robin first wrote Dreiser on 22
October 1908 to praise *Sister Carrie.* According to Dreiser, Robin was the model for the central
character in " 'Vanity, Vanity,' Saith the Preacher" *(Twelve Men).* Under the name "Odin
Gregory," Robin published *Caius Gracchus* (1920), a verse tragedy for which Dreiser wrote the
introduction.
"Mame" is Dreiser's sister Mary Frances.
"L" is either Lillian Rosenthal or Louise Campbell.

Boul and so home. The girls dress and we go to the Blue Front for dinner. Mr. Siler—casting director for Fox. His friends. This movie world. Afterward we drive a little way and then return home and to bed.

Sunday, July 3—1921 —Hollywood
We leave 3:15 P.M. for Santa Barbara. All that time spent in getting ready. Trouble in Cahuenga Ave—when we go to Imai & Co for some eggs. No gas in tank. Take car finally to Studio Garage—Helens friend. The long ride up. We average 30 miles an hour, Helen driving. Trouble on hills—or she thinks there is. Jumps out once & begins to push car back in sand. No room in Santa Barbara. We sleep in the car near the El Mira Sol. Beauty of the beach beyond Ventura.

Monday, July 4—1921—Hollywood.
Wake in motor car—4 A.M.—Santa Barbara. Go down town for something to eat. No place open. We cruise around. Go to see Boyland—now the Samarkand. Then to beach—Ambassador burned. Then back up State Street for a drink. We stay to see the parade. The different floats. The Jap Dragon God. Leave at 11. Lie on Beach near Ventura & eat. Helens lusty talk, and Myrtles. On home. Very hot. Get here at 6. We eat. Tire gives out just as we get here. We go to bed—too tired to do a thing.

Tuesday, July 26—1921—Hollywood
We bath at 6 P.M. this day in new open air pool at Bimini—first time. I have been working all day on the article. Am full of taking new house in Glendale.

Thursday—July—28—1921—Hollywood.
Bright as usual. Helen working at Goldwyn. Car in repair shop. (Pickering) This makes 3rd day. Helen & I ride accross town to 16th & Vermont. I leave & walk out Washington to about Larchmont. Then accross. See how L.A. is building. Walk for a sweat & get it. Tremendously impressed with growth & beauty of city. The wonderful houses about Windsor Square. I see faces in clouds. Think of doing the South Sea novel—[unreadable word]— Reach Radium Sulpher Springs. They are just changing name in

paint to Melrose Springs. Take a bath. My funny attendant. Landowner, book salesman, book worm. Hiker. Still a bath rubber. Walk home afterwards. Work on "An Overcrowded Entry Way."[153] Myrtle returns. Has just got job of starter in Meyer-Siegel. 75 per. She tells how she bosses everyone around. Work on. Helen comes. Has been over for car. Didn't get. Myrtle & I go to grocery for steak, bread etc.

Friday, Aug 26, 1921. 652 N. Columbus, Glendale. Helen working at Goldwyn. Location. A big house in Beverly Hills. She gets up at six in order to be at the studio at eight. Myrtle working at Meyer-Seigel, in Broadway. Leaves every morning at seven forty-five. For the present she sleeps in the south east corner of the general living room on the floor. At this stage the room is empty save for the victrola, the curtains and the books in the built in bookcase. Robin is in town, at the Alexandria. I have agreed to meet him or at least call him up before noon. Have also an invitation to come down and see Leadsworth who wishes to make a deal with me anent the Abrams cure. A hot day. It is always hot and bright in the San Fernando valley. I water the lawn, feed the chickens and then take the Red Car down. The crowd waiting to get on at Doran Street. I get off at Sixth and Hill and call up Robin from the American Drugstore. He is most anxious for me to get two movie girls and let him furnish the automobile and the expenses and see some of the beauties of the country. Am in no mood for it. Besides do not know of two girls who would endure such overtures as he might make. Go to Leadsworths office. He isn't there. Won't be till Monday. Go round to the Alexandria. Find Robin in the lobby with some friends. Introduces me to his doctor friend. A man who is crazy about women. We leave him and go into the restaurant for some ice tea and to talk. Robin wants to talk movie production of excellent things but has no great amount of cash. I am bored for he merely wants to get ideas from me. Then he suggest going to Marcelles for lunch, the doctor to be

153. "An Overcrowded Entryway" is a twenty-two-page typescript article among the Dreiser papers at the University of Pennsylvania. It deals with the competition and abuses that young women face as they try to enter the film market in Hollywood. Much of Dreiser's information came from his discussions with Helen about labor conditions at the studios.

included. We go. En route we stop into Hutton and Brothers, brokers, on Spring Street, to meet the manager from N.Y. He has just come on to enlarge the business, the city is growing so. The usual dose of smutty stories for entertainment. Amusing but revealing an innately commonplace and sensual mind. He is just taking a local manager into the firm and the same is introduced to us. A vulgar, slick, sly, oily person who laughs much and tells funny stories but whose eyes are steely points, none the less. We go on to Marcelles. The usual luncheon crowd of a smart[154]

Wednesday, Sept. 21—1921—Glendale—652—North Columbus. Helen out during P.M. I see Leadsworth in AM. Back in Glendale by 10:30. Working on cutting out all data relating to Arbuckle.[155] Also in cleaning up correspondence. Helen returns about 4—with Western proofs of her. A fine set of art photos. Ought to do her a world of good. Afterwards we go to market in car. Bread, milk— tomatoes, Jenna's mayonaise, grapes, jar of cranberry preserves, etc. Then we go for a ride—1st time out to Selvas de Verduga, Mont Rose & Sunland. Beautiful country. Helen wants to build an estate. We return at dusk. Lovely sunset. Delightful Evening. The days go by like a dream. Myrtle comes at 6:30. More talk of Arbuckle. I go to bed early—about 8:15. Helen bows in about nine—"to be wiss oo."

Sunday, Jan 8—1922—Glendale.—652 North Columbus Up at about 11 A.M. My leg—strained knee tendons—very bad. Helen trying Christian Science on me. Helen, Myrtle & I discuss it as everything else. At 3 We leave for drive. Go through Eagle Rock to Pasadena. Then to East to Pasadena dam & lake. (The picnic grounds in the valley.) Then to Flintridge & the golf course. Beautiful. Then to La Canada. Then to Newhall. Then down to P.O. Via Verdugo Rd. No letters. Two bills. Back home. Get milk, bread & salad dressing at little store on Hollywood—near Glendale Boul. Home & get dinner. To bed early because I feel depressed.

154. A page from the diary is missing at this point.
155. Roscoe ("Fatty") Arbuckle (1887–1933), the film comedian, was being tried for manslaughter at this time. The trial, which resulted from the death of a young actress during a party at his home, ended in acquittal.

Am wishing for money & success in my work.

State RR commission complaining of local fares. Settle on my play. Awfully hard to do. Nervous & unable to decide up things. Work —or try to—while Helen calls up California loan, State Bank here & others. She explains how she proposes to get around Stanford. I write these notes. She goes out to get groceries & more fruit to add to a fruit salad of day before. I spend half hour in dark room trying to repeat Experiment of 1909. Help will come. Return to breakfast nook in kitchen to work. The chicken that stoops to be petted. Glorious state of marigolds.

Sunday, April 30, 1922. 652 N. Columbus. Beautiful day. Helen does not want to go to Helen Poles, because of the possible crowd but I finally persuade her to go. We breakfast at home. Helen sleeps in the P.M. I work. We try out the Gardner car which the man brings. (To Montrose and Back. Helen does not like it. At 5:30 we ride over to the Poles. Beautiful house, built by Frank Lloyd Wright, Jr., who is there. He is the man who married Kirah after I left her and from whom she secured a divorce.[156] A fine fellow. Looks like Ed.[157] A charming artistic point of view. We are shown the house. Dinner. The lights. Mrs. Poles litle boy. Jack and his queer friends. We talk until ten,—then motor home. I like Wright so much and wish I might see him again. Helen charming in her grey Bulgarian dress which she dislikes so much and which I and everyone else likes.

Monday, May 1, 1922. Bright day. Helen working at the Fairbanks studio. She leaves at seven-thirty and I go with her, as far as Western and Santa Monica. Am going downtown to find a cap to match my coat. Also to bank, to get laundry etc. Take Western Ave car to Hill St. Go into Oviatt and Alexanders, Wood Bros., in Sixth St., and to Mullen and Bluett. Buy two silk collars,—fifty cents each. Go to two more stores and find no cap. Go to bank (Hellman, Night and Day) and deposit $60 for Helen. Go to Army and Navy store. No cap. Then to another hat store opposite the Rosslyn in Fifth. Find exact match there. Go to Fifth Street store

156. Kirah Markham (see p. 117, n. 1).
157. Dreiser's brother Edward.

and buy Helen three pair stockings. Also four hdkfs for myself. Get box sanitary napkins for Helen at the Owl Drug store, Sixth and Brdwy, then return to bank and draw ten. Go out Sixth to the Pacific Jap laundry and get seven silk shirts of mine. Forget a package with all of my purchases and have to return. The Jap is carefully examining them. Take Glendale car to Doran street. Always admire the wonderful mountain view beyond Silver Lake. Come home, (652 N. COLUMBUS) and water the lawn and feed the chickens. Also get myself some breakfast. Then to work and work until six on <u>Lolita</u> (A Gallery of Women.)[158] Have all sorts of wandering thoughts about life which can never be written down. Am so fond of Helen who is really a great person in her way. She comes at six full of excited chatter about "the lot" and the ten beauties of whom she is one. The story of Allen Dwan, Dick Rossyn, Art, and camera man, the actor who plays the king, Rita, Margie, Dorothy, Miss Hughes, and I know not who else. The rivalries. The jealousies. The terrible wardrobe woman. The young electrical assistant, OBrien, whose father is a director and who is so brilliant. ("I wish I could play that part. I'd have your telephone number in about a minute.") How Dwan was angry with a girl who would not come to his house because he had not troubled to send a car for her. What he said to Helen about having burned up all her energy the night before,—and all because he was angry at her for ignoring him.

We go down town to the P.O. in the car. Helens chatter, en route. Letters from Lengel, Louise and the Century Co. A check for A Traveler at Forty.[159] No word from Ditrichstein who is playing at The Mason.[160] We dine at the Marine Cafe. The bad Lobster a la Newburg. We shift to Chicken a la King. Then home. Stop at the Mason and try for seats to see The Great Lover but the box office is closed. We motor out to Cahuenga to get some cosmetics for Helen but the drug store there is closed. Then back to house and to bed. Helen very much pleased with the new light overcoat and cap.

158. "Lolita" did not appear in *A Gallery of Women* (1929); it remains in manuscript at the University of Pennsylvania.
159. The Century Co. was paying Dreiser royalties for *A Traveler at Forty,* which it had published in 1913.
160. Leo Ditrichstein (1865–1928), actor, playwright. He and Dreiser were planning a dramatization of *The "Genius"*—a project which was never realized.

Tomorrow is her birthday. One of her remarks in the night. "Hold me, Teddie. We have such a little time on earth and we will never have each other any more in any other world forever."

So poignant the thought. And so poignant the mood.

Friday. May—5—1922 (652 N. Columbus—Glendale) Dinner today at 7 with Ettinge and "June"—(Papoose) at the Rex Arms. Bacardi Cocktails & wine. Excellent meal. Ettinge tells of Mexico & Havana. Talks of Al Jennings "Through the Shadows With O. Henry."[161] Wants me to read it. I tell what I knew of Henry. Helen sick during meal. She is working out at Fairbanks & very much wrought up by the pursuit of Allen Dwan. Peggy, Margie, Rita, Dorothy, Miss Hughes, Miss Rossyn & some others annoy her. We leave early—at 10. I have been working all day on Lolita.[162]

Saturday, May 6—1922. Glendale—652 N. Columbus. Get up early. Ride over to studio (Fairbanks) with Helen. Leave her at gate—then walk all around it. The lovely old French (Norman) Castle. The old English castle. Wagon load of dogs. Caparisoned horses. All the old costumes. The fellows outside at the gate. The nine five dollar checks. The two officious assistants. The old man with the long hair who wouldnt work for less than 7⁵⁰. Walk back (accross) to Hollywood Boul & down to Highland. Take bus to Glendale. Very pleasent gay day. Work all day on Lolita. Eat P.M. Myrtle & ⌐ ⌐ stop by—she is going to Portland Monday. Later she comes out to see Helen. We dine at the Glen Inn & take her down town. Then home. Myrtles story of the old man who had to prove to the doctor that he was not impotent in order to know whether the girl had decieved him or not: arm in sling.

161. *Through the Shadows with O. Henry* (1921) by Alphonso J. Jennings (1863– ?). On 16 May 1922, Dreiser wrote to Mencken saying, "I tried to read the other day Al Jennings on O. Henry. What swill."

162. At this point in the diaries Dreiser affixed a clipping of a newspaper article entitled "Peggy Not to Blame." The piece begins, "The most powerful personal factor is charm. Women who have charm are generally irresistible; women who have charm and beauty are rare and are always irresistible." Above the clipping Dreiser has written, "This applies to Helen."

Tuesday—May 9—1922 (652 N. Columbus—Glendale) Helen working at Fairbanks. Canned the day before. Very nervous & angry. I work all day on story. (Ida Hauchawout)[163] Finish it at 6 to my satisfaction. It is cloudy all day with flaws of sun. I expect a rainbow all P.M. & at 6—slipping out, one is staged for me—a double rainbow clear accross the heavens in each case. "I shall set my sign in the heavens". The children over the way playing & shouting. Helen comes. Discharge has been cancelled at Fairbanks request. She does not know whether to stay on or not. We go down town to eat. I here all of the days developments—how Dwan said "Come over here now. I'll tell you something nice"—and how she took it. How the girls acted. The astonishment of Rita. Her description of Margie.

Thursday. May 11—1922 (652 N. Columbus) try to get Morce Petchnikoff. Can't. Mrs. Snodgrass calls up. Wants to know how Ditrichstein thing has come out. I tell her it hasnt come out. No letter from D that day.

Saturday, May 13—1922. Glendale. Helen & I have slight row over money. She apologizes. Very hot, bright day. I water & clip the lawn. Feed chickens. Neighbor who says "well, I see your still on the job. But its beautiful. Am now trying to do a short story— the Shadow,[164] for Mary Stewart Cutting, Jr.[165]

Sunday—May—28—1922 (Glendale)
Helen & I motor to Lebec (the Durant Inn—via the Ridge Route to Bakersfield). We do it in the new Maxwell. The great valleys & peaks. The ease with which the car takes them. Newhall. Saugus. The Inns en route. Helen enthusiastic over my joy in the scenery.

Tuesday—May 30—1922—Glendale
Work all day on Shadow— & mail. Helen gets home 5. P.M. We dine at The Tavern—Hollywood. Then drive to P.O. Then out to

---

163. "Ida Hauchawout" was published in *Century* 106 (July 1923): 335–48; it was later reprinted in *A Gallery of Women* (1929).

164. "The Shadow" was published (as "Jealousy") in *Harper's Bazaar* 59 (August 1924): 84–85, 92, 94, 96; it was reprinted as "The Shadow" in *Chains* (1927).

165. Mary Stewart Cutting (1850–1924), novelist, editor.

Beach—via Wilshire Boul. No stars. The sea. The black waves. Old sea moods come back. I think of Long Beach & Manhattan in Paul's days.[166]

Friday. Aug 11—1922. Glendale—Cal. Leaving for S.F. The bags. Helen, Myrtle, Helens mother. We drop Myrtle at Hollywood Boul. Out Hollywood Boul to Universal City. Then north. The Hay wagons. The different towns. See map. Handsome Ventura. Old mission. The beach. Santa Barbara by 11 A.M. On to San Luis Obispo. Reach there at 6. On to Paso Robles. Helens mother. The chickens. Dinner in Paso. The hotel & stores. No public Parking after 1 A.M. The sea-going bed.

Saturday Aug 12—1922. All day in car en-route to Oakland. Beautiful Salinas Valley. Cattle. Nice & cool. King City. Salinas. The Shell Oil Co. Restaurant in Salinas (11 Aug). On to San Jose. San Juan Mission. Detour. Helens mother, the dogs & the chicken. Eat in San Jose. On to Oakland. We dine under trees at Hayward. Oakland in P.M. The Key Route Inn. Lake. Dinner. Helens mother off at depot. Row over tip. Helens tears. We put car up & walk. Then back to Hotel. A good bed. Good Rest.

Sunday, Aug 13—1922. Oakland
We get up at 8.30. Get clean car at garage. Go to the fish place in the business heart & I have an abalone steak. We start for S.F. Drive out around Lake Merritt, to see it. Then out on Mole to take ferry. Ferry charge $1.22 for a car & two persons. We decide to move all our things to S.F. before crossing. Go back & get bags. The cross over. Beautiful day. Gulls. The lovely bay. We drive out to Golden Gate Park & see the museum there. Horrible pictures— the gift of the publisher of the Chronicle, H. De Young. Drive along the sea. Then back to Seal Rocks & around the Presidio. Find the other museum & the beautiful water colors. Also the etchings by Zorn. Very fascinating. Too many pictures. We leave. Take

166. Dreiser's brother Paul Dresser.

rooms at Virginia. Dinner at Fish Place. At night we walk down to the old Barbary Coast but it is all blown up. Nothing there. Destroyed bars. We return to bed.

Monday—Aug 14—1922 Hotel Virginia Post at Mason—San Francisco. Up at 8:30. Breakfast at cafeteria foot of Mason, on Market. Much talk & joy in S.F. Decide to do worlds Fair museum (Presidio) thoroughly & so return there. We are there until one P.M. Water colors, etchings, Japanese prints, paintings. At one we quit & go to lunch. Decide to drive South of Market & do. The factories, docks, cars, pidgeons, boats. The gull seated on the raft which the man was making. We go through Chinatown looking for a lamp. Thence to a theatre to see a picture Helen was in. Then to room. Afterwards we hunt out a fine French restaurant & dine. To bed at about 11.

Tuesday—Aug 15—San Francisco
We breakfast—cafeteria. Thence to Tamalpais. Mill valley. Once more the wonderful bay, ships, gulls—the fun of being with Helen. I ask about trees 800 feet high! We ride back. Helen buys perfume. She had some shopping to do & I walk South of Market—my dream-land. Back at 5:30. I call on Newbegin. He sends me a bottle of whiskey—We are out. We dine at the St. Francis. Walk & then to bed.

Wednesday—Aug. 16—1922. Hotel Virginia—Mason at Post—San Francisco. Up at 8. Breakfast at cafeteria in Market. Helen goes to 478 Market to get money (50$\underline{^{00}}$ from Bank By Wire). Back to hotel. We descide to drive, get out car & drive South to S. San Francisco. The Hills. Fog. Fine view of bay. Back at 2 via South S.F. to Casina to see La, La Lucile. Winnie Baldwin. (Looks like Florence De Shon) Good show. Afterwards to room. Then to Newbegins. Propose dinner. He agrees. We decide to get Sterling. In Newbegins car to Taits. Georges Humor. I name Newbegin Benedict XVIth. The story of Commodus—Emperor of Rome.[167]

167. Dreiser is probably thinking of Benedict XV (1854–1922), who was Pope from 1914 to 1922. Commodus (A.D. 161–192) was the Roman emperor whose brutal misrule ended in his assassination and in civil war.

Helen dances much. On to Bagdad. Thence to the Sheik. The commonplaceness of Jazz—muscicians. The freshness of the sea air. Through the park to Lilly Pond. George goes in after lillies. Newbegin holds the light. On to Georges girls place. Then to Bob's. The poor dancing. Back to hotel. To bed.

Thursday—17<u>th</u>—1922—Aug. <u>San Francisco</u> Up at 8. Round with H——. Gray. Cold Bath. We breakfast at Cafeteria at foot of Mason St on Market. George Sterling is coming at 9 A.M. to take me to the sculptor Von Sabern studio (Clay & Taylor) to meet Gustave Frennsen the German novelist (Herlinglie, Jorn Uhl, Klaus Heinrich Bass).[168] In cafeteria we see the boy who wanted a job as dish washer. Helen pities him so. Wants to go back & give him money. Walk up Mason. Meet Sterling. Go with him to Von Saberns. <u>Frennson.</u> His attendants. Tells me of present conditions in Germany. Also how well a minister has to be educated there. Is collecting money for German children. Von Saberns studio. His work. Busts of George Douglas, Sterling & others. Rents studio for 40 a month. Spent $1500 fixing it up. His wife. Her pet gopher snake. She beats a tin pan to quiet it. The little cat. Von Sabern models Frennsen as we talk. He goes. Von Sabern wants to model me. Agrees to a sitting at 8 P.M. Then makes it dinner before. Helen, Sterling & I walk out Taylor to Russian Hill. Then down to Jules who looks like Ceaser. The fine lunch. <u>Jules.</u> We ride back to Sutter. See Newbegin, the bookseller. He gives me a California map for Helen. Back to Hotel. She is taking bath. Tells of Sterlings efforts to seduce her. We play about till 4 P.M. Sick at stomach. Helen cries because I say she is not high spirited enough to improvise a white under skirt to wear with her white dress. I suggest making one out of a sheet. I soothe her. We walk to two stores (City of Paris & another in Market) & get one. Back up Powell to room. I take a bromo-seltzer. Make these notes. Helen dresses for the Von Sabern dinner. Sterling comes at 6:15. We go & after dinner I pose for a head. The funny critic. Why Lal[169]—the Hindo, couldnt get in. Helen & Sterling dance & flirt. At twelve

168. Gustave Frenssen (1863–1945), German novelist. Dreiser is referring to *Hilligenlei* (1905), *Jörn Uhl* (1901), and *Klaus Hinrich Bass* (1909).
169. Gobind Behari Lal, the Hearst science editor.

we are taken home in some ones car. The swift driving on those hills.

Friday. Aug 18—1922—More posing for Von Sabern at his studio. Helen shops. I walk with Frennsen. Picture of us taken together. Critics again there. Leave at 11 to return at 2 & pose more. Helen & I fight about nothing. Lunch at a cafeteria. We ride out to Von Saberns, 1398 Jackson Street. I pose till four. Then we go. Take car to hotel. Get bags. Cross—via ferry to Oakland. Dine there— Erff-Zurland restaurant—then out 14<u>th</u> St to Hayward. Dublin, Livermore, Tracy & Stockton. The fine night air. The fun of riding. We stop at the hotel Lincoln. Stockton. The chinese. The charming room.

Saturday, Aug 19—1922. Stockton, Cal
Wake in Hotel Lincoln, Room overlooks local Chinatown. Never knew California inland towns were such a compost of Asiatics and Americans. Chinese, Japs, Mexicans, Spaniards and various types of Americans on hand. We breakfast in a cafeteria, then to Lincoln garage for the car. Then to hotel for bags and to pay bill. The boy finds Helens shoes left in the room and comes carrying them into the street. A tip of course. On to Manteca. Gas 24 1/2 cents, here. On to Ripon, Salida, Riverbank, Oakdale, Knights Ferry, Chinese Camp, Jacksonville, Groveland, etc. A flat, dry country for which water would do much. Oakdale a town in which Mark Twain is said to have held forth. The fierce detour beyond Knights Ferry. No sign of anything to ferry over. The bear, desert-like hills. The lonely birds. Beyond Jacksonville the real climb begins. Fierce roads. We pick up a hiker. The story of his life. Helen gets down on him for being a faker. We get run into on the ridge above Jacksonville. Arrive at Buck Meadow and stop for a sandwich. The prices. Arrive at Carlin and stop for the night. Room and breakfast, 7.50. The tent. How we got rid of the hiker for the night. The tent. The tall trees. The stars. The camp fire. The cool night air. A delicious place to sleep. Waitresses at this place very snippy and uppish for some reason. Leave car in front of tent door and slumber.

Sunday, Aug 20—1922—Yosemite, Cal

Didnt know it was Sunday until next day. Climbing all day from the Carlin Inn to Yosemite. The big trees—(Pride of California and <u>Fallen Giant.</u> That hiker we picked up is with us. His talk. His character. Helen & I quarrel about her refusing to put the top down. At Yosemite I get out & walk. <u>Yosemite.</u> El Capitan. The Inn. The village. The stream. The people. The cafeteria. The fakery. We see it all. Decide to motor to Wawona. The fierce climb. Last view of Valley. The shadowy forrest. The broken down Chevrolet & family. It gets dark. The girl & boy with the donkey. The thrill of beauty. Car insulation threatens to burn. Helen strikes wheel & knocks air tube lose. We limp into Wawona. $11 for room for 1 night with breakfast. That dinner! Dancing. We sit in the car & look at the stars.

Monday, Aug. 21—1922—Riding from Wawona to Merced—from Merced to Fresno and Fresno to Bakersfield.[170]

Tuesday. Aug. 22—1922. Riding from Bakersfield to La. The garage. The breakfast & local paper. The beautiful drive to Tejon. Lebec & Saugus. Los Angeles crowds. Hot weather again. Burbank. Kotex—Home. Helen discovers that Myrtle lived here with Catharine. A row. I water the lawn. We go to P.O. Lots of mail. Get a bite to eat in Hollywood. Then on and to bed. A wonderful, wonderful trip—really.[171]

$$\begin{array}{r} 25 \\ \underline{24} \quad 2 \\ 100 \\ \underline{50} \\ 600 \\ \underline{350} \\ 9.50 \\ 55 \end{array} \quad \text{—Lunch—1}^{\underline{st}} \text{ day}$$

170. Here Dreiser inserted the typescript of a poem by Sterling and a clipping which comments on the wealth of California and the necessity of protecting it from Asiatics.

171. After this entry in the diary, Dreiser inserted a letter from a correspondent whose signature is indecipherible. The letter suggests that its writer was mentally unbalanced. He speaks of accosting Dreiser at the door of Von Sabern's studio, and he continues, "Do you want to be a party to a bad mixture of human chemicals? . . . Then take my counsel . . . I as a chemist have merely set you aside from within reach of an explosive combination."

1.45	Dinner Paso Robles
95	Breakfast
55	Milk etc.—Salinas
.20	San Jose
13.20	
3.50	Oakland Room
1.45	Dinner
1.22	Ferry
$5.00	—Room
1.50	Garage
6.00	Meal
31.87	

Sept. 11, 1922. Glendale, Cal. Allen Benson in town.[172] Have an appointment with him at the Alexandria. Due at ten. Helen and I go down but have difficult time in finding a parking. Quite warm. B—— doesn't know whether he wants to stay over a day or go east. Finally decides to stay. We breakfast at Petifils then go back to hotel for his mail. After delay we make tour of beaches with him, going west on Pico to Venice and then south. His talk of old California. Will not believe the amount of new fine roads everywhere. Doesn't like anything much till he comes to Glendale and sees the little house and the mountain just north of it. We take him through Selvas de Verduga and the Dahlia Garden to Montrose. Doesn't like Montrose as well as Glendale. We take him down to P.O. and then to hotel. Helen has appointment with Burd. She buying a lot in Montrose. I leave her and Allen. He has a dinner engagement. Walk up to hotel and then take Glendale car. The sudden depression. Bad news from Cosmo anent sketches.[173] Ride out to Glendale and dine at the Cafeteria on North Brand. Then home. Soon Helen comes while I am watering the grass. She has had a quarrel with Burd and is glad of it. Her description of his point of view, his manner and his method of living. Personally feel very much depressed and soon go to bed. At the moment see no very clear way out of money troubles or that I am making any real artistic headway with work. The relentless push against the individual on and away into dissolution hangs heavy on me.

172. Allen Benson was the editor of the monthly *Reconstruction* in 1922.
173. *Cosmopolitan Magazine.*

[Dreiser's despondent mood continued, and by early October he and Helen returned to New York. He began the diary again on 12 January 1923.]

Friday, Jan 12—1923—16 St. Lukes Pl. New York City. Spent A.M. hearing Dr. Coué—the French Auto-Suggestionist.[174] Visited Brill (A.A.) 1 W. 70th St. first to get ticket.[175] Helen & I very much pleased with Coue's personality. Discuss his mental force & charm. Afterwards—1 P.M. return & find card in box from Clara S & Mrs. Grushlow.[176] Out in a car & want to go riding. Leave Helen & go to see Lengel about new Boni & Liveright contract. He makes some good suggestions. Leave him at 3 & visit Liveright. Have an hours session there. We all but agree. Another meeting at 1 on Monday. Return here. Meet Bob Mackay on street.[177] Old time editor of Success. Gives his history. To house. Then to Syls— 15 Wadsworth Ave where I listen to her spout C.S. & eat bread pudding.[178] Then home. H——who has been to vaudeville with F.D., arrives at 1 A.M.

Friday, Jan—19—1923—16 St. Lukes Place A bright day. First thing a telephone call from Lengel saying that at last he has sold serial rights of The "Genius" for $2,500.[179] I am to see him. Must see Liveright first & get release from him. Helen & I dress & breakfast in the little lunch place in Greenwich Ave west of the Sheridan Sq. theatre. I go to L's office. Sale ok. Then to Lengels & arrange there. Then call up Hume.[180] (Not in) Call up Edward Dodd.[181] (Not in) Call up Hoyns at Harper's.[182] (Gone to

---

174. Philip Emile Coué (1856–1926), French mental healer who toured America in 1923.

175. A. A. Brill (1874–1948), psychiatrist, author. Brill's translations of Freud first made Freud's work available to many Americans, including Dreiser. He and Dreiser maintained a life-long correspondence from the time of their first meeting in 1917.

176. Clara Samuels and Mrs. Grushlow, Dreiser's old New York friends.

177. Robert MacKay, who was editor of Orison S. Marden's *Success* in 1906–08.

178. Dreiser's sister Sylvia (?–1945). "C. S." is Christian Science.

179. William Lengel sold the serial rights of an abridged version of The "Genius"; it appeared in *Metropolitan Magazine* 56 (February–March, 1923); 57 (April–September, 1923); 58 (October–November, 1923).

180. Arthur Carter Hume (1870–1942), an attorney who served as Dreiser's legal advisor in his dealings with publishers.

181. Edward H. Dodd (1869–1965) of the publishing firm Dodd, Mead. Dreiser was at this time trying to interest him in reissuing The "Genius."

182. Henry Hoyns (1868–1945), editor, publisher. In 1923 Hoyns was vice-president of Harper and Brothers; in 1931 he became chairman of the board.

California) Return here & first put $650⁰⁰ in Greenwich bank at 402 Hudson Street. Then come to house. Helen packing. We discuss this move. I do not want her to go. The pathos of it. She goes to her music lesson. I autograph all my books for her. Start revising.

Jan 20—1923—Saturday. 16 St. Lukes Pl N.Y. A gray day. Helen gets telegram accepting her offer to take $1,000 clear profit on her two Montrose lots. I get letters from Carl Van Vechten[183] telling me where I can buy boot-leg, and from a little theatre in Minneapolis wanting to do Old Ragpicker.[184] Have an appointment here with Theodore Simpson—a medallion sculptor who is to begin a study of me. We go to breakfast. When we return Helen begins to pack & then I realize that actually she is leaving. The sinking sensation in the pit of my stomach. The sense of loss. I can hardly believe that she is going. So many scraps of many & beautiful things that we have done together come to me. Mr. Simpson comes —a very clean featured, pale & artistic fellow. I wish now that no one would come. He shows me reproductions which I show Helen behind closed doors at the back. Yewdale comes. We discuss many persons and things. In order that Helen may get her things out I suggest that we adjourn to the Civic Club for lunch. The medallionist suggests sketching for 20 minutes anyhow. To lunch— walking along Le Roy to Sixth & accross Washington Square. Mr. Simpsons wife comes—a fat wife. We lunch, but I am brooding about Helen. What will the future be like now. So they slip away from me, one by one, & periods close . . . forever. I pose after lunch for an hour in the gallery—yet anxious to go. Finally get rid of the worker. Return here. The empty studio. Call up B & L. Then Helen calls. Says she will come to dinner. Also come down. I am cheered a little—but not much. The beginning of the end.

Wednesday. Jan 24—1923—16 St. Lukes Place, N.Y.C.
Helen recovering from her illness night before. Stays in bed all day. I work—3:30 visit Jacques Loeb at Rockefeller Institute. Find him quite old—very positive that all is accidental—no thought, no

183. Carl Van Vechten (1880–1964), novelist, critic, photographer.
184. "The Old Ragpicker" was never produced in Minneapolis.

plan—no intelligence and great danger of dark ages returning.
Thinks intelligensia ought to hold together in a kind of brother
hood.

Wretched day. Gray, dark slop & slush underfoot. Rain & snow
alternating. Awful subway crush. Helen & I dine—about 8 at
Brazilian Coffee House—43rd St. N.Y.

Thursday—Feb. 1—1923—Atlantic City. The Ritz-Carlton—Room
818 Rains. Not feeling well. Breakfast at a little place in
Pennsylvania Ave. Ride down in a Nash jitney. Return to hotel,
same way. Walk a little on Board Walk in rain. The waves, shells,
gulls, dead crabs. Sit in main parlor for a time. Arrange for chair
car to N.Y.—8:50 P.M. Dine at the Green Front in Atlantic Ave.
Take train at 8:50. Change at N. Philadelphia. Very foggy. Much
delayed. Arrive N.Y. 1:30 A.M.! The Jewish vaudeville troupe. The
praying priest. The hail fellow from Newark. I meet Fitzgibbons—
Peter's old friend.[185] He tells his story.

Saturday—Feb. 3—1923—New York.
16 St. Lukes Place. Very cold & gray. Helen and I decide to see
Hunting Wild Animals in Africa—a movie exhibit at the Lyric. It
turns out to be very interesting. Up to date whaling. Penguins. The
De Beers Mine. Elephants, Rhinoceri, Hippapotami, Wart hogs.
Hyenas. Baboons. The drinking pools. A puff adder. Gnus, Zebras,
Dik-Diks. Giraffes. The long list of African animals. Poor country.
Scant vegetation. Wild tribes. Lions. Hawks. The up-to-date Ford.
Am impressed with the terror of death in which every animal
appears to live.

Wednesday, Feb. 7—1923—N.Y. City
16 St. Lukes Place. Clear & bright. 11:30 meet Liveright & sign
new contracts for Genius, Titan, Hoosier Holiday, Plays Natural &
Supernatural.[186] 1 P.M. meet Fulton Oursler & Bernarr McFadden

185. T. C. Fitzgibbons was a journalist and a friend of Peter McCord (the "Peter" of
Twelve Men). He had been connected with the Sharon Herald in Pennsylvania.
186. As part of the new contract, Liveright agreed to buy The "Genius," The Titan, A
Hoosier Holiday, and The Plays from Dodd, Mead; to pay Dreiser's remaining debt to the firm;
and to reissue the books.

of the McFadden Publications.[187] Rather interesting talk. 4 P.M. Outline Mildred My Mildred, a musical comedy to Susan Connally who is to do it under my direction.[188] 6:30 P.M. dine at little French Place—40th & 7th Ave. Then go to see Jitto's Atonement— at the Comedy. Very good. A play inspired by Shaw & his ideas & done by one of his faithful disciples. Imitaters get the key to anything that has once been done. Home. Meet Mencken & Nathan on the street.

Friday, Feb. 9—1923—16 St. Lukes Place N.Y.C. Clear. Melting snow on ground. After looking in A.M. for electric fittings for stove & breakfasting at Papas in 14th Street at 8th Ave., work all day on sketch for A Gallery of Women. Evening Helen & I go to see Liza —a negro musical comedy at 63rd St. theatre. Quite good. Afterwards, in 42nd Street, meet Young now a professor in N.Y. University.[189] He wants to come down & see me. P.M. Went to see Rosenthal about my lungs—
Also Emma.[190] The medicine he gives me helps almost at once.

Wednesday. Mch—14—1923—N.Y.
16 St. Lukes Place. Walk with Mrs. H—— in Hoboken. Tea in the ferry House. We discuss the poems. Only a few changes. Walk here & there. The lovely sunlight on the river & boats coming back. I leave her at Christopher & 7th Ave. She has talked much of the Moscow Art Theatre. Helen & I go to see The Lower Depths— Gorky the same evening. How depressed she would have been if she had known that I had walked with Mrs. H—— in the afternoon.

Friday. Mch 16—1923—16 St. Lukes Pl Helen decides to leave because I am going to dinner at Mrs. Howeys. Her rage. She packs her bags. I go. The bland, colorless evening. We talk of the

187. Fulton Oursler (1893–1952), critic, novelist, editor; Bernarr MacFadden (1868–1955), author, publisher.
188. Susan Cornelia Connolly was a playwright who collaborated with Dreiser on "Mildred My Mildred," a three-act comedy among the Dreiser papers at the University of Pennsylvania. The plot is absurd: the action describes the pursuit by two suitors of a girl named Mildred; their travels take them to Egypt, China, and the Gobi Desert; and the play involves encounters with African natives.
189. Art Young (1866–1943), political cartoonist, writer, editor.
190. Dreiser's sister Emma.

Moscow Art Theatre Players—principally. I return. My thoughts on being alone. To bed. At two Helen comes. I let her in. Her surprise. Half intoxicated. We sleep.

Sunday, March 18—1923—(16 St Lukes Pl) Helen & I go to Asbury Park. Beautiful day. We hurry to catch the 11.10. Breakfast in Pennsylvania Station. The ride down. Newark, Elizabeth, Red Bank. The inlets. The pretty houses. We walk about Asbury. Then lunch at the Cake Shop. All the Christian Americans at the hotels. After lunch we walk through Ocean Grove. The statue of Mr. Stark. Helen tells the story of Rain.[191] We pass through Bradley Beach & Avon by the sea. I think of Jug, Kirah, Estelle.[192] The lagoons. The pretty houses. The new shore road to Belmar. We go on to Belmar & take car back to Asbury. Train just leaving. Decide to wait for the 7:32. Helen enthuses over a pretty child. Back to the beach. The new moon. We both wish over our right shoulders. The walk on the board walk. The walk by the lagoon. The lighted town— The moon above it. The dogs barking in the dusk. The silver light. The children playing. A momentary heartache because of beauty. The 7:32 Pennsylvania Station 10:10. Childs. The Studio. To bed.

Saturday—April 7—1923—16 St Lukes Pl N.Y.
Saturday afternoon Helen & I go to Long Beach. She has a new dress. We are disappointed. No life there. Restaurants all closed. The Nassau Hotel almost deserted. We go back to Brooklyn. Dine there. Then Home.

Sunday, April 8th—1923. N.Y. 16 St. Lukes Pl
Helen & I go to Bronx Park & spend the day. Warm & pleasent. Most interesting animals. We are fascinated by a white pea fowl, an ant eater, a group of wild swine, the kangeroos, giraffes, rhinocerae, wild zebras, asses, the seals & birds. Discuss nature & the intelligence of animals all the way. Leave at 5:30. Dine in Greenwich Village—the little place at 10th & 7th. Then to see a moving picture.

---

191. Probably W. Somerset Maugham's story "Rain."
192. These are women with whom he had had long-term relations: his wife Sara ("Jug") Dreiser, Kirah Markham, Estelle Kubitz.

Wednesday, April 11—1923. N.Y.—16 St. Lukes Pl
See Anathema at the 48<u>th</u> St theatre with Robin.[193] My going out
this night with him is the cause of Helens moving again—this time
to 60 W. 49<u>th</u>. I am depressed by that but cannot help it. A
wonderful play. Very interpretative of life.

Saturday, April 14—1923—N.Y. 16 St. Lukes Pl
Helen living up town. 60 W. 49<u>th</u> St. Work all day alone. Rather
depressed. Recieve first copies of the French translation of Twelve
Men (Douz Hommes).[194] Send copies to Mencken, Rascoe, Van
Vechten & Mrs. Kubitz. Evening Helen calls up, wants to come
down. She does, for an hour. Dine with Mr & Mrs John K.
Williams & some of their friends at 428 Lafayette Street. Interesting
talk. Home at 11:30. Helen stays all night with me.

Sunday—April 15—1923—16 St. Lukes Pl
Helen & I go to Newark. Walk through the old portion of the city,
talking all the while. Take car finally to Springfield, then to So.
Orange, then back to N.Y. Chocolate there & then train to N.Y.
Go to Sheridan Theatre to see what is there. It is raining.
Nazimova in ⌐   ⌐. We dont like her so dont go in. Take subway
to 42nd. See <u>Down to the Sea in Ships</u>—another lemon. Then to
dinner—42nd & Broadway. German place. Then walk to 18th
along 7th Home. She is very loving again. Doesn't want to leave
me.

Sunday, June 10—1923—N.Y. City
Helen & I motor out to Lake Ronkonkoma returning via Islip. We
row on the lake. Have tea at the inn. Visit several road houses near
Islip. Beautiful day. Return via 59th St Bridge—very late. Hot in
town. Crush of automobiles delays us almost hours.

Saturday, June 30—1923—N.Y. City
Helen & I start for Cortland & Big Moose Lake. Get 3 bottles of
gin from Mame. Cross at Christopher Street to Hoboken. Go all
through Passaic, Paterson, Pompton Lake, Newfoundland, Franklin

---

193. "Anathema," by Leonid Andreyev, opened at the 48th Street Theatre on 10 April
1923 and ran for 23 performances.
194. *Douze Hommes,* trans. Fernande Hélie (Paris: F. Rieder, 1923).

Furnace, Sussex & Port Jervis to Monticello. Four miles this side find a vacant cottage & we are allowed to stay there. (Charles Haas) The spring. The woods. We go into Monticello to get things for breakfast. Helen delighted.

Sunday, July 1—1923—Monticello, N.Y.
We motor from here to Binghamton & Cortland. Follow East Branch of the Delaware River almost to Binghamton. Beautiful scenery. Bright, cool day. No car trouble. At Cortland, 7 P.M. Stop at the Cortland House. The fine house. A good room but we resent being compelled to stay in town. The beautiful Glen just south of Cortland. Greeks running restaurants everywhere.

Monday, July 2—1923—Cortland N.Y.
We motor from here first to Little York Lake—thence back via Homer & Cortland to South Otselic (McGraw, Solon, East Freetown, Cincinnatus, Pitcher, N. Pitcher). The farmer who knew Frank Brown.[195] The old house. Four trees. Armenian farmers. We walk about it. Back to DeRuyter. The lost French Ball. Helen imitates a cat & it cries. The Tobes house, DeRuyter. We motor on toward Cazanovia where we stop. Beautiful homes. The strawberry farmer. We dine at the Locklaen House. Delightful room in a country home.

Tuesday. July 3—1923—Cazanovia N.Y.
Raining, slightly. We motor from here to Utica & Big Moose Lake. I get a hair cut & shave. The lovely country to Utica. The Adirondack Gate beyond it. Price of lots on other lake—$500 to $1000. The Campus. Old Forge. The Inn there. We loaf an hour. The run-a-way horse. Thence on to Eagle Bay and from there to Big Moose. Put up at the Glenmore on the lake. 10\frac{00}{}$ for room, dinner & breakfast. No bath. We row on the lake & listen to the music & watch the dancers. It rains from 3 A.M. till dawn.

July 4—1923. Big Moose Lake, N.Y.
Bright, cool day. Talk to the guide who found Grace Browns body. His recollections of Gillette & her. We motor back to Eagle Bay.

---

195. Frank Brown was the father of Grace Brown, the murdered girl in the Gillette case of 1906, which Dreiser used as the basis for the story of Clyde Griffiths in *An American Tragedy*.

Car gets mired & has to be hauled out by another. $2<u>00</u>. Halfway to Old Forge one tire gets a puncture. Repairs & changes at Old Forge Garage. Lunch. Thence on to Herkimer. About half way we swing a hammock in the woods & rest. The wood peckers. Blue jays. Helen sees a blue bird. The beauty of the run from Barneveld to Herkimer (Trenton, Falls, Poland, Newport Fairfield). Inns, streams, hills, pretty towns—a beautiful simple, life. Visit court house & County Jail, Herkimer. On to Canajoharie. We dine there —Wagner house. Back to Ft. Plain to stop at an old house we saw. Lovely room. Beautiful view of Mohawk river. Lose a bottle of gin. Fireworks. A small town parade. The many trains of the N.Y. Central & Big Four. Sleep.

July 5—1923 (Thursday) Ft. Plain N.Y.
Motor from here to N.Y. City—leaving at 10.30 A.M. Wretched road to Albany. No worthwhile scenery. Breakfast in Amsterdam. Turn South, west shore of Hudson, at Albany. Stop to loaf on river near Cedar Hill. Enormous ice houses. On to Ravena, Coxsakie, Athens, Catskill & Kingston. Helen likes Kingston. Arrive at Newburgh at 6:30 and dine. Take the road around Storm King & West Point. Bear Mountain Park. The Lake. Beautiful Scenery. Arrive Nyack about 9. Forty Second Street about 11. Put up car & get to bed about 12.50. Beautiful ride but very tired.

Nov. 9—1923—New York City.
Living at 118 W. 11th St. Saw The Hunchback of Notre Dame in evening at the Astor Theatre— with Helen. Like Lon Chaneys interpretation of the hunchback very much. Helen & I bought some candy & then returned to 35 W. 50th Street—her apartment.

Nov. 12—1923—New York City
Had dinner with Sallie K—at Mouquins—28th & 6th Ave.[196] From there went to see the Vanities of 1923 at the Earl Carroll.[197] Very much amused by ⌞   ⌟and his buffooneries. Six naked women shown in this show behind very transparent screens.

---

196. Sallie Kusell, Dreiser's secretary and mistress who, with Louise Campbell, helped him in the editing of *An American Tragedy.*
197. Dreiser is referring to the Ziegfeld Follies of 1923 at the Earl Carroll Theater.

Nov. 13—1923—118 W. 11th St. N.Y.C.
Stopping with Helen at 35 W. 50th St. Up at 8 A.M. in order to keep appointment below.[198] Had teeth cleaned & one tooth filled. Return to room at 118 W. 11th & worked for rest of day.

Nov. 21—1923—Washington D.C.
(stopping with R.D. Heine—2400 California St)
Jane Cowl in Peleas & Melisande.[199] Saw it with Jesse A. Hildebrand.[200] 934 New Jersey Ave. S.E. Wash. D.C. Not an unintelligent interpretation but Miss Cowl not sufficiently satisfactory for the role. Afterwards returned with Heine to 2400 California St where I spent the night.

Wednesday, Nov. 28—1923—N.Y. 118 W. 11th
Helen & I go to see a comedy "Time" by Arthur Henry.[201] Only fair. Old time stuff. Supposed to be a success. Helen likes it. I am glad for Henry's sake. Not otherwise.

Tuesday, Dec. 11—1923—N.Y.—118 W. 11
Helen & I go to see the Music Box. A good musical comedy.

Sunday, Dec. 23—1923. New York
Helen & I decide to go to Atlantic City in the car. She is a little irritated because I went out Friday evening. It is grey & threatening rain. We get everything ready, breakfast in the apartment & then— about 1 P.M. start. I forget glasses and at Liberty Street ferry have to turn & go up to 118—then to 50th. Find them there. We start again. Down 5th & 7th to Liberty. Ferry to J.C. Straight road to Newark, Elizabeth & Rahway. At Rahway we go to New Brunswick—then Dayton, Cranberry & Heightstown. (wrong road) It begins to rain. Very early dark. We turn east at last toward Freehold. Helen cries thinking of Friday. Outside Freehold tire goes bad. Cant fix. We limp in. Sunday in country garages dont

---

198. At the bottom of this page of the diary Dreiser has pasted an appointment card from Arthur G. Croker, D.D.S., for 9:30 A.M., 13 November 1923.
199. Jane Cowl (1884–1950), actress.
200. Jesse A. Hildebrand (1888–?), writer, editor.
201. Arthur Henry's play "Time" opened at the 39th Street Theatre on 26 November 1923 and ran for fifty-one performances.

work—some of them. I borrow tools & change wheel. Then on to next town—Adelphia. It pours rain. Very dark. Another wheel goes flat. We return to Adelphia. Bill of $5.20—to buy a cheap tube & change tires. On to Lakewood—next town. Moon comes out. It clears up. We dine. Laurel in Pines wants 32\underline{00}$ for room with bath for 1 night. Laurel House wants $28. The Jewish invasion. Burst of Jew Hotels. We call up ten of them. Nothing less than $9 per night —for room with bath for two. Finally find a small American hotel on Main Street. Excellent. Rate 5$\underline{00}$. We stay there. Helen likes it & is happy again.

The one room with the three beds in it. "Vell—you can sleep in vun of dem".

Monday Dec. 24—1923—Lakewood—N.J. We breakfast in this small hotel. I fix a gin rickey. Go out to buy a tire. Helen & I canvas all stores. Finally get a Silvertown Cord 31 × 4—for 19$\underline{00}$. Tube for 3$\underline{00}$ & three to put it on. Then we return, get car & change the tire. Then send Helen's presents home from P.O. Then on down coast to Toms River, Lanoka, Forked River, Waretown, Barnegat, Manahawkin, West Creek, Parkertown, Tuckerton, Bass River, New Gretna, Leeds, Oceanville, Absecon. Atlantic City. Beautiful road. Pines, inlets. Delightful air. We leave Lakewood at 12. Arrive Atlantic City 4. Call up various hotels. This is Christmas eve. No rooms at Traymore, Shelburne, Marlborough—Blenheim. Rooms at Ritz (no meals— per day) $16, Ambassador (no meals, 14. Chelsea—$18. Haddon Hall offers room with bath, meals—$20 per day. We go there. Fine view of sea. We walk on the board walk. Then dine. Buy dozens of oranges & make orange juice. Bed about 11. (I had to go out & buy black tie, silk socks & silk collar —all forgotten)

Tuesday December 25—1923. (Christmas) Atlantic City.
Very bright day. Fine view of ocean. We breakfast at 9. Walk out to High School & then west. Outside Hotels Atlantic City is drear. The dubs who stopped all traffic to let a sail boat through the bridge. Back to Hotel for lunch. We call up Shelburne & decide to move at end of day. Can get room for 10$\underline{00}$—dine where we please. We return to Haddon Hall, pack & move. Delightful new room. Interesting orchestra. We dine here. Then walk & finally go to bed. Helen loves loafing & enjoying hot salt water baths.

Wednesday Dec. 26—1923—Atlantic City. The Shelburne
We loaf another day. Up at 10:30. Walk to inlet on Atlantic Ave.
Then breakfast. More oranges. We ride out to Longport nearly.
Then walk back. Wonderful walk. Dinner at the Shelburne. Listen
to concert afterward. Finally to bed.

Thursday, Dec 27—1923. Atlantic City
Hotel Shelburne. We decide to return to N.Y. Breakfast in Hotel.
Then pack & get car. Garage rate in A.C. $1⁵⁰ per night. Look for
"air" & distilled water for battery. Then by same route to Toms
River. Cold & grey today. But we are comfortable & happy. Reach
Toms River by one. Turn there to Seaside Park. Then north to
Point Pleasant, Manasquan, Sea Girt, Spring Lake, etc to Long
Branch. Then via Red Bank, Keyport & South Amboy to Perth
Amboy, Elizabeth & Newark. Helen tired. We dine in Newark.
Then home—via Lackawanna Ferry. Leave my bags here 118. Then
go up to her place.

Friday, Dec 28—1923. N.Y.C. Stayed at Helens all night. Worked
at 118 during day. Glad to be back & working.

Wednesday, Jan 2—1924—New York City
Living at 118 W. 11th St. Working on An American Tragedy.
Chapter 33. Night previous spent with Helen—35-W. 50. We
breakfasted in the cafe on Sixth Ave. near 50th. I stopped in at
Boni & Liveright—61 W. 48th on way down to see about re issue
of Titan & Jennie Gerhardt.[202] Then here to work. Mame & Mrs.
Freeman worrying over their tea-room. Percy Stickney Grant calls
up in P.M. & wants to come to see me.[203] Also T.C. Fitzgibbons—
Peter's old friend—now conducting the (Pa) Sharon Herald. Wants
me to sign a copy of the "Genius". For old times sake agree to
meet him at the Brevoort. —5 P.M. Meet two friends of his. We
have an hour of pleasant reminiscences. Upon persuasion I agree to
get Helen & join them for dinner. Also to see Little Jesse James.
We seperate. Fitzgibbons & I go to the 8th Street book shop where

202. Boni & Liveright reissued *Jennie Gerhardt* in 1924 and *The Titan* in 1925.
203. Dr. Percy Stickney Grant (1860–1927), pastor of the Church of the Ascension at
Fifth Avenue and 10th Street. He admired Dreiser's work and sympathized with him in his
struggle for literary freedom.

he buys 2 "Genius's" and 1 Color of a Great City. Come to 118 & find Helen waiting. Thence, in taxi, to Commodore hotel. We drink in their room (1941). Then down to dinner in the grill. Afterwards to the 48th Street theatre. Vulgar, sexy musical comedy, but not wholly unamusing. During show it begins to rain. Afterward Helen does not want to go back to Commodore. I make apologies & we go to 35 W. 50th. I read last year of Lincolns life in Ida Tarbells Life of him.[204] Then to bed. Helen thinks she is caught. Has passed her period & is worrying.

Friday—Jan 4—1924—N.Y.—118 W. 11
Helen & I go to see the Covered Wagon at the Criterion. Not bad as a movie. The wagon train pictures rather interesting.

Thursday—Jan 31—1924—N.Y. 118 W. 11th.
Helen gets two tickets from some friend for <u>The Miracle.</u> A trashy bit of religion fol-de-rol—all wrong in the dogmatic interpretation of life. Good for boob-trimming. Interesting as a bit of stage craft but barely that. We both felt the same about. Dinner before hand at the new hotel Empire—Brodwy 65th. A cold night. We use the car.

Monday, Feb. 4—1924—N.Y.—118 W. 11th St.
Helen away—on one of her spells. I go alone in the evening to see Walter Hampden in Cyrano de Bergerac.[205] Only a fair production. Nothing arrestingly brilliant or moving. The idea is better than the interpretation. Recall the great excitement concerning another version of it 20 years before. Misting, cold & cloudy when I come out. On way down 7th Ave. I compose "Tall Towers."[206] To bed after midnight.

---

204. Ida Tarbell (1857–1944), author, editor, journalist. Dreiser began reading Tarbell's *Early Life of Abraham Lincoln,* 2 vols. (1900), in 1903, and it remained one of his favorite books. See p. 97, n. 38.
205. Walter Hampden (1879–1955), actor.
206. Dreiser's poem "Tall Towers" was published in the *New York Evening Post Literary Review,* 20 December 1924. It was later reprinted in *Moods: Cadenced and Declaimed* (1926).

Saturday Feb—9—1924. N.Y.C.—118 W. 11th St
Helen & I go to see a negro show at the Colonial, Brdwy & 63rd.
Very amusing. Two negros. "De Dudy got 'em" ("Deducts $10")
Afterward we walk down Brdwy to 50th & stay at her place.

Tuesday—Feb 12—1924. N.Y.C.—118 W. 11th
Lincoln's birthday. (Working on novel) In the evening Helen & I
go to see St. Joan at the Theatre Guild Theatre, 35th St & 6th Ave.
Fine drama. Bit of Shavian Buffoonery at the end. Very much
impressed with the mans brilliant interpretation of the probabilities.
Helen very enthusiastic. Before this we have dinner at Keans Chop
House—36th St. Not very good. I hear two medics in the wash
room fixing up their charges against a luckless devil who has had
the poor sense to employ the two of them. A fine bit of robbery.

Thursday. March 20—1924—118 W. 11th & 35 W. 50th N.Y.
Helen getting ready to go west. The storage people are coming
tomorrow for the furniture. I am very much depressed for Helen is
the only one I really care for now, anymore. We quarrel over
something in the A.M. but at 3 P.M. she comes round with the car
& I ride with her out in Brooklyn. We return. Put up car & go to
see Douglas Fairbanks in The Thief of Bagdad. Not bad.
Afterwards we go to 35 West & I hold close to Helen all night
because I feel so gloomy about her leaving me. It is for the 1st
time in 4 years—over four years really—(Since Sept 11—1919.)

Wednesday, April 2—1924—118 W. 11th St NY
Very clear, pleasant day. Snow still on ground but melting fast.
Walk about Washington Sq. in A.M. Work all day on book. At 5:30
S.K. comes over & stays until 6:30.[207] I shake her & get away by
7:15 and go around to Mrs. H—— (60 W. 12) Her peculiar
husband. He gives me a drink. We go to a Syrian restaurant in
Washington Street. She tells me about her father the famous
surgeon. Also about ∟   ⌟ and her sister. (A typical English
intellectual cad & ass.) After dinner we walk South to the Battery—
then all through the financial district & north along South Street to

207. S.K. is Sallie Kusell.

Williamsburgh Bridge. D. H.'s peculiar attitude toward her children. Morally she is beginning to hedge. We take bus accross Delancey to 7th Ave & walk north to my place. When I invite her in & close the door she immediately begins to undress—which makes me laugh. I hadn't assumed that copulation naturally followed. However—always willing to oblige. We talk of Masters & his present drift. Finally I walk home with her & immediately return here. My mood in regard to her is always peculiar. I may not see her again & would not care, really.

Thursday—April 3—1924—118 W. 11th St N.Y.
Clear warm day. Usual routine here. Breakfast & then to work. Am having trouble with the book. At 5 P.M. a Miss Joffe of The Day—a Jewish Daily, calls to interview me. She proves interesting & tells me not a little about the East Side. At 6:15 she leaves & I call up S.K. She has tickets for Poppy a musical comedy.[208] It is at the Apollo Theatre in 42nd St. We go & I enjoy it much—especially W.C. Fields—as the incorrigible old time circus shill and short change man. Suggest "Old Hoss" Hoey very much. Afterwards we walk down 8th to Greenwich Village. S.K. rather gloomy but cheers up. Leave her at her steps at 12:30 & return here & to bed.

Saturday, April 5—1924—118 W. 11th St. N.Y.C.
Beautiful day—clear & warm. Up early. No letter from Helen. Get rolls & milk for Mame & have breakfast here. Her garden at back needs some work. I reset two posts for her. Work on book from 10:30 on but not very successfully. Stop & answer a number of letters. Call up S.K. (78 Washington Pl) who—at 12.30 brings around some corrected chapters. She is to be off at 2 and wants me to spend P.M. with her. But I work on until 3 when May Brandstone shows up—after one year of absence.[209] Has married & already is some what disillusioned. Wants to work for me again. She remains until 5:30 when I go about to S.K.s. We leave for Newark for dinner. The beauty of the park there. Visit the new

208. "Poppy" by Dorothy Donnelly, opened at the Apollo Theatre on 3 September 1923, and ran for 346 performances.
209. May Branstone's correspondence with Dreiser shows that she typed for him and that she knew him socially.

market, built farther east. Dine in a restaurant overlooking the
square. Then go to see Magnolia at a movie house. The picture is
not as good as the play. We leave early & come back to N.Y. It is
11 but I stay until 12.30. We have a heavy round. Then home & to
bed.

Sunday, April 6—1924—118 W. 11th St. N.Y.
Raining hard all day. Very dark. Not feeling very good. Gertie
seriously ill at Em's and Mame decides to go up there. S.K. living
at 78 Washington Place. Have agreed to invite her to breakfast but
my mood is against it. Call her up & meet her at 8th & 6th Ave
long enough to give her Chapter 17 of An American Tragedy to
type. She is planning to visit some woman friend who lives out at
Jackson Heights in order to get news of her own mother. Return &
start working on the book again. Write Llona, a French critic, about
my books over there.[210] He has a publisher for them. Ross
Freeman comes down to visit. He is an engineer and ex-bull fighter
in Mexico. At 3:30 S.K. comes back with the chapter. Stays a half
hour & leaves. And Ross leaves too. I work again till 8 without
interruption. Finish chapter 18. Then go to little restaurant at 14th
& 7th Ave & have two hot dogs & a cup of coffee. Walk in rain to
59th Street. Many odd thoughts about the city. Return at 10 & go
to bed. Wrote Helen who is with her mother in Portland, Oregon.

Wednesday, May 14—1924. 118 W. 11th N.Y.C.
Working on An American Tragedy. Bright weather. Mrs. Guitteau
agrees to come down today. At 6$\underline{30}$ she arrives & after talking here
an hour we go to Mame's (Greenwich Village Inn) for dinner. She
appears more charming than on previous visits. We talk of N.Y. &
literature & her family life. After dinner walk back here & she
remains until 12. The windows facing the court back of Mames all
lighted. They make enough light for us. Instead of being so
determined with me as at first she is now very simple & yeilding. I
never saw anyone with a prettier body. She suggests some one in a
musical comedy & proves to have been connected with The Show
Girl. Appears to be completely overawed & subdued by the power

210. Victor Llona was the French critic who translated Dreiser's works.

of a name. Once more life seems so purely based on position or luck which permits achievement. Without the fame of my books I personally could not acheive this relationship at all.

At 12$\frac{30}{}$ I take her to her apartment on Riverside Drive & leave her. The big dog. The books. The whiskey.

Wednesday. May 28—1924—118 W. 11th St N.Y.
Magdalene Davis[211] & I go to hear Lemon & Sumner debate Censorship at Civic Club. Before that we dine at Mame's. Run into Gertie & Robin. Delightful spring evening. Walk over past St. Marks Church. Afterwards we walk past this house but on to her place—4 Grove Street. Tells me about the girls & boys in Ebensburg, Pa. Agrees to come over Friday night which she does. A most interesting & colorful mind. I am sure she will write some day.

Sunday. June 1—1924—N.Y. 118 W. 11th St
Magdalene & her sister Leone & I spend Sunday on Canal. We meet in Lackawanna Station Hoboken at 11. Get back to Newark 8 P.M. Same day. Go to Boonton & walk between there & Dover—to Denville. Canal being dried up & turned into an automobile highway. Breakfast in Boonton. Flowers. We bath our feet in the Passaic. Home by midnight. Dinner in Newark. A most delightful day.

Tuesday, June 3—1924—118 W. 11th St. NY
Magdalene & I meet here at 10$\frac{30}{}$ P.M. for pleasure.

Wednesday, June 4—1924. 118 W. 11th N.Y.
S.K. & I walk in Prospect Park, Brooklyn. Dine there. Go home together.

Thursday, June 5—1924—118 W. 11th St N.Y.
Another warm, pleasent spring day. Have an appointment today with Maud Guitteau for 6$\frac{30}{}$ P.M. here.

---

211. Magdalen Davis is identified in a letter that Dreiser sent to Helen (18 June 1924) as "connected with the Greenwich Village Theatre & the Standard Oil Company."

Friday, June 6—1924—118 W. 11th St. NY

Clear warm day. Work all day long on book. Lengel calls up. Wants me to go to dinner with him & his wife. I dont want to & get out of it. Send, at his request, 2 stories & 8 studies of women to the Cosmopolitan. S.K. calls up. Has an appointment with her Chicago friend. We agree to meet at her place at 9 P.M. I work on here till 7³⁰. Finish 29. Get a sandwich at Coffee Pot. Magdalene calls up, we agree to meet Saturday at 3 for an outing. At 9³⁰ I go over. S.K. & I talk & finally go to bed together. I stay until 2³⁰—sleeping. Then get up & come here. S.K. & I do some heavy work. We agree to meet again Sunday at 2 P.M.

Saturday, June 7—1924—118 W. 11th St

Beautiful, warm clear day. Finest yet, this spring. Up at 8³⁰. Cold bath. Breakfast at little Coffee Pot around the corner. Then to bank (406 Hudson) Stans & Co refuse to pay coupons until June 15. Return here. Work on Chapter 29. Part time in yard, downstairs. Brennan making a screen door. Mrs. Guitteau calls up. Wants to come down but I refuse. Arrange possibly for Sunday. Call up S.K. She has gone to Larchmont. At 2⁵⁰ Magdalene (Davis) calls up. Says she'll be here at 3. She comes in great spirits. Dances to Whispering record. We decide to go to Staten Island. Stop in Coffee Pot around the corner—(6th Ave) & have a sandwich. Then take 6th Ave L. to Battery. Try to get a boat to some where but cant. The pidgeons flying low. Take boat to Staten Island. She tells about some of her past affairs. Also how much Leone likes me. At St. George take train for Pleasent Plains. Delightful ride. Much talk of characters. Her work in different cities—(Lancaster Pa., Evansville, Ind.) The woman in Buffalo whose life was like a Gorky novel.[212] Get off at Pleasent Plains. Have a soda. Get weighed. She weighs 123. I 200. Walk to Loretto Beach & sit on sand. The lovely bay. The 3 boys going out to light in a row boat. The 4 old women. Magdalene teases them by hugging me. We try to copulate on the beach. Too many watching. Play in the sand. At 7³⁰ start walking south along shore road to Toltenville. The stars. A new moon. I see it over my right shoulder. Frogs, tree toads, gnats. We

212. Maxim Gorki (1868–1936), Russian novelist and dramatist.

admire pretty cottages alight in the dark. I walk with my hand on M's hip. Teases me with sensuous motions. Tells me the story of her mother & village life in Ebensburg, Pa. Her father. Why she left home. Why she came to N.Y. We stop & dance in the dark. On to St. Marys Beach. Find an old house not open yet for season. Lie on steps & screw, Magdalene sitting astride my knees. Lovely walk back to train. Miss the 11. Make the 11$\frac{37}{}$. The small lunch car. The trackless trolley. M wants me to be nice to Leone (her sister). We talk of books—her job with the Standard Oil Co. The Chicago case. At 6th Ave & 8th   Have supper at 1$\frac{30}{}$ A.M. I leave her at her door. (4 Grove St)

Sunday, June 8—1924—118 W. 11th St.

Rainy, last night with Magdalene Davis on Staten Island. Didnt get to bed till 3. Up at 11. Sallie Kussell calls up. I arrange to go over there at 2. Breakfast with Mame & Brennan.[213] She has more to tell of Ross Freeman & the Greenwitch Inn. He is over there now in charge for his mother. Come up to rooms & work until 2. Then go over to S.K. On way—42th—7th—) call up Mrs. Guitteau. She is waiting. Get out of going up there. At S.K.'s (79 W.12) we talk of the Nathan Leopold—Louis Loeb case in Chicago.[214] Also of perversions, Kraft-Ebbing, Freud etc. The K's have just bought a copy of Psychopathia Sexualis.[215] S.K. reads Chapter 29—Part II, decides its fine. I sleep an hour. Then we have a heavy round. Afterwards we quarrel over the number of women I have. Makes a remark about my back which infuriates me. I want to quit. She hangs on & we go to dinner at the Tavern. Hardly speak. I feel very down. At 9$\frac{15}{}$ we leave. I look in on Helens car in the Annabeck garage in 50th St. We take 6th Ave. L to 14th. Walk to

213. Austin Brennan was a salesman who married Dreiser's sister Mame. The Brennans lived next door to Dreiser at his 118 West 11th Street apartment, and they served as the rental agents for his building.

214. Dreiser is referring to Nathan Leopold and Richard Loeb, who kidnapped and murdered fourteen-year-old Bobby Franks in Chicago on 21 May 1924. The two men were convicted in a famous trial in which Clarence Darrow represented them. On 5 June 1924, Dreiser wrote to Helen that the case "interests me enormously": "It's one of those fantastic things that seems to hold so much more than is on the surface. Just a desire to kill doesn't seem to explain it. There must be something more it seems to me. A great novel there somewhere."

215. Baron Richard von Krafft-Ebing (1840–1902), German neurologist and psychiatrist; Dreiser refers to his *Psychopathia Sexualis* (1886); Sigmund Freud (1856–1939).

12th in silence & I leave her there. Wants me to go to room but I refuse. Come here. Pen these notes. Then to bed. Very cold, gray & rainy today.

<u>Wednesday, July 2nd 1924, N.Y.—118 W. 11th</u>
Breakfast with S.K. Bright day. Work here until 3. When Mrs. Guitteau comes. Her new dress & hat. We play until 5. Then dress & go to Pennsylvania Station. Tickets to Long Beach. We walk on board walk & dine at the Nassau. The gay dancers. I miss Helen dreadfully. Walk on board walk after dinner. Then back to N.Y. at 11:20—arriving 12.26. Her house at 1. I leave & get off at 23rd in order to drop an air-mail letter for Helen in air-mail box at 23rd & 5th. Walk home from there. To bed. 1.30. At Long Beach Mrs. Guitteau tells story of her girlhood life with 1st & 2nd husbands. The disappearing act. Her stage career.

MOTORING TO FLORIDA
1925-26

On 8 December 1925, nine days before formal publication of *An American Tragedy,* Dreiser and Helen decided to take an automobile trip south to Florida. Both were weary after the long labor of completing the novel, and Dreiser wanted to be away from New York so that he might escape the winter cold and the reactions to the *Tragedy.* Consequently, the diary is less erotic and exotic than those before 1925, but it reveals, among other things, Dreiser's eye for social and natural details. His descriptions of the new South and of Florida, then in the midst of a land boom, and his notes on the physical aspects of the landscape solve no biographical cruxes; but they provide a glimpse of Dreiser's bent as an observer, offering us scene after scene of rapidly rendered snapshots. We also begin to observe the changes in his life with Helen, as their relationship acquires the note of strain and mutual dependence that will characterize their next twenty years together.

JANUARY 1926   15 CENTS

THE MAGAZINE OF FLC

Suniland

THE MAGAZINE OF FLORIDA

CHARLES·A·WINTER

Magazine Purchased in Florida

Tuesday—Dec. 8—1925— (New York) Stopping at Hotel Empire —63nd & Bdway. We decide to leave for Florida today. License tag problem. I have to see Mame, M.K.[1] Car is in a garage at 64th & 11th Ave. Breakfast in the hotel. A letter from Maurice Richmond who has Paul's songs, telling me he is going to go over the list & select.[2] Go for the car. Pack all bags— 9. Leave for B & L. first.[3] Then to Pennsylvania Hotel. See M.K. Helen waiting in 6th Ave. Then to Mames. She has a plan to get me to pay a 75 bill for furniture. I give her $20 on account. Then to South Ferry. We get there at 2 P.M. The gulls going accross. A quick run to Tottenville. Then to New Brunswick. I wire Robin concerning The Will—and disappointing him.[4] We run on to Trenton. Dark. Poor restaurant where we pay 2$\frac{50}{}$. Then on to Phila. Arrive at 9. Broad Street is torn up. They are building a new subway. Try to get Louise on phone.[5] No go. We stop at The Commodore in 15$\underline{th}$ St. A charming room. Helen has a bad cold. Worries about dying! At 10$\frac{30}{}$ we go out for a late snack. Call up Esherick.[6] He wants us to come on out to Paoli. Helen is too tired. Then to bed.

Wed. Dec 9—1925. Philadelphia. Raining. Helen decides to drive out to the Eshericks. I plan to see Louise & come out after dinner. Breakfast at 18th & Market. Expensive & poor. Helen goes. I call up Louise. She arranges to meet me at her sisters apartment, The Concord—45th & Spruce at noon. Walk about old Philly. 3nd St. Library Street. The quaint old atmosphere. Along Market to Broad Street Station. Call a taxi, get two packages from package room & drive out. Louise very glad to see me. Gets lunch. We go over the

1. M. K. is Maud Karola, who first wrote Dreiser on 6 February 1924, and shortly after became an intimate friend.
   Mame is Dreiser's sister Mary Frances (1861-1944).
2. Maurice Richmond (1880-1965), music publisher and distributor. Richmond was the president of Richmond Music Supply Corporation, which held the distribution rights to a number of Paul Dresser's songs.
3. B. & L. is Boni & Liveright, Dreiser's publisher since 1918.
4. James G. Robin (see p. 381, n. 152). At this time Robin was an editor at the Colony Publishing Co., the firm with which Dreiser was negotiating on behalf of John Milo Maxwell's book on the authorship of Shakespeare's plays.
5. Louise Campbell, who recently had helped Dreiser edit *An American Tragedy*. (see p. 150, n. 7).
6. Wharton Esherick was an artist and a friend of Dreiser, to whom he had been introduced by Kirah Markham in 1924. At that time Dreiser stayed with Esherick and his wife, Letty, at their country home in Paoli, Pennsylvannia.

stuff that needs to be done. Toward 4³⁰ P.M. walk into Philly along Spruce & Chestnut. The size of the U. of P.[7] Enormous. The Christmas shops. We go to a quaint inn. The Pheasant. Louise tells me the story of Laura. Her mother a successful department head in Wanamaker. After dinner we go to the Art Alliance to see an art Exhibit. Then I leave for Paoli. Esherick at the station. Helen a little grouchy because I did not get out to dinner. I have a cold & take a whiskey Toddy. To bed at 11.

Thursday, Dec 10—1925. Paoli—Pa. The Eshericks. His studio. Helen paints a hat. Mary. E presents me with a cane. We go for a walk. The country side. The fox hounds baying down a fox. I cut some wood. A fine dinner before the fire.

Friday, Dec. 11th 1925— Paoli. The Eshericks. Helens attitude toward E. I loaf the day away reading The Diary of a Forty-Niner.[8] Bad cold. Break it by fasting. Cut much wood late in P.M. H. quarreling. To bed at 10.

H. L. Mencken in Baltimore

7. The University of Pennsylvannia.
8. *The Diary of a Forty-Niner* (1906), edited by Chauncey de Leon Canfield (1843–1909).

Saturday—Dec. 12—1925. Paoli. Off for Balto & Washington.
Leave at 9. The run to Balto. Chadds Ford. (I was there in 1897.)
Kennett Sq. (ditto) The charm of Maryland. We cross the
Susquehanna. Havre de Grace. Balto. I wire Komroff.[9] Call on
Mencken. He furnishes me a bottle of booze. His mother is very
ill.[10] On to Washington. Arrive at about 8. Helen & I quarrel. I
threaten to blow the trip & frighten her. We stop at the capitol. I
eat alone in the Union Station at about 11. Still a bad cold.

Sunday Dec 13—1925 Washington. Breakfast at Childs. Try to see
S.S. Peter & Pauls Cathedral. Cold wind blowing. We return &
start for Richmond. Poor character of Virginia country. The towns.
Famous names. Manassas. Chickahominy. Alexandria.
Fredericksburg. The poor sandwiches! Richmond. Scarcely any
towns. Country beautiful & a little sad. We stop at the Richmond.
Six for a room. The southern dialect. Attitude to northerners. A
reserved & repressed town I fear. Helen & I go for a walk after
dinner. Telegraph B & L. To bed about midnight.

Monday. Dec 14— 1925— Richmond. We look it over in the car.
Breakfast in a cafeteria. Helen tells of her Charleston experiences.[11]
Start for Durham N. Carolina. Roads not very good. Petersburg.
Post cards. Helen still a little sick. Cotton & tobacco in fields to
south. We reach So. Hill. The Southern dame who had turned to
boarding house keeping. Two quail. The crowd on the way to
Florida. And from Flushing. A good stove. A nights sound sleep.

Tuesday, Dec. 15—1925. South Hill, N.C. Raining. We start for
Durham & Winston Salem. Fine roads in N.C. Very cold. Oxford!
(The Sunshine City! in a cold rain.) Durham. The American
Tobacco Co. The Washington-Duke Hotel. Also Duke University.

---

9. Manuel Komroff, editor of Liveright's Modern Library series. With Tom Smith, he
was responsible for editing *An American Tragedy* for Boni and Liveright.

10. Mencken's mother died the next day, on 13 December 1925. This visit occasioned
a split in the friendship of the two men. Although they had been increasingly at odds over
literary and philosophical issues since 1916, Mencken took to heart what he saw at the time as
Dreiser's insensitivity to his mother's final illness.

11. Helen's husband, Frank Richardson, was from Charleston; she lived there for some
months before she left him and came to New York in 1918.

Very striking. We stop for sandwiches & a map. Next Greensboro. Marvelous roads. Many mill towns— Cotton. Furniture, tobacco. Greensboro & the O. Henry Hotel. A 14-story office bldg. Life & vigor everywhere. The old south gone. On to Winston-Salem. A breakdown of a truck. A negro rides with us. We fix our car. The Moravians of Winston-Salem. The Robert E. Lee hotel. Another $6 room. Mail from N.Y. A good dinner. We buy Christmas cards & I send off 160 in checks. To bed at midnight. Roosters crowing.

Wed. Dec. 16—1925. Winston-Salem. Gray. Not so cold. Not raining. We breakfast in a southern cafeteria. The look of the town. The R. J. Reynolds Co. The big tobacco markets—The bidding. Two negroes entertaining others—for cash—about the factories. The poor white. The negro boy with two sizes of shoes. Mr. Tramet wont let me in. I post these notes. Theme in the papers. N.C. is discussing 8 as opposed to six months schooling for children if it can afford it. (The good roads.) A restaurant man stages a fight between a rat & a rattler.[12] Greek Restaurant keepers. Southern aliveness as manifested by Chrysler-Maxwell Garage. Dinner in the boarding house next door. Southern. Also factory. In every city one is affected by the living relationship—the exquisite, frail moment of pure conjunctive contact. One senses the life around one, so multiplex & inarticulate—but so moving or devastating. So here. A thousend thoughts, moods, dreams spring up. One wishes this & that. Understands this & that, suspects this & that. But does not know. So here. I am reminded of the mill towns in the north of England.

After dinner we go to Postal Telegraph. I complain, by wire, of mail delay. Then to a movie. Two new movie stars in a high-flown love romance. He blind & a soldier (The Dark Angel). She left behind but united at last. All probabilities have ended of course. A vile little theatre. Then a walk. The fine houses built on tobacco. We return to hotel & to bed.

12. Dreiser clipped a detailed and gruesome account of this event from an unknown newspaper and kept it with the diary. The battle took place over a period of several days, with the rattler eventually killing and swallowing the rat. There are similarities between this newspaper account and the story of the lobster and the squid in Chapter I of *The Financier* (1912).

Thursday. Dec. 17—1925—<u>Winston Salem</u> Cold & raw. We leave
for Columbia South Carolina. Go out the wrong road of course. To
Lexington first—via Elles & Welcome. Small towns—but each with
cotton mills. Fine roads. One can feel this is high ground. Houses
good looking. Schools not bad. Cotton. Tobacco. Lexington a big
mill town. The Yadkin river & bridge. A fine bridge. New & good
houses. Same at China Grove, Landis, Kannapolis where are
enormous mills. One can see Fall River being destroyed. Pretty
girls waving to us as we pass. Same at Concord, Harrisburg &
Newell. Small towns. The sun comes out. We reach Charlotte.
Southern, but commercial. The talkative South Carolinian. We eat
rabbit for lunch. Mills, mills, mills on every hand. Hear of one with
20,000 employes! The bad roads of S.C. are predicted—&
rightly.

Leave Charlotte & go South to Pineville. Big signs urging claims
of different routes. We go via Ft. Mill, Rock Hill, to Chester. Long
detour. Poor cabins like road. <u>Chester.</u> A typical Southern town.
The tin garages. No lock. The business of trying to get the garage
locked. Chicken, buscuit, gravy & molasses. Poor shops. Oil lamps
for sale in most windows. Any amount of corn-cob & wooden pipes
—2 for 5. A typical Arizona hick town. The stage drivers. I read
parts of D. H. Lawrence Essays. Also in An American Tragedy—
which we got at Winston. Nice rooms—2$\underline{^{50}}$ with bath. Bed at
about 10.

<u>Friday, Dec. 18—Chester, So. Carolina</u> The Chester House.
Breakfast in hotel. Typical southern atmosphere. We get all bags.—
we think. Garage not locked after all. We hear of bad roads to
South & are advised to go via Augusta. The man & wife in the Star
Car. The genial oil station man. Pretty fine drive to Augusta. Bright
& not cold. No mill towns to speak of. No paved roads. To
Lexington, to Batesburg, to Laketown, Croft & Aiken. High
ground. Fine views. The inn with the peafowls & palms. We get to
Aiken. Rear left break goes on the bum. Also speedometer. Get
break taken off at Aiken by Negro. Then on into Augusta. Fierce
roads. Swampland. The vegetation grows more tropic. Live Oaks.
Some moss. 12$\underline{^{50}}$ for car repairs. The Richmond Hotel. The fine

restaurant Stubbs (best fried chicken, ever.) I learn about Augusta. Helen & I quarrel over S.K.[13] A bad night.

Saturday, Dec. 19—1925. Augusta Ga. It rains. Hard feelings. How they spoil everything. Breakfast at Stubbs. We go & get the car. Quarrel over charges. Get the bags at hotel. Helen misses brown bag. $400 in dresses gone. We call up Chester. Deny any knowledge there. Go back to garage. No word. To police department. The two detectives. It rains hard. We write to Chester. Also description for police. At 3 P.M. Start out. It rains. A tire picks up a nail. We go back. 1$\underline{00}$ for repairs there. 6$\underline{00}$ for room at Augusta. 12$\underline{50}$ to first garage bag. Helen down & out. We motor on to Waynesboro, Ga. Hellish roads. We nearly mire. A passing car deluges us with mud. We pick up an old house at 6 P.M. It is quite dark. Large rooms. The Heatrola. The talkative landlady. We learn of Florida. The coffee shop. The irritated lady owner. The fierce stores. A warm summer thunder storm. Some flowers—though cold in the A.M. Live oaks. The druggist who explained that Ga. was as good as Florida. Home & to bed. Myself very unhappy, really. Seven trucks going South to Miami with lumber from North Carolina!

Sunday— Dec 20—1925—Waynesboro. Ga I think it is Saturday. We get up & hurry out. Cloudy & cold. The car a sight! We motor to Millen— 21 miles. "You will like Millen". En route we almost mire. The streets of Millen. No restaurant but the dirty Greeks, opposite station. The Southern atmosphere. Arizona to the life. The stores. No oil for sail on Sunday or gas. Churches surrounded by cars! We motor to Sylvania. En route it clears up. Beautiful. The long aisles of pines. Swamps. Live oaks. Trailing moss. We mire. But we get the car out. Scarcely any cars. Cabins & huts en route. Pigs, goats, sheep, chickens, cotten & cane. At Newington Helen chases a little pig in her fur coat. At Sylvania I get oil & gas from a low Greek who admits he is low. All the young life of the town about his place. On to Kildare, Springfield, Rincon. The streets in the towns are the worst of all. The bleeding pine trees.

13. S.K. is Sally Kusell, Dreiser's secretary and mistress.

(Turpentine.) I bleed with them. At last— at 4 P.M.—only 80 miles done we strike a decent road 21 miles from Savannah. Summer at last. A soft wind. Pines, Palms, Dismal Swamps. Bright jays & mockers. We reach Savannah—Negroes. The Desoto. The Hicks hotel. Helen wildly enthusiastic. A good cafeteria. An "odah of Ostahs."[14] A good room. We walk along Main Street & out Bull. No change. The beautiful squares & churches. A good dinner. Negro Street. A negro arrested for offering a white woman 5⁰⁰. The excitement. Prosperity of the Southern negro. He is the only one who works apparently. Beautiful girls. Thoughts as to life. Youth Moonlight

Monday— Dec 21—1925. Savannah Rain, Rain. The little restaurant girl. Been to Philly—once. Patterson just over the river from N.Y. The garage man. Car stuck. Water on generator. Our row. Three white men bossing one Negro at work. The sensual girls always working for someone. I bawl the man out—tell him about garages—about putting a rubber over an engine while washing it. (Generator, carburetor, spark plugs—all wet.) He tells me not to get "hard boiled." Finally stir him to action. He drives us to the De Soto. The flooding rain—almost a cloud burst. Into the old Independent Presbyterian church.[15] (So beautiful.) To P.O. A letter for Helen. To Market to see Negroes. Back to hotel. I catch up on my notes. This hotel is mostly patronized by Southern men—planters—who smoke & chew—and are ungainly & wasp-like & wear ungainly clothes. Finally—at 3 we finally go for the car. Nothing done. Didnt have key. I row again. We take off spark plugs & dry them. Then get a blow pipe & dry the wires. Finally it goes & we get out. On a sign outside was "Washing" Polishing 1⁵⁰. Washing 1⁰⁰. The car was only washed & he charged me—or tried to—1⁵⁰. I called him. A drive to Tybee. The miles of Palms. I think we are out of gas. Back in time for dinner. Afterward we go to get the car fixed. The talkative man in Drayton St. "I'm just going to my lodge now. Come around in the morning. I'm from the North." We put up car. Then go for a walk along the levee. The Savannah

14. Dreiser's rendering of an "order of Oysters" in Southern pronunciation.
15. Dreiser had visited the Independent Presbyterian Church during his stay in Savannah in 1916 (see p. 137, n. 35).

by night. Like Thames & the London of Dickens. The yacht with fruit & flowers on the table. The four-master—suggestive of all the seven seas. We come up, walk into another portion. The old negro with a hat like an East Side Jew washing old clothes in a tub. He cleaned & sold old suits. The various Dickensian houses & people. Mr. Robenstine, his wife & daughter before a rag shop in the evening warmth. Tablets to show that the first iron ship in the world war built here out of plates shipped from Scotland. Also the first steamer that ever crossed the Atlantic was built & launched here in 1819. To bed.

Tuesday, Dec. 22—1925— Savannah. Raining again in the night. The chorous of birds. We decide to get out just the same. Breakfast in Cafeteria. $1.24. We go to the Board of Trade. Go to garage for car. .50 cents. To electrician. Get speedometer & transmission gear fixed. Then to electrician for a light. A nigger is sent to accompany us. He gets 15 cents out of me. .40 cents for a rear light globe. Are told to go via Route 20— Beyond Jencks bridge left turn— Claxton, Reidsville, Glenville, Baxley—Alma. The old huts out of Savannah. Oil & gas. The woods. A colored boy driving an ox cart. The first of the railroad-like road-beds through the pines—straight as an arrow. It grows cold. Threatens a cyclone. Morasses. Moss. Palms. Low unpainted cottages. Convicts in a wagon. We get lost. Wait for convict wagon. Get lost again. I knock at an empty house. The old Southerner on the buckboard. "Go down thar to Pembroke. There you'll be in tech with the best roads. Ask for Colonel Duke." We go toward Pembroke. The saw mill & turpentine camp. We come to a river crossing a road back. The two men in the Ford. "You can go accross. Keep in the middle of the road". We start. The car floats. Thernos Aycock—Brooklet, Ga. Route 1. Jeflison to the life. A long humped nose like Emerson. He gets us out. Is going to Pembroke to see a lawyer. "Me an my Partner. You may not think it to look at me but I'm from the North too. Yes sir. I only come down here two years ago from N. Carolina!" I learn of Crocken Turpentine. "Hit dont hurt the trees. They dont die. No sir. Hit jest stops their growth. They live on for fifteen years". Each tree yeilds $5 a year. 25 a keg for turpentine. How negro help is retained. "Theres a lot in talkin & book-keepin. A nigger he's like this. He buys moren he needs. Mostly you can talk him into it. Once he owes you five he cant git away. Five the law & you can hold him on that fer a year or so." The man with the 500 acres. Contract for $9,000. Talked into it. "We're a goin to get it away from him. Yes sir. Thats what we're agoin to do. We're a goin to see the lawyer. We talked him into signin onto it & now we're goin to make him stick. Fine trees. Worth $8,000 if its worth anything." Morality. "I've been arrested four times for been with women. I been arrested three times for drinkin." Fines 35 to $50. "They dont have nothin to do with any just their own women." All hard shell Baptist. All they know is cotton & corn. Goes to Savannah "over yere" for niggers. 1.50 a day. We get to Pembroke. Then to Groveland. The route to Glenville. The painter who painted the restaurant. The man who wanted a hamburger sandwich for a nickle. "You all want to much." The beautiful woman in the Ford. More pine woods. A fair road. The sky reddens. At dusk we reach Glenville. Decide to stay. Rear end trouble. A Georgia mechanic. The Kennedy house. Terrible rooms & beds. The Moreland House. Better. But so bare & cold. A family living room. A beautiful married daughter from Savannah. A Babel of Tongues. Dreadful stories of rains, wrecked cars. We get frightened. The old man from Sebring. The hot, vain, sensuous, strutting, stuffy girls. Where is the farm girl of twenty years ago. No sewers. No toilets inside. A wonderful dinner for 50 cents. What are the fine parts of Florida. The old man makes plain he is rich. Has picture cards of crocodiles. Why he left Augusta. "I told em we didnt have no divorce in S.C. anyhow. I just thot I'd hit him with that though it wouldnt do no good." Clear & cold outside. The stars. Orions Belt. The feel & mood of a back woods Georgia town. A cold bed in a cold room.

Wed. Dec. 23rd 1925—
Glennville, Geo. A babel of tongues. Are the roads impassable or are they not. We decide that they are. I rise at 6. Walk about the town. The young drug clerk yelling as he came to work. The man dressed. We get car fixed. Speedometer, etc. The young girls of Glennville. The old farm girl has gone. Painted cheeks. Rolled stockings, a bursting sense of sex. Sex mad— beauty mad. Crazy about Florida. The drug store. "The Melody That Made You Mine." Tall pines. Yellow roads. Cheap stores. Jews dealing with

niggers & poor whites. "How do you spell Louise". Arizona—or
Cowboy types. The old man who lived at Sebring at breakfast. The
road out. We get the car fixed. Groceries. Helen buys a pair of
garters & shocks the clerk. More lonely roads through pines. The
little pond. A road built like a railroad bed. The Altamaha River.
Lances bridge. Toll 1.25. Jessup. Lunch. I buy a nut. The country
boys. "Pa wont let me. He'd find me." We cant make up our
minds which road to take. 91 miles to Jacksonville or 130 via
Waycross. Choose Waycross. Only fair road. Four streams to ride
through. The red berries. Screvan. Another long, straight
railroad-like road bed through the Pines. The various swamps.
Moss. Palms. Satilla River. Beautiful reddish marble bridges.
Offerman, Patterson Owen—Blackshear—Waycross—all along the
Atlantic Coast Line. The Hotel Munson. $4 a night. No negro. No
elevator. We stop in a small beanry. Decorating for Christmas "Do
you want 'er twisted." (Referring to color bands of paper.) We
bath, Rest. Out to see Waycross. The other hotel. Moving Picture.
"An Idyl of the Ghetto." The five & ten cent store. Poor stocks.
The Railway Station. Blacks & Whites. The bus lines. The "Nifty"
Caferteria and run by two old sisters. Excellent food. Ham and
"grits". More tourists. We are accosted by a man from Springfield
Mass— just up from Miami. No trouble about rooms. Prices fair.
Florida a bedlam. Too much construction. State Road to
Jacksonville open. Fishing in Flagler Street—Miami. Tents 15 miles
out. St. Petersburg nice. Daytona & Palm Beach best. He expects
to make Augusta—186 miles—in his Chrysler yet tonight! We
return to hotel & discuss the Florida rush. It is too remarkable for
words.

> The man in the automobile
> selling fireworks for
> Xmas

Thursday, Dec. 24— 1925. Waycross, Ga.   In the Munson Hotel.
Frost on all the cars. We dress. Go to the Nifty Caferteria. A man
hands me a Savannah paper. Go back. Car is stalled. We think
water frozen. The thin ice. The boy who finally finds out the
trouble. The wire bracing the ∟   ⌐ is shorting it. Off to the
Maxwell Garage. Southern dubs mechanics. Finally at 10:30 on to
Jacksonville. Waycross a homely town. The Dixie Highway.
Wretched. Goats, sheep, pigs. 21 Buzzards in a flock. We put the

top down. Folkston. Detours of the day before. St. Marys River. 25 cents each to get out. Floor-eye-day. A good road all the way into Jacksonville. The seepy ground. Jacksonville. We go right through. 18 cents to get over the bridge. A hot dog place with hot dogs for a dime despite all the reports. The Road to St. Augustine. San Jose. Frank Croissant[16]—"Crossantania. My Masterpeice" signed Frank Croissant, Architect. The mixture of good & bad roads to St Augustine. Roadside water. The distroyed pier. Much building. Lots $294. We reach St. Augustine. 1st impressions. Old defensive gate. The fort built by the Spaniards. The P.O. Old governors place. Mail. Letters from Louise, Kussell, Liveright, Petronelle.[17] She wants me to come to France & live with her. The house in San Marco St. An Englishman. A room for 2.50. 25 cents extra for an oil stove. 25 cts extra for a bath. Room to be vacated by noon. The old gent wouldnt give one N.Y. for 50 St. Augustines though his wife likes it. We wander down the principal narrow street, ⌐   ⌐ to Western Union. The crowd of helpers. Where are the Floridians? I inquire of one quaint old hotel for rooms. It is being run by Kykes. Another by New Englanders. Helen gets her bag back. Excitement. Dinner at a cafeteria. Host & hostess drunk. "Were going to have cocktails! Not around the world for nothin." 45 years with a circus & without a bath. We walk around the town. A man from Eastport Maine. Clerk in a hotel. Colder down here than he ever was in Eastport. "All of Georgia is down here but two & theyre up there trying to fix up the roads". Basketball between Nashville & the Y.M.C.A. A negro section. Where are the poor negroes? Churches. Smart shops. Good clothes. A gay life. The Alcazar! The colored fountain. The Ponce-de-Leon—not even open yet. A worth while Presbyterian & Baptist church. The dog, the bone & the sandwich. Home & too bed.

Friday Dec. 25 —1925— Christmas. St. Augustine Florida

A California morning. Warmer. Blue birds. Poincianas. A red roof. We get up & eat at 9.30. French pancakes—nit. The Alcazar— Ponce-de-Leon by day. Palms. Florida better than Calif. It has

---

16. G. Frank Croissant (1887–1956), land developer. In 1924 Croissant bought one hundred acres near Fort Lauderdale and developed it into Croissant Park, a project that made him a fortune.

17. Petronelle Sombart (see p. 167, n. 43).

Horace Liveright (1886–1933) was publisher of *An American Tragedy.*

warmth, tropic vegetation & plenty of water. Greater hotels. I never saw such hotels anywhere. We visit old Spanish fort. Back to room. Pack & leave. Ride out to Fountain of Youth. A chance sign directs us. The lady who is in danger from Principalities & Powers. Poisoned by watermelon. Poisoned by gas! Poisoned by Cocoa-Cola. Garilla—a great writer. The new Messiah is to land at the Fountain of Youth. Two millions of rare documents in her house. The Church! Baptistry. Fountain. We drink. Society for Conservation of American Women. England plotting with India to rule world. Broke Germany. Now finance will rule through religion. Great plots—Very old. Her odd cane. We get away. Ride down. I write these notes sitting on a stone wall looking at the water & hearing the gulls squeak. We ride around St. Augustine. Negro quarter. Oldest house. A cocoa-cola. The sailor who had been down to the South Seas. Kusaie, Easter Island. Phillipines. Luzon. The Hessian fly. Spitting cobra—grass or ribbon snake. Moving picture man. Drug stores not open here on Sunday. The hotel opposite the Alcazar. Jews. Room with two beds $14 per day without board. No elevator. No telephone. No push button. Walk through three rooms to get to floor above. We ride out to beach. Cars run up & down sand. Real Estate schemes everywhere. Four or five here. "Davis Shores", "Santa Roses", "A Residential Masterpiece". Gates usually—and then signs— Or chalk marks showing lots. It turns grey. We come back to the Doreta. Room without a telephone, push button or heat 6$\frac{00}{}$ for the night. No elevator. Stay in six. Go round to Cafeteria. A Xmas dinner was to have been served. Drunkeness shut it up. And all the moral signs tacked over the place. We dine at another place. Go to the Alcazar & listen to the music. The clerk of the Doreta tells of Southern life. 1000 carpenters leave Miami in 1 day for want of work. Ditto 600 plumbers. A man killed for stealing two loaves of bread. No trade wanted. "We sell sunshine down here." His interest in curing & packing mullet & some other fish. A good as salmon. To bed.

Saturday, Dec 26 —1925—St. Augustine, Fla. Clear. Bright. We go to the cafeteria. The old showman is back on the job—much the worse for wear. To the express office. Helens bag not likely to be here for a week. The Constant line at the P.O. General Delivery.

No boxes for rent. We visit the old fort. (See cards.) Back to hotel
& pack. These notes. Then out on Dixie Highway. No towns. Poor
road in part. Warm. The through buses to Coral Gables. Palms in
groves. The Old Engine. A town site for sale, Hotel & all. "Wilson
Street." "Roosevelt Street." Water & bare fields. We arrive at
Hastings. A few shacks like Folkston, Ga. Next Bunnell. A beanry.
Food cheap so far. The realtor from Orlando. Tells of
developments around this town. What can be grown. Tobacco, rice,
sugar. Mentions a new 100-mile drive from St. Augustine to
Orlando & Daytona. Tells of hotel scenes in August in Miami.
Developments without houses. Street signs Roosevelt St. Wilson St.
We go into Daytona along Halifax river? Jungles of Palms. Men
fishing. We enter Daytona. Not impressed at first. Copying Calif.
Then we see waterfront business street. I buy a bolt for the car.
Helen greatly impressed. We take a room at the Ridgewood.
8$\underline{00}$ per night. A charming hotel. Next to "Luthers" to eat. After
that a walk. Tired. Where to put the car. Leave it out.

Sunday, Dec. 27— 1925. Daytona, Fla. A California morning.
Sunlight like gold. Warm. We go to a good restaurant. Then walk
on the beach. Yachts from everywhere. Wild ducks & gulls. We
feed them. Get the car & put top down. Someone took a bolt
holding the bumper. To Dixie highway. A new cemetery. How
made. Piling sand in a swamp. Back to Orlando Beach. 14 cents to
get across. 27 miles of Sand Boulevard. We see a man drive his car
in the water. A Scotch garage man from Schenectady. Land values.
$5,000 a front foot for beach lots. Two to three thousend a front
foot for town lots. No sewerage. Cesspools. $250. rent for a
garage. Workingmen 60 per cent of what they earn. He makes
$100 a week clear. Booze 12 a quart at Xmas. $4 a bottle other
times—and plentiful. We return to Daytona. Dine at Caltanea's.
Telegram to N.Y. Telegraph man tells of business. More to square
miles in Fla. than anywhere else in U.S. Park car. I read in "A
Young Girls Diary."[18] Write letter to Karola. Petronelle, Gas Co.,
Bank, etc.

18. *A Young Girl's Diary* by Grete Lainer Von Lainsheim.

Monday Dec 28—1925— Daytona Fla. Cold—very. We get up at 10. Buy bolts. Vicks, cold cream. Stamps. I give Helen fifty. Car to garage man in Ormond. Couldnt fix. On to De Land. The various developments in 15 miles. About 20. Textile City. Plans grand. Nothing done. Volusia County farm lands. We reach De Land. Take car to be fixed. 4$\underline{00}$ for a room without heat or bath. We finally pay 3$\underline{00}$. Loaf about. See Thomas Meighan in Officer Donahue. To bed. Bright moon. Very cold. Orions Belt straight ahead. 11.95 for car repairs. 11 for a Florida license.

Tuesday, Dec. 29—1925. De Land Fla. Warmer. Bright. Breakfast at the White House Cafe. 70 cents. Get front fender fixed. To Eustis. Beautiful road. St. Johns River. Steamer of Jacksonville. Black water. The Blue Heron—Eustis. Mt. Dora and Lake Apopka (The Fern City.) Royella. The men at Eustis. Eustis Lake. 200 miles to Jacksonville by water. Mr. Callahan. He describes middle central Florida conditions. Car 2$\underline{00}$ to fix. (It breaks next day). The lakes of this region. Land subdivisions. Oranges in plenty. Orlando. 25,000. Six or seven lakes in the city. The San Juan Hotel. The Angbilt. (What a name.) We dine. On by moonlight to Mt. Dora, Tavares (a charming court house), Leesburg. Lakes on either hand. The black shadows cast by the moon. 25 miles to Mt. Dora. 6 to Tavares. 12 1/2 to Leesburg—45 to Ocala.—90 all told & we arrive at 10 oclock. Vile hotels! No heat! No private bath. Yet 5$\underline{00}$ per night! The conference in the lunch counter over hot milk! All Floridians are honest. Its the outsiders who are the crooks. To bed at 11.

Wed. Dec. 30—1925 — Ocala, Florida Up & out of Ocala at 9$\underline{30}$. Gas & oil $2.55. Long road to Palatka. About 60 miles. Citra. Hawthorne. I see a red bird. Fine pine groves—all bleeding. The Kaolin bed east of Hawthorne. It is raining. Palatka. The cafteria. The real estater. A tire blows up. No tire under 28 in the town. Put on the spare. The extra tire rack breaks. I think of soldering it on. We get to Hastings. Then to St. Augustine. Express Office. No bag for Helen. To P.O. No letters except two from M.K. We get laundry. Take a room at the Doreta. I buy a tire for 20\underline{00}$. To the telegraph office. To the negro laundry. To the Alcazar. To a restaurant. The band in the public square. I send S.K. a telegram.

Trouble with Helen at once. We return to hotel. Angry—I go downstairs in lobby & I read M.K.s letters. Post these notes. Still cloudy but not raining. Travel with rain & car trouble & a lost bag is not so much.

Thursday, Dec 31—1925— St. Augustine, Fla Helen still sore. We dont speak. Dress & go to wretched restaurant in oldest street. Cakes & ham. The tourists who expect to see St Augustine in 30 minutes. To the Western Union. 2 telegrams from Chester, S.C. Cost $1.42. Havent even sent back. Great trouble. One message back. Cost .72 cts. We decide to leave St. Aug. for Fort Lauderdale. Go & take car to be fixed. He agrees to have it ready by 3 P.M. Cost $7⁰⁰. Leave it. Go & see about getting laundry at 3. Negro life here. "Lincoln City". Laundry will be ready. Back to Alcazar Court to rest. Helen angry, leaves to get shoe fixed. I sit till 2. Go to Charlies in oldest street. Hot dogs & coffee. The Mexican proprietor & his Florida girls. To room. H & I go for car. It is ready. Go for laundry. It is ready. Go to hotel. Get bags. No negro to carry anything out. "On at four". We leave for Daytona. No hardware store. At Hastings (20 miles) buy bolts. The negro & his green crops. On to Daytona. It gets warmer. Moon comes up. Dinner in Daytona Cafeteria. Drive to New Smyrna. The Palms Hotel. The hotel keeper from Baltimore. He tells of climate. 88 all summer. Summer 8 months long. Heavy rains. Okeechobee overflows its banks. Norwesters rock coasts. Rush began June 1— 1925. Nothing before then. 1300 real estaters in Daytona in September. But a few now. Long heat is wearing. Plenty of money being made. He is getting rich. No New Year bells or whistles here.

+

Friday, Jan 1—1926. New Smyrna, Fla The Palms hotel. The Indian River. We walk down to it. Pelicans fishing. Wild ducks. Porpoises. Beautiful flowers. Warm & delightful. To a cafeteria. Nothing but ham & eggs. The thirty alligators owned by a plumber. The shore road to Titusville. More developments! A blue crane. A palm jungle. More Pelicans. We come to Oak Hill. A sugar cane mill. We get off & go in. "Pull it Don. Pull it." Don

WESTERN UNION TELEGRAM

562MZ 32 BLUE

NEWYORK NY 617P DEC 31 1925

THEODORE DREISER 656
GEN DLY FTLAUDERDALE FLO

DEAR DREISER I THINK IT IS GOING TO BE A HAPPY NEW YEAR FOR US
AN AMERICAN TRAGEDY HAS STARTED BRAVELY STOP I WISH YOU WERE HERE
TONIGHT TO CELEBRATE WITH US
HORACE LIVERIGHT
717P

Horace Liveright Telegram Reporting on the Tragedy

was a horse. The bees. Florida crackers. We drink fresh cane juice. Are given a bottle of marvellous cane syrup. Air plants. Mistletoe. Oranges. Grapefruits. Orchards. Grapefruit brings 2$\underline{00}$ a box. Oranges ditto. Lots here—650. Crackers coining money. They know the price of rooms in Miami. Palms 60 feet high. One cracker tent. A free lunch. Wild hogs. Wild deer. On to Titusville. More developments. A dead cow. The "causeway" to De Soto Beach. Blue & white cranes. Beautiful. Crested woodpeckers? Plenty of fish. The Beauty of the Indian River. Carleton Terrace. Well developed. California stuff. Cocoa. An old Fla. Hick town, Rockledge. Nothing there. Valencia. Nothing at most developments. Eau Gallie. Indian river hotel. We arrive at Malabar. A room for 3$\underline{50}$. Its wretchedness. I post these notes. Sit out & look at stars & moon. The beauty of the night here. Wild ducks.

Saturday, Jan 2—1926— Malabar. This was a series of rooms along the shore—with a lunch counter attached. The fine, sanitary arrangements. No bath. A small tin bowl. 3$\underline{00}$. On at about 9. A fine, clear day. Valkyrie, Micco, Rossland, Sebastian, Wabasso, Reams, Vero. The usual land development schemes. "You are now entering"— Then only signs & street names. But Vero! The bright shops & houses. We breakfast there. I cash a check. Have a talk with the owner of the Vero Gardens. "Come & help us make a town". She had only been there a month. The husband looked like Wilson Mizner.[19] Oslo. Indrio! The signs all the way down. Not a thing there but horses & wagons grading streets. St. Lucie. We stop on the shore & see them making orangade. Below there are cranes fishing. The fish leaping out of the water—for joy in sun, only to be snapped up by gulls & cormorants. The new, big red flower. Ft. Pierce. (Very cheap.) We do not go to Okeechobee. Eldred. Ankona, Waveland. (Where four presidents fished.) Picture City. Nothing there. We stop & eat sardines & grape fruit. Kelsey City. Palm Beach. The noise & bustle. Smallness of streets. Roar of trucks. We cross the St. Lucie navigation canal to Palm Beach proper. The fine stores The general beach. Unable to find the great hotels at first. Ride down the coast. Return & finally stop at the El Verano. 12$\underline{00}$ per night. We are really opposite a general East coast bus depot. The noise. A wretched restaurant with high prices & no menu worth a dam. To bed.

Sunday, Jan 3rd 1926— Palm Beach, Fla Cloudy, warm morning. Helen picks gray hairs out of my eyebrows. I change to a light gray suit. Post these notes. This is a poor hotel in the matter of cleanliness. Plan—rather charming. We get out about 10^{30} for breakfast. An excellent cafeteria. To garage for my cane. Then ferry over to Palm Beach proper to see the hotels. The small, crowded ferry boat. The Royal Poinciana. Very large—very old. In the best style of the great old hotels. North & South two new ones in modern style. No grounds—no vistas, no verandahs. No seeming love of out door beauty. All in door grandioseness. Shops & show all about. The Royal Daniello. Rates 30 to 50 per day for two. We walk to Ocean. New kind of sea life. A blue ∟　 ⌏ . Many jelly fish. The gay parasols & chairs. Back to Royal Poinciana. A walk around. Then to the El Verano. Lunch. Our car locked in the

19. Wilson Mizner (1876–1933), playwright, author. Mizner married the widow of Charles T. Yerkes, the original for Dreiser's character Cowperwood. In 1926 Mizner took part in the Florida land boom as the director of the Mizner Development Corporation, the firm that developed Boca Raton.

garage for the day! We walk about. The better state of negros. Greeks & Italians here. Arcades. Due to heat. Brash, eager sensuous, restless young America. Sabbath work & all hotels & buildings! Styles up to the minute. Prices low. Cocoanuts that fell in the street. White yachts in blue water. Great Honey colored hotels rising above green palms. I meditate on life & work. Sigh for N.Y. At five we try for car! Not open! At 6 we get it. A row! Pay out at hotel & take road for Ft. Lauderdale. The sea side road at night. Rain! Stars. A delicious run. The hotel at Delray. We find the Los Olas at Ft. Lauderdale. Senator Watsons old home.[20] The sea. Palms. Moonlight. A wonderful room. A delightful nights rest.

Monday, Jan 4—1925. Ft. Lauderdale, Fla The Las Olas Inn. Sun over the sea at dawn. A fresh window. We bath & breakfast here. To P.O. We picked this to avoid a P.O. rush & there is a queu a half a block long! No mail. All mail two to three weeks late! Helen in despair. We breakfast. Return to Los Olas. A row because I suggest returning to N.Y. Decide to drive on to Miami. The moving developments here. A new Venice! Sea land lots $12,000 each. And thousands of houses representing 50 to $100,000 invested. The giant excavating cranes. Digging canals. For the first time in America I see cities being built to a plan! A lesson to U.S. The quest for beauty. It will remake America! The high spirits of everyone. Dania. New street lights. Business Lots 25,000. We see Hollywood. Enormous hotel. A smaller one opening just this day. The stranded boat. The negroes work by song! Another development just below! Fifty white & blue cranes in one pond. Hallandale, Fulford, Ojus, Miami Shores. To Miami City. A wretched road of shacks & gas stations & camps & junk & garages —with millions being spent on the seaside everywhere. Enormous canal to Okeechobee! The city proper! The camps. Great buildings. Helen buys a dress, hat & stockings at Burdines. I buy stockings. A bit of lunch. Then to Miami Beach. Helen gets greatly excited. We drive out to Deauville & back. More city planning. The paradise of

20. Thomas E. Watson (1856–1922), populist politician, author, editor, senator from Georgia, and vice-presidential candidate for the People's Party in 1904 and 1908. In 1905 he founded in New York *Tom Watson's Magazine* (later called *Watson's Magazine*) which published Dreiser, Masters, and Gorky, among others.

the western world. The contrast with California. Here wealth builds. Out there is the world of moderate means. A quick run back. We arrive at nine. To bed at 10.

Tuesday, Jan 5, 1926—Ft. Lauderdale, Fla Las Olas Inn. Up at dawn for a dip. Spend over an hour in sea. The warmth of sands & water. Sunrise! Gulls. I talk with a carpenter. This inn to be replaced by a $2,000,000 structure at once! Negroes in vans riding to work & singing. To P.O. A bundle of mail. Helen buys a belt. Get car cleaned. The car-cleaning man from Seattle & Texas. Proposes to live on Long Island. Man is now at last as free as birds. This man works in Texas oil fields in summer—here in winter. Tells me of boom in Seattle & Long Beach Calif. Cleans car beautifully. Tells me of new method of painting them. I send two telegrams. Helen grouchy. Return here & read mail. S.L. fails to see any great value in new book.[21] I read all mail. Post these notes. Wrote some letters. We go into city for lunch. Ride through cheaper development of Ft. Lauderdale. Cute houses at about $5,000. The colors. Get back into same road leading out here. I read. Go for a walk up beach—The stars over the sea. Music & dancing in the small pavilion. Return & find Helen sitting outside alone. At midnight Helen decides to make up.

Wednesday, Jan 6—1926—Las Olas Inn, Ft Lauderdale, Fla. Up at sunrise & into the sea. The ship. Gulls. 5 pelicans. The water warm. Bathers. We dress & go down town to breakfast & P.O. Helen buys a yellow hat—for $8. No mail. No bag. We ride out to Seminole Indian camp. South Sea Island type of hut. Colors suggest same. Fly bitten deer meat. An accordian, a victrola. Ironing board. Oil lamps. Still cooking in a pot over the fire. Dirt, no baths. Disgusting. Come back. Park car. Decide to go on New

---

21. Sinclair Lewis, who did not like *An American Tragedy* and refused to review it. Dreiser is probably reading a letter from Tom Smith, the editor at Boni & Liveright who sent Lewis proofs of the novel and received a negative response. Dreiser likely expected Lewis's reaction. On 4 November 1925, Dreiser had written Mencken, complaining about the state of the proofs that Smith had sent to Lewis (and to Mencken): "This is not fair to me. Those very proofs have since been cut and revised in such a way as to eliminate many weaknesses. If the book is to be read for criticism it should be read from the final page proofs which should be available in about a week."

River-Everglades boat trip. It leaves at 2 P.M. The houses on new river. The Morang Canals. The Sound. Lake Mabel. Quarrel between Hollywood & Morang. Tom Taggart.[22] Why are so many Indianians here? The Flagler canal. Banyan beer. The Dania Canal. Looking for alligators. Cranes. Great derricks. In 1910 drainage of Okeechobee by canals begun. Okeechobee having no outlet made Everglades. Now being drained. Glades are commonplace farm lands. Trees growing up. An alligator. A 15,000,000 electric plant near by. The Dania Canal gives places to new river canal. Real swamps. Floating hyacinths. Cranes. The new river again. A great floating crane comes up. Old boats sunk. Royal Palms. Where Joe Jefferson fished back in 1900.[23] Ross Clarks Place. A great yacht dock miles up stream. Beautiful houses with yachts anchored at shore. Safe Southern waters. We get back at 5$\frac{30}{}$. Return to Las Olas. Then down for dinner. Real Estate officer giving lectures to music. A furniture store giving a concert. The beach & a swim & to bed. Thousands of real estaters.

Thursday, Jan 7—1926 Las Olas Inn Fla Up at Sunrise. Wonder of sea here. Water perfectly still. Sands at bottom clear. At nine we start for down town. Car trouble. Mr. Collins. A proposed trip to Miami with him. A change of plans. Breakfast at the Glades. The waitress from N.Y. who is going to start a tea room. Two letters. One from Louise. One from S.K. We start for Miami. Hollywood Inn. I read S.K.'s letter. On to Miami by Biscayne Bay road. Mir-a-Mar district. Over the cause way. Looking for Frank Richardson. Oil man who didnt know where Coral Gables were. Had only been here 3 days. On to Atlantic shores in search of Boca Raton. Chisholm & Richardson. Beautiful hotels. B.M.T. Roney. Taline Brothers. Golden Shores. We return to Miami. Mad beauty of Biscayne Bay side of Miami. Distant view of Miami. We inspect a house. The weak roof. On to Coral Gables. Miami crowds & cars. Administration Bldg of Gables. Feel of air. Tall Pines. A hotel— with typical westerners in it. A proposed dancing club. A theatre.

22. Thomas Taggart, Jr. (1886–1949), a businessman and the son of Senator Thomas Taggart of Indiana.
23. Joseph Jefferson III (1829–1905), actor, producer. Jefferson is mentioned several times in Dreiser's *Sister Carrie.*

Many houses. A hot dog. We return to Miami. Flagler St. A furniture store. More real estate offices with lectures & orchestras. And crowded. On over causeway to Atlantic Shores. Beauty of night. Hollywood. A new road into Lauderdale. Home at 9$\underline{30}$ dead tired & to bed.

Friday, Jan 8—1926— Las Olas Inn, Fla Sunrise. Fawn colored gray clouds tipped with pink—an electric blue-gray sky above. Green-blue waters below. We get up & plunge into sea. An old dying dog. Breakfast here. Mr. Collins arrives. We decide not to go. Walk to inlet in rear. Hibiscus. I post these notes. First letters about the book—Ficke.[24] Et alia. I get all the special edition papers to sign.[25] We start for Boca Raton. The fan belt causes trouble. Florida congestion according to newspapers—31 ships of Miami unable to unload. It begins to rain. Boca Raton. Not a thing of all the advertised stuff except an inn and a few paved streets and some unattractive looking homes. Back to Lauderdale by the main road. No cheap lots anywhere. Beach lots 17,500 & up. Look at various subdivisions. North Lauderdale. Its all growing. Dine at the Glades cafe. Rent $30,000 a year. Very few customers. Dinner poor. Home & I sign first bunch of special editions & to bed early. Its cold & raining hard.

Saturday—Jan 9— Ft. Lauderdale It clears off in the morning & we decide—after breakfast down town, to go to Miami. But before going write various letters. Leave for Miami about noon. The fan belt breaks. We go to the Maxwell company in Miami. Then on to Coral Gables. Rain. The Venetian Pool at last. The Miami-Biltmore and Country Club. The old Spanish church. Beauty, age, romance made to order & sold at so much a lot. It gets dark. Back to town. See a working man knocked down by a Ford which escapes. I go to the man. Raining hard. Dine in a wretched restaurant. Attend a Hollywood real-estate lecture. The history of Florida. Chisholm & Richardson. Home in the rain. This trip is boresome to me.

---

24. Arthur Davidson Ficke (1883–1945), lawyer, poet, novelist.
25. Leaves for the limited signed issue of *An American Tragedy* were mailed to Dreiser for his signature. They were later bound into the special copies of the book.

<u>Sunday, Jan 10—1926—Ft. Lauderdale</u> It rains all day. Stay in bed till 1$\underline{30}$. Get up and go down to the Glades. A poor meal. Trouble with the engine but fix it. On up the coast to look at the 5,500 lot. Like it. Back & to a moving picture. <u>A Kiss for Cinderella.</u> Very poor & silly. Home & to bed.

<u>Monday Jan 11—1926 — Ft. Lauderdale</u> Up at nine. Cold but clear. Feel wretched. Down town for breakfast. Finish signing special edition. A walk on the shore. Decide to paint car & do—all the rusty spots. Wretched days with someone I really dont care to be with. Fix packages & take down town. P.O. closed. A line a mile long at General Delivery. We give up & eat at the Brower. A wretched dinner. See <u>Phantom of the Opera.</u> Fair. Home & to bed. Cold. But promises to be clear tomorrow.

<u>Tuesday, Jan 12—1926 Ft. Lauderdale</u> Fair & warmer. Shave. A telegram from S.K. saying book has sold 17,000. A letter from M.K. Breakfast here. Go to P.O. & mail packages. 2 $\underline{35}$ charges. To P.O. no mail. Buy a can of car paint. Decide to leave for Florida City & Royal Palm 40 miles below Miami. I post these notes. Write some letters. We start. Coast route Miami. Coral Gables.

Thursday[26]—Jan. 12

  Drove down from Ft. Lauderdale to and through Miami on way to Coral Gables and Homestead. Helen stopped to ask at stand about man. He had not been killed. Only 3 ribs broken. Was in hospital. Then through Coral Gables on to Homestead. Nicest stretch of road anywhere since road leading into Vero. Clean stretch of beautiful pines and no buildings. Subdivisions continue to Homestead—40 miles south of Miami. Dismal swamp described as extending from Perrine 110 miles South and 45 miles across. Florida City—Homestead: Local hotel has no heat. The N.Y. jew running a restaurant and selling lots in his own subdivision 400 miles north at Ocala. Here—as elsewhere, everyone a stranger to the country. We return to Coral Gables. Stopping to warm up by a forest fire. <u>La Reine</u> Hotel. Stone floors and iron balustrades after Spain and Italy. No heat—no bath tubs. Only joint showers. Walls

26. The passage "Thursday ... Helen writes my notes." at 438.20–439.33 is in Helen's hand.

of paper. 9$\underline{^{00}}$ a day. Main topic of conversation throughout lobby—hog raising. To bed to keep warm.

<u>Wed.</u> Jan 13—1926. Coral Gables—Fla. The La Reine Hotel. I am sick and stay in bed until 2 P.M. Helen goes to buy drugs and orders lunch served in room. Bright and warm outside but room remained cold. We walk around Coral Gables. What is the matter with Coral Gables? A cut and dried commercial proposition. Poetry and art manufactured to order. The mass told how and what to do. Woman asking for a party. Clerk told her to look in the patio. Woman guest goes out and returns shortly from patio. Asks clerk where she had been told to look and the clerk says "Why—right there—in that open space." The General Delivery line here as well as elsewhere. We start for Lauderdale. The long negro street. The Biscayne Bay development. Teatro _____. A detour to Dania. A 5 ton sugar truck wrecks a bridge. Back to Las Olas about 9 P.M. Same room. Very cold.

<u>Thursday</u> —Jan 14—26. Las Olas Inn. Had breakfast at Inn. Went down town to Ft. Lauderdale. Walked both ways. 4 miles. Stopped to look at fish catch at the little inlet. Large sail fish weighing 57 lbs. length 7 feet. The attendant in charge informs us that Zane Grey caught the largest one on record in lower California in Pacific.[27] 135 lbs. Not edible or good for any use. He also tells us how they kill their food with long sword by going into a school of fish and hitting to the right and left—then eating the fish at its leisure. The rainbow made by spray of water. We buy fishing lines and hooks and fish off bridge but catch nothing. I come home to tie up finger and write letters. About 5 P.M. we go to Chinese restaurant for tea. On return past fishing point we again see two more beautiful sail fish dead. We walk out on beautiful point—inlets on both sides. Light on the water. Beautiful sky. Palms outlined against sky. Strong suggestion of tropics. Harmonious—quiet—soothing. Nature! Home to chicken dinner. I to bed to get warm. Helen writes my notes.

---

27. Zane Grey (1875–1939), novelist. Grey was noted for his success at deep-sea fishing and for many tales based on his adventures as a fisherman. He is remembered today as a writer of Western stories.

Friday—Jan 15—1926—Ft. Lauderdale Breakfast down town. Buy fishing tackle. Fish. Later swim. It is warmer. In the evening see Hoot Gibson whom Helen says looks like me in a vile cowboy movie.[28] To bed at 11 P.M.

Saturday—Jan 16—1926— Ft. Lauderdale Warmer. We swim in sea at dawn. Very fine. Breakfast here. Very bad & very expensive. Decide to go to Lake Okeechobee & Tampa—(the latter maybe). Leave at 1 P.M. Up coast to Lake Worth & accross through a town called " ⌞   ⌟ " to Connors Okeechobee road. A good road 53 miles long— along the Lake Worth-Lake Okeechobee Canal. Toll 2$\frac{00}{}$. Loxahatchee! Industrial City! Canal Point. Hoppin' John. Helen plays a slot machine & wins 3 times running. Sugar Cane fields & a sugar refinery. Lake Okeechobee! A primal world. Wild ducks. Game. We go on towerd Okeechobee City. A blow out. 2\frac{10}{}$ & 2 hours to patch a tire. A native Floridian. (God what types.) Evening on the lake. Waterfowl in profusion. The shell like beauty of it all. End of Connors highway. We reach Okeechobee! High priced hotel. We try an auto camp. 2$\frac{50}{}$ for a room without conveniences of any kind. A restless night.

Sunday, Jan 17—1926. Okeechobee, Fla Because of impossibility of getting new tire on Sunday we decide to return to Ft. Lauderdale. Up at 7 & on our way. Beauty of lake in A.M. Soft, spring like quality. Eagles, heron, owls, red birds, ducks, cranes, mud hens—a great variety— Travelers in cars with guns. We arrive at canal. Here of drowning of one—maiming of two. (Steering gear of a car broke precipitating all in canal.) Back to Industrial City. The fine car of four drunks in ditch. West Palm Beach. A good breakfast. We buy a tire 25\frac{00}{}$. The man from Hermosa Beach. We compare California & Florida. He is going back. On down coast. Sunday crowds. We get to the short run on the dirt road above the light. From peace to difficulties & danger. Stuck. Bad feeling among motorists. Every man for himself. Out safely. On to Lauderdale. A swim in sea after dark. Down town to principal Cafe. The music. We return. To bed.

28. Edward "Hoot" Gibson (1892–1962), American cowboy star of silent films.

Monday, Jan 18—1926. Ft. Lauderdale. Up late. 10 A.M. Swim in sea. Very beautiful. Helen is going down to Miami. Breakfast at Glades. I see her off. Make trip on boat around Lauderdale Isles. A $16,000 dollar lot. Cant get up any enthusiasm. Back to room. Big bunch of mail. Many fine letters about book. A love note from Fermor. Decide to write her & K.[29] Helen returns. Comments on my writing. A quarrel. Bad night. We go down town to noisy restaurant.

Tuesday, Jan 19, 1926— Ft. Lauderdale Rose late. Swim in sea. Clear & balmy. Afterwards to stores for various things—scissors— suit to be pressed, laundry etc. A big bundle of mail—Wilder[30]— Fermor, etc The high cost of laundry. To Glades Cafe where I had a wretched chicken-liver omelet. (Made with some disgusting cooking oil which made me sick.) Afterwards read mail. Much applause from many cities. To Las Olas Inn. Then up walk to small stand for a hot dog. Then we walk to Lauderdale by Sea. Beautiful day. 1st sail ship seen on this coast. The nature of the natural vegetation here—hardy plants that clatter & rattle in the wind. Palmettos, cactus— We lie on sand at Lauderdale By Sea. The woman with the French bull. He misbehaves by paying attention to us. Stinggrees dead on shore. We walk back. Convicts on road. Meaninglessness of stripes & chains in these days. Too many crooks on the outside. We take a dip in sea. Warmth of water. New moon. We decide to go down town to see an Elks show in a bit. But deciding to lie down for a few moments before, we fall asleep & do not wake until 10^{30}. Then retire for good.

+

Thursday, Jan 21—1926— Ft. Lauderdale, Fla Sea bath. New restaurant out on Dixie. Chops & coffee—$2 bucks. Go back into town. Tell real estater deal on lot is off. Home. I paint car. Local book store man & asst-cashier 1st national bank arrive to congratulate me on book (An American Tragedy). Tell me of

29. K. is Kirah Markham (see p. 117, n. 1).
30. George Wilder, who hired Dreiser as chief editor of the Butterick Publishing Co. in 1907.

Wildwood & Bayou tree. They go & Helen & I go to see
Wildwood. Enormously impressed. Bananas growing in bunches.
The bayou. A field of cabbages. A row of Royal Palms. We walk
about. I crack a old stale cocoanut. Lapwings flying over fields.
Farming in Florida impresses me. We talk about the meaning of the
soil. Back to Las Olas. Dinner there. The girl who had been to
Australia. To bed.

Friday, Jan 22—1926—Ft. Lauderdale Into Lauderdale. Breakfast
in the Shelley breakfast shop. Send telegram to Sat. Eve. Post.
Change 50 at bank. See the asst cashier. Decide to take lot & pay
200. Go to Miami to see Deering Estate. On south to Royal Palms
& pretty inlet. Back to Miami to fix car. Proposed charge 75$\underline{00}$. We
dine at the Royal Palm. Florida crawfish! Out Dixie to Ft.
Lauderdale & to bed. S.E.P. refuses Florida article.[31]

Saturday—Jan 23 — — 1926. Ft. Lauderdale Breakfast at Shelley.
The womans troubles. Pier at 90 cents. We decide to leave for
N.Y. Go out & pack. To Miami. Clyde liner gone. We catch
Kroonland.[32] Fares for car & us two $200. Put car on board. Go to
W$\underline{m}$ Penn Inn, Miami Beach. $14 per day for a room. Dine in the
Congo Dining room. Gay Florida Plate Dinner for two 6$\underline{00}$. We sit
outside. Visit the Fleetwood. Yachts. Jazz. I frighten a rat. To bed.

Sunday. Jan 24— 1926. Miami Beach W$\underline{m}$ Penn Inn. Breakfast in
a small tea room. 50 cents to sit an hour in a chair by the sea. The
character of Miami Beach. Back to hotel. I wire the World. Very
hot. Bath. Sit below. Smart jewesses. Miami life. To boat at 2$\underline{30}$.
Two dollars to ride 3 blocks. The Sheenie code. Comments by
passengers on Miami. Out to the Kroonland. I see a meteor fall. A
cross-eyed man. A man loses a bag overboard. Berth 343. Dinner
at seats 14–15—Table 9. Sit out on deck. Bright moon. Very warm.
The belt. To bed.

---

31. "S.E.P." is the *Saturday Evening Post.* Dreiser's article, entitled "This Florida Scene,"
was eventually published in two installments in *Vanity Fair* 26 (June 1926): 43, 98, 100; and
26 (July 1926): 63, 94, 96.
32. Dreiser had sailed on the *Kroonland* before. On his return from Europe in 1912, he
had switched at the last moment from the *Titanic* to the *Kroonland.*

Monday, Jan 25—1926—At sea—<u>Kroonland</u> Up at 9^{30}. No breakfast. Bath in hot salt. Watch games on deck. Recover lost books & laundry. Post these notes in card room.

APPENDIX:
DIARY FRAGMENTS, 1914-18

Preserved at the beginning of the "Helen" diary of 1919–25 are three diary fragments—one from April 1914 in Philadelphia, one undated and unlocated, and one from June to July 1918 in Harford County, Maryland. These entries are isolated. They may belong to now lost journals, but there is no concrete evidence to support this hypothesis. These fragments are included here to complete the record of Dreiser's American diaries.

FRAGMENT 1

April 20 (Monday) 1914 Went down town to Adelphia.[1] Trying to cross south to see residence streets. Pocketed by 39th St. & thrown back on Girard Ave. Dinner at Adelphia.

April 21—1914—(Tuesday) Luncheon Franklin Inn—Dinner—8 at Jenkintown. Snellenburgs.[2] 39th Street sloppy—Clean up work most shown here. Various hunchbacks.

April 22—Letter from Cryhon[3]—N.Y. Letter from Jones, (Lane) for picture.[4] Letter from Mrs. ⌐ ¬. Decide to go to Altantic City. Various hunchbacks—one on car going down. Horse shoe—very large in 13th St. Coates cashes check (20).[5] Bright Day. I mail picture to Lane. Home. More H. Br—— Pack bag—to train. At ferry (Camden) see cross eyed man—slightly cross-eyebrows— Incidents disconnecting me with M.C.[6] Two women in booths. Looking for Laurelton instead Stanton. Cant get in booth. Walk & walk. Cant find store. When do number not in—2 phone systems. Take car. Miss M. C. by 3 or 4 minutes. Had premonition this would happen. Train late.

April 23rd (A.C.) 1914. Hotel Lorraine. Bath window contained Paraclete & Cockatrice—both crowned. First thought crown represented Victory over Cockatrice. Then—a crown for each— either way. Then a crown as a result of conflict between them! Which is it. To understand this meaning of Paraclete & Cockatrice

1. Dreiser is in Philadelphia; the Adelphia was a hotel in that city.
2. A department store in Philadelphia.
3. "Cryhon" is a name Dreiser used for Kirah Markham (see p. 117, n. 1).
4. J. Jefferson Jones (1880–1941), the American director of the British publishing house of John Lane Co., which would publish *The Titan* on 22 May 1914, one month from the date of this entry. Jones is asking Dreiser for a picture for publicity purposes.
5. Probably Dreiser's old friend, the editor and author Joseph H. Coates (see p. 58, n. 5).
6. M.C. is Mabel Cheyney.

(symbolic) should be looked up.[7] Represented in small diamond panes—thus— ◇ — Slept till 3. To Stanton. M. C. tall, dark, 38, slender like Mary A. Fanton-Roberts.[8] Intellectual—artistic. We go to end of Board walk. Then to Belmont inn.—Belmont cocktail. Then to big hotel. Dinner 5<u>00</u>. Then to Lorraine to hold bag. Then to Stanton. Feel her body. We unite in reception room 1—A.M. Fierce screw. First time for her. I finally get it in. Comment when completed—"so thats the way its done"—Talk of colleges, mother, Christian Science. My aims, her experiences with me. First impulse not to do it at all.

Friday. April 24—1914. Awake 7—Bath & dress by 8. 9 A.M. train to Phila. Hotel with beautiful clattering kitchen. Bright Day. Hammonton. Camden. Boat to Phila. Man back from Reno. Small boys boat on Delaware. Subway to Broad St. Station. Breakfast 70 cents. Car home. 8 or 9 letters—one from Cryhon. Phone messages day before. I try to get her. Write Jones, Lengel (just married), Lill & Hale.[9] Very stiff & sore. Get to work on "Dawn—chapter 13."

FRAGMENT 2

The blab of the poor. A hunchback in a greasy overcoat & blue trousers. A negro who stops & stares idly at dirty photos. A boy selling papers & rivals. The cars. Two women in an automobile. No good looking girls of any kind. A hard man, looking eagerly at what—faces & more faces—married women who looked pinched & peaked. Young men & middle aged men who suggest futility run to seed. In so far as I can see the world has changed no whit since I was ten or fifteen. The vast majority of the people at the bottom are futile—nondescript. Their ideas are reflected in their dress,

7. The religious symbolism of the window attracted Dreiser's attention. The Paraclete (the comforter, helper) is another name for the Holy Ghost; the Cockatrice, a mythical serpent with the power to kill by its glance, was reputed to have been hatched from a cock's egg.

8. Mary Fanton Roberts, editor (see p. 143, n. 41).

9. William C. Lengel (1888–1965), lawyer, editor, author (see p. 186, n. 78). Lill is Lillian Rosenthal (see p. 150, n. 8). Ralph T. Hale, editor at Small, Maynard & Co., a Boston publisher interested in Dreiser's work.

shoes, hats—the tawdriness of their make up. This street with its small buildings, its clap trap, fighting signs, its minute businesses is enough to make one weep for life and yet—if the burning within is sufficient it is worthwhile and only so. If the burning within is sufficient—the hungers, hopes, lust, fears, then & then only (like life to the grass & flowers) is it worthwhile.

FRAGMENT 3

June 1 to July 1—1918— Spent with Bert[10] in Havre-de-Grace—Harford County, Maryland. The Cooleys. Hal & John—the old mother. The Church festival! The school festival. The flying machines. The hotel at H. de G. (Harford House) Two trips to Balto. The Southern Hotel. Rooms 908 & 1001. The old market & rambles with Bert. Saturday walks into H-de G. The Park there. I do the Essays (The King is Naked).[11] Revise ("Free & Other Stories").[12] Get Bert to pay Marian[13] a visit at the end.

---

10. "Bert" is Estelle Bloom Kubitz.
11. "The King is Naked" was one of the titles Dreiser considered for *Hey Rub-a-Dub-Dub* (1920).
12. *Free and Other Stories* was published on 16 August 1918. Dreiser is probably correcting final proof.
13. Marion Bloom (1888–?), the sister of Estelle Bloom Kubitz (see p. 149, n. 3).

TEXTUAL APPARATUS

SELECTED EMENDATIONS
IN THE DIARY TEXTS

The table below records significant editorial emendations made in the texts of the original diaries in order to produce the texts published in this edition. In each entry the page-line reference is followed by the emended reading printed in this volume. Then follows a left-pointing bracket which should be read as "emended from." To the right of the bracket is the original reading from the diary. Below is a sample entry:

67.7 reduces me] reduces

This entry indicates that at page 67, line 7, of this edition the reading "reduces" from Dreiser's original diary has been emended to "reduces me".

Philadelphia

59.18	having] have
61.1	after having] after
65.12	latter] later
67.4	working order] working
67.7	reduces me] reduces
67.8	might be] might
67.9	affliction] affection
68.16	it being] being
72.26	my] might
73.8	at four] and four
73.15	rose and] rose
75.28	became] began
76.27	town and] town
76.28	Ate] and ate
78.22	moved] my
79.4	beginning] being

79.6	where] when
81.10	walk. Got] walk get
81.23	try] tried
82.22	than] that
83.16	quite quiet] quite quite
86.4	Hydroscin] Hyorcin
86.19	took] to
89.17	when] went
90.13	hydroscin] hyoscin
92.1	so many] some money
92.20	it is,] it
92.20	am ill] am
92.24	mood, but I am] mood and
92.28	in the] the
92.31	Italian's shoe shop] Italian
92.33	shoes] shoe
92.34	half-soled] have ∧soled
94.3	not what] not
94.15	and felt] and
96.9	they] I
96.11	me a] me
97.16	come] home
98.19	found] could
98.23	mine] my
99.5	mine] my
99.7	about it] about
101.28	my eye] my
102.3	and when] and
102.11	sleepy] sleep
102.35	and I] and
105.8	safely] shapely
105.14	it is] it
106.3	the river] river
106.5	plaintive note] plaintive
106.16	see] seen
106.28	walking] walk
107.12	are] or
107.31	slightly sore,] slightly∧
107.36	reached] revd

108.11	in it] in
109.7	are] or
110.23	and read] and
110.28	we could] we call
111.8	covered] covers
111.24	today, and] today
111.24	account is] account
112.6	would] would not
112.8	newspaper men] newspaper
112.23	had written] written

Savannah and the South

124.3	has an] an
124.27	are] a
125.2	note] not
125.18	who] whose
135.13	begin] being
137.3	Eat] Each
137.5	Put on] Put

Greenwich Village

177.4	Hurst] Eurst
179.13	Lead] Lend
205.4	have had] have
206.31	at] of
218.32	tea] ten
229.27	steadily on] steady of
238.22	the government] and government
247.18	stuck] struck
252.2	where] when

Home to Indiana

263.11	boats] boths

A Trip to the Jersey Shore

271.8	off] of

Helen, Hollywood, and the _Tragedy_

278.10	deduction] deducation

281.11	gloom took] gloom
284.24	what the] the
294.22	watch] was
304.3	ninth] night
304.15	down town] down down
306.12	old mission] old
308.12	becomes] beyonds
309.11	for] from
309.30	essays the] essay—the
310.27	Earle'] Eearle∧
313.14	tells me] me
316.35	some on chapters] on some chapter
328.2	Nazimova] Lazinova
330.14	but] by
335.17	I come] I
338.30	screen right] right screen
347.14	Helen at] Helen
353.6	back] black
360.11	golf] gold
360.27	meet] me
362.16	motif] motive
372.11	been] being
378.36	car and] car
378.10	meal] me
388.9	does not] does

Motoring to Florida

421.13	bad roads] roads
428.37	line] 9
429.8	100-mile] 100
433.7	see them making] making
433.7	there are] there
433.15	stores] stories
433.23	get out] get
443.3	card] car

Emendations in Dates

| 71.19 | Dec 7$^{\underline{th}}$] Dec 8$^{\underline{th}}$ |
| 82.18 | 1903] 1902 |

144.3	Feb 17] Feb 14
277.1	July 19] July 20
278.32	Sept 13] Sept 11
280.8	Sept. 14] Sept. 12
281.18	Sept 17] Sept 14
282.13	Sept. 19] Sept. 16
282.16	Sept 20th] Sept 17th
283.4	Sept 21] Sept 18
283.12	Sept 28] Sept 25
292.1	Nov. 14] Nov. 15
318.3	Tuesday] Monday
321.27	June 22] June 21
322.7	June 23] June 24
322.22	June 24] June 25
330.7	July] June
334.6	Aug 22nd] Aug 23rd
334.13	Aug 23] Aug 24
337.3	Sept—10] Sept—9
337.15	Sept 11] Sept 10
349.5	Nov. 29] Nov. 28
353.4	April 24] April 23
354.1	April 25] April 24
365.14	May 6] May 7
365.30	May 7th] May 8th
384.23	Jan 8] Jan 9

INDEX

Abdy, H. Bennett, 339
Abdy, Rowenta Meeks, 339
Abrams, Dr. Albert, 372, 375, 383
Addicks, John Edward, 100
Ade, George, 28
Adelphia Hotel, The (Philadelphia), 447
Aeschylus, 238
Ainslee's Magazine, 60n, 61n, 105n, 204n
Aldis, Mrs. ——, 320
Allen, Ben, 227
Allison, May, 329
Amick, Robert, 213
Anderson, Sherwood, 127, 225n, 363n
Andreyev, Leonid: "Anathema," 400
Angell, Norman B., 349
Arabian Nights, The, 152–53, 172, 178–79, 181, 198–99
Arbuckle, Roscoe ("Fatty"), 384
Armstrong, Rella Abell, 151, 196, 235–36
Arnold, Charles, 259, 263
Ashurst, John, 237
Associated Magazines, 215–16
Auerbach, Joseph S., 157, 253–54
   Essays and Miscellanies, 157n
Author's League of America, 23, 138n
Avebury. *See* Lubbock, Sir John
Babbitt, Irving, 241n
Baer, George F., 109
Baker, May Calvert, 28, 257, 259, 260, 262–63, 265–66
Baldwin, Winnie, 390
Balzac, Honoré de, 33, 310, 371, 378
   Beatrix, 371, 378
   La Peau de Chagrin, 310
Bara, Theda, 177, 219–20
Barr, Amelia E., 83n
Barrymore, John, 255n
Barthelmes, Richard, 323
Baudelaire, Charles, 6
Baus, Simon P., 28, 266
Bebber, ——, 104
Beckley, Zoë, 250–51
   A Chance to Live, 250n
Beerman, Herman and Emma S., 3n, 55n

Behr, Mrs. ——, 203, 225, 231
Belasco, David, 123n
Belmont, August, 254n
Belmont, Major August, 254
Benedict XV (Pope), 390
Bennett, René, 366
Benson, Allen, 252
Benson, Arthur, 244, 394
Berkhardt, Carl, 188n
Berkman, Alexander, 247
   Prison Memoirs of an Anarchist, 247n
"Bert." *See* Kubitz, Estelle Bloom
Bible, The, 355
Bierce, Ambrose, 28
Big Moose Lake (New York), 35, 400–401
Bizozer, Charles, 224
Blood, Benjamin Paul: *Pluriverse,* 375
Bloom, Marion, 24, 47, 147, 149, 156, 158, 165, 171, 180, 198, 201, 222, 224–25, 228, 232, 235, 237–38, 245–46, 251, 272, 449
Blythe, Betty, 350
Blythe, Samuel G., 136
"Bo." *See* Kubitz, Estelle Bloom
Boca Raton (Florida), 433n, 436–37
Bohemian Club (San Francisco), 38, 299n, 365
Bohemian Magazine, 188n, 197n, 213n
Boni, Albert, 177n
Boni and Liveright, 39, 42n, 173, 177n, 209, 251, 254, 280n, 288, 307n, 395–96, 405, 419, 435
Booklovers and Tabard Inn Libraries of the United States, 63n
Booklovers Magazine, 63n, 83n, 84, 100, 112
Bookman, The, 195
Boone, J. Allen, 214
Booth, Franklin, 28, 213, 237, 257, 259, 266n
Booth, Fred, 22, 213, 222, 234, 236
Borgia, Lucrezia, 136
Borrow, George: *The Bible in Spain,* 250–51, 253–55
Boston Transcript, 310n

Bourne, Randolph, 22, 24, 181, 198, 209, 225n, 242
  "The Art of Theodore Dreiser," 181n
Bowler, J. E., 19
Bradley, Anna D., 83
Brann, W. C.: *Iconoclast*, 289
Branstone, May, 408
"Brave Mr. Dreiser," 314n
Brennan, Austin, 411–12
Brevoort Hotel, The (New York), 24, 117, 151, 159, 164, 171, 182, 193, 208–10, 220, 230–32, 244–45, 282, 405
Brill, A. A., 395
Broadway Magazine, 155n, 359n, 374n
Brooks, Gerald, 178
Brooks, Van Wyck, 225n
Brown, Curtis, 334n
Brown, Demetra Vaka: *Haremlik: Some Pages from the Life of Turkish Women*, 184, 189–90
Brown, Frank, 401
Brown, Glenn, 263
Brown, Grace, 35, 401
Bryant, William Cullen, 366
Bryce, James (Viscount): *The American Commonwealth*, 80, 86
Budweiser Garden, 166
Bulletin, The, 63, 65
Burke, Claire, 309
Burrows, Dr. ———, 376–77
Bush, Winifred: LETTER TO DREISER, 142
Butler, Samuel: *Erewhon*, 348
Butterick Publishing Co., 13, 177, 178n, 186n, 196, 374n, 441n
Butterick's *Designer*, 158n
Cady, Agnes ("Ducky"), 201, 209, 219, 239, 241
Cahan, Abraham, 244–45, 247–48, 251, 253, 255
  The Rise of David Levinsky, 244
Cain, Muriel, 263–64, 271
Caine, Hall, 56
Call Magazine, 242n
Calvert, George Chambers, 265
Calvert, May, 29. *See also* Baker, May Calvert
Campbell, Heyworth, 234–35
Campbell, Louise, 18, 25, 147–256 *passim*, 281, 283–84, 304, 349n, 355, 381n, 386, 402, 417–18, 427, 436
  LETTERS TO DREISER, 174–75, 212, 230–31
  Letters to Louise, 150n
Canfield, Chauncey de Leon: *The Diary of a Forty-Niner*, 418
Cardiff, Mary, 303
Carnegie, Andrew, 188

Carus, Paul, 296
Castle, Irene, 249
Caswell, J. Wallace, 260
Catholicism, Roman, 9–10, 96, 261, 266, 285, 352
Century Company, 15, 160n, 218, 386
Century Magazine, The, 89n, 223n, 224, 388n
Chambers, Robert W., 205
Chaney, Lon, 402
Chaplin, Charlie, 192, 235, 350
Chaplin, Mildred Harris, 350
Chapman, Pat, 262
Charles Ray Studio, 315–16
Cheating Cheaters (theatrical company), 167
Chekhov, Anton P., 239, 242–43
chemism, 337
Chester Mystery Plays, The, 237–38
Cheston, Dorothy, 167, 189, 191–92, 226, 238
Cheyney, Mabel, 447n
Chicago American, 195, 230
Chicago Daily Globe, 28, 264n, 271n
Chicago Dial, The, 253
Chicago Globe-Democrat, 289n
Chipman, Walter, 261
Christian Science, 260n, 341, 384, 395, 448
Christopher Columbus, 122
Chronicle, The, 389
Churchill, Allen, 17, 117
Churchill, Winston: *The Inside of the Club*, 351
Clark, Ross, 436
Clemens, Samuel L., 14, 292, 392
  Adventures of Huckleberry Finn, 300, 323
  "Huck Finn," 361
  Life on the Mississippi, 322n
  What is Man, 292
Coates, J. H., & Co., 58n
Coates, Joseph H., 7, 11, 58, 65, 67, 81, 83–87, 89–90, 91, 94, 99–101, 104–7, 111–13, 447
Cobb, Irwin, 136, 273
Colbert, Jessica, 368
Coleridge, Samuel T.: "Kubla Khan," 368
Collier's, 219, 237
Commodus (Emperor), 390
Comstock, Anthony, 211
Connolly, Susan Cornelia, 398
Conroy, Frank, 238
Cook, George Cram, 117n
Cortez, "Andy," 122, 128
Cosmopolitan, 15, 177, 200, 205, 223, 227, 394, 411
Coué, Philip Emile, 395
Courton, Madame ———, 201
Cowan, Percy, 213
Cowl, Jane, 403

Cowley, Malcolm, 21
Exile's Return, 21n
Cox, Mrs. ———, 224–25
Cox, Phil "Chicken," 122, 125
Crabbe, George: "The Village," 119
Crane, Hart, 21
Crane, Stephen, 29, 265n
Maggie: A Girl of the Streets, 161n
Crocker, Bosworth. *See* Lewisohn, Mary Arnold Crocker
Croissant, G. Frank, 427
Croker, Arthur G., 403n
Crosman, Henrietta, 68
Cross, R. Nicoll: *Socrates: The Man and His Mission,* 371
Crowley, Aleister, 246
"Cryhon." *See* Markham, Kirah
Cudlipp, Thelma, 179n, 186, 374
Culver Military Institute, 262
Cummings, E. E., 21
Cutting, Mary Stewart, 388
Daggett, Mabel Porter, 197
Daly, Arnold, 246–47, 253–54
Daly, Augustin, 68n
Danby, Frank, 334
Daniels, Bebe, 326, 350, 373
Darrow, Clarence, 108, 412n
Darty, Pete, 263
Darwin, Charles, 129, 130
Voyage of H.M.S. Beagle, 128
Daskan, Josephine Dodge: *Smith College Stories,* 81
Davenport, Butler, 252n
Davis, ———, 209, 215, 230, 255
Davis, Leone, 410–12
Davis, Magdalene, 410–12
Davis, Robert, 205–6
Dawson, N. P., 23
Debs, Eugene, 248n
De Cassenes, Benjamin, 137
Delineator, The, 177n, 191, 197n
Dell, Floyd, 22, 117n
Love in Greenwich Village, 18
DeMille, Cecil B., 320
Demorest's Family Magazine, 143n
Dempsey, Jack, 267
Deshon, Florence, 347n, 349, 390
DeYoung, H., 389
Dial, The, 181
Dickens, Charles, 424
Dies, Carl, 364
Dillman, Willard, 134, 137
Ditrichstein, Leo, 386, 388
Dix, Leon, 360–61
Dodd, Mead, and Company, 194–95, 395, 397n

Dodge, B. W., & Co., 178n
Dodge, Ben W., 127, 216
Dole, President ———, 219
Donna, Norah, 217
Donnelly, Dorothy: "Poppy," 408
Dorr, Rheta Childe, 27, 208
Inside the Russian Revolution, 210n
A Woman of Fifty, 27, 208n, 210
Dorsey, John, 40
Dos Passos, John, 21
Dostoyevsky, Fyodor, 33
Crime and Punishment, 128, 132, 137, 247
Doty, Douglas, 27, 223–24, 227–28, 329
Doubleday, Frank N., 6
Doubleday, Neltje deGraff (Mrs. Frank N.), 6
Doubleday, Page, & Co., 8n, 172n
Doubt, 223n
Douglas, George, 38, 275, 339, 359, 366, 368
Draper, John W.: *History of the Conflict Between Science and Religion,* 312
Dreiser, Edward Minerod (Dreiser's brother Ed Dresser), 76n, 166, 207–8, 280–81, 292–93, 385
Dreiser, Emma Wilhelmine (Dreiser's sister), 151, 160n, 322n, 398, 409
Dreiser, Helen Richardson (Dreiser's second wife), 14, 31–41, 269, 275, 278–442 *passim,* 445, 453–54
LETTERS FROM DREISER (excerpts), 33, 39
LETTERS TO DREISER, 316, 341–42, 345, 346
My Life with Dreiser, 33n, 34n, 35n, 36, 37n, 39, 41n
NOTE TO DREISER, 347
Dreiser, John Paul (Dreiser's father), 7–10, 16
Dreiser, John Paul, Jr. (Dreiser's brother Paul Dresser), 13, 28, 221, 227, 263, 281, 317n, 374n, 389, 417
"On the Banks of the Wabash," 28, 263n
Dreiser, Mai Skelley (Dreiser's sister-in-law), 207–8, 281, 292–93
Dreiser, Marcus Romanus (Dreiser's brother Rome), 29
Dreiser, Mary Francis (Dreiser's sister Mame), 132, 143, 207–8, 181–82, 184, 212, 216–17, 221–22, 225, 227–30, 237, 245, 247, 250, 252–53, 255, 381, 400, 408–10, 412, 417
Dreiser, Mary Theresa (Dreiser's sister), 280
Dreiser, Sarah Schänäb (Dreiser's mother), 15–16, 29, 32, 110, 280n
Dreiser, Sara Osborne White (Dreiser's first

wife, "Jug"), 3, 8n, 11–12, 34, 46–47, 53, 60, 63n, 64–65, 68–69, 75–80, 83n, 86–88, 94, 101, 106, 111, 179n, 191, 204, 208, 214, 336, 399

Dreiser, Sylvia (Dreiser's sister), 395

Dreiser, Theodore, writings:

"The Almighty Burke," 132n

"An Amateur Laborer," 13, 69n

"Ambling Sam," 322

"America," 19, 158

"American," 149

"American Idealism and German Frightfulness," 22, 167

An American Tragedy, 14–15, 20, 29–30, 34, 36–37, 39, 41–42, 144n, 265n, 275, 299n, 336–37, 347, 350–51, 363n, 381, 401n, 402n, 405, 409, 415, 417n, 419n, 421, 427n, 435n, 437n, 441, 453

"As a Realist Sees It," 135

"Bleeding Hearts," 316

A Book About Myself, 150n, 307n

"Bridget Mullanphy," 26

The Bulwark, 15, 20, 25, 28, 33, 35, 37, 132n, 144, 150n, 153n, 154, 163, 173n, 230n, 232, 288n, 292, 298, 304, 309–10, 314, 318, 334n

"Chains," 25, 155n

Chains, 155n, 206n, 249n, 311n, 335n, 388n

"Change," 22, 242

"Choice, The," 327, 329, 333

The Color of a Great City, 20, 406

"A Country Doctor," 231, 248, 250, 253

"The Cruise of the Idlewild," 197

Dawn, 7, 9, 16, 22, 29, 37, 150n, 192n, 202, 208, 217, 259n, 307n, 448. See also A History of Myself

"De Maupassant, Jr.," 155n

"The Door of the Butcher Rogaum," 196–97

"The Door of the Trap," 329

Douze Hommes (Twelve Men, tr.), 400

"Down Hill and Up," 13

"The Dream," 162, 225n

Dreiser Looks at Russia, 42

"Elizabeth," 18n, 25, 132n. See also This Madness

"Ernita," 26

"Esther Norn," 220n, 244n

"The Father," 230

The Financier, 58n, 119n, 151n, 160, 162n, 254n, 317, 321, 340, 420n

"The Financier" (play), 151n

"Force," 186, 192

"Free," 221, 223–26, 229–31, 234, 238

Free and Other Stories, 177n, 197n, 200n, 202n, 204n, 205n, 221n, 449

"Fulfillment," 35–36, 311, 314, 316–18, 320

A Gallery of Women, 24–27, 36, 155n, 158n, 180n, 186n, 220n, 244n, 303n, 386, 388n, 398

"Geddo Street," 351

The "Genius," 8n, 11, 14–15, 20–21, 23, 28, 37, 118n, 128, 133, 138n, 151n, 153n, 157n, 158n, 166, 179, 181, 183n, 186n, 192, 196, 211n, 215, 246n, 251, 267, 296, 310n, 333, 335–36, 342, 349, 359, 374, 386n, 395, 397, 405–6

"Giff," 180n

The Girl in the Coffin, 190, 202, 206, 215–17, 226–29, 241, 251, 253, 314

"Gloom," 26

"Glory Be! McGlathery," 206n

The Hand of the Potter, 20, 23, 25, 156n, 161, 200, 233–34, 236, 242, 247, 251, 253–55, 280, 338, 342

"Her Boy," 29, 30n, 265, 323, 326, 330

Hey Rub-a-Dub-Dub, 20, 162n, 242n, 247n, 312, 314, 449n

"His Annual Appearance," 77

A History of Myself, 7, 9, 24, 192–93. See also Dawn

The History of Myself, II, 8n. See also Newspaper Days

"Hollywood Now," 372, 375

A Hoosier Holiday, 14–16, 19, 28, 37, 118n, 132, 136–39, 143, 162n, 213n, 257, 259, 397

"Ida Hauchawout," 388

"In the Dark," 222

"The Investigations of Mr. Buckley, Reporter," 75–76

"Irrepressible Edward," 189, 191–92

"Jealousy," 388n

Jennie Gerhardt, 3–4, 7–9, 14, 91, 101, 105n, 111, 119n, 132n, 150n, 160, 182, 209, 216n, 310n, 321, 339n, 342, 405

"The King is Naked," 449

"Kismet," 149–50, 152, 154, 159, 160

"Lady Bountiful, Jr.," 307–8, 310

Laughing Gas, 28, 188, 265, 266n

"Life, Art and America," 21, 225n

"Lilly Edwards: An Episode," 161n

"Lola," 249

"Lolita," 386–87

"The Long, Long Trail," 294

"The Lost Phoebe," 211

"Love," 155, 159–60, 232, 235, 237–39, 241–42, 244, 246, 248, 251, 332

"McEwen of the Shining Slave Makers," 204, 206, 209–11. See also "The Shining Slave Makers"

"Married," 177

"A Mayor and His People," 58n, 99n, 234

"Mea Culpa," 37, 369, 371, 377, 379

"The Mighty Burke," 217n. *See also* "The Mighty Rourke"

"The Mighty Rourke," 217, 219, 221–22, 226, 228

"Mildred My Mildred," 398

Mirage, 351

"Mirage," 351

Moods: Cadenced and Declaimed, 351n, 406n

"The Mystic Hand," 249

"Nemesis," 322

"Neurotic America and the Sex Impulse," 17–18

Newspaper Days, 16, 37, 171–73, 177, 182, 189, 199, 201n, 202–3, 212, 219, 223, 233–34, 242, 264, 307, 308n, 309, 312–15, 317, 323, 332. *See also The History of Myself,* II

"Nigger Jeff," 19

"The Nobody," 232

"The Old Neighborhood," 249

"Old Ragpicker," 117, 145, 396

"Old Rogaum and His Theresa," 197n, 251, 253

"Old Rogaum's Door," 199–200

"Olive Brand," 158n, 303n

"An Overcrowded Entryway," 34, 383

"Peter," 239n, 323n, 329n, 397n

"Phantasmagoria," 247, 249–50, 255

"Phantom Gold," 335–36

Plays of the Natural and the Supernatural, 15, 117, 118n, 151, 222n, 235, 241, 247n, 397

"The Problem of Distribution," 105

"The Problem of the Soil," 58n, 99n

The Rake (1900), 8

The Rake (1915), 37, 123n

"Regina C—," 155n

"Reina," 36

"The Return," 181

"The Right to Kill," 250

"Rona Murther," 186n

"St. Columba and the River," 206

"The Second Choice," 25, 205–6

"The Shadow," 388

"The Shining Slave Makers," 204n

"Sidonie," 25

Sister Carrie, 4–7, 8n, 9, 14–15, 23, 37, 53, 58n, 63n, 95n, 105n, 115, 127n, 160, 172–73, 177n, 178n, 182, 186n, 201n, 209, 217, 223, 227, 235, 339n, 359n, 381n, 436n

The Stoic, 254n

"A Story of Stories," 24, 184, 186–87, 189, 192–93, 196, 198–201, 209, 219

"A Summer in Arcady," 303

"Tall Towers," 406

"This Florida Scene," 42, 442n

This Madness, 18n, 25, 132n

The Titan, 15, 23, 118n, 132n, 151n, 213–14, 218n, 223n, 227, 340, 397, 405, 447n

A Traveler at Forty, 15, 160–62, 256, 386

"True Art Speaks Plainly," 63n, 83n, 100n

"A True Patriarch," 234

Twelve Men, 14, 20, 155n, 217n, 231n, 234n, 239n, 254n, 296n, 303n, 323n, 329n, 375, 381n, 397n, 400

" 'Vanity, Vanity,' Saith the Preacher," 381

"The Victim," 214

"The Weavers," 254

"What's the Matter with the [American] Newspapers," 172, 175

"When the Old Century was New," 202

"Will You Walk into my Parlor?", 200–201, 208

Dreiser, Vera, 207n

Dresser, Ed. *See* Dreiser, Edward Minerod

Dresser, Mai Skelley. *See* Dreiser, Mai Skelley

Dresser, Paul. *See* Dreiser, John Paul, Jr.

Drexel Biddle Press, The, 70

Dudley, Caroline, 294

Dudley, Dorothy, 9, 23, 38n, 294, 365

Forgotten Frontiers: Dreiser and the Land of the Free, 8n, 23n, 294n. *See also* Harvey, Dorothy Dudley

Duffield Co., The, 192, 197

Duffy, Richard, 8–9, 61–62, 213

Duhring, Louis A., 3, 11, 47, 53, 55, 59, 65, 71–72, 74, 78, 83–84, 93, 96–97

Dunkards, 261

Dwan, Allen, 386–88

Earle, Ferdinand, 304–5, 310

Eastman, Crystal, 350

Eastman, Mabel, 347n, 359

Eastman, Max, 22, 349–50

Eaton, Seymour, 63–64, 83

Economic Club of New York, The, 215

Edison, Thomas, Jr., 244n

Edwards, Carlo, 233

Edwards, Gus, 302

Elder, Paul, 338

Elias, Robert H., 5n, 8n, 10n, 15n, 25n, 26n, 117n, 151n, 156n, 341n

Ellis, Havelock, 17

Emerson, Ralph Waldo, 424

Episcopalianism, 9, 85

Era, 58n, 99n, 107n, 234n

Esherick, Letty, 417n

Esherick, Wharton, 417–18
Esperanto, 224
Esquire, 149n, 186n
Ettinge, James A., 381, 387
Euripedes, 238
Everleigh Club of Chicago, The, 161
Fahnstock, Mrs. ———, 219
Fairbanks, Douglas, 34, 192, 217, 312, 373, 388, 407
Farrar, Geraldine, 215
Fayette Review, The, 265n
Ferguson, Elsie, 206, 326
Fermor, ———, 441
Ficke, Arthur Davidson, 437
Field, Sarah Bard, 366
Fields, W. C., 408
Fiske, Minnie Maddern, 189
Fitzgibbons, T. C., 397, 405
Flagg, Jared: *The Crimes of Jared Flagg,* 259
Foerster, Norman, 241n
Forgue, Guy J., 41n
Forster-Nietzsche, Elizabeth: *The Young Nietzsche,* 333
Fort, Charles H., 224, 235
   The Outcast Manufacturers, 223
   X, 223
   Y, 223
   Z, 223
Fortean Society, The, 223n
Four Horsemen of the Apocalypse, The (film), 338
Francis, Governor David R. (Missouri), 239
Frank, Waldo, 21, 225n
   Memoirs of Waldo Frank, 21n
   Time Exposure, 21n
Franklin, Benjamin, 143
Franklin Inn, The (Philadelphia), 112, 447
Franks, Bobby, 412n
Frazer, James George, 219
Frederic, Harold, 6
   The Damnation of Theron Ware, 86
   March Hares, 85
Freeman, Helen, 227
Freeman, Mrs. ———, 405
Freeman, Ross, 409, 412
Freeman, The, 377
Frennson, Gustave, 391–92
   Hillingenlei, 391
   Jörn Uhl, 391
   Klaus Hinrich Bass, 391
Freud, Sigmund, 6, 17, 31, 33, 395n, 412
Friars Club, The, 233
Frick, Henry C., 247n
Fuessle, Newton A., 158–59
Fuller, Henry Blake, 6
   The Cliff Dwellers, 86n, 105–6, 110–11
   With the Procession, 86–87

Fussells, Dr. ———, 77
Gaither, Kyra Markham, 117n. *See also* Markham, Kirah
Gallant, Barney, 256
Gallimard, Gaston, 374
Garland, Hamlin, 6, 83n
   Rose of Dutcher's Coolly, 95
   Ulysses S. Grant: His Life and Character, 112n
Gates, John W., 123
George, Henry, 99n
Germans, 22–23, 28, 133, 139, 164, 183, 196–98, 202, 206, 213, 217, 244, 246, 249, 253, 266, 365, 391
Gibson, Edward ("Hoot"), 440
Gillette, Chester, 35–36, 401
Gish, Lillian, 373
Glaenzer, Richard Butler, 195n
Gleason, ———, 244
Gleason, Lieutenant ———, 86
"Gloom." *See* Kubitz, Estelle Bloom
Goethe, Johann Wolfgang von, 166
Gogol, Nicholas: *Taras Bulbos,* 118
Gold, Mike: *Jews Without Money,* 246n. *See also* Granich, Irwin
Goldman, Emma, 17, 219, 247
Goldman, Ida, 296
Goldwyn, Samuel, 375
Goodman, Edward, 202, 206, 216, 226, 232
Goodman, Lillian Rosedale, 150n. *See also* Rosenthal, Lillian
Gordinnier, M. E., 4
Gordon, Brig. Gen. William Washington, 135
Gorky, Maxim, 398, 411, 434n
Gould, George Milbrey, 205
   Anomalies and Curiosities of Medicine, 205n
   Concerning Lafcadio Hearn, 205n
Granich, Irwin, 246. *See also* Gold, Mike
Grant, Percy Stickney, 405
Grant, Robert: *Unleavened Bread,* 90–91, 93
Grant, Ulysses S., 112, 299
Gray, Charles N., 76, 94, 98, 100, 104–5, 112
Grey, Zane, 439
Griffiths, D. W., 136, 287, 323, 350
Grote, George: *A History of Greece,* 277
Grushlau, Bella, 228, 250–52, 254–55, 298, 395
Guitteau, Maud, 409–13
Haas, Charles, 401
Haeckel, Ernst Heinrich, 33, 129
   The Riddle of the Universe at the Close of the Nineteenth Century, 311
Haggart, Sewell, 166n, 232, 253
Hale, Ralph T., 127, 448
Hale, William H., 134, 143

Halley, Paul, 192
Halloran, Bertha, 27, 162, 173–76, 184–85, 187, 188–90, 192, 204, 209, 211–12, 217, 219, 224, 227, 231, 238–39, 249, 251
Hampden, Walter, 406
Hampton, Benjamin B., 374
Hapgood, Hutchins, 17, 24, 26, 164, 166, 171, 184, 205, 218, 220–21, 224, 226, 230, 233, 245, 247–48, 250–51
  "An Anarchistic Woman," 119–20, 220
  The Spirit of Labor, 121–22
  A Victorian in the Modern World, 24n, 119n, 220n
Harben, William N., 203
Hardy, Thomas, 119n
Harper and Brothers, 182, 183n, 212, 214, 247–48, 395
Harper's Bazaar, 388n
Harper's Monthly Magazine, 75n, 172n, 183n, 231n, 250, 253
Harriman, Raymond Lee, 158–59
Harris, Frank, 10n, 11, 18, 314
  "A Word to Dreiser," 314n
Harrison, James A.: Life of Edgar Allan Poe, 348
Hart, W. B., 235
Hartridge, Clifford, 134, 136, 143, 251
Hartridge, Walter, 134–36, 138, 140
Harvey, Colonel ———, 254
Harvey, Dorothy Dudley, 365. See also Dudley, Dorothy
Hauptmann, Gerhart, 118–19, 154n, 219, 234, 242
  The Teamster, 242
  The Weavers, 118
Haviland, Florence Earle, 303
Hawthorne, Hildegarde: Rambles in Old College Towns, 375
Hawthorne, Nathaniel, 25
Hay, John: The Bread-Winners, 89–90
Hearst, William Randolph, 361
Hearst's International-Cosmopolitan, 18n, 132n, 166, 196–97, 199, 232
Hedrich, ———, 225, 230
Heine, R. D., 403
Heinz, ———, 188
Hélie, Fernande: Douze Hommes, 400. See also Dreiser, Theodore: Twelve Men
Henry, Arthur, 4, 8n, 25, 172n, 186–88, 403
  An Island Cabin, 4, 186n
  "Time," 403
Henry, O., 183n. See also Porter, William Sydney
Hermitage, The (Savannah), 135–36
Herrick, ———, 359

Hersey, Harold, 138, 143, 184–85, 249
Hilder, Julius, 374
Hirsch, ———, 195
History of Chinese Literature, 209
Hoey, "Old Hoss," 408
Hohl, ———, 222, 226
Holden, Alfred, 57, 61, 80, 87
Holland's Magazine, 311n
Holt, Vivian, 154, 178–79, 344
Holy Trinity Church (Philadelphia), 64
Home Journal, 193
Hope, Lawrence (Mrs. Malcolm Nicolson): India's Love Lyrics, 159
Hopkins, Arthur, 156, 158, 231, 233, 236, 242
Howells, William Dean, 6, 89–90
Howeys, Mrs. ———, 398, 407–8
Hoyns, Henry, 182, 395
Hubbard, Elbert, 267
Huebsch, Benjamin W., 216, 320
Hume, Arthur Carter, 395
The Huntington Press: "Dreiser Favors Federal Control: Hits Financiers," 260n
Hurst, Fannie, 177
  Anatomy of Me, 27, 177n
Huxley, Thomas, 10
Hylan, John F., 199
Ince, Alexander, 136, 303
Independent Presbyterian Church, The (Savannah), 137–38, 436
Indiana Club of Chicago, The, 5
Indianapolis News, The, 260n
Indianapolis Star, The, 28, 264n, 265, 267
  "Noted Novelist Visits in City," 265n
Ingram, Rex, 338
International, The, 246n
Jackson, Gen. Henry R., 135n
Jackson, Joseph, 79n
Jacobs, ———, 233
Jacobson, Norman, 244
  "Every Little Bit Helps," 244n
James, Henry, 26
Jarmuth, Edith DeLong, 158, 160, 202, 218–19, 224–25, 229, 251
Jefferson, Joseph III, 436
Jennings, Alphonso J.: Through the Shadows with O. Henry, 387
Jesberg, Dr. Simon, 348
Jesus Christ, 104, 110
Jewett, Rutger B., 5, 105
Jewish Forward, The, 245
Joffe, ———, 408
Johnson, Margaret, 38n, 359, 374
Johnson, Samuel (The Life of Sam Johnson), 128
Jones, Bessie, 253

Jones, J. Jefferson, 118, 143–44, 183, 192, 215, 251, 298, 447–48
Jordan, David Starr, 353
Josephson, Matthew, 21
Joyce, Alice, 302
"Jug." *See* Dreiser, Sara Osborne White
K——. *See* Markham, Kirah
Kafka, Franz, 14
Kalich, Madame Bertha, 209
Karola, Maud, 417, 429–31, 438
Karner, Mrs. ——, 341
Karsner, David, 248, 250–52, 254
 Sixteen Authors to One, 248n
Kauffman, Reginald W., 60, 72
Kaufman, Al, 315
Kazin, Alfred, 22n
Keller, Helen, 254
Keller, Madame, 191
Kelley, Ethel M., 359
Kemp, Harry, 17, 26, 220n, 244
Kennell, Ruth, 26, 42
Kerensky, Alexander, 202
"Kitty Wiggles" House (Philadelphia), 229
Kleckner, ——, 90
Kleinschmidt, Carl, 177
Kloster Glocke (New York), 192, 196, 198, 200, 206, 211, 230, 232, 234, 242
Knopf, Alfred A., 189, 205, 216, 223
Komroff, Manuel, 419
Korgues, Rose, 349n
Kraft-Ebbing, Baron Richard von, 17
 Psychopathia Sexualis, 412
Krog, Fritz, 213
Kroonland, The, 42, 442–43
Kropotkin, Peter, 247
Kubitz, Estelle Bloom ("Bert," "Bo," "Gloom," "Little Bill"), 17–18, 24, 26, 30, 47–48, 147–256 *passim,* 259, 262, 271, 277, 281–82, 284–85, 288, 290–91, 313, 315, 317, 399–400, 449
Kummer, Clare, 188
Kusell, Sallie, 41, 402, 407–13, 422, 427, 430, 436, 438
L——. *See* Rosenthal, Lillian
Ladies Home Journal, 63
Lainsheim, Grete Lainer von: *A Young Girl's Diary,* 429
Lal, Gobind Behari, 391
Lamb's Club, The (New York), 242, 299n
Lane, John, Co., 15, 117n, 118, 132n, 144n, 153n, 169n, 185, 192n, 292, 321n, 447
Lasky, Jesse L., 287
Lasky Studios, The (Hollywood), 292
Latour, Marion, 341
Laurie, ——, 197
Lawrence, Carolyn, 201, 209, 217, 219, 227

Lawrence, D. H., 421
Leadsworth, Dr. ——, 369, 371–72, 375–76, 379–81, 383–84
Leeds, ——, 191
Lengel, William, 186, 204, 222–23, 232, 243, 246, 248, 253, 332, 336, 386, 395, 411, 448
 "The 'Genius' Himself," 186n
Lenin, V., 350
Leopold, Nathan, 412n
Leopold-Loeb case, 412
Lesh, Eben, 263
Levy, Louis, 349
Lewis, Sinclair, 41, 435
Lewis and Clark expedition, 360
Lewisohn, Ludwig, 21–22, 27, 134, 185, 192, 195, 200, 215, 217, 221, 228, 231
 Cities and Men, 185n
 Don Juan, 27, 188n
 Expression in America, 21n, 185n
 Mid-Channel: An American Chronicle, 185n
 Up Stream: An American Chronicle, 185n
Lewisohn, Mary Arnold Crocker (Mrs. Ludwig Lewisohn), 27, 195, 215, 217, 221, 234, 242
 The Last Straw, 242
Liberal Club, The (New York), 17
Liberator, The, 349
Lieber, H. P., 265–67
Lincoln, Abraham, 10, 81, 89n, 97n, 102, 104, 108, 110–11, 406–7
Literary Digest International Book Review, 363n
Little, Nayan, 135, 137, 143, 151
"Little Bill." *See* Kubitz, Estelle Bloom
Little Theatre Society of Indiana, 188n, 265n
Liveright, Horace, 33, 189, 292, 299n, 307–8, 313–14, 320, 330, 359, 374, 381, 395, 397, 427
Liveright, Horace, Co., 7n
Live Stories, 332, 335–36
Llona, Victor, 409
Lloyd George, [David], 313
Loeb, Jacques, 33, 267, 291, 396
 Comparative Physiology of the Brain and Comparative Psychology, 267
Loeb, Richard, 412n
Lopez, Marguerite, 310, 333
Loti, Pierre, 166, 219
Lubbock, Sir John [Avebury]: *The Scenery of England,* 66, 68, 70
Lüchow's (New York), 24, 150, 171, 183, 201, 226
Lunden, Rolf, 42n
Lyon, Harris Merton, 155n
Lyon, Mrs. Harris Merton, 155
McAdoo, William Gibbs, 325

McAlpin, Henry, 135n
McCall's, 372n, 375
McCardell, Roy L., 298
McClure's, 217n, 234n
McCord, Donald, 323, 329, 330
McCord, Peter, 239, 323n, 329, 397, 405
MacDonald, Katherine, 326
McDonald, Mrs. D. H., 351
MacFadden, Bernard, 397–98
MacFadden Publications, 398
McFee, ———, 372, 375
Machar, J. S.: *Magdalen,* 230
Mackay, Robert, 395
McKinley, William, 361
McQuaid, ———, 369
Maitland, Arthur, 190n
Malleson, Miles: "Youth," 255
"Mame." *See* Dreiser, Mary Frances
Marden, Orison S., 395n
Markham, Kirah ("Cryhon"), 18, 22, 25,
    115, 117–18, 127, 132–39, 143–45,
    149, 151, 170–71, 175, 177, 182, 184–
    87, 191–92, 207, 210, 226, 230, 239,
    241, 247, 252, 281, 288, 338, 385, 399,
    417n, 441, 447–48
Masses, 15, 22, 134, 227n, 349n
Masters, Edgar Lee, 20, 24, 145, 231, 247–
    48, 408, 434n
Matthews, Brander, 83n
Maugham, W. Somerset
    The Moon and Sixpence, 285, 292
    Of Human Bondage, 135
    Rain, 399
Maupassant, Guy de, 216
Maurier, George du: *Peter Ibbetson,* 161n
Maxwell, John M., 28, 264–65, 271, 338,
    417n
May, Lola, 247
Medical Review of Reviews, 242
Meighan, Thomas, 430
Melville, Herman: *Typee,* 334
Mencken, H. L., 15, 20, 22–24, 25–26, 41n,
    47, 138–39, 143–45, 147, 149, 151n,
    153n, 155n, 156n, 169, 171–72, 173n,
    180, 181n, 182, 195, 205, 223n, 225n,
    246, 253, 272, 296–97, 298n, 312, 374,
    387n, 398, 400, 419, 435n
    Book of Prefaces, 23, 181, 231n
    "The Dreiser Bugaboo," 172n
    Heathen Days, 325n
    LETTER TO DREISER, 139
    A Mencken Chrestomathy, 40n
    "More Notes from a Diary," 315n
    "Orf'cer Boy," 149
    The Philosophy of Friedrich Nietzsche, 334
    Prejudices: Second Series, 348

"Romantic Intermezzo," 325n
"Sabbath Meditation," 40n
"Sister Carrie's History," 172n
"Theodore Dreiser," 181n
Ventures into Verse, 149n
Methodism, 272n
Metropolitan Magazine, 249n, 395n
Millay, Edna St. Vincent, 17
Miller, Kenneth, 317
Minter, Mary Miles, 302
Mitchell, John P., 199
Mizner, Wilson, 433
Modernist, The, 296
Moers, Ellen, 9n, 36
Molineux, Roland Burke, 37, 123
    "The Man Inside," 123n
Mooney, Tom, 247n
Moore, George: *The Lake,* 340
Moore, Marianne, 21
Moore, Owen, 314
Moravians, 420
Mordell, 202–3, 241
More, Paul Elmer, 22, 241
    The Demon of the Absolute, 241n
Morgan, John Pierpont, 109
Mormonism, 190
Morris, Jud, 261
Mott, Frank Luther, 63n
Mouquin's (New York), 152, 248, 252, 402
Mower, Margaret, 151, 156, 266
Muldoon, William I., 13, 317, 374
Mummers parade, 79
Munsey's, 206n
Myers, Gustavus
    The History of the Great American Fortunes,
        220
    *The History of the Supreme Court of the United
        States,* 220
Nathan, George Jean, 19, 149, 156n, 171,
    180n, 245n, 398
    The Intimate Notebooks of George Jean Nathan,
        19n, 245n
Nation, The, 22n, 228, 281
Nazimova, Alla, 328, 350, 400
Negri, Gaetano: *Julian the Apostate,* 172
Negro, The, 128–30, 407, 423–25, 427–28,
    430–31, 434–35, 439
Neilan, Marshall, 371–74
Nelson, Gertrude, 160, 164–65, 322, 409–10
Newbegin, John, 368, 390–91
New Republic, 281
New York Call, The, 242, 248n, 250, 254
New York Day, The, 408
New York Evening Globe, 23n
New York Evening Mail, 172, 180–81, 191,
    208n, 210, 250–51

New York Evening Post, The, 228, 239n, 406n
New York Evening Telegram, The, 226
New York Globe and Commercial Advertiser, The, 229, 231–32
New York Herald, 226
New York Morning Telegraph, 339n
New York Review, 314n
New York Society for the Suppression of Vice, 15, 157n, 166n, 211n
New York Sun, 229
New York Sunday Telegraph, 298n
New York Times, The, 200
New York Tribune, 155n, 232n, 332n
New York World, The, 160, 211, 442
Nicholas, Anna, 264, 267
Nicholsen, Meredith, 28, 290–91
Nicolay, John George: *A Short Life of Abraham Lincoln,* 81
Nietzsche, Friedrich, 333–34
Nin, Anaïs, 14
Nixon, Ellen, 137n
Norris, Frank: "Trilogy of the Wheat," 63n
Notice, 321
N. P. D., 231
    "Dreiser and Mencken," 231n
O'Brien, ———, 386
O'Day, ———, 368
Oglethorpe Club, The (Savannah), 135, 138, 143
Older, Fremont, 8n
O'Neill, Eleanora R., 310, 312–13, 317, 321, 369
O'Neill, Eugene, 117n, 225n
Oppenheim, James, 225n
Ordynski, Richard, 170
Orren, ———, 261
Ott, Mary Louise, 374
Oursler, Fulton, 397–98
Outlook, The, 105, 112
Padden, Sarah, 187–88
Pagan, 242n
Pagany, S., 143
Page, Walter H., 5
Palmer, Harold Lincoln, 305
Parks, Esther Schänäb, 280n
Parmelee, Maurice Farr: *The Science of Human Behavior: Biological and Psychological Foundations,* 334
Parry, Addison, 262, 264n, 265–66
Parry, Elizabeth, 263–67
Parry, Hessie Daisy, 264–66
Parry, Isabell, 264n, 271
Parry, Maxwell, 264
Pater, Walter, 219
Patges, Mrs. ——— (Helen Dreiser's mother), 318–19, 328, 357, 359–60, 364, 389

Patges, Myrtle (Helen Dreiser's sister), 36, 307, 328, 351, 355–56, 359–60, 369–72, 374–77, 379, 382, 384, 387, 389, 393
Peacock, Thomas Love: *Maid Marian,* 111
Pearson, Nita, 26, 185, 190–91
Pearson's Magazine, 202n, 314
Pell, Arthur, 42n
Petchnikoff, Morce, 388
Philadelphia Record, The, 70
Philadelphia Times, The, 70
Pickford, Mary, 34, 297, 307, 310, 312, 314, 373
Pictorial Review, 206n
Pixley, Frank, 299
Pizer, Donald, 20n, 30n, 100n, 144n
Poe, Edgar Allan, 6, 33, 341–42, 348, 380n
Poles, Helen, 385
Polly's Restaurant (New York), 17, 282
Porter, Eleanor Hodgman: *Pollyanna,* 292
Porter, William Sydney: "The Halberdier of the Little Rheinschloss," 183n
Post, C. M., 264
Powell, R. E., 99
Powys, John Cowper, 24, 143n, 183, 211, 226n, 234, 237–38, 245, 366, 368
Powys, Llewellyn, 366, 368
Powys, Marion, 143, 226
Preston, ———, 61
Prince Hopkins, 306
Provincetown Players, The, 220n
Przybyszewski, Stanislaw: *Homo Sapiens,* 118
Pulitzer, Joseph, 254
Putnam, Nina Wilcox, 16, 208–10, 244
    "Every Little Bit Helps," 244n
Putnam, Robert F., 208n
Pyne, Mary, 25–26, 220, 226, 244n, 250
Ramsey, C. T., 183, 214, 241, 271
Randall, David A., 46
Raphael, John N.: *Peter Ibbetson,* 161–62
Rascoe, Burton, 271, 375, 400
    Theodore Dreiser, 271n
Ray, Charles, 291, 325
Reconstruction, 394n
Red Book, 200, 209
Reedy's Mirror, 197n
Richards, Grant, 143n, 374
Richardson, Frank, 280n, 319, 321, 351–53, 355, 361, 369, 377, 419n, 436
Richardson, Helen Patges. *See* Dreiser, Helen Richardson
Richesen, Clarence, 37
Richmond, Maurice, 417
Riley, James Whitcomb, 28
Roberts, Mary Fanton, 143, 448

Robertson, John W., 380
  Poe: A Study, 380n
Robin, James G., 381, 383, 400, 410, 417
  Caius Gracchus, 381n
Robins, Helen, 234, 238
Robinson, ———, 242
Rockefeller, John D., 188
Rockefeller Institute, The, 396
Rodick, ———, 303
Rodman, Henrietta, 208n
Roeder, Ralph, 238
Rolland, ———, 255–56
Roosevelt, Theodore, 108n, 361
Rosanoff, Lillian, 277, 317
Rosenthal, Eleanor, 220
Rosenthal, Elias, 150, 162, 179, 214, 248
Rosenthal, Lillian, 18, 25, 48, 117, 127, 133–
  35, 137–39, 143–44, 147–256 *passim,*
  262, 264, 281, 283–85, 291, 297–99,
  303, 307, 319–21, 323, 338, 344, 346,
  381n, 448
Rossyn, Dick, 386
Rothapfel, Samuel L., 233, 242
Rothwell, Walter Henry, 292
Rowan, Ernest, 250
Ruggles, Walter, 342
Ruggles, Wesley, 338
Russia, 202, 210–11, 247–48, 263
Rykins-Culp, Mevrouw Julia, 143–45
Sabern, Henry von, 364, 366, 392, 393n
Sacagawea, 360
St. Francis Little Theatre (San Francisco),
  190n, 314n
Salisbury, William, 22, 209, 215, 220, 251
  The Career of a Journalist, 220, 255
Salzman, Jack, 23n
Samuels, Clara, 395
Sand, George, 371
San Francisco Bulletin, 339n
Sanger, Margaret, 17
Santayana, George: *Shelley: or, The Poetic Value
  of Revolutionary Principles,* 377
Sapp, Arthur H., 263
Saturday Evening Post, 15, 42, 196, 198, 221n,
  238, 242, 244
Sayler, Oliver, 28, 260, 263
Scarborough, Dorothy: *The Supernatural in
  Modern English Fiction,* 241n
Scheffel Hall (New York), 183
Scott, Howard, 281
Scott, Lillian Fulton, 63, 87, 111
Seaman, "Judge," 216
Seven Arts, 15, 21–22, 162, 172, 218, 225–26,
  230, 247
Shakespeare, William, 264, 352, 417n
Shapiro, Charles, 22n

Sharon Herald (Pennsylvania), 397n, 405
Shaw, George Bernard, 398, 407
Shawn, Ted, 373
Shay, Frank, 160, 173, 209
Shay, Frank, & Co., 173n
Shelley, Percy Bysshe, 377
Shepard, Mrs. ———, 160, 225
Sherman, Stuart, 22, 228, 232, 253
  "The Barbaric Naturalism of Mr. Dreiser,"
  22n, 228n
  On Contemporary Literature, 228n
Sherwin, Louis, 229n
  "The New Play: Theodore Dreiser and
  Others at the Comedy," 229n
Shipman, Ernest, Agency, 201
Short, Mr. & Mrs. Charles, 261
Shoup, John, 261
Sigourney, Lydia Howard, 300
Siler, ———, 382
Simpson, Theodore, 396
Sinclair, Upton: *The Brass Check: A Study of
  American Journalism,* 312
Small, Maynard & Co., 127n, 448n
Smart Set, 149n, 161n, 180n, 190n, 222n, 315
Smith, Edward H., 28, 33, 158n, 245–47,
  251, 253–54, 303, 317, 366, 381
Smith, Harry Baile, 173n
Smith, Mary, 180
Smith, Tom, 419n, 435n
Smith's, 223n
Society for Certification and Endorsement,
  225–26, 250
Sombart, Petronelle, 167, 173, 180, 198–
  201, 209, 217–19, 239, 241, 427, 429
Sophocles, 238
Spafford, Jessie, 180, 200, 239
Speck, Benny, 353
Spencer, Herbert, 10, 20, 33, 129
Springer, Mrs. ———, 302
Stafford, Henrietta, 26
Stanchfield, John B., 349
Stanford, Leland, 353
Sterling, George, 24, 38, 275, 338–39, 344,
  354, 359, 365, 367–68, 390–91
Stevens, Harold, 319–20
Stevenson, Robert L.: *Treasure Island,* 334
Stewart, Mary, 203, 219, 239
Stoddard, Joseph, Jr., 107, 111
Storm, ———, 315
Stradivari, Antonio, 235n
Strindberg, August, 243
Success, 395
Sullivan, Madelaine, 236–37
Sullivan, "Red," 30
Sumner, John, 23, 157n, 211
Sunday, Billy, 30

Sunhart, J. L., 260–61
Swanberg, W. A., 8n, 191n
Swanson, Gloria, 348
Taggart, Sen. Thomas, 436n
Taggart, Thomas, Jr., 436
Tanquay, Eva, 187
Tarbell, Ida: *Early Life of Abraham Lincoln,* 97, 102, 104, 108, 110–11, 406
Tarkington, Booth, 28, 223n
Tatum, Anna, 18, 25, 33, 132, 138, 145, 203, 207–8, 230n, 248, 313–14
Taylor, J. F., & Co., 4–5, 105
Taylor, Joseph F., 216
Taylor, Miriam, 26, 155–56, 196, 239
Technical Alliance (New York), 281
Terry, Dr.———, 366
Thaw, Harry, 37, 123
Theatre Magazine, 242
Thimble Theatre (New York), 244
Thomase, Olive, 337
"Three New Plays Given at Comedy," 229n
Titanic, The, 42, 441n
Tobenkin, Elias, 186, 188
   Witte Arrives, 186
Toledo Blade, 186n
Tourneur, Maurice, 296, 334, 350
Trimble, ———, 188
Troland, Leonard Thompson: *The Chemical Origin and Regulation of Life,* 291
Tully, Jim, 363
   "Mr. Dreiser Writes an American Tragedy," 363n
Turgenev, Ivan
   The Jew, 222
   A King Lear of the Steppes, 245, 250
Twain, Mark. *See* Clemens, Samuel L.
Uecke, Claire, 119, 143, 209, 211, 214–15, 218, 222, 252
University of Pennsylvania, The, 3, 90, 418
   Free dispensary, 10, 95–96, 98, 100–101, 103
   Free Museum of Science and Art, 91, 95
Valentino, Rudolf, 338
Vallance, C. E.: *The Sword of the King,* 68n
Van Dine, S. S. *See* Wright, Willard Huntington
Vanity Fair, 42, 351n, 442n
Van Nosdall, ———, 369
Van Vechten, Carl, 396, 400
Veblen, Thorsten, 349
Vidyarthi, Guru Datta: *The Terminology of the Vedas and European Scholars,* 300
Viereck, George Sylvester, 22, 246
Vivian, Decima, 151
Wagner, Richard, 333
Walker, Stuart, 266

Wallace, Lew: *The Fair God,* 215
Warren, Frederick Blount, 339–40
   "Reviews of Some of the Season's New Books," 339n
Warwick, Mrs. ———, 367
Washington, Martha, 366
Washington Square Players, 198, 202, 226, 238, 241, 242n, 253, 255n
Watson, Senator Thomas E., 434
Watson's, Tom, Magazine (later *Watson's Magazine*), 434n
Wells, Thomas Bucklin, 183, 248
Westley, Helen, 226
Weyburn, Ned, 302
Wharton, Edith, 20
White, Carlotta, 69
White, Richard (Dreiser's brother-in-law), 68–69
White, Stanford, 123n
Whitlock, Brand: *The 13th District: A Story of a Candidate,* 94
Whitman, Walt, 10
Who's Who (1901–02), 5
Wilder, George W., 177, 441
Wilkinson, Louis, 155, 164, 188, 214–15
   The Chaste Man, 215
Willard, Jess, 267
Williams, ———, 256
Williams, John D., 255
Williams, John K., 400
Willis & Inglis Motion Picture and Theatrical Enterprises, 327
Wilson, Edmund, 21
Wilson, Harry Leon, 136
Wilson, Woodrow, 133, 137n, 244, 249, 313–14
Wood, Charles Erskine Scott, 366
Woodward, William E., 339
Woollcott, Alexander, 223n
Woolworth, F. W., 176
World War I, 22–23, 133, 166–67, 171, 179, 184, 188, 196–98, 201–2, 204, 206, 212–15, 217, 224, 236, 238–39, 249, 253
Wright, Frank Lloyd, 171, 230
Wright, Frank Lloyd, Jr., 230, 385
Wright, Mrs. Frank Lloyd, Jr., 170. *See also* Markham, Kirah
Wright, Willard Huntington, 180, 191, 302, 304–5, 309–10
Wrigley, ———, 188
Writers Club, The (New York), 351
Yerkes, Charles, 58n, 100n, 254, 433n
Yewdale, Merton S., 23, 117, 169, 173, 181, 183–84, 189, 251, 253, 255, 321, 323, 396

Yost, Charles E., 265n
Yost, Gaylord, 28, 265–67
Young, Art, 22, 398
Young, Clara Kimball, 214, 323

Ziegfield Follies, 402n
Zola, Emile, 319
Zorn, ———, 389